Lecture Notes in Computer Science   13519

More information about this series at https://link.springer.com/bookseries/558

Masaaki Kurosu · Sakae Yamamoto ·
Hirohiko Mori · Dylan D. Schmorrow ·
Cali M. Fidopiastis · Norbert A. Streitz ·
Shin'ichi Konomi (Eds.)

HCI International 2022 - Late Breaking Papers

Multimodality in Advanced Interaction Environments

24th International Conference on Human-Computer Interaction
HCII 2022, Virtual Event, June 26 – July 1, 2022
Proceedings

Springer

Editors
Masaaki Kurosu
The Open University of Japan
Chiba, Japan

Sakae Yamamoto
Tokyo University of Science
Tokyo, Saitama, Japan

Hirohiko Mori
Tokyo City University
Tokyo, Japan

Dylan D. Schmorrow
Soar Technology Inc.
Orlando, FL, USA

Cali M. Fidopiastis
Katmai Government Services
Orlando, FL, USA

Norbert A. Streitz
Smart Future Initiative
Frankfurt am Main, Germany

Shin'ichi Konomi
Kyushu University
Fukuoka, Japan

ISSN 0302-9743   ISSN 1611-3349 (electronic)
Lecture Notes in Computer Science
ISBN 978-3-031-17617-3   ISBN 978-3-031-17618-0 (eBook)
https://doi.org/10.1007/978-3-031-17618-0

This Springer imprint is published by the registered company Springer Nature Switzerland AG
The registered company address is: Gewerbestrasse 11, 6330 Cham, Switzerland

Foreword

Human-computer interaction (HCI) is acquiring an ever-increasing scientific and industrial importance, as well as having more impact on people's everyday life, as an ever-growing number of human activities are progressively moving from the physical to the digital world. This process, which has been ongoing for some time now, has been dramatically accelerated by the COVID-19 pandemic. The HCI International (HCII) conference series, held yearly, aims to respond to the compelling need to advance the exchange of knowledge and research and development efforts on the human aspects of design and use of computing systems.

The 24th International Conference on Human-Computer Interaction, HCI International 2022 (HCII 2022), was planned to be held at the Gothia Towers Hotel and Swedish Exhibition & Congress Centre, Göteborg, Sweden, during June 26 to July 1, 2022. Due to the COVID-19 pandemic and with everyone's health and safety in mind, HCII 2022 was organized and run as a virtual conference. It incorporated the 21 thematic areas and affiliated conferences listed on the following page.

A total of 5583 individuals from academia, research institutes, industry, and governmental agencies from 88 countries submitted contributions, and 1276 papers and 275 posters were included in the proceedings that were published just before the start of the conference. Additionally, 296 papers and 181 posters are included in the volumes of the proceedings published after the conference, as "Late Breaking Work". The contributions thoroughly cover the entire field of human-computer interaction, addressing major advances in knowledge and effective use of computers in a variety of application areas. These papers provide academics, researchers, engineers, scientists, practitioners, and students with state-of-the-art information on the most recent advances in HCI. The volumes constituting the full set of the HCII 2022 conference proceedings are listed in the following pages.

I would like to thank the Program Board Chairs and the members of the Program Boards of all thematic areas and affiliated conferences for their contribution and support towards the highest scientific quality and overall success of the HCI International 2022 conference; they have helped in so many ways, including session organization, paper reviewing (single-blind review process, with a minimum of two reviews per submission) and, more generally, acting as good-will ambassadors for the HCII conference.

This conference would not have been possible without the continuous and unwavering support and advice of Gavriel Salvendy, Founder, General Chair Emeritus, and Scientific Advisor. For his outstanding efforts, I would like to express my appreciation to Abbas Moallem, Communications Chair and Editor of HCI International News.

July 2022   Constantine Stephanidis

HCI International 2022 Thematic Areas and Affiliated Conferences

Thematic Areas

- HCI: Human-Computer Interaction
- HIMI: Human Interface and the Management of Information

Affiliated Conferences

- EPCE: 19th International Conference on Engineering Psychology and Cognitive Ergonomics
- AC: 16th International Conference on Augmented Cognition
- UAHCI: 16th International Conference on Universal Access in Human-Computer Interaction
- CCD: 14th International Conference on Cross-Cultural Design
- SCSM: 14th International Conference on Social Computing and Social Media
- VAMR: 14th International Conference on Virtual, Augmented and Mixed Reality
- DHM: 13th International Conference on Digital Human Modeling and Applications in Health, Safety, Ergonomics and Risk Management
- DUXU: 11th International Conference on Design, User Experience and Usability
- C&C: 10th International Conference on Culture and Computing
- DAPI: 10th International Conference on Distributed, Ambient and Pervasive Interactions
- HCIBGO: 9th International Conference on HCI in Business, Government and Organizations
- LCT: 9th International Conference on Learning and Collaboration Technologies
- ITAP: 8th International Conference on Human Aspects of IT for the Aged Population
- AIS: 4th International Conference on Adaptive Instructional Systems
- HCI-CPT: 4th International Conference on HCI for Cybersecurity, Privacy and Trust
- HCI-Games: 4th International Conference on HCI in Games
- MobiTAS: 4th International Conference on HCI in Mobility, Transport and Automotive Systems
- AI-HCI: 3rd International Conference on Artificial Intelligence in HCI
- MOBILE: 3rd International Conference on Design, Operation and Evaluation of Mobile Communications

Conference Proceedings – Full List of Volumes

http://2022.hci.international/proceedings

24th International Conference on Human-Computer Interaction (HCII 2022)

The full list with the Program Board Chairs and the members of the Program Boards of all thematic areas and affiliated conferences is available online at:

http://www.hci.international/board-members-2022.php

HCI International 2023

The 25th International Conference on Human-Computer Interaction, HCI International 2023, will be held jointly with the affiliated conferences at the AC Bella Sky Hotel and Bella Center, Copenhagen, Denmark, 23–28 July 2023. It will cover a broad spectrum of themes related to human-computer interaction, including theoretical issues, methods, tools, processes, and case studies in HCI design, as well as novel interaction techniques, interfaces, and applications. The proceedings will be published by Springer. More information will be available on the conference website: http://2023.hci.international/

General Chair
Constantine Stephanidis
University of Crete and ICS-FORTH
Heraklion, Crete, Greece
Email: general_chair@hcii2023.org

http://2023.hci.international/

Contents

Human-Robot Interaction

Brain-Computer Interfaces

Multimodal Interaction
and Psychophysiological Computing

3D Hand Pose Recognition Over a Wide Area Using Two Omnidirectional Cameras with Field-of-view Division

Yuta Abe🆔 and Takashi Komuro(✉)🆔

Graduate School of Science and Engineering, Saitama University,
255 Shimo-Okubo, Sakura-ku, Saitama 338-8570, Japan
y.abe.796@ms.saitama-u.ac.jp, komuro@mail.saitama-u.ac.jp

Abstract. In this paper, we propose a method for 3D hand pose recognition using two omnidirectional cameras that enables users to perform proximity gesture operations in the entire range in front of a display. In this method, we use a technique of FOV division, which transforms an input omnidirectional camera image into multiple perspective projection images with virtually rotating the camera, in order to avoid distortion in the peripheral area of a perspective projection image. We also introduce two-stage skeleton detection, which uses the results of whole-body skeleton detection for determining the range of hand skeleton detection to reduce false detections. We evaluated the detection rate with and without FOV division. The detection rate with FOV division is higher than that without FOV division, and complex poses can be detected. In addition, the effectiveness of the two-stage skeleton detection was confirmed by comparing the results with and without the two-stage detection.

Keywords: Design methods and techniques · Gesture recognition · Mid-air gestures · Gesture-controlled large display · Omnidirectional camera

1 Introduction

In the medical field such as surgical simulation and remote medical system, there is increasing demand to manipulate three-dimensional (3D) objects displayed on a screen. However, touch panel displays and other input devices that involve physical contact have hygiene problems. Moreover, it is difficult to intuitively manipulate objects in 3D space with conventional input devices such as a mouse and a touch panel display.

In order to solve these problems, technologies that allow mid-air gesture operations using a motion-aware device have been proposed [1, 2]. However, these methods require a user to wear a device, which is inconvenient for the user.

On the other hand, there are studies on gesture recognition using 3D sensors such as depth camera [3, 4] and LeapMotion [5, 6], or from camera images using deep learning-based pose estimation methods [7] such as OpenPose [8]. However,

ⓒ The Author(s), under exclusive license to Springer Nature Switzerland AG 2022
M. Kurosu et al. (Eds.): HCII 2022, LNCS 13519, pp. 3–17, 2022.
https://doi.org/10.1007/978-3-031-17618-0_1

these methods have the limitation that the recognizable range is limited to the detection range of the 3D sensor or the camera's field-of-view (FOV).

In this paper, we propose a method for 3D hand pose recognition using two omnidirectional cameras that enables users to perform proximity gesture operations in the entire range in front of a display. In this method, we use a technique of FOV division, which transforms an input omnidirectional camera image into multiple perspective projection images with virtually rotating the camera, in order to avoid distortion in the peripheral area of a perspective projection image. We also introduce two-stage skeleton detection, which uses the results of whole-body skeleton detection for determining the range of hand skeleton detection to reduce false detections.

2   3D Hand Pose Recognition Using FOV Division and Two-Stage Skeleton Detection

In this section, a method for skeleton detection and 3D hand pose recognition from omnidirectional camera images is shown. As shown in Fig. 1, two omnidirectional cameras are installed on both sides of a large display, and entire range in front of the display is within the FOV of both cameras, enabling a wide-range 3D pose recognition.

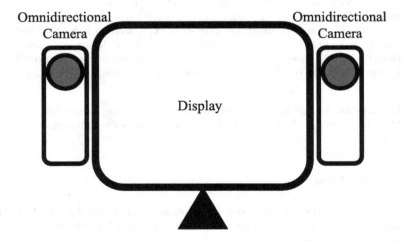

Fig. 1. System configuration

2.1   Geometric Transformation of Omnidirectional Camera Images

The omnidirectional camera image has a specific distortion as shown in Fig. 2. In order to suppress the distortion, the omnidirectional camera images are converted into perspective projection images that are similar to image seen by a human eye or a standard camera.

The perspective projection image is obtained by performing a geometric transformation centered on an arbitrary coordinate in the omnidirectional image. The geometric transformation equation is formulated by the following.

$$\cos c = \sin \phi_0 \sin \phi + \cos \phi_0 \cos \phi \cos(\theta - \theta_0) \tag{1}$$

$$\phi = \arcsin \left(\cos c \sin \phi_0 + \frac{y \sin c \cos \phi_0}{\rho} \right) \tag{2}$$

$$\theta = \theta_0 + \arctan \left(\frac{x \sin c}{\rho \cos \phi_0 \cos c - y \sin \phi_0 \sin c} \right) \tag{3}$$

$$\rho = \sqrt{x^2 + y^2} \tag{4}$$

$$c = \arctan \rho \tag{5}$$

The (x, y) is the coordinate on the perspective projection image corresponding to the coordinate (θ, ϕ) in the omnidirectional image. In the perspective projection image, the center coordinate is determined by the arbitrary coordinate (θ_0, ϕ_0) in the omnidirectional image. c [rad] is the angular distance from the center of the projection at the coordinate where the geometric transformation is performed.

An omnidirectional camera image is shown in Fig. 2, and the image obtained by transforming the coordinates from the center of Fig. 2 to the perspective projection within a horizontal viewing angle of 150 [deg] is shown in Fig. 3.

Fig. 2. The image obtained from an omnidirectional camera

Fig. 3. The image with geometric transformation to perspective projection for Fig. 2

2.2 FOV Division

While the distortion of an omnidirectional camera image is suppressed by the geometric transformation to the perspective projection image, the perspective projection image is stretched at the periphery. This is because omnidirectional camera image captured with a spherical lens is transformed to planar coordinates. At this time, a technique of FOV division is used, which transforms an input omnidirectional camera image into multiple perspective projection images with virtually rotating the camera, in order to avoid distortion in the peripheral area of a perspective projection image. By integrating the results of skeleton detection into each of multiple perspective projection images, skeleton detection can be performed over a wide area with suppression of the effect of distortion.

In addition, for the omnidirectional camera images on the spherical surface, projection from the center of the sphere to the planar coordinates is performed, and thus it is not possible to project a point more than 90 [deg] away from the center point of the projection. Therefore, the maximum possible projection range is less than 180 [deg]. If the conversion to perspective projection is performed without FOV division, it is difficult to fit the entire range in front of the display into the FOV. By generating multiple narrow FOV through FOV division, it is possible to keep the user within the FOV.

The FOV division is performed in such a way that there is an overlapping area in each FOV. This can prevent false skeleton detection in the case where the entire hand is not visible from either FOV due to the hand appearing on the borderline between the FOV. Figure 4 shows a schematic representation of FOV division, and also shows an example of the FOV division for Fig. 2, in which the FOV is divided into three parts at a viewing angle of 90 [deg].

2.3 Two-Stage Skeleton Detection

Skeleton detection is performed from the generated perspective projection images. OpenPose is used for skeleton point detection. OpenPose uses a bottom-up pose estimation model, which can perform whole-body and hand skeleton detection in real-time by deep learning. Using this model, 3D hand pose estimation is performed from the skeleton point information.

Fig. 4. Schematic diagram and example of FOV division by 90 [deg] for an omnidirectional camera

When OpenPose is used to estimate the hand skeleton for the whole image, especially when the size of the hand in the image is small, false detections may occur. Thus, for hand skeleton point detection, a two-stage skeleton detection method is used as shown in Fig. 5, in which the hand detection area is cut out using the hand position information in the image obtained by the whole-body skeleton detection. This method reduces the possibility of false hand skeleton point detection and enables correct hand skeleton point detection even when the hand is small in the image. The hand detection area is determined using the hand, elbow, and shoulder skeleton points obtained by whole-body skeletal detection. The distances between the skeleton points from the hand to the elbow and from the elbow to the shoulder are calculated, and the larger distance is set as the length of one side of the rectangle of the detection area. Using the obtained size of the detection area, hand skeleton points are obtained by hand skeleton detection using the area centered at the hand coordinates as input.

Hand skeleton detection is also performed at the same time. By comparing this with the number of hand skeleton points obtained by the two-stage detection, it is possible to deal with false detections in the case that the whole-body skeleton detection did not work well.

2.4   3D Hand Pose Estimation Using Two Cameras

By detecting the skeleton points from the images taken by the two omnidirectional cameras, the positions of the hand skeleton points are obtained and the hand pose is recognized in 3D space.

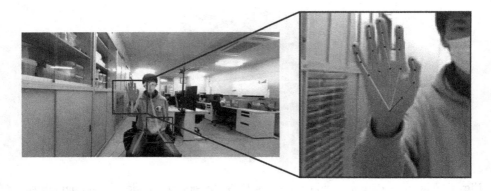

Fig. 5. Hand skeleton point detection by two-stage skeleton detection

For the detected skeleton point coordinates (x, y), it is necessary to convert the detected skeleton point coordinates in other than the front FOV to the coordinates (x', y') in the front camera, because multiple views are generated from one camera due to the FOV division. The coordinate axes are rotated horizontally and then vertically to match the axes of the front FOV. Then, geometric transformation to (x', y') is performed using the equations for geometric transformation to perspective projection. f [pixel] is the focal length of the camera, and θ [rad] and ϕ [rad] are the horizontal and vertical rotation angles to the coordinate axis of the front FOV.

$$x' = f\frac{x}{z} = f\frac{x\cos\theta - f\sin\theta}{x\sin\theta\cos\phi - y\sin\phi + f\cos\theta\cos\phi} \tag{6}$$

$$y' = f\frac{y}{z} = f\frac{x\sin\theta\sin\phi + y\cos\phi + f\sin\phi\cos\theta}{x\sin\theta\cos\phi - y\sin\phi + f\cos\theta\cos\phi} \tag{7}$$

The 3D coordinates (X, Y, Z) is calculated from the skeleton points (x', y') detected by the two cameras. The parallel stereo formula is used for the transformation. The Y coordinates used in parallel stereo are the average of the Y coordinates obtained by the left and right cameras. b [cm] is the baseline length between cameras, (x_r, y_r) are the coordinates obtained from the camera placed on the right side from the user's viewpoint, and (x_l, y_l) are the coordinates obtained from the camera placed on the left side from the user's viewpoint.

$$y_{ave} = \frac{y_r + y_l}{2} \tag{8}$$

$$X = \frac{b(x_r + x_l)}{2(x_r - x_l)} \tag{9}$$

$$Y = \frac{by_{ave}}{2(x_r - x_l)} \tag{10}$$

$$Z = \frac{bf}{2(x_r - x_l)} \tag{11}$$

3 Performance Evaluation

The omnidirectional camera used in this experiment can output a 360 [deg] panoramic image directly from the image. In our experiments, we used 180 [deg] of the 360 [deg] field of view. We used RICOH THETA V, which had a resolution of 1920 × 960 [pixels] and a maximum frame rate of 29.97 [FPS].

3.1 Procedure

In the experimental environment, the height of the omnidirectional camera was set at 38 [cm] from the platform, and the distance between the omnidirectional cameras was set at 90 [cm] in order to evaluate the proximity operation in the situation where the omnidirectional cameras are set at both ends of the large display.

As shown in Fig. 6, the video images were taken by moving the hand in a straight line with a depth of 30 [cm] from the two cameras while performing various gestures within a range of 90 [cm] horizontally. The gesture consists of five patterns: three basic gestures as shown in the Fig. 7 were performed with the hands facing the front of the display, and then each hand gesture was switched to the other three basic hand gestures and also with the hand facing random directions. We evaluated the hand detection rate of each pattern in the captured videos. There was one subject, and the breakdown of the number of input images is shown in Table 1.

Table 1. Images used for input

Input pose	Number of input images
Opened hand	68
Clasped hand	42
Peace-sign gesture	41
Three basic gestures switching	86
Random gesture	140
Total	377

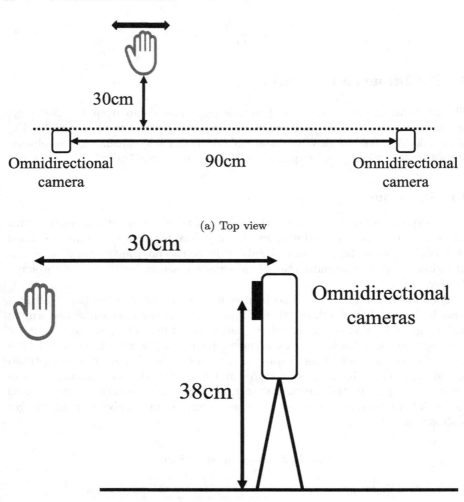

(a) Top view

(b) Side view

Fig. 6. Schematic diagram of the experiment

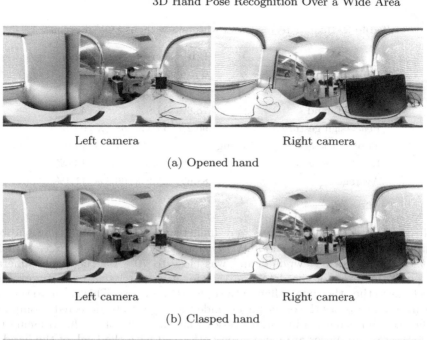

Left camera	Right camera

(a) Opened hand

Left camera	Right camera

(b) Clasped hand

Left camera	Right camera

(c) Peace-sign gesture

Fig. 7. Examples of input images

3.2 Results

Table 2 shows the hand detection rates with and without the FOV division for the left and right viewpoints.

The detection rate was calculated from the number of images that could be detected, the number of input images for each pattern, and the total number of input images. For each pattern, correct detection was defined as the number of images in which at least 15 hand skeletons were detected and the hand pose was not obviously different from the pose of the input image.

Figure 8 shows the detection results when the FOV division is performed and when it is not performed.

Table 2. Hand detection rates with and without FOV division

	Left camera		Right camera	
FOV division	w/	w/o	w/	w/o
Opened hand	98.5%	30.9%	79.4%	7.4%
Clasped hand	78.6%	11.9%	73.8%	4.8%
Peace-sign gesture	90.2%	17.1%	68.3%	9.8%
Three basic gestures switching	97.7%	17.4%	51.2%	14.0%
Random gesture	80.7%	22.9%	67.9%	13.6%
Average	88.6%	21.2%	66.8%	11.1%

In most cases, detection rates were higher with FOV division than without it. In the total results with the FOV division, the detection rate exceeded 80% for the left camera's viewpoint, and was close to 70% for the right camera's viewpoint. In terms of the detection rate for each pose, there were more false detections in the other poses than in the opened hand pose. This is due to the fact that in complex poses the other fingers hide the finger to be detected. Compared to the skeleton detection in various poses with the palm of the hand facing the front, the random poses are more often performed with the back of the hand or the side part of the hand facing the front of the display. Since the detection rate in random poses is lower than in the other poses, it can be assumed that the hand is more correctly detected when the palm is facing the front of the display. One of the reasons for the difference in the detection rate between the right and left viewpoints is assumed to be the effect of manipulating with the right hand only.

In the case of without FOV division, the skeleton detection failed due to the strong projective distortion at the edges of the image. In addition, there were many cases where the whole-body skeleton detection did not work and failed to cut out the hand detection area.

Figure 9 shows a comparison of hand skeleton detection with and without two-stage detection for images with FOV division. As shown in Fig. 9b, without the two-stage detection, the detection of the hand position close to the camera succeeded, but the detection at the other camera failed in many cases. As shown in Fig. 9a, the two-stage detection enabled us to correctly perform skeleton detection for both cameras. In most of the cases, the two-stage detection method was more effective in correct skeleton detection.

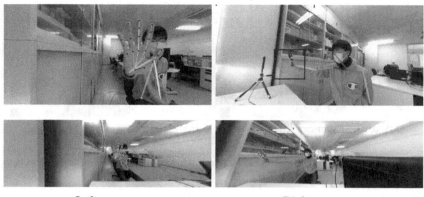

Left camera   Right camera

(a) Result of skeleton detection in opened hand

Left camera   Right camera

(b) Result of skeleton detection in peace signs

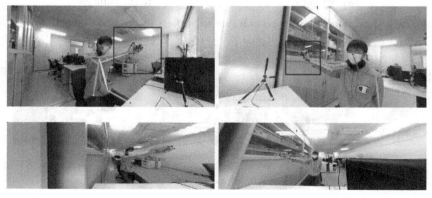

Left camera   Right camera

(c) Result of skeleton detection in clasped hand

Fig. 8. Output examples with and without FOV division

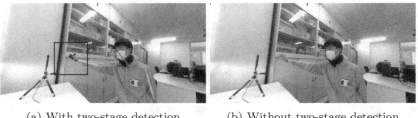

(a) With two-stage detection   (b) Without two-stage detection

Fig. 9. Effects on hand skeleton detection with and without two-stage detection

Left camera   Right camera

(a) False hand skeleton detection due to hand occlusion

Left camera   Right camera

(b) False detection of hand skeleton due to outliers in the hand detection area

Left camera   Right camera

(c) Failure of whole-body skeleton detection

Fig. 10. Failures of hand skeleton detection in two-stage detection

(a) Left camera(right FOV)   (b) Right camera(center FOV)

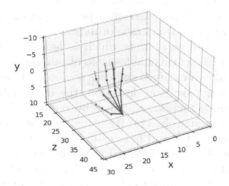

(c) Output of 3D viewed from an oblique upper viewpoint

Fig. 11. 3D hand pose estimation with opened hand

Figure 10 shows examples of false hand skeleton detection in two-stage detection. The most common case of false detection is due to occlusion.As shown inFig. 10a, the detection failed due to cases where the fingertips were hidden by the palm or fingers. In Fig. 10b, the hand slightly protrudes from the hand detection area. In some cases, the detection area of the hand skeleton in the two-stage detection was too small, which caused the false detections. As shown in Fig. 10c, when hand could not be detected by whole-body skeleton detection, only the hand skeleton detection was performed using the entire image as input, and there were cases in which irrelevant parts were detected.

The coordinates of skeleton points in 3D space were estimated using their coordinates with the FOV division. As shown in Fig. 11, the 3D hand pose estimation could be performed correctly in many cases in the opened hand. However, in some cases, the detection did not work well because one finger hid the other finger. when either camera failed to detect, the 3D hand pose estimation also failed.

4   Conclusion

In this paper, we propose a 3D hand pose recognition method to enable users to perform gesture operations in a wide area in front of a large display. By using the omnidirectional cameras, the entire area in front of the display can be covered within the FOV of both cameras, thus achieving 3D recognition over a wide area. The distortion caused by the omnidirectional cameras and the problem of skeleton detection when the size of the hand in the image is small are solved by using FOV division and two-stage skeleton detection.

In the FOV division method, the center position of the panoramic image is shifted and perspective projection transformation is performed multiple times, and the center part of the viewpoint, which is less affected by distortion, is treated as the input image, which enables us to obtain images equivalent to those taken with a normal camera rotated, and thus to detect skeletal points with high accuracy. In the two-stage skeleton detection, the hand detection area was set by whole-body skeleton detection, and thereby reduced the possibility of false detection due to surrounding objects. By using the skeleton point information detected by each method, 3D hand pose estimation was enabled.

There are three issues to be addressed in the future.

The first is to evaluate the accuracy of skeleton detection in 3D space. By comparing the estimated coordinates of skeleton points in 3D space with those obtained by using 3D sensors such as LeapMotion and Kinect, it is possible to evaluate the accuracy of the skeleton detection in this system.

The second is to construct a system that can be operated in real time. Because the proposed method requires a lot of time for image recognition, it is difficult to use the system in real time. This is due to the fact that the process of skeleton detection for the hand itself is time-consuming and that the skeleton detection is performed multiple times along with the FOV division. In order to construct a system that enables real-time operation, it is necessary to speed up the processing in the system. To speed up the process, we can consider methods such as using the hand position coordinates of the previous frame to track the hand movements, limiting the range of the hand skeleton point detection, and reducing the size of the input image.

The third is to deal with cases where multiple persons and both hands are in the FOV. In this experiment, we assumed that only one person using the right hand is the target of operation. As a result of expanding the FOV by the omnidirectional cameras, it is expected that more than one person or more than one hand are detected in the screen at the same time. When multiple users are the target of operation, it is difficult to distinguish the same user from the left and right camera images. It is necessary to distinguish the same users from each other and to estimate the skeleton of each user in 3D space from the results of hand skeleton detection.

References

1. Kumar, P., Verma, J., Prasad, S.: Hand data glove: a wearable real-time device for human-computer interaction. Int. J. Adv. Sci. Technol. **43**, 15–26 (2012)
2. Pietroszek, K., Tahai, L., Wallace, J.R., Lank, E.: Watchcasting: freehand 3d interaction with off-the-shelf smartwatch. In: Proceedings of 2017 IEEE Symposium on 3D User Interfaces (3DUI), pp. 172–175 (2017)
3. Mäkelä, V., James, J., Keskinen, T., Hakulinen, J., Turunen, M.: " It's natural to grab and pull": retrieving content from large displays using mid-air gestures. IEEE Pervas. Comput. **16**(3), 70–77 (2017)
4. Raj, M., Creem-Regehr, S.H., Rand, K.M., Stefanucci, J.K., Thompson, W.B.: Kinect based 3d object manipulation on a desktop display. In: Proceedings of the ACM Symposium on Applied Perception, pp. 99–102 (2012)
5. Bizzotto, N., Costanzo, A., Bizzotto, L., Regis, D., Sandri, A., Magnan, B.: Leap motion gesture control with Osirix in the operating room to control imaging: first experiences during live surgery. Surg. Innov. **21**(6), 655–656 (2014)
6. Fanini, B.: A 3D interface to explore and manipulate multi-scale virtual scenes using the leap motion controller. In: Proceedings of ACHI 2014, the Seventh International Conference on Advances in Computer-Human Interactions, pp. 258–263 (2014)
7. Yam-Viramontes, B.A., Mercado-Ravell, D.: Implementation of a natural user interface to command a drone. In: Proceedings of 2020 International Conference on Unmanned Aircraft Systems (ICUAS), pp. 1139–1144 (2020)
8. Cao, Z., Hidalgo, G., Simon, T., Wei, S.E., Sheikh, Y.: Openpose: realtime multi-person 2d pose estimation using part affinity fields. IEEE Trans. Pattern Anal. Mach. Intell. **43**(1), 172–186 (2019)

Towards a Dynamic Model for the Prediction of Emotion Intensity from Peripheral Physiological Signals

Isabel Barradas[1]([✉])(iD), Reinhard Tschiesner[2](iD), and Angelika Peer[1](iD)

[1] Faculty of Science and Technology, Free University of Bozen-Bolzano,
Bolzano, Italy
isabel.barradas@unibz.it
[2] Faculty of Education, Free University of Bozen-Bolzano, Brixen, Italy

Abstract. Natural human-system interaction can facilitate the acceptance of technological systems. The ability of emotion recognition can hereby provide a significant contribution. Surprisingly, the field of emotion recognition is dominated by static machine learning approaches that do not account for the dynamics present in emotional processes. To overcome this limitation, we applied nonlinear autoregressive (NARX) models to predict emotion intensity from different physiological features extracted from galvanic skin response (GSR), heart rate (HR) and respiration (RSP) signals. NARX models consider the history of both the exogenous inputs (physiological signals) and the output (intensity). Emotions of different intensities were induced with images, while the physiological signals were recorded and the participants assessed their subjectively felt intensity in real-time. The intensity changes were analysed for three different emotion qualities: Happiness/Joy, Disappointment/Regret, Worry/Fear. While models were obtained for each individual, only the best set of parameters across individuals was considered for evaluation. Overall, it was found that the NARX models performed better than a sliding-window linear regression for all qualities. Furthermore, relevant features for the prediction of intensity and "ideal" delays between physiological features and the felt intensity to be captured by the model were identified. Overall, results underline the importance of considering dynamics in emotion recognition and prediction tasks.

Keywords: Emotion recognition · Emotion dynamics · Appraisal models · Electrophysiological signals · Emotion intensity

1 Introduction

Natural human-system interaction can facilitate the acceptance of innovative technological systems. Hereby, also recent advancements in Affective Computing can contribute by achieving more desirable and realistic Human-Machine/Computer interactions that have the ability to recognise the user's

M. Kurosu et al. (Eds.): HCII 2022, LNCS 13519, pp. 18–35, 2022.
https://doi.org/10.1007/978-3-031-17618-0_2

emotional state and to react accordingly [3]. Over the last decades significant advances in emotion modelling for emotion recognition and prediction have been made considering different types of modalities, such as facial expressions, gestures, and electrophysiological signals, eventually also combined in a multimodal approach [24]. Among those, electrophysiological signals are spontaneous, involuntary, and not constrained by social protocols.

Emotion theories often recognise the dynamic nature of emotions, but still, the field of emotion recognition is dominated by linear statistics and static models [8]. In fact, in most emotion recognition studies, an affective state is detected within a time window by employing static machine learning approaches [21] that can either be traditional statistical methods [4,10] or deep learning approaches [11]. These models, however, are not able to fully capture the dynamic nature of emotions, though they have been useful to provide information related to emotional processes.

The emergence of the so-called *appraisal models* emphasised the dynamic nature of emotions, since emotions are defined as processes and involve their different components and respective interactions over time [15]. However, literature focusing on such computational models is still rare. Here we aim at contributing with the development of dynamical, nonlinear autoregressive exogenous (NARX) models to predict emotion intensity from different peripheral electrophysiological signals (galvanic skin response, heart rate, and respiration). As a step towards a multimodal approach, we present results of an individual analysis of different physiological signals. Moreover, we introduce a method for the dynamic assessment of the subjectively felt emotion, a prerequisite for dynamic studies.

This paper is structured as follows: Sect. 2 reviews the state of the art in the field; Sect. 3 explains the architecture of the model studied; Sect. 4 reports the setup and design of our experiment; Sect. 5 introduces how we processed the data and estimated emotion intensity; Sect. 6 explains how we evaluated the model and reports our results; and Sect. 7 contains conclusions and future directions.

2   Related Work

Only few studies account for the dynamics nature of emotions, at least indirectly. For instance, even though Valenza *et al.* (2011) [25] applied a Quadratic Discriminant Classifier to simply discriminate among 5 classes of valence and arousal, they considered nonlinear dynamic methods for feature extraction from galvanic skin response (GSR), heart rate (HR) and respiration (RSP). They compared the same classifier for standard features and for nonlinear dynamic features, concluding that dynamic features allowed the classifier to better recognise different levels of valence and arousal. Similarly, dynamic features have also been used to feed deep learning approaches, as in the case of Liu *et al.* (2021) [12]. They extracted dynamic differential entropy from electroencephalogram (EEG) signals that then were used to classify emotional states into positive or negative with convolutional neural networks.

Other approaches again considered applying deep neural networks that account for temporal dynamics. For instance, nonlinear autoregressive networks with exogenous inputs (NARX networks) were applied by Alazrai and Lee (2012) [1] to detect emotions from facial expressions (analysing videos). These networks are of "NARX-type", in which there are two types of inputs: the present and past values from the exogenous input, and the delayed values of the output signal. In this way, these models consider the temporal dynamics by taking into account the history of the signals. The method performed better than baselines, both in terms of average recognition rate and number of emotional states able to be distinguished. In turn, Mithbavkar and Shah (2019) [14] used different types of neural networks to detect emotions from EMG signals. They found that even though Elman neural networks also present an architecture suitable to study time varying dynamics (due to an undertake layer that works as memory), NARX-type networks reached the best accuracy distinguishing between anger, joy, pleasure, and sadness. It is worth mentioning that, even though the architecture of these deep networks also considers the time history of the signals as inputs, here we overcome issues related to a limited amount of training samples by using a dynamical system approach inspired by the field of system identification (as better described in Sect. 3) instead of a neural network.

While the subjective feeling is characterised by its quality, intensity and duration, aforementioned works exclusively focused on recognizing or predicting emotion quality. In this work, we are particularly interested in studying the dynamics related to intensity, since it is an important characteristic to define an emotion (*e.g.*, "I am *very* happy", "I am *slightly* disappointed") and therefore important to fully comprehend the concept of emotion.

Works like Sonnemans and Frijda (1994) [22], Verduyn *et al.* (2009) [26] and Heylen *et al.* (2015) [6]) studied intensity profiles over time, but still lack a connection between the subjective feeling and neurophysiological responses.

A first attempt in this direction was made by Jenke and Peer (2018) [7], who used GSR to dynamically model emotion intensity over time. They took advantage of Scherer's Component Process Model to develop a grey-box model for intensity estimation based on the Dynamic Field Theory (DFT), a mathematical and conceptual framework that relies on the concept of Dynamic Neural Fields (DNFs) [20]. Moreover, the subjectively felt intensity was measured in real-time during the exhibition of IAPS images [9]. This study was pioneer in the introduction of a dynamic model to predict emotion intensity from physiological signals. However, just information contained in GSR was included.

We believe that the analysis of additional physiological signals is required to gain a more comprehensive understanding of the dynamics of emotion intensity. Thus, in this work we evaluate emotion intensity over a series of peripheral physiological signals and model their dynamics.

3   Models

3.1   NARX Dynamic Model

System identification is a widely used field that aims to build mathematical models of dynamic systems by trying to capture the relationship between the input and output as accurately as possible [13]. One of the approaches used for modelling nonlinear systems is the nonlinear autoregressive exogenous (NARX) model, that can be expressed as follows:

$$y(t) = f(y(t-1), ..., y(t-n_y), u(t), u(t-1), ..., u(t-n_u)) + e(t), \qquad (1)$$

where t is the discrete time-index, $u(t)$ the input, $y(t)$ the output, $e(t)$ the equation error, and n_y and n_u the maximum lags for the system output and input, respectively, and f can be a multiple-input single-output nonlinear function.

The output y is explained through its past values $y(t-1)$, $y(t-2)$, ..., $y(t-n_y)$ – and therefore is an autoregressive model – as well as past values of the input $u(t-1)$, $u(t-2)$, ..., $u(t-n_u)$ – which represent the exogenous variables of the model. Moreover, the model permits the introduction of a delay. If n_k represents the input delay, the input of the system $z(t)$ will be:

$$z(t) = [y(t-1), ..., y(t-n_y), u(t-n_k), u(t-n_k-1), ..., u(t-n_k-n_u)]. \quad (2)$$

In this work, NARX models are estimated through a wavelet network function that uses a combination of linear weights, an offset and a nonlinear function (containing wavelet unit functions that operate on a radial combination of inputs) to compute its output. This is done through the following relationship:

$$y(t) = y_0 + (z(t) - \bar{z})^T PL + W(z(t)) + S(z(t)), \qquad (3)$$

in which $z(t)$ is the vector of regressors with mean $\bar{z}$, y_0 the output offset (a scalar), P a projection matrix, L a vector of weights, and $W(z)$ and $S(z)$ the nonlinear functions of the wavelet network. $W(z)$ is a sum of dilated and translated wavelets, $S(z)$ is a sum of dilated and translated scaling functions.

Equations 1 and 2 just show linear inputs; however, the order of these models can be increased by the introduction of polynomial regressors. This is particularly relevant to predict emotions through physiological signals, since their relationship is known to be nonlinear [18, 25].

3.2   Self-assessment

To self-assess the subjective feeling, the Self-Assessment Manikin test [2], a picture-oriented questionnaire developed to measure an emotional response based on the scales of valence (from positive to negative), perceived arousal (from calming to agitating), and dominance (from submissive to dominant), is typically adopted. These dimensions, however, are considered abstract for most subjects, since they do not correspond to the way people communicate emotions. As an alternative, we investigate the Geneva Emotion Wheel (GEW) –

that distributes emotions according to their valence and control dimensions –
and represents a more convenient way to report the subjective feeling. This
because, on one hand, it contains labels that are closer to our communication
style, and on the other hand, the bi-dimensional structure helps to locate the
discrete emotions on the instrument [16].

It should be noted that the GEW evaluates emotions in the valence-control
space even though literature is dominated by self-assessment in the valence-
arousal space [21]. Scherer (2009) [18], however, claims that, after valence, control is more important than arousal for emotion quality distinction. Valence is
directly related to how much an individual considers an event conductive or
obstructive to reaching their goals (goal conduciveness), and control is a reflex
of how well the individual can cope or adjust to the event consequences (coping
potential).

Looking at the GEW (Fig. 1), it is possible to locate 20 emotion families
with 40 emotion terms according to their valence and control. In here, and
following the idea of polar coordinates, the angle of each of these emotion families
represents the *emotion quality*, and the proximity to the border of the wheel the
emotion intensity.

3.3   Proposed Approach

We use physiological signals (exogenous inputs) to predict changes in emotion
intensity (single output) through NARX models, assuming that the quality is
fixed over a trial. Even though NARX models are a black-box time series modelling approach, finding the best combination of parameters for each physiological
signal gives us an insight about how fast our perception of the subjectively felt
emotion follows physiological signals.

We extract distinct physiological features from galvanic skin response, heart
rate, and respiration signals (see Subsect. 5.2 for more details). Each resulting
feature time series is evaluated separately and used as exogenous input of a
NARX model with the subjectively felt emotion intensity as output. We considered linear regressors of the physiological feature u and the intensity y, polynomial (quadratic) regressors of the physiological feature u, and the existence of a
delay in the physiological feature u. The amount of linear and polynomial regressors for a specific physiological feature u was always the same. Mathematically,
this means that the output $y(t)$ is predicted by:

$$y(t) = f(y(t-1), ..., y(t-n_y), u(t-n_k), u(t-n_k-1), ..., u(t-n_k-n_u)$$
$$u(t-n_k)^2, u(t-n_k-1)^2, ..., u(t-n_k-n_u)^2) + e(t). \tag{4}$$

4   Experiment and Data Acquisition

4.1   Participants

An experiment was conducted with 9 healthy individuals (6 males and 3 females)
aged between 19 and 32 ($M = 28.2, SD = 7.3$). Subjects were screened with

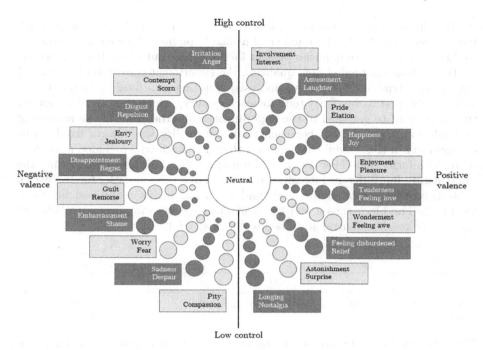

Fig. 1. Version of the Geneva Emotion Wheel (GEW) with 40 emotion terms arranged in 20 emotion families [16]. These families are aligned according to two dimensions – valence and control. With this tool, subjects provided us information about the emotion quality (the angle) and intensity (low intensity: towards the centre of the wheel; high intensity: towards the circumference of the wheel).

questionnaires to exclude participants with any sign of somatization, obsessive-compulsive disorder, interpersonal sensitivity, depression, anxiety, hostility, phobic anxiety, paranoid ideation, and psychoticism (Brief Symptom Checklist [5]) as well as posttraumatic stress disorders. The questionnaires were made available in three different languages (English, Italian, German) and thus, to ensure the validity of responses, only participants with these languages as mother tongue were accepted[1].

4.2 Experimental Design

To analyse intensity profiles for different emotion qualities, we chose qualities that are representative of the quadrants of the Geneva Emotion Wheel (GEW) [16], namely Happiness/Joy (quality of the 1st quadrant, Q1), Disappointment/Regret (quality of the 2nd quadrant, Q2), and Worry/Fear (quality of the 3rd quadrant, Q3).

---

[1] Ethical approval was obtained from the Research Ethics Committee of the Free University of Bozen-Bolzano.

To stimulate these emotions, pictures of the IAPS database [9] were used. Please note that due to the number of available pictures for each quadrant, we could select pictures of qualities present for only three out of the four quadrants.

For each of the final chosen qualities, the experiment consisted of 8 trials (1 "practising" trial and 7 trials for analysis) resulting in a total of 24 trials. The order of the first 3 was fixed (one for each quality), since they were meant for the participant to get used to the experiment, while the order of the remaining 21 trials were randomized. For each trial, the quality was always fixed, while the intensity of stimuli changed over the trial. Each trial included a message with the information "New Trial" (exhibited for 2 s), 3 images representing the same quality but different intensities (exhibited in a random order for 15 s each), a black screen (exhibited for 30 s), and a neutral image (exhibited for 30 s), see Fig. 2. The black screen and the neutral image were important to help the subjects to reach a neutral state before the next trial.

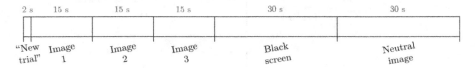

Fig. 2. Emotion induction protocol for each trial. It contains a message informing about the beginning of the new trial, three images meant to induce emotions of different intensities, a black screen and a neutral image. All the images are from the IAPS database [9].

4.3   Experimental Setup and Procedure

First, an online pre-screening meant to assess the inclusion criteria mentioned in Subsect. 4.1 was performed. Participants who met our inclusion criteria were then invited to come to our laboratory and continue the experiment. Once they arrived, they were introduced to the study and tasks. After obtaining written consent, the biosensors to collect electrophysiological signals were placed. In particular, galvanic skin response (GSR) was recorded with a g.tec *g.GSRsensor* of which two small electrodes were placed on middle finger and ring finger. The pulse was measured with a g.tec *g.SpO2* sensor placed on the index finger. The respiration (RSP) was recorded with a belt system that works as a respiration effort sensor. This belt was placed around the chest of the participants. Electroencephalogram (EEG) was also measured, but these signals were not included in this analysis. All these sensors were connected with a g.tec *g.HIamp* amplifier and the signals were recorded with the help of a laptop with the g.tec toolbox *g.HIsys* for Simulink compatible with MATLAB R2020a. The amplifier was set to record the data at a sampling frequency of 256 Hz.

The stimuli presented were part of the IAPS database [9] and were displayed on a monitor in front of the participants. The participants provided real-time information about the perceived quality and intensity of the emotion with the help of a polar device with the GEW [16]. By adjusting a knob, subjects provided the felt quality (the angle of the GEW) and intensity (according to the proximity to the border of the GEW). The knob determined the resistance of a linear potentiometer, measuring intensity, and a rotary potentiometer, measuring quality. They were connected to the laptop through an Arduino UNO, which enabled their recording with Simulink.

As explained in Subsect. 4.2, the quality was fixed over a trial. Therefore, participants were supposed to fix the felt quality at the beginning of the first picture of the trial and, after that, just adjust the intensity according to their subjective feeling.

5   Data Processing

5.1   Pre-processing

We used the g.tec toolbox *g.HIsys* to pre-process the signals as recommended for these sensors. In particular, we applied a low-pass filter at 30 Hz and a notch filter at 50 Hz to the signals from the *g.GSRsensor* and from the *g.SpO2sensor*. In the case of the respiration signals, we used a notch filter at 50 Hz, but also a band-pass filter with cut-off frequencies of 0.1 Hz and 30 Hz.

To account for the time the participants needed to adjust the quality at the beginning of the trials, we did not include the first 2 s of each trial in the analysis.

5.2   Feature Extraction

Besides the filtered galvanic skin response (GSR), heart rate (HR), and the respiration (RSP) rate (respiration cycles per minute), we extracted other features that also gave information about these physiological measurements over time. These are GSR derivative, GSR running rate[2], HR derivative, HR running rate, RSP rate derivative, RSP running rate, inspiration time, expiration time, inhalation depth, and exhalation depth. Besides the derivatives, these features were obtained using blocks meant for feature extraction from the g.tec toolbox *g.HIsys*. Due to the quality of the RSP signal, inspiration time could not be obtained for 5 participants (Subject002, Subject004, Subject005, Subject007 and Subject009).

After extracting these signals, we downsampled them by a factor of 100 – with a resulting frequency of 2.56 Hz. We did this to obtain orders of our models that still have a physiological meaning.

5.3   Intensity Prediction

We used each of the physiological features mentioned in Sect. 5.2 as exogenous variables to predict emotion intensity with a NARX model. We used one exogenous variable per model, which means that in total we aimed to achieve 13 models (one per feature) for each emotion quality. To train each of those models, we

---

[2] The running rate is computed with respect to a reference interval that is moving along with the evaluation window as time proceeds.

used the intensity reported by the participants in real-time as the ground-truth. Taking the nomenclature of Subsect. 3.3, intensity is y and each of the features u. The regressors used for y were linear, while the ones for the physiological signals u were both linear and quadratic.

To find the best model, we trained NARX models with different parameters related to the number of regressors of each signal and to the delay of u in reference to y. This means that, considering Eq. 4, we examined combinations of the values that the parameters n_y, n_u and n_k can take. We considered the three parameters could take values between 1 and 11. Since the data frequency is 2.56 Hz, these values correspond to time intervals between 0.39 and 4.29 s.

We tested these models with a leave-one-out cross-validation (LOOCV) [17]. Particularly, since we had 7 available trials for each emotion, we used 6 trials as the training set and the remaining trial as test set. This process was repeated 7 times, so all trials made once part of the test set.

We repeated this process for the 9 subjects individually.

6 Evaluation

6.1 Methods

Performance: We used the correlation coefficient R between the predicted output and the ground-truth to measure the performance of our models, since we wanted to assess how close the shape of our results is to the ground-truth.

The NARX models computed here are individual. Nonetheless, we aim for an approach giving insights across subjects. To do so, for each combination of parameters, we computed the average R for all participants as explained in more detail in the following paragraph.

For all subjects, qualities and physiological features, we have in total 9317 models (leave-one-out cross-validation, with $N = 7$, of all the combinations of the 11 possible values of n_y, n_u and n_k). For each of these models, we computed the correlation between the predicted output and our ground-truth (the subjectively felt intensity). For each combination of the parameters (e.g., $\{1, 1, 1\}$, $\{1, 1, 2\}$, $\{1, 1, 3\}$, ...), we obtained 7 correlations resulting from the LOOCV. For each participant, we calculated the mean of these 7 correlations. Finally, we calculated the mean of these values across subjects.

After computing this, we have a mean correlation for every combination of values that n_y, n_u and n_k can take. For each physiological feature u, we considered the parameters with the highest R across trials and across subjects.

Additionally, we compared the correlation obtained for each one of those "best" combinations with the results obtained with a sliding-window linear regression. In this linear regression, we used a window length of 13 time points (approximately 5 s) with a step of 3 time points (approximately 1 s) to capture both fast and slow changes of different physiological signals. In each time window, we considered the mean intensity of that window as the output and the following features as inputs: maximum, minimum, mean, and standard deviation. We again adopted LOOCV. Once again, we calculated the correlation coefficient R between the output of the models and the ground-truth and we used these values to compare the two methods. We performed this comparison with a Wilcoxon signed-rank test, assessing whether the correlation obtained for each physiological feature was higher when using NARX models than when using a traditional sliding-window approach. Both p-values and Wilcoxon effect size r are reported[3]. Results are significant when $p < 0.05$ and effect size is considered moderate $(r > 0.30)$ or large $(r > 0.50)$ [23].

Analysis of the Physiological Delay: With NARX models, it is possible to introduce delays in the response variable (intensity) and in the exogenous variables (physiological signals). In our model, this delay is only considered in the exogenous variables. This can actually complement information from the Component Process Model [18,19], since this model takes into consideration the sequential influence of the neurophysiological component on the subjective feeling. For this reason and for each quality separately, we analysed the optimal delay of each physiological feature for intensity prediction.

6.2 Results

Performance: The results for Happiness/Joy (Q1), Disappointment/Regret (Q2) and Worry/Fear (Q3) are displayed in Tables 1, 2 and 3, showing the best results for NARX models across subjects, as well as the corresponding parameters (n_y, n_u, n_k), the results for the sliding-window linear regression, and finally the results of the Wilcoxon signed-rank test with p-value and Wilcoxon effect size r.

Looking at these three tables, we verify that NARX models lead to higher mean correlations across subjects than the sliding-window regression. This happens to every single feature for the three different qualities. When analysing the significance of the results (considering a significance level of 5%), one can see that: for Q1, for eight out of thirteen features a significantly higher correlation is obtained with NARX models; for Q2, all except GSR running rate, inspiration time and RSP running rate show significantly higher correlations for NARX models than for the sliding-window linear regression; and for Q3, the result is more mixed with several features not reaching statistical significance.

Overall, we can conclude that NARX models outperformed the sliding-window linear regression. Differences were more significant for Q1 (Happiness/Joy) and Q2 (Disappointment/Regret) than for Q3 (Worry/Fear). When looking at the Geneva Emotion Wheel, this means that NARX models worked better for emotions characterised by a high control.

Figure 3 also shows prediction results when using the NARX model for an individual trial obtained for a participant using parameters that reached the highest correlation either for this subject in particular (at the top) or across

---

[3] For the purpose of obtaining the z-score necessary to compute r, the approximate method is used. However, the reported p-values are always obtained with the exact method adequate for a small sample size.

subjects (at the bottom). The results in the image were obtained with GSR derivative (in yellow), HR running rate (in red) and RSP running rate (in blue). As expected, the results using subject-dependent optimal parameters are closer to the shape of the reported intensity (ground-truth). This is specially evident for the results obtained with the RSP running rate, in which the intensity predicted with subject-specific optimal parameters is seen to be "prompted" and then accompanies the shape of the ground-truth (just missing the sudden peaks), while this does not happen to the one obtained with optimal parameters across subjects for the same feature.

Physiological Delay: Figures 4, 5 and 6 show the optimal input delay for Q1, Q2 and Q3, respectively. Physiological features related to GSR are represented in yellow at the bottom, HR in red in the middle, and RSP in blue at the top of the figures.

Regarding Happiness/Joy (Q1), it is possible to observe that filtered GSR, GSR derivative, HR derivative, inspiration time, inhalation depth, exhalation depth and RSP running rate take less time to influence the subjectively felt intensity ($n_k \leq 4$, which corresponds to less than 1.6 s), followed by GSR running

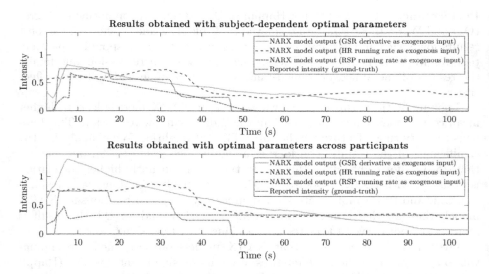

Fig. 3. Example of intensity predictions with NARX models using GSR derivative (in yellow), HR running rate (in red) and RSP running rate (in blue) for Subject006 in the case of Worry/Fear (Q3). The prediction at the top is obtained with the optimal parameters for this subject in particular (GSR derivative: $n_y = 2, n_u = 10, n_k = 5$; HR running rate: $n_y = 5, n_u = 8, n_k = 7$; RSP running rate: $n_y = 3, n_u = 8, n_k = 11$), while the one at the bottom were obtained with the optimal parameters across participants (GSR derivative: $n_y = 4, n_u = 11, n_k = 4$; HR running rate: $n_y = 11, n_u = 11, n_k = 5$; RSP running rate: $n_y = 2, n_u = 9, n_k = 4$). The ground-truth (in grey) corresponds to the subjectively felt intensity reported by the participant. (Color figure online)

Table 1. Summary of the comparison between intensity models for Happiness/Joy (Q1): number of observations, mean (standard deviation) of the highest correlation across subjects obtained with NARX models and the corresponding parameters, mean (standard deviation) of the correlation obtained with sliding-window linear regression, and results of the Wilcoxon signed-rank test (p-value and effect size) between these 2 variables for each physiological feature.

Physiological feature	N	NARX models				Sliding-window linear regression	Wilcoxon signed-rank test statistics	
		n_y	n_u	n_k	Correlation across subjects	Correlation across subjects	p-value	Wilcoxon effect size r
Filtered GSR	9	8	2	4	0.306 (0.274)	0.0996 (0.245)	0.0820	0.474
GSR running rate	9	10	7	6	0.273 (0.167)	0.140 (0.250)	0.125	0.395
GSR derivative	9	3	11	3	0.365 (0.193)	0.0955 (0.0672)	0.0313	0.629
Filtered HR	9	9	2	5	0.452 (0.188)	0.0159 (0.111)	3.91e−03	0.829
HR running rate	9	9	9	6	0.276 (0.224)	0.0360 (0.130)	0.0137	0.711
HR derivative	9	3	11	3	0.360 (0.191)	0.0329 (0.138)	1.95e−03	0.869
RSP rate	9	7	2	5	0.312 (0.225)	0.0569 (0.0678)	9.77e−03	0.750
Inspiration time	4	4	1	1	0.401 (0.137)	−0.0165 (0.191)	0.125	0.668
Expiration time	9	9	4	6	0.321 (0.105)	0.0582 (0.106)	0.0156	0.704
Inhalation depth	9	2	7	1	0.241 (0.175)	−0.0788 (0.170)	0.0156	0.704
Exhalation depth	9	6	4	4	0.285 (0.200)	−0.0248 (0.125)	0.0625	0.549
RSP running rate	9	1	11	2	0.301 (0.287)	0.0105 (0.0149)	1.00	−0.596
RSP derivative	9	3	8	8	0.250 (0.114)	−0.00145 (0.133)	1.95e−03	0.869

Table 2. Summary of the comparison between intensity models for Disappointment/Regret (Q2): number of observations, mean (standard deviation) of the highest correlation across subjects obtained with NARX models and the corresponding parameters, mean (standard deviation) of the correlation obtained with sliding-window linear regression, and results of the Wilcoxon signed-rank test (p-value and effect size) between these 2 variables for each physiological feature.

Physiological feature	N	NARX models				Sliding-window linear regression	Wilcoxon signed-rank test statistics	
		n_y	n_u	n_k	Correlation across subjects	Correlation across subjects	p-value	Wilcoxon effect size r
Filtered GSR	9	8	3	3	0.359 (0.215)	0.161 (0.197)	0.137	0.7108
GSR running rate	9	10	10	5	0.215 (0.220)	0.0970 (0.108)	0.0820	0.474
GSR derivative	9	3	11	4	0.377 (0.150)	0.0103 (0.151)	3.91e−03	0.817
Filtered HR	9	8	1	8	0.485 (0.154)	−1.12e−03 (0.175)	1.95e−03	0.869
HR running rate	9	5	9	6	0.238 (0.212)	0.0927 (0.0.0976)	0.0273	0.632
HR derivative	9	2	11	4	0.377 (0.160)	0.147 (0.101)	1.95e−03	0.869
RSP rate	9	3	7	3	0.283 (0.236)	−0.0337 (0.128)	0.0137	0.711
Inspiration time	4	6	2	6	0.553 (0.110)	0.0102 (0.0882)	0.250	0.447
Expiration time	9	1	3	1	0.381 (0.181)	0.0254 (0.0754)	7.81e−03	0.761
Inhalation depth	9	3	6	3	0.375 (0.144)	−0.0337 (0.0913)	0.0156	0.699
Exhalation depth	9	2	9	1	0.290 (0.193)	−0.0602 (0.0437)	0.0313	0.629
RSP running rate	9	2	11	2	0.216 (0.230)	0.0988 (0.222)	0.156	0.349
RSP derivative	9	7	10	5	0.341 (0.138)	0.0809 (0.0915)	1.95e−03	0.869

Table 3. Summary of the comparison between intensity models for Worry/Fear (Q3): number of observations, mean (standard deviation) of the highest correlation across subjects obtained with NARX models and the corresponding parameters, mean (standard deviation) of the correlation obtained with sliding-window linear regression, and results of the Wilcoxon signed-rank test (p-value and effect size) between these 2 variables for each physiological feature.

Physiological feature	N	NARX models				Sliding-window linear regression	Wilcoxon signed-rank test statistics	
		n_y	n_u	n_k	Correlation across subjects	Correlation across subjects	p-value	Wilcoxon effect size r
Filtered GSR	9	8	2	6	0.285 (0.243)	0.0704 (0.234)	0.102	0.434
GSR running rate	9	11	1	10	0.200 (0.118)	0.105 (0.183)	0.125	0.395
GSR derivative	9	4	11	4	0.339 (0.139)	0.0173 (0.0877)	3.91e−03	0.817
Filtered HR	9	7	2	7	0.387 (0.142)	0.0581 (0.185)	1.95e−03	0.869
HR running rate	9	11	11	5	0.122 (0.0815)	0.0899 (0.146)	0.545	−0.0395
HR derivative	9	4	11	4	0.302 (0.163)	0.0550 (0.126)	1.95e−03	0.869
RSP rate	9	7	2	7	0.247 (0.194)	−0.0350 (0.126)	5.86e−03	0.790
Inspiration time	4	6	1	1	0.367 (0.163)	−0.189 (0.119)	0.25	0.447
Expiration time	9	2	6	2	0.345 (0.141)	0.0172 (0.0488)	0.0625	0.548
Inhalation depth	9	3	5	5	0.292 (0.202)	0.0509 (0.182)	0.109	0.423
Exhalation depth	9	2	6	2	0.292 (0.186)	0.0636 (0.0786)	7.81e−03	0.761
RSP running rate	9	2	9	4	0.225 (0.163)	0.0267 (0.0812)	0.188	0.304
RSP derivative	9	8	5	11	0.208 (0.166)	0.0769 (0.190)	0.248	0.237

rate, filtered HR, HR running rate, RSP rate, expiration time and RSP derivative ($4 < n_k \le 8$, which corresponds to 1.6 s to 3.1 s).

When considering Disappointment/Regret (Q2), filtered GSR, GSR derivative, HR derivative, RSP rate, expiration time, inhalation depth, exhalation depth and RSP running rate are the features taking less time to influence the subjectively felt intensity ($n_k \le 4$, which corresponds to less than 1.6 s), followed by GSR running rate, filtered HR, HR running rate, inspiration time and RSP derivative ($4 < n_k \le 8$, which corresponds to 1.6 s to 3.1 s).

Finally, in the case of Worry/Fear (Q3), GSR running rate, GSR derivative, inspiration time and exhalation depth are the features taking less time to influence the subjectively felt intensity ($n_k \le 4$, which corresponds to less than 1.6 s), followed by filtered GSR, HR running rate, RSP rate, expiration time and inhalation depth ($4 < n_k \le 8$, which corresponds to 1.6 s to 3.1 s), and by filtered HR, HR derivative, RSP running rate and RSP derivative ($n_k \ge 9$, which corresponds to more than 3.5 s).

As can be observed, filtered GSR, GSR derivative, HR derivative inhalation depth, exhalation depth and RSP running rate show a small delay for the qualities characterised by a higher control (Q1 and Q2). GSR derivative, HR derivative and exhalation depth also have a short delay in Q3, suggesting that the delay of these physiological features with respect to the felt intensity is not dependent on the emotion quality. On the other hand, GSR running rate, filtered HR, HR running rate and RSP derivative presented a medium delay for both Q1 and Q2 (qualities with higher control); for Q3 just HR-related features (filtered

HR and HR running rate) presented the same medium delay, while the remaining ones (GSR running rate RSP derivative) reached extremes of high delays. It is also noticeable that, for the qualities characterised by a negative valence (Q2 and Q3), expiration time presented a short delay. Finally, inspiration time has a short delay for Q1 and Q3.

Overall, we observe a rather invariant cluster for HR-based features characterised by medium delays across features. For GSR-based features, both filtered GSR and GSR tend to present short to medium delays. Delays for RSP-related features were found to vary more with the chosen quality.

Emotion appraisal models provide a mean to combine both theoretical concepts and empirical findings. In particular, Scherer's Component Process Model (CPM) considers the appraisal of an event that is highly pertinent to the needs, goals and values of an individual [18,19]. This model is especially relevant to interpret our results, since it considers the effects of a multilevel appraisal on other emotion components. This appraisal is built upon a set of sequential criteria, the so-called "stimulus evaluation checks" (SECs), which are: relevance, implications, coping potential, and normative significance. These SECs influence all the emotion components, including the neurophysiological component and the subjective feeling; therefore, following different SECs, physiological changes are provoked and the individual gets aware of the changes in their affective state. Different SECs can influence the same physiological parameter, as we will explain in the next paragraph.

Considering the influence of the different SECs on both the neurophysiological component and the subjective feeling, some of these processes can be related to the delays we obtained. As mentioned, relevance is the first SEC; under this SEC, the individual assesses the intrinsic pleasantness of the event. This check has an effect in the inhalation (measured from the RSP signal) [18]. Since intrinsic pleasantness is directly related to valence, it is worth mentioning that the only quality with positive valence that we assessed (Q1, Happiness/Joy) is exactly the one in which there is a shorter delay between the physiological feature (inhalation depth) and the felt intensity ($n_k = 1$, which corresponds to 0.4 s, see Fig. 4). The very same SEC also influences the heart rate (decelerates in case of a pleasant event, accelerates in case of an unpleasant event) [18], so a short delay could also be expected in HR-related features. However, HR is also affected in all posterior SECs, so it is not surprising that the optimal delay in the felt emotion intensity is larger than this. Regarding GSR-related features, the delays are expected to be overall slightly shorter than HR-related features, since GSR stops being affected after the second SEC. This is evidenced in our results, expect for GSR running rate in Q3. Lastly, it is also not surprising that the results vary more among them and across qualities for the remaining RSP-related features, since many different outcomes of the different SECs cause changes in both RSP depth and speed.

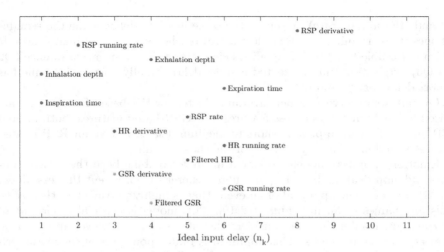

Fig. 4. Ideal input delay across subjects obtained with NARX models for Happiness/Joy (Q1). Physiological features related to galvanic skin response are represented in yellow at the bottom, to heart rate in red in the middle, and to respiration in blue at the top. (Color figure online)

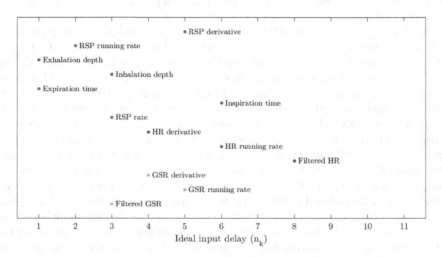

Fig. 5. Ideal input delay across subjects obtained with NARX models for Disappointment/Regret (Q2). Physiological features related to galvanic skin response are represented in yellow at the bottom, to heart rate in red in the middle, and to respiration in blue at the top. (Color figure online)

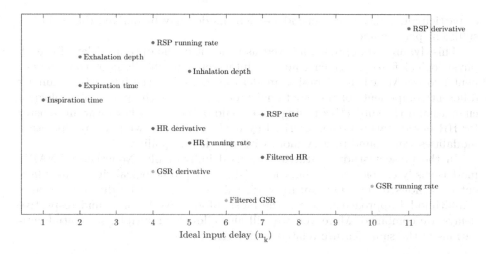

Fig. 6. Ideal input delay across subjects obtained with NARX models for Worry/Fear (Q3). Physiological features related to galvanic skin response are represented in yellow at the bottom, to heart rate in red in the middle, and to respiration in blue at the top. (Color figure online)

7 Conclusion and Future Directions

The field of Human-Computer Interaction is advancing fast to keep up with users' needs and expectations. Predicting users' emotional states is considered an important ingredient in this context. Nonetheless, the majority of research on emotion prediction still focuses on static approaches that neglect the dynamic nature of emotions. In this work, we applied nonlinear autoregressive exogenous (NARX) models to predict the dynamic behaviour of emotion intensity.

Thirteen physiological features extracted from galvanic skin response (GSR), heart rate (HR) and respiration (RSP) signals were used as exogenous inputs to predict emotion intensity with NARX models. These models incorporate information about the time history of the physiological signals in the form of linear and quadratic regressors, as well as the emotion intensity with linear regressors. In general, the introduced dynamic approach showed better performance when compared to a sliding-window linear regression for all the emotion qualities analysed, but specially for Happiness/Joy (Q1) and Disappointment/Regret (Q2). This shows that considering the past history of each variable already gives more clues about the emotional process than a static approach that just considers different features within a time window.

Overall, we observed that meaningful features are very subjective, which is expected as an emotion process is highly dependent on the individual and their needs, goals and values. However, there were many relevant features that were common among participants and thus, we expect that, by increasing the number of participants, also a subject-independent model may be derived that achieves sufficient performance.

This dynamical approach allowed us to identify the optimal delays for each physiological feature, which could be interpreted in the light of the Component Process Model (an appraisal model that considers the interactions among different components of the emotional process, such as the psychophysiological changes and the subjective feeling). We could observe a rather invariant cluster for HR-based features (characterised by medium delays), while delays for other modalities were found to vary more with the chosen quality.

In the present study, features were used individually. Nonetheless, NARX models easily enable the combination of different physiological signals as different exogenous inputs. Our future work will consequently be directed towards a multimodal approach in which the most informative features and respective delays are combined. Moreover, we will also allow for multiple, sequential activations of the same feature related to different SECs.

Acknowledgements. This work is supported in part by a research assistant position of the Free University of Bozen-Bolzano.

References

1. Alazrai, R., Lee, C.G.: An narx-based approach for human emotion identification. In: 2012 IEEE/RSJ International Conference on Intelligent Robots and Systems, pp. 4571–4576. IEEE (2012)
2. Bradley, M.M., Lang, P.J.: Measuring emotion: the self-assessment manikin and the semantic differential. J. Behav. Therapy Exp. Psychiat. **25**(1), 49–59 (1994)
3. Brave, S., Nass, C.: Emotion in human-computer interaction. In: The Human-Computer Interaction Handbook, pp. 103–118. CRC Press (2007)
4. Chang, C.Y., Chang, C.W., Lin, Y.M.: Application of support vector machine for emotion classification. In: 2012 Sixth International Conference on Genetic and Evolutionary Computing, pp. 249–252. IEEE (2012)
5. Derogatis, L.R.: Symptom checklist-90-revised, brief symptom inventory, and bsi-18. In: Handbook of Psychological Assessment in Primary Care Settings (2017)
6. Heylen, J., Verduyn, P., Van Mechelen, I., Ceulemans, E.: Variability in anger intensity profiles: structure and predictive basis. Cognit. Emotion **29**(1), 168–177 (2015)
7. Jenke, R., Peer, A.: A cognitive architecture for modeling emotion dynamics: intensity estimation from physiological signals. Cognit. Syst. Res. **49**, 128–141 (2018)
8. Kuppens, P., Verduyn, P.: Emotion dynamics. Curr. Opin. Psychol. **17**, 22–26 (2017)
9. Lang, P.J.: International affective picture system (IAPS): affective ratings of pictures and instruction manual. Technical report (2005)
10. Li, M., Xu, H., Liu, X., Lu, S.: Emotion recognition from multichannel EEG signals using k-nearest neighbor classification. Technol. Health Care **26**(S1), 509–519 (2018)
11. Lin, W., Li, C., Sun, S.: Deep convolutional neural network for emotion recognition using EEG and peripheral physiological signal. In: Zhao, Y., Kong, X., Taubman, D. (eds.) ICIG 2017. LNCS, vol. 10667, pp. 385–394. Springer, Cham (2017). https://doi.org/10.1007/978-3-319-71589-6_33

12. Liu, S., Wang, X., Zhao, L., Zhao, J., Xin, Q., Wang, S.H.: Subject-independent emotion recognition of EEG signals based on dynamic empirical convolutional neural network. IEEE/ACM Trans. Comput. Biol. Bioinf. **18**(5), 1710–1721 (2020)
13. Ljung, L.: Perspectives on system identification. Annu. Rev. Control **34**(1), 1–12 (2010)
14. Mithbavkar, S.A., Shah, M.S.: Recognition of emotion through facial expressions using EMG signal. In: 2019 International Conference on Nascent Technologies in Engineering (ICNTE), pp. 1–6. IEEE (2019)
15. Moors, A., Ellsworth, P.C., Scherer, K.R., Frijda, N.H.: Appraisal theories of emotion: state of the art and future development. Emotion Rev. **5**(2), 119–124 (2013)
16. Sacharin, V., Schlegel, K., Scherer, K.R.: Geneva emotion wheel rating study (2012)
17. Sammut, C., Webb, G.I. (eds.): Leave-One-Out Cross-Validation, pp. 600–601. Springer, Boston (2010). https://doi.org/10.1007/978-0-387-30164-8_469
18. Scherer, K.R.: The dynamic architecture of emotion: evidence for the component process model. Cognit. Emotion **23**(7), 1307–1351 (2009)
19. Scherer, K.R., Schorr, A., Johnstone, T.: Appraisal Processes in Emotion: Theory, Methods, Research. Oxford University Press (2001)
20. Schneegans, S., Schöner, G.: Dynamic field theory as a framework for understanding embodied cognition. In: Handbook of Cognitive Science, pp. 241–271 (2008)
21. Shu, L., et al.: A review of emotion recognition using physiological signals. Sensors **18**(7), 2074 (2018)
22. Sonnemans, J., Frijda, N.H.: The structure of subjective emotional intensity. Cognit. Emotion **8**(4), 329–350 (1994)
23. Sprent, P., Smeeton, N.C.: Applied Nonparametric Statistical Methods. CRC Press (2016)
24. Torres-Valencia, C.A., Garcia-Arias, H.F., Lopez, M.A.A., Orozco-Gutiérrez, A.A.: Comparative analysis of physiological signals and electroencephalogram (EEG) for multimodal emotion recognition using generative models. In: 2014 XIX Symposium on Image, Signal Processing and Artificial Vision, pp. 1–5. IEEE (2014)
25. Valenza, G., Lanata, A., Scilingo, E.P.: The role of nonlinear dynamics in affective valence and arousal recognition. IEEE Trans. Affect. Comput. **3**(2), 237–249 (2011)
26. Verduyn, P., Van Mechelen, I., Tuerlinckx, F., Meers, K., Van Coillie, H.: Intensity profiles of emotional experience over time. Cognit. Emotion **23**(7), 1427–1443 (2009)

Introduction to the 2nd Edition of "Semantic, Artificial and Computational Interaction Studies"

Cornelia Ebert[1], Andy Lücking[2,3]([⊠])(iD), and Alexander Mehler[2]

[1] Department of Linguistics, Goethe University Frankfurt, Frankfurt, Germany
ebert@lingua.uni-frankfurt.de
[2] Text Technology Lab, Goethe University Frankfurt, Frankfurt, Germany
{luecking,mehler}@em.uni-frankfurt.de
[3] Université Paris Cité, Paris, France

Abstract. "Behavioromics" is a term that has been invented to cover the study of multimodal interaction from various disciplines and points of view. These disciplines and points of view, however, lack a platform for exchange. The workshop session on "Semantic, artificial and computational interaction studies" provides such a platform. We motivate behavioromics, sketch its historical background, and summarize this year's contributions.

Keywords: Multimodal interaction · Behavioromics · Semantics · Human-computer interaction

1 Motivation

Manual gestures, facial expressions, head movements, shrugs, laughter, body orientation, speech, pauses, intonation: they all contribute to constituting what is called *multimodal interaction*. Aiming at natural (for humans) interfaces, the field of HCI paid attention to this social fact early on [10,55]. It is also a vital topic in Conversation Analysis [32,65] and the Cognitive Sciences [31,61] and begins to percolate to theoretical linguistics [28,50] and (formal) semantics [19,66]. Simultaneously, due to the digital turn, work on multimodal communication is expanded by data analytics, that is, statistical means to describe the form of communication [33,56,59,69] or to ground distributional semantics in visual [6], auditory [44], or even olfactory [43] perception to eventually arrive at multimodal distributional semantics. However, while conjoint in investigating a common empirical domain, there is little exchange between these fields. The session on "Semantic, artificial and computational interaction studies" aims at bringing these branches together. Potential goals are to delineate experimental studies, computational methods, resource building, and exploration to integrate symbolic, statistical, laboratory, field, and corpus-based approaches – a joint methodological endeavor that might be called *behavioromics*.

M. Kurosu et al. (Eds.): HCII 2022, LNCS 13519, pp. 36–47, 2022.
https://doi.org/10.1007/978-3-031-17618-0_3

Behavioromics has various and diverse precursors. We name some of them in Sect. 2 before we provide an overview of the contributions of the 2022 session (Sect. 3). A synthesis is given against this backdrop in Sect. 4.

2   Selected Historical Background

One of the finest considerations of gesture and multimodal interaction is probably to be found in the arts. As is well-known, paintings by Giotto di Bondone stand out due to the expressive body language of the participants of the subject scenes depicted in his paintings [5]. Another famous historical root attending at co-verbal gesture is its vital use in giving speeches and is dealt with within the ancient rhetoric instructions given by Quintillian [60].[1] So, while there is a lot of fuss about spoken and written language (and rightly so, see, e.g., [18,34]), human everyday life and culture is deeply shaped by "whole body communication". In fact, multimodal interaction is regarded the ecological niche of language – a recent such claim has been made again in [35]. This view of natural language starts to spread in theoretical linguistics, too [16], contributing to overcoming a "written language bias" [47] and leading to the current "coming of age of sign language and gesture studies" [31]. One can dare to say that this development would please two of the founding figures of modern language sciences, Gottlob Frege and Ferdinand de Saussure: De Saussure [17] always emphasized the primacy of spoken over written language; Frege [23] was clear that in order to express a complete thought, circumstances accompanying speech such as finger points and glances need to be taken into account.

Accounting for (spoken) language as an inherently multimodal phenomenon imposes on a very basic level observational and representational challenges. While the gestures (using the term in a broad sense) mentioned at the beginning of this paper are uncontradictedly communication means, this is less clear with respect to smell (but see [43] for grounding smell terms in chemical structures) or clothing (clothing might be regarded a sociolinguistic style, developing as part of, e.g., signaling games [11]). In any case, studying multimodal behavior requires to represent multimodal behavior, like phonetics requires to represent speech sounds, for which the *International Phonetic Alphabet* (https://www.internationalphoneticalphabet.org) provides a standardized notation system. An early, encompassing account in this respect is the *kinesics* program developed by Ray Birdwhistell [8,9], which comes with alphabets for various articulators like gaze, speech, and body movements. Kinesics failed to gain wide acceptance (see [38] for a critical appreciation), but the observational and representational duties remain. Nowadays representation systems focusing on relative temporal relations instead of articulator alphabets like the *Behavior Markup Language* [67] prevail; a recently initiated workshop series on *Multimodal Semantic Representations* (MMSR, https://aclanthology.org/events/mmsr-2021/) takes up the

---

[1] For an overview of the history of gesture studies and its precursors see the first chapters of [41].

issue in question *expressive verbis* (and is partly also represented in the 2022 Behavioromics session, see Sect. 3).

Studies from fields as diverse as anthropology, behavioral psychology, Conversation Analysis (CA) and related disciplines were interested in the total of human behavior early on and provided foundational insights [3, 14, 15, 20, 21, 32, 39, 40, 65]. A particular impetus for a gestural turn furthermore came from more psychologically oriented work [52, 53]. Taxonomies and observational regularities due to these and related approaches are still prolific.

Advances in formal grammar theory, however, initiated in computer science, most notably by the development of multichart parsers [36] and multimodal finite-state parsing [37]. Multicharts are still used in more recent constraint-based grammar implementations [1] – An overview of formal, multimodal grammar architectures is given in [51]. A formal grammar is the – implicitly assumed or explicitly mentioned – algorithmic backbone for multimodal grammars as diverse as [2, 24, 30, 46, 48], which implement an extended notion of language in the "heart of linguistics". These developments fit in with extended notions of grammar as declarative systems characterizing talk in interaction [28]. Currently, we also see new algorithmic approaches beyond "grammar proper" coming up such as $\lambda\Psi$-algebra [64].

Arguably the first computational system for speech–gesture integration has been developed in the context of human–computer interaction [10], where a pointing gesture has been modeled in terms of pen input on a computer screen and interpreted as a placing command. Pointing gestures also are the type of gesture that received the earliest attention from semantics and pragmatics [62], but also formal structure-mapping approaches for the semantics of iconicity have been developed [29]. Within two-dimensional semantics it is discussed how gestures interact with proffered and presupposed, at-issue and non-at-issue content [19, 66].

The strong interest from computer science in the entirety of body behavior is most evident at *Conversational Agents*, be they embodied or not [13, 58] (to name just two sources from a vast field, which are also partly represented in the 2022 session on Behavioromics). The reason for the importance of non-verbal behavior for physical or virtual artificial agents is obvious: in order for an interaction with a robot to appear *natural*, the robot has to communicate naturally, that is, with all sorts of gestures.[2]

Even a quick look at the (necessarily) partial background on work on multimodal interaction shows that it has been a multi-disciplinary enterprise from the outset, including symbolic, statistical, laboratory, field, and corpus-based approaches. This multi-disciplinary, multimodal perspective also frames Behavioromics and the contributions of the current issue.

---

[2] An attempt of an overview of the range of communicative gestures is given in [49].

3   Overview of Contributions

A dynamic semantics for multimodal communication, Jeremy Kuhn. In combining descriptive and depictive information from sign language, Kuhn aims at developing a dynamic semantic system for anaphora resolution in sign languages to capture order phenomena such as $John_i$ entered the room. He_i began to sing. vs. *He_i began to sing. $John_i$ entered the room. or binding phenomena with quantifiers (Nobody received [a prize]$_i$ and bragged about it$_i$. vs. *Nobody recieved [a prize]$_i$. It$_i$ was made of gold.). The main claim he makes is that, since anaphoric relations are expressed via the iconic use of space in sign languages, a dynamic semantic system must be built on this insight and a pictorial discourse referent must be introduced at a certain locus before it can be retrieved. In other words, "one must create a picture before one can point to it". This, so it is argued, building on [45], is also the reason why we do not observe phenomena of backwards anaphora as often in sign languages as in spoken languages. Furthermore, Kuhn develops a theory that makes reference to the well-established concept of a *local context* that describes the immediate scope in which an expression is interpreted and broadens this to capture phenomena that rely on iconic space. This way, the author develops a formal semantic system that does justice to the modality-specific visual-gestural properties of sign languages.

Towards Situated AMR: Creating a Corpus of Gesture AMR, Lucia Donatelli, Kenneth Lai, Richard Brutti, James Pustejovsky. The authors present Gesture-AMR, an extension of *Abstract Meaning Representation* (AMR) [4], which covers manual gestures. To this end – and thoroughly building on previous gesture work on annotation and multimodal meaning – gestures are represented according to a template which basically provides four slots: (i) type of gesture, (ii) agent of gesture, (iii) content of gesture, and (iv) addressee of gesture. The type of gesture is filled by the classical taxonomy which distinguishes *iconic, deictic,* and *emblematic* gestures. Agent and addressee are given by the utterance situation (the authors apply Gesture-AMR to the EGGNOG corpus [68]). The content depends on the gesture type: deictic gestures contribute a location, the content of emblems can be obtained from a lexicon, iconic gestures are described in terms of action predicates taken from PropBank [57]. Note that gestures which exhibit multiple meaning components (like a deictic gesture which simultaneously draws the shape of the object pointed at) are represented as mixed types, initiating the basic template more than once. Temporal alignment and "affiliation" [65] (see also Sect. 2) are expressed on the level of communication acts. Here, speech and gesture can be coupled into *ensembles* [41], co-referential or in some other ways semantically coordinated communicative multi-tier pairs.

Incremental Unit Networks for Distributed, Symbolic Multimodal Processing and Representation, Mir Tahsin Imtiaz, Casey Kennington. Natural language processing happens incrementally. Incremental interpretation, however, is usually not a feature of *Spoken Dialogue Systems* (SDS), leading to inadequacies in their speed and responsiveness. The paper by Imtiaz and Kennington presents a framework of an SDS which is *modular, multimodal, dis-*

tributive, incremental and *temporally aligned* and thus meets *five core requirements* for such systems. This is achieved by extending the *Incremental Unit* (IU) framework of [42]. One of the shortcomings of this framework concerns the simultaneous processing of data originating from multimodal sensors which is physically distributed. To address this challenge, the authors develop a framework to enable cross-modal information exchange. In doing so, they go beyond related work that only meets proper subsets of the five core requirements. A central IU-related component of their approach is a network model of information units interconnected by horizontal (same-level) and vertical (grounded-in) links, with the processor having access to all units to update or revise processing steps as needed. Units can be organized into modules, resulting in the representation of multimodal data in a multimodal network such that grounded-in links concern dependencies of units of different modes. To enable temporal alignment and information fusion, the authors extend the *Platform for Situated Intelligence* (PSI) in such a way that its representation format is IU-compliant. Finally, to make IUs accessible across distributed modules, they develop a query language, thereby providing a database-driven technology to address the above challenge. The resulting architecture is extensively evaluated and thus represents a promising example of how IU-related approaches can be combined with those based on parallel processing (PSI) in an environment that makes all relevant multimodal data accessible to the central processor.

The interaction space: Considering speaker-hearer location in co-speech gesture analysis and annotation, Schuyler Laparle. It's a truism that manual gesture is a visuo-spatial phenomenon. Laparle shows that this truism actually gives rise to a spatial structure in dialogue she calls *interaction space* (IS); the IS, it is then argued, is essential for understanding discourse management. Thus, the IS extends or complements the non-interactive gesture space [52], which is used for describing extent and movement of hand-and-arm gestures. The IS emerges by conversational engagement, that is by turning *toward* an addressee. In interview situations (the examples mainly discussed by Laparle) there are even two possible interaction spaces for each interview partner, one between the interview partner and its interlocutor, and one between the interview partner and the audience. Interestingly, using empty spaces, dialogue agents can also create virtual ISs, for instance, toward an imagined audience. The IS is the "pitch" for interlocutors' gesture-based management of discourse topics; Laparle gives examples for PRESENT, REFER, CONTRAST, and REMOVE.[3] From the perspective of the researcher, the IS turns out to be an essential interpretive means for understanding and analyzing interactive actions in dialogue. Hence,

---

[3] In a footnote, Laparle remarks that one can think of interaction spaces in terms of conceptual or mental spaces [22]. However, there is another apparent connection, namely thinking of interaction spaces as parts of *dialogue gameboards* [25]. This construal would immediately connect interaction spaces to dialogue semantic frameworks and management action could be modeled as effects of conversational moves, as has been shown for some interactive pointing gestures [26].

the IS should become part of the standard inventory for gesture annotation and linguistic interpretation.

Interruption multimodal analysis, Liu Yang, Catherine Achard, Catherine Pelachaud. Turn-taking is often initiated by interruptions, i.e., by a listener attempting to take over the turn while his or her interlocutor is still holding it, thus violating the '*one person speaks at a time*' rule. Knowing how to handle such interruptions or initiating them is an important part of our conversational competence. Modeling this competence from a computational perspective aims to enable *Embodied Conversational Agents* (ECA) to successfully perform or manage interruptions in dialogic communication. To this end, ECAs must be able to distinguish interruptions from both back-channel behavior and smooth turn-takings. In order to train corresponding classifiers, one needs sufficiently rich data on interruptions in dialogues, which are annotated using an annotation scheme that captures their multimodal signals. Providing and instantiating such a scheme (by example of the French part of the NoXi corpus [12]) is the subject of the paper by Yang et al. Using their scheme, they identify prosodic features, facial and body movement features (related to hand and head activity) that signal interruptions. The annotation is done with respect to the audio and video streams of both interlocutors. The features are accompanied by distribution analyses that provide initial insights into the respective feature dynamics under the specific scenario of the NoXi corpus. The annotation scheme goes beyond related work in that it considers a broader range of interruptions (e.g., during silence) in addition to smooth turn-taking and backchannel behavior while distinguishing between successful and failed interruptions. In conjunction with the opposition of cooperative and competitive interruptions, this distinction opens the field for a detailed analysis of interruptions. Interestingly, the work shows that interruptions are both frequent and usually successful, indicating the importance of modeling this type of dialogic behavior in the context of ECAs.

Laughter meaning construction in development, Chiara Mazzocconi. "Laughter", as Mazzocconi demonstrates, is a term which covers a variety of non-verbal vocalizations, both formal and functional. Laughs occur standalone or overlapping with verbal utterances (speech laughter); they appear before, in between, or following speech; they exhibit very different acoustic profiles (F_0, duration and arousal), and, most importantly, they show a range of semantic and pragmatic functions. In particular, Mazzocconi argues that laughter is a proper subject of *linguistic* analysis.[4] At the core of her analyses is the finding that laughter is *propositional* and *exophoric*: laughter has propositional content that arises from a "laughable". The laughable triggers laughing because it is pleasant and/or incongruous to some of the speaker's/laugher's expectations or assumptions. Based on empirical investigations, Mazzocconi comes up with an "incongruity taxonomy" alongside congruent laughs: incongruity can be *pleasant* (e.g., a punchline), *social* (violation of a social norm), or *pragmatic* (a clash

---

[4] In considering "laughter as language" [27], Mazzocconi can be seen as joining in McNeill's famous question "So You Think Gestures are Nonverbal?" [52].

between literal and intended meaning, e.g., irony). These sophisticated adult uses develop ontogenetically from vocalizations which emerge in babies around the third month of life. Mazzocconi makes the point that especially antiphonal laughter (laughter in response to laughter by an interlocutor) is a core ingredient of parent-child conversation. Not only is (shared) laughter deeply embedded in social bonding interactions, it is also systematically involved in the child's first one-word utterances. On the view spread out by Mazzocconi, laughter is part and parcel of natural language communication, and therefore, as she continues, also has to be a feature of naturally interacting Spoken Dialogue Systems (SDS) and Embodied Conversational Agents (ECA): Laughter can be used to detect (in developmental and conversational studies) and to model (SDS and ECA) semantic and pragmatic competencies beyond telling jokes like failure detection and socially engaged feedback learning. By example of laughter Mazzocconi demonstrates that one cannot study or engineer language without studying or engineering gesture, too.

In addition to the above papers, the 2022 session on Behavioromics saw two additional presentations:

Regularities in multimodal behaviour patterns as the basis for human-artificial agent interaction, Judith Holler. Holler focuses on regularities in multimodal utterances, as opposed to idiosyncratic behavior. That is, Holler aims at finding stable, channel-crossing form-meaning patterns. This includes repeated uses within and across interlocutors (as has been attested with respect to co-verbal manual [54]), uniformities across visual form variations as known from gesture fields or families [24], but also specific single gestures exhibiting coherent functions. These multimodal regularities are functionally integrated into conversation: they take part in regulating discourses and "modulate" illocutionary force. However, they immediately also raise questions about context-dependency and compositionality, as is discussed by Holler. Such patterns are not only of interest for multimodal interaction studies *per se*, they are also important for the generation and comprehension of naturalistic behavior of artificial conversational agents.

Multimodal Corpus Linguistics with the TV News Archive: Prospects and Challenges, Bodo Winter, Greg Woodin. Winter and Woodin advocate and exemplify a corpus-based approach to study multimodal utterances. They point out the *TV News Archive* (https://archive.org/details/tv), a platform that makes all American TV news as well as some international channels (e.g., Al Jazeera, BBC) available several hours after broadcasting. The archive not only collects the news video clips, but because all American TV is captioned, also speech transcription is available. Hence, the data base can be searched for specific verbal expressions, which can then be interpreted in the visual context of the news video. As a case study, the authors look at verbal description and video clips of people using quantificational expressions such as "tiny number" and "huge number". They found that gesture rates were very high and that gestures are semantically congruent with speech: for instance, the pincer grip (letter "G" in the letter signing alphabet of America Sign Language, that is, thumb in parallel to your index finger, but not touching, the rest three fingers closed like in forming a fist) is used for small quantities (which is in line with depictive strategies observed in direction-giving dialogues [7,63]) The authors conclude that the TV News Archive provides naturalistic data from an ecologically valid setting.

4 Conclusion

As illustrated in Sect. 2, the study of multimodal communication has been a multidisciplinary (though not necessarily a joint) endeavor. This year's session on *behavioromics* aims, among others, at bringing these different disciplines, which nonetheless share large parts of their empirical domain, together. By this means, semantics (Kuhn), computational linguistics (Donatelli et al.), natural language processing (Imtiaz and Kennington), discourse studies (Laparle), conversational agents (Yang et al.), cognitive sciences (Mazzocconi and Holler), corpus research (Winter and Woodin) have the seldomly enabled but needed opportunity to get into discussion.

References

1. Alahverdzhieva, K., Flickinger, D., Lascarides, A.: Multimodal grammar implementation. In: Proceedings of the 2012 Conference of the North American Chapter of the Association for Computational Linguistics: Human Language Technologies, pp. 582–586. NAACL-HLT 2012 (2012)
2. Alahverdzhieva, K., Lascarides, A., Flickinger, D.: Aligning speech and co-speech gesture in a constraint-based grammar. J. Lang. Model. **5**(3), 421–464 (2017)
3. Argyle, M.: Bodily Communication, 2nd edn. Routledge, London, New York (1988)
4. Banarescu, L., et al.: Abstract meaning representation for sembanking. In: Proceedings of the 7th Linguistic Annotation Workshop and Interoperability with Discourse, pp. 178–186 (2013)
5. Barasch, M.: Giotto and the Language of Gesture. Cambridge University Press, Cambridge (1987)
6. Baroni, M.: Grounding distributional semantics in the visual world. Lang. Linguist. Compass **10**(1), 3–13 (2016)
7. Bergmann, K., Kopp, S.: Verbal or visual? How information is distributed across speech and gesture in spatial dialog. In: Schlangen, D., Fernández, R. (eds.) Proceedings of the 10th Workshop on the Semantics and Pragmatics of Dialogue, pp. 90–97. Brandial'06, Universitätsverlag Potsdam, Potsdam (2006)
8. Birdwhistell, R.L.: Kinesics and Context. Conduct and Communication Series. University of Pennsylvania Press, Philadelphia (1970)
9. Birdwhistell, R.L.: Background to kinesics. ETC Rev. Gen. Semant. **40**(3), 352–361 (1983)
10. Bolt, R.A.: "Put-that-there": voice and gesture at the graphics interface. SIGGRAPH Comput. Graph. **14**, 262–270 (1980). https://doi.org/10.1145/965105. 807503

11. Burnett, H.: Signalling games, sociolinguistic variation and the construction of style. Linguist. Philos. **42**(5), 419–450 (2019). https://doi.org/10.1007/s10988-018-9254-y
12. Cafaro, A., et al.: The Noxi database: multimodal recordings of mediated novice-expert interactions. In: Proceedings of the 19th ACM International Conference on Multimodal Interaction (ICMI 201207), pp. 350–359. Association for Computing Machinery, New York (2017). https://doi.org/10.1145/3136755.3136780
13. Cassell, J.: Embodied conversational interface agents. Communun. ACM **43**(4), 70–78 (2000). https://doi.org/10.1145/332051.332075
14. Clark, H.H.: Using Language. Cambridge University Press, Cambridge (1996)
15. Clark, H.H.: Pointing and placing. In: Kita, S. (ed.) Pointing: Where Language, Culture, and Cognition Meet, chap. 10, pp. 243–269. Lawrence Erlbaum Associates Inc, Mahwah (2003)
16. Cooper, R.: Charting a way through the trees. Theor. Linguist. **43**(1–2), 121–128 (2017). https://doi.org/10.1515/tl-2017-0009
17. de Saussure, F.: Course de linguistique générale. In: Bally, C., Sechehaye, A. (eds.) Bibliothèque Scientifique Payot, Payot, Paris (1916)
18. Deacon, T.: The Symbolic Species. Penguin Press, London (1997)
19. Ebert, C., Ebert, C., Hörnig, R.: Demonstratives as dimension shifters. Proc. Sinn Bedeutung **24**(1), 161–178 (2020). https://doi.org/10.18148/sub/2020.v24i1.859
20. Efron, D.: Gesture and Environment. King's Crown Press, Morningside Heights (1941)
21. Ekman, P., Friesen, W.V.: The repertoire of nonverbal behavior: categories, origins, usage, and coding. Semiotica **1**(1), 49–98 (1969)
22. Fauconnier, G.: Mental Spaces: Aspects of Meaning Construction in Natural Language. Cambridge University Press, Cambridge (1994)
23. Frege, G.: Der Gedanke. Beiträge zur Philosophie des deutschen Idealismus **1**(2), 58–77 (1918)
24. Fricke, E.: Grammatik multimodal. Wie Wörter und Gesten zusammenwirken. No. 40 in Linguistik - Impulse und Tendenzen, De Gruyter, Berlin and Boston (2012)
25. Ginzburg, J.: The Interactive Stance: Meaning for Conversation. Oxford University Press, Oxford (2012)
26. Ginzburg, J., Lücking, A.: I thought pointing is rude: a dialogue-semantic analysis of pointing at the addressee. In: Grosz, P., Martí, L., Pearson, H., Sudo, Y., Zobel, S. (eds.) Proceedings of Sinn und Bedeutung, vol. 25, pp. 276–291. SuB 25 (2021). https://ojs.ub.uni-konstanz.de/sub/index.php/sub/article/view/937. Special Session: Gestures and Natural Language Semantics
27. Ginzburg, J., Mazzocconi, C., Tian, Y.: Laughter as language. Glossa **5**(1), 104 (2020). https://doi.org/10.5334/gjgl.1152
28. Ginzburg, J., Poesio, M.: Grammar is a system that characterizes talk in interaction. Front. Psychol. **7**, 1938 (2016). https://doi.org/10.3389/fpsyg.2016.01938
29. Giorgolo, G.: A formal semantics for iconic spatial gestures. In: Aloni, M., Bastiaanse, H., de Jager, T., Schulz, K. (eds.) Logic, Language and Meaning. LNCS (LNAI), vol. 6042, pp. 305–314. Springer, Heidelberg (2010). https://doi.org/10.1007/978-3-642-14287-1_31
30. Giorgolo, G., Asudeh, A.: Multimodal communication in LFG: gestures and the correspondence architecture. In: Proceedings of LFG11, pp. 257–277 (2011)
31. Goldin-Meadow, S., Brentari, D.: Gesture, sign, and language: the coming of age of sign language and gesture studies. Behav. Brain Sci. **40**, e46 (2017). https://doi.org/10.1017/S0140525X15001247

32. Goodwin, C.: The intelligibility of gesture within a framework of co-operative action. In: Seyfeddinipur, M., Gullberg, M. (eds.) From Gesture in Conversation to Visible Action as Utterance, pp. 199–216. John Benjamins, Amsterdam and Philadelphia (2014)

33. Gurion, T., Healey, P.G., Hough, J.: Comparing models of speakers' and listeners' head nods. In: Proceedings of the 24th Workshop on the Semantics and Pragmatics of Dialogue. SEMDIAL (2020)

34. Hauser, M.D., Chomsky, N., Fitch, W.T.: The faculty of language: what is it, who has it, and how did it evolve? Science **298**(5598), 1569–1579 (2002). https://doi.org/10.1126/science.298.5598.1569, review

35. Holler, J., Levinson, S.C.: Multimodal language processing in human communication. Trends Cognit. Sci. **23**(8), 639–652 (2019). https://doi.org/10.1016/j.tics.2019.05.006, opinion

36. Johnston, M.: Unification-based multimodal parsing. In: Proceedings of the 36th Annual Meeting on Association for Computational Linguistics - Volume I, Montreal, Quebec, pp. 624–630 (1998)

37. Johnston, M., Bangalore, S.: Finite-state multimodal integration and understanding. Nat. Lang. Eng. **11**(2), 159–187 (2005)

38. Jolly, S.: Understanding body language: Birdwhistell's theory of kinesics. Corp. Commun. Int. J. **5**(3), 133–139 (2000). https://doi.org/10.1108/13563280010377518

39. Kendon, A.: Some relationships between body motion and speech. An analysis of an example. In: Siegman, A.W., Pope, B. (eds.) Studies in Dyadic Communication, chap. 9, pp. 177–210. Pergamon Press, Elmsford (1972)

40. Kendon, A.: Gesticulation and speech: two aspects of the process of utterance. In: Key, M.R. (ed.) The Relationship of Verbal and Nonverbal Communication, pp. 207–227. No. 25 in Contributions to the Sociology of Language, Mouton, The Hague (1980)

41. Kendon, A.: Gesture: Visible Action as Utterance. Cambridge University Press, Cambridge (2004)

42. Kennington, C., Schlangen, D.: Incremental unit networks for multimodal, fine-grained information state representation. In: Proceedings of the 1st Workshop on Multimodal Semantic Representations, pp. 89–94. MMSR, Association for Computational Linguistics, Groningen, Netherlands (Online) (2021). https://aclanthology.org/2021.mmsr-1.8

43. Kiela, D., Bulat, L., Clark, S.: Grounding semantics in olfactory perception. In: Proceedings of the 53rd Annual Meeting of the Association for Computational Linguistics and the 7th International Joint Conference on Natural Language Processing (Volume 2: Short Papers), pp. 231–236. Association for Computational Linguistics, Beijing (2015). https://doi.org/10.3115/v1/P15-2038

44. Kiela, D., Clark, S.: Learning neural audio embeddings for grounding semantics in auditory perception. J. Artif. Intell. Res. **60**, 1003–1030 (2017)

45. Koulidobrova, E., Lillo-Martin, D.: A 'point' of inquiry: the case of the (non-) pronominal IX in ASL. In: Grosz, P., Patel-Grosz, P. (eds.) Impact of Pronominal Form on Interpretation. Studies in Generative Grammar. De Gruyter Mouton, Berlin and Boston (2016)

46. Lascarides, A., Stone, M.: Formal semantics of iconic gesture. In: Schlangen, D., Fernández, R. (eds.) Proceedings of the 10th Workshop on the Semantics and Pragmatics of Dialogue, pp. 64–71. Brandial'06, Universitätsverlag Potsdam, Potsdam (2006)

47. Linell, P.: The Written Language Bias in Linguistics: Its Nature. Origins and Transformations. Advances in Communication and Linguistic Theory. Routledge, New York (2005)
48. Lücking, A.: Modeling co-verbal gesture perception in type theory with records. In: Ganzha, M., Maciaszek, L., Paprzycki, M. (eds.) Proceedings of the 2016 Federated Conference on Computer Science and Information Systems. Annals of Computer Science and Information Systems, vol. 8, pp. 383–392. IEEE (2016). https://doi.org/10.15439/2016F83
49. Lücking, A., Pfeiffer, T.: Framing multimodal technical communication. With focal points in speech-gesture-integration and gaze recognition. In: Mehler, A., Romary, L. (eds.) Handbook of Technical Communication, chap. 18, pp. 591–644. No. 8 in Handbooks of Applied Linguistics, De Gruyter Mouton, Berlin and Boston (2012)
50. Lücking, A., Pfeiffer, T., Rieser, H.: Pointing and reference reconsidered. J. Pragmat. **77**, 56–79 (2015). https://doi.org/10.1016/j.pragma.2014.12.013
51. Lücking, A., Rieser, H., Staudacher, M.: Multi-modal integration for gesture and speech. In: Schlangen, D., Fernández, R. (eds.) Proceedings of the 10th Workshop on the Semantics and Pragmatics of Dialogue, pp. 106–113. Brandial'06, Universitätsverlag Potsdam, Potsdam (2006)
52. McNeill, D.: So you think gestures are nonverbal? Psychol. Rev. **92**(3), 350–371 (1985)
53. McNeill, D.: Hand and Mind - What Gestures Reveal about Thought. Chicago University Press, Chicago (1992)
54. Mehler, A., Lücking, A.: Pathways of alignment between gesture and speech: assessing information transmission in multimodal ensembles. In: Giorgolo, G., Alahverdzhieva, K. (eds.) Proceedings of the International Workshop on Formal and Computational Approaches to Multimodal Communication Under the Auspices of ESSLLI 2012, Opole, Poland, 6–10 August (2012)
55. Oviatt, S.L.: Multimodal interfaces. In: Jacko, J.A., Sears, A. (eds.) The Human-Computer Interaction Handbook, chap. 21, pp. 286–304. L. Erlbaum Associates Inc., Hillsdale (2003)
56. Özkan, E.E., Gurion, T., Hough, J., Healey, P.G., Jamone, L.: Specific hand motion patterns correlate to miscommunications during dyadic conversations. In: 2021 IEEE International Conference on Development and Learning, pp. 1–6. ICDL (2021). https://doi.org/10.1109/ICDL49984.2021.9515613
57. Palmer, M., Gildea, D., Kingsbury, P.: The proposition bank: an annotated corpus of semantic roles. Comput. Linguist. **31**(1), 71–106 (2005). https://doi.org/10.1162/0891201053630264
58. Poggi, I., Pelachaud, C.: Performative faces. Speech Commun. **26**(1), 5–21 (1998). https://doi.org/10.1016/S0167-6393(98)00047-8
59. Pouw, W., Dixon, J.A.: Gesture networks: introducing dynamic time warping and network analysis for the kinematic study of gesture ensembles. Discourse Processes **57**(4), 301–319 (2020). https://doi.org/10.1080/0163853X.2019.1678967
60. Quintilian, M.F.: Institutio oratoria. http://thelatinlibrary.com/quintilian/quintilian.institutio.shtml (1 Century)
61. Rasenberg, M., Özyürek, A., Dingemanse, M.: Alignment in multimodal interaction: an integrative framework. Cognit. Sci. **44**(11), e12911 (2020). https://doi.org/10.1111/cogs.12911
62. Rieser, H.: Pointing in dialogue. In: Proceedings of the Eighth Workshop on the Semantics and Pragmatics of Dialogue, pp. 93–100. Catalog '04, Barcelona (2004)

63. Rieser, H.: On factoring out a gesture typology from the *Bielefeld* speech-and-gesture-alignment corpus (SAGA). In: Kopp, S., Wachsmuth, I. (eds.) GW 2009. LNCS (LNAI), vol. 5934, pp. 47–60. Springer, Heidelberg (2010). https://doi.org/10.1007/978-3-642-12553-9_5

64. Rieser, H., Lawler, I.: Multi-modal meaning - an empirically-founded process algebra approach. Semant. Pragmat. **13**(8), n/a (2020). https://doi.org/10.3765/sp.13.8

65. Schegloff, E.A.: On some gestures' relation to talk. In: Atkinson, J.M., Heritage, J. (eds.) Structures of Social Action. Studies in Conversational Analysis, chap. 12, pp. 266–296. Studies in Emotion and Social Interaction. Cambridge University Press, Cambridge (1984)

66. Schlenker, P.: Gesture projection and cosuppositions. Linguist. Philos. **41**(3), 295–365 (2018). https://doi.org/10.1007/s10988-017-9225-8

67. Vilhjálmsson, H., et al.: The behavior markup language: recent developments and challenges. In: Pelachaud, C., Martin, J.-C., André, E., Chollet, G., Karpouzis, K., Pelé, D. (eds.) IVA 2007. LNCS (LNAI), vol. 4722, pp. 99–111. Springer, Heidelberg (2007). https://doi.org/10.1007/978-3-540-74997-4_10

68. Wang, I., et al.: EGGNOG: a continuous, multi-modal data set of naturally occurring gestures with ground truth labels. In: The 12th IEEE International Conference on Automatic Face Gesture Recognition, pp. 414–421. FG 2017 (2017). https://doi.org/10.1109/FG.2017.145

69. Wohltjen, S., Wheatley, T.: Eye contact marks the rise and fall of shared attention in conversation. Proc. Natl. Acad. Sci. **118**(37), e2106645118 (2021). https://doi.org/10.1073/pnas.2106645118

Towards Efficient Odor Diffusion with an Olfactory Display Using an Electronic Nose

Miguel Garcia-Ruiz[1]([✉]) [ID], Laura Gaytan-Lugo[2] [ID], Pedro Santana Mancilla[3] [ID], and Raul Aquino-Santos[3] [ID]

[1] Algoma University, Sault Ste. Marie, ON P6A 2G4, Canada
miguel.garcia@algomau.ca
[2] University of Colima, 28400 Coquimatlan, Colima, Mexico
laura@ucol.mx
[3] University of Colima, 28040 Colima City, Colima, Mexico
{psantana,aquinor}@ucol.mx

Abstract. Olfactory displays (human-computer interfaces that generate and diffuse odors to a user with a purpose) have been researched to complement or supplement other human sensory modalities, as well as using odors as effective sensory stimuli. We developed an olfactory display with a commonly-used microcontroller board and off-the-shelf components. A challenge in olfactory displays is diffusing the right odor concentration to a user. We developed and applied an electronic nose (e-nose) to determine if an intended odor is not lingering, otherwise our olfactory display will generate an excessive amount of odor. As a proof of concept, we developed a virtual environment that activates our olfactory display when a virtual lemon is visible on it, diffusing a lemon odor if the odor is not already present around the user, detected by our e-nose. Our informal prototype tests shown that it is feasible to use an e-nose to control the odor concentration generated by an olfactory display, thus avoiding an excess of odor that may produce a negative user experience. The Evolutionary Prototyping methodology was very useful for developing our olfactory display system and electronic nose.

Keywords: Olfactory display · Electronic nose · Smell · Odor · Virtual environment · Microcontroller board

1 Introduction

Since the 1990s [1, 2], computer-based olfactory displays have been proposed and researched in a number of domains, with the purpose of complementing and supplementing sensory modalities with the use of the olfactory modality. An olfactory display is a computer system with a human-computer interface that generates, controls and diffuses one or more odors towards a user with a purpose [2, 3], providing an olfactory stimulus to its user. In the nineties, olfactory displays were initially researched as a technology that could incorporate the sense of smell in multimodal virtual reality (VR)

[4]. For example, [5] explored the use of smell in a virtual reality simulation to support firefighters training, exposing them to possible smoke smells. Odors in virtual reality and virtual environments may support training transfer and immersion [6]. Recent research on odors in VR include support for well-being and relaxation (e.g. [7]) and for supporting education and training [8], among other applications. Olfactory display research has been conducted on odor generation and delivery technologies [9], including research about how users perceive and interact with the diffused odors generated by olfactory interfaces. The sense of smell has been underused in human-computer interaction [2], although recent advances in microcontroller boards (small self-contained computers used for controlling sensors and actuators) have facilitated the prototyping of olfactory display applications [8]. For instance, [10] used an ATMega2560 microcontroller to control the fan speed of an olfactory display system.

A major challenge in olfactory displays is removing the odor from the environment after its use. Many odors tend to linger, and in some applications they need to be removed quickly [8], for example, when they are used in video games [11]. Some olfactory display systems include a mechanism for removing the diffused odor when it is no longer used or needed, such as fans and air filters [12]. A way to overcoming this challenge is to produce the right concentration of odor in an olfactory interface to avoid olfactory adaptation or over-saturation [13, 14]. Other problems with lingering odors may occur, such as masking (an odor suppresses another one) and multiplicity (an odor enhances another one) [9]. In this paper, we describe a method to produce a controlled odor diffusion in an olfactory display system using an electronic nose, or e-nose. An e-nose is an electronic sensing system that detects one or more specific odors, and their concentration in the environment [15]. An e-nose can be used to analyze one or more specific gases or volatile organic compounds (VOCs) and their concentration in the air [16, 17]. This can be useful to avoid an excess of odor production that may affect the user's odor perception. The e-nose analyzes the air surrounding the user and the olfactory display generates a particular odor if that odor is not lingering around the user. There is previous research on olfactory display systems using e-noses. [18] successfully used an e-nose for evaluating the accuracy of odor concentration diffused by an olfactory display. [2] and [9] describe a number of techniques for storing, generating and diffusing odors in olfactory displays. Scented essential oils have been used in olfactory displays [19], where the odors can be diffused towards the user with the help of a fan [20].

2 Statement of the Objective

The objective of this paper is to demonstrate the use of an e-nose for controlling the odor diffusion of an olfactory display that is activated by a virtual environment. In our prototype, the e-nose analyzes the air surrounding the user and the olfactory display generates a particular odor if that odor is not lingering around the user, thus avoiding an excess of odor production that may affect the user's odor perception.

3 Our Olfactory Display System + Electronic Nose Prototype

We describe in this section the technical aspects of our olfactory display and our e-nose. An Arduino Uno [21] microcontroller board was used for controlling a computer fan and an odor generator (an off-the-shelf Honeywell Mini Mist humidifier [22]), containing an essential oil reservoir. The microcontroller board also controls a computer fan that suctions air through a filter that we made with an activated carbon sheet. The frame holding the air filter was 3D printed to give it robustness. Another Arduino Uno microcontroller board obtains data from a Keyestudio SEN-CCS811 odor sensor module [23]. This microcontroller board and the sensor module makes up the e-nose. The SEN-CCS811 sensor module measures the concentration of total volatile organic compounds (TVOC) in the environment. TVOCs are human-made organic chemicals that evaporate at room temperature, used in many household products such as aromatizers and essential oils [24], although VOCS are also present in nature [25]. The SEN-CCS811 odor sensor module used in our prototype can detect TVOC concentrations from 0 to 32,768 parts per billion (PPB). We used in our olfactory display the Ellia 100% pure lemon (Citrus Limon) essential oil, developed by Homedics [26], by placing 10 drops of the essential oil in the humidifier's reservoir. After a number of trials and as part of the prototyping process, we found that this number of drops was optimal for its diffusion using the humidifier. Lemon odors have been successfully used in olfactory displays, providing an effective olfactory sensory stimulus [27].

Figure 1 shows the main components of our designed olfactory display system and our e-nose. We decided to use the Arduino Uno microcontroller board because it is easy to program and to interface with, and is powerful enough to control the PC fans, the odor sensor module and the odor generator. We used a special electronic circuit with transistors and a 12v external power source for controlling the fans. The microcontroller board interfaces through a USB cable with a MacBook Pro laptop computer with 16 GB

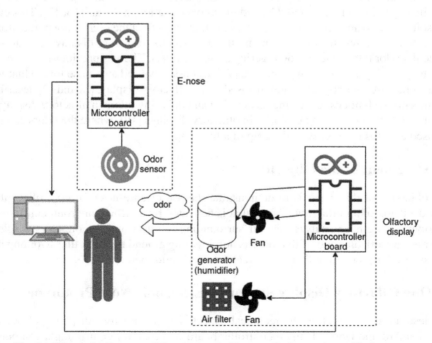

Fig. 1. Schematic diagram of the proposed olfactory display system with the e-nose.

of RAM, containing the M1 microprocessor. This computer is used to read data from the e-nose to activate the humidifier and fans, and to run a 3D virtual environment created as a proof of concept for testing the olfactory display system and the electronic nose.

The Honeywell humidifier that we selected for our olfactory display is low-cost and easy to operate, facilitating our prototype development. The Ellia lemon essential oil that we used in our olfactory display is easily available from many department stores and online distributors, as well as the activated carbon sheet used for the air filter.

The algorithm that runs on the laptop computer for activating the olfactory display and the e-nose is listed as follows:

1. If the virtual lemon is visualized on the computer screen, do the following:

   1a. Read the odor sensor data.
   1b. If the lemon odor is detected in the environment, do the following:

       1b.1 Do not activate the olfactory display.
       1b.2 Activate the air filter.

2. If the lemon odor is not detected in the environment do the following:

   2a. Activate the olfactory display (fan + humidifier) for some seconds.
   2b. Activate the air filter.

3. Go to step 1.

We coded the algorithm in a Python program, which access the Arduino microcontroller board through a laptop's USB port. In order to run the virtual environment more efficiently, all the e-nose data acquisition and processing is done on one of the microcontroller boards to free up computational processing power from the laptop computer.

Fig. 2. The complete olfactory display + electronic nose set up.

We developed and improved the olfactory display and the e-nose following an adaptation of the Evolutionary Prototyping methodology [28]. Figure 2 shows our prototype containing the olfactory display and the electronic nose.

As Fig. 2 shows, A solid-state relay was used for turning the humidifier on and off with one of the Arduino Uno microcontroller boards. The PC fan (also controlled by the microcontroller board) placed on top the humidifier diffused the odor towards the user.

4 The 3D Virtual Environment

We developed a 3D virtual environment made in Godot [29, 30], a popular video game engine. A Godot script from the virtual environment sends a digital signal to the Python program. This program activates the microcontroller board that controls the humidifier and the fan when a virtual lemon is displayed on the center of the computer screen, generating and diffusing the lemon odor by turning on the humidifier containing the essential oil. Figure 2 shows the virtual environment that we developed for our proof of concept, running on the laptop computer. The lemon 3D model that is displayed on the virtual environment was downloaded from [31]. We also created and displayed more than 200 virtual crates in the virtual environment to give the illusion of perspective and to show 3D models other than the virtual lemon to deactivate the olfactory display when the virtual crates were displayed. The crates were procedurally generated in Godot and placed randomly in the virtual environment.

5 Preliminary Results

We informally tested the virtual environment, the olfactory display and the electronic nose a number of times, navigating in the virtual environment in 3D using the computer's arrow keys. As expected, our olfactory display was activated every time the virtual lemon appeared at the center of the computer screen, while we captured the electronic nose data

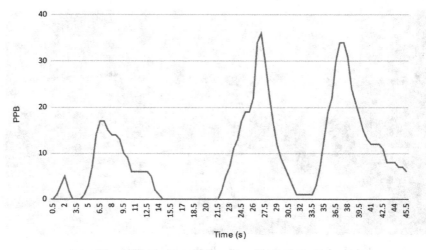

Fig. 3. Data obtained from the electronic nose.

for 45.5 s. Figure 3 shows the data that we sampled from the SEN-CCS811 odor sensor module once every 0.5 s. According to the sensor manufacturer, this is the minimum time required for reading data from the odor sensor. The sensor data was obtained through the Arduino IDE's Serial Monitor.

As Fig. 3 shows, the valleys are the periods where the virtual lemon was not displayed on the screen, and no lemon odor was present or it was barely present in the environment, when the sensor read very low odor concentrations from the environment. In addition, the low PPB readings indicated that the air filter was operating effectively during those periods. The peaks happened during the olfactory display activation, where two of them are values greater than 30 PPB. During the peaks, the lemon odor was distinctive. We will need to conduct further user studies to confirm this. There is a small peak at the beginning of the readings. We believe that it happened because the sensor required an initial self-calibration adjustment, according to the sensor module's specifications [23]. We found in a number of trials that TVOC concentrations of the lemon odor of less than 20 PPB were barely noticeable, but we will need to confirm that in further user testing. We then set up the program for stopping the olfactory display when the electronic nose obtained values of 20 PPB or less. A video recording showcasing the olfactory display, the electronic nose data and the virtual environment is shown in [32].

6 Conclusions

This paper presented an olfactory display system and an e-nose, with the objective of diffusing the right amount of odor to a user, avoiding an excess of odor production in the **user's** environment that may affect user's odor perception. Both the olfactory display and the e-nose were interfaced to a laptop computer using microcontroller boards. A 3D virtual environment running on the laptop computer activated the olfactory display system when a 3D model of a lemon was displayed on the screen. The Evolutionary Prototyping methodology was very useful for developing our olfactory display system and our e-nose.

Our paper demonstrated the application of easy-to-use electronic components, and a low-cost yet capable microcontroller board for developing a rapid prototype of an olfactory display and an e-nose. In addition, the Godot game engine facilitated the virtual environment prototyping. We found that the SEN-CCS811 odor sensor module was effective for measuring the concentration of the essential oil odor in the environment. Our informal prototype tests shown that it is technically possible to use an e-nose to measure the odor concentration generated by an olfactory display, thus avoiding generating an excess of odor that may produce a negative user experience. Further user studies are needed to corroborate this.

For future work, we will adapt the virtual environment made in Godot to run on a virtual reality headset. We are planning to send the activation data from the virtual reality environment to the microcontroller board controlling our olfactory display using the Message Queuing Telemetry Transport MQTT protocol [33]. In addition, we plan to develop and test an array of two or more VOC odor sensors connected to the virtual environment and the olfactory display. The array should provide more sensor data accuracy [34], since individual e-noses performance and data results may have false or unreliable odor classifications, provided that an optimal classification pattern algorithm is applied to them. The array may be needed because sensors sometimes present an inherent problem of sensor signal drift and other technical issues. In addition, environmental factors such as humidity and temperature may affect sensor's performance [35]. These problems should be minimized by getting data from an array of sensors, where one or more sensors will compensate for any affected odor sensor.

References

1. Kaye, J.N.: Symbolic olfactory display (2001). https://dspace.mit.edu/handle/1721.1/16788
2. Kaye, J.: "Jofish": making scents: aromatic output for HCI. Interactions. **11**, 48–61 (2004). https://doi.org/10.1145/962342.964333
3. Yanagida, Y., Tomono, A.: Basics for Olfactory Display. In: Human Olfactory Displays and Interfaces: Odor Sensing and Presentation. pp. 60–85. IGI Global, Hershey (2013). https://doi.org/10.4018/978-1-4666-2521-1.ch003
4. Barfield, W., Danas, E.: Comments on the use of olfactory displays for virtual environments. Presence: Teleoper. Virtual Environ. **5**, 109–121 (1996). https://doi.org/10.1162/pres.1996.5.1.109
5. Cater, J.P.: Smell/taste: odors in reality. In: Proceedings of IEEE International Conference on Systems, Man and Cybernetics. p. 1781 vols.2-. IEEE (1994). https://doi.org/10.1109/ICSMC.1994.400108
6. Howell, M.J., Herrera, N.S., Moore, A.G., McMahan, R.P.: A reproducible olfactory display for exploring olfaction in immersive media experiences. Multimedia Tools Appl. **75**(20), 12311–12330 (2015). https://doi.org/10.1007/s11042-015-2971-0
7. Serrano, B., Baños, R.M., Botella, C.: Virtual reality and stimulation of touch and smell for inducing relaxation: a randomized controlled trial. Comput. Hum. Behav. **55**, 1–8 (2016). https://doi.org/10.1016/j.chb.2015.08.007
8. Garcia-Ruiz, M.A., Kapralos, B., Rebolledo-Mendez, G.: An overview of olfactory displays in education and training. MTI. **5**, 64 (2021). https://doi.org/10.3390/mti5100064
9. Yanagida, Y.: A survey of olfactory displays: making and delivering scents. In: Presented at the Sensors, Taipei, Taiwan (2012)
10. Batch, A., Patnaik, B., Akazue, M., Elmqvist, N.: Scents and sensibility: evaluating information olfactation. In: Proceedings of the 2020 CHI Conference on Human Factors in Computing Systems. pp. 1–14. Association for Computing Machinery, New York, NY, USA (2020)
11. Tsaramirsis, G., Papoutsidakis, M., Derbali, M., Khan, F.Q., Michailidis, F.: Towards smart gaming olfactory displays. Sensors **20**, 1002 (2020). https://doi.org/10.3390/s20041002
12. Kato, S., Nakamoto, T.: Wearable olfactory display with less residual odor. In: 2019 IEEE International Symposium on Olfaction and Electronic Nose (ISOEN), pp. 1–3 (2019). https://doi.org/10.1109/ISOEN.2019.8823231
13. Sugimoto, S., Okada, K.: Olfactory display based on ink jet printer mechanism and its presentation techniques. In: Human Olfactory Displays and Interfaces: Odor Sensing and Presentation, pp. 401–414. IGI Global, Hershey (2013). https://doi.org/10.4018/978-1-4666-2521-1.ch020
14. Kadowaki, A., Sato, J., Bannai, Y., Okada, K.: Presentation technique of scent to avoid olfactory adaptation. In: 17th International Conference on Artificial Reality and Telexistence (ICAT 2007), pp. 97–104 (2007). https://doi.org/10.1109/ICAT.2007.8
15. Davide, F., Holmberg, M., Lundstrm, I.: Virtual olfactory interfaces: electronic noses and olfactory displays. In: Communications Through Virtual Technology: Identity, Community and Technology in the Internet Age, Amsterdam, The Netherlands, pp. 193–220. IOS Press (2004)

16. Kauer, J.S., White, J.: Electronic Nose. In: Squire, L.R. (ed.) Encyclopedia of Neuroscience, pp. 871–877. Academic Press, Oxford (2009). https://doi.org/10.1016/B978-008045046-9.01694-6

17. Al-Dayyeni, W.S., et al.: A review on electronic nose: coherent taxonomy, classification, motivations, challenges, recommendations and datasets. IEEE Access **9**, 88535–88551 (2021). https://doi.org/10.1109/ACCESS.2021.3090165

18. Hu, Y.-Y., et al.: aBio: active bi-olfactory display using subwoofers for virtual reality. In: Proceedings of the 29th ACM International Conference on Multimedia. pp. 2065–2073. Association for Computing Machinery, New York (2021)

19. Covington, J.A., Agbroko, S.O., Tiele, A.: Development of a portable, multichannel olfactory display transducer. IEEE Sens. J. **18**, 4969–4974 (2018). https://doi.org/10.1109/JSEN.2018.2832284

20. Herrera, N.S., McMahan, R.P.: Development of a simple and low-cost olfactory display for immersive media experiences. In: Proceedings of the 2nd ACM International Workshop on Immersive Media Experiences, pp. 1–6. Association for Computing Machinery, New York (2014). https://doi.org/10.1145/2660579.2660584

21. UNO R3 | Arduino Documentation. https://docs.arduino.cc/hardware/uno-rev3. Accessed 20 May 2022

22. Mini Cool Mist Humidifier. https://www.honeywellpluggedin.com/mini-cool-mist-humidifier-hul525. Accessed 20 May 2022

23. KS0457 keyestudio CCS811 Carbon Dioxide Air Quality Sensor - Keyestudio Wiki. https://wiki.keyestudio.com/KS0457_keyestudio_CCS811_Carbon_Dioxide_Air_Quality_Sensor. Accessed 23 Mar 2022

24. Nematollahi, N., Weinberg, J.L., Flattery, J., Goodman, N., Kolev, S.D., Steinemann, A.: Volatile chemical emissions from essential oils with therapeutic claims. Air Qual. Atmos. Health **14**(3), 365–369 (2020). https://doi.org/10.1007/s11869-020-00941-4

25. Vivaldo, G., Masi, E., Taiti, C., Caldarelli, G., Mancuso, S.: The network of plants volatile organic compounds. Sci. Rep. **7**, 11050 (2017). https://doi.org/10.1038/s41598-017-10975-x

26. Ellia Lemon Essential Oil. https://www.homedics.ca/lemon-essential-oil/. Accessed 20 May 2022

27. Berna, A.: Metal oxide sensors for electronic noses and their application to food analysis. Sensors. **10**, 3882–3910 (2010). https://doi.org/10.3390/s100403882

28. Garcia-Ruiz, M., Santana, P.: Design, evaluation and impact of educational olfactory interfaces. In: 19th Americas Conference on Information Systems, AMCIS 2013 - Hyperconnected World: Anything, Anywhere, Anytime, pp. 1053–1059. AMCIS, Chicago (2013)

29. Godot Engine - Free and open source 2D and 3D game engine. https://godotengine.org/. Accessed 28 Mar 2022

30. Dhule, M.: Getting started with Godot. In: Dhule, M. (ed.) Beginning Game Development with Godot: Learn to Create and Publish Your First 2D Platform Game, pp. 17–33. Apress, Berkeley (2022). https://doi.org/10.1007/978-1-4842-7455-2_2

31. Lemon Free 3D Model - .blend - Free3D. https://free3d.com/3d-model/lemon-72357.html. Accessed 20 May 2022

32. Miguel Garcia-Ruiz: New video by Miguel Garcia. https://photos.google.com/share/AF1QipOE3A_H2GWV644ZksnaYD8sHDWQvQBM2oywd6gIvRRmBb9LXp6PeznvDxsKC-SBBQ?key=Q2RTdmozbTdDQmpncXQzN2R0bXZpUGo5YWNMNWln. Accessed 21 Apr 2022

33. Al Enany, M.O., Harb, H.M., Attiya, G.: A comparative analysis of MQTT and IoT application protocols. In: 2021 International Conference on Electronic Engineering (ICEEM), pp. 1–6 (2021). https://doi.org/10.1109/ICEEM52022.2021.9480384

34. He, J., Xu, L., Wang, P., Wang, Q.: A high precise E-nose for daily indoor air quality monitoring in living environment. Integration **58**, 286–294 (2017). https://doi.org/10.1016/j.vlsi.2016.12.010
35. Goodner, K.L., Dreher, J.G., Rouseff, R.L.: The dangers of creating false classifications due to noise in electronic nose and similar multivariate analyses. Sens. Actuators, B Chem. **80**, 261–266 (2001). https://doi.org/10.1016/S0925-4005(01)00917-0

Rendering Personalized Real-Time Expressions While Speaking Under a Mask

Akira Hashimoto[1], Jun-Li Lu[1,2]([✉]), and Yoichi Ochiai[1,2]

[1] Research and Development Center for Digital Nature, University of Tsukuba, Tsukuba, Japan
[2] Faculty of Library, Information and Media Science, University of Tsukuba, Tsukuba, Japan
jllu@slis.tsukuba.ac.jp

Abstract. During COVID-19, people often wear masks in daily activities or communication. To solve the problem of generating faces with expressions under masks, we propose a framework of methods, including detecting the shape or locations of masked faces, generating the facial expressions under masks. Further, due to synthesizing quality facial expressions, we propose to optimize the merging of sub-results with useful face information such as key points of face. Further, we propose a framework for customization or personalization of user-preferring AI-generation results. We showed the system capable of running real-time and discussed the development in multiple aspects of research, interface, and applications.

Keywords: Generation of faces with expressions · Frameworks of methods · Interfaces · Customization

1 Introduction

During COVID-19, people often wear masks in daily activities or communication. To improve the difficulties or increase the perception of users on people who wears mask during the communication of activities, we propose a framework or methods to resolve the problems by providing the AI-rendering results of faces with expressions when users speak under mask. The benefits, applications, or researches related to this research can be valuable in multiple aspects, including the communication related, e.g., online meeting, meeting under wearing masks, the algorithms or methods related to generation, recognition, or detection of facial image or spoken voices under masks.

To solve the problem of generating faces with expressions under masks, we propose a framework consisting of three main methods. First, we detect the shape or locations of mask on the masked face, especially towards multiple faces, masks, or spoken behaviors under masks. Second, we generate the facial expressions under masks. Specifically, this involves the correlation between the facial

M. Kurosu et al. (Eds.): HCII 2022, LNCS 13519, pp. 57–66, 2022.
https://doi.org/10.1007/978-3-031-17618-0_5

expression and the spoken voices of conversation for users. Further, due to the quality of synthesizing facial expressions under masks, we also utilize additional and critical information of face, including the detection of landmark points of face, and models of faces or expressions, or considering the factors of multiple users.

To further improve the quality of AI-generation results or the application possibility, we propose a framework for customization or personalization. In customizing AI results with user preference, first, the definition or description of data including faces, masks, voices of conversation, or user-related factors are flexible and can be defined by users or situations. Further, with these above data and the results of AI-generation, the modification or novel understandings could be applied by the annotation of users. In rebuilding the user-preferring AI generation results, we apply self-supervised or unsupervised machine learning to train or retrain the models. Specifically, we apply contrastive learning on the face image or spoken voices of conversations to improve and find suitable features of facial image or spoken voices under certain users or situations.

In the current experimental results, we implemented the proposed system by referencing the latest methods or models. In our experiments, we found that the generation quality could be affected by the appearance of users or masks. Further, the suitable merging method of multiple sub-results of detected mask shapes, generated facial expressions, or key locations of face, was critical for the quality generation of users. With the proposed frameworks of facial expressions under masks, the customization or personalization, the related applications, interfaces, or data, resolving the appearance of masked faces might be useful or valuable in multiple directions of research, communication, or applications.

2   Related Work

2.1   GAN-Based Rendering and the Limitations

As the current AI drawing capabilities might be limited on specific parameters or usages, we aim to create diverse AI-generated visual contents from the unlimited and interesting expressions, which can contribute or improve on valuable applications such as information visualization of user's written documents, creation tools for visual arts, novel ways of accessible communication between normal and disabilities, and even used to increase marketing effect by meaningful generated visual contents. Further, the effective customization or personalization on huge and various text-image data by advanced self-supervised learning will be studied since the current literature may be limited. We compare our proposals or modeling for generating flexible or diverse visual expressions from textual expressions, with limitation of existing GAN-based generation of rendering [1, 7, 12, 17, 28, 30], and further showing applications or interfaces of human or social factors.

2.2   Customization or Personalization by Machine Learning

To customize or personalize the rendering results of face with expressions, there are some aspects of methodologies as follows. One aspect is to provide flexible or

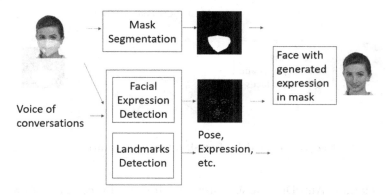

Fig. 1. System: Generating the faces with possible expressions when under the masked faces.

selective parameters for users to select and generate their preferring results. In the system with models, the used data or records of AI-generation of users can be utilized to rebuilt the intelligence of the system towards personalized usage or preferring AI results. Furthermore, the algorithms or methods in machine learning are useful in assisting training or retraining the system with accuracy or efficiency.

2.3   Multicultural and Diverse Face Masks During COVID-19

The coronavirus pandemic has significantly changed the cultures of masks in the world. Therefore, we survey multicultural masks and compare masks on features, functionality, design, and entertainment, especially focusing on the varying points between before and during COVID-19 pandemic. In our work, knowing the design patterns of various masks can be useful in brining ideas of mask design and fabrication. For example, in Asia, Japan people usually wear mask prevent hay fever and influenza. In design of masks, there might be few variations of mask in the market, but after Corona, people are seem to wear not only normal masks but also masks of various colors or patterns. Another example, people wear mask for healthy concerns, such as protecting themself from exhaust fumes or sunburn, such as in Taiwan. Further, wearing mask may be concerned with critical issues. For example, in some regions of Europe, such as Austria, it is prohibited to cover your face to the extent that cannot be recognizable in public institutions. Another different cultures or impression in Europe or United States are that in some cases wearing a mask is regarded as non-cool, a sign of weakness or ill persons. Overall, mask cultures has changed and the attention or importance of masks from people has significantly increased, which is a motivation that we need to investigate the changes of mask cultures for designing mask used during COVID-19.For AI rendering, applying machine learning to generate facial or related images [3, 5, 6, 8, 10, 13–15, 20, 23, 24, 27] by learning the characteristics of a specific clothing brand, and then created patterns from the images

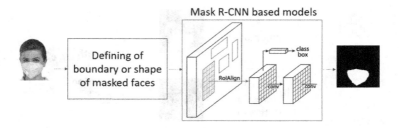

Fig. 2. The models of masked face segmentation.

to create clothes. AutoDraw assists users in drawing by combing drawings of artists with machine learning. These technologies of fabrication and machine assisted rendering bring powerful tools for novel mask design.

3   Generating Facial Expressions from Masked Faces

In Fig. 1, we show the system of generating facial expressions of a user when under the masked faces. There are multiple components of methodologies in the system, which are mask segmentation, facial expressions detection, landmarks detection, and generation of face with expressions. Further, to customize or personalize the generation results, we propose to the components of collecting personal data or data annotation and the methods of retraining models by self-supervised or unsupervised learning. In retraining models, we utilize the contrastive learning approaches to improve the estimation results or accuracy towards the preference or interest of the users.

3.1   Masked Face Segmentation

To locate the shape or positions of the masked part of a face, we segment the shape of a masked face. To achieve the accurate segmentation, we utilize the method, Mask R-CNN based models, which are proved to be capable in accurate detection in multiple experiments. Further, to locate the shape of masked faces, we define the shape of masked faces and prepare the training dataset. Specifically, we define which kinds of masks should be detected by using the training dataset. In the method of Fig. 2, given an image of a face with mask, the proposed Mask R-CNN based models detects the shape of the mask in the face.

$$f' = Definition\ of\ mask\ shape(f),$$
$$f_{mask} = Mask\ RCNN\ based\ model(f').$$

3.2   Facial Expression Generation

We generate the expressions of a face while the user is speaking under the masked face, In Fig. 3, we utilize the Encoder-Decoder based models to generate the facial

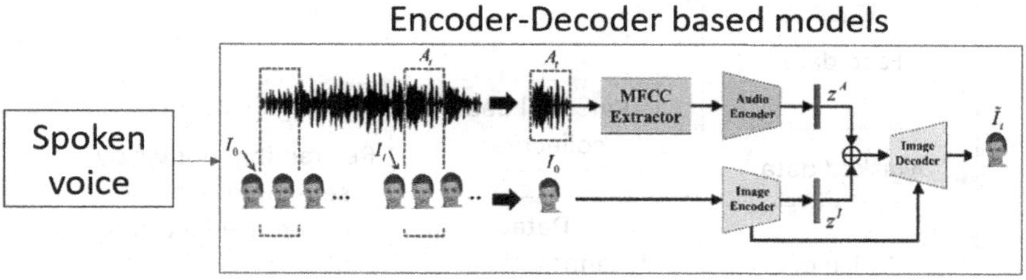

Encoder-Decoder based models

Fig. 3. The models of facial expression generation.

expressions by given a sequence of spoken voices. In the modeling, we utilize the sequence of the pairs of spoken voices and face images as the training data to generate the facial expressions.Specifically, in the models of Fig. 3, the given spoken voices and facial images are encoded, and thus these encoded features are used to generate the facial expressions by decoder.

$$f'_t = Decoder(Encoder(f_t) \oplus Encoder(v_t)),$$

where the generated face f'_t is decoded by the encoded feature of face f_t and the encoded feature of spoken voice v_t.

3.3 Landmarks Detection Within Face

To accurately synthesizing the generated face with multiple sub-results, by using the located key points of a face, we apply the method of landmark detection in the face, and detect and get the detected landmark points.

$$P = Landmark\ points\ detection(f),$$

where P is a set of detected landmark points in the face f.

3.4 Generating Faces with Expressions for Masked Faces

With multiple sub-results, we generate the face with expression while speaking under mask. As shown in Fig. 1, the generated face is combined by multiple sub-results including the segmented mask, the generated facial expressions, and the detected landmark points of face. Note that we also build and train neural networks that generate the merged face with expressions.

4 Customizing or Personalizing Facial Expressions Under Masked Faces

Further, to customize the rendering results with personalized facial expressions, we propose a framework describing the three main components for customizing the personalized results. In the framework of Fig. 4, first, we consider that

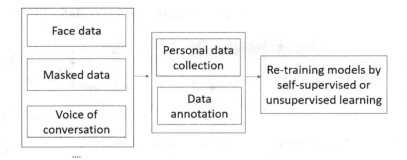

Fig. 4. The framework of customizing the generation of faces with expressions including definition and annotation of data, interfaces, and retraining methods.

the dataset or definition of faces, masked faces, masks, or the voice of conversation, can be re-defined or annotated based on personal usage situation or other purposes. Second, in the context of application, we require interfaces where user's input parameters are needed or provided. That is, users can have multiple parameters to input to fit personal preferential results, e.g., the level of changing of facial expressions. Third, given the data of multiple parameters, we require the method or models that can learn the customized generation results of facial expressions. Therefore, we utilize the machine learning of self-supervised or unsupervised approaches to re-train the proposed neural network models.

4.1   Contrastive Learning

In retraining models by using self-supervised or unsupervised learning, we utilize the approaches of contrastive learning [4,9,11,16,18,19,21], which have been showed to be effective in multiple contexts or models or types of data. The face images or spoken voices of conversation of users are expected to be improved. In Fig. 5, in the contrastive learning approaches, the variability or diversity of face images are augmented, and the features of augmented face images are encoded by CNN models and trained by the losses of contrastive learning. Thus, the improved features of face images are used in the existing models to generate more customized or diverse results. Similarly, the spoken voices of conversations will be augmented under the similar process or models as in the face images. For the computation of loss, a common loss function for computation of contrastive loss, which is Normalized Temperature-scaled Cross Entropy Loss (NT-Xent) [25].

$$l_{i,j} = -log \frac{exp(sim(z_i, z_j)/\tau)}{\sum_{k=1}^{2N} 1_{k \neq i} exp(sim(z_i, z_k)/\tau)}.$$

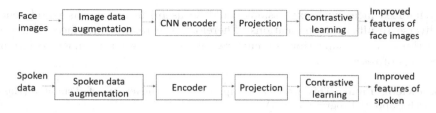

Fig. 5. Contrastive learning on face images and spoken voices of conversations for improving the features of face images or spoken voices.

Fig. 6. Some experimental results of real-time processing.

5   Experimental Results, Discussions, and Conclusions

We showed the implementation of the system, the used data, current experimental results, and the related analysis or discussion as follows. In the reference of implementation, For the segmentation of face masks, we used a latest model that was Mask RCNN based models [29]. For the generation of faces, we used some generation methods including the face generation using key points of face [26]. For the detection of landmark points in face, we referenced the methods [2,22]. About the data or training data used in the work, we used some dataset of face with masks and applied the annotation by ourself or the way of the crowdsourcing (Fig. 6).

In the current experimental results, we showed that our models can be run in real-time to detect the mask, located the mask shapes, and replaced with the specified rendering with accuracy and efficiency. In the detection of masked faces, we observed that the appearance of users might be some factors affecting the performance. E.g., some mask similar appearance in face could be recognized as parts of a mask. Thus, we applied additional information such as locations or relative positions of face or the key parts of face (e.g., mouth, ear, eye). For the generation of faces, we applied the GAN-based models and observed that the synthesis of facial expressions were not quality as expected or natural for the user. Therefore, we applied some merging computations by using other information related to human face or their expressions, e.g., the averages or models of typical faces or expressions, the detected locations of the parts of faces, and the recognized materials of the user's faces.

From the current experimental results, we discussed some ongoing works and future directions of research as follows. For generating quality facial expressions under mask, the suitable merging of the sub-results from detected mask shapes, key points of face, or generated faces or expressions, was critical and might need optimization for merging. For the related research directions or works, as described in customization or personalization of this work, the customization of

AI-generated faces with expressions could be useful in making user-preference or diverse results and applications. Therefore, the related interfaces, dataset, algorithms of customization, or cultures of users or wearing mask, could be directions of research.

Acknowledgement. This work was supported by University of Tsukuba (Basic Research Support Program Type A).

References

1. Cherepkov, A., Voynov, A., Babenko, A.: Navigating the GAN parameter space for semantic image editing. In: IEEE Conference on Computer Vision and Pattern Recognition, CVPR 2021, virtual, June 19–25, pp. 3671–3680. Computer Vision Foundation / IEEE (2021)
2. Eskimez, S.E., Maddox, R.K., Xu, C., Duan, Z.: Noise-resilient training method for face landmark generation from speech. IEEE ACM Trans. Audio Speech Lang. Process. **28**, 27–38 (2020)
3. Glowacka, N., Ruminski, J.: Face with mask detection in thermal images using deep neural networks. Sensors **21**(19), 6387 (2021)
4. He, H., Zha, K., Katabi, D.: Indiscriminate poisoning attacks on unsupervised contrastive learning. CoRR abs/2202.11202 (2022)
5. Hemathilaka, S., Aponso, A.: A comprehensive study on occlusion invariant face recognition under face mask occlusion. CoRR abs/2201.09089 (2022)
6. Hong, J.H., et al: A 3D model-based approach for fitting masks to faces in the wild. CoRR abs/2103.00803 (2021)
7. Hong, Y., Niu, L., Zhang, J., Zhao, W., Fu, C., Zhang, L.: F2GAN: fusing-and-filling GAN for few-shot image generation. In: Chen, C.W., Cucchiara, R., Hua, X., Qi, G., Ricci, E., Zhang, Z., Zimmermann, R. (eds.) MM '20: The 28th ACM International Conference on Multimedia, Virtual Event / Seattle, WA, USA, October 12–16, pp. 2535–2543. ACM (2020)
8. Khamlae, P., Sookhanaphibarn, K., Choensawat, W.: An application of deep-learning techniques to face mask detection during the COVID-19 pandemic. In: 3rd IEEE Global Conference on Life Sciences and Technologies, LifeTech 2021, Nara, Japan, March 9–11, pp. 298–299. IEEE (2021)
9. Kim, D.H., Song, B.C.: Contrastive adversarial learning for person independent facial emotion recognition. In: Thirty-Fifth AAAI Conference on Artificial Intelligence, AAAI 2021, Thirty-Third Conference on Innovative Applications of Artificial Intelligence, IAAI 2021, The Eleventh Symposium on Educational Advances in Artificial Intelligence, EAAI 2021, Virtual Event, February 2–9, pp. 5948–5956. AAAI Press (2021)
10. Koklu, M., Cinar, I., Taspinar, Y.S.: CNN-based bi-directional and directional long-short term memory network for determination of face mask. Biomed. Signal Process. Control. 71(Part), 103216 (2022)
11. Lee, T., Yoo, S.: Augmenting few-shot learning with supervised contrastive learning. IEEE Access **9**, 61466–61474 (2021)

12. Liu, D., Nabail, M., Hertzmann, A., Kalogerakis, E.: Neural contours: Learning to draw lines from 3d shapes. In: 2020 IEEE/CVF Conference on Computer Vision and Pattern Recognition, CVPR 2020, Seattle, WA, USA, June 13–19, pp. 5427–5435. Computer Vision Foundation / IEEE (2020)
13. Mallol-Ragolta, A., Liu, S., Schuller, B.W.: The filtering effect of face masks in their detection from speech. In: 43rd Annual International Conference of the IEEE Engineering in Medicine & Biology Society, EMBC 2021, Mexico, November 1–5, pp. 2079–2082. IEEE (2021)
14. Mare, T., et al.: A realistic approach to generate masked faces applied on two novel masked face recognition data sets. CoRR abs/2109.01745 (2021)
15. Martínez-Díaz, Y., Méndez-Vázquez, H., Luevano, L.S., Nicolás-Díaz, M., Chang, L., González-Mendoza, M.: Towards accurate and lightweight masked face recognition: an experimental evaluation. IEEE Access **10**, 7341–7353 (2022)
16. Peng, X., Wang, K., Zhu, Z., You, Y.: Crafting better contrastive views for siamese representation learning. CoRR abs/2202.03278 (2022)
17. Richardson, E., et al.: Encoding in style: A stylegan encoder for image-to-image translation. In: IEEE Conference on Computer Vision and Pattern Recognition, CVPR 2021, virtual, June 19–25, pp. 2287–2296. Computer Vision Foundation / IEEE (2021)
18. Roy, S., Etemad, A.: Spatiotemporal contrastive learning of facial expressions in videos. In: 9th International Conference on Affective Computing and Intelligent Interaction, ACII 2021, Nara, Japan, September 28 - Oct. 1, pp. 1–8. IEEE (2021)
19. Soni, P.N., Shi, S., Sriram, P.R., Ng, A.Y., Rajpurkar, P.: Contrastive learning of heart and lung sounds for label-efficient diagnosis. Patterns **3**(1), 100400 (2022)
20. Vadlapati, J., S, S.V., Varghese, E.: Facial recognition using the opencv libraries of python for the pictures of human faces wearing face masks during the COVID-19 pandemic. In: 12th International Conference on Computing Communication and Networking Technologies, ICCCNT 2021, Kharagpur, India, July 6–8, 2021. pp. 1–5. IEEE (2021)
21. Wang, H., Xiao, R., Li, Y., Feng, L., Niu, G., Chen, G., Zhao, J.: Pico: Contrastive label disambiguation for partial label learning. CoRR abs/2201.08984 (2022)
22. Wang, J., et al.: Deep high-resolution representation learning for visual recognition. IEEE Trans. Pattern Anal. Mach. Intell. **43**(10), 3349–3364 (2021)
23. Wang, Z., et al.: Masked face recognition dataset and application. CoRR abs/2003.09093 (2020)
24. Wei, Y., et al.: MagGAN: high-resolution face attribute editing with mask-guided generative adversarial network. In: Ishikawa, H., Liu, C.-L., Pajdla, T., Shi, J. (eds.) ACCV 2020. LNCS, vol. 12625, pp. 661–678. Springer, Cham (2021). https://doi.org/10.1007/978-3-030-69538-5_40
25. Weng, L., Elsawah, A.M., Fang, K.: Cross-entropy loss for recommending efficient fold-over technique. J. Syst. Sci. Complex. **34**(1), 402–439 (2021)
26. Yang, Y., Guo, X.: Generative landmark guided face inpainting. In: Peng, Y., Liu, Q., Lu, H., Sun, Z., Liu, C., Chen, X., Zha, H., Yang, J. (eds.) PRCV 2020. LNCS, vol. 12305, pp. 14–26. Springer, Cham (2020). https://doi.org/10.1007/978-3-030-60633-6_2
27. Yao, C., et al.: rPPG-based spoofing detection for face mask attack using efficientnet on weighted spatial-temporal representation. In: 2021 IEEE International Conference on Image Processing, ICIP 2021, Anchorage, AK, USA, September 19–22, pp. 3872–3876. IEEE (2021)
28. Ye, M., Shen, J., Lin, G., Xiang, T., Shao, L., Hoi, S.C.H.: Deep learning for person re-identification: A survey and outlook. CoRR abs/2001.04193 (2020)

29. Yu, C., Gao, C., Wang, J., Yu, G., Shen, C., Sang, N.: Bisenet V2: bilateral network with guided aggregation for real-time semantic segmentation. Int. J. Comput. Vis. **129**(11), 3051–3068 (2021)
30. Zheng, Z., Zheng, L., Yang, Y.: Unlabeled samples generated by GAN improve the person re-identification baseline in vitro. In: IEEE International Conference on Computer Vision, ICCV 2017, Venice, Italy, October 22–29, pp. 3774–3782. IEEE Computer Society (2017)

Applying Generative Adversarial Networks and Vision Transformers in Speech Emotion Recognition

Panikos Heracleous[(⊠)], Satoru Fukayama, Jun Ogata, and Yasser Mohammad

National Institute of Advanced Industrial Science and Technology (AIST),
2-3-26 Aomi, Koto-ku, Tokyo 135-0064, Japan
{panikos.heracleous,s.fukayama,jun.ogata}@aist.go.jp, yasserm@aun.edu.eg

Abstract. Automatic recognition of human emotions is of high importance in human-computer interaction (HCI) due to its applications in real-world tasks. Previously, several studies have been introduced to address the problem of emotion recognition using several kinds of sensors, feature extraction methods, and classification techniques. Specifically, emotion recognition has been reported using audio, vision, text, and biosensors. Although, using acted emotion signals, significant improvements have been achieved, emotion recognition still faces low performance due to the lack of real data and limited data size. To address this problem, in this study data augmentation is investigated based on Generative Adversarial Networks (GANs). For classification the Vision Transformer (ViT) is being used. ViT has originally been applied for image classification, but in the current study is being adopted for emotion recognition. The proposed methods have been evaluated using the English IEMOCAP and the Japanese JTES speech corpora and showed significant improvements when data augmentation has been applied.

Keywords: Speech emotion recognition · Vision Transformer · CycleGAN

1 Introduction

Speech emotion recognition plays an important role in HCI and its real-world applications [1]. Speech emotion recognition can be applied in robotics, call centers, education, and health care. Due to the high importance of speech emotion recognition and its applications, many studies have investigated and reported methods and results in this research area [2–8]. Studies in emotion recognition using visual modality have also been reported [9,10].

Several neural architectures have been used for speech emotion recognition over the years with state of the art results being achieved using Bidirectional LSTMs followed by an attention layer applied directly to raw acoustic data [11]. ResNet applied to spectrograms of acoustic data [12], Bidirectional LSTMs and self-attention mechanisms applied to the decoder component of an automatic

© The Author(s), under exclusive license to Springer Nature Switzerland AG 2022
M. Kurosu et al. (Eds.): HCII 2022, LNCS 13519, pp. 67–75, 2022.
https://doi.org/10.1007/978-3-031-17618-0_6

speech recognition model (ASR) model combined with raw acoustic features [2]. Also, a GRU model applied to acoustic statistical features including MFCCs [13]. The proposed method differs from all these approaches by using a pre-trained deep model for feature extraction.

Wav2vec [14] feature extraction in the context of speech emotion recognition also has been reported in [15] who compared wav2vec and HuBERT pre-trained models for speech emotion recognition (among other tasks) with and without ASR fine-tuning. In that study, only a simple classifier consisting of average time pooling and one linear layer was used. Moreover, they allowed the transformer blocks of the feature extractor to be fine-tuned during speech emotion recognition training.

The current study introduces experiments and results on speech emotion recognition based on state-of-the-art Deep Neural Network (DNN)-based classification methods. Specifically, we address the problem of the lack of large realistic and labeled emotional data and the problem of unbalanced data across emotional states [16]. The proposed method applies Generative Adversarial Networks (GANs) [17] and Vision Transformers (ViT) [18]. The GANs are able to generate target synthetic data of a specific domain. GANs consist of two networks namely, the generator and the discriminator. The generator is trained with random data (e.g., neutral speech) and generates samples of the target domain (e.g., emotional speech). The discriminator receives the synthetic samples along with real target samples, and decides whether the synthetic sample is accepted as real or not. Both the generator and discriminator are trained together. A specific architecture of GAN is the CycleGAN [19], which has been introduced for image-to-image translation. The main difference between GAN and CycleGAN is that the latter operates in two-directions with two generators and discriminators. As a result, CycleGAN can transfer from two sources to samples of two targets using unpaired input data. Several researchers have reported results on speech conversion [20] by taking advantage of the GAN and CycleGAN. Regarding speech emotion recognition, few studies introduced methods based on CycleGANs using different classifiers and feature extraction techniques [21].

In the current study, a method based on the integration of CycleGAN and ViT classifier is introduced. ViT is a simplified architecture of the standard Transformers [22], originally applied to natural language processing and computer vision. In contrast, in the current study ViT is being adapted to speech emotion recognition. As far as our knowledge goes, this is the first time when ViT is applied in a speech emotion task, or integrated with CyCleGAN.

2   Methodology

2.1   Data

For the evaluation of the proposed methods, two emotional corpora have been used. Specifically, the English Ryerson Audio-Visual Database of Emotional Speech and Song (RAVDESS) [23] and the Twitter-based emotional speech (JTES) have been used.

The RAVDESS database consists of 7356 files in total, and each file was rated 10 times on emotional validity, intensity, and genuineness. Ratings were provided by 247 non-professional annotators. High levels of emotional validity, interrater reliability, and test-retest intrarater reliability were reported. The audio-visual RAVDESS database has been produced by 24 actors (12 males and 12 females). In the current study, speech samples only are being used.

Two experiments have been conducted using RAVDESS namely, for the classification of four and for eight emotions. In the case of four emotions, angry, happy, sad, and neutral have been considered. In the case of eight emotions, calm, happy, sad, angry, fearful, surprise, and disgust have been considered. For training and testing 80% and 20% of the 1440 speech samples have been used, respectively. The features consist of RGB color melspectrogram images.

The JTES Japanese corpus uses Twitter tweets to produce speech samples. The speech samples were produced by 50 female and 50 male non-professional speakers. The labeling is based on the contents of the tweets, and tweets are categorized into for emotions, namely neutral, angry, joy, and sad. From all produced speech samples, 50 phonetically and prosodically balanced sentences for each emotion were selected. These sentences were used to produce the emotional JTES corpus, which consists of 20,000 speech samples.

The creators of the JTES corpus have used dataset for speech recognition and speech emotion recognition. When speech recognition experiments have been conducted, 23.05% word error (WER) have been achieved when using speaker adaptation. In the case of speech emotion recognition, 70% weighted accuracy (WA) on average has been obtained. The features used were log mel-filter bank features and the log power in 25-dimensional vector. Moreover, the delta and delta-delta features are calculated from the 25-dimensional feature vectors, to obtain a 75-dimensional features vectors. For classification, a feed-forward deep neural network (DNN) [24] has been used.

2.2   Feature Extraction

In the current study, mel spectrograms extracted for raw speech samples have been used as features. From each speech file, a color image (3-channel RGB image), representing the mel spectrogram, has been extracted. The original size of each image was 300×300, but for training and testing the images have been resized to 72×72. Figure 1 shows two cases of the spectrograms for the emotions angry, joy, neutral, and sad in the case of using the JTES corpus. As can be observed, the spectrograms are clearly distinguished across the emotions. Also, the two cases show the similarities of the same emotions.

2.3   Description of CycleGAN

CycleGAN consists of two Generators and two Discriminators. The two neural networks and training together, and the training samples being unaligned. In this architecture, the Generator tries to create fake samples that cannot be

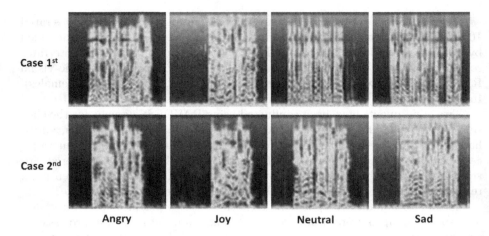

Fig. 1. Examples of mel spectrograms used as features in the case of the JTES corpus.

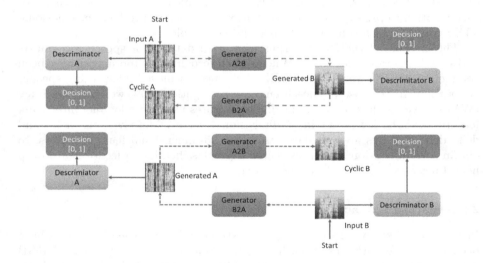

Fig. 2. The architecture of the CycleGAN.

distinquished from the real samples. On the other hand, the Discriminator will decide whatether the created fake sample can be accepted or not.

Figure 2 shows the architecture of the CycleGAN applied in the current study. The architecture shown is the case of the two-directional CycleGAN and consists of two Generators and two Discriminators. In the case of JTES, for the *Input A* 4000 normal speech samples have been used. Specifically, 4000 samples from the LibriSpeech [25] have been used to train the generator and create synthetic RAVDESS and JTES samples. The training data of the RAVDESS and of the JTES have beeen used for the discriminator. The *Generator A2B* is trained with

2000 speech samples from LibriSpeech. As a result, transformed GAN-samples (*Generated B*) are greated, which contain emotional information. Additionally, the *Generator B2A* create fake samples similar to the input. The lower part of the Fig. 2, shows the reverse case.

2.4 Vision Transformer

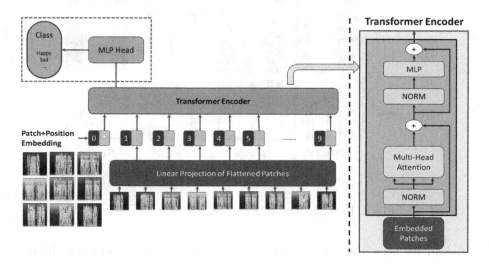

Fig. 3. The architecture of Vision Transformer (ViT).

Figure 3 shows the architecture of the ViT, along with the applied decoder. ViT is a simplified version of transformers adopted for image classification. In the current study, applying ViT in speech emotion recognition using mel spectrograms features is being investigated. Because in both cases images are used as features, it is assumed that nature of the two problems are similar.

In order to apply the ViT for speech emotion classification, the following steps have been followed:

– Each image is split to patches
– The patches are flattened
– lower-dimensional linear embeddings from the flattened patches are produced
– Positional embeddings are added
– A standard transformer encoder is fed with the sequence as input.

Figure 4 shows examples of CycleGAN-transformed LibriSpeech neutral-normal speech to fake JTES emotional speech. It can be observed that real and fake feature are very similar. Also, the transformed samples differ across different emotions. In the classification experiments, JTES, RAVDESS emotional

Real neutral

Fake emotion

Real emotion

Fake neutral

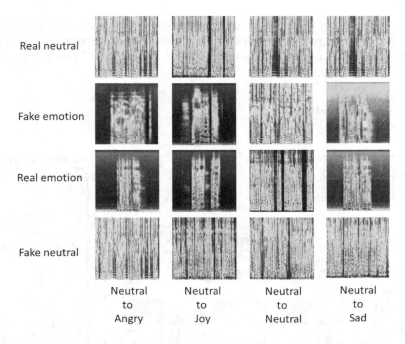

Neutral to Angry   Neutral to Joy   Neutral to Neutral   Neutral to Sad

Fig. 4. Examples of CycleGAN-transformed samples.

samples have been used. Also, the two corpora have been augmented with fake emotional dataset produced by the CycleGAN. In this stage, only one-directional CycleGAN has been used.

3   Results

As previously mentioned, CycleGAN is able to operate in two-directions. In our experiments, however, one-direction operation was applied. As for the ViT, a similar architecture as in [18] with few differences was used. Specifically, the batch size was set to 64, the transformer layers to 4, and the epochs to 400. These parameters may be not optimal, and higher accuracies can be achieved by hyperparameters tuning. Note that the current study does not primarily aim at optimizing the performance of the classifier. Instead, the main goals are to demonstrate and confirm the effectiveness of using CycleGAN in speech emotion recognition, and to investigate whether ViT can also be used in speech emotion recognition and not only in image classification.

Table 1 shows the results obtained when using the RAVDESS corpus. Three experiments have been conducted to evaluate the proposed methods. In the first experiment, both training and test data consist of real RAVDESS samples. In the second experiment, real RAVDESS samples for testing, and for training CycleGAN-transformed samples (2000 out of the 4000 thousands CycleGAN-transformed) have been used, respectively. Finally, in the third experiment, the real RAVDESS training data have been augmented with the training CycleGAN-transformed (remaining 2000 thousand CycleGAN-transformed samples). For testing, the real test RAVDESS samples have been used. As shown, when using transformed + real as training data, and real as testing data the accuracy improves in both 4-class and 8-class experiments. Specifically, in the case of 4 classes, the accuracy improves from 74.5% to 77.0%, and in the case of 8 classes from 61.0% to 63.5%. These results indicate that the transformed data are rich in emotional information, and that when adding them to the real training data, the emotion recognition accuracy improves. Table 2 shows the results obtained when using the JTES corpus and the proposed methods. In the case of using real training and testing data, the accuracy was 63.32%. When CycleGAN-transformed samples have been used for training, and real samples for testing, a 60.6% accuracy has been obtained, which is closely comparable to the previous one (real case). Finally, when for training the real JTES samples have been augmented with CycleGAN-converted samples, a 66.05% accuracy has been achieved, which is the highest among the three cases.

The results obtained in both RAVDESS and JTES show that CycleGAN effectively produces emotional samples from neutral-normal speech. The transformed samples can be used to augment limited emotional corpus such as the RAVDESS.

Table 1. Accuracy for 4-class and 8-class speech emotion recognition using RAVDESS and the proposed method.

Conditions		Classes	
Training	Testing	4 classes	8 classes
Real	Real	74.5	61.0
Transformed	Real	61.0	41.5
Transformed and real	Real	77.0	63.5

Table 2. Accuracy for 4-class speech emotion recognition using JTES and the proposed methods.

Conditions		Classes
Training	Testing	4 classes
Real	Real	63.3
Transformed	Real	60.6
Transformed and real	Real	66.1

4   Conclusions

In the current study, we conducted experiments on speech emotion recognition based on CycleGAN and ViT architectures. The aim of the study was to investigate whether CycleGAN is able to transfer acoustic features from natural speech to emotional speech, and how a ViT can deal with speech emotion recognition. The methods evaluated on two emotional datasets, namely the English RAVDESS and the Japanese JTES. Speech samples from the LibriSpeech normal speech corpora has been used to create fake RAVDESS and fake JTES emotional samples. The obtained results show that the fake emotional samples can be used to augment emotional data and improve the accuracy. This is of high importance especially in the case of limited emotional corpus, such as RAVDESS. The results demonstrate the effectiveness of the proposed methods in speech emotion recognition using RAVDESS and JTES corpora. Currently several methods are being designed and applied to achieve higher accuracy for this task. Specifically, hyperparameters tuning, comparison with other architectures, and applying 1-dimensional features are in progress.

Acknowledgments. This work was supported by Council for Science, Technology and Innovation, "Cross-ministerial Strategic Innovation Promotion Program (SIP), Big-data and AI-enabled Cyberspace Technologies" (funding agency: NEDO).

References

1. Busso, C., Bulut, M., Narayanan, S.: Toward effective automatic recognition systems of emotion in speech. In: Gratch, J., Marsella, S. (eds.) Social Emotions in Nature and Artifact: Emotions in Human and Human-Computer Interaction, pp. 110–127. Oxford University Press, New York, November 2013
2. Feng, H., Uno, S., Kawahara, T.: End-to-end speech emotion recognition combined with acoustic-to-word ASR model. In: INTERSPEECH, pp. 501–505 (2020)
3. Huang, J., Tao, J., Liu, B., Lian, Z.: Learning utterance-level representations with label smoothing for speech emotion recognition. In: Proceedings of Interspeech, pp. 4079–4083 (2020)
4. Jalal, M.A., Milner, R., Hain, T., Moore, R.K.: Removing bias with residual mixture of multi-view attention for speech emotion recognition. In: Proceedings of Interspeech, pp. 4084–4088 (2020)
5. Jalal, M.A., Milner, R., Hain, T.: Empirical interpretation of speech emotion perception with attention based model for speech emotion recognition. In: Proceedings of Interspeech, pp. 4113–4117 (2020)
6. Stuhlsatz, A., Meyer, C., Eyben, F., Zielke1, T., Meier, G., Schuller, B.: Deep neural networks for acoustic emotion recognition: raising the benchmarks. In: Proceedings of ICASSP, pp. 5688–5691 (2011)
7. Han, K., Yu, D., Tashev, I.: Speech emotion recognition using deep neural network and extreme learning machine. In: Proceedings of Interspeech, pp. 2023–2027 (2014)
8. Lim, W., Jang, D., Lee, T.: Speech emotion recognition using convolutional and recurrent neural networks. In: Proceedings of Signal and Information Processing Association Annual Summit and Conference (APSIPA) (2016)

9. Rawat, W., Wang, Z.: Deep convolutional neural networks for image classification: a comprehensive review. Neural Commun. **29**, 2352–2449 (2017)
10. Huynh, X.-P., Tran, T.-D., Kim, Y.-G.: Convolutional neural network models for facial expression recognition using BU-3DFE database. In: Information Science and Applications (ICISA) 2016. LNEE, vol. 376, pp. 441–450. Springer, Singapore (2016). https://doi.org/10.1007/978-981-10-0557-2_44
11. Jalal, M., Milner, R., Hain, T.: Empirical interpretation of speech emotion perception with attention based model for speech emotion recognition. In: INTER-SPEECH, pp. 4113–4117 (2020)
12. Padi, S., Sadjadi, S.O., Sriram, R.D., Manocha, D.: Improved speech emotion recognition using transfer learning and spectrogram augmentation. In: ICMI, pp. 645–652 (2021)
13. Xu, Y., Xu, H., Zou, J.: HGEM: a hierarchical grained and feature model for acoustic emotion recognition. In: ICASSP 2020–2020 IEEE International Conference on Acoustics, Speech and Signal Processing (ICASSP), pp. 6499–6503. IEEE (2020)
14. Baevski, A., Zhou, H., Mohamed, A., Auli, M.: wav2vec 2.0: a framework for self-supervised learning of speech representations. arXiv preprint arXiv:2006.11477 (2020)
15. Wang, Y., Boumadane, A., Heba, A.: A fine-tuned Wav2vec 2.0/Hubert Benchmark For Speech Emotion Recognition, Speaker Verification and Spoken Language Understanding. arXiv preprint arXiv:2111.02735 (2021)
16. Schuller, B., et al.: Paralinguistics in speech and languagestate-of-the-art and the challenge. Comput. Speech Lang. **27**(1), 4–39 (2013)
17. Ian, G., et al.: Generative adversarial nets. In: Advances in Neural Information Processing Systems (2014)
18. Dosovitskiy, A, et al.: An image is worth 16x16 words: transformers for image recognition at scale. arXiv:2010.11929v2 (2020)
19. Zhu, J.Y., Park, T., Isola, P., Efros, A.A.: Unpaired image-toimage translation using cycle-consistent adversarial networks. In: Proceedings of the IEEE International Conference on Computer Vision, pp. 2223–2232 (2017)
20. Kaneko, T., Kameoka, H.: Parallel-data-free voice conversion using cycle-consistent adversarial networks. In: 26th European Signal Processing Conference arXiv:1711.11293, November 2017 (2018)
21. Bao, F., Neumann, M., Vu, N.T.: Cyclegan-based emotion style transfer as data augmentation for speech emotion recognition. In: Proceedings of Interspeech 2019, pp. 2828–2832 (2019)
22. Vaswani, A., et al.: Attention is all you need. arXiv:1706.03762 (2017)
23. Livingstone, S.R., Peck, K., Russo, F.A.: RAVDESS: the ryerson audio-visual database of emotional speech and song. In: 22nd Annual Meeting of the Canadian Society for Brain, Behaviour and Cognitive Science (CSBBCS) (Kingston, ON) (2012)
24. Hinton, G., et al.: Deep neural networks for acoustic modeling in speech recognition: the shared views of four research groups. IEEE Signal Process. Mag. **29**(6), 82–97 (2012)
25. Panayotov, V., Chen, G., Povey, D., Khudanpur, S.: Librispeech: an ASR corpus based on public domain 382 audio books. In: IEEE International Conference on Acoustics, Speech and Signal Processing, pp. 5206–5210 (2015)

Development of a Web-Based Interview Support System Using Characters Nodding with Various Movements

Yutaka Ishii[1][✉], Satoshi Kurokawa[2], Miwako Kitamura[2], and Tomio Watanabe[1]

[1] Okayama Prefectural University, Kuboki 111, Soja, Okayama, Japan
{ishii,watanabe}@cse.oka-pu.ac.jp
[2] Graduate School, Okayama Prefectural University, Kuboki 111, Soja, Okayama, Japan
satoshi@hint.cse.oka-pu.ac.jp

Abstract. In contrast to conventional face-to-face interviews, web-based interviews may cause additional tension due to the lack of a sense of unity and difficulty in sharing the rhythm of dialogue, in addition to the tension of job interviews. First, we conducted a questionnaire survey on job interviews to find out what kind of interview format and environment actually reduces nervousness. The questionnaire included questions about interview methods and emotions during interviews for fourth-year university students who had experienced job interviews. The results showed that many of the respondents felt that the explanations and interviews before the interviews helped to alleviate their anxiety and nervousness. In addition, many respondents said that they had casual conversations with their friends and interviewers before the interview to ease their tension. Furthermore, the presence of a familiar person at the interview or not may have helped to alleviate the nervousness of the interviewees. Based on these results, we propose a web interview support system using the communication support character called Inter-Actor which is a speech-driven embodied entrainment character that automatically generates body movements based on speech. We developed a web interview support system using the nodding patterns grouped by cluster analysis based on the impressions. The effectiveness of the developed system was demonstrated in an evaluation experiment using a role-play interview task.

Keywords: Web-based interview · Communication enhancement · Auto-generated motions

1 Introduction

Due to the spread of the new coronavirus (COVID-19), it has become difficult to hold face-to-face job interviews, and the number of companies conducting web interviews has increased rapidly. In contrast to conventional face-to-face interviews, web-based interviews may cause additional tension due to the lack of a sense of unity and difficulty in sharing the rhythm of dialogue, in addition to the tension of job interviews. In face-to-face communication, non-verbal information such as nodding and gestures promotes

M. Kurosu et al. (Eds.): HCII 2022, LNCS 13519, pp. 76–87, 2022.
https://doi.org/10.1007/978-3-031-17618-0_7

smooth information sharing. In web interviews, supplementary nonverbal information may also promote rhythmic synchronization and support smooth communication.

As a method to support online communication, a system that shares a virtual dialogue space such as the metaverse via avatars and supplements nonverbal information can be mentioned. In a previous study, InterActor, a speech-driven embodied entrainment character that automatically generates body movements based on speech, has been developed [1]. InterActor is a Computer Generated (CG) character that has functions of both a listener and a speaker. The listener performs embodied entrainment behaviors, such as nodding and other body motions, to a user's voice. The speaker performs rhythmical sympathetic motions to a user's voice. InterActor responds to utterances with an appropriate timing by means of its entire body motions and actions in the manner of a listener and a talker. In addition, InterActor can transmit the talker's message to a partner by generating a body motion similar to a speaker on the basis of a time series of speech, presenting both the speech and the entrained body motions simultaneously. The information transmitted and received by this system is only through speech. Thus, the InterActor generates the entrained communicative movements and actions based on speech input and supports the sharing of mutual embodiment in communication. The use of such a character that expresses embodied rhythms is expected to ease the tension of examinees and promote their speech.

Various interview training systems have been developed to reduce tension in interviews and to improve the impression of the interviewer [2, 3]. We have shown the effect of virtual face-to-face projection of self-images in video interviews [4]. We have also developed an embodied video communication system, called'E-VChat' that superimposes a user's own avatar and communication support characters on the partner's image for enhancing remote communication using a video image [5]. This system is constructed by the partner's video image using interactive CG characters including user's own avatar and virtual audience characters. We have confirmed the effectiveness of the system by an experiment under free conversation. Furthermore, we developed an embodied entrainment audience characters system with partner's face to relate audience characters with the partner. This system could bring about more active interaction by virtual audience even if the remote partner does not respond to user's speech. In addition, we confirmed the effectiveness of the system in which face images of partner's face are superimposed on audience characters under free conversation with friends. However, this system is not always evaluated effectively in all situations including nervous situations such as a job interview [6]. Then, as online job interviews are becoming more common, we are investigating more effective methods of presenting the characters.

In this study, we propose a system that replaces the interviewer's image with a CG character for users who feel nervous about communicating with the frontal camera image of the interviewer. The CG character is a voice-driven embodied entrainment character that has been developed in our previous research. The nodding of the character is based on the impressions of various motions, which are being studied in another research [7]. A web interview support system is developed using the nodding patterns grouped by cluster analysis based on the impressions. In addition, the effectiveness of the developed system was demonstrated in an evaluation experiment using a role-play interview task.

2 Web-Based Interview Support System Using Characters Nodding with Various Movements

2.1 Questionnaire Survey on Web-Based Interviews

We conducted a questionnaire survey of fourth-year undergraduates who have had job interviews in order to examine a system that can ease the tension of examinees in web interviews. In this questionnaire, we prepared questions about the interview format, emotions during the interview, experiences eased the nervousness, and so on.

The purpose of this study is to develop an effective system to ease the tension of examinees in web interviews. First, we conducted a questionnaire survey on job interviews to find out what kind of interview format and environment actually reduces nervousness. The questionnaire included questions about interview methods and emotions during interviews. The subjects were 51 fourth-year university students who had experienced job interviews. The results of the questionnaire indicated that chatting, speaking with gestures, and moving the body before the interview helped to alleviate the tension. In addition, we compared the four items of "Relief," "Stress," "Nervousness" and "impatience" when there was a person who was familiar with the interview, such as the person who explained the interview before the actual interview, and when there was no such person. As shown in the Fig. 1, there was a significant difference at the 1% significance level in the Wilcoxon's signed rank test for the item of "Relief," and it was confirmed that people felt relieved when there was a person who was familiar with the interview.

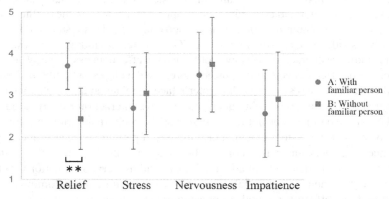

Fig. 1. The result of the comparison in the four items of relief, stress, nervousness, and impatience when there was a person who was familiar with the interview (A) and when there was no such person (B).

2.2 System Prototype with Interaction Model for Auto-generated Entrained Motion

Based on the results of the questionnaire, we developed a prototype of a system in which the interviewer himself acts as a character agent to give explanations during the break time before the interview, and also acts as a communication support character on the examinee's screen during the actual interview. The system uses InterActor, a character that automatically generates speaker and listener actions based on the speaker's voice according to the following interaction model. A prototype of the system is shown in the Fig. 2.

Fig. 2. A prototype of the system using a video image and InterActors.

A LIStener's Interaction Model

A listener's interaction model of the CG character includes a nodding reaction model [1] that estimates the nodding timing from a speech ON-OFF pattern and a body reaction model linked to the nodding reaction model. A hierarchy model consisting of two stages, macro and micro (Fig. 3), predicts the timing of nodding. The macro stage estimates whether a nodding response exists or not in a duration unit that consists of a talkspurt episode $T(i)$ and the following silence episode $S(i)$ with a hangover value of 4/30 s. The estimator $M_u(i)$ is a moving-average (MA) model, expressed as the weighted sum of unit speech activity $R(i)$ in (1) and (2). When $M_u(i)$ exceeds the threshold value, the nodding $M(i)$ is also an MA model, estimated as the weighted sum of the binary speech signal $V(i)$ in (3). The body movements are related to the speech input at a timing over the body threshold. The body threshold is set lower than that of the nodding prediction of the MA model that is expressed as the weighted sum of the binary speech signal to nodding. The mouth motion is realized by a switching operation synchronized with the burst-pause of speech. In other words, when the InterActor works as a listener for generating body movements, the relationship between nodding and other movements is dependent on the threshold values of the nodding estimation.

$$M_u(i) = \sum_{j=1}^{J} a(j)R(i-j) + u(i) \qquad (1)$$

$$R(i) = \frac{T(i)}{T(i) + S(i)} \qquad (2)$$

$a(j)$: linear prediction coefficient
$T(i)$: talkspurt duration in the i-th duration unit
$S(i)$: silence duration in the i-th duration unit
$u(i)$: noise

$$M(i) = \sum_{k=1}^{K} b(j)V(i-j) + w(i) \qquad (3)$$

$b(j)$: linear prediction coefficient
$V(i)$: voice
$w(i)$: noise

The body movements of the speaker are also related to the speech input by operating both the neck and one of the other body actions at a timing over the threshold, which is the speaker's interaction model estimates as its own MA model of the burst-pause of speech to the entire body motion. Because speech and arm movements are related at a relatively high threshold value, one of the arm actions in the preset multiple patterns is selected for operation when the power of speech is over the threshold.

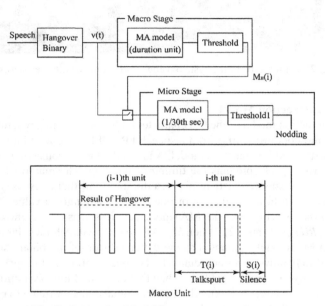

Fig. 3. Interaction Model for auto-generated motions.

2.3 Characters Nodding with Various Movements

In the results of the questionnaire in Sect. 2.1, many respondents mentioned that they were nervous in job interviews because they were basically meeting the interviewer for the first time. In this study, we develop a web-based interview support system that replaces the interviewer's own image with a character agent. In order to support more effective interaction, the character agent automatically generates various nodding motions. So, we have evaluated impressions of three nodding components: the number of nods, the angle, and the time required for each nod [7]. In the experiment, we used the various nodding motion output system shown in the Fig. 4 and evaluated the impressions of 19 different nodding motions with the characteristics shown in Table 1. We used the 30 adjective pairs shown in Table 2 to evaluate the impressions. In this experiment, a standard nodding behavior (500 ms, 0.35 rad, 1 time: "standard nod") was set and evaluated relative to the standard nod. Thirty students (21 males and 9 females) participated in the experiment.

Table 1. Nodding motions with the characteristics.

Nodding components	Values
Number of nods [times]	1, 2, 3
Angle [rad]	0.2, 0.35, 0.5
Time required for each nod [msec]	250, 500, 1000

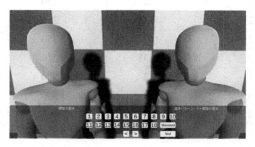

Fig. 4. The various nodding motion output system for the experiment.

Table 2. 30 pairs of adjectives.

light	dark		sober	drunk
soft	hard		responsible	irresponsible
hot	cold		settle	restless
positive	negative		rational	emotional
strong	weak		ambitious	lethargic
calm	excitable		lovely	hateful
active	passive		leisurely	impatient
like	dislike		gentle	severe
kind	unkind		bullish	timid
pleasurable	painful		considerate	selfish
reliable	undependable		extroverted	introverted
serious	humorous		energetic	tired
pleasant	unpleasant		sensitive	insensitive
stable	changeable		agreeable	attitude
chatty	quiet		friendly	unfriendly

Hierarchical cluster analysis (Euclidean distance, Ward's method) was performed to categorize the 19 nodding behaviors in Table 1 using the calculated factor score means. Table 3 shows the nodding movements classified when three clusters are extracted. The standardized scores in each cluster are shown in Fig. 5. The impression of each nodding motion classified in clusters A to C is characterized.

Table 3. Motion patterns based on the analysis classified into three clusters.

Mode	Values for components		
	Number of nods	Nodding angles [rad]	Time for each nod [msec]
A	1	0.2	250
	1	0.35	250
	2	0.2	250
	2	0.35	250
	3	0.2	250
	3	0.35	250
B	1	0.2	500
	3	0.2	500
	2	0.2	500
	1	0.35	1000
	1	0.5	1000
	2	0.35	1000
	2	0.5	1000
C	1	0.35	500
	1	0.5	500
	2	0.35	500
	2	0.5	500
	3	0.35	500
	3	0.5	500

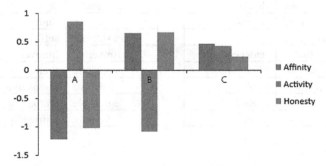

Fig. 5. Standardized scores of the analysis classified into three clusters.

2.4 Web-Based Interview Support System

We have been developing a system that automatically generates nodding motions based on voice input. However, in a web interview situation, the interviewee needs to be quiet while the interviewer is speaking to avoid speech collisions. In such cases, the character does not perform any actions, so we developed a system that responds based on the interviewee's gaze toward the character. In the experimental environment, two monitors were set up in front of the interviewee as the evaluation target. The front monitor displayed a system with agents behaving according to the conditions of each mode in a virtual space. The other monitor displayed the Zoom screen of the teleconferencing system used to conduct the call. However, the interviewee does not see this Zoom screen. Unity was used to construct the virtual space, and Tobii Pro nano was used to measure eye movement. An example of communication scene using web-based interview support system is shown in Fig. 6.

Fig. 6. Example of communication scene using the web-based interview support system.

3 Evaluation Experiment

3.1 Experimental Setup

We conducted a role-play interview experiment to confirm the impressions of different nodding motions. The interviewee underwent an online role-play interview for about 15 min, watching the agent on a monitor instead of the interviewer's image. Five modes were used in the experiment: "calm and leisurely" and "humorous and emotional" nodding, which were prepared according to previous studies. Mode 1 uses a non-nodding agent as a control condition. In modes 2 and 3, the agents made "calm and leisurely" nods and "humorous and emotional" nods based on gaze, and in modes 4 and 5, based on voice, respectively as shown in Table 4. For each mode, the interview was paused at about 3 min for a questionnaire.

The questionnaire of 13 items consisted of 9 items based on previous studies [7]: Agreeable/Attitude, Like/Dislike, Friendly/Unfriendly, Active/Passive, Energetic/Tired, Light/Dark, Reliable/Undependable, Responsible/Irresponsible and Serious/Humorous, and 4 items related to the web interview: interaction, relief, stress and usability. The questionnaire was examined using a seven-point bipolar rating scale based on SD method. The order of evaluation was switched for each participant in the experiment for counterbalance. Finally, the participants were asked to describe the experiment freely. There were 18 participants in the experiment, 9 male and 9 female students. The interviewers were required to attend a one-hour training course provided by the university's Job Hunting Advisor prior to the interview, and to dress uniformly in suits during the experiment.

Table 4. Comparison mode in the experiment.

Mode	Input	Motion	Cluster type
1	---	Not move	---
2	Gaze	Move	A
3	Gaze	Move	B
4	Voice	Move	A
5	Voice	Move	B

3.2 Experimental Results

Friedman tests were conducted to determine whether the effect of nodding movements was based on impression ratings for each of the 7-level sensory evaluation items. Furthermore, Wilcoxon signed-rank tests were performed between modes 2 and 3 and between modes 4 and 5, which differ in nodding behavior for multiple comparisons. In addition, to investigate differences between eye and voice input information, we also evaluated between modes 2 and 4, and between modes 3 and 5. The results are shown in Figs. 7 and 8. Figure 7 shows that there was a significant difference between modes 2 and 3 using eye gaze at the 0.1% significance level for "Serious/Humorous," 1% for "Agreeable/Attitude," "Like/Dislike" and "Responsible/Irresponsible" and 5% for "Friendly/Unfriendly" and "Reliable/Undependable." For the four additional items, significant differences were found between Modes 2 and 3 using eye gaze at the 1% level for all items of "Interaction," "Relief," "Stress" and "Usability."

Next, Table 5 shows the results of the pairwise comparisons. Mode 4 (Voice A) was rated the highest, followed by Mode 2 (Mode A), indicating that the motion character based on voice input was highly rated, although there was no significant difference in the 7-level evaluation. Based on these results, it is considered that the "friendly" and "sincere" nodding behavior of Group A is connected to communication support in the Web interview.

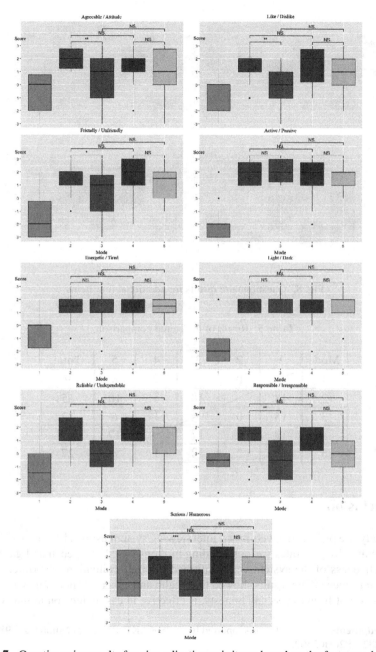

Fig. 7. Questionnaire results for nine adjective-pair items based on the factor analysis.

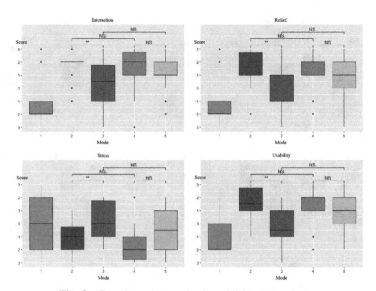

Fig. 8. Questionnaire results for additional four items.

Table 5. Result of the paired comparison.

Mode	1	2	3	4	5	Total
1		0	3	0	6	9
2	18		18	3	10	55
3	15	0		1	6	22
4	18	15	17		17	67
5	12	2	12	1		27

4 Conclusion

In this study, we proposed a web-based interviewing system using a humanoid 3D agent that automatically generates various nodding motions based on speech and gaze input. The effectiveness of the system was confirmed through evaluation experiments using role-play interviews. The results showed that "calm and leisurely" nodding, which gives an impression of friendliness and honesty, is effective in easing tension in interviews.

Acknowledgments. This work was supported by JSPS KAKENHI Grant Number JP19K12067, JP20H04232, JP20H05569.

References

1. Watanabe, T.: Human-Entrained Embodied Interaction and Communication Technology, pp. 161–177. Emotional Engineering, Springer (2011). https://doi.org/10.1007/978-1-84996-423-4_9
2. Anderson, K., et al.: The TARDIS framework: intelligent virtual agents for social coaching in job interviews. In: Reidsma, D., Katayose, H., Nijholt, A. (eds.) ACE 2013. LNCS, vol. 8253, pp. 476–491. Springer, Cham (2013). https://doi.org/10.1007/978-3-319-03161-3_35
3. Tanaka, H., et al.: Automated social skills trainer. In: IUI '15 Proceedings of the 20th International Conference on Intelligent User Interfaces, pp. 17-27 (2015)
4. Ishii, Y., Watanabe, T.: Evaluation of embodied interaction on a virtual face-to-face projection in a tele-communication Interview. Trans. Human Interface Society **10**(2), 1–10 (2008, in Japanese)
5. Ishii, Y., Watanabe, T.: E-VChat: a video communication system in which a speech-driven embodied entrainment character working with head motion is superimposed for a virtual face-to-face scene. In: Proc. of the 21st IEEE International Symposium on Robot and Human Interactive Communication (RO-MAN2012), pp.191–196 (2012)
6. Kunita, S., Ishii, Y., Watanabe, T.: Evaluation of a video communication system using embodied entrainment audience characters by a simulated job interview. Proc. of Human Interface Symposium **2018**, 558–561 (2018). (in Japanese)
7. Kitamura, M., Kurokawa, S., Ishii, Y., Watanabe, T.: Impression evaluation of various nodding movements by humanoid 3D model, correspondences on human interface. Human Interface Society **23**(6), 1–8 (2021, in Japanese)

Emotion Recognition from Physiological Signals Using Continuous Wavelet Transform and Deep Learning

Lana Jalal[✉][iD] and Angelika Peer[iD]

Free University of Bozen-Bolzano, 39100 Bolzano, Italy
{lanadalawrjalal.jalal,angelika.peer}@unibz.it

Abstract. In recent years, emotion recognition has received increasing attention as it plays an essential role in human-computer interaction systems. This paper proposes a four-class multimodal approach for emotion recognition based on peripheral physiological signals that uniquely combines a Continuous Wavelet Transform (CWT) for feature extraction, an overlapping sliding window approach to generate more data samples and a Convolutional Neural Network (CNN) model for classification. The proposed model processes multiple signal types such as Galvanic Skin Response (GSR), respiration patterns, and blood volume pressure. Achieved results indicate an accuracy of 84.2%, which outperforms state-of-the-art models on four-class classification despite of being only based on peripheral signals.

Keywords: Emotion recognition · Convolutional neural network · Deep learning · Physiological signals · Wavelet transform

1 Introduction

Emotional states influence people's perceptions, thoughts, and decisions. Thus, recognition of different emotional states has widespread use in distance learning, medical care, intelligent systems, and human-computer interaction (HCI) as manifested in an increasing interest in this field over recent years [1].

Emotion recognition from physiological signals has gained significant attention as these signals cannot easily be masked compared to other signals such as facial expressions, gestures, or speech [2]. Physiological signals can be subdivided into Electroencephalogram (EEG) signals and peripheral physiological signals. Peripheral physiological signals include electromyogram (EMG) signals, electrocardiogram (ECG) signals, galvanic skin resistance (GSR) signals, etc. We intentionally excluded EEG signals from this study given the increase in methodological complexity in terms of data acquisition and analysis of such signals [3] that may not be compliant with many real-life applications and also since we believe that a robust classification of human emotion should be possible also based on peripheral physiological signals without explicitly involving EEG [2,4].

M. Kurosu et al. (Eds.): HCII 2022, LNCS 13519, pp. 88–99, 2022.
https://doi.org/10.1007/978-3-031-17618-0_8

While the most straightforward way to represent emotions is to use emotion-labels (e.g., joy, fear), this representation has some disadvantages. The main one is that labels are not cross-lingual as emotions do not have exact translations in different languages [5]. Psychologists, therefore, often represent emotions or feelings using dimensional models (generally 2 or 3-dimensional) [6]. The most famous dimensional model is the 2D valence-arousal or pleasure-arousal model [7] (see Fig. 1). The valence scale ranges from pleasant to unpleasant, the arousal scale from calm to excited.

Previous studies have performed independent valence and arousal classification, resulting in a two-class classification, i.e., distinguishing high valence (HV)/low valence (LV) and high arousal (HA)/low arousal (LA). However, independent classification fails to consider arousal and valence correlations and does not allow implementation of end-to-end learning since classification results must be mapped onto a 2D plane for emotion judgment [8].

In this work, we propose a four-class, multimodal approach to emotion recognition that combines i) time-frequency domain features based on a Continuous Wavelet Transform calculated from three physiological signals (galvanic skin response (GSR), respiration patterns, and blood volume pressure), ii) a data augmentation technique called overlapping sliding window to generate more data samples, and iii) a Convolutional Neural Network (CNN) model for emotion classification. We evaluate our proposed model on a public multimodal dataset called DEAP.

This paper is organized as follows. Section 2 discusses related work. Section 3 describes methodological details. Section 4 analyzes results and compares them with state-of-the-art models. In Sect. 5, we conclude our work and discuss directions of future work.

2   Related Work

Emotion recognition from physiological signals has received significant attention in recent years. Among others feature extraction is considered an essential step of emotion recognition [9]. The wavelet transform is widely used for feature extraction and allows transforming time series of EEG and physiological signals into images. Alharbey et al. [10] used CWT for ECG arrhythmias detection and employed standard deviation (SD) and Shannon entropy (SE) for feature extraction, while a safe threshold has been used for classification to discriminate between the different arrhythmias. Boronoyev et al. [11] used CWT for the analysis of pulse model signals. They described a new wavelet-based detection method for physiological pressure signal components and found that wavelet analysis is capable of defining local characteristics of a signal and helps investigating changes in the spectral distribution of a pulse signal. A wavelet-transform-based feature extraction method was proposed by Long et al. [12] to recognize emotions through ECG signals. A threshold value was set to classify two emotional states. Cheng and Liu [13] adopted the wavelet transform to analyze surface EMG signal features. Surface EMG signals were decomposed by discrete wavelet transform (DWT), then the extracted wavelet features were inputted to a back-propagation neural network to identify four emotional states. Summarizing, several studies propose CWT as an efficient time-frequency analysis method for EEG and ECG signals. Motivated by these works we consider the use of CWT for feature extraction from peripheral physiological signals.

Several approaches have been proposed in the literature for classifying emotional states, i.e., Support Vector Machines (SVM), Fine Gaussian Support Vector Machines (FGSVM) or multimodal residual networks. Verma et al. [14] proposed a multimodal approach, whereby 25 features were extracted from EEG and peripheral signals by DWT and used SVM for the classification of thirteen affective emotional states. Hassan et al. [4] extracted features from peripheral signals by applying an unsupervised deep belief network (DBN) and combined them in a feature fusion vector; they used FGSVM for classification. Ma et al. [15] proposed a multimodal residual network for detecting emotional states. This network can learn the correlation between EEG and other physiological signals by sharing weights between the modality of each layer.

Recently, CNN models have been proven to be extremely successful for signal detection, image denoising, image classification, and emotion classification. For example, a 2D CNN classifier that automatically extracts features from correlation matrices was proposed by Mei et al. [16] for emotion recognition of four classes. Lin et al. [17] transformed different frequency bands of EEG signals into six gray images and extracted hand-crafted features of other peripheral physiological signals; these images and features were then fed into a pre-trained deep convolutional AlexNet to classify two emotional states. Liu et al. [18] used linear-frequency cepstral coefficients (LFCC) as features from raw EEG signals and pre-trained a deep convolutional ResNet to classify the emotional states. Kwon et al. [8] used wavelet transform as a pre-processing method for EEG signals; then, they designed a four-class classifier that takes two extracted features as input of the first layer of a fully connected CNN model.

Despite the demonstrated success achieved with CNNs for signal classification involving physiological signals, their generalization ability is known to be poor in case of an insufficient sample size. Thus, in order to amplify the emotion samples an overlapping sliding window mechanism similar to [19,20] is used in this work to obtain a larger amount of data as recommended for achieving efficient recognition with deep learning methods [21].

We finally propose a multimodal CNN model for the recognition of four emotions in the valence-arousal space that processes physiological signals and that combines CWT as an efficient time-domain method for feature extraction as well as a sliding window approach for data expansion to increase the average of the classification rate.

3   Methods

3.1   Emotional State Classification

While classification of physiological signals into two classes (HV/HA) and (LV/LA) is straightforward [22], increasing the number of classes allows not only end-to-end learning, but also capturing possible correlations between the arousal and valence dimensions. In the present study, we classify the emotional state in the valence-arousal plane [6] into four emotional regions, which are: high valence and high arousal (HVHA), high valence and low arousal (HVLA), low valence and low arousal (LVLA), and low valence and high arousal (LVHA), as illustrated in Fig. 1.

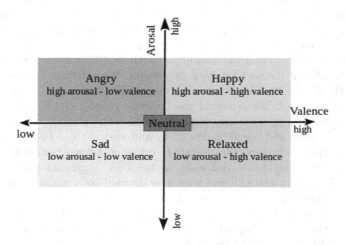

Fig. 1. Valence-arousal plane.

3.2   Dataset

The DEAP dataset [23] is widely used for studying emotion classification from physiological signals. It contains EEG and peripheral signals that include GSR, respiration, EMG (muscle movement), EOG (eye movements), temperature, and blood pressure. These signals are available with a sampling rate 512 Hz

In DEAP, 32 subjects watched 40 music videos with different emotions, and each video was approximately one-minute long. For each video, the subjects rated arousal, valence, like/dislike, and dominance/familiarity on a scale from 1 to 9. Thus, a median of 5 is used as the threshold to divide emotional regions into four labels, namely, *happy*, *sad*, *angry*, and *relaxed* (see Fig. 1). For example, if the score of a video in the valence and arousal dimension is found to be greater than 5, it is assigned to HVHA "happy". If the valence score is found to be greater than 5 and the arousal score smaller or equal to 5, it is assigned to HVLA "relaxed". If the score on valence and arousal is found to be smaller or equal to 5, it is assigned to LVLA "sad"; otherwise, it is assigned to LVHA "angry".

For our study we used three peripheral physiological signals from this dataset to study emotion classification, namely GSR, respiration patterns, and blood volume pressure. We analyzed only the first 23 subjects of the DEAP dataset as two significantly different groups could be observed after calculating the wavelet transform (group one for subjects 1–23, group two for the rest of subjects). While it is not entirely clear from where this effect comes based on the online documentation provided on the dataset, it may be connected to the two hardware setups used to record the dataset or different signal conditioning procedures adopted.

3.3   Sliding Window Mechanism

Training a CNN requires a large amount of training data, and a sufficient amount of such data is often not available. The limited amount of data makes the model prone to overfitting [24]. Thus at present, researchers usually adopt methods such as expanding datasets, removing features as well as regularizing and terminating the training in advance to prevent model overfitting [25].

We apply a sliding window technique with 96.67% overlap to the source signals of the DEAP dataset for data expansion. We consider a sliding window with a length of $L = 30$ s to slide with a step of 1 s from $t_0 = 3$ s to $t_f = 63$ s, as illustrated in Fig. 2. We removed the baseline part of the first 3 s and only retained the remaining 60 s experimental data. The sliding window initially (blue rectangle with red lines) starts at t_0 and ends at $t_0 + L$, segmenting the signal S_1. In the next step, the updated sliding window (rectangle with blue dashed lines) starts at $t_0 + 1$ and ends at $t_0 + L + 1$, segmenting the signal S_2 (see Fig. 2). This way the original signal is divided into multiple sets of one-dimensional segments. The list of obtained segments is finally collected in $S_i = [S_1, S_2, ..., S_{30}]$, whereby the subscript i indicates the experiment/video number. The signal is then downsampled 128 Hz; therefore, the number of samples per segment is 3840 (128 samples/second $\times$ 30 s). The number of segments for each subject is finally given by 1200 (40 experiments $\times$ 30 segments). For each subject consequently 1200 emotion labels are created.

The dataset for all considered peripheral physiological signals (37–39 channels: GSR, respiration, and plethysmograph) can finally be expressed with $r_i = [S_i^{37}, S_i^{38}, S_i^{39}]$ for each experiment/video number. The total dataset for one subject over all experiments is then collected in $R_j = [r_1, r_2, ..., r_{30}]$ with j the subject number. For 23 out of 32 subjects of the DEAP dataset, the total number of segments is 27.600 (23 subjects $\times$ 1200 segments). The number of segments per label and their percentage of the total number of segments is reported in Table 1.

Table 1. Number of segments (expanded sample points).

Label	No of segments	Percentage of total number of segments
Happy	9450	34.24%
Relaxed	5760	20.87%
Sad	5910	21.41%
Angry	6480	23.48%

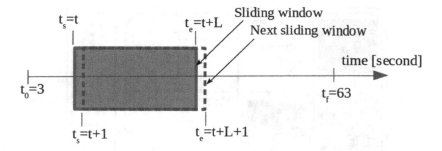

Fig. 2. Sliding window

3.4 Signal Transformation Using CWT

Wavelet transforms are useful for a multi-resolution analysis, where signals can be analyzed at different frequencies and time scales [14]. We used MATLAB's function cwtfilterbank to create a CWT filter bank. The default wavelet used in the filter bank is the analytic Morse (3,60) wavelet. The CWT was applied to extract information from 1D peripheral physiological signals and the coefficients were arranged to form a CWT scalogram, which defined the visual representation of the processed signal in time, scale and coefficient values. It identifies signals having low frequency components or signals whose frequency component changes rapidly; an example of a scalogram is shown in Fig. 3. Each colored image was saved with a size of $(227 \times 227 \times 3)$ pixels. The total transformed data includes 27600 scalograms for each channel (GSR, respiration, and plethysmograph). Then, we concatenated the images from the three channels into a single image, and passed them as input to the classifier, as discussed in the following subsection.

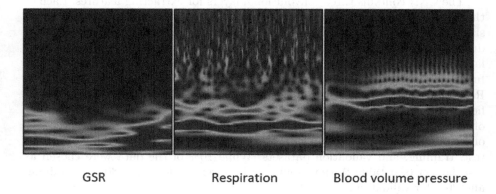

| GSR | Respiration | Blood volume pressure |

Fig. 3. Wavelet transformed scalogram.

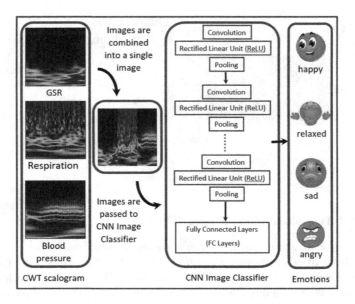

Fig. 4. Convolutional neural network model

3.5 Convolutional Neural Network Model

In order to recognize the emotional state, we trained a 9-layer CNN model based on three physiological signals. As explained in the previous subsection, the CWT was used to transform the physiological signals into images. Then, the obtained three images were combined into a single image ($227 \times 227 \times 3$), which was used as input of the first layer of the proposed CNN. A detailed illustration of the CNN architecture is given in Fig. 4.

The CNN contains three convolutional layers for extracting features. Each of them is followed by a max-pooling layer to reduce the data size, and the kernel size of the convolutional layer is (3×3). A batch normalization layer is introduced to speed up model convergence and prevent overfitting. The full connection layer is used to obtain classification results before updating the weights. The cost function is used to update the weights based on the classification results. The ReLu function is selected as the activation function and Softmax as the classifier. The output size was chosen to be 4 classes, which is equal to the number of labels in the task. The network was trained using 50 epochs and a batch size of 32 samples with a learning rate of 0.001. The data was randomly split into test, training, and validation datasets. While 10% of the data were chosen as test dataset (see Table 2), the remaining data were divided into 80% for training and 20% for validation.

Table 2. Training and test data

Label	Training data (Data quantity)	Test data (Data quantity)
Happy	8505	945
Relaxed	5184	576
Sad	5319	591
Angry	5832	648

4   Results and Discussions

4.1   Performance Evaluation

This section reports on the performance of the proposed model for human emotion recognition based on peripheral physiological signals. The confusion matrix is used as the generalized metric to evaluate and present the performance of the proposed method. The confusion matrix used gives the actual (target) class and predicted (output) class of four basic emotions in rows and columns. Each of the shown black cells of the confusion matrix indicate the number and the percentage of correctly predicted emotion classes, while white cells of the confusion matrix indicate the number of misclassified emotion classes and their percentage.

Figure 5 shows the accuracy achieved during the training phase using the validation data. The results from the test data are shown as a confusion matrix in Fig. 6. The 'relaxed' emotion is correctly classified with 88.2%, which is the highest among the emotional states, and the lowest classification accuracy is obtained for the 'sad' emotion with 79.2%. The overall classification accuracy for all emotional states was found to be 84.24%.

Table 3. Comparison with state-of-the-art models evaluated on DEAP dataset

Model	Signals	Accuracy
Zhang et al. [26]	EEG(8)	71.62%
Martínez et al. [27]	EGG(32)	72.50%
Kwon et al. [8]	EEG(32), GSR	73.43%
Huang et al. [29]	EEG(32), EOG, GSR, Respiration	82.92%
Proposed methed	**GSR, Respiration, Blood volume pressure**	**84.20%**
Bagherzadeh et al. [28]	EEG(32), EOG, EMG, GSR, Respiration, Temperature, Blood pressure	93.60%

4.2   Comparison with Existing Models

We compared the performance of the proposed model with state-of-the-art models that performed a four-class classification on the DEAP dataset. As shown in

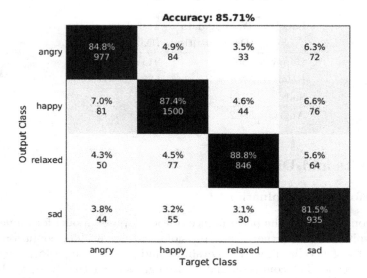

Fig. 5. Confusion matrices for the CNN evaluated over validation data.

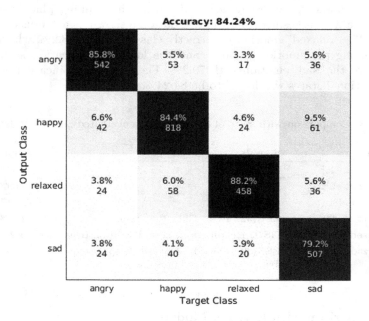

Fig. 6. Confusion matrices for the CNN evaluated over the test data.

Table 3, the proposed model outperforms the state of the art in the field, except for Bagherzadeh et al. [28]. They used EEG and all the peripheral physiological signals of the DEAP dataset, while the proposed model used only parts of the peripheral physiological signals. Thus, it can be reasonably assumed that the obtained classification accuracy can be further improved by incorporating all sensor data [8]. Zhang et al. [26] used wavelet feature extraction based on a smoothed pseudo-winger-ville distribution and SVM for classification. Martínez-Rodrigo et al. [27] used quadratic sample entropy for extracting biological signal features and SVM for classifying the extracted features; Kwon et al. [8] used a 2D CNN model for feature extraction and classification by tuning the hyper-parameters in convolution filters. Huang et al. [29] proposed an Ensemble Convolutional Neural Network (ECNN), which could automatically recognize various signals' correlations and employed the plurality voting strategy for affective state recognition. Bagherzadeh et al. [28] extracted spectral and time features from EEG and peripheral signals and used the majority voting method for classification.

The observed increase in accuracy over the majority of state-of-the-art implementations can be explained by two main factors: Firstly, the overlapping sliding window mechanism that was used to increase data samples for each class resulted in an improvement of the CNN model's capacity to classify the emotional state. The approach helped to overcome the available limited amount of data, which otherwise paired with an increase in the number of classes would have led to a reduction of the accuracy of the model. Secondly, part of the performance enhancement can also be attributed to the feature extraction that considered a time-frequency approach based on CWT.

5   Conclusions

This work proposed a four-class multimodal approach to emotion recognition using peripheral physiological signals that uniquely combined a Continuous Wavelet Transform (CWT) for feature extraction, an overlapping sliding window approach to generate more data samples and a Convolutional Neural Network (CNN) model for classification.

The results showed that the proposed model outperformed state-of-the-art models in four-class classification tasks despite of being only based on peripheral signals. We consequently conclude that a powerful classification of human emotion is also possible based on peripheral physiological signals. The improved performance can be explained by i) the increased number of data samples due to the sliding window mechanism and ii) the choice of a time-frequency approach for feature extraction based on CWT, that better characterized emotional patterns than traditional methods.

Despite of the good obtained results, further research is needed to verify the model's universality on different datasets. We also aim to investigate the combination of peripheral and EEG signals.

Acknowledgement. The work is supported in part by the 'MELANIE' project funded by the European Regional Development Fund (ERDF), project No. FESR1138.

References

1. Liao, J., Zhong, Q., Zhu, Y., Cai, D.: Multimodal physiological signal emotion recognition based on convolutional recurrent neural network. In: IOP Conference Series: Materials Science and Engineering, pp. 032005. IOP Publishing (2020)
2. Zhao, Y., Cao, X., Lin, J., Yu, D., Cao, X.: Multimodal affective states recognition based on multiscale CNNs and biologically inspired decision fusion model. IEEE Transactions on Affective Computing (2021)
3. Puce, A., Hämäläinen, M.S.: A review of issues related to data acquisition and analysis in EEG/MEG studies. Brain Sci. **7**(6), 58 (2017)
4. Hassan, M.M., Alam, M.G.R., Uddin, M.Z., Huda, S., Almogren, A., Fortino, G.: Human emotion recognition using deep belief network architecture. Inf. Fusion **51**, 10–18 (2019)
5. Russell, J.A., Mehrabian, A.: Evidence for a three-factor theory of emotions. J. Res. Pers. **11**(3), 273–294 (1997)
6. Soleymani, M., Pantic, M. and Pun, T.: Multimodal emotion recognition in response to videos (Extended abstract). In: 2015 International Conference on Affective Computing and Intelligent Interaction, pp. 491–497 ACII (2015)
7. Russell, J.A.: Culture and the categorization of emotions. Psychol. Bull. **110**(3), 426–450 (1991)
8. Kwon, Y.H., Shin, S.B., Kim, S.D.: Electroencephalography based fusion two-dimensional (2D)-convolution neural networks (CNN) model for emotion recognition system. Sensors **18**(5), 1383 (2018)
9. Wu, D., Zhang, J., Zhao, Q.: Multimodal fused emotion recognition about expression-EEG interaction and collaboration using deep learning. IEEE Access **8**, 133180–133189 (2020)
10. Alharbey, R.A., Alsubhi, S., Daqrouq, K., Alkhateeb, A.: The continuous wavelet transform using for natural ECG signal arrhythmias detection by statistical parameters. Alex. Eng. J. **61**(12), 9243–9248 (2022)
11. Boronoyev, V.V., Garmaev, B.Z., Lebedintseva, I.V.: The features of continuous wavelet transform for physiological pressure signal. In: Fourteenth International Symposium on Atmospheric and Ocean Optics/Atmospheric Physics, pp. 693611. International Society for Optics and Photonics (2008)
12. Long, Z., Liu, G., Dai, X.: Extracting emotional features from ECG by using wavelet transform. In: 2010 International Conference on Biomedical Engineering and Computer Science, pp. 1–4. IEEE (2010)
13. Cheng, B., Liu, G.: Emotion recognition from surface EMG signal using wavelet transform and neural network. In Proceedings of the 2nd international conference on bioinformatics and biomedical engineering, pp. 1363–1366. ICBBE (2008)
14. Verma, G.K., Tiwary, U.S.: Multimodal fusion framework: a multiresolution approach for emotion classification and recognition from physiological signals. Neuroimage **102**, 162–172 (2014)
15. Ma, J., Tang, H., Zheng, W.L., Lu, B.L.: Emotion recognition using multimodal residual LSTM network. In: Proceedings of the 27th ACM International Conference on Multimedia, pp. 176–183. ACM (2019)
16. Mei, H., Xu, X.: EEG-based emotion classification using convolutional neural network. In: 2017 International Conference on Security, Pattern Analysis, and Cybernetics (SPAC), pp. 130–135. IEEE (2017)
17. Lin, W., Li, C. and Sun, S.: Deep convolutional neural network for emotion recognition using EEG and peripheral physiological signal. In: International Conference on Image and Graphics, pp. 385–394. Springer, Cham (2017)

18. Liu, N., Fang, Y., Li, L., Hou, L., Yang, F., Guo, Y.: Multiple feature fusion for automatic emotion recognition using EEG signals. In: 2018 IEEE International Conference on Acoustics, Speech and Signal Processing (ICASSP), pp. 896–900. IEEE (2018)
19. da Silva, M.A.F., de Carvalho, R.L., da Silva Almeida, T.: Evaluation of a Sliding Window mechanism as DataAugmentation over Emotion Detection on Speech. Acad. J. Comput. Eng. Appl. Math. **2**(1), 11–18 (2021)
20. Garg, S., Patro, R.K., Behera, S., Tigga, N.P., Pandey, R.: An overlapping sliding window and combined features based emotion recognition system for EEG signals. Appl. Comput. Inform. (2021)
21. Zhou, J., Wei, X., Cheng, C., Yang, Q., Li, Q.: Multimodal emotion recognition method based on convolutional auto-encoder. Int. J. Comput. Intell. Syst. **12**(1), 351–358 (2019)
22. Karyana, D.N., Wisesty, U.N., Nasri, J.: Klasifikasi sinyal EEG menggunakan deep neural network dengan stacked denoising autoencoder. eProc. Eng. **3**(3), 5296–5303 (2016)
23. Koelstra, S., et al.: Deap: a database for emotion analysis; using physiological signals. IEEE Trans. Affect. Comput. **3**(1), 18–31 (2012)
24. Zhang, X.-Y., Wang, W.-R., Shen, C.-Y., Sun, Y., Huang, L.-X.: Extraction of EEG components based on time - frequency blind source separation. In: Pan, J.-S., Tsai, P.-W., Watada, J., Jain, L.C. (eds.) IIH-MSP 2017. SIST, vol. 82, pp. 3–10. Springer, Cham (2018). https://doi.org/10.1007/978-3-319-63859-1_1
25. Sanjar, K., Rehman, A., Paul, A., JeongHong, K.: Weight dropout for preventing neural networks from overfitting. In: Proceedings of the 8th International Conference on Orange Technology (ICOT), pp. 1–4. IEEE (2020)
26. Zhang, Y., Cheng, C., Zhang, Y.: Multimodal emotion recognition using a hierarchical fusion convolutional neural network. IEEE Access **9**, 7943–7951 (2021)
27. Martínez-Rodrigo, A., García-Martínez, B., Alcaraz, R., Fernández-Caballero, A., González, P.: Study of electroencephalographic signal regularity for automatic emotion recognition. In: Ochoa, S.F., Singh, P., Bravo, J. (eds.) UCAmI 2017. LNCS, vol. 10586, pp. 766–777. Springer, Cham (2017). https://doi.org/10.1007/978-3-319-67585-5_74
28. Bagherzadeh, S., Maghooli, K., Farhadi, J., Zangeneh Soroush, M.: Emotion recognition from physiological signals using parallel stacked autoencoders. Neurophysiology, **50**(6), 428–435 (2018)
29. Huang, H., Hu, Z., Wang, W., Wu, M.: Multimodal emotion recognition based on ensemble convolutional neural network. IEEE Access **8**, 3265–3271 (2019)

Surrogate Sensory Feedback of Grip Force in Older and Younger Participants only Influences Fine Motor Control, but Not the Object Weight Perception

Jai Prakash Kushvah and Gerhard Rinkenauer[✉]

Leibniz Research Centre for Working Environment and Human Factors, Ardeystr. 67, 44139 Dortmund, Germany
{kushvah,Rinkenauer}@ifado.de

Abstract. Successful execution of motor commands dealing with the object variabilities is realized by the somatosensory feedback during the dexterous object manipulation. These feedback inputs are slow in general; however, responsible for corrective mismatch process and motoric execution. Aging induced reduction in concentration of tactile afferents and mechanoreceptors and consequently, the reduced skin sensitivity may further impair the slow feedback process and manual dexterity. Regardless of the fact that aging is associated with diminished tactile functioning and affected hand dexterity, however, studies have shown no marked differences in perceptual abilities. In the present study, we re-investigated the aging effects on skin physiological (skin sensitivity and hydration measures) and object manipulation task measures. Further, a novel attempt was made to support the affected somatosensory feedback process by providing an additional online grip force related acoustic surrogate feedback. We evaluated the object-hand kinematic and psychophysical data of 16 young and 16 elderly participants collected during a classical weight discrimination task, allowing object shape-weight manipulation. Results showed clear aging effects on hand skin physiological measures. As expected, aging and object shape overall influenced the precision-grip measures and discrimination ability. Skin sensitivity measures were not found correlated with weight discrimination task measures in the elderly group. Aging did not affect the object weight perception. Importantly, the acoustic feedback strengthened the somatosensory feedback process and speed up the corrective mismatch process by shortening the object loading phase and later the force application, but it did not help the perceptual system to improve the object weight perception.

Keywords: Somatosensory feedback · Aging · Skin sensitivity

1 Introduction

Grasping and moving the objects in routine life seem so automatized that we even ignore the common accidental situations like object displacement, slip and breakage. These object-hand interactions are performed based on pre-constructed/updated motor

M. Kurosu et al. (Eds.): HCII 2022, LNCS 13519, pp. 100–112, 2022.
https://doi.org/10.1007/978-3-031-17618-0_9

commands to achieve a balanced grip-lift force scaling at the object-digit-interface. However, the frictional changes at the object-digit-interface arising because of variable object properties (i.e., shape, size, mass) and operational conditions can disturb such grasp stability. In order to deal with such variabilities, our perceptual system uses the visual and haptic sensory channels [21–24, 26]. Here, the visual cues are used for antici- pated force parameterization in an almost automatized manner and indirectly observing the mechanical events [22]. Importantly, the haptic cues assess the actual sensory state by providing distinctive perceptual estimates of object properties and contact event information, i.e., finger pressure, time, power, distribution of contact forces, frictional properties [21]. Such somatosensory feedback is crucial for evaluating the actual and anticipated sensory states [22]. Any mismatch leads to an update of motor command to compensate for an anticipated destabilization. Thus, a corrective motoric execution is expressed by the grip-lift force scaling at object-digit interface. In this way, we avoid the object slip from the hand and later, search for the optimal grip force application during adaptation. Since the somatosensory feedback is slow in general (~100ms) which delays updating the pre-constructed motor plan and force accommodation while dealing with the object variabilities [22–24, 26]. Such limitation of the somatosensory mechanism in combination of affected tactile afferents functioning might further deteriorate the object manipulation task performance [4]. Aging is one of the such factors, which are linked with the reduced sensory-motor and kinesthetic process.

Aging studies have shown the sensory decline in terms of biophysical and discrimina- tion abilities. Age related reduction in concentration of tactile afferents and mechanore- ceptors [1, 13, 20] and consequently, the reduced skin sensitivity in terms of two-point discrimination [33, 37] and touch-pressure threshold [10, 29] in older adults has been well documented. Sensory deterioration because of aging may further impair the slow feedback process and therefore may hamper the manual dexterity in elderly age group. Studies have shown aging effects on vision acuity [14, 32], haptic acuity [30], reach to grasp contact [6, 35] and grip force efforts [4, 8, 9]. Further, aging significantly affects the discrimination threshold [31] and object weight-ratio [19]. Regardless of the fact that aging is associated with diminished tactile functioning and affected hand dexterity, however, the aging effects are unable to produce marked perceptual differences [10, 30]. Older and younger adults showed no differences while the 3-D object shape perception. Aging showed no impact on the sensorimotor adaptation during visual-haptic conflict [12]. Despite having the sensory decline, older adults did not differ in the perceptual performance compared to the younger adults. Holmin and Norman (2012) suggested that aging effects introduced in the weight perception studies are task dependent [19]. Depending on the task specificity, the probable reasons have been derived as extra pre- caution [25], muscular reorganisation [9], insufficient tactile information [10], reliance on sensorimotor prediction [42].

In the present study, we are aiming for two main objectives. First, we are re- investigating the aging effects on hand skin physiological parameters and then on force kinematic and perceptual measures during a standard object lifting weight discrimination task. The task utilised in the study is a prototypic object manipulation task [22–24, 26] which offers a unique opportunity to address the aging effects on object-hand kinematics and perceptual abilities (perceived heaviness and difference limen (DL)). Based on literature available, we hypothesize that aging should impact the hand skin physiological measures and force scaling during various phases of the object manipulation task. Additionally, hand physiological measures and manipulation task measures might share the correlation between them as the haptic sense is involved. Second, we are adopting a novel strategy to support the slow feedback process to maintain grasp stability during variable object properties. We are adding a sensory channel along with the somatosensory feedback to strengthen the mismatch resolution process by providing an online grip force feedback through auditory sense. It has been well studied now that events implementing multi-modalities followed by spatiotemporal correspondence allow for multisensory integration and improve the sensorimotor correlations [15, 23]. Thus, we hypothesize that online acoustic feedback should improve the somatosensory feedback loop and force prediction to accommodate at the object-digit-interface and should improve the object weight estimation while dealing with the object variabilities.

2 Method

2.1 Participants

Groups of young (n = 16, Mage = 24.27 years, SD = 3.32 years) and elderly (n = 16, Mage = 69 years, SD = 8.08 years) healthy, right-handed participants took part in the study. Background questionnaire ensured that none of participants had colored blindness, any neurological disorder and hand function limitation. Inclusion criterion of normal hearing and normal or corrected-to-normal vision was followed. Participants were compensated with either course credits or monetary reward (€10 / hour) for their participation in the study. Participants' willingness to take part in the study was obtained in form of the written informed consent prior to the study.

2.2 Experimental Tools and Task

Semmes-Weinstein Monofilament Test. The test was used to measure the tactile sensitivity in terms of touch-pressure thresholds (TPT) of the right-hand thumb and index finger [36]. Test procedure was conducted as per recommended by Bell-Krotoski and colleagues (1993) [5]. Participants were instructed to close the eyes and to respond 'YES' when a monofilament touch stimulus was perceived on thumb or index finger pulp. Monofilament was touched 3 times on the pulp. Each time it was applied for approximately 1.5 s, held for approximately 1.5 s and lifted over by approximately 1.5 s.

Two-Point Discrimination (2PD). A test device Distcrim-A-GonTM was used to measure tactile sensitivity of right-hand thumb and index finger in terms of spatial acuity. The Semmes-Weinstein monofilaments measure only the superficial sensations of touch and pressure, which does not conclude tactile sensitivity. The 2-PD test assesses cutaneous innervation and central somatosensory function [38, 39]. Participants were instructed to respond by saying 'one' if they feel one point or 'two' if they feel 2 points against the test site while keeping the eyes closed.

Skin Hydration Test. Object handling is influenced by skin-object friction. Finger-tip moisture/hydration optimizes hand-object interaction by minimizing the required grip force while griping, lifting or transportation [2]. Thus, a certain level of skin hydration is essential for successful hand-object interactions. Right-hand thumb and index finger skin hydration levels were assessed using the eight hydration pin probes provided by DermaLab, Cortex Technology. Participants were simply asked to press the spring-loaded pin-probes 8 times against each thumb and index finger and the average hydration scores were noted.

Weight Discrimination Task and Procedure. Test objects with different surface angles (A, B and C cf. Fig. 1, left side) and a reference object (Fig. 1, left side) in two feedback conditions (with and without acoustic feedback) were implemented each in total 6 blocks of a standard two-alternative-forced-choice weight discrimination task. Sequence of object and feedback conditions was randomized to avoid the carryover effect on the task performance. Weights for the reference object kept constant at 220 g, whereas the test objects weights were varied on a trial-by-trial basis. Test objects weight were controlled by an electric linear motor functioning based on a staircase algorithm with two randomly sequenced interleaved staircases procedures [11]. The algorithm approximated the 75th and 25th percentile response probabilities for the object heaviness on two points of the psychometric function using the weighted up/down 3-step rule [27]. Participants were instructed for the task as to first briefly lift the reference object and then the test object to a certain height using the precision grip. Middle portion of the task objects was marked with a gripping area. Afterwards, they were asked to give their perceived heaviness response for the test object: if the test object was heavier than the reference one, press "ja"; otherwise, press "nein" on the response pad. Participants were guided on the computer screen to ensure the proper execution of the task trials. Object lift trials were kept free from any time constraint and holding period in between. Thus, the grip force applied during object lifts and movements was genuine.

Grip force while lifting the surface objects was continuously measured using strain gauges in a customized set up. The measured grip force values were converted into a sound whose frequency increased/ decreased as per the grip force applied in the acoustic feedback condition. Such acoustic feedback was presented on external speakers to participants.

Task Measures. Grip force data was processed using customized MATLAB scripts (MathWorks Inc., USA) to calculate the psychophysical measures. Point of subjective equality (PSE) was measured using a maximum likelihood procedure. A logistic psychometric function [7] was used for this:

$$\text{Prob ("heavier"|Wi)} = \frac{1}{1 + \frac{e^{(PSE - Wi)}}{0.91.DL}}$$

It indicates the probability whether the test object is judged heavier than the reference object, in the ith trail. Difference limen (DL) denotes the steepness of the psychometric function (weight difference between the 75th and 25th percentile). Perceived heaviness

(PH) of the test objects was calculated by a transformation rule suggested by Rinkenauer et al. (1999) [34]: $PH = refw + (refw - PSE)$. Here, refw denotes the reference object weight.

Movement profile points were derived from the displacement recorded in the electric linear motor, whereas the force profile was derived from the strain gauge signals during the object lifting. Movement and force profiles representing the object lift trials were superimposed to mark the points for (1) force onset time, (2) force peak amplitude, (3) movement onset time, (4) movement onset force, (5) movement peak amplitude, and (6) movement offset force (as shown in Fig. 1, right side). Precision grip parameters of force peak amplitude, latency (movement onset force time – force onset time) and movement onset force were calculated and analyzed in R.

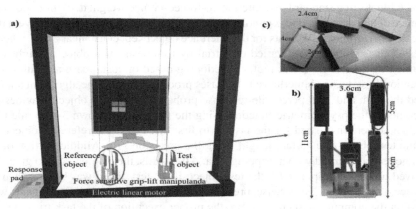

Fig. 1. (A) Schematic depiction of the customized experimental set-up used for the weight-discrimination-task. (B) The setup comprised with the two force-sensitive grip-lift manipulanda for reference and test object. (C) 3 types of experimental objects (surface angle: 0°, + 10° and -10°) with equal weight and dimensions were designed.

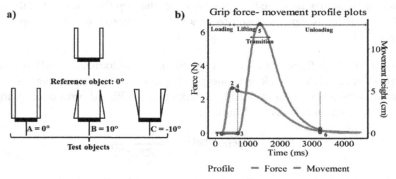

Fig. 2. a) Schematic presentation of the experimental objects: reference object and test objects with their respective surface angles. b) Schematic depiction of averaged experimental grip force and movement profiles and the measured data points. For details see the main text.

3 Results

3 x 2 x 2 mixed factorial ANOVAs were calculated to explore the main effects of within-subjects factors: *object* shape (A vs. B vs. C) and *feedback* (without acoustic feedback vs. with acoustic feedback) and between-subjects factor of *age* (young vs. old) on psychophysical measures and precision grip parameters for test objects. In case when the sphericity assumption was violated, degrees of freedom and p values were adjusted using Greenhouse-Geisser (F_{GG}, $\varepsilon > .75$) and Huynh-Feldt corrections (F_{HF}, $\varepsilon < .75$). Statistical analysis was performed using R and the open-source statistical software JASP.

3.1 Psychophysical Measures

Perceived Heaviness. Perceived heaviness was significantly modulated by the within-subjects factor *object* shape [F_{HF} (1.63, 48.89) = 25.75, $p < .001$, $\omega^2 = .19$]. Bonferroni corrected post hoc pairwise comparisons revealed highest perceived heaviness for test object B (M = 240.43 g, SD = 31.04 g) compared to object A (M = 218.4 g, SD = 20.9 g, $t = 5.39$, $p < .001$) and object C (M = 212.65 g, SD = 24.82 g, $t = 6.80$, $p < .001$). Thus, variation in object surface angle contributed in the object heaviness responses. Importantly, grip force related acoustic *feedback* was not helpful to improvise the perceived heaviness ($p = .09$) and we did not see the *age*-related differences ($p = .94$).

Difference Limen (DL). DL was affected by *object* shape [F_{GG} (1.24, 38.03) = 10.32, $p < .01$, $\omega^2 = .18$]. Bonferroni-corrected post hoc pairwise comparisons revealed that DL was higher for object B (M = 22.08 g, SD = 14.45 g) compared to object A (M = 11.56 g, SD = 5.77 g, $t = 4.13$, $p < .001$) and object C (M = 12.45 g, SD = 6.45 g, $t = 3.17$, $p < .001$). *Age* significantly affected the discrimination sensitivity [F (1, 30) = 7.68, p = .01, $\omega^2 = .10$]. Elderly group was less sensitive (M = 16.78 g, SD = 12.82 g) compared to the young one (M = 16.78 g, SD = 6.68 g) for object weight discrimination. DL scores remained unaffected by the acoustic *feedback* ($p = .7$).

3.2 Precision Grip Measures

Grip-Force Peak Amplitude. Test object peak force amplitudes were affected by *object* shape [F_{GG} (1.27, 38.12) = 143.73, $p < .001$, $\omega^2 = .65$]. Grip-force peak amplitude increased with increase of the object surface angle i.e., C < A < B; ($M_C = 4.64$ N, SD = 1.53 N; $M_A = 7.01$ N, SD = 1.88 N; $M_B = 10.85$ N, SD = 2.62 N; B-A: $t = 10.38$, $p < .001$, B-C: $t = 16.79$, $p < .001$; A-C: $t = 6.41$, $p < .001$). Grip force peak was affected by *age* [F (1, 30) = 5.21, $p = .03$, $\omega^2 = .06$] as elderly participants applied higher peak grip force (M = 8.09 N, SD = 3.49 N) than the young ones (M = 6.92 N, SD = 2.96 N) while lifting the test objects. Results did not show the effect of grip force related auditory *feedback* on test peak force application ($p = .23$). Two - way interaction effect of *feedback* and *age* was significant on the grip force measure [F (1, 30) = 5.23, $p = .03$, $\omega^2 = .01$] (Fig. 2 a).

Movement Onset Force (MOF). Grip force applied at the movement onset was influenced by main effects of *object* shape [F_{GG} (1.19, 35.60) = 141.38, $p < .001$, $\omega^2 = .69$], *feedback* [F (1, 30) = 10.93, p < .01, $\omega 2 = .02$] and *age* [F (1, 30) = 4.12, $p = .05$, $\omega^2 = .05$]. Grip force application increased with increase of the object surface angle [B (M = 10.13 N, SD = 2.83 N) > A (M = 5.82 N, SD = 1.32 N) > C (M = 3.90 N, SD = .99 N); B-A: $t = 11.35$, $p < .001$; B-C: $t = 16.42$, $p < .001$; A-C: $t = 5.07$, $p < .001$]. Further, in presence of auditory feedback the force values were dropped significantly (M = 6.44 N, SD = 3.25 N) compared to when it was absent (M = 6.8 N, SD = 3.19 N). Elderly participants applied higher grip force (M = 7.07 N, SD = 3.41 N) compared to the young ones (M = 6.16 N, SD = 2.96 N). Two - way interaction effect of feedback and age was significant on MOF [F (1, 30) = 4.55, $p = .01$, $\omega^2 = .01$] (Fig. 2 b).

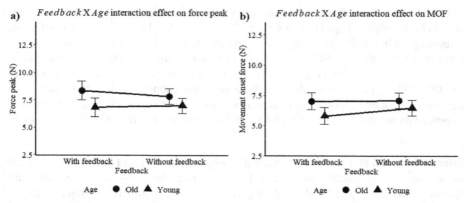

Fig. 3. Plot showing the mean comparisons associated to the interaction effects of *Feedback* and *Age* on peak force amplitudes (a) and on movement onset force measure (b). Here, mean points are presented with 95% confidence interval (CI) error bars.

Latency. Test object latency got affected by *object* shape [F_{GG} (1.35, 40.62) = 49.21, $p < .001$, $\omega^2 = .40$]. Bonferroni-corrected post-hoc pairwise comparisons showed that latency for object B (M = 336.05 ms, SD = 128.67 ms) was greater than object A (M = 207.27 ms, SD = 69.31 ms; $t = 8.20$, $p < .001$) and object C (M = 195.63 ms, SD = 63.72 ms; $t = 8.94$, $p < .001$). Importantly, main effect of *feedback* was also significant [F (1, 30) = 54.14, $p < .001$, $\omega^2 = .18$]. Application of grip force synchronized auditory feedback reduced the test object latency (M = 217.67 ms, SD = 91.49 ms) compared to when it was absent (M = 274.96 ms, SD = 122.52 ms). Latency differences were significant due to the *age* effect [F (1, 30) = 7.66, $p = .01$, $\omega^2 = .10$]. Elderly group took longer time (M = 274.92 ms, SD = 115.33 ms) than the young one (M = 217.72 ms, SD = 100.42 ms). Two - way interaction effect of *object* and *feedback* emerged significant on latency measure [F_{HF} (1.72, 51.65) = 6.11, $p = .01$, $\omega^2 = .02$]. Therefore, latency was significantly improved the latency while lifting the test object in presence of auditory feedback and such reduction of latency increased with increasing the object surface angle (Fig. 4).

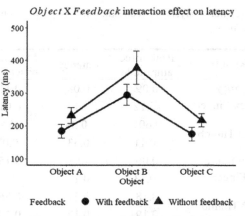

Fig. 4. Plot showing the mean comparisons associated to the interaction effects of *Object* and *Feedback* on latency measure. Here, mean points are presented with 95% confidence interval (CI) error bars.

3.3   Aging Effects on Hand Skin Sensitivity-Hydration Measures

Group differences explaining the aging effects on skin sensitivity and hydration were simply calculated using Student t-tests. Both skin sensitivity measures (2PD and TPT) and hydration measures showed significant group differences. Skin sensitivity thresholds were higher for older aged group [2PD index finger: t (30) = 5.27, p < .001; 2PD thumb: t (30) = 5.28, p < .001; TP index finger: t (30) = 7.21, p < .001; TP Thumb [t (30) = 10.61, p < .001]. Thus, aging showed negative impact on skin sensitivity measures. Further, younger participants had higher skin hydration levels for both thumb and index finger compared to the elderly ones [Index finger: t (30) = 6.77, p < .001; Thumb: t (30) = 8.61, p < .001]. The differences in skin hydration levels could have a negative effect on surface adhesion friction between the finger and the object surface in the older participants.

3.4   Correlation Between Hand Physiological Parameters and Weight Discrimination Task Measures

Correlation analysis was performed using the Pearson correlation coefficient to explore the relative functioning of thumb and index finger in terms of skin sensitivity (2PD and TPT) and hydration measure within the two groups. Significant positive correlation between thumb and index finger for 2 PD [r (30) = .69, p < .01)] and hydration measure [r (30) = .82, p < .001)] was observed among the young participants. Besides that, in elderly group, only the skin hydration measure found correlated for thumb and index finger [r (30) = .81, p < .001)]. Further, correlation analysis was performed to see the relationship between hand physiological measures (skin sensitivity and hydration measure) and weight discrimination task measures. Results revealed that both skin hydration and 2 PD measures associated to thumb in young age group were positively correlated with the peak force amplitude and movement onset force. No such correlations were observed in the elderly group (Table 1).

Table 1. Pearson's correlation analysis between skin sensitivity-hydration measures and weight-discrimination task measures

Age-group	Variables	Peak force amplitude	Latency	Movement onset force	Perceived heaviness
Young	2PD	0.09	0.08	0.11	-0.01
Old	Index Finger	-0.12	0	0.01	-0.13
Young	2PD Thumb	0.60*	-0.34	0.54*	0.2
Old		-0.11	0.33	-0.07	-0.39
Young	TP Index Finger	0.06	-0.2	0.15	-0.1
Old		-0.13	0.13	-0.13	0.04
Young	TP Thumb	0.18	0.21	0.36	-0.02
Old		0.19	0.17	0.37	-0.17
Young	Index Finger Hydration	-0.49	-0.24	-0.64**	0.11
Old		-0.39	-0.15	-0.37	0.16
Young	Thumb Hydration	-0.53*	-0.24	-0.65**	0.09
Old		-0.22	-0.28	-0.17	0.18

$* p < .05, ** p < .01, *** p < .001$

4 Discussion

Present study was conducted to explain two main research questions. Initially, how does aging affect the hand skin sensitivity-hydration and object discrimination task measures? Is there any relationship between skin sensitivity-hydration and object-hand-kinematics of the manipulation task? Second, we explored effect of additional sensory channel on the force and movement dynamics of the object manipulation. Here, we will discuss the findings in the context of our research questions one by one. We assessed the skin sensitivity measures of 2PD and TPT and skin hydration to ensure the functioning of the cutaneous mechanoreceptors and moisture levels. Participants could only use their thumb and index finger (implementing precision grip) in the main experiment task. Thus, it was important to take measures for both index finger and thumb. Functional variability among digits may influence the configuration and grip force application at the object-digit-interface. Results revealed that index finger and thumb were correlated for hydration measure but not for the TPT measure within both the groups. Further, both the digits for 2PD were only correlated in the young age group. It shows that relative firings of cutaneous mechanoreceptors (FA-1 and SA-1) mostly in the elderly group had individual differences.

Results showed the clear differences in index finger and thumb related skin sensitivity measures of TPT and 2PD and skin hydration between the young and elderly groups. Further, repeated-measures ANOVAs also followed the aging effects on force kinematics measures in terms of precision-grip parameters. Higher peak grip forces, longer latency period and higher movement onset force were associated with the elderly group. Effects of tactile afferents functioning on hand dexterity within the context of aging was explored in the correlation analysis (see Table 1). Correlation between thumb 2PD and grip force measures (peak force and MOF) in young age group supporting the that firing in tactile afferents has possible consequences on object grasp and lift. However, such correlation was absent in the elderly group. Also, the TPT measure did not show any correlation with the task measures in both the groups. Such discrepancy can be explained within the context of tactile afferents firing during different task conditions [18, 40]. TPT is associated with the minimal firing of tactile afferents, involving a small number of cutaneous innervations (FA-1 and SA-1). Whereas, the nature of applied contact forces during object grasps and lift is different from a slight touch while performing TPT. Applied contact forces during 2PD shares similarity to some extent as both superficial and deeper cutaneous innervations are involved. Next, a certain level of moisture between object-digits is always essential to resolve the frictional changes [3]. In young age individuals, grip forces (peak force, MOF) at different task phases were regulated as per the thumb fingertip hydration. Such correlation was absent in the elderly group. Our results agree that aging induced skin hydration reduction changed skin properties and increased grip force application and latency measure are associated with overcompensation strategy [2, 3].

Haptic sense mainly contributes in the somatosensory feedback during object-hand interaction, where these cutaneous afferents provide the object surface information (shape, friction, material) at the beginning of the preload phase; based on which the brain predicts required force to execute the updated motor command. It seems reasonable that reduced/impaired functioning of tactile afferents could severely affect the hand dexterity [4]. The weight discrimination task employed in the study was featured with the variable object weight in combination with object shape manipulation. Within the framework of object variabilities, it is always crucial to get the somatosensory feedback as soon as the contact with the object. So that the restructured motor plan could be updated. Here, we implemented the auditory surrogate sensory feedback to strengthen the slow somatosensory feedback. We evaluated the feedback strategy for elderly group to see the impact in context of aging. ANOVA results showed an overall impact of object surface angle on weigh-discrimination task measures. Increase in object surface angle found associated with higher grip force efforts and longer time duration to lift the object. It suggests that participants made substantial force efforts during loading and lifting phases to accommodate the object shape variability. Also, the perceived heaviness and difference limen increased with higher surface angle object. These findings are in line with previous research [16, 21]. Grip force related online auditory feedback showed significant impact on limited precision grip parameters. We hypothesized that effective feedback process could support the delayed somatosensory feedback process by improving the force adjustments at the object-digit interface while dealing with the object shape-weight variabilities. Auditory feedback gained no impact on test object perceived heaviness and weight discrimination. Similarly, the peak grip force application during the loading phase showed no effect of the employed feedback strategy. Interestingly, grip force related auditory feedback reduced the latency and movement onset force application. These findings support our hypothesis. While dealing with the object variabilities, auditory feedback speeds up the delayed somatosensory feedback loop, which resultant into the shortening of the loading phase. Further, the accelerated feedback process leads to corrective force parameter specification by updating the pre-constructed motor commands. Updated force parameters guide for improved force application. We observed this in form of the lowered movement onset force application. Previously, various feedback strategies have shown the positive impact on grip force application [17, 28, 41]. However, these studies did not implement the object variabilities in grasping and tactile assistive paradigms. Further, object weight perception remained unaffected in the presence of grip force related auditory feedback. This could be possibly because of the different processing pathways of the tactile signals [18]. In our findings, the feedback strategy only worked for the sensorimotor control and the perception/cognition processing remained intact.

In brief, our study investigated the significant aging effects on hand skin physiology and object manipulation task related psychophysical and precision grip parameters. Our study only reported with the loading-lifting phase measures. Further analysis of the transition and unloading phase measures might provide more insights on effects of object shape, aging and feedback strategy. The present study suggests that auditory surrogate feedback on grip force is a promising strategy for improving fine motor control, but not for improving the object weight perception.

References

1. Abdouni, A., Djaghloul, M., Thieulin, C., Vargiolu, R., Pailler-Mattei, C., Zahouani, H.: Biophysical properties of the human finger for touch comprehension: influences of ageing and gender. Royal Society open Sci. 4(8), 170321 (2017)
2. André, T., Lefevre, P., Thonnard, J.L.: Fingertip moisture is optimally modulated during object manipulation. J. Neurophysiol. 103(1), 402–408 (2010)
3. André, T., Lévesque, V., Hayward, V., Lefèvre, P., Thonnard, J.L.: Effect of skin hydration on the dynamics of fingertip gripping contact. J. R. Soc. Interface 8(64), 1574–1583 (2011)
4. Augurelle, A.S., Smith, A.M., Lejeune, T., Thonnard, J.L.: Importance of cutaneous feedback in maintaining a secure grip during manipulation of hand-held objects. J. Neurophysiol. 89(2), 665–671 (2003)
5. Bell-Krotoski, J., Weinstein, S., Weinstein, C.: Testing sensibility, including touch-pressure, two-point discrimination, point localization, and vibration. J. Hand Ther. 6(2), 114–123 (1993)
6. Bennett, K.M., Castiello, U.: Reach to grasp: changes with age. J. Gerontol. 49(1), P1–P7 (1994)
7. Bush, R.R.: Estimation and evaluation. Handbook of Mathematical Psychology 1, 429–469 (1963)
8. Carmeli, E., Patish, H., Coleman, R.: The aging hand. J. Gerontol. A Biol. Sci. Med. Sci. 58(2), M146–M152 (2003)
9. Cole, K.J., Beck, C.L.: The stability of precision grip force in older adults. J. Mot. Behav. 26(2), 171–177 (1994)
10. Cole, K.J., Rotella, D.L., Harper, J.G.: Tactile impairments cannot explain the effect of age on a grasp and lift task. Exp. Brain Res. 121(3), 263–269 (1998)
11. Cornsweet, T.N.: The staircase-method in psychophysics. Am. J. Psychol. 75(3), 485–491 (1962)
12. Couth, S., Gowen, E., Poliakoff, E.: How does ageing affect grasp adaptation to a visual–haptic size conflict? Exp. Brain Res. 236(8), 2173–2184 (2018)

13. Decorps, J., Saumet, J.L., Sommer, P., Sigaudo-Roussel, D., Fromy, B.: Effect of ageing on tactile transduction processes. Ageing Res. Rev. **13**, 90–99 (2014)
14. Elliot, D.B., Yang, K.C., Whitaker, D.: Visual acuity changes throughout adulthood in normal, healthy eyes: seeing beyond 6/6. Optom. Vis. Sci. **72**(3), 186–191 (1995)
15. Ernst, M.O., Banks, M.S.: Humans integrate visual and haptic information in a statistically optimal fashion. Nature **415**(6870), 429–433 (2002)
16. Flanagan, J.R., Bandomir, C.A.: Coming to grips with weight perception: effects of grasp configuration on perceived heaviness. Percept. Psychophys. **62**(6), 1204–1219 (2000)
17. Gibo, T.L., Bastian, A.J., Okamura, A.M.: Grip force control during virtual object interaction: effect of force feedback, accuracy demands, and training. IEEE Trans. Haptics **7**(1), 37–47 (2013)
18. Goodwin, A.W., Wheat, H.E.: Sensory signals in neural populations underlying tactile perception and manipulation. Annu. Rev. Neurosci. **27**(1), 53–77 (2004)
19. Holmin, J.S., Norman, J.F.: Aging and weight-ratio perception. PLoS ONE **7**(10), e47701 (2012)
20. Iwasaki, T., Goto, N., Goto, J., Ezure, H., Moriyama, H.: The aging of human Meissner's corpuscles as evidenced by parallel sectioning. Okajimas Folia Anat. Jpn. **79**(6), 185–189 (2003)
21. Jenmalm, P., Johansson, R.S.: Visual and somatosensory information about object shape control manipulative fingertip forces. J. Neurosci. **17**(11), 4486–4499 (1997)
22. Johansson, R.S.: Sensory input and control of grip. Sensory Guidance of Movement **218**, 45–63 (1998)
23. Johansson, R.S., Flanagan, J.R.: Coding and use of tactile signals from the fingertips in object manipulation tasks. Nat. Rev. Neurosci. **10**(5), 345–359 (2009)
24. Johansson, R.S., Westling, G.: Roles of glabrous skin receptors and sensorimotor memory in automatic control of precision grip when lifting rougher or more slippery objects. Exp. Brain Res. **56**(3), 550–564 (1984)
25. Johansson, R.S., Westling, G.: Signals in tactile afferents from the fingers eliciting adaptive motor responses during precision grip. Exp. Brain Res. **66**(1), 141–154 (1987)
26. Johansson, R.S., Westling, G.: Coordinated isometric muscle commands adequately and erroneously programmed for the weight during lifting task with precision grip. Exp. Brain Res. **71**, 59–71 (1988). https://doi.org/10.1007/bf00247522
27. Kaernbach, C.: Simple adaptive testing with the weighted up-down method. Percept. Psychophys. **49**(3), 227–229 (1991)
28. King, C.H., et al.: Tactile feedback induces reduced grasping force in robot-assisted surgery. IEEE Trans. Haptics **2**(2), 103–110 (2009)
29. Murata, J., Murata, S., Hiroshige, J., Ohtao, H., Horie, J., Kai, Y.: The influence of age-related changes in tactile sensibility and muscular strength on hand function in older adult females. Int. J. Gerontol. **4**(4), 180–183 (2010)
30. Norman, J.F., Kappers, A.M.L., Beers, A.M., Scott, A.K., Norman, H.F., Koenderink, J.J.: Aging and the haptic perception of 3D surface shape. Atten. Percept. Psychophys. **73**(3), 908–918 (2010)
31. Norman, J.F., Norman, H.F., Swindle, J.M., Jennings, L.R., Bartholomew, A.N.: Aging and the discrimination of object weight. Perception **38**(9), 1347–1354 (2009)
32. Pitts, D.G.: Visual acuity as a function of age. J. Am. Optom. Assoc. **53**(2), 117–124 (1982)
33. Ranganathan, V.K., Siemionow, V., Sahgal, V., Yue, G.H.: Effects of aging on hand function. J. Am. Geriatr. Soc. **49**(11), 1478–1484 (2001)
34. Rinkenauer, G., Mattes, S., Ulrich, R.: The surface—weight illusion: on the contribution of grip force to perceived heaviness. Percept. Psychophys. **61**(1), 23–30 (1999)

35. Runnarong, N., Tretriluxana, J., Waiyasil, W., Sittisupapong, P., Tretriluxana, S.: Age-related changes in reach-to-grasp movements with partial visual occlusion. PLoS ONE 14(8), e0221320 (2019)
36. Semmes, J., Weinstein, S., Ghent, L.: Teuber Hl. Semmes-Weinstein Aesthesiometer Monofilament Test. North Coast Medical, California (1960)
37. Shimokata, H., Kuzuya, F.: Two-point discrimination test of the skin as an index of sensory aging. Gerontology 41(5), 267–272 (1995)
38. Sullivan, S.B., Thomas, J.: A Text Book of Physical Rehabilitation. FA Davis Company publication, 5th edition, 720–721 (2007)
39. Tong, J., Mao, O., Goldreich, D.: Two-point orientation discrimination versus the traditional two-point test for tactile spatial acuity assessment. Frontiers in human neuroscience, 7 (2013)
40. Vallbo, A.B., Johansson, R.S.: Properties of cutaneous mechanoreceptors in the human hand related to touch sensation. Hum. Neurobiol. 3(1), 3–14 (1984)
41. Verner, L.N., Okamura, A.M.: Effects of translational and gripping force feedback are decoupled in a 4-degree-of-freedom telemanipulator. In: Second Joint EuroHaptics Conference and Symposium on Haptic Interfaces for Virtual Environment and Teleoperator Systems (WHC'07), pp. 286–291. IEEE (2007)
42. Wolpe, N., et al.: Ageing increases reliance on sensorimotor prediction through structural and functional differences in frontostriatal circuits. Nat. Commun. 7(1), 1–11 (2016)

Laughter Meaning Construction and Use in Development: Children and Spoken Dialogue Systems

Chiara Mazzocconi[1,2]([✉]) [iD]

[1] Aix-Marseille University, CNRS, Laboratoire Parole et Langage, Aix-en-Provence, France
chiara.mazzocconi@univ-amu.fr
[2] Institute of Language Communication and the Brain, Aix-en-Provence, France
https://scholar.google.com/citations?user=ASyZ81EAAAAJ&hl=en&oi=ao

Abstract. In the current work a brief overview of some studies conducted on laughter taking a multidisciplinary perspective will be presented. The integration of analyses of corpus data, theoretical and formal insights, behavioural experiments, machine learning methods, and developmental data, turned out to be fruitful to gain insight into laughter behaviour and on how its production contributes to our conversations. A crucial claim emerging from the studies presented is that laughter conveys propositional meaning interacting with other modalities, in a manner akin to other content bearing words. The implications that such results have for the implementations of more competent, from a semantic and pragmatic perspective, spoken dialogue systems will be outlined. Especially the qualitative and quantitative analysis of developmental data will offer the basis for the proposal of some specific applications.

Keywords: Laughter semantics · Multimodal communication · Pragmatic development · Communication feedback · Spoken dialogue systems

1 Introduction

Laughter has for long been dismissed by the field of semantics, on the wave of a markedly speech- and text- oriented analysis of meaning. By now awareness that meaning is conveyed multimodally is granted and semantic formal accounts of behaviour or features that used to be considered out of the remits of linguistics, or anyway out of those of semantics, (e.g. gestures, facial expressions, prosody, disfluencies) are flourishing (e.g. [4,5,38,48,54,96]).

Embracing the spirit of the workshop, inviting for exchange of methods and insights across disciplines, in the current work a brief overview on some of the

This work, carried out within the Labex BLRI (ANR-11-LABX-0036) and the Institute Convergence ILCB (ANR-16-CONV-0002), has benefited from support from the French government, managed by the French National Agency for Research (ANR) and the Excellence Initiative of Aix-Marseille University (A*MIDEX).

M. Kurosu et al. (Eds.): HCII 2022, LNCS 13519, pp. 113–133, 2022.
https://doi.org/10.1007/978-3-031-17618-0_10

investigations conducted on laughter will be presented, showing how a quantitative and qualitative analysis of cross-linguistic corpus data, in triangulation with theoretical and formal insights, behavioural, machine learning methods, and developmental data turn out to be beneficial for the understanding of laughter behaviour and of how it contributes to our conversations. The multidisciplinary investigations conducted points to the need to integrate laughter in frameworks aimed at modelling meaning in interaction, stressing the importance of a multimodal approach to the study of dialogue semantics, having therefore important implications for the design of Spoken Dialogue Systems.

The paper is structured as follows: in the first part, a corollary of studies related to the use of laughter in adult conversation supporting the idea that laughter should be treated in a manner akin to language and on how its meaning interacts with other modalities will be presented; in the second part, the attention will be shifted to studies on laughter behaviour development, focussing especially on two aspects: (1) a quantitative and qualitative analysis of caregivers' responses to child laughter in development, highlighting similarities with studies in language acquisition; (2) the use of laughter in relation to potentially discomforting situations (e.g. criticising/correcting the interlocutor, asking a favour, apologising). Those will constitute further ground for a concluding discussion about the implications and potential applications that the results presented have for the implementation of more competent Spoken Dialogue Systems (SDS) and Embodied Conversational Agents (ECAs), spotlighting especially on aspects related to natural language processing. Explicitly, in what follows some elements aimed at answering (at least partially) the following questions will be presented:

- Does laughter convey meaning? How does it affect dialogue?
- How does it interact with other modalities in terms of time-alignment and function?
- How do children learn laughter meaning?
- What do adult and developmental studies of laughter can contribute to the implementation of spoken dialogue systems?

NOTE: When reporting extracts of conversations, for laughter transcriptions we will use the annotation guidelines used in the DUEL corpus [49]. Especially relevant will be these two conventions: < laughter/ > to tag standalone laughter not overlapping with speech (e.g., "that's cool < laughter/ >") and < laughter > < /laughter > to tag speech-laughter (e.g., "< laughter >yeah< /laughter >"). Through out the paper, whenever an extract of the interaction is reported, this is provided with an hyperlink to a video-clip of the original recording.

2 Laughter as Language: Triangulating Methods and Insights

2.1 A Multi-layered Framework for Laughter Analysis

Laughter is a universal [88,89] and ancient, both phylogenetically [23,56] and ontogenetically [76,93], non-verbal vocalization; one which is pervasive in our interactions (5.8 (sd = 2.5)/10 mins [102]; speed-dating 21(sd = 9.28)/5 min [33]; DUEL French 45/10 m, DUEL Chinese 26/10 m; BNC 5/10 m [71]). It is so deep-rooted that it is one of the behaviours for which contagious effects can be observed, fostering bonding and affiliation [44]. Despite mostly associated to funniness, laughter does not occur only in response to humour. Especially studies in Conversation Analysis have shown its crucial role in managing conversations at several levels: dynamics (turn-taking and topic-change), lexical (signalling problems of lexical retrieval, imprecision in the lexical choice), pragmatic (marking irony, disambiguate meaning, managing self-correction) and social (to smooth and soften difficult situations, to show (dis)affiliation and mark group boundaries) [40,51,80,104]. It is not surprising therefore that laughter has been object of scholar investigation since millennia from many different disciplines (for reviews see [55] and [14]). Nevertheless, the taxonomies available and the theories proposed, especially for what concerns the classification of laughter uses, resulted hard to integrate. The reasons for the difficulty can be assigned partly to the fact that the different taxonomies were created from different perspectives and for different aims, partly, as argued in [71], might be related to the fact that often different levels of analysis were considered, and inconsistencies or overlap between those could be identified even within the same framework (e.g. acoustic characteristics, spontaneity, triggers and functions). Therefore, in order to comprehensively integrate insights from previous studies, and effectively characterise laughter use, a framework that would clearly distinguish different levels of analysis has been proposed [71]. Making an analogy with speech, it has been argued that for the study of laughter it is likewise fruitful to differentiate aspects relative to the form, the positioning, the meaning, the effects on dialogue and the resulting social dynamics. A pivotal node to highlight is therefore that laughter has meaning, which can be spelled out in propositional form and multimodally interact with speech and other modalities.

The foundations of this claim come from the analysis of adult dialogic corpus data in different languages (French, Chinese and English) and contexts [71] and on attested examples of: successful standalone laughter uses to perform a dialogue act (e.g. answering a question) (as in 1 – and in 7 later in the manuscript), elicitation of propositional clarification requests or rebuttals (as in 4 and 5), laughter reversal meaning (i.e. ironic use of laughter[1]) (2), derivation of pragmatic implicatures (1), and displacing of laughter affecting the meaning of the uttered speech (3) (see [71] and [39] for more examples and detailed discussion).

(1) [Buying ingredients for Carbonara Pasta]
    A: Do we need sour cream?
    B: < laughter/ >

(2) *Example Providence Corpus, Lily 030010* – Ironic use of laughter.
    C (Child): Who's this from?
    M (Mum): Um... that is from the swim club.

---

[1] This is typically marked by peculiar acoustic features, a characterisation of which is still underexplored.

C: What is it?
M: It says we havta have to pay them. < laughter/ >
C: We have to pay them?
M: Yeah.
C: What .. what do you havta have to pay ?
C: What do you havta pay what do you have to pay mommy ?
M: Well we have to pay so we can go to the swim club this summer.

(3) *Example from Ginzburg et al. 2020*
   (i) Jill is John's, < laughter/ > long-term friend.
   (ii) A: She is John's long-term < laughter/ > friend

[71] and [39] propose that laughter has propositional content that arises from the *laughable* (i.e. the entity the laughter is related to – regardless of the presence of a humourous element), exhibiting certain similarity in behaviour with eventive anaphors. This is constituted by a core simple meaning of type $P(l)$ which could be expressed as "The laughable l having property P triggers a positively valenced shift of arousal of value d within A's emotional state e". The laughable therefore is a crucial element for laughter meaning interpretation, being a constituent of laughter content, which can be incongruous and/or pleasant. In Example 2, an example of ironic use of laughter, is provided where both of these properties are negated: having to pay for being allowed to access the swimming pool is not incongruous, neither pleasant for the economy of a family.

This core meaning then, when aligned with contextual reasoning gets enriched and nuanced as a function of the type of laughable it is related to, the type of incongruity appraised, and the context, being able to generate the wide variety of functions observed in adult conversations. Specifically, [71] distinguish four main classes of laughables depending on the presence (or absence) of incongruity and on its type: *Pleasant incongruity* (cases in which a clash between the laughable and certain background information is perceived as witty, rewarding and/or somehow pleasant, ca. humour), *Social incongruity* (instances involving a clash between social norms and/or comfort and the laughable, e.g. criticism to the interlocutor, asking a favour, apologising for a mistake, etc.), *Pragmatic incongruity* (when there is a clash between what is said and what is meant, e.g. irony and scare-quoting) and cases where no incongruity can be identified and the laughable seems to reside solely in a sense of *pleasantness* felt or aimed to be shown to the interlocutor. A structured classification of laughter pragmatic functions has been proposed in [71] in the form of a binary decision tree. It has to be noted that despite the core meaning and phylogenetic origin of laughter are related to pleasantness and affiliation, laughter can also have a negative valence being produced at the expenses of others. The framework proposed in [71] and [39] account also for such uses taking as a starting point the same basic meaning previously stated. The cooperative or non-cooperative goal of the laughter production pertains indeed to another level of analysis. In the case of mocking for example, what in the literature has been often referred to as superiority laughter, would be analysed as laughter related to a laughable appraised as *incongruous* and *pleasant* (someone's misfortune in this case), produced with a hostile attitude towards the target. Due to space constraints, we defer to [39] for a detailed description of the formal representation of laughter meaning proposed, embedded in a framework for dialogue modelling (KoS) [37] (formulated within the framework of Type Theory with Records (TTR) [19]), able to capture the interplay of contextual, as well as cognitive and emotional (i.e. mood) elements, which influence meaning and implicatures derivation.

2.2 Positioning Laughter

The distinction of different levels of analysis pertaining to the analysis of laughter, similarly to speech, and the structured annotation of its argument, proved to be fruitful especially for what concerns insights on how meaning is coordinated and aligned across modalities. Specifically, the data presented in [98] disconfirmed the common sequential adjacency assumption (i.e. laughter always follows what it is related to) (e.g. [102]), showing that laughter can follow, but also overlap or precede its argument. In addition, we observed that laughter does "interrupt" and does overlap with own and others' speech, invalidating thus the claim that laughter occurs exclusively during pauses and at phrase boundaries (Laughter punctuation effect [82]). The patterns observed resemble therefore those reported for manual gesture in relation to speech [2, 86].

2.3 Characterising Different Laughter Functions: Gaze and Accompanying Dialogue Acts

Regarding the pragmatic functions performed by laughter, the statistical analysis reported in [70] suggests that they cannot be reliably predicted from a single factor of the analysis, but that they are rather characterised by specific (partly language-dependent) cluster of features. A further analysis, exploring in detail acoustic features, showed that acoustics, taken in isolation, cannot be considered a reliable cue of the laughter function [66, Chapter 6].

In the same attempt to characterise different laughter uses, [69] investigates whether laughs performing different pragmatic functions would be accompanied by different gaze patterns at the interlocutor. A multimodal corpus of dialogical interactions is analysed [92] in order to conduct an event-related analysis centered around laughter onset and offset from both participants. The results show that laughs performing different pragmatic functions are related to different gaze patterns, both for the laugher and her partner, corroborating with studies reporting different gaze patterns depending on the accompanying dialogue act [52]. Data reported in [7] come in support of this conclusion. Becker-Asano and Ishiguro [7], evaluating the role of laughter in perception of social robots, found that when the robot was gazing directly at the participant while laughing, that led to the perception of the robot's laughter as "laughing at someone" rather than "laughing with someone". Moreover, it has been observed that gaze is an important cue exploited by interactants when reciprocating laughter, similarly to what can be observed in speech-turn taking [6,87]. Those data stress therefore the importance of integrating laughter and gaze for modelling of meaning construction and coordination in interaction, especially highlighting how the combined consideration of different modalities can help in the respective interpretation and classification, and even prediction when desirable [69].

From the corpora studies reported, it emerges that laughter is able to perform or accompany a variety of dialogue acts. This led to an investigation on how laughter is distributed across the different dialogue acts, as annotated in the Switchboard Dialogue Act Corpus [63]. The analysis shows how different dialogue acts are characterised by different laughter patterns, both from the participant performing the act and from the partner, and showed that laughs can positively impact the performance of Transformer-based neural networks models (BERT [26]) in a Dialogue Act Recognition task. These results highlight the importance of laughter for meaning construction and disambiguation in interaction [63].

3   Learning to Laugh: Developmental Data and Communicative Feedback

While on one hand we observe a quite pragmatically sophisticated use of laughter in adulthood, on the other we know that laughter is a rather old behaviour, emerging in babies around the third month of life [76,93]. At this early age, the neuropsychological infrastructure that would be necessary for an adult-like use is not yet available, suggesting therefore that it is a vocalisation the use of which must undergo development. According to [28], laughter emerges as an unconscious vocalisation reflex to a positive inner-state and, through the modelling and influence of the environment [3,60], it becomes an important and varied form of non-verbal communication, one that is crucially social in its nature.

Several scholars have pointed out how laughter can be important from a socio-cognitive perspective in the development of infants [73,85] and how its occurrences could be informative from very early on about the underpinning neuropsychological development [64,72,81], but nevertheless a structured longitudinal characterisation of laughter use in the early years was still lacking. Indeed laughter has been often excluded by fascinating and thorough studies on preverbal infant vocalisations, partly because these were mostly focused on speech-like production, partly because of its putative reflexive nature (e.g. [50,59]). Far from being a reflex behaviour (stereotyped and unconditioned by the environment [79]), laughter is actually importantly affected by the contextual and social circumstances, both in production and perception [1,22,101], and can be carefully positioned in our utterances [41]. Furthermore, it is a peculiarly valuable means for a developing young communicative partner at several levels.

Like other vocalisations produced in the first months of life it is a means to get practice with turn-taking [45,95] and engage in the first reciprocal communicative exchanges. What is special about laughter is that it is a vocalization typically involving positive affect which induces the same effect in the partner [77,78], being particularly effective in initiating, engaging and maintaining interactions with caregivers [85], and in setting off the virtuous dynamic circle of meaning construction and social coordination as described in [34,35]. It is moreover one of the first means available to children to attract attention, first to the self and then to external targets [95], but especially to contribute to the conversation, respond, occupy a dialogical turn and conveying meaning with the same level of proficiency of an adult. It is moreover a signal that supports the comprehension of non-literal or not sincere meaning very early on, e.g. humourous intentions [47]. It may therefore be a crucial means in helping to scaffold abilities which form the basis for further complex mentalising processes.

In order to compensate for the lack of structured insights about laughter development, a longitudinal observation of laughter behaviour in four typically developing (North-American English) children in interaction with their mothers from 12 to 36 months of age has been conducted [66,67] (Providence Corpus, [25]) using the multi-layered framework proposed in [71]. Significant changes over time have been observed both in laughter use (in terms of frequency, laughable and function) and in behaviour in response to the partner's laughter both in children and mothers, mirroring the neuro-psychological development of the child on different levels (especially linguistic, pragmatic and attentional) and the mother's attunement to it [66,67].

What follows will be focused specifically on a quantitative and qualitative analysis of some caregiver responses to child laughter observed in our longitudinal study, that might model and influence the construction of laughter meaning in interaction. Notably, it will be highlighted how those patterns/behaviours identified mirror what has been observed and studied in relation to the first speech-like vocalisations and speech utterances produced by children, namely: contingent responses [8,50,59], reformulations [9], and clarification requests [20,58].

3.1 Contingent Responses

Multiple studies investigated mother responsivity to speech-like pre-verbal vocalisations in infants and their effect on the successive vocalisations. These studies all highlight the tendency of caregivers to reply contingently to speech-like vocalisations (either in the same modality or in another one – e.g. gesture, body posture, facial expressions) [8,43,50,59] and the beneficial role of these contingent responses on successive language production and learning [42,65,97]. Those works though, being focused strictly on speech acquisition, systematically excluded laughter – viewed as non-speech and deemed as a reflex.

Data from the longitudinal exploration of laughter development from 12 to 36 months of age show though that mothers give important value to its infants' laughter productions especially up until 24 months of age showing similar responses to those observed for speech-like vocalisations [67]. Figure 1 presents the reciprocal contingent responses (within 1 s from laughter offset) to the partner's laughter as observed in the Providence Corpus with 6 months interval.

On the left, Fig. 1a illustrates the transition probabilities[2] of laughter mimicry (laughter produced in response to laughter – as in 6), while on the right, Fig. 1b presents the contingent explicit responses occurring also in other modalities (e.g. gaze, smile, exclamations and clarification requests).

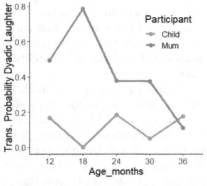 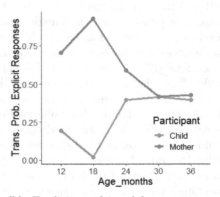

(a) Laughter Mimicry (Antiphonal laughter)

(b) Explicit multimodal response to partner's laughter

Fig. 1. Responses to each other's laughter: children and mothers. – Transitional Probabilities (TP) (taken from [67]).

We observe high transitional probabilities of mothers being contingently responsive to child laughter (within 1 s). The urge to respond contingently to child laughter is particularly high at the earliest time points of interest (12 and 18 months), while it decreases over time (24, 30, and 36 months) (Fig. 1a). The transitional probabilities of contingent responses to child's laughter is even higher if we consider other multimodal reactions (i.e. exclamation, smile, orienting look, clarification requests) (Fig. 1b).

While allowing the earliest equitable exchanges, a systematic contingent response from the caregiver (either aligning with or providing a response in other modalities) teaches the child that his/her contribution is meaningful, communicatively relevant and helps them shape its use [21,24,34]. The decrease observed in contingent alignment from mothers, can be explained by the fact that over time laughter is not anymore one of the few means the child has to engage in interaction, by 24 months indeed the repertoire of communicative abilities is much broader, including speech, and the mother might therefore have a lower urge to reinforce laughter production specifically. In detail, it is worth noting that around 36 months contingent responses constituted by pure laughter mimicry have lower transitional probabilities compared to explicit multimodal responses. This is in line with [59] and [32], who observed that as the child

---

[2] Transition Probabilities are calculated as a proportion of the count of behaviour x to occur from participant A over the total of laughter productions from partner B.

grows older mothers diversify the type of their responses, being therefore more variegated and less consistent, both in the form of response provided and in the timing.

The variation in laughter alignment and contingent multimodal explicit responses over time in mothers might therefore be one of the features of caregivers' adaptation to the communicative development of their children, similarly to the well known characteristics of child directed speech [57,90,105]. The data presented also matches results from other studies suggesting that when interacting with simpler systems, e.g., virtual agents or robots, human behavioural alignment is particularly marked [12,13]. The same seems to apply also to very young children, partly motivated by the will to be at the same level and partly (even unconsciously) aiming to reinforce behaviour, offer explicit feedback, contingent response, and helping scaffolding a functional communication development. The dynamic nature of mothers' responsiveness to laughter (similar to what has been observed in the context of play, exploration, and vocalization) (e.g. [10]), adapting to the neuro-psychological development of the child, supports a dynamic view of interaction [21,34]. Such a view distance itself from a perspective where interaction is only modelled in terms of a sender and a receiver, but where children themselves play an active role in eliciting caregivers behaviour.

The high responsivity of caregivers to laughter and the observation of similar dynamics to those observed in relation to speech, stress the high importance of laughter in early interactions, as well as, once again, highlighting how speech and laughter meaning are similarly treated, constructed and negotiated in interaction, pointing to the fact that they should also be modelled and accounted for their semantic import similarly.

3.2 Reformulation and Clarification Requests

Of particular interest are the cases when the contingent response to child laughter from the mother is a verbal reformulation of the non-verbal laughter vocalization, asking for confirmation or a clarification request (as in 4 and 5). In so doing the mother makes explicit that laughter has a communicative value, propositional content [68], and shows availability to negotiate jointly its meaning and reference.

Similar patterns have been for long studied also for what concerns the earliest speech productions: adult reformulations of child utterances or clarifications requests constitute feedback from caregivers which allows them to correct and/or refine their knowledge [15–17,91].

(4) *Example from Providence Corpus – Lily 010611*
    M: There's miss spider. She's eating a piece of cake!
    C: < laughter/ >
    M: Yeah .
    C: < laughter/ >
    M: < laughter/ > Is that silly ? Whada [: what do] you think the spider should do on her birthday ?

(5) *Example from Providence Corpus – Naima 02004*
    M: March eighteenth.
    C: [non-word vocalisations]
    M: Can you say that?
    C: < laughter/ >
    M: Can you say March eighteenth?
    C: < laughter/ >
    M: < laughter > Is that funny? < /laughter >
    C: < laughter/ >

It is worth noting that all the clarification requests presented assume as default the most basic meaning of laughter, i.e. expressing the appraisal of a *pleasant incongruity* (ca. funniness). This is in fact the most common use of laughter also in adult dialogue [71] and it is, until 24 months of age, the only use observed in children [66]. Nevertheless, in (6) we observe also a propositional reformulation in the form of a confirmation request which addresses rather the pleasantness component of laughter meaning, alluding to the positively valenced appraisal it can be sign of, regardless of the appraisal of an incongruity ("Isn't that good?").

(6) Example from Providence Corpus – William 010605
    (finishing reading a book and closing it)
    M: now everybody was beautiful.
    C: < laughter/ >
    M: < laughter/ > isn't that good ? here, what's in here!

In Example (7) we then see an instance of laughter produced by Naima (18 months old) as a response to the mother's clarification request. The mother interprets it clearly as an affirmative answer (instantiating therefore a case in which laughter performs effectively a complete dialogue act in its standalone use) and makes explicit one of the most common implicatures that can be derived when a laughter is produced accompanying an utterance patently incongruous, i.e. the utterance contains a pleasant incongruity and it is intended not seriously (i.e. doing/saying the "wrong" thing on purpose [47] with humorous intentions).

(7) *Example from Providence Corpus – Naima 010604* – Reformulation
    M: Where did you make the coffee?
    C: Tea.
    M: Tea? there was no tea ! did you make the coffee in the bathroom ? no! Where did you make the coffee ? where did you make the coffee this morning?
    C: < smiling > upstairs.
    M: upstairs !? that's a joke, right ?
    C: < laughter/ >
    M: < laughter >yeah< /laughter >, you're making a joke ! you know that coffee ... there's no kitchen upstairs !

In Example (8) we can nicely observe the process of laughter meaning and reference clarification and negotiation between mother and child, coming to a final agreement. We see the child laughing and the mum responding contingently to the child laughter with a laugh, but her production sounds particularly posed and aimed only at imitating the child, potentially mocking her. The child then, probably felt misunderstood, rephrases her laughter making explicit its propositional content "It is a funny one!", which triggers a sequence of clarification requests about the laughter meaning and the laughable, finally coming to an agreement by the end of the extract.

(8) *Example Providence Corpus – Lily 020004* – Meta-linguistic laughable
   M: Hello *Jessica!* Can you say that?
   C: < laughter/ >
   M: < laughter/ > [laughter from the mother, imitating/mocking the child]
   C: This is a funny one!
   M: < laughter/ > It's a funny one? < laughter/ >
   C: It's a funny word!
   M: It's a funny word? "Jessica" is a funny word?
   C: Yes! M: Ok!

These pieces of data are interesting from two perspectives: on one hand they support, again, the claim that laughter has propositional content, being object of clarification requests like other content bearing words [68, 83]; on the other hand they show that dynamics akin to those observed in relation to speech, in terms of meaning clarification [57, 91] and negotiation [11], are at play also for laughter, reinforcing its semantic relevance, and shedding light on how its meaning and use can be shaped and modelled through interaction.

4   Laughter to Correct

This section will be focused on two laughter uses: (i) laughter production in relation to *social incongruities* and (ii) laughter production in the appraisal of *pleasant incongruities* related to mistakes. The term *social incongruity* has been used to refer to situations where there is a clash between social norms and/or comfort and the laughable. In these cases laughter can come in handy to smooth the potential discomfort (e.g. embarrassment), function as a face-saving device (e.g. apologising, dispreferred answer), softening a potential face-threatening or intrusive action (e.g. criticising and asking a favour) [41, 51, 66, 80, 84].

Despite mother use of laughter in terms of pragmatic functions differs from the distribution observed in adults [66], children are exposed since the first years to a variety of laughter uses. In (9) we have an example of a laugh produced by the mother which is classified as *social incongruity*. The mother is indeed reproaching the child for his disproportionate negative reaction, and the laugh softens her request to stop behaving loudly and being naughty. Her laughter proves to be very successful in helping the child regulate, and (maybe realising he was being funnily distressed) he even joins the mother's laughter.

In particular, in mother-child interaction it is observed a rather relevant percentages (8%) (equally distributed in the different dyads analysed) of cases where laughter resulted hard to classify being at the limit between laughter related to a *pleasant incongruity* and a *social* one. These are most often cases where the mother is laughing at her baby making a mistake, a clumsy movement or mispronouncing a word (whether the mother added a successive correction or not). The mother seems to laugh at the incongruous/imprecise behaviours partly because she finds them funny, but at the same time she is also smoothing the situation and reassuring the child that everything is fine and that s/he can go on with her/his activities/strivings, and in some cases she also softens a co-occurring correction. An example is proposed in (10). In these cases therefore laughter can be considered as a negative feedback, or, when the mum explicitly reformulates or corrects the child, as accompanying one.

(9) *Example Providence Corpus – Alex 030103* – Social incongruity
    C: [non-word vocalisations] try this. No this one !
    M: alright could I use the pen ?
    C: nope [no] . *Nooo! [screaming]*
    M: < laughter > stop it < /laughter >.
    C:< laughter/ >

(10) *Example Providence Corpus – William 010412* – Mislabelling
    M: what's that ?
    C: [non-word vocalisations].
    M: nose. Where's your nose ?
    C: *eye !*
    M: < laughter > that's your nose, this is your eye. < /laughter >
    < laughter/ > You're funny.

These cases stress the importance of laughter in managing interaction and softening potential criticalities from a very early age, and its important role in social referencing, reassuring and encouraging the child as s/he learns to cope with the first challenges [31,94], having potentially evolutionary benefits [46].

Laughter in relation to social incongruity is crucial in our interaction and in managing the impression of the interlocutor, in its use indeed it reassures the interlocutor that the situation is not to be taken too seriously and at the same time, in induce a positive disposition in the partner [77,78,84]. In the latter part of the next section it will be proposed how taking in account such uses of laughter might have useful applications for SDS and ECAs.

5   Implication for Spoken Dialogue Systems

The multi- and inter- disciplinary work (sketchily) overviewed stresses with little doubt the necessity to integrate laughter, and other non-verbal social signals [39], in any framework aimed to model meaning in interaction, not only for what concerns aspects related to affecting computing [7,74], but also for aspects related to natural language processing [71]. The studies overviewed have shown indeed how laughter conveys meaning and how it can affect the meaning of speech utterances and the unfolding of the dialogue.

The investigations conducted, offered empirical relevant insights for the implementation (either in perception or production) of SDS at several levels:

- Laughter conveys meaning which needs to be integrated and treated in interaction with speech and other modalities.
- Laughter can co-occur with speech from the laugher herself and from the partner, and can interrupt speech utterances.
- Its positioning in relation to the argument can be rather free, occurring most often after, but also during or before the argument it is related to; mirroring patterns observed in manual gestures [86].
- In order to interpret the laughter functions performed, acoustics in itself is not sufficient, since they seem rather characterised by a language-dependent cluster of features: positioning in relation to speech, in relation to others' laughter, position in relation to the laughable, characteristics of the laughable, and contingent gaze patterns from the laugher and from the partner.
- Taking in account laughter, ideally in synergy with other modalities (e.g. gaze and facial expressions), can help in tasks of Dialogue Act Recognition and discrimination, disambiguating illocutionary forces and social meaning.

It is here embraced a view that sees computational models useful to study human behaviour and language development (e.g. [99]), but also a view that the other direction can also be valuable (e.g. [18]). The patterns observed in development can tell us a lot about the behaviour object of analysis in itself and can help designers of SDS teach their algorithms how to have a better grasp about what is going on in conversation, getting inspired by the most efficient conversation learners ever: babies. The patterns observed in mother-child interaction brought us to propose two possible applications for SDS.

5.1   Communicative Feedback Learning for Laughter Meaning Adjustments

Currently there are not SDS able to process or produce efficiently laughs with different pragmatic functions. There have been work aimed at aligning with human laughter behaviour [29,100], as well as work in order to implement laughing avatars mainly focused on laughter as a reaction to jokes [27]. Interpreting laughter meaning or producing it in a pragmatically appropriate way is still an important challenge for SDS, since it requires crucially the identification of the laughable entailing rich multidimensional contextual processing. Maraev et al. [62] present a suggested programme to achieve an efficient integration of laughter into SDS highlighting most importantly three essential components: (i) an incremental interface that would operate word by word to enable the speech and laughter to be appropriately positioned and compose the online meaning of an utterance, (ii) appraisal techniques that would infer emotion reaction from the incrementally processed utterance, (iii) local pragmatics that would enable online pragmatic reasoning needed for evaluating incongruity.

The reflections raised about the importance of caregivers' communication feedback for child laughter use learning, showing patterns akin to those observed in relation to language learning, can lead to the proposal of a line of application related to the implementation of SDS able to take in account communicative feedback from the user to adjust laughter interpretation and use. In models of automatic language learning it has been shown that the alternation of Cross Situational Learning and Communicative Feedback is the most effective training setting to have better performances in a simulated ideal language learner [75]. We can imagine a similar algorithm to be applied specifically in relation to laughter: where its production get reinforced by contingent mimicry or explicit multimodal responses, its meaning and argument is discussed, clarified and negotiated similarly to what happens with speech utterances. Positive and negative feedback provided by the user in relation to agent's laughter, might help the system in the negotiation of laughter meaning and in the identification of the laughable. Moreover, we can also imagine such a system to be useful for tuning the SDS to the users' personal or culture-influenced laughter use preference [36,40,71]. This would necessarily need to be implemented in a framework able to represent laughter meaning, as well as shared and private informational and emotional states, in order to account for grounding and clarification requests, as proposed in [61] within the KoS framework [37].

A similar idea has been implemented in a robot producing jokes, where contingent laughter was considered as a positive reinforcement feedback to accommodate the user's personal humour taste [103]. The application proposed here would relate to the accommodation of laughter meaning and use, requiring a more complex semantic representation of the dialogic interaction situated in context [61]. It is worth mentioning that the empirical data provided by [98], i.e. laughter alignment in relation to the laughable is rather free, would have been beneficial in the study of [103]. The authors indeed report how the fact that laughter might occur with a rather free misalignment in relation to the punch line (even before the end of the joke or several seconds after its offset) had a negative impact on the reliability of their feedback measure, causing their robot to miss some of the laughter responses from the users given that it was programmed to detect them only shortly after the punchline offset.

5.2   Failure Detection and Failure Management

In caregiver-child interaction, it has been observed a particular use of laughter from mothers, who often laugh in response to mistakes produced by the child (in terms of phonetics, phonology, semantics, pragmatics, or kinematics) [66]. Similarly also in adult conversation we can observe laughter to be produced in the context of incongruous misunderstanding. Taking into account laughter user's production might therefore be a valuable piece of information to be integrated in SDS, being a potential indicator to support failure detection: when not expected indeed, laughter from the user might signal that the generated behaviour or utterance has been appraised as incongruous by the user in relation with the contextual interaction. Some exploratory work in this direction is being conducted in the context of chat bot interactions, analysing the occurrence of laughter reaction to the automatically generated messages [30].

Moreover, as observed in numerous corpus studies, laughter is not exclusively related to humour and can be used to smooth potentially unpleasant situations, where the incongruity resides in the clash between the ideal flow of a conversation or social comfort and the current situation. This can occur for example in cases where the interlocutor is criticising the partner's proposal or action, is disagreeing, is offering a dispreferred answer, or is feeling embarrassed, or is somewhat intruding the space of the interlocutor asking for a favour or apologising. When a failure is detected, a SDS might therefore exploit laughter in order to manage the failure or the breakdown. This would therefore expand recent investigations on user perceptions of different artificially inserted failures of communication in robots [53]. Analysing the user perception and cooperativeness when laughter is inserted in comparison to when it is not, will offer moreover good experimental data to test the possible co-option psychological explanation advanced in [66, 71].

Similar considerations have been put forward by Maraev and colleagues [61] who present in detail how SDS would benefit from the integration of specific laughter uses at different levels, proposing a proof-theoretic architecture of a dialogue manager based on KoS framework [37].

6   Conclusion, Limitations and Further Directions

It is important to acknowledge various limitations of the studies presented especially in terms of sample size and languages and cultures considered, as well as the numerous questions that are still open. Nevertheless, the studies overviewed show with little doubt the importance of taking a multimodal approach in the modelling of dialogue meaning in interaction. Triangulating methodologies and different approaches it has been shown that laughter has propositional content which interacts with speech and other modalities creating meaning incrementally. This helped in understanding laughter behaviour in itself, allowing to construct, on this pivotal assumption, a structured and reliable framework of analysis, which resulted fruitful to capture patterns in adult conversation and to characterise trajectories in development at different level of analysis, but also in integrating laughter import in a formal representation of meaning in dialogue.

In particular in the current manuscript reflections on the responses produced by caregivers to child laughter were presented. The analysis of those, mirroring behaviours observed in responses to speech like production, once more, goes in support of the importance of laughter meaning in dialogue modelling and sheds light on how it is constructed and negotiated in interaction similarly to other content bearing words.

Taken all together, the data acquired constitute useful empirical material for the implementation of SDS and ECAs more competent from a semantic and pragmatic perspective, both for what concerns processing and production. We outlined the most important clear implications that we envisaged, and proposed some possible suggestions for further applications.

References

1. Addyman, C., Fogelquist, C., Levakova, L., Rees, S.: Social facilitation of laughter and smiles in preschool children. Front. Psychol. **9**, 1048 (2018)
2. Alahverdzhieva, K., Lascarides, A., Flickinger, D.: Aligning speech and co-speech gesture in a constraint-based grammar. J. Lang. Model. **5**(3), 421–464 (2018)
3. Argyle, M.: Social cognition and social interaction. Psychologist **1**(5), 177–83 (1988)
4. Bavelas, J., Gerwing, J., Healing, S.: Hand and facial gestures in conversational interaction. In: The Oxford Handbook of Language and Social Psychology, pp. 111–130 (2014)
5. Bavelas, J.B., Chovil, N.: Visible acts of meaning: an integrated message model of language in face-to-face dialogue. J. Lang. Soc. Psychol. **19**(2), 163–194 (2000)
6. Bavelas, J.B., Coates, L., Johnson, T.: Listener responses as a collaborative process: the role of gaze. J. Commun. **52**(3), 566–580 (2002)
7. Becker-Asano, C., Ishiguro, H.: Laughter in social robotics-no laughing matter. In: International Workshop on Social Intelligence Design, pp. 287–300. Citeseer (2009)
8. Bloom, K.: Distinguishing between social reinforcement and social elicitation. J. Exp. Child Psychol. **38**(1), 93–102 (1984)
9. Bohannon, J.N., Stanowicz, L.B.: The issue of negative evidence: adult responses to children's language errors. Dev. Psychol. **24**(5), 684 (1988)
10. Bornstein, M.H., Tamis-LeMonda, C.S., Hahn, C.S., Haynes, O.M.: Maternal responsiveness to young children at three ages: longitudinal analysis of a multidimensional, modular, and specific parenting construct. Dev. Psychol. **44**(3), 867 (2008)
11. Van den Branden, K.: Effects of negotiation on language learners' output. Lang. Learn. **47**(4), 589–636 (1997)
12. Branigan, H.P., Pickering, M.J., Pearson, J., McLean, J.F.: Linguistic alignment between people and computers. J. Pragmat. **42**(9), 2355–2368 (2010)
13. Branigan, H.P., Pickering, M.J., Pearson, J., McLean, J.F., Brown, A.: The role of beliefs in lexical alignment: evidence from dialogs with humans and computers. Cognition **121**(1), 41–57 (2011)
14. Chafe, W.L.: The Importance of Not Being Earnest: The Feeling Behind Laughter and Humor, vol. 3. John Benjamins Publishing (2007)
15. Chouinard, M.M., Clark, E.V.: Adult reformulations of child errors as negative evidence. J. Child Lang. **30**(3), 637–669 (2003)
16. Clark, E.V.: Conversation and language acquisition: a pragmatic approach. Lang. Learn. Dev. **14**(3), 170–185 (2018)
17. Clark, E.V.: Conversational repair and the acquisition of language. Discourse Process. **57**(5–6), 441–459 (2020)
18. Colas, C., Karch, T., Moulin-Frier, C., Oudeyer, P.Y.: Language as a cognitive tool: Dall-e, humans and vygotskian RL agents, March 2021
19. Cooper, R.: From perception to communication: an analysis of meaning and action using a theory of types with records (TTR). Manuscript (2020)
20. Corsaro, W.A.: The clarification request as a feature of adult interactive styles with young children. Lang. Soc. **6**(2), 183–207 (1977)
21. Cuffari, E.C., Di Paolo, E., De Jaegher, H.: From participatory sense-making to language: there and back again. Phenomenol. Cogn. Sci. **14**(4), 1089–1125 (2014)

22. Curran, W., McKeown, G.J., Rychlowska, M., André, E., Wagner, J., Lingenfelser, F.: Social context disambiguates the interpretation of laughter. Front. Psychol. **8**, 2342 (2017)

23. Davila-Ross, M., Dezecache, G.: The complexity and phylogenetic continuity of laughter and smiles in hominids. Front. Psychol. **12**, 2065 (2021)

24. De Jaegher, H., Di Paolo, E.: Participatory sense-making. Phenomenol. Cogn. Sci. **6**(4), 485–507 (2007)

25. Demuth, K., Culbertson, J., Alter, J.: Word-minimality, epenthesis and coda licensing in the early acquisition of English. Lang. Speech **49**(2), 137–173 (2006)

26. Devlin, J., Chang, M.W., Lee, K., Toutanova, K.: BERT: pre-training of deep bidirectional transformers for language understanding (2018)

27. Ding, Y., Prepin, K., Huang, J., Pelachaud, C., Artières, T.: Laughter animation synthesis. In: Proceedings of the 2014 International Conference on Autonomous Agents and Multi-agent Systems, pp. 773–780 (2014)

28. Ekman, P., Friesen, W.V.: Unmasking the face: a guide to recognizing emotions from facial cues (1975)

29. El Haddad, K., Chakravarthula, S.N., Kennedy, J.: Smile and laugh dynamics in naturalistic dyadic interactions: intensity levels, sequences and roles. In: 2019 International Conference on Multimodal Interaction, pp. 259–263 (2019)

30. Farah, J.C., Spaenlehauer, B., Lu, X., Ingram, S., Gillet, D.: An exploratory study of reactions to bot comments on Github. In: Pre-print. Association for Computing Machinery (2022)

31. Fawcett, C., Liszkowski, U.: Social referencing during infancy and early childhood across cultures. In: International Encyclopedia of the Social & Behavioral Sciences, pp. 556–562 (2015)

32. Fogel, A.: Social play, positive affect, and coping skills in the first 6 months of life. Topics Early Childhood Spec. Educ. **2**(3), 53–65 (1982)

33. Fuchs, S., Rathcke, T.: Laugh is in the air? In: Proceedings of Laughter Workshop 2018, Paris, France, pp. 21–24 (2018)

34. Fusaroli, R., Raczaszek-Leonardi, J., Tylen, K.: Dialog as interpersonal synergy. New Ideas Psychol. **32**, 147–157 (2014)

35. Fusaroli, R., Tylen, K.: Carving language for social coordination: a dynamical approach. Interact. Stud. **13**(1), 103–124 (2012)

36. Gavioli, L.: Turn-initial versus turn-final laughter: two techniques for initiating remedy in English/Italian bookshop service encounters. Discourse Process. **19**(3), 369–384 (1995)

37. Ginzburg, J.: The Interactive Stance: Meaning for Conversation. Oxford University Press, Oxford (2012)

38. Ginzburg, J., Fernández, R., Schlangen, D.: Disfluencies as intra-utterance dialogue moves. Semant. Pragmatics **7**, 1–9 (2014)

39. Ginzburg, J., Mazzocconi, C., Tian, Y.: Laughter as language. Glossa J. Gen. Linguist. **5**(1), 104 (2020)

40. Glenn, P., Holt, E.: Introduction. In: Glenn, P., Holt, E. (eds.) Studies of Laughter in Interaction. Bloomsbury (2013)

41. Glenn, P.: Laughter in Interaction, vol. 18. Cambridge University Press, Cambridge (2003)

42. Goldstein, M.H., Schwade, J.A.: Social feedback to infants' babbling facilitates rapid phonological learning. Psychol. Sci. **19**(5), 515–523 (2008)

43. Goldstein, M.H., Schwade, J.A., Bornstein, M.H.: The value of vocalizing: five-month-old infants associate their own noncry vocalizations with responses from caregivers. Child Dev. **80**(3), 636–644 (2009)

44. Hatfield, E., Cacioppo, J.T., Rapson, R.L.: Emotional Contagion. Studies in Emotion and Social Interaction (1994)
45. Hilbrink, E.E., Gattis, M., Levinson, S.C.: Early developmental changes in the timing of turn-taking: a longitudinal study of mother-infant interaction. Front. Psychol. **6**, 1492 (2015)
46. Hogan, P.C.: Laughing brains: on the cognitive mechanisms and reproductive functions of mirth. Semiotica **2007**(165) (2007)
47. Hoicka, E., Gattis, M.: Do the wrong thing: how toddlers tell a joke from a mistake. Cogn. Dev. **23**(1), 180–190 (2008)
48. Holler, J., Levinson, S.C.: Multimodal language processing in human communication. Trends Cogn. Sci. **23**(8), 639–652 (2019)
49. Hough, J., Tian, Y., de Ruiter, L., Betz, S., Schlangen, D., Ginzburg, J.: DUEL: a multi-lingual multimodal dialogue corpus for disfluency, exclamations and laughter. In: 10th edition of the Language Resources and Evaluation Conference (2016)
50. Hsu, H.C., Fogel, A.: Infant vocal development in a dynamic mother-infant communication system. Infancy **2**(1), 87–109 (2001)
51. Jefferson, G.: On the organization of laughter in talk about troubles. Struct. Soc. Action Stud. Conversation Anal. **346**, 369 (1984)
52. Kendrick, K.H., Holler, J.: Gaze direction signals response preference in conversation. Res. Lang. Soc. Interact. **50**(1), 12–32 (2017)
53. Kontogiorgos, D., Tran, M., Gustafson, J., Soleymani, M.: A systematic cross-corpus analysis of human reactions to robot conversational failures. In: Proceedings of the 2021 International Conference on Multimodal Interaction, pp. 112–120 (2021)
54. Kotz, S.A., Paulmann, S.: When emotional prosody and semantics dance cheek to cheek: ERP evidence. Brain Res. **1151**, 107–118 (2007)
55. Kozintsev, A.: The Mirror of Laughter, vol. 1. Transaction Publishers, New Brunswick (2011)
56. Kret, M.E., Venneker, D., Evans, B., Samara, I., Sauter, D.: The ontogeny of human laughter. Biol. Lett. **17**, 20210319 (2021)
57. Kunert, R., Fernández, R., Zuidema, W.: Adaptation in child directed speech: evidence from corpora. In: Proceedings of SemDial, pp. 112–119 (2011)
58. Leech, K.A., Salo, V.C., Rowe, M.L., Cabrera, N.J.: Father input and child vocabulary development: the importance of WH questions and clarification requests. In: Seminars in Speech and Language, vol. 34, pp. 249–259. Thieme Medical Publishers (2013)
59. Leonardi, G., Nomikou, I., Rohlfing, K.J., Raczaszek-Leonardi, J.: Vocal interactions at the dawn of communication: the emergence of mutuality and complementarity in mother-infant interaction. In: 2016 Joint IEEE International Conference on Development and Learning and Epigenetic Robotics (ICDL-EpiRob), pp. 288–293. IEEE (2016)
60. Malatesta, C.Z., Haviland, J.M.: Learning display rules: the socialization of emotion expression in infancy. Child Dev. **53**, 991–1003 (1982)
61. Maraev, V., Bernardy, J.P., Howes, C.: Non-humorous use of laughter in spoken dialogue systems. In: Linguistic and Cognitive Approaches to Dialog Agents (LaCATODA 2021), pp. 33–44 (2021)
62. Maraev, V., Mazzocconi, C., Howes, C., Ginzburg, J.: Integrating laughter into spoken dialogue systems: preliminary analysis and suggested programme. In: FAIM/ISCA Workshop on Artificial Intelligence for Multimodal Human Robot Interaction, Stockholm, Sweden (2018)

63. Maraev, V., Noble, B., Mazzocconi, C., Howes, C.: Dialogue act classification is a laughing matter. In: Proceedings of the 25th Workshop on the Semantics and Pragmatics of Dialogue (2021)
64. Martin, R.A.: The Psychology of Humor: An Integrative Approach. Elsevier, Amsterdam (2010)
65. Masek, L.R., McMillan, B.T., Paterson, S.J., Tamis-LeMonda, C.S., Golinkoff, R.M., Hirsh-Pasek, K.: Where language meets attention: how contingent interactions promote learning. Dev. Rev. **60**, 100961 (2021)
66. Mazzocconi, C.: Laughter in interaction: semantics, pragmatics, and child development. Ph.D. thesis, Université de Paris (2019)
67. Mazzocconi, C., Ginzburg, J.: A longitudinal characterisation of typical laughter development in mother-child interaction from 12 to 36 months: formal features and reciprocal responsiveness. J. Nonverbal Behav. (2022)
68. Mazzocconi, C., Maraev, V., Ginzburg, J.: Laughter repair. In: Proceedings of SemDial 2018 (AixDial), The 22nd Workshop on the Semantics and Pragmatics of Dialogue, Aix-en-Provence (France) (2018)
69. Mazzocconi, C., Maraev, V., Somashekarappa, V., Howes, C.: Looking for laughs: gaze interaction with laughter pragmatics and coordination. In: Proceedings of the 2021 International Conference on Multimodal Interaction, pp. 636–644 (2021)
70. Mazzocconi, C., Tian, Y., Ginzburg, J.: A multi-layered analysis laughter. In: Proceedings of the SemDial 2016: JerSem: The 20th Workshop on the Semantics and Pragmatics of Dialogue (2016)
71. Mazzocconi, C., Tian, Y., Ginzburg, J.: What's your laughter doing there? A taxonomy of the pragmatic functions of laughter. IEEE Trans. Affect. Comput. **13**(3), 1302–1321 (2020)
72. McGhee, P.E., Pistolesi, E.: Humor: Its Origin and Development. WH Freeman, San Francisco (1979)
73. Mireault, G.C., Reddy, V.: Humor in Infants: Developmental and Psychological Perspectives. Springer, New York (2016)
74. Nijholt, A.: Embodied agents: a new impetus to humor research. In: The April Fools Day Workshop on Computational Humour, Proceedings of Twente Workshop on Language Technology, vol. 20, pp. 101–111 (2002)
75. Nikolaus, M., Fourtassi, A.: Modeling the interaction between perception-based and production-based learning in children's early acquisition of semantic knowledge. In: Proceedings of the 25th Conference on Computational Natural Language Learning, pp. 391–407 (2021)
76. Nwokah, E.E., Hsu, H.C., Dobrowolska, O., Fogel, A.: The development of laughter in mother-infant communication: timing parameters and temporal sequences. Infant Behav. Dev. **17**(1), 23–35 (1994)
77. Owren, M.J., Bachorowski, J.A.: Reconsidering the evolution of nonlinguistic communication: the case of laughter. J. Nonverbal Behav. **27**(3), 183–200 (2003)
78. Patterson, M.: The evolution of a functional model of nonverbal exchange: a personal perspective. In: Sequence and Pattern in Communicative Behavior, pp. 190–205 (1985)
79. Pedroso, F.: Reflexes. In: Haith, M.M., Benson, J.B. (eds.) Encyclopedia of Infant and Early Childhood Development, pp. 11–23. Academic Press, San Diego (2008)
80. Petitjean, C., González-Martínez, E.: Laughing and smiling to manage trouble in French-language classroom interaction. Classroom Discourse **6**(2), 89–106 (2015)
81. Piaget, J.: Play, Dreams and Imitation in Childhood, vol. 25. Psychology Press (1999)

82. Provine, R.R.: Laughter punctuates speech: linguistic, social and gender contexts of laughter. Ethology **95**(4), 291–298 (1993)
83. Purver, M., Ginzburg, J.: Clarifying noun phrase semantics. J. Semant. **21**(3), 283–339 (2004)
84. Raclaw, J., Ford, C.E.: Laughter and the management of divergent positions in peer review interactions. J. Pragmat. **113**, 1–15 (2017)
85. Reddy, V.: How Infants Know Minds. Harvard University Press, Cambridge (2008)
86. Rieser, H., Lawler, I.: Multi-modal meaning-an empirically-founded process algebra approach. Semant. Pragmat. **13**, 8 (2020)
87. Rossano, F.: Gaze in conversation. In: Sidnell, J., Stivers, T. (eds.) The Handbook of Conversation Analysis, Chapter 15, p. 308. Wiley (2013)
88. Ruch, W., Ekman, P.: The expressive pattern of laughter. In: Emotion, Qualia, and Consciousness, pp. 426–443 (2001)
89. Sauter, D., Eisner, F., Ekman, P., Scott, S.K.: Universal vocal signals of emotion. In: 31st Annual Meeting of the Cognitive Science Society (CogSci 2009), pp. 2251–2255. Cognitive Science Society (2009)
90. Saxton, M.: The inevitability of child directed speech. In: Foster-Cohen, S. (eds.) Language Acquisition, pp. 62–86. Springer, Heidelberg (2009). https://doi.org/10.1057/9780230240780_4
91. Saxton, M., Houston-Price, C., Dawson, N.: The prompt hypothesis: clarification requests as corrective input for grammatical errors. Appl. Psycholinguist. **26**(3), 393–414 (2005)
92. Somashekarappa, V., Howes, C., Sayeed, A.: An annotation approach for social and referential gaze in dialogue. In: Proceedings of the 12th Language Resources and Evaluation Conference, pp. 759–765 (2020)
93. Sroufe, L.A., Wunsch, J.P.: The development of laughter in the first year of life. Child Dev. **43**, 1326–1344 (1972)
94. Stenberg, G.: Does contingency in adults' responding influence 12-month-old infants' social referencing? Infant Behav. Dev. **46**, 67–79 (2017)
95. Stevenson, M.B., Ver Hoeve, J.N., Roach, M.A., Leavitt, L.A.: The beginning of conversation: early patterns of mother-infant vocal responsiveness. Infant Behav. Dev. **9**(4), 423–440 (1986)
96. Stewart, D.: Semantic Prosody: A Critical Evaluation. Routledge, London (2010)
97. Tamis-LeMonda, C.S., Bornstein, M.H., Baumwell, L.: Maternal responsiveness and children's achievement of language milestones. Child Dev. **72**(3), 748–767 (2001)
98. Tian, Y., Mazzocconi, C., Ginzburg, J.: When do we laugh? In: 17th Annual Meeting of the Special Interest Group on Discourse and Dialogue, p. 360 (2016)
99. Tsuji, S., Cristia, A., Dupoux, E.: Scala: a blueprint for computational models of language acquisition in social context. Cognition **213**, 104779 (2021)
100. Urbain, J., et al.: AVLaughterCycle. J. Multimodal User Interfaces **4**(1), 47–58 (2010)
101. Van Hooff, J., Preuschoft, S.: Laughter and smiling: the intertwining of nature and culture. In: Animal Social Complexity: Intelligence, Culture, and Individualized Societies, pp. 260–287 (2003)
102. Vettin, J., Todt, D.: Laughter in conversation: features of occurrence and acoustic structure. J. Nonverbal Behav. **28**(2), 93–115 (2004)
103. Weber, K., Ritschel, H., Aslan, I., Lingenfelser, F., André, E.: How to shape the humor of a robot-social behavior adaptation based on reinforcement learning. In: Proceedings of the 20th ACM International Conference on Multimodal Interaction, pp. 154–162 (2018)

104. Wessel-Tolvig, B.N., Paggio, P.: Can co-speech gesture change the perception of ambiguous motion events? In: 4th European and 7th Nordic Symposium on Multimodal Communication, vol. 141, pp. 56–65 (2017)
105. You, G., Daum, M.M., Stoll, S.: Adults adapt to child speech in semantic use (2021)

Skeleton-Based Sign Language Recognition with Graph Convolutional Networks on Small Data

Yuriya Nakamura and Lei Jing[✉]

Aizu-Wakamatsu, Fukushima 965-8580, Japan
leijing@u-aizu.ac.jp

Abstract. Sign language is an important means of communication for people with speech or hearing impairments. On the other hand, it is difficult for normal people to understand sign language. Therefore, We need technology to support communication between people with speech or hearing impairments and normal people, and sign language recognition (SLR) is important to facilitate communication. In this work, we propose an approach to recognize sign language from dynamic skeletons using graph convolutional networks (GCNs). In this method, the convolution is performed by capturing the complex dynamic skeleton of sign language as graph structures. In addition, we suggest a skeleton data augmentation method, which uses MediaPipe and 3D motion data to create a new skeleton dataset for SLR from small data. We use 20 signs from Kogakuin University Japanese Sign Language Multi-Dimensional Database (KoSign) and achieve an average accuracy of 44.6% on top1 and 90.2% on top5 for two subjects.

Keywords: Sign language · Graph Convolutional Networks · Data augmentation

1 Introduction

Sign language is a visual language expressed by the movements of the entire body, including hands, fingers, facial expressions, and mouth shapes. For people with speech or hearing impairments, sign language is a useful tool for daily interaction instead of spoken language. Sign language can reduce barriers to communication with people who are speech or hearing impairments. On the other hand, it is not easy for normal people to understand sign language. Therefore, we need a platform built with algorithms to recognize various sign languages, which is called Sign Language Recognition (SLR) [1]. It is a technique that assists communication between people with speech and hearing impairments and normal people.

In general, human actions can be recognized from various data modalities, such as RGB, depth, and skeleton [2]. Among them, skeleton data for action recognition are easy to acquire using depth sensors, and highly accurate human pose estimation methods have been realized, such as OpenPose [3] and

© The Author(s), under exclusive license to Springer Nature Switzerland AG 2022
M. Kurosu et al. (Eds.): HCII 2022, LNCS 13519, pp. 134–142, 2022.
https://doi.org/10.1007/978-3-031-17618-0_11

MediaPipe [4]. In recent years, a method using Graph Convolutional Networks (GCNs) was quoted in action recognition using skeleton data as input [5]. GCNs is a convolutional neural network that input is graph structures represented by a matrix. If the skeleton data is a graph structure, nodes correspond to body joints and edges correspond to segments between body joints. This makes it possible to consider the relationships segments between body joints and to recognize complex actions.

A main issue for SLR is how to collect training datasets. Currently, there is no large dataset consisting of a large number of people in Japanese Sign Language. Another main issue of our research is what methods of GCNs to use. We use 3D motion data to make a 3D human model do sign language to cover the small amount of training data and capture it from different view directions. Additionally, we use the MediaPipe to collect the skeleton data from the acquired videos. We use Spatial-Temporal Graph Convolutional Networks (ST-GCN) [5] to recognize the actions of the sign language. In this work, I suggest a new approach for SLR using GCNs that can recognize the complex movements of sign language based on the human skeleton. Additionally, we present a new dataset of human skeletons for SLR using a skeleton data augmentation method.

2   Related Works

Skeleton-based action recognition has received increasing attention in recent years. Yan et al. quoted Spatial-Temporal Graph Convolutional Networks (ST-GCN) [5]. As shown in Fig. 1, ST-GCN can go beyond the limitations of conventional methods and automatically learns both spatial and temporal patterns from the data, resulting in higher expressive power as well as stronger generalization capability. The same graph structure is used for all layers, and only the positions of the joints are given as information in ST-GCN. The source code of ST-GCN is open to the public on GitHub.

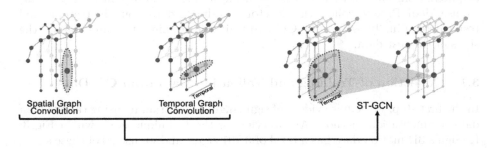

Fig. 1. ST-GCN combines convolutional processing for spatial graphs and temporal graphs.

In addition, a highly accurate skeleton estimation method has been realized. Lugaresi et al. quoted MediaPipe, which is machine learning (ML) solutions for live and streaming media [4]. It offers sixteen different solutions on six different platforms. Python platform can estimate skeleton data such as the face, hands, and body of persons in images.

Kogakuin University Japanese Sign Language Multi-Dimensional Database (KoSign) [6] was quoted as a database of various data on Japanese Sign Language by Nagashima. This database consists of sign language video data (MXF, MP4), 3D motion data (BVH, C3D, FBX), and depth data (XEF) taken from two native speakers of the Japanese Sign Language. Additionally, KoSign provides Multi-dimensional data Annotation support Tool for Sign Language Dialogue (MAT) with its source code. MAT can be used for the word data it provides, for drawing, and as a tool to assist in phonetic and morphological analysis.

Most of the sign language datasets provided consist of a small number of subjects, and the number of data for a sign is small. In KoSign, the average number of RGB videos per sign is 6. The American Sign Language Lexicon Video Dataset (ASLLVD) is a dataset consisting of 1–6 native ASL signers and 2742 signs [7]. It is an imbalanced dataset, and the average number of RGB videos per sign is 3.6. LSE-Sign is a dataset consisting of 2 native signers of Spanish Sign Language and 2400 signs [8]. The average number of RGB videos per sign of the dataset is 1. Therefore, all datasets have an average number of RGB videos per sign of less than 10. Samples of some signs in these datasets are insufficient. Our skeleton augmentation method allows us to increase the number of data from a small dataset using 3d motion data.

3   System Design

Figure 2 shows the system architecture. First, we apply the skeleton data augmentation method. We use KoSign's 3D motion data and MAT to make a 3D human model do sign language in Unity and capture it from different view directions. We use the videos for training. For the test, we use RGB videos are acquired from two non-native signers using a single Azure Kinect DK. Next, we use MediaPipe to collect the skeleton coordinate data from the training and test videos. Finally, we use ST-GCN to train the training data and classify the signs of the test data.

3.1   Collection of Training and Validation Data from CG Data

In the first step, we acquire videos of sign language for training using the skeleton data augmentation method. An overview of the technique is shown in Fig. 3. KoSign's 3D motion data has a total of 3,701 signs, and we use 20 of these signs. The 3D motion data in the BVH format of KoSign is used to acquire the videos for training. BVH consists of skeleton data and motion data.

In this work, we use MAT to load the BVH file and make the 3d human model to do the selected 20 signs. We set the frame rate of the videos to 30fps and use Unity Recorder to capture it. There is no shadow on the 3D human model in the default settings of MAT. Therefore, when the hand and face are the same

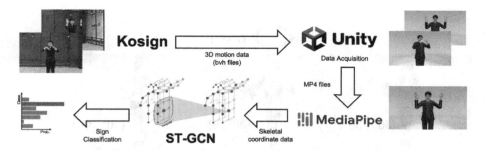

Fig. 2. Overview of the system architecture

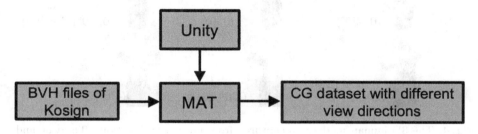

Fig. 3. Skeleton data augmentation method

color and they overlap, MediaPipe is unable to recognize between the hand and face, which affects the skeleton estimation. In this way, we change the material of the 3D human model to add a shadow. We capture nine different views from the same sign in Unity. As shown in Fig. 4, the human model is captured at the same distance but from nine different yaw angles and pitch angles: $-30°$, $0°$, $30°$.

The training videos are segmented to generate videos with only the sign language part and label the segmented videos. The dataset of CG is split into training and validation. We assign a proportion of 80% of the samples for training and 20% for validation.

3.2 Collection of Test Data

In the second step, we acquire videos of the sign language for the test. RGB videos for the test are captured by a single Azure Kinect DK. The test dataset consists of one front view captured from two non-native signers using the camera. We set the frame rate of the Azure Kinect DK to 30 fps, the same as the training videos. We collect the test data indoors. Finally, we generate videos of sign language parts only of the test videos as well as the training videos and label the segmented videos.

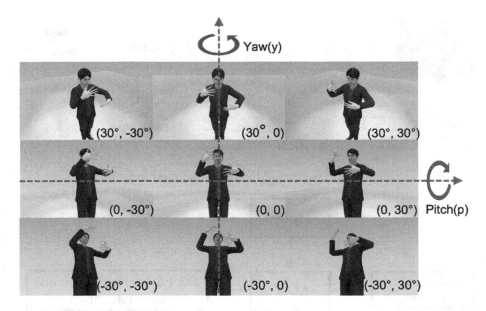

Fig. 4. The 3D human model was captured from nine view directions. The yaw and pitch of each view direction are represented by (p, y).

3.3 Skeleton Estimation with MediaPipe

In the third step, we estimate skeletons from all frames of segmented videos using MediaPipe. We use MediaPipe Hands and Pose to estimate the coordinates of training and test videos for all frames in segmented videos. MediaPipe Hands is a high-fidelity hand and finger tracking solution that uses ML to infer 21 3D key points of the hand from RGB videos frames. MediaPipe Pose is an ML solution for high-fidelity body pose tracking, inferring 33 3D key points from RGB videos frames. Therefore, Media Pipe Hands and Pose consist of a total of 75 key points as shown in (a) and (b) of Fig. 5.

Default of MediaPipe includes the coordinates of joints that are not used for sign language, such as hip and legs. In addition, the joints of the body, mouth, and eyes are not connected and there are three graph structures. They need to be made into a single graph structure for GCNs. For this reason, we adjust the key points of MediaPipe. We add nodes at the center of the shoulder and mouth and edges between the shoulder, mouth, and nose to create a single graph. We select the 59 key points, of which 5 refer to the shoulders and arms, 21 refer to each hand and 12 refer to a face. In other words, the pause was changed from 33 key points to 17 key points as shown in (c) of Fig. 5. Finally, we save the estimated key points in CSV files.

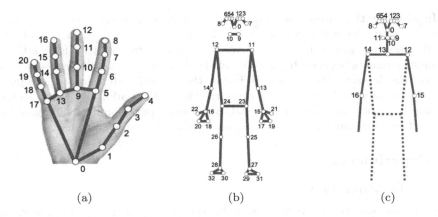

(a)   (b)   (c)

Fig. 5. MediaPipe's default Hands (a) and Pose (b). Key points of MediaPipe Pose after the adjustment (c).

3.4   Sign Language Classification Using ST-GCN

In the final step, we use the training and validation data to create an SLR model and evaluate the model with the test dataset. Figure 6 shows an overview of the SLR using ST-GCN. We make changes to the ST-GCN source code to be able to train and test the dataset we have created.

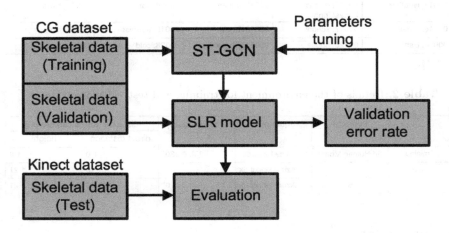

Fig. 6. Overview of SLR using ST-GCN

First, we create an array of (number of samples, xyz coordinates, number of frames, number of joints, maximum number of bodies drawn) from the dataset in the CSV files to accommodate the ST-GCN input. In this process, we unify the frame length of all the data. In this work, the number of fixed frames adopted is

80. In addition, the number of bodies joints and the maximum number of bodies drawn is always 59 and 1. Second, we serialize the data and save it in a binary file. We use NPY files as binary files. We define a new graph layout for ST-GCN to adapt segments between body joints of the dataset. This setting allows for 59 joints of the dataset to be supported. We set the training batch size to 8, dropout to 0.2, optimizer to Adam, and learning rate to 0.01. In addition, we finish the training at Epoch 500. Each joint is labeled using a partitioning strategy called Spatial Configuration Partitioning [5] during convolution operations.

4   Experiments

4.1   Data Acquisition

The 20 signs selected from KoSign to be used as training data are shown in Table 1. Since the sign language of the 3d human model is captured from 9 directions, 9 videos were acquired for each sign and we acquire a total of 180 samples. In the test data acquisition, there are two non-native signers, and the height and distance are the same. We capture 5 videos for each sign. The number of samples acquired in the test data is 200. Details of the training and test videos environment are shown in Table 2.

Table 1. Selected signs for the experiments.

00006: TV	00007: camera	00008: father	00009: human	00010: free
00011: weather	00012: correct, honest, right	00013: Japan	00014: ear	00015: bright
00016: bread	00017: school	00018: book	00019: address	00023: high
00024: Earth	00026: house	00027: Christmas	00028: cold	00029: now

Table 2. Details of the environment for training and test video acquisition.

	subjects	equipment	angle [degree]	distance from a camera [m]	
				direct distance	height
Training	3d Human Model	Unity Recorder	-30°, 0°, 30°	1.0	1.0
Test	A	Azure kinect dk	0°	1.10	1.21
	B	Azure kinect dk	0°	1.10	1.21

4.2   Skeleton Estimation

We save the x,y,z coordinates of the joint data estimated using MediaPipe, the number of frames, and the number of joints in a CSV file. Finally, dropped frames could not be estimated when estimating the skeleton with MediaPipe. We dropped frames for which either Hands or Pose estimation was not possible and removed the files with dropped all frames. As a result, the final sample size was 173 for the training and validation data and 193 for the test data.

5   Result

Figure 7 shows the accuracy of our approach in recognizing the 20 signs selected from KoSign. The top k accuracy corresponds to the accuracy based on the k most likely responses presented by the model. In this approach, we achieve an average accuracy of 44.6% for the top 1, 79.8% for the top 3, and 90.2% for the top 5.

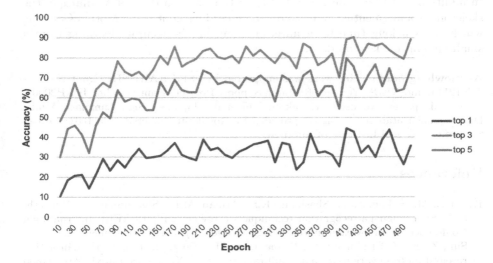

Fig. 7. Sign Language Recognition in this work performance on the test dataset. We report the accuracies on top1, top3, and top5.

As shown in the results, Our SLR model does not achieve high accuracy. MediaPipe may not be able to correctly estimate the skeleton of the hand movements overlap. In addition, when the frame rate is low, if the hand movements are too fast, the image becomes blurred and the skeleton cannot be recognized correctly. When these things happen, we can't acquire the skeleton information from the frame and the frame is dropped as a missing frame. In my research, we remove files that have had all their frames dropped. There are 14 files in total in the CG and Kinect datasets that were removed. This may be the reason for the low accuracy. It is also possible that there is simply not enough data. One way to improve these is to simply increase the frame rate of the dataset for training and test. Additionally, using data augmentation to increase the total number of data may solve this problem.

6   Conclusion

We presented our approach to SLR using the skeleton data augmentation method and ST-GCN. This research uses many key points that are different from traditional studies [9]. The use of 42 key points for both hands combined has the potential to accommodate the complex finger movements of sign language. In addition, the inclusion of facial skeleton data may allow for the correct recognition of signs with few differences. The skeleton data augmentation method will help to solve the problem of imbalanced data of skeleton data.

For future work, we consider improving our data acquisition method. For example, using a highly accurate human pose estimation method than MediaPipe or increasing the frame rate of the videos might improve the SLR performance. In addition, if CG can be generated from the skeleton data of MediaPipe, the skeleton data augmentation method can be used without using Motion Capture, which takes a long time to acquire, enabling highly accurate learning from a small amount of skeleton data.

Acknowledgments. This work was supported by JSPS KAKENHI Grant Number 22K12114, and NEDO Younger Research Support Project Grant Number JPNP20004.

In this paper, we used "Kogakuin University Japanese Sign Language Multi-Dimensional Database (KoSign)" provided by Kogakuin University via IDR Dataset Service of National Institute of Informatics.

References

1. Safeel, M., Sukumar, T., Shashank, K.S., Arman, M.D., Shashidhar, R., Puneeth, S.B.: Sign language recognition techniques- a review. In: 2020 IEEE International Conference for Innovation in Technology (INOCON). IEEE, November 2020
2. Sun, Z., Ke, Q., Rahmani, H., Bennamoun, M., Wang, G., Liu, J.: Human action recognition from various data modalities: a review. arXiv preprint arXiv:2012.11866 (2020)
3. Cao, Z., Simon, T., Wei, S.-E., Sheikh, Y.: Realtime multi-person 2D pose estimation using part affinity fields. arXiv preprint arXiv:1611.08050 (2016)
4. Lugaresi, C., et al.: MediaPipe: a framework for building perception pipelines. arXiv preprint arXiv:1906.08172 (2019)
5. Yan, S., Xiong, Y., Lin, D.: Spatial temporal graph convolutional networks for skeleton-based action recognition. arXiv preprint arXiv:1801.07455 (2018)
6. Nagasima, Y.: Kogakuin University Japanese Sign Language Multi-Dimensional Database (KoSign). Informatics Research Data Repository, National Institute of Informatics (2021). https://doi.org/10.32130/rdata.5.1
7. Neidle, C., Thangali, A., Sclaroff, S.: Challenges in development of the American Sign Language Lexicon Video Dataset (ASLLVD) corpus (2012)
8. Gutierrez-Sigut, E., Costello, B., Baus, C., Carreiras, M.: LSE-sign: a lexical database for Spanish Sign Language. Behav. Res. Methods **48**(1), 123–137 (2015). https://doi.org/10.3758/s13428-014-0560-1
9. Correia de Amorim, C., Macêdo, D., Zanchettin, C.: Spatial-temporal graph convolutional networks for sign language recognition. arXiv preprint arXiv:1901.11164 (2019)

Gesture Elicitation for Augmented Reality Environments

Francisco Vinicius Nascimento da Silva[1]([⊠]),
Francisco C. de Mattos Brito Oliveira[1], Robson de Moraes Alves[1],
and Gabriela de Castro Quintinho[2]

[1] Ceara State University, Avenue. Dr. Silas Munguba, 1700 - Itaperi,
Fortaleza, CE, Brazil
{vinicius.silva,fran,robson.moraes}@dellead.com,
viniciunascimento1@gmail.com
[2] PUC - RS, Porto Alegre, Brazil
grabriela.quintinho@dellead.com

Abstract. The study of gesture elicitation in Human-Computer Interaction (HCI) aims to improve the interaction with the computational environment, providing improved usability and a consequent increase in performance in executing their tasks. In environments using augmented reality, gestures are preferable over eye gaze, as, in the former, the user does not take the focus off the field of work. However, unnatural motions are more difficult to memorize, and their use puts any gains from using the technique at risk. Thus, it is necessary to elicit gestures to discover which incorporated movement appears naturally when the user is asked to send a specific command to the interface. This work aims to elicit natural gestures for an augmented reality environment. During the elicitation process, research subjects were presented with stimuli to which they should react by performing gestures that represent commands for the interface in an augmented reality environment, such as, for example, moving forward, backward and changing zoom (scale). As a result, 434 movements were found, with an average of 18 movements per person, where nine actions for the right hand and nine for the left hand were separated. In addition, the movements made by the participants were categorized into bi-manuals, those that were worked with both hands to carry out the interaction, uni-manual movements, which is when the participant used only one hand, and symmetrical bi-manual, when the participant performed a move with one hand that depended on the other hand to complete the interaction. After these analyzes of individual movements, an average of 3 movements considered natural for each interaction were obtained, in which the researchers chose the two most performed by each participant; each movement resulted from an analysis carried out considering the naturalness in which the gesture was performed and also the ease that the participant had to do so. The gesture chosen for each command was the one whose category had the highest number of natural occurrences, the one that had the most performed category by the participants.

© The Author(s), under exclusive license to Springer Nature Switzerland AG 2022
M. Kurosu et al. (Eds.): HCII 2022, LNCS 13519, pp. 143–159, 2022.
https://doi.org/10.1007/978-3-031-17618-0_12

1   Introduction

Since the studies initiated by Jacob O. Wobbrock, the elicitation of gestures is a technique that allows the collection of input preferences, in their symbolic value, by end-users [22]. This method makes it possible to discover between the input of manual gestures in the computational context, which acts as a popular tool for exchanging information between users and a [19] interface.

The use of gestures proves to be beneficial in performing tasks, especially when the stimulus for their execution is linked to the daily life of users, providing more enriched information, especially when the task requires maintaining focus on the activity while using the application. This is particularly important for Augmented Reality (AR) cases, where movements are performed in an embodied [21] manner.

Gestures have great importance in human communication, as they are considered an extension of their expressions. The movement of the hands during a person's speech, in most cases, presents propositional aspects to the true meaning of the speech that the individual is performing [8]. Human gestural communication can be characterized as natural interaction with its speakers. Each gesture performed can be considered idiosyncratic; for some authors such as [7] this happens due to the state of each person in each person is submitted to the execution of these gestures, such as anger, love, lie, truth, among other feelings.

This work aims to elicit gestures in augmented reality environments. The process of discovering gestures must occur naturally so that each person can learn the proposed gestures to interact with virtual objects such as rotation, translation, zoom. Gestures learned naturally facilitate their identification to carry out the tasks proposed for each user. The elicitation process consisted of experimenting with 25 participants, aged between 18 and 40 years and by male and female gender, 15 men and ten women. The research subjects performed the gestures that best expressed their intentions during the tests and made them aloud. For example, the researcher asks which gesture the participant would perform if he wanted to change the size to scale of a given 3D object immersed in the AR environment, the participant, in turn, would perform a gesture that he thought was appropriate for that proposed interaction, which we call elicitation. Open, where participants had complete freedom to perform any movements that were relevant to them.

In the following section, information about gestures in augmented reality and accessibility environments is shown. In Sect. 3, the theoretical basis for the construction of the work is demonstrated. Section 4 introduces related works. This work methodology is presented in Sect. 5. Section 6 refers to data collection. Data analysis is discussed in Sect. 7. We present the gestures elicited in section eight. The ninth and last section is reserved for discussions and future work.

2   Gestures and AR

The study helped identify two new parametric categories for classifying gestures. Exclusive to AR: while [23] featured gestures in terms of Shape, Nature, Connection, and Flow. In some studies, the authors observed that the size of the AR object affected the number of hands used to manipulate the objects (e.g., for palm-sized or smaller objects, just one hand; for larger objects, two hands) [12].

One result of an elicitation study is the production of a mapped set of inputs called a consensus set ([1], and [2]). Most More useful than a single set of mapped inputs is observational data that comes from elicitation studies. This includes insights into the formation of inputs, the times surrounding input generation, and trends in user preferences for inputs and input modalities. An example of these extended benefits is the finding that the size of a proposed gesture is impacted by the size of the displayed object [16]. This work extends previous studies of gesture elicitation in AR [13] by testing additional modalities of isolated speech and multimodal interactions of gesture and speech and allowing gesture proposals for each referent. Furthermore, the set of interactions presented here shows the main proposals allowing a better interpretation of trends in the formation of the gesture [21].

3   Theoretical Foundation

3.1   History of Gestures

Among the fundamental characteristics of human language, learning through interaction is transmitted over generations and varies according to the types of existing human societies. For some authors found in the literature such as [14], the origin of gestures are discussed with four proposed hypotheses, namely: phylogenetic ritualization, which is a process in which communication is displayed as a sign of dominance, which may emerge due to the lack of movements body as they are borrowed from other contexts which are where a communication signal is created by two individuals shaping the behavior of both in repeated instances of interaction over time, ontogenetic ritualization which refers to situations where observers acquire parts from the gestural representation of copying the gestures that are directed to them, social learning by imitation and social learning through negotiation that takes into account the shared understanding of gestural meaning originated from a mutual construction in real-time for both members.

However, speech extends beyond what can be considered an expression of content, a social form of action where gesture plays an important role. One of the first psychological approaches to the modern study of gestures can be found in the work of David McNeill *"Do you think gestures are nonverbal"* [6]. In this work, David McNeill approaches the conceptual content aspects of the utterance, observing through an examination the hand movements considered as components integrated into the utterance produced.

Thus, gestures are an indecomposable part of speech, where McNeill recognized that people, when gesturing, express what he called pragmatic content; that is, gestures are always in conjunction with speech. McNeill further considered that gestural movements conceive a kind of mental image form of the components that people are gesturing about in their speech and conclude in his book *"Hand and mind: What gestures reveal about thought"*, that gestures reveal about thinking, involving cognitive processes in the production of utterances rather than considering gestures as the final component of an utterance in the process of social interaction [7].

3.2 Gesture Elicitation

GES emerged from the need for the importance of understanding different devices and environments; this premeditates the increase in the user's ability to interact with more complex environments [11]. Some studies found in the literature demonstrate that gestures can be elicited by experts such as [3,20], while others demonstrate precedence for gestures created by the experiment users themselves, such as the works of [1,10,23].

This study aims at mapping the input of technologies through an interactive design, in which these inputs must be discovered by the users of the [21] systems. GES aims at a better understanding of users' behavior, as, for example, gestures performed on the upper parts of the body are preferred; GES has also seen use for various input domains where it can be found on multi-touch surfaces. As in [1] and mobile devices in [15].

3.3 Concepts and Terminology

Figure 1 shows how the gesture elicitation process takes place. The experiment is conducted by each participant individually, where sessions can last up to 20 min. Participants are submitted to CAD modeling tasks, images, or videos, and later their actions will be captured and analyzed by external researchers.

Some terminology about GES found in the works of [5], and [19] will be shown below.

- Navigation: Navigation refers to the tasks of moving the participant's viewpoints. The user can perform tasks like zoom and orbit. The participants are positioned so that their field of vision is in a panoramic way in relation to the interactions that are submitted;
- Manipulation: This term refers to methods in which an object's parameters are changed, such as positioning, orientation, and scale. The categories that were denoted in Fig. ?? were rotated, resized (scale), copied, and moved. For this technique, the participants also positioned themselves so that their vision was in panoramic mode;
- Primitives: In this group are concentrated forms free of manipulation, such as cone, prism, and box. Usually, in this group, static images are shown to the participants. The term freeform is used to refer to 2d objects that contain lines and curves as components;

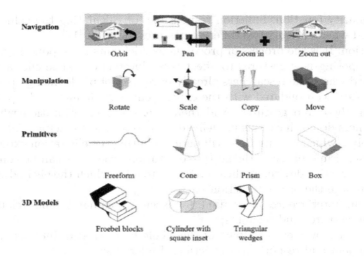

Fig. 1. Methods for the process of eliciting gestures - available in [5]

- Models: Refers to the objects used during the execution of the experiments with the participants. Models can be in either 2D or 3D format and serve as a method of interaction between the interface and users;
- Agreement: Occurs when you have a situation where the gestures of two or more participants are evaluated as being identical according to the rules, criteria, or similarity function. For example, the researcher may consider that the direction of the gesture and the speed are important factors for evaluation in the process of eliciting gestures;
- Agreement Rate: It is the numerical measure that has the function of quantifying the agreement between the elicited gestures of the participants. Example: Of the 20 study participants, three subgroups of sizes 9, 7, and 5 appear for the "Dim illuminates' so that all participants in each subgroup They Agree. The agreement score [22] calculates $(9/20)^2 + (7/20)^2 + (5/20)^2 = 388$ and according to [18], $(9 * 8 + 7 * 6 + 5 * 4) = (20 * 19) = 353$;
- Command: It is the action that activates the execution of the functionalities in the user interface. It can also be known as a gesture command, where the gesture is represented as an input action for interactions. For example, the researcher asks the participant which gesture can be used to rotate a 3d object, the participant, in turn, would propose a gestural movement that he/she found convenient to perform that task;
- Consensus Rate: A measure of agreement found in [17] that employs dissimilarity and tolerance functions;
- Set of Gestures: It is the set considered with the highest number of the agreement for the referents proposed to the participants. For example, in an experiment with 20 people, 15 participants concluded that hand rotation, with the fingers pointing forward, rotating clockwise, was considered an appropriate gesture to rotate an object;

- Dissimilarity function: Function responsible for calculating the value that is reflected when eliciting two different gestures found in [17];
- Elicitation: It is the process of provoking participants to respond to referents and proposing new gestures to affect these interactions. The elicitation can be closed where the researchers already have a set of predefined gestures that will be later consolidated with the experiment participants in the process of eliciting these and gestures. And then, there is open elicitation where the researchers do not have this predefined set and let the participants decide for themselves which gesture they will perform during the elicitation experiment;
- End User: Final phase of the gesture elicitation process, it can be considered as an interactive device, application, or system for which the elicited gestures will compose the user interaction part;
- Function: Interface resource used to execute commands and relationship between gestures and referents;
- Gesture: A movement of a part of the whole body used to interact with the environment and respond to the action of referents;
- : Interface feature that can be controlled using an automated command or the execution of an elicited gesture. Such as, for example, rotating a 3D object in the augmented reality environment;
- Symbol: Any action that makes sense to evoke a referent in its function form, for example, air gestures, dash-shaped gestures, voice commands, icons, button labels, menu items;
- Participant: Subject who volunteers to participate in the gesture elicitation experiment.

4   Related Work

Multimodal interaction techniques using gestures and voice offer architects and engineers a natural way to create computer-aided design models. The work of [5] conducted an experiment with 41 participants to obtain gesture and speech preferences for references and making these models. The authors presented a compilation of gestures evaluated by experts as the most suitable for articulation, as well as a set of terms and commands extracted from the participants' speech. And finally, they provide recommendations for the design of a CAD modeling system based on gestures and voice for projects.

The work of [21] establishes a better understanding of syntax choices in the types of multimodal interactions reproduced by users' speech and gestures in augmented reality environments. The paper presents a multimodal elicitation study carried out with 24 participants. The canonical referents for translation, rotation, and scaling were used along with some abstract referents (create, destroy, and select). In this study, time windows for multimodal interactions of gestures and speech are developed using the start and stop times for gestures and speech, as well as trigger times for gestures. Finally, trends in the most common proposals for each modality are examined. They are showing that the disagreement between the proposals is often caused by a variation in the posture or syntax of the hand. This allows you to present aliasing recommendations to increase the percentage of natural user interactions captured by future multi-modal interactive systems.

The study by [11] looks at how to find a set of gestures for 3D travel using a multitouch screen and a mid-air device to improve user interaction. A user study was carried out with 30 subjects, concluding that users prefer simple gestures to multitouch. Furthermore, the researchers found that the legacy of the multitouch user is carried over by mid-Air interaction. Finally, the work proposes a set of gestures for both types of interaction.

In the work of [9], a gesture elicitation study is carried out with 25 visually impaired users. Quantitative classification analysis is performed with them, and an ideal set of gestures is obtained. Furthermore, typewriting is proposed using which visually impaired users can interact with computers. In this work, an overview of the gesture selection method is presented, and some important facts about ideal gestures are revealed.

What differentiates our research from other works is the fact that we carried out an open elicitation with the participants, guaranteeing their freedom during the experiment and allowing the gestures to be elicited in the most natural way possible.

5   Our Methodology for Gesture Elicitation in RA Environments

5.1   Test Scenario

The Test Scenario consists of setting up an environment that simulates the interface of an application, with the purpose that the user starts from a questionnaire containing the available functions to interact with the AR environment. The functions are FORWARD, BACK, POUNDS, CLOSE, ROTATE, SCALE, AND RECORD. The complete environment contains a smartphone application, virtual reality glasses, and a camera to capture the gestural movements of the participants. As shown in Fig. 2.

With the application in hand, the user will be submitted to the questionnaire where each question concerns the gesture in which the interaction with the application will be used. All questions will be answered in the form of gestures; that is, each answer consists of a gesture performed naturally. During this stage of answers, the process of open elicitation was carried out, where the user has complete freedom to make a gesture that he/she finds plausible to answer the questions. While the user performs the gestures to answer the questions of the questionnaire, his hand movements will be captured where later, after performing a common factor with the other participants, the assignment of each gesture to the functions contained in the AR application. The capture of the hands is done from the top of the participant so that it simulates their vision. Performing this process, the gestures tend to be performed naturally, making the interaction with the application easier making the participant more comfortable and familiarized while using the application.

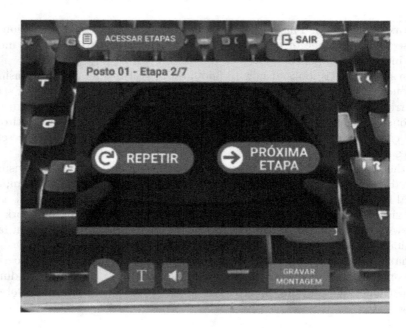

Fig. 2. Application for test scenario and capture of participants' hand movements

The target audience is people with/without knowledge about virtual and augmented reality concepts, as long as they follow the questionnaire didactically. It is not necessary to have extensive knowledge about this area, as the main purpose of this scenario is the process of eliciting the gestures to be used in the AR application. For this, the movements of several hands are captured during the execution of the test scenario.

5.2   Questionnaire for the Gesture Elicitation Process

The applied questionnaire contains questions related to the interaction functions of the AR environment that are present in both video interfaces and 3D models (FORWARD, BACK, POUNDS, RECORD, and CLOSE), where the response form is a gesture performed by the user. Each question consists of a different scenario, where the function intended for the question and the gesture that the user would like to perform to interact with the application are described.

Scenario 01 - Gesture Elicitation for the FORWARD function (Steps) of the AR environment. Question 01: Which gesture would you perform to advance to the next video? Given that: There is a forward function in the application. When: The user performs a gesture that he/she finds coherent for the function to advance. Then: This gesture would be captured.

Scenario 02 - Gesture Elicitation for the BACK function (Steps) of the AR environment. Question 02: What gesture would you perform to go back to the previous video? Given that: There is a back function in the application When: The user performs a gesture that he/she finds coherent for the function to return. Then: This gesture would be captured.

Scenario 03 - Gesture Elicitation for the POUNDS function of the AR environment. Question 03: What gesture would you perform to activate the video pounds function? Given that: There is a function to enable video library in the application When: The user makes a gesture that he/she thinks is coherent for the function to activate video pounds. Then: This gesture would be captured.

Scenario 04 - Gesture Elicitation for the RECORD function of the training carried out within the AR environment. Question 04: What gesture would you perform so that the system could start recording your actions? Given that: There is a function of recording training in the application When: The user performs a gesture that he/she finds coherent for the function of recording training. Then: This gesture would be captured.

Scenario 05 - Gesture Elicitation for the CLOSE function of the training carried out in the AR environment. Question 05: What gesture would you perform so that you could EXIT the augmented reality application? Given that: There is a function to close training in the application When: The user performs a gesture that he/she thinks is coherent for the function of closing training. Then: This gesture would be captured.

Scenario 06 - Gesture Elicitation for ZOOM/SCALE function in 3D objects in the Ar environment. Question 06: What gesture would you perform to zoom in and out of the 3D object displayed on the interface? Given that: There is a pause function in the application. When: The user makes a gesture that he/she thinks is coherent for the zoom function. Then: This gesture would be captured.

6   Data Collection

The elicitation process consisted of carrying out an experiment with 25 participants, aged between 18 and 40 years, and also by male and female gender, 15 men and ten women. During the tests, the research subjects performed the gestures that best expressed their intentions and made them out loud. For example, the researcher asks which gesture the participant would perform if he wanted to change the size to scale of a given 3D object immersed in the AR environment, the participant, in turn, would perform a gesture that he thought was appropriate for that proposed interaction, which we call elicitation. Open, where participants had complete freedom to perform any movements that were relevant to them.

Figure 3 represents a graph with the ages of the participants. Participants were divided into groups of 18–29 years, 30–39 years, 40–49 years, and over 50 years.

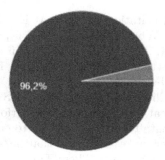

Fig. 3. Age of participants

Figure 4 represents data with participants who have already used devices that work with virtual/augmented reality shown in blue and participants who have never used these devices shown in red.

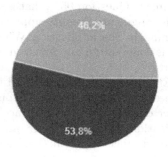

Fig. 4. Use of virtual/augmented reality devices (Color figure online)

As a result, a total of 434 movements were found, with an average of 18 movements per person, where nine movements for the right hand and nine movements for the left hand were separated. In addition, the movements made by the participants were categorized into bi-manual, those that were worked with both hands to perform the interaction, uni-manual movements, which is when the participant used only one hand, and symmetrical bi-manual, when the participant performed a movement with one hand that depended on the other hand to complete the interaction.

7   Data Analysis

After completing the questionnaire and capturing the participants' hand movements, the videos were submitted on situated analysis techniques added to the Elan program. ELAN is the acronym for EUDICO Linguistic Annotator; this tool was created for multimodal analysis, for complex labeling of audiovisual resources. It has a layer-based data model that supports multi-level annotations, and multi-player time-based media [4].

With Elan, it was possible to add annotations during the execution flow of each video. The notes contain descriptions of the movements made by each participant, such as for the gesture of moving forward, descriptions were made of how the participant performed the movements of his hands from the beginning to the end when he lowered his hands to perform the next movement. See Fig. 5.

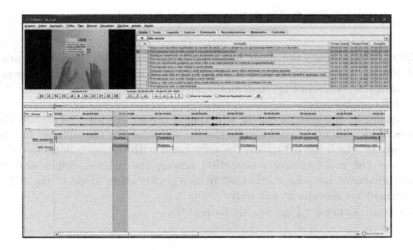

Fig. 5. Elan annotation interface

Figure 6 represents an example of how annotations are extracted from participants' videos. Participants were renamed Research Subject (SP), where each SP has its respective referents, such as the forward function and, for this function, the description of the movements of each of the hands. Each hand has its own distinctive character, where we color the movements categorized through a common factor derived from the videos capturing the movements of the hands of the SPs as well as the notes extracted from Elan.

The researchers organized by color each movement performed by the SPs. And after this separation, the elected movements were those that obtained the greatest common factor on the part of the participants. The descriptions were separated for each hand individually, showing from the beginning of the elicitation where the SP starts by raising the hand until the end when he lowers it at rest.

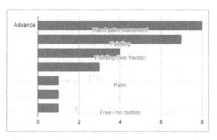

Fig. 6. Annotations extracted from videos

Figure 7a represents the most common hand movements performed among all SPs during the execution of the gesture elicitation experiment representing the forward referent, and Fig. 7b demonstrates the common factor of annotations for the referent return.

For example, the gesture for the function of advancing, the researchers chose six types of movements in common by the participants. For the advance function, the gesture in which the SP makes the movement with the open hand from right to left was the most common execution among the others, demonstrating a natural movement because it emerged from a provocation made to the SP, and he performed his movement naturally.

The same occurs for Figs. 8a, 8b, 9a and 9b.

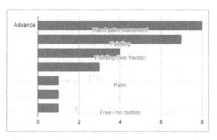

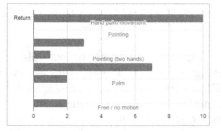

(a) Forward gesture　　　　　　　　(b) Return Gesture

Fig. 7. .

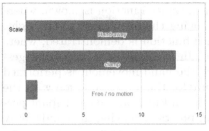

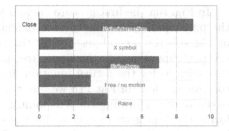

| (a) Scale Gesture | (b) Close Gesture |

Fig. 8. .

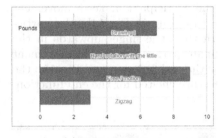

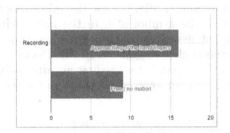

| (a) Pounds Gesture | (b) Recording Gesture |

Fig. 9. .

8   The Gestures Elicited

After analyzing the individual movements, an average of 2 movements considered natural for each interaction were obtained, in which the researchers chose the two most performed the participant; each movement resulted from an analysis performed considering the naturalness in which the gesture was performed and also the ease of use. That the participant had in doing so. The gesture chosen for each command was the one whose category had the highest number of natural occurrences, the one that had the most performed category by the participants.

Next, we have the demonstration of the main gestures elicited from the application of this elicitation experiment. The images contain the name of the gesture and its movement being performed. The choice of the two most elected movements is due to the Libras referent having been elicited only two movements, so for the sake of standardization; the researchers decided to leave only the two most common movements for each gesture.

In Fig. 10a the first gesture elicited for the advance function is shown, where the participant performs the movement of moving the open hand to the right, in Fig. 10b the second gesture for the advance function is demonstrated, where the participant points the finger to the right. In Fig. 11a there is the first gesture elicited for the return function, in which the hand movement is performed towards the left, in Fig. 11b we find the gesture for the return function with the participant performing the left-pointing motion. In Fig. 12a, the participant performs the first gesture elicited for the scaling function, moving his hands away in opposite directions, while in Fig. 12b, the participant performs the second gesture elicited with pinch movements. In Fig. 13a, the participant performed the first gesture elicited for the recording function, joining the index and thumb fingers of the hands, and in Fig. 13b the second gesture elicited for the recording function. In Fig. 14a for the Libra function, the participant makes a movement with the symbol of L in the first elicited gesture, and in Fig. 14b, the participant makes an anticlockwise movement with the little finger upwards in the second elicited gesture. In Fig. 15a the participant performs a zig-zag movement with his hands for the first gesture elicited for the end function and Fig. 15b the participant lowered his hands in the second gesture elicited for the end function.

(a) forward gesture 1

(b) forward gesture 2

Fig. 10. .

(a) Return gesture 1

(b) Return gesture 2

Fig. 11. .

(a) Scale gesture 1

(b) Gesture scale 2

Fig. 12. .

(a) Record gesture 1

(b) Record gesture 2

Fig. 13. .

(a) Pounds gesture 1

(b) Pounds gesture 2

Fig. 14. .

(a) Close gesture 1

(b) Close gesture 2

Fig. 15. .

9   Discussion and Future Work

It is concluded that the elicited gestures occurred naturally; that is, each gesture was generated from a stimulus caused by the methodology of the experiment applied to the participants. The researchers' analysis also showed more than one gesture for each task proposed by the questionnaire while recording the videos; that is, each task can be performed by more than one elicited natural gesture, the open elicitation process provided more naturalness and ease during the execution of gestures by the participants, making the interaction process as comfortable as possible during the application of the experiment and the use of this type of interaction in augmented reality applications. As future works, we propose the expansion of gesture research with the PCD public (person with disabilities) so that we can elicit other types of gestures and also prove the accessibility of gestures currently discovered.

Acknowledgment. This study was an initiative of Dell Computers and Universidade Estadual do Ceará. In addition, developed by Lead - Research, Development and Innovation Center Dell.

References

1. Buchanan, S., Floyd, B., Holderness, W., LaViola, J.J.: Towards user-defined multi-touch gestures for 3D objects. In: Proceedings of the 2013 ACM International Conference on Interactive Tabletops and Surfaces, pp. 231–240 (2013)
2. Cohé, A., Hachet, M.: Understanding user gestures for manipulating 3D objects from touchscreen inputs. In: GI 2012-Graphics Interface, pp. 157–164. ACM (2012)
3. Freeman, D., Benko, H., Morris, M.R., Wigdor, D.: ShadowGuides: visualizations for in-situ learning of multi-touch and whole-hand gestures. In: Proceedings of the ACM International Conference on Interactive Tabletops and Surfaces, pp. 165–172 (2009)
4. Fuldain, J.S.: Elan analisi multimodalerako lanabesa. In: I. Jardunaldiak Ondareaz eta Hezkuntzaz (2012)
5. Khan, S., Tunçer, B.: Gesture and speech elicitation for 3D CAD modeling in conceptual design. Autom. Constr. **106**, 102847 (2019)
6. McNeill, D.: So you think gestures are nonverbal? Psychol. Rev. **92**(3), 350 (1985)
7. Mcneill, D.: Hand and Mind: What Gestures Reveal About Thought. Bibliovault OAI Repository, vol. 27. The University of Chicago Press, Chicago (1994). https://doi.org/10.2307/1576015
8. Müller, C.: How recurrent gestures mean: conventionalized contexts-of-use and embodied motivation. Gesture **16**, 277–304 (2017). https://doi.org/10.1075/gest.16.2.05mul
9. Modanwal, G., Sarawadekar, K.: A gesture elicitation study with visually impaired users. In: Stephanidis, C. (ed.) HCI 2018. CCIS, vol. 851, pp. 54–61. Springer, Cham (2018). https://doi.org/10.1007/978-3-319-92279-9_7
10. Morris, M.R., Wobbrock, J.O., Wilson, A.D.: Understanding users' preferences for surface gestures. In: Proceedings of Graphics Interface 2010, pp. 261–268 (2010)
11. Ortega, F.R., et al.: Gesture elicitation for 3D travel via multi-touch and mid-air systems for procedurally generated pseudo-universe. In: 2017 IEEE Symposium on 3D User Interfaces (3DUI), pp. 144–153. IEEE (2017)

12. Pham, T., Vermeulen, J., Tang, A., MacDonald Vermeulen, L.: Scale impacts elicited gestures for manipulating holograms: implications for AR gesture design. In: Proceedings of the 2018 Designing Interactive Systems Conference, pp. 227–240 (2018)

13. Piumsomboon, T., Clark, A., Billinghurst, M., Cockburn, A.: User-defined gestures for augmented reality. In: Kotzé, P., Marsden, G., Lindgaard, G., Wesson, J., Winckler, M. (eds.) INTERACT 2013. LNCS, vol. 8118, pp. 282–299. Springer, Heidelberg (2013). https://doi.org/10.1007/978-3-642-40480-1_18

14. Prieur, J., Barbu, S., Blois-Heulin, C., Lemasson, A.: The origins of gestures and language: history, current advances and proposed theories. Biol. Rev. **95**(3), 531–554 (2020)

15. Ruiz, J., Li, Y., Lank, E.: User-defined motion gestures for mobile interaction. In: Proceedings of the SIGCHI Conference on Human Factors in Computing Systems, pp. 197–206 (2011)

16. Tarre, K., Williams, A.S., Borges, L., Rishe, N.D., Barreto, A.B., Ortega, F.R.: Towards first person gamer modeling and the problem with game classification in user studies. In: Proceedings of the 24th ACM Symposium on Virtual Reality Software and Technology, pp. 1–2 (2018)

17. Vatavu, R.D.: The dissimilarity-consensus approach to agreement analysis in gesture elicitation studies. In: Proceedings of the 2019 CHI Conference on Human Factors in Computing Systems, pp. 1–13 (2019)

18. Vatavu, R.D., Wobbrock, J.O.: Formalizing agreement analysis for elicitation studies: new measures, significance test, and toolkit. In: Proceedings of the 33rd Annual ACM Conference on Human Factors in Computing Systems, pp. 1325–1334 (2015)

19. Villarreal-Narvaez, S., Vanderdonckt, J., Vatavu, R.D., Wobbrock, J.A.: A systematic review of gesture elicitation studies: what can we learn from 216 studies. In: Proceedings of ACM International Conference on Designing Interactive Systems (DIS 2020) (2020)

20. Wigdor, D., Wixon, D.: Brave NUI World: Designing Natural User Interfaces for Touch and Gesture. Elsevier, Amsterdam (2011)

21. Williams, A.S., Garcia, J., Ortega, F.: Understanding multimodal user gesture and speech behavior for object manipulation in augmented reality using elicitation. IEEE Trans. Visual Comput. Graphics **26**(12), 3479–3489 (2020)

22. Wobbrock, J.O., Aung, H.H., Rothrock, B., Myers, B.A.: Maximizing the guessability of symbolic input. In: CHI 2005 Extended Abstracts on Human Factors in Computing Systems, pp. 1869–1872 (2005)

23. Wobbrock, J.O., Morris, M.R., Wilson, A.D.: User-defined gestures for surface computing. In: Proceedings of the SIGCHI Conference on Human Factors in Computing Systems, pp. 1083–1092 (2009)

A Systematic Procedure for Comparing Template-Based Gesture Recognizers

Mehdi Ousmer[1]([✉]) [iD], Arthur Sluÿters[1] [iD], Nathan Magrofuoco[1] [iD],
Paolo Roselli[2] [iD], and Jean Vanderdonckt[1] [iD]

[1] Université catholique de Louvain, LouRIM, Louvain-la-Neuve, Belgium
{mehdi.ousmer,arthur.sluyters,nathan.magrofuoco,
jean.vanderdonckt}@uclouvain.be
[2] Università degli Studi di Roma, Roma, Italy
roselli@mat.uniroma2.it

Abstract. To consistently compare gesture recognizers under identical conditions, a systematic procedure for comparative testing should investigate how the number of templates, the number of sampling points, the number of fingers, and their configuration with other hand parameters such as hand joints, palm, and fingertips impact performance. This paper defines a systematic procedure for comparing recognizers using a series of test definitions, *i.e.* an ordered list of test cases with controlled variables common to all test cases. For each test case, its accuracy is measured by the recognition rate and its responsiveness by the execution time. This procedure is applied on six state-of-the-art template-based gesture recognizers on SHREC2019, a gesture dataset that contains simple and complex hand gestures tested and is largely used in the literature for competition in a user-independent scenario, and on JACKKNIFE-LM, another challenging dataset. The results of the procedure identify the configurations in which each recognizer is the most accurate or the fastest.

Keywords: Gestural interaction · Gesture recognizer · Hand gesture recognition · Real-time recognition · Template matching

1 Introduction

Miniaturized sensors are today incorporated into almost any everyday object or wearable object, such as smart watches and smart glasses, offering new sources of input for new forms of interaction [3]. Touchless user interfaces enable end users to view, control, and manipulate any type of digital content [18], such as an object, an item, a scene, without physically touching the device, with fingers [7], hands [1,34]. They are explored in a wide range of demanding contexts of use to the point that touchless interaction becomes a requirement. A comparative study is a research approach to evaluate a group of two or more instances of a tool, process, or software system. It relies on a framework to compare different systems that must be described in detail [17]. It is a test that differs from *benchmarking*, which evaluates performance against standard values on a group of metrics. While a significant body of knowledge exists for gesture recognition using sophisticated Machine Learning (ML) techniques, this article focuses on the family of template matching recognizers, which recognize a candidate gesture that matches a gesture class represented by a limited set of training templates. We consider this family of recognizers for their important properties [19]:

1. End users wish to interact by gesture in real time with their associated data with a discrete or continuous control. This interaction requires a low response time (*e.g.*, 0.1 s according to Nielsen [21]) and a high accuracy (*e.g.*, a recognition rate of $\geq 90\%$ [20,31]).
2. For designers, gesture vocabularies should be straightforward to design, to prototype [4], to edit, and to expand, particularly for user-defined gestures [32].
3. For a developer, these recognizers do not require extensive expertise in artificial intelligence as they are easy to train, modify, understand, compute, and interpret [6]. Their incorporation into a development cycle is clear. Pattern matching based on templates is widely used in system development [6].

The remainder of this paper is structured as follows: an introduction addresses the topic of existing surveys and other comparative testing focusing on the Leap Motion Controller (LMC). Section 3 presents some related works of comparative studies. Section 4 defines and applies the systematic procedure for comparative testing. Section 5 discusses the results. Finally, the document concludes with future research efforts and perspectives.

2 Related Work

Much work has been done on gesture recognition and particularly during the last decades, mainly on algorithms to effectively and efficiently recognize 2D gestures [5,11,26,28] (see [18] for a survey), then 3D gestures in general [33] and for LMC in particular [14], mainly inspired by Artificial Intelligence (AI), Machine Learning (ML) [14] and computer vision [8,23].

At the same time, many comparative studies were carried out in gesture recognition and related fields. The comparative study of Khan *et al.* [16] concerns various vision-based hand gesture recognition systems based on three main characteristics: segmentation, detection of features, and extraction phases. While another comparative study evaluates the effectiveness of a proposed feature selector method by comparing it with three other methods based on four performance measures and the prediction time; in order to demonstrate the impact of the feature selector in the performance of data fusion in activity recognition [30]. A comparative study between different devices to evaluate them in a game design context [15]. Despite the presence of numerous comparative testing for gesture recognition and related topics, there are none for hand gesture recognition using an LMC. Ferrer *et al.* [13] made a comparative study of a number of features for predicting human motion based on the minimum curvature variance. Although there are many comparative trials for gesture recognition and related topics, there are none for hand gesture recognition using the LMC.

3   Evaluation

The comparative testing performed in this paper aims at filling this gap in the literature. As such, we selected two available datasets for a number of reasons, including reproducibility. We evaluated the described recognizers in a user-independent scenario. We tested them on full hand gestures provided by the LMC skeletal hand model (Fig. 1a) to show the efficiency of these recognizers.

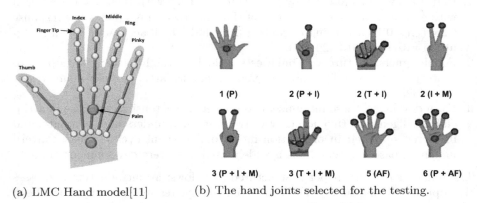

(a) LMC Hand model[11]   (b) The hand joints selected for the testing.

Fig. 1. Overview of the LMC Hand model and joints

3.1   Experiment

Design. Our evaluation was within factors with five independent variables:

1. RECOGNIZER: nominal variable with 6 conditions, representing the various recognizers implemented for recognizing 3D gestures P^3+ [22], F [22], Jackknife [25] and $3Cent$ [9]. And the two new recognizers are described in Appendix A: $P^3 + X$ and *PennyPincher3D*.
2. DATASET: nominal variable with 2 condition, representing the datasets considered, *i.e.* SHREC2019 [10] and Jackknife-LM [25] described in Appendix B.
3. JOINTS: Nominal variable with 8 conditions, representing the hand joints used. Since the fingers contain several joints, we decided to use the information provided by the tips of the fingers (Fig. 1b): "**1(P)**" = {Palm}, "**2(P+I)**" = {Palm, Index}, "**2(T+I)**" = {Thumb, Index}, "**2(I+M)**" = {Index, Middle}, "**3(P+I+M)**" = {Palm, Index, Middle}, "**3(T+I+M)**" = {Thumb, Index, Middle}, "**5(AF)**" = {Thumb, Index, Middle, Ring, Pinky}, "**6(P+AF)**" = {Palm, Thumb, Index, Middle, Ring, Pinky}.
4. NUMBER OF TEMPLATES: numerical variable with 5 conditions, representing the number of templates per gesture for training: $T = \{1, 2, 4, 8, 16\}$.
5. SAMPLING: numerical variable with 5 values representing the number of points per gesture: $N = \{4, 8, 16, 32, 64\}$.

Apparatus. We used a hexa-core Intel Core i7 2.20 GHz CPU and a Windows 10 Home Edition operating system. The RAM was 16 GB DDR4 memory with 2400 MHz.

3.2   Procedure and Measures

We compute the *recognition rate* (computed as the ratio of positive recognitions divided by the total number of trials) for the 6 (RECOGNIZER) × 2 (DATASET) = 12 basic configurations following the typical method used in the literature to evaluate gesture recognizers [2, 4, 5, 22, 28, 29, 32]: the *user-independent scenario* evaluates the recognition on gestures produced by users who are different from those used for training the recognizer. In this scenario, the basic configurations are refined depending on A, the number of joints, on T, the number of templates and depending on N, the number of resampling points to train the recognizer. A template is randomly selected for each gesture class from all participants and saved for testing. Then, a training set is obtained by randomly choosing T templates for each gesture class for all remaining users. They should be different from the templates previously selected for testing. Then, the recognizer is trained on the resulting training set. This operation is repeated $R = 100$ times for each template of the T set.

4   Results and Discussion

Overall, we performed 2 (DATASET) × 8 (JOINTS) × 5 (SAMPLING) × 5 (NUMBER OF TEMPLATES) × 100 (repetitions) × 6 (RECOGNIZER) = 240,000 recognition trials for each dataset. In the end, the number of recognized gestures is averaged to get the recognition rate and formatted as a percentage. We use GraphPad Prism to perform statistical computations.

4.1   SHREC2019 Dataset

Overall Recognition Rate. Figure 2 shows the average recognition rate for all tests under all conditions, with the recognizers displayed in descending order. The \$$P^3$+ has the best average recognition rate ($M = 85.90\%$, $SD = 15.44\%$), followed by \$$P^3 + X$ and Jackknife with, respectively ($M = 84.90\%$, $SD = 16.45\%$) and ($M = 82.11\%$, $SD = 14.06\%$), while the average value of the recognition rate of *PennyPincher3D* is equal to ($M = 80.02\%, SD = 12.38\%$),

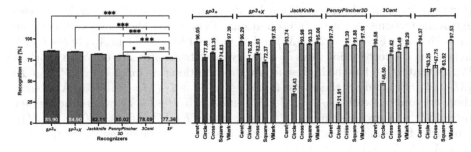

Fig. 2. Recognition rates of all recognizers for the SHREC2019 for all conditions. Error bars show a confidence interval of 95%.

for the last two recognizers, the average rates do not exceed 80% with $3Cent$ ($M = 78.09\%$, $SD = 18.12\%$) and $\$F$ ($M = 77.36\%$, $SD = 19.27\%$). We calculated the four normality tests for the RECOGNIZER variable: K sample's Anderson-Darling test, D'Agostino's K2 test and Kolmogorov-Smirnov's KS. None of the recognition rates followed a normal distribution, while for the Shapiro-Wilk test, the number of samples was too large to test for normality. Next, we calculated a Kruskal-Wallis test with Dunn's multiple comparisons on the measures. The overall difference between the recognizers is very significant ($p<.001^{***}$). Figure 2 shows that $\$P^3+$ is the most accurate Recognizer, and it significantly outclasses all other recognizers. $\$P^3+$ is better than $\$F$ with a highly significant difference ($Z = 48.84, p<.001^{***}$) and significantly better than Jackknife ($Z = 27.86$, $p<.001^{***}$). Also, $\$P^3+$ significantly outperforms $\$P^3 + X$ ($Z = 5.247, p<.001^{***}$). However, $\$F$ is not significantly different from $3Cent$ ($Z = 1.928, n.s.$), while this later is significantly outperformed by $PennyPincher3D$ ($Z = 3.055, p<.05^*$).

Furthermore, the overall recognition rate per gesture class indicates that the gestures "Caret" (/\) and "V-mark" (V) have average rates greater than or equal to 90%. Similarly to the average recognition rates of the other classes, they vary from one recognizer to another. While the "Cross" (X) is better recognized than the "Square" ([]) and the "Circle" (O) by the $\$F$, $\$P^3+$ and $\$P^3 + X$ recognizers. The best average recognition rate for "Cross" (X) gesture class is achieved by Jackknife ($M = 93.98\%$); this value goes down respectively to ($M = 83.35\%$) for $\$P^3+$ and to ($M = 67.75\%$) for $\$F$ with a difference of 10.53% and 26.45%. For Jackknife and $PennyPincher3D$, the "Square" ([]) and "Cross" (X) classes have similar average recognition rates. On the contrary, the gesture class "Circle" (O) has a very low average recognition rate for Jackknife ($M = 34.43\%$), $PennyPincher3D$ ($M = 21.91\%$) and $3Cent$ ($M = 46.50\%$). Detailed recognition rate tables of each condition are reproduced in Appendix C.2. A color-coding scheme reveals to what extent the recognition rate satisfies the rate expected by end users: $\tau \geq 90\%$ [20, 31]. Some recognizers hold few or almost no green cells, such as $PennyPincher3D$, $3Cent$ and $\$F$, whereas $\$P^3+$ and $\$P^3 + X$ have frequent green cells, indicating that many conditions tested gave high recognition rates. Since the goal is to perform a comparative test of recognizers in the SHREC2019 dataset, we refined the results by relaxing the aforementioned constraint: $\tau \geq 80\%$.

Recognition Rates by Number of Joints. Figure 3 shows the average recognition rates for each value of condition JOINTS (A), each recognition rate is the average of the recognition rates of all conditions (T) and (N). The values vary between $M = 75.5\%$ for $\$F$ in $A = 2(I+M)$ and $M = 87.04\%$ for $\$P^3+$ in $A = 3(P+I+T)$. In general, the recognition rates do not vary much from one value of (A) to another. We see that $\$P^3+$ has the highest average recognition rate for $A = 3 : (P+I+T)$ ($M = 87.04\%$) and $\$F$ the lowest for $A = 2 : (M + I)$ ($M = 75.58\%$). Although, there are some conditions $A = 2(I+M)$ and $A = 3(P+I+T)$, where the average rate of $\$P^3 + X$ exceeds that of $\$P^3+$ (e.g. $A = 2(I+M)$ and $A = 3(P+I+M)$). Similarly, for some values of (A), $3Cent$ has a lower recognition rates than $\$F$ (e.g. $A = 1(P)$ and $A = 2(T + I)$).

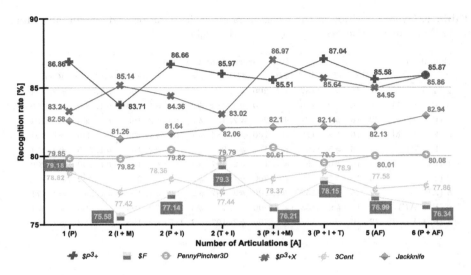

Fig. 3. Recognition rates of all recognizers for the SHREC2019 dataset [10], the plot shows average rates by joint $A = \{1\,(P), ..., 6\,(P + AF)\}$.

As a way to help understand the behavior of the recognizer with respect to both the number of points as well as the number of joints. Figure 11 in Appendix C.4 is an overview of recognizers ranked by recognition rate. This ranking is presented along two axes, the number of joints (A) and the number of sampling points (N). It shows which recognizers are better than the others for each pair of conditions (A, N). To respect the restriction on the recognition rate that we have defined above, all recognizers in this figure comply with two criteria: **1)** the recognizer must achieve a recognition rate > 80%. **2)** The recognition rate must be the highest value among the conditions of (T). Globally, the position of the recognizers varies a lot according to the defined conditions, and few recognizers keep a constant ranking by varying the number of joints or the number of points (*e.g.*, *PennyPincher3D* for $N = 16$ and $N = 32$). For $N = 4$, we observe that some recognizers do not appear, because of the first criterion defined, except for *3Cent*, which has at least a recognition rate that respects the criterion. We notice that for several conditions, the $\$P^3+$ recognizer takes the first place, except for the condition where $A = 2\,(P + I)$ and $A = 2\,(I + M)$ where $\$P^3 + X$ is designated as the best recognizer. In contrast to $\$P^3+$, the *PennyPincher3D* often achieves the lowest recognition rate and is ranked last.

Recognition Rate for the Optimal Conditions. To evaluate the efficiency of the recognizers, we planned to test them in a precise scenario where the conditions are well defined. For this reason, we determine which values of the variables JOINTS (A), SAMPLING (N), and NUMBER OF TEMPLATES (T) allow an optimal comparison of the different recognizers in the recognition rate measure. We completed a de Borda ranking of all combinations of conditions for each recognizer, and the result is reported in the Table 1. The de Borda ranking

Table 1. Overall position of the recognizers for each condition and overall, according to de Borda method across all recognizers (the higher, the better).

Condition				Recognizer (#Rank, Score)					
A	N	T	Overall	P^3+	F	PP3D	Jackknife	$P^3 + X$	3Cent
2 (T + I)	32	16	#1, 1187	#1, 200	#1, 200	#2, 196	#1, 200	#1, 200	#2, 191
3 (P + I +M)	32	16	#2, 1180	#1, 200	#3, 184	#2, 196	#1, 200	#1, 200	#1, 200
2 (P + I)	32	16	#3, 1177	#1, 200	#2, 197	#2, 196	#2, 193	#1, 200	#2, 191
3 (P + I +M)	16	16	#4, 1175	#1, 200	#3, 184	#1, 200	#1, 200	#1, 200	#2, 191
2 (I + M)	32	16	#5, 1166	#2, 186	#1, 200	#2, 196	#2, 193	#1, 200	#2, 191
1 (P)	64	16	#6, 1161	#2, 186	#2, 197	#3, 185	#2, 193	#1, 200	#1, 200
2 (T + I)	16	16	#7, 1158	#1, 200	#1, 200	#3, 185	#1, 200	#2, 182	#2, 191
5 (AF)	32	16	#8, 1157	#1, 200	#2, 197	#2, 196	#2, 193	#1,200	#3, 171
6 (P + AF)	32	16	#9, 1153	#1, 200	#3, 184	#3, 185	#2, 193	#1, 200	#2, 191
3 (P + I + T)	32	16	#10, 1148	#1, 200	#2, 197	#3, 185	#2, 193	#2, 182	#2, 191
...	...	...	...	...	...	...	...	...	...

selects the best combination of conditions the one with the highest overall Borda score. This implies that the elected combination of values has a high recognition rate with many recognizers. Furthermore, we notice that many conditions share the same rank and score in the ranking for each recognizer. This situation is due to a defined sensitivity value of 2% in the recognition rate. We determine the case of a tie between the last ranked combination of conditions and the following combination to be ranked on a specific recognizer, if the difference between their recognition rates is less than the defined sensitivity value. According to the Table 1, the result of the Borda ranking gives this combination of conditions $(A = 2\,(T + I)/\ N = 32/\ T = 16)$ as the best.

Based on de Borda's results, we evaluate the recognizers on the SHREC2019 dataset under the elected conditions. The left part of Fig. 10 in Appendix C.1 shows the average recognition rate for the defined conditions. According to these results, the P^3+ has the best average recognition rate ($M = 97.00\%$, $SD = 7.18\%$), followed by the $P^3 + X$ ($M = 95.20\%$, $SD = 8.59\%$) and the F ($M = 94.20\%$, $SD = 9.55\%$), while $PennyPincher3D$ is the least accurate recognizer ($M = 87.80\%$, $SD = 13.30\%$), for the other two recognizers, the average rate of Jackknife ($M = 93.2\%$, $SD = 10.34\%$) and 3Cent ($M = 90.80\%, SD = 13.16\%$). Like for the overall recognition rate on all conditions in the part 4.1, we calculated the four normality tests: K sample's Anderson-Darling test, Shapiro-Wilk W test, D'Agostino's K2 test and Kolmogorov-Smirnov's KS. None of the recognition rates followed a normal distribution. Then, we calculated a Kruskal-Wallis test with Dunn's multiple comparisons. The high difference between the recognizer P^3+ and $PennyPincher3D$ (10%) is statistically highly significant ($Z = 5.736$, $p<.001^{***}$). Same thing for $P^3 + X$ that is significantly better than $PennyPincher3D$ ($Z = 4.420$, $p<.001^{***}$). Moreover, P^3+ is significantly more accurate than 3Cent by 6.2% ($Z = 3.699$, $p<.01^{**}$). F is superior by 6.4% to $PennyPincher3D$ with a high significant difference ($Z = 3.788$, $p<.01^{**}$). However, P^3+ is not significantly better than Jackknife ($Z = 2.581$, $n.s.$), while this later is significantly better than $PennyPincher3D$ ($Z = 3.156$, $p<.05^*$).

In the same figure, the bar chart on the right shows the number of recognized gestures per gesture class on 100 repetitions, noting that all recognizers achieve a perfect score for at least one gesture class. Among the gesture classes in question, there is the "Caret" (/\) for *PennyPincher3D* and *3Cent* recognizers, and also the "V-mark" (V) gesture class for $P^3 + X$, F recognizers. While P^3+ achieves an accuracy rate of ($\frac{100}{100}$) for two gesture classes : the "V-mark" (V) and the "Cross" (X). Although Jackknife achieves a flawless recognition for three gesture classes: 'Caret" (/\), "Cross"(X) and 'V-mark" (V), its recognition of the "Circle"(O) gesture class is weak ($\frac{75}{100}$). This difficulty is also encountered by *PennyPincher3D* for the same gesture class ($\frac{59}{100}$) as for *3Cent*. However, the latter achieves the best accuracy rate for the "Square"([]) gesture class ($\frac{99}{100}$) which means that *PennyPincher3D* is well designed to recognize this gesture class, especially when the other recognizers perform less well in recognizing it.

Overall Conditions Execution Time. In Fig. 4a the average execution times of the different recognizers for all conditions varied between ($M = 0.047$ ms, $SD = 0.060$ ms) for the *PennyPincher3D* and ($M = 1.611$ ms, $SD = 3.328$ ms) for the P^3+. The execution times do not follow a normal distribution, we calculated a Kruskal-Wallis test which indicates a significant difference in the execution times of the recognizers. After that, the Dunn's multiple comparisons, show significant differences for all pairs of recognizers except between *3Cent* and $P^3 + X$. The *PennyPincher3D* ($M = 0.047$ ms, $SD = 0.060$ ms) is significantly faster than other recognizers; It is significantly better than Jackknife ($M = 0.195$ ms, $SD = 0.2457$ ms) with a difference of 148 µs ($Z = 73.62$, $p<.001^{***}$), and outperforms significantly the slowest recognizer P^3+ ($Z = 147.7$, $p<.001^{***}$).

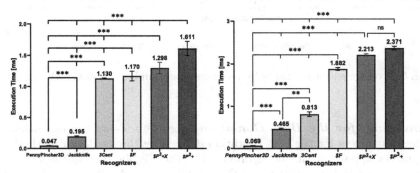

(a) Execution times for all conditions.

(b) Exec. times for the optimal conditions.

Fig. 4. Average execution times by recognizer. Error bars show a confidence interval of 95%.

Overall Execution Time by Number of Joints. The graphs in Fig. 5 show the execution times according to the values of the variable JOINTS (A). The smallest value in the graphic is the averaged execution time of *PennyPincher3D* for the condition $A = 1$ (P) ($M = 0.017$ ms, $SD = 0.020$ ms), while the longest execution time is achieved by $\$P^3+$ for $A = 6$ $(P + AF)$ ($M = 3.204$ ms, $SD = 5.936$ ms). The *PennyPincher3D* is the fastest recognizer and is ahead of the Jackknife. According to the results, we distinguish two groups of recognizers with regard to their execution times. The one formed by Jackknife ($M = 0.195$ ms, $SD = 0.246$ ms) and *PennyPincher3D*; with a small slope, they are not much affected by the variation in the number of articulations. The second group consisting of $3Cent$($M = 1.130$ ms, $SD = 0.683$ ms), $\$F$ ($M = 1.170$ ms, $SD = 3.328$ ms), $\$P^3 + X$($M = 1.298$ ms, $SD = 2.731$ ms) and $\$P^3+$ in order from fastest to slowest recognizer; All the recognizers are significantly impacted by the variation of number of joints ($p<.001^{***}$).

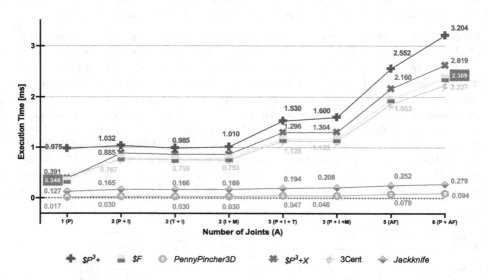

Fig. 5. Average execution times by recognizer per number of joints (A).

Execution Time for the Best Condition. Figure 4b shows the execution time of the recognizers for the best condition defined by the de Borda method. The recognizers appear in the same order as in the Fig. 4a. *PennyPincher3D* remains the fastest ($M = 0.069$ ms, $SD = 0.005$ ms) and $\$P^3+$ the slowest ($M = 2.371$ ms, $SD = 0.213$ ms). The Kruskal-Wallis shows significant differences between all the recognizers except between the $\$P^3+$ and $\$P^3 + X$ ($Z = 1.910, n.s.$).

4.2   Jackknife-LM Dataset

Overall Recognition Rate. The Jackknife-LM dataset has more gesture classes than SHREC2019, mainly complex gestures where different joints can move independently of the hand movement. Figure 6a sums up the averaged recognition results of each of the recognizers for all tests under all conditions. The results give an overview of the results with this dataset which are different from the results obtained for the SHREC2019. In general, none of the recognizers went beyond the 80%. The Jackknife recognizer ($M = 73.60\%$, $SD = 19.75\%$) takes the lead and outperforms significantly other recognizers, followed by the P^3+ ($M = 68.75\%$, $SD = 19.73\%$), which is slightly better than $P^3 + X$ ($M = 68.15\%$, $SD = 20.51\%$) by (0.60%). They are followed by $3Cent$ and F with respectfully ($M = 63.66\%$, $SD = 18.29\%$) and ($M = 62.96\%$, $SD = 20.12\%$) which are significantly better than $PennyPincher3D$ the least efficient of the recognizers ($M = 56.87\%$, $SD = 19.99\%$).

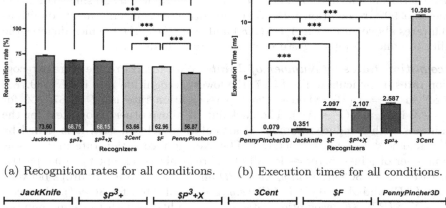

(a) Recognition rates for all conditions.   (b) Execution times for all conditions.

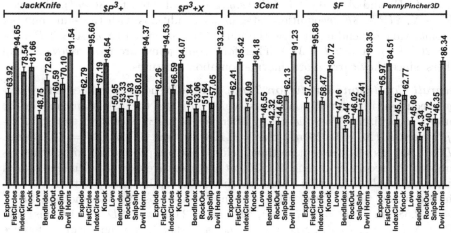

(c) Overall recognition rates for all conditions by gesture class.

Fig. 6. Recognition rates and execution times of all recognizers for the Jackknife-LM for user independent scenario. Error bars show a confidence interval of 95%.

Three gesture classes ("FistCircles", "Knock" and "Sideways") are well recognized for all the recognizers (*i.e.* $\tau \geq 80\%$ - Fig. 6c, bottom). An exception to this is *PennyPincher3D* where the "Knock" gesture has an average recognition rate of ($M = 62, 77\%$). However, the "Love", "BendIndex", "DevilHorns" and "SnipSnip" have the worst average recognition rates for most recognizers (*i.e.* $\tau \leq 60\%$), except for Jackknife, where the "SnipSnip" and "BendIndex" are above 70%. These results indicate that for many recognizers, many conditions perform very well with gestures where the fingers remain static, regardless of hand movements, whereas the recognition rate drops down for many conditions with gestures that include finger movements. From the table in the Appendix C.3 which details the average recognition rates for the different conditions. The orange cells are the predominant ones in the table for majority of the recognizers, which express a low recognition rate for many conditions $\tau \leq 80\%$ (*e.g. PennyPincher3D*, $3Cent$ and $\$F$). For *PennyPincher3D*, $3Cent$, no single condition achieves a 90% recognition rate. While for other recognizers, many conditions reach rates above 90% with $A = 5\,(AF)$ and $A = 6\,(P + AF)$, which denotes the ability to handle complex gestures under certain conditions.

Recognition Rates by Number of Joints. With respect to the average recognition rates by articulation in Fig. 7, the lowest recognition rate is $M = 39.78\%$ for $\$F$ in $A = 1\,(P)$, whereas the top recognition rate is $M = 87.78\%$ for $\$P^3 + X$ in $A = 6\,(P + AF)$. The Jackknife is above other recognizers for the conditions with a reduced number of articulations ($A \leq 3$), then it is joined by $\$P^3+$ and $\$P^3 + X$ at $A = 5\,(AF)$. The average recognition rate increases as the number of joints increases for all of the recognizers, except for some particular cases, as for $3Cent$, *PennyPincher3D* and $\$P3+$ whose rate drops between $A = 5\,(AF)$ and $A = 6\,(P + AF)$ (*e.g.* a drop of 2.6% for $3Cent$). However, $\$P^3 + X$, $\$P^3+$, $\$F$ recognition rates under conditions with the same number of joints vary depending on how the joints are configured (*e.g.*, $A = 2(P + I)$, $A = 2(T + I)$, $A = 2(I + M)$). Therefore, some joints are more relevant than others, since they carry more information about gestures.

Overall Conditions Execution Time. Figure 6b shows the values of the average execution times for all conditions, which indicates the execution time for the various recognizers. There is a big difference between execution time of *PennyPincher3D* ($M = 0.079$ ms, $SD = 0.108$ ms) and $3Cent$ ($M = 10.585$ ms, $SD = 5.911$ ms). The execution time includes the pre-processing time of the gesture and the recognition time. For $3Cent$ the excessive execution time is caused by the resampling function based on the Cubic Spline interpolation method. The execution times of the other recognizers are close to one another, $\$P^3+$ ($M = 2.587$ ms, $SD = 4.371$ ms), $\$F$ ($M = 2.097$ ms, $SD = 4.184$ ms) and $\$P^3 + X$ ($M = 2.107$ ms, $SD = 4.371$ ms) and there is no significant difference between the latter two ($Z = 1.772, n.s.$). Jackknife, which has the highest recognition rate, is also a fast recognizer ($M = 0.351$ ms, $SD = 0.508$ ms). Thus, it makes it well suited to this dataset.

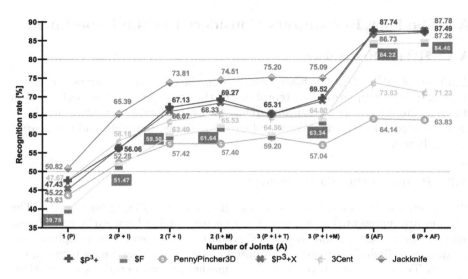

Fig. 7. Recognition rates of all recognizers for the Jackknife-LM dataset [25], the plot shows average rates by joint $A = \{1\ (P), ..., 6\ (P + AF)\}$.

5 Conclusion

The objective of this comparative study on LMC-based gestures is to fill a gap in the literature. For this reason, we evaluated in a user-independent scenario six gesture recognizers on two LMC-Based datasets composed of simple and complex gestures (*i.e.* SHREC2019 and Jackknife-LM). Overall, for the SHREC2019, $\$P^3+$ achieved the best recognition rate and is significantly better than the other recognizers and it was confirmed under particular optimal conditions, while $\$F$ is the worst for this dataset. We also noticed that some recognizers are more adapted to recognize certain gestures than others. For the Jackknife-LM dataset, the Jackknife recognizer achieves overall good recognition rates under certain conditions, but does not satisfy the high accuracy property for many other conditions. We have seen that many recognizers are impacted by the nature of the gesture performed. Furthermore, some recognizers are slow to process long gestures, which makes them less attractive. This procedure is a good contribution to designers who wish to choose a reliable and efficient recognizer and thus guide them to meet their needs. The limitation of this study is that it only includes one type of gesture recognition algorithm based on the template matching technique. A solution to be implemented in the future would be to extend the tests with new machine learning algorithms and new gestures related to specific application fields by including more datasets.

A   The New Recognizers Considered in the Experiment

A.1 P^3+X Recognizer

A variant of P^3+ [27], that takes into account the direction-invariance by tracking conflicting templates (*i.e.*, templates of the same gesture but performed in different directions). If a gesture matches with a conflicting template, its direction is compared with the direction of each conflicting template and the nearest one is chosen.

A.2   PennyPincher3D Recognizer

PennyPincher3D is an adaptation of the 2D recognizer *PennyPincher* [24]. The gestures are represented as a set of $N-1$ vectors linking between N equidistant points. The recognizer matches the candidate gesture with the template that maximizes a dissimilarity score, computed as the sum of the angles between the vectors. The computation relies on basic mathematical operations as additions and multiplications. The gestures require just a resampling as prepossessing. This recognizer is scale- and position- invariant as most of the $-recognizers.

B   The Datasets Considered in the Experiment

B.1   SHREC2019 [10]

The **SHREC2019** dataset [10] contains a sequence of 3D points and quaternions for each hand's joint designating one of five gesture classes (Fig. 8): "Cross" (X), "Circle" (O), "V-mark" (V), "Caret" (/\), and "Square" ([])). It served in (SHREC) track, a contest on online gesture recognition to detect command gestures from hands' movements in a virtual reality context. The proposed dataset consists of 195 3D movements performed by 13 participants with the whole hand. The dataset contains unsegmented gestures, the training set and the testing set were merged to create a unique dataset in which, unnecessary hand movements were removed from the gestures.

Cross "X"   **Circle "O"**   **V-mark "V"**   **Caret "^"**   **Square "[]"**

Fig. 8. The SHREC2019 gesture classes.

B.2   Jackknife-LM [25]

The **Jackknife-LM (Jackknife-LeapMotion)** dataset [25] contains 3D complex gestures of the hand and saved as 3D skeleton which is provided by the LeapMotion. We used the segmented gestures composed by 360 samples of 9 different gesture classes for example "Fist Circles", "Snip Snip", "Explode" (Fig. 9). It was used to test a rejection approach of non-gesture sequences from a continuous data stream. While segmented gestures make up the training set, authors employ unsegmented sessions of samples in the test [25].

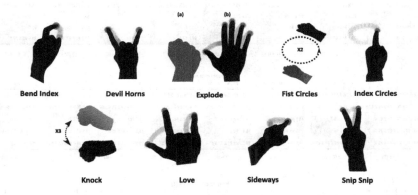

Fig. 9. The Jackknife-LM gesture classes [25].

C   Recognition Rates

C.1   Recognition Rate for Best Condition for the SHREC2019

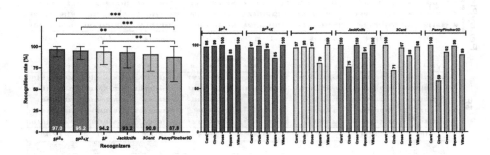

Fig. 10. Recognition rate (left) and the number of recognized gestures per class over 100 trials (right) of all recognizers for user independent scenario, for the optimal conditions defined by the de Borda ranking: $A = 2\,(T + I)$, $N = 32$, $T = 16$. Error bars show a confidence interval of 95%.

C.2   Recognition Rates Tables for the SHREC2019

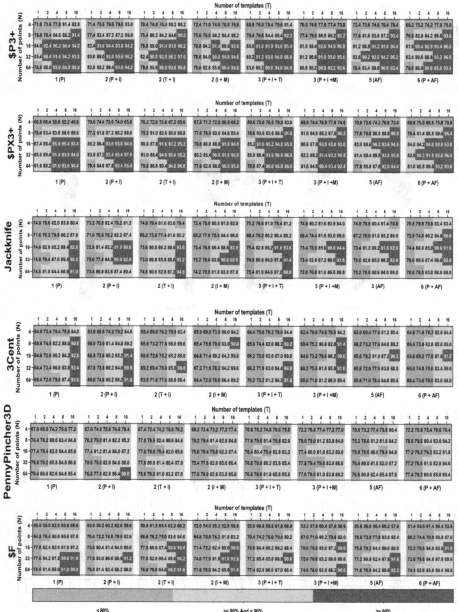

C.3   Recognition Rates Tables for the Jackknife-LM

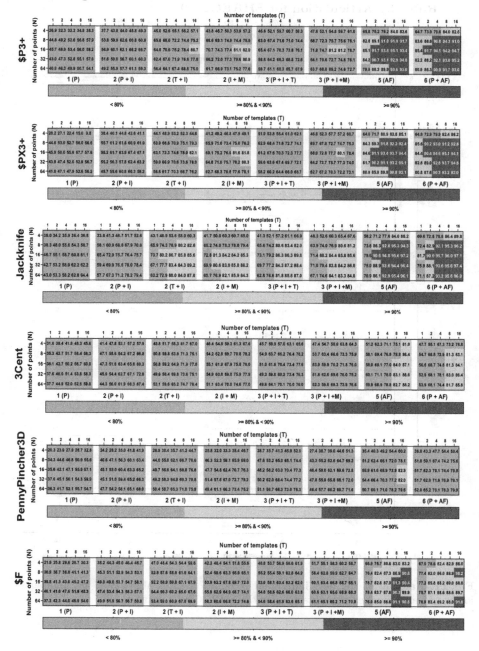

C.4   The Ranking of the Recognizers Based on the Best Individual Rates by Articulation for SHREC2019

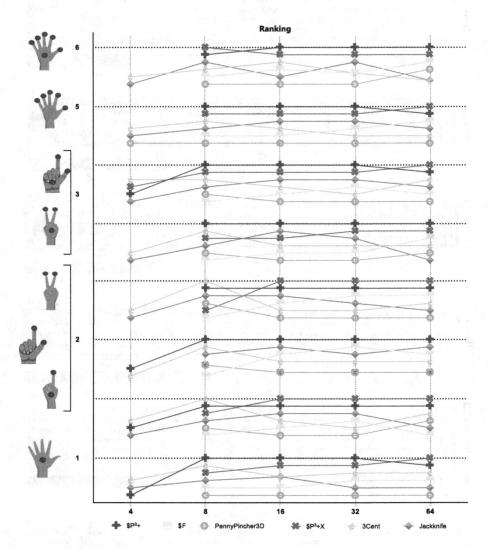

Fig. 11. Ranking of the best individual recognition rates above 80% by number of joints (A) and number of points (N) for the SHREC2019 dataset.

References

1. Abraham, L., Urru, A., Norman, N., Wilk, M.P., Walsh, M.J., O'Flynn, B.: Hand tracking and gesture recognition using lensless smart sensors. Sensors **18**(9), 2834 (2018). https://doi.org/10.3390/s18092834
2. Akl, A., Valaee, S.: Accelerometer-based gesture recognition via dynamic-time warping, affinity propagation, & compressive sensing. In: 2010 IEEE International Conference on Acoustics, Speech and Signal Processing, pp. 2270–2273 (2010). https://doi.org/10.1109/ICASSP.2010.5495895
3. Aliofkhazraei, M., Ali, N.: Recent developments in miniaturization of sensor technologies and their applications. In: Comprehensive Materials Processing, pp. 245–306. Elsevier, Oxford (2014). https://doi.org/10.1016/B978-0-08-096532-1.01309-1
4. Anthony, L., Wobbrock, J.O.: A lightweight multistroke recognizer for user interface prototypes. In: Proceedings of Graphics Interface 2010 (GI 2010), pp. 245–252. Canadian Information Processing Society, Toronto (2010). https://dl.acm.org/doi/10.5555/1839214.1839258
5. Anthony, L., Wobbrock, J.O.: $N-ProTractor: a fast and accurate multistroke recognizer. In: Proceedings of Graphics Interface 2012 (GI 2012), pp. 117–120. Canadian Information Processing Society, Toronto (2012). https://dl.acm.org/doi/10.5555/2305276.2305296
6. Aquino, N., Vanderdonckt, J., Pastor, O.: Transformation templates: adding flexibility to model-driven engineering of user interfaces. In: Shin, S.Y., Ossowski, S., Schumacher, M., Palakal, M.J., Hung, C. (eds.) Proceedings of the 2010 ACM Symposium on Applied Computing (SAC), Sierre, Switzerland, 22–26 March 2010, pp. 1195–1202. ACM (2010). https://doi.org/10.1145/1774088.1774340
7. Benitez-Garcia, G., Haris, M., Tsuda, Y., Ukita, N.: Finger gesture spotting from long sequences based on multi-stream recurrent neural networks. Sensors **20**(2), 528 (2020). https://doi.org/10.3390/s20020528
8. Brunelli, R.: Template Matching Techniques in Computer Vision: Theory and Practice. Wiley, New York (2009)
9. Caputo, F.M., et al.: A 3 cent recognizer: simple and effective retrieval and classification of mid-air gestures from single 3D traces. In: Proceedings of the Conference on Smart Tools and Applications in Computer Graphics (STAG 2017), p. 9–15. Eurographics Association, Goslar, DEU (2017). https://doi.org/10.2312/stag.201
10. Caputo, F.M., et al.: Online gesture recognition. In: Biasotti, S., Lavoué, G., Veltkamp, R. (eds.) Eurographics Workshop on 3D Object Retrieval, pp. 93–102. The Eurographics Association (2019). https://doi.org/10.2312/3dor.20191067
11. Coyette, A., Schimke, S., Vanderdonckt, J., Vielhauer, C.: Trainable sketch recognizer for graphical user interface design. In: Baranauskas, C., Palanque, P., Abascal, J., Barbosa, S.D.J. (eds.) INTERACT 2007. LNCS, vol. 4662, pp. 124–135. Springer, Heidelberg (2007). https://doi.org/10.1007/978-3-540-74796-3_14
12. Davis, A.: Getting Started with the Leap Motion SDK (2014). https://blog.leapmotion.com/getting-started-leap-motion-sdk/
13. Ferrer, G., Sanfeliu, A.: Comparative analysis of human motion trajectory prediction using minimum variance curvature. In: Proceedings of the 6th International Conference on Human-Robot Interaction (HRI 2011), pp. 135–136. Association for Computing Machinery, New York (2011). https://doi.org/10.1145/1957656.1957698

14. Filho, I.A.S., Chen, E.N., da Silva Junior, J.M., da Silva Barboza, R.: Gesture recognition using leap motion: a comparison between machine learning algorithms. In: ACM SIGGRAPH 2018 Posters (SIGGRAPH 2018). Association for Computing Machinery, New York (2018). https://doi.org/10.1145/3230744.3230750

15. Khalaf, A.S., Alharthi, S.A., Dolgov, I., Toups, Z.O.: A comparative study of hand gesture recognition devices in the context of game design. In: Proceedings of the 2019 ACM International Conference on Interactive Surfaces and Spaces (ISS 2019), pp. 397–402. Association for Computing Machinery, New York (2019). https://doi.org/10.1145/3343055.3360758

16. Khan, R.Z.: Comparative study of hand gesture recognition system. Comput. Sci. Inf. Technol. **2**, 203–213 (2012). https://doi.org/10.5121/csit.2012.2320

17. Leach, R.J.: Introduction to Software Engineering, 2nd edn. Chapman & Hall/CRC (2016)

18. Magrofuoco, N., Pérez-Medina, J.L., Roselli, P., Vanderdonckt, J., Villarreal, S.: Eliciting contact-based and contactless gestures with radar-based sensors. IEEE Access **7**, 176982–176997 (2019). https://doi.org/10.1109/ACCESS.2019.2951349

19. Magrofuoco, N., Roselli, P., Vanderdonckt, J.: Two-dimensional stroke gesture recognition: a survey. ACM Comput. Surv. **54**(7), 155:1–155:36 (2022). https://doi.org/10.1145/3465400

20. Marin, G., Dominio, F., Zanuttigh, P.: Hand gesture recognition with jointly calibrated Leap Motion and depth sensor. Multim. Tools Appl. **75**(22), 14991–15015 (2015). https://doi.org/10.1007/s11042-015-2451-6

21. Nielsen, J.: Usability Engineering, Interactive Technologies. Elsevier Science (1994)

22. Ousmer, M., Sluÿters, A., Magrofuoco, N., Roselli, P., Vanderdonckt, J.: Recognizing 3D trajectories as 2D multi-stroke gestures. In: Proceedings of the ACM on Human-Computer Interaction 4(ISS) (2020). https://doi.org/10.1145/3427326

23. Rautaray, S.S., Agrawal, A.: Vision based hand gesture recognition for human computer interaction: a survey. Artif. Intell. Rev. **43**(1), 1–54 (2012). https://doi.org/10.1007/s10462-012-9356-9

24. Taranta, II, E.M., LaViola, Jr., J.J.: Penny pincher: a blazing fast, highly accurate $-family recognizer. In: Proceedings of the 41st Graphics Interface Conference (GI 2015), pp. 195–202. Canadian Information Processing Society, Toronto (2015). https://dl.acm.org/doi/10.5555/2788890.2788925

25. Taranta II, E.M., Samiei, A., Maghoumi, M., Khaloo, P., Pittman, C.R., LaViola Jr., J.J.: Jackknife: a reliable recognizer with few samples and many modalities. In: Proceedings of the 2017 CHI Conference on Human Factors in Computing Systems (CHI 2017), pp. 5850–5861. ACM, New York (2017). https://doi.org/10.1145/3025453.3026002

26. Vanderdonckt, J., Roselli, P., Pérez-Medina, J.L.: !FTL, an articulation-invariant stroke gesture recognizer with controllable position, scale, and rotation invariances. In: Proceedings of the ICMI 2018, pp. 125–134. ACM, New York (2018). https://doi.org/10.1145/3242969.3243032

27. Vatavu, R.D.: Improving gesture recognition accuracy on touch screens for users with low vision. In: Proceedings of the 2017 CHI Conference on Human Factors in Computing Systems (CHI 2017), pp. 4667–4679. ACM, New York (2017). https://doi.org/10.1145/3025453.3025941

28. Vatavu, R.D., Anthony, L., Wobbrock, J.O.: Gestures as point clouds: a $P recognizer for user interface prototypes. In: Proceedings of the 14th ACM International Conference on Multimodal Interaction (ICMI 2012), pp. 273–280. ACM, New York (2012). https://doi.org/10.1145/2388676.2388732

29. Vatavu, R.D., Anthony, L., Wobbrock, J.O.: $Q: a super-quick, articulation-invariant stroke-gesture recognizer for low-resource devices. In: Proceedings of the MobileHCI 2018, pp. 23:1–23:12. ACM, New York (2018). https://doi.org/10.1145/3229434.3229465

30. Wang, A., Chen, G., Yang, J., Zhao, S., Chang, C.Y.: A comparative study on human activity recognition using inertial sensors in a smartphone. IEEE Sens. J. **16**, 1 (2016). https://doi.org/10.1109/JSEN.2016.2545708

31. Wang, C., Liu, Z., Chan, S.C.: Superpixel-Based Hand Gesture Recognition With Kinect Depth Camera. IEEE Transactions on Multimedia **17**(1), 29–39 (2015). https://doi.org/10.1109/TMM.2014.2374357

32. Wobbrock, J.O., Wilson, A.D., Li, Y.: Gestures without libraries, toolkits or training: a $1 recognizer for user interface prototypes. In: Proceedings of the 20th Annual ACM Symposium on User Interface Software and Technology (UIST 2007), pp. 159–168. ACM, New York (2007). https://doi.org/10.1145/1294211.1294238

33. Yasen, M., Jusoh, S.: A systematic review on hand gesture recognition techniques, challenges and applications. PeerJ Comput. Sci. **5**, e218 (2019). https://doi.org/10.7717/peerj-cs.218

34. Zengeler, N., Kopinski, T., Handmann, U.: Hand gesture recognition in automotive human-machine interaction using depth cameras. Sensors **19**(1), 59 (2019). https://doi.org/10.3390/s19010059

An Elderly User-Defined Gesture Set for Audio Natural Interaction in Square Dance

Jiayu Su[✉]

Central South University, Changsha, China
sujiayu0224@163.com

Abstract. Mid-air gestures have long been used as a natural way to control electronic products such as smart audio. However, due to the differences between designers and elderly users, the elderly's use of mid-air gestures is still limited. To make gesture-based interaction more natural for elderly users, the study aimed to find user-defined gestures suitable for elderly users in square dancing sound. We conducted a structured process based on participatory design. Older participants were invited to design gestures and evaluate the quality of gesture vocabulary. We collected the gestures and evaluated them based on older participants' preferences. Six gestures were obtained that were most suitable for controlling the audio target commands of square dancing. These gestures were designed by elderly users. Most of them were one-handed, flat palm or single index finger gestures. These gestures also had obvious directional indicators, including vertical (up/down) lines and counterclockwise circular motion. We designed a set of gestures using these gestures. Data analysis also showed that the best gestures scored relatively high in ease of execution and memorability. This suggests that the older participants placed greater value on ease of use and good memory when choosing gestures.

Keywords: Elderly · Mid-air gesture interaction · User defined · Participatory design · Square dance sound

1 Introduction

Data from the Bulletin of China's Seventh National Population Census (No.5) show that the aging population will become the long-term fundamental reality of the country, and it will be further deepened. China has come into the age of silver economy, and the aging interaction design has gradually become a hot topic. Square dancing is a daily recreational, fitness and social activity for most elderly people in China. The sound interaction design in this scene has yet to be explored. Prior research on the mid-air gesture interaction of square dance audio equipment is also lacking.

In square dancing, sometimes the keys and remote control of traditional audio equipment are not convenient or feasible. At this point, gestures, especially mid-air gestures, enable intuitive and natural interactions. Mid-air gestures allow elderly users to interact without obstacles during exercise. It is more inclusive than traditional interaction. Thus, mid-air gesture interaction may create huge potential when properly designed.

M. Kurosu et al. (Eds.): HCII 2022, LNCS 13519, pp. 180–191, 2022.
https://doi.org/10.1007/978-3-031-17618-0_14

Mid-air gestures have long been used as a natural way to control electronic products such as smart audio. However, due to the differences between designers and elderly users, the elderly's use of mid-air gestures is still limited. This may also lead to poor acceptance and use confidence among the elderly.

Therefore, some studies collect user-defined gestures by involving older end-users. These gestures are then analyzed by the system designer. Gesture elicitation study, which is a technique that has emerged from the field of participatory design, has attracted increasing attention and been widely used to collect end-users' requirements and expectations regarding the target system in the gesture design of various HCI applications [1]. However, this approach is plagued by problems of legacy bias [2] and disagreement [3]. It may not be able to generate the best gesture for the target task and system in practice. Additionally, research has no further insights into the solutions.

In this research, we work through the structured design process based on participatory design. This study is structured as follows: First, we analyzed the requirements of gesture interaction for square dance audio equipment and defined the set of tasks. Through a gesture elicitation study, a set of elderly user-defined gestures was established. Next, we extracted candidate gestures and evaluated gesture vocabulary based on the elderly participants' experience and preferences. Finally, we established a suitable set of elderly user-defined gestures for square dance audio equipment and analyzed the factors that may affect the gesture preferences of elderly users.

2   Related Work

2.1   Age-Appropriate Gesture Interaction Study

The research fields of aging interaction are becoming increasingly wider, including medical apps [4], smart homes [5], car interfaces [6], exercise games [7], shopping carts [8], electronic products [9] and so on. The mid-air gesture interaction suitable for the elderly has also been applied to some fields, such as smart bedrooms [10], living spaces for the elderly [11], automotive applications [12], etc.

It is possible and significant to find mid-air gestures that are better suited to elderly users for specific tasks. Research has shown that elderly users can accept mid-air gesture interaction, and their response to mid-air gesture interaction is more active than touch interaction [13]. Mid-air gesture interaction can not only overcome some barrier-free problems arising with age, but also make the interaction process more pleasant and improve their experience [14].

Mid-air gesture interaction is easy to learn. The rules and definitions of gestures come from users' daily cognition and are less restricted by product attributes, so they are easy for users to accept and learn [15]. Easy-to-learn gestures are more likely to motivate older people to use them positively. However, making gestures more cognitive and inclusive requires their active participation.

2.2 Gesture Elicitation Study

With the widespread use of mid-air gesture interaction, designers are increasingly applying gesture elicitation to help them confirm the appropriate gesture set for the application. However, approximately half of the population of participants in previous studies came from academic settings. Therefore, they may not represent all user groups. Additionally, there is not much discussion about the representativeness of participants in gesture elicitation study. The other half were mostly adults between the ages of 18 and 60. Gesture elicitation studies using mainly elderly participants are relatively scarce [16]. There are even fewer studies on gesture elicitation for elderly users in square dancing.

In addition, legacy bias is a major concern of gesture elicitation studies. It refers to "the prior experience with interfaces and technologies, that makes it hard to uncover new gestures for an emerging medium". Researchers suggest requiring users to propose many gestures for each referent and recruiting users in groups to leverage their ideas [17]. Although legacy bias is considered a factor that may not produce originality in gesture proposals, sometimes it is considered to have positive effects in elicitation studies [16]. Some researchers argue that, in most cases, biased gestures have the advantage of simplicity, and they do not need to spend too much time on learning and guessing, to obtain higher consistency scores in gesture elicitation studies [18]. Therefore, when the user has no spare time or willingness to learn new interactive technologies and methods, or when the user's cognitive ability is overwhelmed, this gesture may just be the most appropriate.

2.3 Summary

In general, prior studies have explored the theory of gesture interaction for aging and gesture elicitation. However, the research on gesture elicitation for elderly users aiming at interacting with audio devices in square dance needs to be expanded. To solve this problem, this study carried out experiments, optimized the results, and finally designed an acoustic gesture set of square dance defined by elderly users.

3 Experiment 1: Gesture Elicitation

The square dance sound has many functions, and the elderly only need to operate several common functions when using it. Therefore, we analyzed and summarized the functions of the square dance sound and defined the tasks that interact most often. Then, two experiments were conducted to elicit and evaluate gestures. The first experiment aimed to elicit one gesture from every elderly participant for each task. The second experiment aimed to evaluate the gesture vocabulary and verify the popularity of the collected mid-air gestures.

3.1 Requirement Analysis and Task Definition

To design friendly and natural gestures for the elderly in square dance, it is necessary to determine the use environment of the equipment, end-users and target tasks. We extensively collected common command task feedback from elderly users and studied the function of square dance audio equipment. Through the analysis, we determined 6 tasks of the audio equipment. (Table 1 lists these 6 tasks.) There were three pairs of homologous and basic functions of the audio equipment (pause music, play music, last song, next song, turn up the volume, turn down the volume). By investigating the key settings of the audio equipment, the functions of pause and play music are mostly integrated with one key. This interaction mode may also be more consistent with the original cognition and usage habits of elderly users. Therefore, to simplify the interaction and reduce the cognitive load of elderly users, pause and play are integrated into a single task, such as pause/play.

In summary, these tasks can meet the basic needs of elderly users to operate square dance audio and cover common functions. To keep the memory burden of the elderly users at a low level and avoid negative efficiency, the number of target tasks is finally limited to six. These tasks lay the foundation for follow-up research.

Table 1. Target Tasks

No	Task name
A	Pause/Play
B	Turn up the volume
C	Turn down the volume
D	Last song
E	Next song
F	Single cycle

3.2 User-Defined Gesture Naming Principle

To summarize the collected gestures more efficiently, it is necessary to name each user-defined gesture. The naming principle is "gender number - subject number - command group number - gesture number".

For example, the female number is W, and the male number is M. The serial numbers of subjects are 1, 2, 3, 4…. The six operation commands are listed as pause/play -A, turn up the volume -B, turn down the volume -C, last song -D, next song -E, single cycle -F. Gestures designed by the subjects are arranged as follows: 1, 2.

Example: The third female subject designed the first gesture for the "last song" command, named W3-D-1.

3.3 Gesture Interaction Video Preparation

We have fully considered the cognition and acceptance of the elderly. Then, we selected a mid-air gesture interaction video of smart audio within 1 min.

3.4 Preliminary Experiments

Purpose. To make the formal experiment of gesture elicitation go smoothly, enhance the reliability and effectiveness of the experimental results. We conducted a preliminary experiment to solve these difficulties and improve the experimental scheme.

Method. We follow a structured process of participatory design experiments. Each subject was tested once. Then, we recorded the difficulties and problems encountered in the process. It is convenient for subsequent adjustment and supplementation of the scheme.

Subjects. We recruited 5 subjects (2 males, 3 females) aged over 60 years. All of them have participated in square dancing activities and have experience with square dancing sound. The subjects were all in good health. Their dominant hand is right-handed. They have clear cognition and can clearly understand the task and process of the experiment.

Procedures and Methods

1. Subjects were recruited through offline contact.
2. Briefly explained the purpose and background of the study for the elderly participants. Then, we explained the basic requirements and operation methods of mid-air gesture interaction.
3. A mid-air gesture interaction video was played within 1 min to help them understand.
4. The next experiment was conducted after confirming that they understood the operation process and requirements.
5. Each task was shown on PowerPoint to the participants. It includes the task name and the audio of sound state change.
6. The elderly participants were asked to come up with 2 suitable gestures for the corresponding tasks.
7. After all 6 tasks were completed, the experiment was ended.
8. Conducted a brief interview afterward.

Results and Problems. Through the gesture elicitation study with 5 participants and 6 tasks, we collected a total of 48 ($3 \times 6 \times 2 + 2 \times 6 \times 1$) gestures. The gestures with the same shapes and trajectory were integrated into one gesture and the nonstandard gestures were removed. Finally, we obtained a gesture set with 29 elderly user-defined gestures.

In the preliminary experiment, we found that the task of designing two gestures for each command seemed to exceed the cognitive load of older participants. Their performance is not very positive. The collected gestures are not valid enough. Three of them thought it was difficult to design two gestures per command. Two subjects failed to complete the task (only one gesture was designed for each instruction). Therefore, in the formal experiment, we changed the requirement to design one suitable gesture for each of the six tasks.

3.5 Formal Experiment

Purpose. To make gesture-based interaction easier to use for the elderly, this experiment aims to find a set of elderly user-defined gestures suitable for controlling the square dance audio equipment.

Methods. The structured process of a participatory design experiment scheme was followed, and each subject was tested once.

Subjects. We recruited 30 subjects (14 males, 16 females) aged over 60 years. All of them have participated in square dancing activities and have experience with square dancing sound. The subjects were all in good health. Their dominant hand is right-handed. They have clear cognition and can clearly understand the task and process of the experiment. However, none of them had any experience with mid-air gesture-based interaction.

Procedures and Methods

1. Subjects were recruited through offline contact.
2. Briefly explained the purpose and background of the study for the elderly participants. Then, we explained the basic requirements and operation methods of mid-air gesture interaction.
3. A mid-air gesture interaction video was played within 1 min to help them understand.
4. The next experiment was conducted after confirming that they understood the operation process and requirements.
5. Each task was shown on PowerPoint to the participants. It includes the task name and the audio of sound state change.
6. The elderly participants were asked to devise 1 suitable gesture for the corresponding tasks.
7. After all 6 tasks were completed, the experiment was ended.
8. Conducted a brief interview afterward.

Experimental Instructions. The experiment lasted approximately 25 min on average. To eliminate the influence of the order of 6 tasks, the order of all tasks was randomly set. The experiment adopted the method of vocal thinking and asked the elderly participants to explain their ideas of designing. There was no time limit for the whole experiment so that all elderly participants had enough time to understand tasks and design gestures. The whole experimental process is recorded by video. (Fig. 1 shows the experimental setup.)

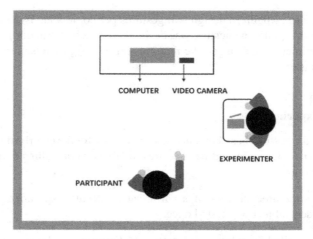

Fig. 1. Experimental setup

Results and Discussion. Through the gesture elicitation study with 30 participants and 6 tasks, we collected a total of 180 (30 × 6 × 1) gestures. The gestures with the same shapes and trajectory were integrated into one gesture and the nonstandard gestures were removed. Finally, we obtained a gesture set with 48 elderly user-defined gestures.

We found that the gestures defined by most elderly participants have a high repetition rate and low quality of shapes and trajectories. This may be related to the traditional behavior habits, legacy bias and cognitive ability of the elderly.

4   Experiment 2: Gesture Vocabulary Evaluation

4.1   Purpose

For further exploration, this experiment aimed to reduce legacy biases in the gesture elicitation study and filter the most desired gestures of older participants for each task.

4.2   Preparation

First, we extracted candidate gestures from the gesture set. Due to legacy bias, the most appropriate gesture may be another gesture suggested by multiple participants. We invited three experts to compare and evaluate the group's gestures. They chose four candidate gestures for each task. Through expert selection, we obtained 24 candidate gestures for the target task. They include gestures of different hand shapes. Such as thumbs-up, index finger drawing circles in the air, one index finger holding against the other palm (pause), two hands clapping and so on. Then the candidate gestures were coded (group - serial number) for the next experiment.

4.3 Subjects

To avoid data pollution, another 10 elderly participants (4 males, 6 females) over 60 years old were recruited for the study. All of them often take part in square dance activities and have some experience in sound operation.

4.4 Procedures and Methods

1. Subjects were recruited through offline contact.
2. Briefly explained the purpose and background of the study for the elderly participants. Then, we explained the basic requirements and operation methods of mid-air gesture interaction.
3. The next experiment was conducted after confirming that they understood the operation process and requirements.
4. The elderly participants were asked to watch the demo video of the candidate gestures on the PowerPoint, and make the same gestures 3 times by themselves.
5. The elderly participants completed a questionnaire with the help and instructions of the experimenter and scored the quality of the gestures.
6. After all the experiments were completed, the experimenter ended the experiment and appreciated the elderly participants.

4.5 Experimental Instructions

To eliminate the influence of other factors, the demo video was recorded on a white background. The duration of each video was limited to 2–3 s. For each task, the elderly participants were asked to rank the four candidate gestures from the most suitable to the least suitable. The ranking aimed to collect the most suitable gestures selected by elderly users. The questionnaire included aspects with a five-point Likert scale (1 = completely disagree, 5 = completely agree): ease of execution, enjoyment of execution, good match, and memorability [19].

4.6 Experimental Results

We collected responses from all 10 older participants. The six best gestures for the task were then selected. The selection is based on the ranking of the most desired gestures by older users and the score of gesture quality.

The results of the questionnaire are shown in Table 2. In general, the overall quality scores of most candidate gestures were high. The differences between different task groups were also obvious. Task D (last song) had the highest total score. Task B (turn up the volume) had the lowest total score. There were obvious differences in the quality scores of the four candidate gestures among different task groups. We can intuitively select the best gesture for each group.

Table 2. Part of the questionnaire results

Gesture Code	Ease of execution		Enjoyment of execution		Good match		Memorability	
	M	SD	M	SD	M	SD	M	SD
A-1	4.00	0.82	3.80	0.79	4.20	0.92	4.20	0.79
A-2	2.80	1.03	2.90	0.99	2.30	0.68	1.90	0.99
A-3	4.60	0.52	4.70	0.48	4.70	0.48	4.80	0.42
A-4	4.80	0.42	4.70	0.48	4.20	0.79	4.50	0.71
B-1	2.60	1.35	2.60	1.35	2.90	0.88	2.90	1.29
B-2	3.30	1.34	3.50	1.35	3.70	1.16	3.20	1.62
B-3	4.90	0.32	4.90	0.32	4.50	0.53	4.50	0.53
B-4	4.10	0.99	4.20	0.79	2.50	0.71	2.30	0.95
C-1	4.30	0.68	3.60	0.97	3.70	0.48	3.30	0.68
C-2	3.20	1.40	3.40	1.27	3.60	1.27	3.40	1.43
C-3	4.90	0.32	4.80	0.42	4.60	0.52	4.70	0.48
C-4	3.40	1.08	3.20	1.03	2.30	0.82	2.20	0.92

5   Discussion

For ease of execution, the gesture of "keep the palm horizontal and swing the forearm vertically in the air" (A-2, $M = 2.80$, $SD = 1.03$), the gesture of "forefinger and middle fingers together upward" (B-1, $M = 2.60$, $SD = 1.35$) and the gesture of "forefinger and middle fingers together toward the right" (E-1, $SD = 1.35$). These gestures were not easy to perform. Elderly participants tended to view arm movements as complicated. The gesture is difficult to perform in a standard and wide range of motion, resulting in fatigue. Regarding the index and middle finger gestures, they concluded that it was not their usual finger. They preferred five-fingered gestures and a single index finger.

For enjoyment of execution, the elderly participants thought that the gesture of "pulling hands relatively outward" (B-2, $M = 3.50$, $SD = 1.35$) and the gesture of "pushing hands relatively inward" (C-2, $M = 3.40$, $SD = 1.27$) were not comfortable to perform. They preferred a one-handed operation.

For a good match, the thumbs up gesture (B-4, $M = 2.50$, $SD = 0.71$) and thumbs down gesture (C-4, $M = 2.30$, $SD = 0.82$) were not matched with the task of turning up or down the volume. In older participants' habitual cognitive experience, these two gestures were more associated with ratings of "good" and "bad." Interestingly, neither gesture scored high on memorability (B-4, $M = 2.30$, $SD = 0.95$; C-4, $M = 2.20$, $SD = 0.92$). In addition, for the "last song" and "next song" tasks, it seemed that because of the "up" and "down" directional nouns in Chinese names, the older participants were more likely to think that the up and down gestures matched them than the left and right directions (D-1, $M = 3.20$, $SD = 0.79$; E-1, $M = 2.50$, $SD = 0.53$). Similarly, left and right gestures were rated low for memorability (D-1, $M = 3.10$, $SD = 0.99$; E-1, M

= 2.00, SD = 0.82). Thus, for older users, matching and memorability may be closely related. Gestures with higher matching to a task may be more conducive to memory.

For memorability, some elderly users have some common intuitive gestures. They are easier for them to remember. For example, for the "pause/play" task, they first thought of the gesture of "one index finger against the other palm (pause)". The task of "single cycle" was the gesture of "one index finger drawing circles". These gestures all had higher memory scores (A-3, M = 4.80, SD = 0.42; F-1, M = 4.80, SD = 0.63).

Table 3. Frequency of each gesture was chosen

Gesture Code	F	Gesture Code	F
A-1	2	D-1	1
A-2	0	D-2	3
A-3	5	D-3	2
A-4	3	D-4	4
B-1	1	E-1	0
B-2	2	E-2	4
B-3	6	E-3	1
B-4	1	E-4	5
C-1	1	F-1	5
C-2	2	F-2	1
C-3	7	F-3	3
C-4	0	F-4	1

In addition, we analyzed the frequency of each candidate gesture being selected as the best gesture by the elderly participants (see Table 3). For each task, the gestures most favored by elderly users were A-3, B-3, C-3, D-4, E-4 and F-1. For task A, task B, task C, task E and task F, the selection rate of specific gestures exceeds 50%. Compared with other gestures in task D, D-4 had no obvious advantages.

In other words, we obtained the most desired gestures for 6 tasks (see Fig. 2). Most of these gestures are one-handed gestures, which are flat palm or single index finger gestures. They have relatively high scores in ease of execution and memorability. This finding showed that elderly participants attach great importance to ease of execution and good memorability when choosing gestures.

Moreover, these gestures have obvious directional indication features, including vertical (up/down) lines and counterclockwise circular motion. This is the same as the findings of Vorwerg et al. [20]. In the two pairs of homologous tasks, the opposite direction of the same gesture is dominant.

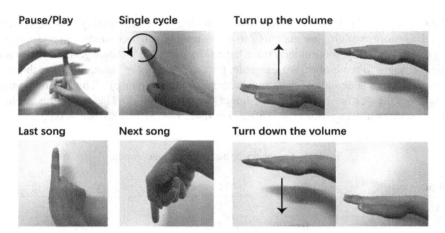

Fig. 2. Elderly user-defined gesture set

6 Conclusion

Mid-air gestures have long been used as a natural interactive method to control electronic products such as smart audio. However, these gestures are mainly defined by designers rather than elderly end-users. The difference between designers and elderly users leads to the limited interaction of elderly people to control audio by mid-air gestures. Moreover, there is a lack of research on the audio gesture interaction among the elderly in square dancing. Therefore, it is necessary to conduct a mid-air gesture elicitation study for square dance sound to obtain the elderly user-defined gesture set.

We conducted research through a structured design process based on participatory design. Starting with defining target tasks, the study conducted experiments that resulted in a set of gestures defined by older users. Experiment 1 invited elderly participants to design gestures, and experiment 2 evaluated gesture vocabulary according to the preferences of elderly participants. The results indicated a series of gestures best suited to the target task. They provided more natural interaction for older users. They can reduce the cognitive load and learning cost of older users.

Finally, We need further research. By evaluating the usage and satisfaction of these gestures in practical applications, we can explore more opportunities and possibilities. In addition, our future work may evaluate the influence of user gender, cultural background, region, sports dance and other factors on mid-air gesture preference. By classifying the elderly users, we can find the best gesture for different types of elderly users. It could help older users personalize their mid-air gesture interaction systems.

References

1. Wu, H., Wang, Y., Qiu, J., Liu, J., Zhang, X.: User-defined gesture interaction for immersive VR shopping applications. Beh. Inf. Technol. **38**(7), 726–741 (2019)
2. Morris, M.R., et al.: Reducing legacy bias in gesture elicitation studies. Interactions **21**(3), 40–45 (2014)

3. Wu, H., Zhang, S., Liu, J., Qiu, J., Zhang, X.: The gesture disagreement problem in free-hand gesture interaction. Int. J. Human-Computer Interaction **35**(12), 1102–1114 (2019)
4. Xu, R., Li, Y., Zhu, L.: Interaction design of the elderly medical APP based on SHERPA and FMEA. Packaging Eng. (04), 213–220 (2019)
5. Chen, X., Xue, L.: Interaction design of elderly-oriented intelligent home products based on QFD/TRIZ. Packaging Eng. **20**, 74–80 (2019)
6. Li, Y., Chen, Z.: Research on automobile human machine interface interaction design of the elderly based on FMEA and FTA. Packaging Eng. **06**, 98–105 (2021)
7. Wang, Y., Wang, T.: Research on interactive design of exergames for the elderly based on flow theory. Design Res. (05), 72–76 (2021)
8. Yu, D., Yi, X., Wang, Y.: Shopping cart design research for elderly based on user experience. Packaging .ineering (12), 99–103 (2017)
9. Cheng, H., Li, Y.: The electronics product design for the aged facing user experience. Packaging Eng. (14), 37–41 (2014)
10. Booranrom, Y., Watanapa, B., Mongkolnam, P.: Smart bedroom for elderly using kinect. In: 2014 International Computer Science and Engineering Conference (ICSEC), pp. 427–432. IEEE. (2014)
11. Basanta, H., Huang, Y.P., Lee, T. T.: Using voice and gesture to control living space for the elderly people. In: 2017 International Conference on System Science and Engineering (ICSSE), pp. 20–23. IEEE. (2017)
12. Trojaniello, D., Cristiano, A., Musteata, S., Sanna, A.: Evaluating real-time hand gesture recognition for automotive applications in elderly population: cognitive load, user experience and usability degree. HEALTHINFO, Nice, France (2018)
13. Znagui Hassani, A., Dijk, B.V., Ludden, G., Eertink, H.: Touch versus in-air hand gestures: evaluating the acceptance by seniors of human-robot interaction. In: International Joint Conference on Ambient Intelligence, pp. 309–313. Springer, Berlin, Heidelberg. (2011). https://doi.org/10.1007/978-3-642-25167-2_42
14. Ferron, M., Mana, N., Mich, O.: Designing mid-air gesture interaction with mobile devices for older adults. In: Perspectives on human-computer interaction research with older people, pp. 81–100. Springer, Cham. (2019). https://doi.org/10.1007/978-3-030-06076-3_6
15. Sun, X., Zhou, B., Li, T.: Design key elements and principles of in-air gesture-based interaction. Packaging Eng. (08), 10–13 (2015)
16. Vogiatzidakis, P., Koutsabasis, P.: Gesture elicitation studies for mid-air interaction: a review. Multimodal Technol. Interaction **2**(4), 65 (2018)
17. Morris, M.R., et al.: Reducing legacy bias in gesture elicitation studies. Interactions, **21**(3), 40–45 (2014)
18. Köpsel, A., Bubalo, N.: Benefiting from legacy bias. Interactions **22**(5), 44–47 (2015)
19. Guérit, R., Cierro, A., Vanderdonckt, J., Pérez-Medina, J.L.: Gesture elicitation and usability testing for an armband interacting with netflix and spotify. In: Rocha, Á., Ferrás, C., Paredes, M. (eds.) ICITS 2019. AISC, vol. 918, pp. 625–637. Springer, Cham (2019). https://doi.org/10.1007/978-3-030-11890-7_60
20. Vorwerg, S., et al.: Requirements for gesture-controlled remote operation to facilitate human-technology interaction in the living environment of elderly people. In: International Conference on Human-Computer Interaction, pp. 551–569). Springer, Cham (2019). https://doi.org/10.1007/978-3-030-22012-9_39

Using Fiducial Marker for Analyzing Wearable Eye-Tracker Gaze Data Measured While Cooking

Miona Tabuchi[1(✉)] and Tetsuya Hirotomi[2]

[1] Graduate School of Natural Science and Technology, Shimane University, Matsue, Shimane 690-8504, Japan
n21m106@matsu.shimane-u.ac.jp
[2] Institute of Science and Engineering, Academic Assembly, Shimane University, Matsue, Shimane 690-8504, Japan
hirotomi@cis.shimane-u.ac.jp

Abstract. The deficits in cognitive functions affect carrying out instrumental activities of daily living. Assistive products oriented to support these activities, e.g., cooking, should predict the user's behavior. The user's areas of interest (AOI) calculated from the eye gaze data measured by a wearable eye-tracker can be used for the prediction. We developed a new AOI estimation method suitable for cooking context based on multiple fiducial markers. The evaluation suggested that our method was more feasible than the use of feature extraction and feature matching for AOI estimation on objects in the kitchen, including cooking utensils with their move and overlap, while cooking.

Keywords: Eye tracking · Gaze analysis · Technology for cognitive well-being

1 Introduction

A traumatic brain injury (TBI) may occur when the head or brain is struck by an external force [6]. Individuals who experience a TBI often exhibit problems with executive functions. Executive functions are higher-level cognitive functions related to goal-setting, planning, organizing, monitoring, and the flexible control of cognition and behavior [23]. These functions affect carrying out instrumental activities of daily living, such as cooking [5,7,15]. For example, Hendry et al. reported that poorer cognitive functions were significantly associated with greater omissions and estimation errors, lack of goal achievement, and longer completion time while cooking [13].

To compensate the cognitive deficits, Arab et al. proposed a special kitchen for a single user equipped with hundreds of sensors and output devices including motion sensors, contact sensors, home energy monitors, flow meters, touch screen, speaker, and Light-Emitting Diodes (LED) [1,2]. In this kitchen, the user's actions are recognized by these sensors. To support following predefined recipes, the output device presents some clues to the user, for example, highlighting the cooker. Such a cognitive assistance can support individuals who experience TBI. However, to use the assistance in real-world settings, a new assistive product should be developed for proactively preventing such error behaviors by using simpler system.

Eye tracking technology has been used for predicting behaviors in a variety of activities, e.g., bicycle and car driving [20,22], store shopping [16], web browsing [21], and construction work [12]. Their approach is based on estimating a single area of interest (AOI) or transitions among AOIs by analyzing the fixation. A wearable eye-tracker can collect gaze data on the wearer's visual attention and record a video of the surrounding environment with sound. The wearer can freely move around the environment. The wearable one is more suitable for the use in real-world settings than stationary ones [4]. Feature extraction and feature matching is well-known object recognition method [8,11,24]. However, applying it to AOI estimation while cooking has the following difficulties:

- The recognition of objects without strong textures, e.g. a plain white cutting board, loses accuracy because feature extractors may fail to match feature points.
- Objects which change their appearance while cooking, e.g. "baked" and "mixed," cannot be tracked.
- Feature extraction and feature matching are time-consuming.

We therefore developed a new AOI estimation method for a wearable eye-tracker. In this method, "multiple" fiducial markers, to be more specific, ArUco markers [10], are attached to each object. These markers are used to calculate object polygons. Then, AOI is estimated by an eye gaze fixation point and these polygons. In this paper, a brief overview of object detection methods with/without markers is introduced in Sect. 2. The implementation of our method is presented in Sect. 3. Prior to applying our method to eye gaze analysis for individuals who experience TBI, we have evaluated its performance by eye gaze data when individuals who did not experience TBI were preparing meals. The results and discussions are described in the latter sections.

2   Related Works

To implement AOI estimation, a given object should be found in a still image or video sequence by object recognition. Object recognition can be classified by the use of markers. The markerless approach is based on feature extraction and feature matching but has above mentioned difficulties for AOI estimation while cooking. Another approach is based on the use of fiducial markers.

To use fiducial markers, the candidates of AOIs should be predefined. It means that each object should be associated with one or a few markers and their data, such as boundaries of the object, should be input prior to the recognition. However, the objects can be recognized by these preparations even if they are without strong textures and their appearance is changed. This approach is brute-force, but less time-consuming than the markerless approach.

Duchowski et al. [9] and Bykowski et al. [3] proposed to use one fiducial marker for each object. In cooking environment, cooking utensils and hands often overlap one another in line of sight. A single marker is easily hidden. Pfeiffer et al. [17,18] used 3D models in combination with 2D fiducial markers to handle the overlap. However, their method cannot be applied to moving objects such as cooking utensils.

3   AOI Estimation Method Using Multiple Fiducial Markers

In this section, an overview of our AOI estimation method using multiple fiducial markers is presented. The method is implemented by using Python 3.7.11 and OpenCV 3.4.15.55.

3.1   Inputting Target Object Data

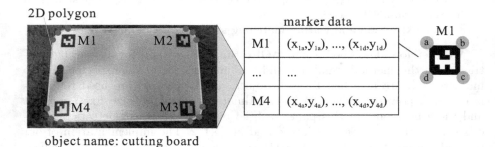

Fig. 1. Target object data

This step is the preparation for AOI estimation. In cooking context, the containers and printed recipes can be AOIs. These objects are named "target objects." Figure 1 shows an example of a cutting board. First, at least one fiducial ArUco marker is attached to a target object. These markers can be laminated. In this example, four markers M1 to M4 are attached to the cutting board. Then one or a few pictures of the object are taken. For better accuracy, all markers should be clearly presented in these pictures. They are stored with an object name, polygons to specify its boundary and subareas, markers' data attached to the object, and a layer to which the object belongs. The object name should be unique. Our method uses 2D polygons. Each marker data includes its ID and location of four vertices. Layers are used for AOI estimation with overlapped objects. In such a case, an object on the topmost layer is selected as AOI.

3.2 Collecting Eye Gaze Data

This step is to collect gaze data by a wearable eye-tracker as shown in Fig. 2. We used Tobii Pro Glasses 2 in this study. It can record the video of 1920 × 1080 pixels and 25 frames per second by a scene camera. The eye gaze data (b) is also recorded in 50 Hz. It includes time stamp, status indicator, and gaze position in the video frame (a). The status indicator becomes 0 if gaze position is available. If not, it becomes 1.

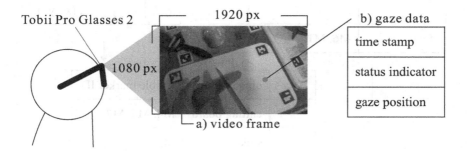

Fig. 2. Gaze data collected by wearable eye-tracker

3.3 Detecting Markers

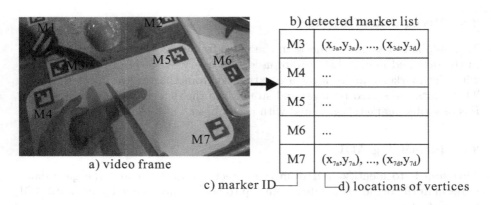

Fig. 3. Marker detection

This step is to detect markers in the video frame. The frame is processed by OpenCV, a set of markers and their four vertices are detected. Figure 3 is an example. In the video frame (a), markers M1 to M7 were available. However, markers M1 and M2 were partly cut off in the frame. OpenCV could detect markers M3 to M7 (c) and the locations of their vertices (d). These data are stored into the detected marker list (b).

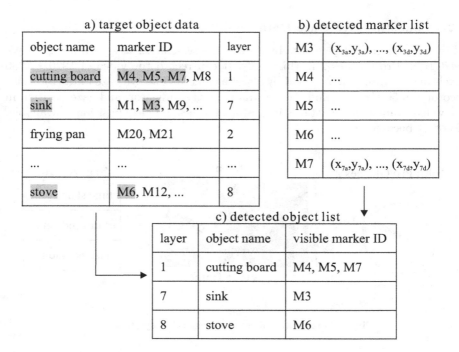

Fig. 4. Object recognition

3.4 Recognizing Objects

This step is to recognize objects in the video frame. As shown in Fig. 4, the IDs in the detected marker list (b) are used as a query. A set of objects associated with the marker and its layer are extracted from the target object data (a). These data are sorted by layer and stored into the detected object list (c) with IDs of visible markers associated with each object.

3.5 Identifying AOI

This step is to identify AOI from the detected object list and the gaze data. Objects in the list are evaluated from top to bottom layers one by one until AOI hit is detected.

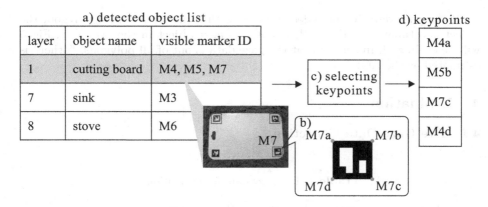

Fig. 5. Selecting keypoints of the object

Figure 5 shows an example. In this case, the topmost object in the list (a) is the cutting board. Its bottom left marker M8 is not visible in the video frame and other three markers, M4, M5, and M7, are visible (see, Fig. 3). Each marker has four vertices, e.g., marker M7 has M7a, M7b, M7c, and M7d, and the cutting board has 12 vertices. All combinations of four vertices among them are evaluated by calculating the sum of the distance between all pairs of vertices. The four vertices with the biggest sum are selected as keypoints (d). Figure 6 shows three examples of combinations of four vertices. Combination (b) has the biggest sum and four vertices represented by red points in (b) are considered as the keypoints.

Figure 7 shows the process of perspective transformation based on the keypoints. Each keypoint has the locations in the image stored in target object data (a) and the locations in the video frame (b). Both locations were used to estimate the homography matrix (c). This matrix (d) is used for perspective transformation (e) of 2D polygons specifying boundaries and subareas of the object stored in target object data in Fig. 1. Then, the polygons are transformed to the video frame as shown in (f).

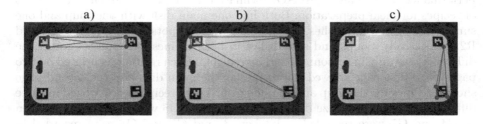

Fig. 6. Examples of combinations of four vertices (Color figure online)

If the gaze data in the video frame is within the transformed polygon, the object is estimated as the AOI. If not, the next object in the list (a) in Fig. 5 will be evaluated. In case of that the gaze data is out of all polygons, "other" is estimated as the AOI.

4   Evaluation

4.1   Eye Gaze Data Collection

Table 1. Eye gaze data for evaluation

ID	Marker	Recipe	Kitchen	Frames
G1	with	R1	α	270
G2	without	R1	α	287
G3	with	R1	α	255
G4	with	R1	β	263
G5	with	R1	γ	222
G6	with	R2	α	250
G7	with	R2	β	254
G8	with	R2	γ	224

Eight time series eye gaze data were used to evaluate the proposed method. Table 1 shows some details of these data. For recording the data, Tobii pro glasses 2 wearable eye-tracker was used. A set of fiducial markers were attached to "containers" which may change their contents while cooking in gaze data G1, G3, G4, G5, G6, G7, and G8. The containers were a cutting board, frying pan, microwave oven, refrigerator, condiment shelf, sink, stove, and sub-table. In addition to them, fiducial markers were attached to printed recipes on the wall. No marker was used in gaze data G2 because this data was for evaluating the performance of the markerless AOI estimation method. We prepared two types of recipes for meal preparation. Both had one main dish with one soup and one simple side dish. Main dishes were keema curry and potsticker in recipes R1 and R2, respectively. Soups and side dishes in both recipes were almost same, the difference was only in seasonings and ingredients. Each recipe was printed on two pages. The first page showed the recipe for the main dish and the second page showed recipes for the soup and the side dish. Three recipes were cooked in three different kitchens. Eye gaze data G1, G2, G3, and G6 were recorded in kitchen α, G4 and G7 were recorded in kitchen β, and G5 and G8 were recorded in kitchen γ. Figure 8 shows apparatus of Kitchen α. Red rectangles indicate AOIs in this experiment. Containers and printed recipes were considered as AOIs. The evaluation was aimed to examine the AOI estimation performance of the proposed method prior to using it for individuals who experience TBI. That is

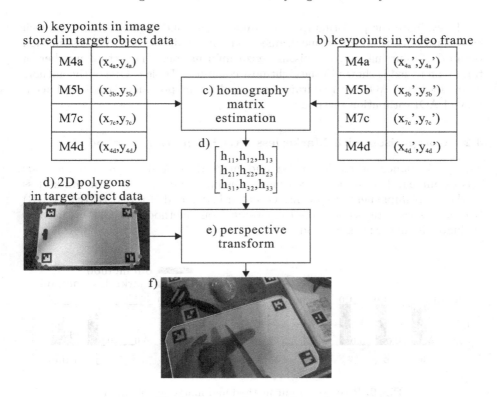

a) keypoints in image stored in target object data

M4a	(x_{4a}, y_{4a})
M5b	(x_{5b}, y_{5b})
M7c	(x_{7c}, y_{7c})
M4d	(x_{4d}, y_{4d})

c) homography matrix estimation

b) keypoints in video frame

M4a	(x_{4a}', y_{4a}')
M5b	(x_{5b}', y_{5b}')
M7c	(x_{7c}', y_{7c}')
M4d	(x_{4d}', y_{4d}')

d)
$$\begin{bmatrix} h_{11}, h_{12}, h_{13} \\ h_{21}, h_{22}, h_{23} \\ h_{31}, h_{32}, h_{33} \end{bmatrix}$$

d) 2D polygons in target object data

e) perspective transform

f)

Fig. 7. Perspective transformation

why, the eye gaze data collection was conducted by four healthy individuals, two males and two females, who did not experience TBI. Prior to the data collection, we explained the study and obtained informed consent from them.

Fig. 8. Apparatus of kitchen α and the following AOIs: a) cutting board, b) frying pan, c) microwave, d) first page of recipe, e) second page of recipe, f) refrigerator, g) shelf, h) sink, i) stove, and j) sub table

To evaluate the performance, 300 frames were randomly selected from each gaze data set. However, some frames were not suitable for AOI estimation because of blurring and/or missing gaze information. The actual number of frames analyzed is shown in the rightmost column in Table 1. One of the authors manually found AOI in these frames to calculate the precision, recall, and accuracy of AOI estimation methods.

4.2 Comparison with Markerless AOI Estimation Method

The performance of marker-based and markerless AOI estimation methods was examined. The marker-based method is our proposed one. The markerless method was implemented by using Oriented FAST and Rotated BRIEF (ORB) [19]. Eye gaze data G1 was used to evaluate our method and G2 was used to evaluate the markerless method.

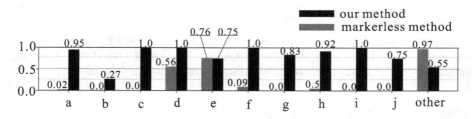

Fig. 9. Precision of our method and markerless method

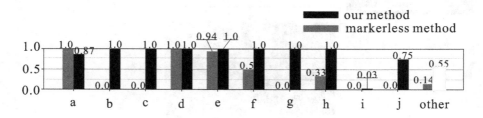

Fig. 10. Recall of our method and markerless method

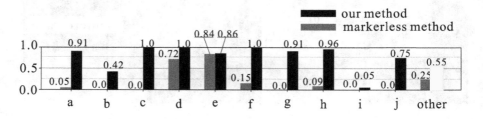

Fig. 11. F-score of our method and markerless method

Figures 9, 10, and 11 show precision, recall, and f-score of their AOI estimation. There were 10 AOIs, from a to j, as shown in Fig. 8. "Other" means that the eye gaze point was out of these AOIs. Our method achieved higher precision for estimating b, c, e, f, g, h, i, j, and other. It also achieved higher recall for estimating a, b, c, d, f, g, h, i, and j. As a result, its f-scores were higher than those of the markerless method for all AOIs. The markerless method achieved very low f-scores except for d and e. These two AOIs were printed recipes. It suggests that our method was rather robust for estimating AOIs with changing contents in comparison with the markerless method. The overall accuracy of our method was 73.7%. That was also better than the accuracy of the markerless method (22.6%).

We used a desktop PC with Intel i7-1060NG7 CPU, Intel Iris Plus Graphics 1536 MB GPU, and 15 GB RAM running on mac OS version 12.3.1. To estimate an AOI in a frame, our method took 48 ± 19 ms and the markerless method took 435 ± 347 ms.

4.3 Applicability to Different Kitchens and Recipes

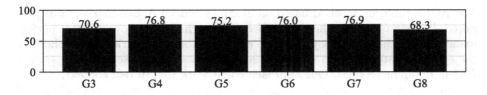

Fig. 12. Overall accuracy for different settings

The applicability of our method to different kitchens and recipes was examined by using eye gaze data G3 to G8. Figure 12 shows the overall accuracy for AOI estimation in different settings. The overall accuracy of our method while following recipe R1 was 70.6% (G3), 76.8% (G4), and 75.2% (G5) in kitchen α, β, and γ. For recipe R2, it was 76.0% (G6), 76.9% (G7), and 68.3% (G8).

5 Discussion

The proposed method achieved better f-score than the markerless method. It suggested that the use of fiducial markers and predefined layers was more feasible than the use of feature extraction and feature matching for AOI estimation on objects in the kitchen, including cooking utensils with their move and overlap, while cooking. The overall accuracy reached around 70% in the eye gaze data collected while preparing meals by following two different recipes in three kitchens. It showed that our method had some level of applicability to different settings. To improve the accuracy, we analyzed the estimation failure when processing eye gaze data G3 to G8. The failure occurred in 26% of 1468 frames. The most frequent failure occurred in detecting markers (23%). Our method failed to detect all markers associated with an AOI object because they were partly visible, in low light, or looked from steep side view, as well as, the AOI object was inside but all markers were outside the frame of the scene camera. Another failure occurred in perspective transformation (3%). The transformation of polygons was not so accurate because the sum of the distance between keypoints was too short.

Our method was approximately nine times faster than the markerless method. AOI estimation methods based on fiducial markers are, in many cases, faster than the markerless method. The time consuming process in these methods is usually homography matrix estimation and perspective transformation. For example, the method proposed in [14] repeated the process by evaluating a set of keypoints until appropriate transformation could be found. In our method, such repetition was avoided by calculating the sum of the distance between keypoints. However, further optimization is necessary for implementing our method because the current implementation could handle approximately 21 fps.

6   Conclusion

The AOI estimation method based on multiple fiducial ArUco markers was proposed. It is simple and rather brute-force approach, but it showed better performance in aspects of accuracy and time efficiency than the markerless method for the eye gaze data collected while cooking. The overall accuracy reached around 70% in different settings. Our approach could work well in real context.

Our future work is to analyze the gaze point transition pattern of individuals who experience TBI to support their meal preparation. Currently, our method processes the frame one by one. We plan to implement a function that compensates the estimation failure by using AOIs detected in a few frames before. Additionally, further optimization is necessary for improving its time efficiency.

References

1. Arab, F., Bauchet, J., Pigot, H., Giroux, A., Giroux, S.: Design and assessment of enabling environments for cooking activities. In: Proceedings of the 2014 ACM International Joint Conference on Pervasive and Ubiquitous Computing: Adjunct Publication, UbiComp 2014 Adjunct, pp. 517–526. Association for Computing Machinery, New York, NY, USA (2014). https://doi.org/10.1145/2638728.2641329
2. Bauchet, J., Pigot, H., Giroux, S., Lussier-Desrochers, D., Lachapelle, Y., Mokhtari, M.: Designing judicious interactions for cognitive assistance. In: Proceeding of the Eleventh International ACM SIGACCESS Conference on Computers and accessibility - ASSETS 2009, p. 11. ACM Press, New York, USA (2009). https://doi.org/10.1145/1639642.1639647, http://portal.acm.org/citation.cfm?doid=1639642.1639647
3. Bykowski, A., Kupinski, S.: Feature matching and ArUco markers application in mobile eye tracking studies. In: 2018 Signal Processing: Algorithms, Architectures, Arrangements, and Applications (SPA), pp. 255–260. IEEE,

September 2018. https://doi.org/10.23919/SPA.2018.8563387, https://ieeexplore.
ieee.org/document/8563387/

4. Carter, B.T., Luke, S.G.: Best practices in eye tracking research. Int. J. Psychophysiol. **155**, 49–62 (2020). https://doi.org/10.1016/j.ijpsycho.2020.05.010, https://linkinghub.elsevier.com/retrieve/pii/S0167876020301458

5. Chevignard, M., et al.: An ecological approach to planning dysfunction: script execution. Cortex **36**(5), 649–669 (2000). https://doi.org/10.1016/S0010-9452(08)70543-4, https://linkinghub.elsevier.com/retrieve/pii/S0010945208705434

6. Cook, A.M., Polgar, J.M.: Cook and Hussey's Assistive Technologies: Principles and Practice. Elsevier Health Sciences (2019)

7. Dawson, D.R., Chipman, M.: The disablement experienced by traumatically brain-injured adults living in the community. Brain Injury **9**(4), 339–353 (1995). https://doi.org/10.3109/02699059509005774, http://www.tandfonline.com/doi/full/10.3109/02699059509005774

8. De Beugher, S., Ichiche, Y., Brône, G., Goedemé, T.: Automatic analysis of eye-tracking data using object detection algorithms. In: Proceedings of the 2012 ACM Conference on Ubiquitous Computing - UbiComp 2012, p. 677. ACM Press, New York, USA (2012). https://doi.org/10.1145/2370216.2370363, http://dl.acm.org/citation.cfm?doid=2370216.2370363

9. Duchowski, A.T., Peysakhovich, V., Krejtz, K.: Using pose estimation to map gaze to detected fiducial markers. Procedia Comput. Sci. **176**, 3771–3779 (2020). https://doi.org/10.1016/j.procs.2020.09.010, https://linkinghub.elsevier.com/retrieve/pii/S1877050920319013

10. Garrido-Jurado, S., Muñoz-Salinas, R., Madrid-Cuevas, F., Marín-Jiménez, M.: Automatic generation and detection of highly reliable fiducial markers under occlusion. Pattern Recogn. **47**(6), 2280–2292 (2014). https://doi.org/10.1016/j.patcog.2014.01.005, https://linkinghub.elsevier.com/retrieve/pii/S0031320314000235

11. Harmening, K., Pfeiffer, T.: Location-based online identification of objects in the centre of visual attention using eye tracking. In: SAGA-International Workshop on Solutions for Automatic Gaze Data Analysis: Proceedings (2013). https://doi.org/10.2390/biecoll-saga2013_10

12. Hasanzadeh, S., Esmaeili, B., Dodd, M.D.: Examining the relationship between construction workers' visual attention and situation awareness under fall and tripping hazard conditions: using mobile eye tracking. J. Constr. Eng. Manage. **144**(7), 04018060 (2018). https://doi.org/10.1061/(ASCE)CO.1943-7862.0001516, http://ascelibrary.org/doi/10.1061/%28ASCE%29CO.1943-7862.0001516

13. Hendry, K., et al.: Cognitive deficits underlying error behavior on a naturalistic task after severe traumatic brain injury. Front. Behav. Neurosci. **10**, Paper ID 190, October 2016. https://doi.org/10.3389/fnbeh.2016.00190, http://journal.frontiersin.org/article/10.3389/fnbeh.2016.00190/full

14. Ondrašovič, M., Tarábek, P.: Homography ranking based on multiple groups of point correspondences. Sensors **21**(17), 5752 (2021). https://doi.org/10.3390/s21175752, https://www.mdpi.com/1424-8220/21/17/5752

15. Penfield, W., Evans, J.: The frontal lobe in man: a clinical study of maximum removals. Brain **58**(1), 115–133 (1935). https://doi.org/10.1093/brain/58.1.115, https://academic.oup.com/brain/article-lookup/doi/10.1093/brain/58.1.115

16. Peng, M., Browne, H., Cahayadi, J., Cakmak, Y.: Predicting food choices based on eye-tracking data: comparisons between real-life and virtual tasks. Appetite **166**, 105477 (2021). https://doi.org/10.1016/j.appet.2021.105477, https://linkinghub.elsevier.com/retrieve/pii/S0195666321003846

17. Pfeiffer, T., Renner, P.: EyeSee3D: a low-cost approach for analyzing mobile 3D eye tracking data using computer vision and augmented reality technology. In: Proceedings of the Symposium on Eye Tracking Research and Applications, pp. 195–202. ACM, New York, NY, USA, March 2014. https://doi.org/10.1145/2578153.2578183

18. Pfeiffer, T., Renner, P., Pfeiffer-Leßmann, N.: EyeSee3D 2.0: model-based real-time analysis of mobile eye-tracking in static and dynamic three-dimensional scenes. In: Proceedings of the Ninth Biennial ACM Symposium on Eye Tracking Research & Applications, pp. 189–196. ACM, New York, NY, USA, March 2016. https://doi.org/10.1145/2857491.2857532

19. Rublee, E., Rabaud, V., Konolige, K., Bradski, G.: ORB: an efficient alternative to SIFT or SURF. In: 2011 International Conference on Computer Vision, pp. 2564–2571. IEEE, November 2011. http://ieeexplore.ieee.org/document/6126544/

20. Rupi, F., Krizek: Visual eye gaze while cycling: analyzing eye tracking at signalized intersections in urban conditions. Sustainability 11(21), 6089 (2019). https://doi.org/10.3390/su11216089

21. Salminen, J., Nagpal, M., Kwak, H., An, J., Jung, S.G., Jansen, B.J.: Confusion prediction from eye-tracking data. In: Proceedings of the 9th International Conference on Information Systems and Technologies, pp. 1–9. ACM, New York, NY, USA, March 2019. https://doi.org/10.1145/3361570.3361577

22. Sodhi, M., Reimer, B., Cohen, J.L., Vastenburg, E., Kaars, R., Kirschenbaum, S.: On-road driver eye movement tracking using head-mounted devices. In: Proceedings of the Symposium on Eye Tracking Research & Applications - ETRA 2002, p. 61. ACM Press, New York, USA (2002). https://doi.org/10.1145/507072.507086, http://portal.acm.org/citation.cfm?doid=507072.507086

23. Tanguay, A.N., Davidson, P.S.R., Guerrero Nuñez, K.V., Ferland, M.B.: Cooking breakfast after a brain injury. Front. Behav. Neurosci. 8, 272 (2014). https://doi.org/10.3389/fnbeh.2014.00272, http://journal.frontiersin.org/article/10.3389/fnbeh.2014.00272/abstract

24. Toyama, T., Kieninger, T., Shafait, F., Dengel, A.: Gaze guided object recognition using a head-mounted eye tracker. In: Proceedings of the Symposium on Eye Tracking Research and Applications - ETRA 2012, p. 91. ACM Press, New York, USA (2012). https://doi.org/10.1145/2168556.2168570, http://dl.acm.org/citation.cfm?doid=2168556.2168570

Using Wearable Devices for Emotion Recognition in Mobile Human- Computer Interaction: A Review

Tao Wang(iD) and Hanling Zhang(✉) (iD)

School of Design, Hunan University, Changsha 410082, Hunan, China
jt_hlzhang@hnu.edu.cn

Abstract. With the popularity of wearable devices, human-computer interaction (HCI) has begun to expand to mobile environments. Since emotion is an essential part of the interaction experience, capturing users' emotional experience in mobile HCI using wearable devices has become a promising research area. We examined research papers in the above-mentioned fields in the past five years (2017–2021) and finally included 29 papers in the review results. We divide these articles by application area, analyze them in terms of several key elements of the experimental process, and give a clear view of the data. This review unravels the current practical applications and research methods of using wearable devices to capture physiological signals for emotion recognition, aiming to provide readers with guidelines for research methods and inspiration for future research directions.

Keywords: Mobile human-computer interaction · Physiological signals · Wearable devices · Emotion recognition

1 Introduction

The proliferation of wearable devices [1] and the development of mobile technologies have enabled the spread of HCI to all areas of daily life. Accordingly, mobile HCI and the corresponding user experience are receiving increasing attention [2].

Emotions, as an important part of the user experience, play a key role in positive human-computer interaction. Many psychologists believe that most human behavior and thinking are driven by emotions [3]. Several studies have also shown that emotions affect human productivity [4, 5], physical and mental health [1, 6], which has a huge impact on human-computer interaction.

Current emotion recognition methods are difficult to meet the requirements of real mobile HCI. Most research stays in the laboratory testing stage, and emotion recognition tests are rarely conducted in outdoor environments. Emotion recognition methods can generally be divided into those based on behavioral performance (expressions, speech, body movements, etc.) and those based on physiological signals. To date, there has been more research on affective computing around the former than the latter [7].

M. Kurosu et al. (Eds.): HCII 2022, LNCS 13519, pp. 205–227, 2022.
https://doi.org/10.1007/978-3-031-17618-0_16

Although behavioral performance-based emotion recognition methods, such as representative facial expression recognition, have the advantage of being intuitive. However, in some cases, expressions are not obvious or can be disguised, which reduces the reliability and accuracy of recognition results [8]. Compared to methods based on behavioral performance, methods based on physiological signals are more advantageous in mobile human-computer interaction. Physiological signals are influenced by the human endocrine system and autonomic nervous system and are less influenced by the subjective human consciousness. Therefore, physiological signals are almost spontaneous and uncontrollable, which makes them a more objective indicator of true emotional response [8, 9].

Cameras in portable devices often capture only part of the facial expressions of users as they move [10, 11] and complex environments lead to unstable lighting conditions, which reduce the accuracy and feasibility of emotion recognition. In addition, behavioral performance-based methods may have problems in terms of device portability, user privacy, and data computation volume [9]. In contrast, wearable devices that measure changes in physiological signals are often user-friendly and consumer-grade, becoming better tools for measuring emotions outside the laboratory [12].

Under the theme of "Emotion recognition through physiological signal acquisition by wearable devices", this paper focuses on practical applications and reports the process and results of the literature review. Specifically, this work focuses on the following research questions:

- RQ1: What wearable devices are used in these emotion recognition methods? What physiological signals are these methods based on?
- RQ2: What are the practical applications of this type of emotion recognition technology in HCI? What are the characteristics of each application?
- RQ3: What are the important links in the specific process of emotion recognition experiments? What are the similarities, differences and innovations?

These research questions address the key elements of emotion recognition in mobile HCI: wearable devices, physiological signals, and application domains, focusing on the testing process of emotion recognition in different application scenarios, including experimental environments, emotion-eliciting materials, emotion classification, and benchmarks for evaluating emotion recognition results. In this review, we visualized the results and related information in graphical form and answered each of the research questions in detail. The main contributions of the review are as follows:

- It provides a comprehensive review and summary of the physiological signals and wearable devices employed for emotion recognition in mobile HCI over the past five years, and can serve as a guide for relevant researchers in their selection and use.
- It categorizes the practical applications of emotion recognition in HCI and sorts out the specific process methods used in testing experiments.
- It summarizes the widespread problems and foreseeable future trends when performing emotion recognition in mobile HCI and provides inspiration for future research.

The paper is organized as follows: Sect. 2 presents the sentiment classification model and related work, and Sect. 3 describes the methodology and research methods used in the review. The review results are presented in Sect. 4 and discussed in Sect. 5. As a final remark, Sect. 6 concludes the paper.

2 Background

2.1 Emotion Models

Since human emotions are complex and variable, psychology has many emotion models to quantify feelings. Currently, two main emotion theories are widely used to classify and represent emotions, discrete emotion theory and dimensional emotion theory [13]. The first category is the basic emotion theory, which classifies emotions into discrete categories. The best known of these is the classification model [14], which divides emotions into six basic emotions: anger, fear, sadness, happiness, surprise, and disgust. These basic emotions combine to form other, more complex, non-basic emotions. Another is the dimensional emotion theory, where emotions are composed of different dimensions and discrete emotional states correspond to regions in a multidimensional space. The most classic is the circumplex model [15], which assesses emotions using two dimensions: arousal and valence. Arousal measures the intensity of the emotion, from low to high, while valence measures the pleasantness of the emotion, from negative to positive.

2.2 Related Work

In the past, several studies have reviewed physiological signal-based methods for emotion recognition. Some surveys related to the topic of our review are shown below, and their limitations are analyzed.

Two reviews [16, 17] have reviewed physiological signal-based emotion recognition methods. Similarly, they both stated that the use of wearable devices to detect heart-related physiological signals is a good way to accurately and inconspicuously measure emotions in real life. The limitation is that their testing environments are restricted to controlled laboratories. One difference is that one study [16] added facial expression recognition to the physiological signal.

Close to our research questions, some reviews [18–20] reviewed studies using wearable devices to measure physiological signals to recognize emotion recognition. The difference is that the wearable devices they summarize cannot all meet requirements such as lightweight and wireless, and the tests mostly stay in controlled laboratories. It is worth noting that they started to focus on emotion recognition in outdoor environments.

A more novel review [7] address non-invasive mobile sensing methods for emotion recognition in smartphone devices. Although cell phones are common mobile devices, cell phone cameras have many limitations in real mobile human-computer interaction.

On the topic of "emotion recognition around physiological signal detection by wearable devices," previous reviews rarely focus on mobile HCI or practical applications. Therefore, we hope to fill the gap in this field with this paper.

3   Review Methodology

This study was conducted according to the systematic literature review guidelines [21, 22]. Following these two guidelines, our literature review was divided into three main steps: (1) information sources and search strategy, (2) study selection and quality assessment, (3) data extraction and synthesis.

3.1   Data Sources and Search Strategy

We searched the Web of Science database in December 2021 using the keywords "emotion recognition AND wearable device". For publication time, we focused on the latest advances and trends in the field, so we only selected research articles from the last five years (2017 to 2021). For document types, we chose "Articles" and "Meeting" to exclude invalid data. For language, we set it to English.

3.2   Study Selection and Quality Assessment

After the initial review, a total of 205 articles potentially relevant to the current research question were shortlisted. Before the formal screening, 7 duplicate articles were excluded, yielding 198 articles. Then 108 articles were excluded based on the exclusion and inclusion criteria review, leaving 90 articles. The following are the inclusion and exclusion criteria we specified:

- Wearable devices. Do they meet the requirements of inconspicuousness and user-friendliness in mobile HCI? Are they consumer-grade products?
- Signal source. Does it mainly rely on capturing physiological signals to identify emotions? Some wearable devices rely on built-in miniature cameras for local facial expression recognition, with physiological signals as a supplement; they are excluded from the scope of this paper.
- Experimental testing. Whether real-life experimental tests have been conducted to test the emotion recognition method. Some articles only present a feasible framework for emotion recognition without actual experimental testing on subjects, which are excluded from this paper.

In addition, to ensure that each article has sufficient and appropriate information to demonstrate the methodology of their studies, we set additional quality criteria:

- Research focus. Does the research focus on practical applications and experimental methods?
- Application potential or value. Does the research have close to real-life use cases or tests in mobile HCI?
- Experiment Introduction. Are the experiments or cases described in detail and clearly? Does it include key elements such as test environment, stimulus materials, equipment, and data processing?

The quality criteria review excluded the remaining articles and the final 29 remaining articles were included in this review. The detailed process is illustrated in the PRISMA flowchart in Fig. 1.

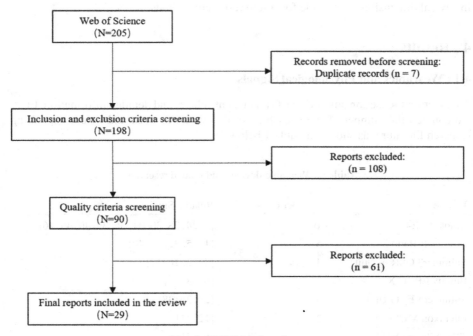

Fig. 1. PRISMA flowchart.

3.3 Data Extraction and Data Synthesis

Each article reviewed was read in more detail to extract the following key data.

- Practical applications of the study
- The wearable device, wireless transmission method, type of device, sensors carried
- Experimental environment
- Emotional stimulus materials
- Emotion classification
- Evaluation benchmark

First, we summarized the realistic application scenarios of emotion recognition in the field of human-computer interaction by classifying different studies according to the attributes of the target population, the experimental environment, and the type of emotion for their practical applications. Then, the experimental methods are organized in several dimensions as a guide for future research methods.

4   Results

4.1   Wearables and Physiological Signals

This section focuses on answering RQ1 using data charts and detailed information. First, we counted the number of times each type of device was used and its corresponding research literature, as shown in Table 1 below.

Table 1. Wearable devices and related research.

Device	Number of uses	Related Studies
Empatica E4	10	[9, 24, 28, 30, 31, 36, 39, 40, 45, 46]
Microsoft Band 2	5	[1, 25, 32, 39, 40]
Shimmer3 GSR + Unit	4	[4, 12, 26, 27]
Emotiv EPOC X	3	[6, 33, 44]
Shimmer3 ECG Unit	3	[24, 26, 38]
Interaxon MUSE	2	[12, 41]
TDK Silmme W20	2	[5, 34]
Emotiv Insight	1	[43]
Algoband F8	1	[8]
Analog ADI-VSM	1	[37]
Mio® alpha	1	[42]
NeuroSky	1	[32]
B-Alert x10	1	[23]

In addition, to provide a reference guide for future researchers in selecting wearable devices and physiological signals, we analyzed which devices researchers would choose more often when using specific signals, as shown in Fig. 2 below.

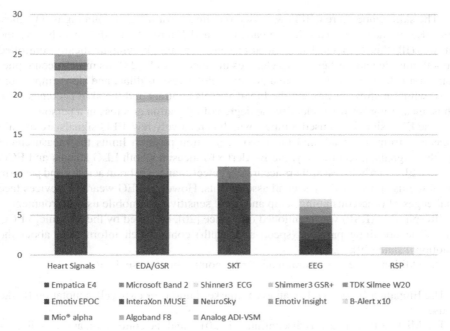

Fig. 2. Equipment usage in each signal.

According to the position of wearing, wearable devices are mainly divided into two types: wristband and headband. A special one, Shimme3 ECG was worn on the chest. Compared to the headband devices, the wristband devices represented by Empatica E4 are more frequently used.

Physiological signals can be broadly classified into five categories: cardiac-related signals, electrical skin signals, skin temperature, electroencephalographic signals, and respiration.

Cardiac-related biosignals are used the most (up to 25 times), which include photo-plethysmography (PPG) and electrocardiography (ECG). The PPG is more commonly used, with 21 times. Its measurement electrodes are usually integrated into smartwatches to make it easier for users to wear and measure while on the move. The ECG method is used less frequently, with only four times. Measurement devices are also only provided by Alert x10 [23] and Shimmer3 ECG units [24–26].

The EDA/GSR was used the second most often, reaching 20 times. Emotional stimuli cause an autonomous activation of the sweat glands of the skin, which in turn causes changes in the electrical activity of the skin [27]. The measurement sensors are usually installed on the finger (Shimmer3 GSR + Unit) or wrist (Empatica E4, Microsoft Band 2, Analog Devices ADI-VSM). Studies [4, 27, 28] have mentioned that GSR signals are more sensitive to the arousal of emotions compared to valence.

The skin temperature (SKT) was used the third most often, amounting to 11 times. The SKT is measured with the Empatica E4 and Microsoft Band 2, which have the infrared (IR) thermometer. The stimulation causes changes in sympathetically controlled smooth muscle and further causes changes in blood vessels [28]. Its more specific phenomenon is that in a relaxed state a person's blood vessels dilate and skin temperature rises, while in stress or anxiety the blood vessels contract and the skin becomes cold. Thus, measuring SKT can identify the degree of relaxation or stress in a person.

The EEG signal was used 8 times, which is relatively few. EEG signals are usually measured from the head, and the fixed acquisition position limits the measurement of other signals. Exceptionally, the B-Alert x10 measures both EEG signals and ECG signals. EEG can help researchers accurately detect changes in brain activity and perform unconscious and second-by-second assessments. However, EEG wearable devices face challenges of time-consuming setup and noise sensitivity in mobile use environments.

Respiration (RSP) was mentioned only once [26], collected by the Shimmer3 ECG Unit. The breathing patterns (speed and depth) contain rich information about the emotional state [29].

In addition, there are several noteworthy points about these devices:

- The Empatica E4 device has an event marker button for easy self-annotation by the user.
- The Microsoft Band 2 was discontinued in 2016, and the companion app was discontinued in 2019. This means that users can continue to use their devices (track heart rate, record exercise, track sleep, etc.), but the features provided by the cloud or mobile apps will no longer work.
- The Emotiv EPOC model mentioned in the studies is the Emotiv EPOC+, which has been discontinued and replaced by the upgraded EPOC X. The main features of both are similar.
- The Silmme W20 can measure pulse rate while moving, but in some cases (strenuous exercise, cold environments, poor blood flow, etc.) the signal may be lost.
- Some studies used other signal characteristics in addition to physiological signals in identifying emotions, including eye-tracking data [9] and acceleration data representing body movement [30].

4.2 Specific Applications

This section answers RQ2, focusing on different application scenarios' concerns and experimental procedures. Twenty-two studies account for specific application scenarios of emotion recognition, while the other seven articles only account for emotion recognition methods and performance without practical applications. To understand the research approaches of researchers in different fields, we divided the 22 articles by application areas into negative emotion detection, context-aware systems, analytical assessment, worker emotion analysis, and communication assistance. We summarized the characteristics of different application scenarios (application meaning, experimental setup, emotional stimulus material, and emotional classification), as shown in Table 2.

Table 2. Experimental procedures for different applications.

Application	References	Environment	Pre-experiment	Stimulation	Emotion Model	Baseline
Negative Emotion Detection	[6]	Labs	Assessment	Psychology Approach	Negative emotion	Self-report
	[36]	Labs	Assessment	Psychology Approach	Negative emotion	Self-report
		Dynamic	n/a	Real Scenes		Self-report
	[24]	Labs	Adjustment	Psychology Approach, Video Clips	Negative emotion	Self-report
	[25]	Dynamic	n/a	Real Scenes	Negative emotion	Self-report
	[26]	Labs	Adjustment	Video Clips	Negative emotion	n/a
	[1]	Labs	Adjustment	Emotional Pictures	Negative emotion	n/a
	[37]	Static	n/a	Real Scenes	Negative emotion	Self-report, Biomarkers
	[38]	Dynamic	n/a	Real Scenes	Negative emotion	n/a
	[27]	Labs	Assessment	Audio Clips	Negative emotion	Self-report
Unclassified	[8]	Labs	n/a	Video Clips	Valence	Emotional labels
	[12]	Labs	Adjustment	Emotional Pictures	Dimensional	Self-report
	[32]	Labs	Adjustment	Video Clips	Valence	Self-report
	[33]	Labs	n/a	Games	Valence	Self-report
	[31]	Labs	Adjustment	Video Clips	Dimensional, Discrete	Self-report
	[34]	Dynamic	n/a	Real Scenes	Dimensional, Discrete	Manual labeling
	[28]	Static	n/a	Audio Clips	Valence	Self-report
Context-aware Systems	[40]	Labs	n/a	Emotional Pictures	Dimensional	Self-report
		Labs	n/a	Games		n/a
	[39]	Labs	n/a	VR	Dimensional	Self-report
		Labs	n/a	Emotional Pictures		Emotional labels
	[41]	Labs	n/a	Video Clips	Dimensional, Discrete	Manual labeling
		Dynamic	n/a	Real Scenes		n/a

(continued)

Table 2. (*continued*)

Application	References	Environment	Pre-experiment	Stimulation	Emotion Model	Baseline
	[42]	Labs	n/a	n/a	Dimensional, Discrete	Self-report
	[43]	Static	n/a	Video Clips	Discrete	n/a
	[30]	Labs	Adjustment	Video Clips	Laughter	Manual labeling
Analysis and Evaluation	[9]	Dynamic	n/a	Video Clips	Dimensional	Manual labeling
	[23]	Labs	Adjustment	Emotional Pictures	Dimensional	Self-report
		Labs	n/a	VR		Self-report
		Dynamic	n/a	Real Scenes		Self-report
Worker Emotion Detection	[5]	Dynamic	n/a	Real Scenes	Dimensional, Discrete	n/a
	[4]	Labs	n/a	Emotional Pictures	Dimensional	Self-report
	[44]	Dynamic	n/a	Real Scenes	Dimensional	Biomarkers
Communication Assistance	[45]	Dynamic	n/a	Real Scenes	Dimensional	Manual labeling
	[46]	Labs	Measurement	Video Clips	Discrete	Self-report

- **Uncategorized.** The seven studies in this category used emotion recognition methods that did not apply to specific scenarios but had potential and value for practical application. Most of these studies were tested in a controlled experimental setting, as no practical application scenarios were specified. Four articles set up a relaxation period before the experiment to allow subjects to maintain a neutral mood. Emotional stimuli relied primarily on visual and auditory stimuli, including still pictures [12], audio clips [28], and video clips [8, 31, 32], and video games [33]. Studies outside the laboratory setting [34] targeted five subjects and collected their physiological signals during 10 weeks of work. All seven studies had a similar feature in terms of mood categorization, all categorizing on the valence dimension (positive and negative). In addition, some of them [8, 35] adding neutral.
- **Negative emotion detection.** Nine articles addressed negative emotion detection: six examined psychological assessment in everyday life [6, 24–27, 36] and three focused on negative emotion detection in specific scenarios, such as work [1], pre-surgery [37] and driving [38]. Studies in this category used a variety of emotionally stimulating materials. Four studies used realistic scenarios for their experiments: vehicle driving [38], pre-surgery [37], classroom lectures [36] and daily life [24, 36]. Six used laboratory simulations, divided into psychological tests [6, 26, 36] and audiovisual materials [1, 25–27]. These studies specifically address the emotion of stress, some of which are also elaborated as anxiety. Anxiety can essentially be explained as chronic

stress [6]. One study [26] classifies stress more carefully into three levels: relaxed, mildly stressful, and moderately stressful. In particular, a study on negative emotions in driving [38] considered both anxiety and anger.

- **Context-aware system (CAS).** Context-aware systems (CAS), including Cognitive assistants [39] and personal assistants [40], provide users with information prompts and decision support services by collecting data from users and the environment. The addition of emotion recognition allows the CAS to understand users' feelings and needs better and provide more humanized services. This type of research has affluent subdivisions: mobile scenarios [39], emotional games [40], life and health logs [41], and music recommendations [42]. Two studies are more specific, Cai et al. [43] studying the relationship between human personality, behavior and emotion; and Di Lascio et al. [30] using physiological signals and body movement data to detect laughter. The emotionally stimulating materials used in these studies were essentially visual and or auditory.
- **Analysis and Evaluation.** Emotions play an essential role in user experience in consumption, travel, and entertainment. Two articles use emotion recognition for targeted assessment tests. One study [9] had subjects walk or stand in a real outdoor scenario while watching video clips. The other [23] was more complex, with a controlled laboratory and an actual pavilion. First, subjects viewed emotional pictures of the IAPS or experienced a VR virtual exhibit in the controlled laboratory. In addition, subjects assessed the show in an actual pavilion. Similarly, both studies used the dimensional emotions model.
- **Worker state detection.** The emotional state of workers affects key production factors such as safety, efficiency, and employee turnover. Therefore, understanding the emotional state of employees at work can help workers do their jobs better, and companies improve their efficiency [4, 5, 44]. Three articles investigated the relationship between mood and working conditions [44] and between mood and productivity [4, 5], respectively. Two studies [5, 44] used different work scenarios in actual workplaces to elicit emotions. Another study in a laboratory setting [4] used photographs of workers' daily lives to evoke emotions. Similarly, all three articles categorized emotions according to an arousal-valence dimensional model.
- **Communication Assistance.** Individuals with autism or developmental delays have difficulty expressing their feelings or seeking help. Unobtrusive wearable devices can identify emotions to address such communication impairments. The study on children with developmental abnormalities or delays [45] conducted experiments in real everyday life; another study on individuals with autism [46] used video clips to elicit emotions under laboratory conditions.

4.3 Experimental Environment

Unlike the previous section, the sections from 4.3 to 4.7 are not limited to individual application areas but focus more on the experimental process in overall mobile HCI to answer RQ3.

We divided the different experimental settings into the controlled laboratory (22 papers) and realistic environment (13 papers). Since multiple experiments in different environments may be conducted in a single study, the cumulative number of experiments exceeds the finalized 29 papers. Based on the motion state of the wearable device, the realistic environments were further divided into static and dynamic categories. Static means that the subjects need to follow regulations to maintain a specific state, similar to a controlled laboratory, while dynamic represents the freedom of movement that the subjects can perform without restrictions. There were 3 static experiments and 10 dynamic experiments. The dynamic experiments in the natural environment are very close to the real mobile human-computer interaction and have guiding and reference values, so we analyzed the wearable devices applied in the naturally dynamic environment, as shown in Fig. 3.

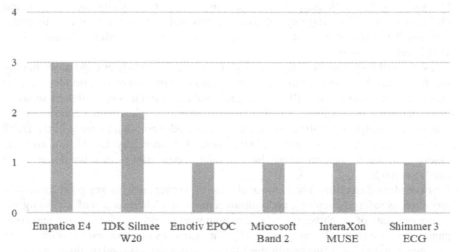

Fig. 3. Wearable device usage in dynamic real-world environments.

Some patterns can be found: these wearable devices in the figure all have the potential for practical application in mobile HCI. Among them, the more used ones are the wristband wearables like Empatica E4 [9, 36, 45], Silmee W20 [5, 34], and Microsoft Band2 [24]. Compared to EEG headbands such as the Emotiv Epoc [44] and InteraXon MUSE [41], wristband wearables are lighter, less conspicuous, measure a wider variety of signals, are more preferred by researchers.

4.4 Pre-experimental Sessions

Many studies will set up a pre-experimental session to measure, assess, or stabilize subjects' emotional baseline (often referred to as a neutral mood or relaxed state). We counted this literature, and the results are shown in Table 3.

The obvious point is that only studies in which the testing environment was in a controlled laboratory (12 studies) arranged some pre-experimental sessions. This was also done for all studies where the application was a negative emotion test and the experimental setting was a controlled laboratory.

Table 3. Specific details of the pre-experimental session.

Application	References	Pre-experiment	Specific operation
Negative emotion detection	[6]	Assessment	The Hamilton Anxiety Rating Scale (HAM-A)
	[36]	Assessment	The Perceived Stress Scale (PSS)
	[24]	Adjustment	Audio for meditation
	[26]	Adjustment	Relaxing video clips
	[1]	Adjustment	IAPS (Non-stress videos)
	[27]	Assessment	The Visual Analogue Scale for Anxiety (VAS-A)
Unclassified	[12]	Adjustment	2 min of relaxation time
	[32]	Adjustment	Rest time (10 s open eyes and 10 s closed eyes)
	[31]	Adjustment	60 s of relaxation time
Context-aware systems	[30]	Adjustment	60 s of relaxation time
Analysis and evaluation	[23]	Adjustment	Watch the white screen for a 4-min break
Communication Assistance	[46]	Measurement	Calculate the average value of ten-second signal

Assessment procedures typically use psychological questionnaires or physiological signal measures to assess the subjects' emotional state to determine whether they are in the desired neutral state. Stabilization procedures often use blank or neutral audiovisual material to relax subjects for 10 s to 4 min to ensure that the emotional state is neutral (relaxed) before the formal experiment.

4.5 Emotionally Stimulating Material

The previous Sect. 4.2 analyzed the stimulus materials used in different application scenarios, while this section will sort, analyze and summarize the emotional stimulus materials as a whole, as shown in Fig. 4.

The video clips were used 10 times and were commonly used in all areas. Six of these were video clips selected by the researchers themselves, and these were more flexible and adapted to the needs of the study. The next most popular video clip was the Database for Emotion Analysis (DEAP) [25, 41], which was used twice.

Real-life scenarios occurred 10 times, and the emotional stimuli faced by subjects in real-life and work scenarios were more complex and could not be specifically counted. Specific to the study of anger anxiety while driving [38], it developed an Android app to capture photos in front of the car. These photos were then manually analyzed to extract potential stimuli that caused changes in driver mood, including traffic density, road complexity, and any obstacles that could cause stress.

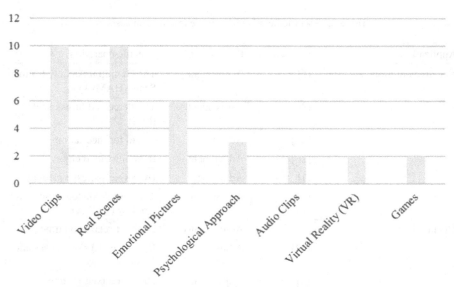

Fig. 4. The use of different emotionally stimulating materials.

Emotional pictures appeared 6 times, commonly using large databases of validated emotional pictures such as the International Affective Picture System (IAPS) and the Nencki Affective Picture System (NAPS). However, different individuals may have biased feelings and assessments of these pictures, so Fortune et al. (2020) chose personal photographs as emotional stimulus material in the hope that they would elicit more realistic and easily measurable emotional responses.

The psychological method was used 3 times, all of them appearing in studies in the category of negative emotion (stress and anxiety) detection. Of these, the Trier Social Test (TSST) [26, 36] was used more often.

The audio material was used 2 times. One was the canonical database the International Affective Digitized Sounds (IADS-2) [28] and the other was a researcher-selected audio clip [27].

Both VR and games were used 2 times, but they do not have canonical databases and were mostly screened by the researchers themselves.

4.6 Emotion Classification

According to Table 2, we count the number of times different emotion classification methods were used. As shown in the Fig. 5, there are broadly four types of emotion classification: dimensional emotions, negative emotions, discrete emotions, and positive-negative emotions. The arousal-potency dimensional model was the most widely used, with 13 studies basing their mood classification on this. Studies in the negative emotion detection category all focused on detecting stress, anxiety, or anger emotions.

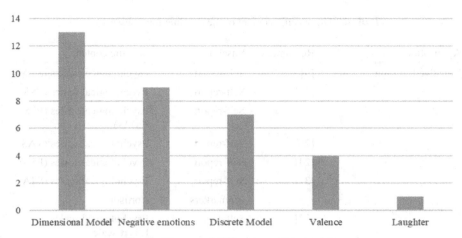

Fig. 5. The use of different emotion models.

The discrete emotion model is not usually used alone. Discrete emotions corresponded to different regions on the two-dimensional plane of arousal-valence, and five of the seven studies used the discrete emotion model together with the arousal-valence dimension model. Only two used the discrete emotion model alone in the classification of emotions.

The categorization of emotions according to valence (negative-positive) is somewhat ambiguous in its definition of different emotions and appears only in studies that do not specify an application scenario, which may indicate its difficulty in adequately describing the user's emotional experience in real emotion recognition applications.

There is only one study on laughter detection [30].

4.7 Baseline for Assessment

The vast majority of experiments established baselines for judging the accuracy of emotion recognition results, including self-reports completed by subjects, emotion labels that came with the emotion stimulus material, manual observation and labeling, and biological benchmarks. Table 4 shows the baseline used for all experiments to determine the accuracy of the emotion recognition results; Fig. 6 reveals the usage of different baselines.

Self-reports were used 20 times, mostly on scales or questionnaires that are widely used in psychology. Of these, the Self-Assessment Manikin (SAM) was used the most (seven times); the Likert scale was used four times; the State-Trait Anxiety Inventory (STAI) was used twice. The Perceived Stress Scale (PSS) was used three times, all in negative emotion detection studies. Nalepa, Kutt, Giżycka, et al. [40] used an off-the-shelf application, the PsychoPy program. Two studies [32, 42] used questionnaires custom-designed by the researchers.

Table 4. The specific content of the baseline for assessment.

Application	References	Baseline	Specific content
Negative Emotion	[6]	Self-report	Psychological scales (SAM)
	[36]	Self-report	Psychological scales (PSS)
		Self-report	Psychological scales (PSS, EMAs)
	[26]	Self-report	Psychological scales (VASS)
	[24]	Self-report	Psychological scales (PSS)
	[37]	Self-report,	Psychological scales (STAI)
		Biomarkers	Cortisol
	[27]	Self-report	Psychological scales (a Likert scale)
Unclassified	[8]	Emotional labels	From video clips
	[12]	Self-report	Psychological scales (SAM)
	[31]	Self-report	Psychological scales (a Likert scale)
	[33]	Self-report	Psychological scales (SAM)
	[32]	Self-report	Psychological scales (Customized questionnaire)
	[34]	Manual labeling	Subjects labeled themselves
	[28]	Self-report	Psychological scales (PANAS, STAI, SSSQ)
Context-aware Systems	[40]	Self-report	Psychological scales (PsychoPy program)
	[39]	Self-report	Psychological scales (a Likert scale)
		Emotional labels	From emotional pictures
	[41]	Manual labeling	By subjects
	[42]	Self-report	Psychological scales (Customized questionnaire)
	[30]	Manual labeling	By professional annotator
Analysis and Evaluation	[9]	Manual labeling	Subjects labeled themselves
	[23]	Self-report	Psychological scales (SAM)
		Self-report	Psychological scales (SAM)
		Self-report	Psychological scales (SAM)
	[4]	Self-report	Psychological scales (a Likert scale)
	[44]	Biomarkers	Cortisol

(*continued*)

Table 4. (*continued*)

Application	References	Baseline	Specific content
Communication Assistance	[45]	Manual labeling	Diary of observations by people around subjects
	[46]	Self-report	Psychological scales (SAM)

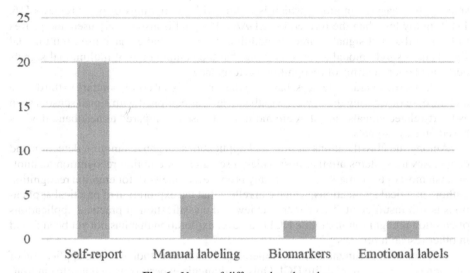

Fig. 6. Usage of different benchmarks.

Manual annotation was usually divided into annotation by the subjects themselves and annotation by professional observers. Subjects' own labeling is usually done in between video clips [9, 41] or when emotions are strong [34]. Professional observer labeling varies depending on the experimental setting. Daily life scenarios relied on people around the subjects, such as in a study of emotional expression in children with autism [45], where family members and teachers observed children's behaviors and activities and labeled them in the form of a diary. In laboratory scenarios, professional observers annotated by watching back video recordings [30].

A novel approach is the detection of cortisol in saliva, a reliable biomarker proven by research to reflect levels of stress, anger and depression [37, 44].

In addition, two studies [8, 39] used mood labels that come with the mood stimulus material as a baseline for testing the identification results. These mood stimulus materials were derived from widely used databases, and using their self-contained mood labels is a more convenient method.

5 Discussion

This section discusses our findings around the review results and research questions, as well as analyzes their similarities and differences with findings in other review articles. Based on the review findings, we discuss the problems and future directions in the reviewed studies.

For the selection of physiological signals, the use of wearable devices to detect cardiac- related physiological signals in real life is a good way to accurately and inconspicuously measure emotions, which is in line with the findings of other reviews [16, 17]. Slightly less than the former, the EDA/GSR signal is also widely used and proves to be a well-suited signal source. In addition, far more studies have used multimodal signals than single-modal signals, proving that the combination of multimodal signals performs better in terms of recognition performance.

In the use of wearable devices, based on the type of signal corresponding to the device and the ease of wearing the device, wristband devices equipped with signal sensors such as heart-related signals and EDA are more widely used, compared to headband devices based on EEG signals.

Among the classifications of practical applications, negative emotion detection and context-aware systems are the most widely used areas of emotion recognition technology, but most of the remaining studies only propose a framework for emotion recognition without practical applications, which can reflect that the exploration of practical applications is still insufficient. This paper's review and classification of practical applications of emotion recognition in mobile HCI is a novel exploration that has not yet been found in other research reviews.

In terms of experimental settings, there are even fewer studies on the application of emotion recognition in real-life HCI. Only 10 dynamic experiments in real-life environments have been conducted, which implies that there are still a large number of issues to be explored and studied in the process of transforming technology into applications.

Before the stimulation begins, studies that place experiments in controlled laboratories usually arrange procedures to keep subjects in a neutral emotional state to ensure the accuracy of the data. Given the complexity of the experimental setting and the time-consuming nature of the pre-experimental phase, real-life experiments usually ignore the pre-experimental phase.

The widely used emotional stimulus materials are video clips, real-life scenes or emotional pictures, which is consistent with the finding of another review [18]. The stimulus materials used in studies on negative emotion detection are noteworthy: some psychological methods are more widely used, such as the Trier Social Test (TSST) [26, 36] which is used to elicit stress or anxiety in subjects.

The dimensional model of arousal-potency is widely used by many studies, in contrast to the claim of another survey [7] (that many studies of mobile affective computing aim to identify discrete emotions). The discrete emotion models in the reviewed studies were mostly used in combination with dimensional models.

In contrast to the study by Saganowski et al. [18] that used only self-reports as a basis for emotion assessment, our work incorporates manual annotation, biomarkers, and emotion labels that come with the stimulus material, providing researchers with more flexible options. Of course, self-report is still the primary source of basic facts about emotions for many researchers, and it includes commonly used questionnaires such as the Likert scale, the Self-Assessment Manikin (SAM), and the State-Trait Anxiety Inventory (STAI).

Despite the progress made, real mobile HCI applications are scarce, with only 1/3 of the studies reviewed attempting emotion recognition applications using wearable devices in real environments. A variety of factors have constrained the progress of research.

First, the user experience of the device. Only a small class of devices such as the Empatica E4 and Microsoft Band 2 have managed to measure inconspicuously, while the rest still suffer from exposed cables [25, 26] and excessive size. EEG headgear such as the Emotiv Epoc and InteraXon MUSE face problems with cumbersome electrode setup processes and interference from motion artifacts, and the headgear limits suitable scenarios. Both Shimmer3 GSR Unit and Shimmer3 ECG have exposed cables, leading to the inevitable interference of human motion in the real environment by them. Second, the problem of equipment setup. Subjects were often asked to undergo a signal stabilization period of 5 to 10 min after putting on the devices [26, 28]. Similarly, subjects were asked to clean the skin on the forehead and behind the ear before wearing the EEG headband to reduce the impedance between the skin and the electrodes [12]. These settings disrupt the coherence and ease of use in real human-computer interaction. In addition, almost all devices inevitably suffer from poor signal quality in mobile conditions.

There are few studies on how to identify the source of stimuli that cause mood changes. T. Zhang et al. [9] attempted to have subjects wear head-mounted eye-tracking devices to collect eye-movement data for video providers to analyze the relationship between video content and users' emotions. Dobbins & Fairclough [38] used a camera to capture the view in front of the driving vehicle to provide a human analysis of the relationship between road conditions and mood changes. In-depth exploration of the user's emotional experience requires clear identification of the source of emotional stimuli in the interaction and then making adjustments, for which we hope and suggest more research be explored in the future.

6 Conclusions

This paper is based on the systematic literature review approach, focusing on the use of wearable devices to measure physiological signals for emotion recognition and highlighting practical applications of emotion recognition in mobile HCI. Closely focused on the above-mentioned topics, we finally obtained 29 articles through a review of the Web of Science database and a rigorous inclusion and exclusion process.

Extracting valid data from these articles and performing statistical analysis, we have the research directions and experimental methods for emotion recognition in mobile HCI, which can be used as a reference guide for future researchers. This review is mainly for researchers who wish to translate emotion recognition technology into practical applications. It is hoped that the results of our review will provide them with references in equipment selection and experimental design, and bring inspiration for their research directions.

The limitations of this review are the number of articles used and the research questions. Due to limited manpower and time, there is a possibility of expanding the scope of the reviewed articles. The research questions focus on research methods and experimental procedures, without sorting out signal processing methods and algorithmic models.

Emotion recognition methods are based on physiological signals only. Some studies were not only based on physiological signals but also incorporated other data sources such as facial expressions, speech, or eye movement signals, for which we can conduct more extensive research in the future.

Acknowledgment. This work was supported by funds for the National Natural Science Foundation of Changsha (kq2202176), Key R&D Program of Hunan(2022SK2104), Leading plan for scientific and technological innovation of high-tech industries of Hunan(2022GK4010), National Key R&D Program of China(2021YFF0900602), the National Natural Science Foundation of China (61672222).

References

1. Khowaja, S.A., Prabono, A.G., Setiawan, F., Yahya, B.N., Lee, S.-L.: Toward soft real-time stress detection using wrist-worn devices for human workspaces. Soft. Comput. **25**(4), 2793–2820 (2021)
2. Landowska, A., Miler, J.: Limitations of emotion recognition in software user experience evaluation context. In: 2016 Federated Conference on Computer Science and Information Systems (FedCSIS). pp. 1631–1640 (2016)
3. Agarwal, A., Meyer, A.: Beyond usability: evaluating emotional response as an integral part of the user experience. In: CHI '09 Extended Abstracts on Human Factors in Computing Systems. pp. 2919–2930. Association for Computing Machinery, New York, NY, USA (2009)
4. Fortune, E., Yusuf, Y., Blocker, R.: Measuring arousal and emotion in healthcare employees using novel devices. In: 2020 IEEE 20th International Conference on Bioinformatics and Bioengineering (BIBE). pp. 835–838 (2020)
5. Kadoya, Y., Khan, M.S.R., Watanapongvanich, S., Binnagan, P.: Emotional status and productivity: Evidence from the special economic zone in Laos. Sustainability **12**, 1544 (2020)
6. Baghdadi, A., Aribi, Y., Fourati, R., Halouani, N., Siarry, P., Alimi, A.: Psychological stimulation for anxious states detection based on EEG-related features. J. Ambient. Intell. Humaniz. Comput. **12**(8), 8519–8533 (2021)
7. Tzafilkou, K., Economides, A.A., Protogeros, N.: Mobile sensing for emotion recognition in smartphones: a literature review on non-intrusive methodologies. Int. J. Human–Computer Interaction. 0, 1–15 (2021). https://doi.org/10.1080/10447318.2021.1979290
8. Shu, L., et al.: Wearable emotion recognition using heart rate data from a smart bracelet. Sensors **20**, 718 (2020)
9. Zhang, T., El Ali, A., Wang, C., Hanjalic, A., Cesar, P.: Corrnet: fine-grained emotion recognition for video watching using wearable physiological sensors. Sensors **21**, 52 (2021)
10. Kwon, J., Kim, D.-H., Park, W., Kim, L.: A wearable device for emotional recognition using facial expression and physiological response. In: 2016 38th Annual International Conference of the IEEE Engineering in Medicine and Biology Society (EMBC). pp. 5765–5768 (2016)

11. Nie, J., Hu, Y., Wang, Y., Xia, S., Jiang, X.: SPIDERS: Low-Cost Wireless Glasses for Continuous In-Situ Bio-Signal Acquisition and Emotion Recognition. In: 2020 IEEE/ACM Fifth International Conference on Internet-of-Things Design and Implementation (IoTDI). pp. 27–39 (2020)
12. Laureanti, R., et al.: Emotion assessment using machine learning and low-cost wearable devices. In: 2020 42nd Annual International Conference of the IEEE Engineering in Medicine Biology Society (EMBC). pp. 576–579 (2020)
13. Zhang, J., Yin, Z., Chen, P., Nichele, S.: Emotion recognition using multi-modal data and machine learning techniques: a tutorial and review. Information Fusion. 59, 103–126 (2020). https://doi.org/10.1016/j.inffus.2020.01.011
14. Ekman, P.: An Argument for Basic Emotions. null. 6, 169–200 (1992). https://doi.org/10.1080/02699939208411068
15. Russell, J.A.: A circumplex model of affect. J. Pers. Soc. Psychol. 39, 1161–1178 (1980). https://doi.org/10.1037/h0077714
16. Egger, M., Ley, M., Hanke, S.: Emotion recognition from physiological signal analysis: a review. Electronic Notes in Theoretical Computer Science 343, 35–55 (2019). https://doi.org/10.1016/j.entcs.2019.04.009
17. Shu, L., et al.: A review of emotion recognition using physiological signals. Sensors 18, 2074 (2018). https://doi.org/10.3390/s18072074
18. Saganowski, S., et al.: Emotion recognition using wearables: a systematic literature review - work-in-progress. In: 2020 IEEE International Conference on Pervasive Computing and Communications Workshops (PerCom Workshops). pp. 1–6 (2020)
19. Schmidt, P., Reiss, A., Dürichen, R., Laerhoven, K.V.: Wearable-based affect recognition—a review. Sensors 19, 4079 (2019). https://doi.org/10.3390/s19194079
20. Wijasena, H.Z., Ferdiana, R., Wibirama, S.: A survey of emotion recognition using physiological signal in wearable devices. In: 2021 International Conference on Artificial Intelligence and Mechatronics Systems (AIMS). pp. 1–6 (2021)
21. Kitchenham, B.: Procedures for performing systematic reviews. Keele, UK, Keele University. 33, 1–26 (2004)
22. Mohamed Shaffril, H.A., Samsuddin, S.F., Abu Samah, A.: The ABC of systematic literature review: the basic methodological guidance for beginners. Qual. Quant. 55(4), 1319–1346 (2021). https://doi.org/10.1007/s11135-020-01059-6
23. Marín-Morales, J., et al.: Real vs. immersive-virtual emotional experience: analysis of psychophysiological patterns in a free exploration of an art museum. PLOS ONE. 14, e0223881 (2019). https://doi.org/10.1371/journal.pone.0223881
24. Dobbins, C., Fairclough, S., Lisboa, P., Navarro, F.F.G.: A lifelogging platform towards detecting negative emotions in everyday life using wearable devices. In: 2018 IEEE International Conference on Pervasive Computing and Communications Workshops (PerCom Workshops). pp. 306–311 (2018)
25. Markova, V., Ganchev, T., Kalinkov, K.: Detection of negative emotions and high-arousal negative-valence states on the move. In: 2018 Advances in Wireless and Optical Communications (RTUWO). pp. 61–65 (2018)
26. Montesinos, V., Dell'Agnola, F., Arza, A., Aminifar, A., Atienza, D.: Multi-modal acute stress recognition using off-the-shelf wearable devices. In: 2019 41st Annual International Conference of the IEEE Engineering in Medicine and Biology Society (EMBC). pp. 2196–2201. IEEE (2019)
27. Gasparini, F., Giltri, M., Bandini, S.: Discriminating affective state intensity using physiological responses. Multimedia Tools and Applications 79(47–48), 35845–35865 (2020)

28. Cosoli, G., Poli, A., Scalise, L., Spinsante, S.: Measurement of multimodal physiological signals for stimulation detection by wearable devices. Measurement **184**, 109966 (2021)
29. Zhang, Q., Chen, X., Zhan, Q., Yang, T., Xia, S.: Respiration-based emotion recognition with deep learning. Comput. Ind. **92**, 84–90 (2017)
30. Di Lascio, E., Gashi, S., Santini, S.: Laughter recognition using non-invasive wearable devices. In: Proceedings of the 13th EAI International Conference on Pervasive Computing Technologies for Healthcare. pp. 262–271. Association for Computing Machinery, New York, NY, USA (2019)
31. Ahn, I.Y., Sung, N.-M., Lim, J.-H., Seo, J., Yun, I.D.: Development of an oneM2M-compliant IoT platform for wearable data collection. KSII Trans. Internet Inf. Syst. (TIIS) **13**, 1–15 (2019)
32. Zhao, B., Wang, Z., Yu, Z., Guo, B.: EmotionSense: emotion recognition based on wearable wristband. In: 2018 IEEE SmartWorld, Ubiquitous Intelligence & Computing, Advanced & Trusted Computing, Scalable Computing & Communications, Cloud & Big Data Computing, Internet of People and Smart City Innovation (Smart-World/SCALCOM/UIC/ATC/CBDCom/IOP/SCI). pp. 346–355. IEEE (2018)
33. Alakuş, T.B., Türkoğlu, İ.: EEG-based emotion estimation with different deep learning models. In: 2019 4th International Conference on Computer Science and Engineering (UBMK). pp. 33–37 (2019)
34. Hayano, J., Tanabiki, T., Iwata, S., Abe, K., Yuda, E.: Estimation of emotions by wearable biometric sensors under daily activities. In: 2018 IEEE 7th Global Conference on Consumer Electronics (GCCE). pp. 240–241 (2018)
35. Apicella, A., Arpaia, P., Mastrati, G., Moccaldi, N., Prevete, R.: Preliminary validation of a measurement system for emotion recognition. In: 2020 IEEE International Symposium on Medical Measurements and Applications (MeMeA). pp. 1–6 (2020)
36. Can, Y.S., Gokay, D., Kılıç, D.R., Ekiz, D., Chalabianloo, N., Ersoy, C.: How laboratory experiments can be exploited for monitoring stress in the wild: a bridge between laboratory and daily life. Sensors. **20**, 838 (2020). https://doi.org/10.3390/s20030838
37. Anusha, A.S., et al.: Electrodermal activity based pre-surgery stress detection using a wrist wearable. IEEE J. Biomed. Health Inform. **24**, 92–100 (2019)
38. Dobbins, C., Fairclough, S.: A mobile lifelogging platform to measure anxiety and anger during real-life driving. In: 2017 IEEE International Conference on Pervasive Computing and Communications Workshops (PerCom Workshops). pp. 327–332 (2017)
39. Nalepa, G.J., Kutt, K., Bobek, S.: Mobile platform for affective context-aware systems. Futur. Gener. Comput. Syst. **92**, 490–503 (2019). https://doi.org/10.1016/j.future.2018.02.033
40. Nalepa, G.J., Kutt, K., Giżycka, B., Jemio\lo, P., Bobek, S.: Analysis and use of the emotional context with wearable devices for games and intelligent assistants. Sensors. **19**, 2509 (2019)
41. Jiang, S., Li, Z., Zhou, P., Li, M.: Memento: an emotion-driven lifelogging system with wearables. ACM Trans. Sen. Netw. **15**, 8:1–8:23 (2019). https://doi.org/10.1145/3281630
42. Chiu, M.-C., Ko, L.-W.: Develop a personalized intelligent music selection system based on heart rate variability and machine learning. Multimedia Tools Appl. **76**(14), 15607–15639 (2017)
43. Cai, R., Guo, A., Ma, J., Huang, R., Yu, R., Yang, C.: Correlation analyses between personality traits and personal behaviors under specific emotion states using physiological data from wearable devices. In: 2018 IEEE 16th Intl Conf on Dependable, Autonomic and Secure Computing, 16th Intl Conf on Pervasive Intelligence and Computing, 4th Intl Conf on Big Data Intelligence and Computing and Cyber Science and Technology Congress(DASC/PiCom/DataCom/CyberSciTech). pp. 46–53 (2018)
44. Hwang, S., Jebelli, H., Choi, B., Choi, M., Lee, S.: Measuring workers' emotional state during construction tasks using wearable EEG. J. Constr. Eng. Manag. **144**, 04018050 (2018)

45. Redd, C.B., et al.: Physiological signal monitoring for identification of emotional dysregulation in children. In: 2020 42nd Annual International Conference of the IEEE Engineering in Medicine & Biology Society (EMBC). pp. 4273–4277. IEEE (2020)
46. Pollreisz, D., TaheriNejad, N.: A simple algorithm for emotion recognition, using physiological signals of a smart watch. In: 2017 39th annual international conference of the ieee engineering in medicine and biology society (EMBC). pp. 2353–2356. IEEE (2017)

Human-Robot Interaction

Human-Robot-Collaboration in the Healthcare Environment: An Exploratory Study

Katharina Gleichauf, Ramona Schmid, and Verena Wagner-Hartl[✉] [ID]

Faculty Industrial Technologies, Furtwangen University, Campus Tuttlingen, Kronenstraße 16, 78532 Tuttlingen, Germany

{katharina.gleichauf,ramona.schmid,
verena.wagner-hartl}@hs-furtwangen.de

Abstract. There is an existing shortage of skilled personnel in the healthcare environment. The growing need for healthcare professionals due to the increasing number of elderly people represents a sociopolitical and economic challenge. It is expected that human-robot collaboration in healthcare will rise in the near future because it could be a great advantage to relieve healthcare professionals with technical systems. To promote the acceptance of such technical systems and digital aids, it is important to involve the health care staff from the very beginning. Therefore, the aim of this study was to examine differences in the acceptance of and the general attitude towards robots in the healthcare sector. In focus was the difference between people working in the health care environment and those who don't. An exploratory study was conducted to find out if - and if yes how - the attitude of people towards robots in the healthcare sector differ and whether the type of robot has an influence on the attitudes towards robots. The results show that participants working in the healthcare sector have a less positive attitude towards robots than those not working in the healthcare sector. Furthermore, significant differences can be shown regarding the assessments of the different robots in the different scenarios. The results of the study should help to understand how people working in the healthcare sector evaluate the potential use of different robots in healthcare.

Keywords: Human-robot collaboration · Healthcare environment · Acceptance

1 Introduction

The proportion of elderly people in the population is increasing around the world. This results in more people needing care [1]. Consequently, there is a growing need for healthcare professionals, which represents a sociopolitical and economic challenge. This challenge exists because the healthcare sector already has a long history of staffing problems, such as staff shortages and turnover rates [2]. Which in result can affect the quality and safety of care [3]. To relieve the burden on professional healthcare workers and make work processes more effective, digital and technical systems are introduced [4]. Those technical systems are not only computer systems but also robots. An interaction

© The Author(s), under exclusive license to Springer Nature Switzerland AG 2022
M. Kurosu et al. (Eds.): HCII 2022, LNCS 13519, pp. 231–240, 2022.
https://doi.org/10.1007/978-3-031-17618-0_17

between a robot and a human being is called human-robot interaction [5]. As of now human-machine interaction in healthcare is primarily used to help patients improve or monitor their health. It is expected that human-machine interaction in healthcare will rise in the near future. In in-home and inpatient care as well as in hospitals, robotic systems are already increasingly being used as support for control, routine, and logistical activities [6]. By incorporating interacting robots, the healthcare sector can improve the quality and accessibility of healthcare services, which in turn may improve the patients' health outcomes for example due to more close monitoring [7]. In addition, the support of robots will increase the time for patients by the healthcare staff itself. This could also improve the well-being of the patients. However, despite the great need for support, human-robot interaction in the healthcare environment faces several challenges. These range from ethical aspects (e.g. awareness of the patients intimate space [8]) and design issues to safety, utility, acceptance, and appropriateness.

Another challenge occurred when in December 2019, the virus SARS-CoV-2, also known as the coronavirus, was discovered in China and developed into a worldwide pandemic [9]. According to the Robert Koch Institute [10] the course of the disease varies. There are cases that remain completely asymptomatic as well as cases where the infection can lead to severe pneumonia with lung failure and death. This disease resulted in major challenges for society as a whole and especially for the staff in the healthcare environment [11]. To protect oneself and keep the virus from spreading one of the main measures for the public is social distancing [10]. For people working in the healthcare environment applying physical distancing is – in many cases - not a valid option. In this regard, the use of robots can have benefits in terms of health and safety for patients and healthcare staff [12].

Yang et al. [13] addressed the question of whether robots could be effective tools in the fight against COVID-19. Today, robots can already be used in many areas of healthcare and serve as support. They have the potential to disinfect, distribute medicines and food, measure vital signs, and keep someone company. With the escalation of a pandemic such as the one caused by Sars-CoV-2, the potential role of robotics is becoming increasingly clear. Since coronavirus viruses can persist for days on inanimate surfaces, the cleaning of surfaces is highly relevant. To prevent the spread of diseases, so-called UV-surface disinfection robots can be used in the hospitals [14]. These are UV-light-devices that are completely robot-controlled and contact-free. They are used to clean contaminated surfaces and thus effectively reduce contamination. Evaluations show that compared to standard room disinfection, non-contact technologies reduce residual contamination more effectively. Furthermore, such systems are able to save costs, perform rapidly and reduce the risk of infection for cleaning staff who are directly exposed to viruses while cleaning, which could be prevented by using these systems [13]. A robot that is used for the disinfections of rooms and surfaces is one of the robots that does not necessarily have to have direct contact to patients when it is used. Examples for such robots are the "Laska" and "Yezhik UVD Robots" by Aitheon [15]. Another robot that is already being used and tested in the healthcare environment today the robot "Moxi" from the company Diligent Robotics [16]. "Moxi" is a one-armed robot for assistance in hospitals. Normally, it does not have direct patient contact. It is designed to assist nurses by performing routine tasks that do not require direct interaction with the patient. For example, its tasks include fetching supplies and lab results.

A robot that can socially interact also seems to be very useful and supportive especially in times of a pandemic where people have very few social contacts because of physical distancing and isolation [17]. It is well known that quarantine and isolation have a significant impact on the mental health and the psychological well-being of people [18]. This is where social robots can be useful.

A study by Aymerich-Franch and Ferrer [11] examined the implementation of social robots in real settings during the COVID-19 pandemic. The results showed that during the crisis an expansion of social robots occurred due to their advantages of facilitating the social distance and palliating the effects of isolation. One example is the "Care-O-Bot" by the Fraunhofer Institute [19]. The "Care-O-Bot" is a mobile robot assistant that is used to actively support humans, for example, it assists them with tasks such as monitoring vital functions or reminders. In addition, the robot "Pepper" by the company Softbank Robotics is already in use [20]. Pepper can recognize people and reacts individually to its environment. It also recognizes moods and things like body posture and facial expressions, which qualifies it for contact with people [21]. Within the healthcare sector pepper is already used, to entertain elderly people needing care.

An important factor in implementing robots into the workplace is the subjective perception of the interaction between humans and robots by the users who get in contact with the robots, in this case the healthcare staff and patients themselves [22]. Since they are supposed to interact directly with the corresponding systems, the attitude, perception, and acceptance of the interacting humans is crucial for the introduction of a successful human-robot interaction. That's why it is important to involve the healthcare staff as well as potential patients from the very beginning when thinking about the implementation of a robot within a healthcare system. In this context, people's opinions and attitudes differ. For example, attitudes towards robots in the different areas of everyday life, work and care were investigated in a former studies of our research group [23, 24]. The results show that attitudes towards robots in everyday life and work are neutral to positive, whereas in the care sector they are neutral to negative. Following Wagner-Hartl et al. [24] the results in the care sector are valid for two different scenarios: To let a robot take care on oneself as well as to let a robot take care on relatives. Furthermore, the results show significant differences regarding the assessment of the need and acceptance of a robot that assists people in different care relevant tasks. For example, the help of a robot was assessed significant better for tasks like transportation or the relocation of patients than tasks like support with body care, assistance with feeding or entertainment. This is also in line with [25] who show that elderly people indicate the help of a robot for tasks like body washing or companionship as not useful.

Aim of the Study

The aim of this study was to examine differences in general attitude towards and the acceptance of robots in the healthcare sector. In the focus was the difference between people working in the healthcare environment and those who don't. An exploratory study was conducted to find out if - and if yes how - the attitude of people towards robots in the healthcare environment differ and whether the type of robot has an influence on the acceptance of robots. Consequently, the following research questions will be investigated:

1. To what extent do the attitudes towards robots in the healthcare environment differ between persons, who work in the healthcare environment and among those who don't?
2. Does the acceptance (usefulness and satisfaction) of different types of robots used within the care sector, differ between persons, who work in the healthcare environment and among those who don't?

2   Method

2.1   Participants

Overall, 115 women and 78 men ($N = 193$) aged between 18 and 74 years ($M = 32.83$, $SD = 14.52$; 2 participants did not report their age) participated in the online study. 33 of the participants work in the healthcare environment and 160 participants work in other occupational fields. Following the results of a t-test, no significant difference regarding age can be shown for the two different working environment groups, $t(190) = 1.42$, $p = .157$ (participants that work in healthcare environment: $M = 36.09$, $SD = 14.48$; participants that do not work in healthcare environment: $M = 32.15$, $SD = 14.49$). All participants provided their informed consent at the beginning of the online study.

2.2   Study Design and Materials

An exploratory study was designed as an online survey with a within-subject design. Overall, the participants needed 10–15 min to complete the questionnaire. The first part of the questionnaire focused on sociodemographic data and possible personal linkages to the work in the healthcare sector as well as general attitudes and previous knowledge about human-robot interaction. In this context, the participants had to assess their general attitude towards robots on a 5-point rating scale [negative (-2) – rather negative (-1) – neutral (0) – rather positive ($+1$) – positive ($+2$)].

In the main part of the questionnaire, the participants assessed four different robots with four different uses (scenarios). The different robots were an assistance robot (Moxi) [16], a disinfection robot (by Aitheon) [15], a care robot (Care-O-Bot) [19] and a social robot (Pepper) [20]. The robots were embedded in a scenario, which should help the participants to understand their possible usage in the context of the healthcare environment. The scenarios contents were adapted from the specific manufacturer websites of the different robots [15, 16, 19, 20]. For each scenario the activity of the robot was described textually (see Table 1).

For a better visual imagination, two additional pictures of each type of robot were presented together with the text to the participants. The pictures used were requested from the specific companies and were used with their consent. One of each pictures showed the robots in a healthcare environment while the other picture showed the robot by itself with a neutral background.

Table 1. Description of the four different scenarios, representing the four different robots in a healthcare environment

Scenario 1: Assistance robot	"Moxi" is an assisting robot in nursing [16]. It helps hospital staff with tasks that are not performed directly on the patient. These include tasks such as delivering bed linen to the patient's room or transport laboratory samples to the laboratory where it is analyzed
Scenario 2: Disinfection robot	Aitheons disinfection robot is used to disinfect rooms [15]. It moves through the room fully automatically and irradiates each surface to be disinfected with UV light. The germs are killed by this process, which prevents the spread of bacteria, viruses, etc. via surfaces
Scenario 3: Care robot	The "Care-O-Bot" is a mobile robot which can provide support in hospitals [19]. Its tasks include monitoring patient monitors, providing information to doctors and triggering alarms in case of an emergency
Scenario 4: Social robot	"Pepper" is a robot that is used in many ways. In the hospital, "Pepper" is a contact point for social contact [20]. For the most part, he serves as a contact person for patients. He cheers them up, entertains them and fulfils their wishes

After each scenario with one of the robots the participants rated their subjectively perceived acceptance using the acceptance scale of Van der Laan et al. [26]. In the acceptance scale nine items (5-point semantic differentials; ranging from -2 to $+2$) represent two subscales of acceptance: Usefulness and satisfaction.

2.3 Statistical Analysis

The software IBM SPSS Statistics was used for the statistical analysis. T-tests and analyses of variance with repeated measures were used as statistical procedure. The evaluation was based on a significance level of 5%.

3 Results

3.1 General Attitudes Towards Robots

The results of an independent samples t-test show significant difference in the general attitudes towards robots between persons, who work in the healthcare environment and those who don't, $t(191) = -3.53$, $p = .001$ (see Fig. 1). Persons who don't work in healthcare ($M = .86$, $SD = .97$) have a significantly more positive general attitude towards robots than people working in healthcare ($M = .18$, $SD = 1.16$).

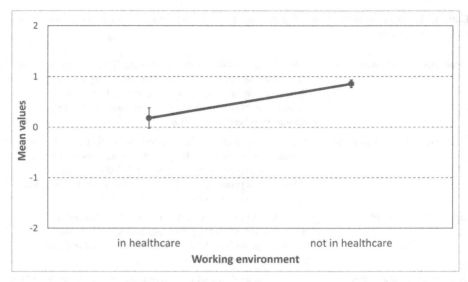

Note. 5-point scale: Negative (-2) – positive (+2); I ... standard error of mean

Fig. 1. General attitudes towards robots – Differences of the two different working environment groups

3.2   Acceptance Regarding Different Robots

Usefulness. Following the results of an analyzes of variance with repeated measures, the different scenarios describing different types of robots (see Table 1) were assessed as significantly different regarding their usefulness, $F_{GG}(2.12, 393.41) = 22.38, p \leq .0001,$ $\eta^2{}_{part} = .107$ (see Fig. 2). The interaction scenario x working environment group, did not reach the level of significance, $F_{GG}(2.12, 393.41) = 2.70, p = .065, \eta^2{}_{part} = .014.$ Post-hoc analyses (Sidak) showed that Scenario 1 describing the use of the an assistance robot like the robot "Moxi" [16] $(M = .52, SD = .50; p \leq .0001)$, Scenario 2 (disinfection robot [24]; $M = .56, SD = .29; p \leq .0001)$ and Scenario 3 representing the usage of a care robot like the "Care-O-Bot" [19] $(M = .53, SD = .54; p \leq .0001)$ were assessed as significantly more useful by the participants than Scenario 4 describing a social robot like the well-known robot "Pepper" [20] $(M = .07, SD = .82)$. In addition, Scenario 2 was assessed significantly more useful than Scenario 3 $(p = .035)$. Furthermore, a significant effect of the working environment group can be shown, $F(1, 186) = 5.37,$ $p = .022, \eta^2{}_{part} = .028$. Overall, participants working in the healthcare environment assessed the different robots as significantly less useful than participants who don't work in healthcare environment.

Satisfaction. The results of an analyzes with variance with repeated measures showed significant difference regarding the perceived satisfaction of the different robots represented in the four different scenarios, $F_{HF}(2.71, 503.46) = 6.46, p \leq .0001, \eta^2{}_{part} = .034$ (see Fig. 3). A significant interaction scenario x working environment, $F_{HF}(2.71, 503.46)$ $= 1.47, p = .224, \eta^2{}_{part} = .008$, as well as an effect of the working environment groups,

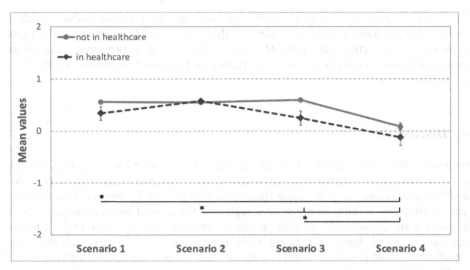

Note. 5-point scale: Negative (-2) to positive (+2); * ... $p \le .05$; I ... standard error of mean

Fig. 2. Perceived usefulness of different robot scenarios.

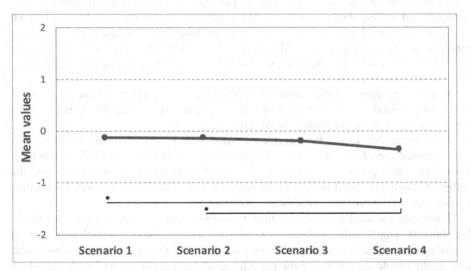

Note. 5-point scale: Negative (-2) to positive (+2); * ... $p \le .05$; I ... standard error of mean;

Fig. 3. Perceived satisfaction of different robot scenarios.

$F(1, 186) = 2.35, p = .127, \eta^2_{part} = .012$, cannot be shown. Post-hoc analyses (Sidak) showed that Scenario 1 (assistance robot [16]; $M = -.13, SD = .48; p = .031$) and Scenario 2 (disinfection robot [15]; $M = -.14, SD = .35; p = .001$) were assessed as significantly more satisfying by the participants than Scenario 4 (social robot [20]; $M = -.36, SD = .71$).

4 Discussion

Following the results, the first research question "(1) To what extent do the attitudes towards robots in the healthcare environment differ between persons, who work in the healthcare environment and among those who don't?" can be answered as follows: The results show significant differences regarding the general attitude towards robots between participants working in the healthcare environment and participants who do not work in this working environment. Persons who don't work in healthcare showed a significantly more positive general attitude towards robots than people working in the healthcare environment.

Furthermore, significant differences can be shown regarding the assessments of the different robots in the different scenarios. Therefore, research question 2 can be answered with: the acceptance (perceived usefulness and satisfaction) of different types of robots used within the care sector, differ between persons, who work in the healthcare environment and among those who don't. The results show that regarding the perceived usefulness of the different robots described in the four scenarios, the social robot was assessed as significantly less useful than all other robots (assisting robot, disinfection robot and a care robot). Furthermore, the disinfection robot was assessed as significantly more useful than the care robot.

In addition, regarding the perceived satisfaction of the participants the social robot was also assessed as significantly less satisfying than the disinfection robot and the assistance robot described within the different scenarios.

Differences due to the two working environment groups can only be shown for the perceived usefulness but not for the perceived satisfaction of the different robots. Therefore, participants who did not work in the healthcare environment assessed the different robots presented in the four different scenarios significantly more useful than participants who work in the healthcare environment.

Following the results, health care professionals seem to be more critical when thinking about working together with robots within their working environment than people not working in this specific working field. One limitation of the study must be considered: Due to the online questionnaire the participants did not really "work" with the robots presented within the different scenarios but only got to imagine how it would be if the robot would support them within the different tasks. From our point of view, it would be important to expand the research. Health care professionals as well as patients and potential future patients should have the possibility to experience to work and actually interact with a robot within the healthcare environment. This would have the benefit of measuring their feeling within this framework.

To sum it up, the results of the study should help to understand how people working in the healthcare sector relate to different robots in healthcare environments. The results emphasize the importance of including this particular group in future research, as the introduction of robots would change their personal workspace. Only if the people who will work with the robots are also convinced that the interaction can support them in their daily work, a good cooperation will succeed.

Acknowledgement. The authors would like to thank all participants who participated in the study.

Author's Statement. The authors state no conflict of interest. Informed consent has been provided from all participants of the study. The study was approved by the ethics committee of the Furtwangen University.

References

1. World Health Organization: Ageing and Health https://www.who.int/news-room/fact-sheets/detail/ageing-and-health Accessed 05 Dec 2021
2. Kaiser Family Foundation https://www.kff.org/coronavirus-covid-19/issue-brief/nursing-facility-staffing-shortages-during-the-covid-19-pandemic/ Accessed 12 May 2022
3. World Health Organization: Health workforce https://www.who.int/health-topics/health-workforce#tab=tab_1 Accessed 12 May 2022
4. Bundesministerium für Gesundheit: Konzertierte Aktion Pflege, Zweiter Bericht zum Stand der Umsetzung der Vereinbarung der Arbeitsgruppen 1 bis 5 [*Concerted Action on Long-Term Care. Second Report on the Status of Implementation of the Agreements of Working Groups 1 to 5*]. Bundesministerium für Gesundheit [*Federal Ministery of Health*]. Berlin, Germany (2021)
5. Goodrich, M.A., Schultz, A.C.: Human-robot interaction: a survey. Foundations Trends Human-Computer Interaction **1**(3), 203–275 (2007)
6. Holland, J., et al.: Service robots in the healthcare sector. Robotics **10**(1), 47 (2021)
7. Olaronke, I., Oluwaseun, O., Rhoda, I.: State of the art: a study of human-robot interaction in healthcare. Int. J. Inf. Eng. Electronic Bus. **3**(3), 43–55 (2017)
8. Parviainen, J., Turja, T., Aerschot, L.: Social robots and human touch in care: the perceived usefulness pf robot assistance among healthcare professionals. In: Korn, O. (eds.): Social Robots: Technological, Societal and Ethical Aspects of Human-Robot Interaction. pp. 187–204. Springer International Publishing, Cham (2019) https://doi.org/10.1007/978-3-030-17107-0_10
9. Robert Koch Institut: Täglicher Lagebericht des RKI zur Coronavirus-Krankheit-2019 (COVID-19) [Robert Koch Institute: RKI Daily Situation Report on the Coronavirus Disease-2019 (COVID-19)]. Berlin, Germany (2020)
10. Robert Koch Institut: Epidemiologischer Steckbrief zu SARS-CoV-2 und COVID-19 [Robert Koch Institute: Epidemiological profile of SARS-CoV-2 and COVID.19], https://www.rki.de/DE/Content/InfAZ/N/Neuartiges_Coronavirus/Steckbrief.html#doc13776792bod Accessed 17 May 2022
11. Aymerich-Franch, L., Ferrer, I.: The implementation of social robots during the COVID-19 pandemic. ArXiv preprint (2020)

12. Tavakoli, M., Carriere, J., Torabi, A.: Robotics, Smart Wearable Technologies, and Autonomous Intelligent Systems for Healthcare During the COVID-19 Pandemic: An Analysis of the State of the Art and Future Vision. Advanced Intelligent Systems. 2 (2020)

13. Yang, G., et al.: Keep healthcare workers safe: application of teleoperated robot in isolation ward for COVID-19 prevention and control. Chinese J. Mechanical Eng. 33(1), 1–4 (2020)

14. Doll, M., Morgan, D.J., Anderson, D., Bearman, G.: Touchless technologies for decontamination in the hospital: a review of hydrogen peroxide and UV devices. Current Infectious Disease Reports 17(9), 1–11 (2015)

15. Aitheon: Reduce infections with UV Disinfection Robots. https://aitheon.com/disinfection-robots Accessed 18 May 2022

16. Diligent Robotics Inc.: Care is a team effort. https://www.diligentrobots.com/moxi Accessed 17 May 2022

17. World Health Organization: Coronavirus disease 2019 (COVID-19) Situation Report 72 (2021)

18. Aymerich-Franch, L.: COVID-19 lockdown: impact on psychological well-being and relationship to habit and routine modifications. PsyArXiv (2020)

19. Frauenhofer IPA: Care-O-bot 4 https://www.care-o-bot.de/de/care-o-bot-4.html Accessed 17 May 2022

20. SoftBank Robotics: Pepper. https://www.softbankrobotics.com/emea/de/pepper Accessed 17 May 2022

21. Humanizing Technologies: Emotionale Ansprache von Kunden durch den humanoiden Roboter Pepper [Humanizing Technologies: Emotional Addressing of Customers by the Humanoid Robot Pepper]. https://humanizing.com/de/pepper-roboter-humanoider-rob oter-von-softbank-robotics-fuer-handel-messen-empfaenge-showrooms-happiness-hero/ Accessed 17 May 2022

22. Görke, M., Blankemeyer, S., Pischke, D., Oubari, A., Raatz, A., Nyhuis, P.: Sichere und akzeptierte Kollaboration von Mensch und Maschine: Integrierte Betrachtung technischer und nicht technischer Gestaltungsfaktoren für die Einführung nachhaltiger und effizienter kollaborativer Montagesysteme [Safe and accepted human-machine collaboration: integrated consideration of technical and non-technical design factors for the introduction of sustainable and efficient collaborative assembly systems]. Zeitschrift für wirtschaftlichen Fabrikbetrieb [J. Economic Factory Operation] 112, 41–45 (2017)

23. Wagner-Hartl, V., Gleichauf, K., Schmid, R.: Are we ready for human-robot collaboration at work and in our everyday lives? - an exploratory approach. In: Ahram, T., Karwowski, W., Pickl, S., Taiar, R. (eds.) IHSED 2019. AISC, vol. 1026, pp. 135–141. Springer, Cham (2020). https://doi.org/10.1007/978-3-030-27928-8_21

24. Wagner-Hartl, V., et al.: Who would let a robot take care of them? - gender and age differences. In: Stephanidis, C., Antona, M. (eds.) HCII 2020. CCIS, vol. 1224, pp. 196–202. Springer, Cham (2020). https://doi.org/10.1007/978-3-030-50726-8_26

25. Mast, M., et al.: User-centered design of a dynamic-autonomy remote interaction concept for manipulation-capable robots to assist elderly people in the home. J. Human-Robot Interaction 1(1), 96–118 (2012)

26. Van Der Laan, J.D., Heino, A., De Waard, D.: A simple procedure for the assessment of acceptance of advanced transport telematics. Trans. Res. Part C: Emerging Technol. 5, 1–10 (1997)

Towards an Active Predictive Relation by Reconceptualizing a Vacuum Robot: Research on the Transparency and Acceptance of the Predictive Behaviors

Peicheng Guo[✉] and Iskander Smit

Department of Industrial Design, Delft University of Technology, Delft, The Netherlands
guopshing@outlook.com

Abstract. With the development of Artificial intelligence, the connected objects are extended with the predictive capabilities and the character of things can change to "things that predict". If a connected device is able to embrace a predictive system that not only profiles for scripted behavior but could also use the knowledge co-created by all the other similar devices and their users that encounter similar situations, the predictions can be generated based on that. In this case, a new type of interplay between humans and things called "predictive relation" is created. However, before this future takes place, it is required to find out appropriate patterns to address challenges such as the transparency and users' acceptance of predictive behaviors of connected products. The research in this article takes a vacuum robot as a reference product for the study. The research starts by collecting users' daily practice with vacuum robots through 4-day diary booklets. And then the booklets serve as sensitizing tools to envision the possible predictive capabilities and lead the discussion on the acceptance and transparency of general predicting things. From the creative sessions we propose 1) design qualities for the acceptance of the predicting things, and 2) a model of generating predictive behavior that enhances the transparency. Eventually, we also propose the idea of "Designers as the facilitators of the human-robot collaboration".

Keywords: Internet of Things · Artificial intelligence · Human-robot interaction · Transparency · Acceptance · Robot autonomy

1 Introduction

1.1 Predictive Relations & Knowledge

For some time now, things are becoming connected, such as electronic consumer products, being able to connect to each other directly and through the Internet, and things can interact without human interference [1]. By implementing sensors, things can exchange data and combine products into a decentralized system. This system of connected objects is referred to as the Internet of Things (IoT). With the development of Artificial Intelligence and Machine Learning capabilities, the connected objects are now extended with

M. Kurosu et al. (Eds.): HCII 2022, LNCS 13519, pp. 241–256, 2022.
https://doi.org/10.1007/978-3-031-17618-0_18

predictive capabilities and the character of these things is changed to "things that predict" [2]. If a connected device is able to embrace a predictive system that not only profiles for scripted behavior but can also use the knowledge co-created by all the other similar devices and their users that encounter similar situations, predictions can be generated based on that. In doing so, a new type of interplay between humans and things called "predictive relation" is created (shown in Fig. 1). Commonly, there will be a feedback loop when users interact with a product or service. According to experiences from the past (t-1), the users will form a mental model (t+1) to understand and foresee in what way the product will perform. For example, a user considers an object as a cleaning tool based on his/her past experience with the tool and expects it to clean up the floor accordingly. When intelligence is added to the object, like sensors and algorithms equipped by the factory and schedule for performing tasks set by the users, this profile will also influence the anticipations of the users. Moreover, as a smart object fed with the predictive knowledge generated from the decentralized system, the profile will be formed by the knowledge on predicted futures and then indirectly shape the user's perception of the product.

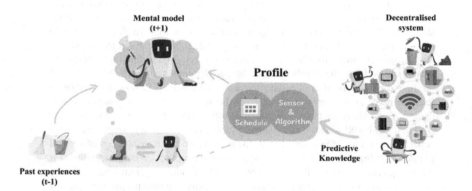

Fig. 1. An image of predictive relations and knowledge [2]

1.2   Current Issues and Related Work of AI & the Connected Objects

Acceptance. When we envision how promising a new concept or a new technology can be to enhance our lives, we still reserve the right to decide for ourselves whether to accept this new technology, especially when it will significantly change our existing lives. As everyday objects are implemented with predictive capabilities and become complex systems, one of the possibilities is that we will lose the control that we currently have on the objects. At that time, how shall we adapt to this shift in role, or how can robots help us accept them equipped with this new technology? Therefore, a successful implementation of a new technology would not be achieved without the investigation of user acceptance.

Apart from the theory such as Technology Acceptance Model (TAM) [3] focusing on the measurable factors of a concrete and realized system like perceived ease-of-use, the Domestication Theory [12–14] uses the metaphor of taming a wild animal into the home environment to investigate how a new technology is being integrated and adopted in users daily life. Thus, the acceptance qualities of an immeasurable and unrealized technology such as things becoming predictive, are easier to be investigated through the Domestication Theory. The Domestication Theory provides a model which is divided into 4 dimensions:

- Practical domestication: This dimension points out the interactions that are physical and observable with the technology. This can refer to how the technology can be used, such as a button on the product to push.
- Symbolic domestication: This refers to what the technology means for the users after having it in their life, illustrating the unobserved after-effects of adopting the technology.
- Cognitive domestication: are the mental practices associated with the use of technology, e.g., how the users learn from and through the technology and how the technology changes the users in return.
- Social domestication: refers to how technology is influenced not only by individuals but also through a diversity of actors who hold agency in how the technology is applied to the lives of users and others around them.

Transparency. When the thing is able to predict and make decisions autonomously as a "black box", it's hard to explain why and how it reached certain outcomes. Sometimes the users can immediately realize that the predictions can perfectly meet their needs, while sometimes its predictive knowledge may achieve users' potential demands that they are not yet aware of. Moreover, the predictive knowledge may take over the decision making and the reasons for the predictive decision are sometimes missing, leaving the user with passive use. To open up the "black box", many have called for creating artificial systems with explainable and transparent qualities that humans can trust [4, 5]. Many well-known digital examples have come up with some solutions on transparency, such as Explainable AI of Google cloud which provide a set of tools and framework to help the customer learn and interpret predictions made by the Artificial Intelligence [18], but cases are few when looking into the IoT products [2].

Robot Autonomy and the Level of Robot Autonomy. Robot autonomy is considered highly relevant to the capability of the smart system to perform its own tasks and actions. In the field of human-robot interaction (HRI), robot autonomy plays a crucial role, since it will influence the performance of the tasks, the way and density of interaction with humans, and the reliability of the performance in an environment. A scientific basis of study on the autonomy of robots can help designers to understand the features and tasks of the smart objects and identify which actions and tasks should be assigned to humans or robots [6]. Over the years, the studies on the definition of robot autonomy have been discussed from the perspective of psychology and engineering [7–9]. The term is applied to characterize varied aspects of robotics, from the ability of the robot to manage itself to the level of required human intervention. In Beer's study [6], they proposed a more detailed definition, which integrates current generally accepted definitions of autonomy and indicates common characteristics of autonomy (i.e., sense, plan, act, task-specific goal, and control): *"The extent to which a robot can **sense** its environment, **plan** based* *on that environment, and **act** upon that environment with the intent of reaching some task-specific goal (either given to or created by the robot) without external control."* This definition helps deconstruct the behavior of an autonomous robot into 3 dimensions—— Sense, Plan, and Act, and indicates that the characteristics should be taken into account when researching robot autonomy. Views on how autonomy impacts human-robot interaction are different. In the case of Huang's research team, they hold the view that the level of robot autonomy (LORA) has a negative linear relationship with the frequency of HRI, which means that the higher LORA, the lower the frequency of HRI [10]. The LORA also reveals that autonomy is not a binary allocation: either human or robot is allocated to a specific goal and action, but a continuous category that splits between the human and robot, indicating the degree of dynamic control of the tasks. Beer's team [6] highlights that the robot's autonomy is in a state of fluctuation, which may switch between levels over time according to the interaction, task, and environment.

1.3   Research Direction

With the predictive knowledge added to the interplay we have with the connected objects, there is no sufficient reference to validate if the interplay meets the requirements when the relation is linked to the future. So, before the future takes place, it is required to find out appropriate patterns to address the challenges such as the transparency and users' acceptance of predictive behaviors of connected products. It is urged to have an active and valid dialogue to understand the now and the future at the same time, and this leads to the question: 'how to design transparent and acceptable predictive relations for the things that predict?' Therefore, to investigate the question, the research in this article takes a vacuum robot as a reference product of the study, including the following contributions:

- From vacuum robots to general predicting things:

  - Design qualities for the acceptance of the predicting things
  - Model of generating predictive behavior that enhances the transparency

- The idea of "Designer as the facilitator of the human-robot collaboration"

2   Methods

A creative session is conducted to dive deep into the context of the user and the vacuum robot to envision what kind of capabilities can be applied to the vacuum robot as predictive capabilities. Taking vacuum robots as the reference products, the research also focuses on exploring the general qualities that can help the predicting robots perform appropriately and integrate into our lives. Besides, based on the envisioned predictive capabilities, we also discuss how the predictive knowledge is being generated in individuals' contexts and how can it be explainable and transparent to the users. In conclusion, three research questions for the qualitative study are set up as follows:

- What predictive capabilities could be applied to the vacuum robot in the future?

- From vacuum robots to general predicting things, what qualities can help the predicting robots become acceptable in our life?
- How does predictive knowledge generate in the individual context that can enhance transparency?

The creative session consists of 2 parts. In the first part, 4 users of vacuum robots and 2 experts from the robotic and design fields were invited and they were provided with a 4-day diary booklet to record their daily individual practices of cleaning and their relationship with the current vacuum robot. After that, they were asked to bring their dairy booklets together to present and discuss their experience with vacuum robots. In the second part, a 1-h creative session was conducted through sketching and discussion to envision the predictive capabilities of vacuum robots and identify the design qualities for acceptance of general predicting robots. Besides, in a holistic view, we summarize the predictive behaviors envisioned in the creative session to a model indicating how a predictive behavior is being generated in the individual context. All participants were provided and asked to sign up for the consent forms before the study (Table 1).

Table 1. The structure of creative session

	Activities	Theories	Outcomes
Part 1	Investigating the daily practices with the vacuum robots through 4-day diary booklets	Path of expression [11]	Daily individual practices of cleaning and their relationship with the current vacuum robots
Part 2	Envisioning the possible predictive capabilities based on the current context of use and identifying the design qualities	The Domestication Theory [12–14]	• Categories of predictive behaviors • Design qualities for the acceptance of the predicting things • Model of generating predictive behavior that enhances the transparency

2.1 Sensitizing the Expression of Participants: Path of Expression

To help the participants envision the predictive knowledge of vacuum robots in the future, the study follows the path of expression [11]——ask about the present and the past before asking about the future. It enables participants to connect to what their concerns are from their past and present experiences and use that to trigger their feelings and ideas about the future. Thus, the study starts by recording participants' experiences and feelings about the present and past through the dairy booklets and then discusses the future scenarios of predictive behavior of vacuum robots. In addition, as a sensitizing tool, the diary booklet also follows the path of expression to help the participants record and present their personal experiences on the booklet. It not only asks about participants' current and past experiences but also requires them to think about the vacuum robots' possible connections with other objects in the future (Fig. 2).

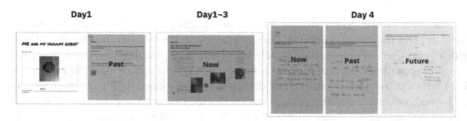

Fig. 2. An example of the diary booklet

2.2 Sensitizing the Findings: Domestication Theory

To answer the research question: what qualities can help the predicting robots perform appropriately and become acceptable in our life, the Domestication Theory [12–14] is applied to lead the questions during the creative session and sensitize the participants to find out the qualities from the predictive capabilities they envisioned that help the predictive behaviors become acceptable.

3 From the Current Vacuum Robot to the Predicting Vacuum Robot

3.1 The Main Tasks of the Current Vacuum Robot

To summarize the daily practices of current vacuum robots, the data collected by the 4-day diary booklets are categorized into groups of main tasks. The tasks are described from the human perspective and clustered as: 1) preparing for the cleaning, 2) opportunistic cleaning, 3) planned cleaning, 4) solving the problems when cleaning, 5) after cleaning.

- Preparing for the cleaning: Usually, before the robot is able to clean, some components, such as an empty dust box, should be installed. Sometimes, users must preclean up the cables scattered on the ground to prevent robots stucking and overturning.
- Opportunistic cleaning is the type of cleaning task that is temporary and unscheduled [15]. Sometimes the users and vacuum robots may need to carry out some unexpected cleaning tasks, such as cleaning up specific areas and rooms that are covered by scattered nuts with spot cleaning and room cleaning mode.
- Planned cleaning: The cleaning activities that are regularly carried out, such as weekly scheduled cleaning, cleaning in the condition of leaving home, are categorized as planned cleaning [15].

- Solve the problems when cleaning: The robot may encounter problems in the cleaning route. Solving problems, such as getting rid of stucking, are common activities in the cleaning routine.
- After cleaning: When the cleaning is complete, the robot will automatically go to the charging base and switch to the Sleep Mode. Also, to maintain the robot and obtain new features, users are required to replace the consumables and update the system regularly.

3.2 Categories of Predictive Behaviors

Summarizing from the perspective of the starting point of the predictive behavior, the scenarios envisioned by the participants can be categorized as follows: 1) Predicting starts from sensing the environment, 2) Predicting directly starts from the knowledge generated from the cloud users.

Predicting Starts from Sensing the Environment. In this situation, the predicting robot first senses the surrounding environment, then matches the collected information with the data from the cloud to trigger the predictive actions. The predictive behaviors in this situation can start from sensing the elements of the scene: the human actions (e.g. users' commands and emotions), and recognizing the object (e.g. dust, etc.).

Predicting Directly Starts from the Knowledge Generated from the Cloud Users. The other way to trigger the predictive knowledge is that the predictions directly start from the cloud. Instead of triggering predictive behavior through the surroundings where the robot is embedded, in this situation, predictions are executed by obtaining knowledge directly from the cloud. For example, the predicting robot performs actions because of weather information and news reports (Fig. 3).

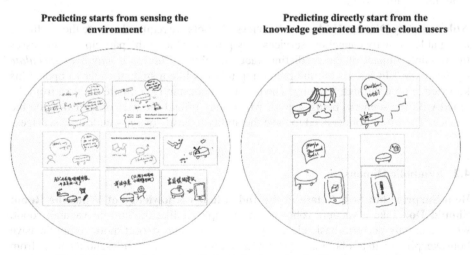

Fig. 3. The categories of predictive behaviors sketched by the participants

4 From Vacuum Robots to General Predicting Things

To identify the qualities that help the predicting robot become acceptable in our daily life, the Domestication theory is applied in the creative session to sensitize the findings. Based on the theory, the findings are classified into 4 dimensions.

4.1 Practical Dimension

Able to Show Context-Related Information. The ability to help the user to learn the reason behind the predictive behavior is crucial for the things that predict [2]. The Human-AI interaction guideline from Microsoft [16] indicates one of the ways to express the reasons for predictions is to show the information that is related to the user's current environment and activity. This also can be proved from the creative session. Without guidance from the interviewer, the interactive dialogues with the predicting robot created by 4 participants all include the contextually relevant information to explain the robot's behavior. For example, the robot provides the information that it is detected from the user's current behavior——smoking, and asks for permission to clean. Another situation that came up from the participants shows that the robot points out the user will have a party and recommends cleaning in advance.

Able to Provide Room for Negotiation on the Decision Made by the Robot. When robots become intelligent or even able to predict, it is inevitable that they will need to make decisions autonomously at various degrees. These decisions may not always fit perfectly with the user's wishes. At this point, robots need to be able to negotiate, to revise their behavior, and even more advanced, to convince users to accept and understand their behavior. The negotiation process can also stimulate the user to provide the robot with more information to learn.

Able to Easily Dismiss Undesired Services. Robots are required to have the quality of being able to easily cancel the services they provide. One of the participants addresses the possible impact of the predicting vacuum robot: *"The robot may over-speculate my behavior."* In his vision, the predicting robot is like a student eager to update his knowledge pool through learning. The robot will constantly compare the data from the cloud with the scenario being served, which may offend the user or over-provide the service. Therefore, robots need to have the ability to easily dismiss undesired services.

4.2 Symbolic Dimension

Be a Surprise but Still Relate to the Individual's Knowledge of What the Robot Should Do. Take a vacuum robot as an example, unlike the current vacuum robot, which can only perform basic cleaning tasks, participants expect more comprehensive housekeeping from a robot that can gain more knowledge about household chores from other users. For example, based on reports of an increase in slip and fall accidents due to slippery floors, the vacuum robot issued a slippery floor warning. Also, one participant drew a scenario describing the vacuum robot that keeps pets away from broken cups, etc. All of these indicate a shift from the robot, which now represents a guarantee of completing basic tasks, to a symbol of providing unanticipated knowledge or even surprises. However, no matter how intelligent and predictive a robot becomes, the predictive behavior should still relate to the individual's knowledge of what the robot is supposed to do.

P6: *"I know that when this technology turns out to be a reality, he will give me a lot of surprises, and even know how to do the cleaning better than I do, but his behavior should still be in line with my key expectations of this product, I mean, like, saving my time on cleaning the floor."*

Able to Foster New Lifestyle. Based on the fact that users now have a need for pre-cleaning (removing the objects that the vacuum robot will easily get stuck) before launching the vacuum robot, one participant suggested that through learning from the cloud, the vacuum robot is able to identify furniture and give suggestions on furniture placement to free up more sweeping space. Another participant proposed that predicting robots can hint and stimulate users to buy more smart devices in a proper time. The participants' expectations for the predicting robot were no longer limited to better work, but extended to suggestions for new lifestyles, such as embracing new home layouts and new smart devices. They also said: *"(...) Compared to the current sweeper, I think if the predictive sweeper recommends new things to me from time to time, this will keep me fresh to him, so that the frequency of use may increase."*

4.3   Cognitive Dimension

Able to Motivate Users to Constantly Participate in Generating Predictive Knowledge for Other Users. Unlike current robots, predicting robot is not only a matter of encouraging users to be more involved, but also a matter of motivating them to pass on the knowledge they co-create with the robot to the cloud in order to enrich the knowledge base of the robot system to serve more people and make predictive behavior more relevant to people's demands. A participant from a robotics company said, *"(...) As a developer of the robot, it is also an important part of our job to effectively collect user preference and feedback to enhance our system (...)"* He added: *"(...) There are many ways to motivate users to donate their data, such as enabling them to understand what parts of the information they are about to share are desensitized. We also build a community of users to make them feel connected, and to let them realize how valuable their data donation is to the community (...)".*

Able to Motivate Users to Provide Feedback in Order to Make the New (Predictive) Behaviors More Suitable in Their Own Context. This expert also said, *"(...) when the robot first predicts a new behavior through the cloud database, for example, that the robot predicts the user may need to clean the floor while smoking, the robot can ask for the user's opinion in a polite and questioning tone, and when this behavior is accepted by the user several times, the robot then performs the task with more initiative (...)"* This process also allows the user to understand the underlying reasons for the predictive behavior of the robot and to adjust the nuances of the behavior to their own situation, e.g., sweeping the floor in a specific area around the user when the user is smoking. Through this process, the user changes from unfamiliar with this predictive behavior to familiar with it, and gradually delegates the initiative to the robot.

4.4 Social Dimension

No Social Comparison. When the robot starts to predict behaviors that it learns from networked users, the user will start to be influenced by social comparison. *"(…) it's like when I'm browsing a certain t-shirt on an online shopping platform, and the website gives me information that the person who viewed this t-shirt also bought this pair of jeans. Then I will start to think….hmmmm…maybe having this pair of jeans to match the t-shirt would be nice. So, when I learn that prediction is learned from someone else, I will start to reflect on my own thoughts".*

If a robot is trying to prove that its predictive behavior is reasonable, it is not a good idea to compare the individual's situation with other users, even though the users know that the information is anonymous.

P7: *"Well, I understand that the robot will try to told me this information so as to make me feel that his decision was reliable and reasonable, but it also made me feel defensive. Why should I do the same just like others?".*
P8: *"It's like he has his own social circle with other robots, and I know he learns a lot from there, but I feel offended if he's always comparing my situation to others".*

5 Discussion

From the study, it is not hard to notice that, in the future, the process of defining products——what the products should do and how to do it, has shifted from the stage of the design process to the stage where users use the product. In the predictive system, the roles of planning the tasks and justifying the appropriate initiative are highly dependent on the knowledge generated from similar and networked users. In this system, users are not only engaged as the ones using the products but also as the ones participating in the evaluation, making the predictive behavior more appropriate and suitable for more people through the involvement of a wide variety of users.

In the following paragraph, we first reflect on the identified design qualities that enable predicting things to become acceptable. Then, in a holistic view, we summarize the predictive behaviors envisioned in the creative session to a model indicating how a predictive behavior is being generated in the individual context. Besides, we also discuss that the proposed model reveals the users' learning and adapting process. And thus, we argue the way to generate the predictive behavior in our proposed model can enhance transparency. Finally, we discuss the shifting role of designers when things become predictive and reflect on the value of the creative session.

Table 2. The design qualities identified from the creative sessions

Dimensions	Qualities
Practical	-Able to show context-related information -Able to provide room for negotiation on the decision made by the robot -Able to easily dismiss undesired services
Symbolic	-Be a surprise but still relate to the individual's knowledge of what the robot should do -Able to foster new lifestyle
Cognitive	-Able to motivate users to constantly participate in generating predictive knowledge for other users -Able to motivate users to provide feedback in order to make the new (predictive) behaviors more suitable in their own context
Social	-No social comparison

5.1 Design Qualities for the Acceptance of the Predicting Things

Our main findings from the creative session are conceptualized in Table 2, where we summarize the qualities that enable predicting things to become acceptable in 4 dimensions.

It can be concluded that, when things become predictive, the predicting thing change the role from a command follower to a collaborator who is expected to have the qualities of bidirectional communication and negotiation. Therefore, in the practical dimension, the predicting robot should provide ways for users to actively argue whether the predictive behaviors are appropriate and easily cancel the undesired services. Besides, reasonable and appropriate information such as context-related information provided by the predicting robots can help users understand how the prediction is being generated and thus and thus enable the predictions more likely to become acceptable.

Different from existing robots that represent performing defined and scripted behaviors, the predicting robots symbolize bringing new and unanticipated knowledge to the user. In this manner, the user can learn about other networked users' daily practices through the predicting robot, thus changing his or her own lifestyle. However, the knowledge of a predicting robot cannot expand without rules. The predictive knowledge still needs to comply with ethics and be restricted to the robot's domain of duties. For example, a domestic predicting vacuum robot should vacuum inside the house instead of going out to the garden to sweep the leaves. Further research is required on how to define the scope of predictive knowledge.

The development of predictive knowledge is co-created by all the networked users and robots. To expand this cloud-based knowledge pool, in the cognitive dimension, the predicting robots need to be able to motivate their users to generate new knowledge continuously and actively for the community in the cloud. Similarly, in the individual context, the predicting robots are required to have the capability to motivate users to provide feedback in order to customize the predictive behaviors more suitable and acceptable to the individual.

When the users are aware that the formation of predictive knowledge is a co-creation process with other users, inevitably, the users may attribute social properties to their relationship with the predicting robots. For example, because of the potential social comparison, the users may resist the robots' predictive behaviors which perform based on networked knowledge. Therefore, as a predicting robot the behavior should be performed in a way that minimizes the impact of social comparisons. For instance, do not argue that the prediction is reasonable with the results of comparing individual situations with the cloud users.

5.2 Model of Generating Predictive Behaviors that Enhances the Transparency

The process of generating predictive behaviors is highly automatic. According to the definition of robot autonomy [6], the process can be divided into 3 parts——Sense, Plan, and Act. With this concept in mind, based on the predictive capabilities summarized from the creative session, we propose a model of generating predictive behavior to reveal how the predictive behavior is being developed in the individual context (shown in Fig. 4).

Sense. In the Sense part of the model, according to the findings in Session 3.2, there are 2 ways to trigger the prediction: 1) starting from robots sensing the environment and the users' command, 2) directly starting from the knowledge generated from the cloud users. As Fig. 4 shows, the only difference between these two processes is that the former has one more step than the latter one, i.e. sensing the user's environment and command.

Plan & Act. After the predicting robot sensing the environment or the prediction directly starts from the cloud, the predicting robot will match the collected information with the data from the cloud to interpret and understand the scene. Based on the cloud knowledge and the user's past experience, the robot will determine the initial autonomy level when this predictive behavior first takes place in the context and perform actions with the corresponding level of automation. The interaction between humans and robots will create a loop of co-performance [17] where human performers and robot performers together judge and shape the appropriate performance under individual situations. Through the co-performance, the predictive behavior will be gradually adjusted and adapted to the specific circumstances, and the data generated from this loop will also feed forward the profile in the cloud.

Kuijer and Giaccardi [17] define the co-performance in the view that things have equal roles with humans to learn and judge the tasks in the interplay. In the traditional procedure of developing smart things, the performances of the devices are determined in the design process. However, in the concept of 'co-performance', the process of defining the performances of the things is shifted to the everyday use practice, which creates an open space for humans and things to learn and adapt to the appropriate performances in their daily practice. The distribution of the agency and the robot's autonomy, however, are the result of this dynamic learning and adapting process.

In the loop of co-performance, humans and robots will learn and adapt to the behavior of each other, and the labor distribution between humans and robots will be dynamically changed throughout the interplay. For instance, the human judges whether a particular predictive behavior is appropriate, and through the interplay with the robot, the predictive behavior becomes more in line with the personal expectations. In this process, the distribution of activities between humans and robots is also changing, thus implicitly affecting robots' autonomy. Also, since the interplay reveals the learning process, the reasoning and the generating process of the predictive behavior can be explained in this loop, thus enhancing the transparency of predictive behaviors.

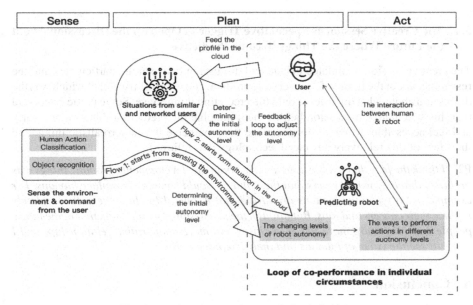

Fig. 4. Model of generating predictive behaviors

5.3 The Shifting Role of the Designer When Things Become Predictive: Designers as Facilitators of Human-Robot Collaboration

The creative session eventually led to discussions and reflections on the shifting roles of designers and developers when designing the predicting things in the future. Some participants thought that the designer should be the one to help the user set up a proper expectation of the robot's capabilities. Admittedly, robots empowered with Artificial Intelligence have great potential, but there are still limitations to what they can accomplish. The designer, therefore, has the responsibility to help the user understand what the predicting robot can do and how well it can do. In addition, when robots are equipped with the abilities of self-awareness and self-determination, their role changes from the command's followers to a collaborator on equal footing with humans. At that time, humans are no longer in the state of outputting one-way commands to robots, but humans and robots are in a state of bidirectional communication, or even bidirectional negotiation and compromise. By then, the focus of designers and product developers will be extended to how to guide the users and the predicting robots to form a well-coordinated partnership and how to lead this partnership to co-create reliable and meaningful knowledge. Therefore, this article proposes the view that: when the connected things become predictive, one of the roles of the designer is to facilitate the collaboration between humans and robots. The designers here are the ones who help to bring in the background knowledge and the patterns of the predictive relation and indicate the ways for humans and robots to co-perform reliable and meaningful daily practice in their partnership.

5.4   The Creative Session as Speculative Trigger to Open up the Discussion About the Future Where the Things Become Predictive

The creative session stimulated debate and discussion between the participants and the researcher about the future of the everyday product, and the most fruitful of which was the discussion about what qualities should the predicting things have. Some participants said that this speculative discussion helped them imagine the predicting thing more clearly and feel accessible, which no longer made them perceive it as a surrealistic thing, and their fear of this relatively advanced technology was relieved.

P2: *"I think the fear that people used to have about the development of robotic things was probably that they would worry that these things would completely replace humans. For example, most typically, humans are afraid that Artificial Intelligence will completely replace their careers and jobs. But through the discussion, I would think that in the future people and robots are more like in a closer and more cooperative relationship, and I can still see the value of humans and their irreplaceability."*

6   Conclusion

This article presents qualitative research on the acceptance and transparency of predicting things by taking vacuum robots as reference products. The qualitative research was shaped in the form of a 2-part creative session that envisioned the possible predictive capabilities of the vacuum robots and discuss their possible impacts.

From vacuum robots to general predicting things, we identify design qualities for acceptance based on the Domestication Theory and are divided into 4 dimensions. Besides, from the creative session, we also propose a model of generating predictive behaviors and argue that the loop of co-performance in the proposed model can reveal the learning and adapting process, thus enhancing transparency. Finally, we propose the idea of "Designers as facilitators of the human-robot collaboration" when things become predictive. In the coming future, the designers can be the ones who help to bring in the background knowledge and the patterns of the predictive relation and indicate the ways for humans and robots to co-perform reliable and meaningful daily practice in their partnership.

Further research can be conducted on evaluating the effect and impact of the proposed design qualities and model. The design qualities and the model can be integrated into the prototype using method such as "Wizard-of-Oz" to engage the participants to experience and test the predictive relation. Besides, regarding the idea of "Designers as facilitators of the human-robot collaboration", there is still much room for more systematic exploration, such as designing a systematic pre-sales and after-sales service system for predicting robots to facilitate collaboration.

Acknowledgements. We would like to thank Nazli Cila for her contribution in the earlier stages of the research. Thanks to Yahong Li and Xuejing Feng for their comments and suggestions during the research and writing, as well as to all the participants for their fruitful insights in the creative session. The research was commissioned by the Cities of Things Delft Design Lab.

References

1. Rowland, C., Goodman, E., Charlier, M., Light, A., Lui, A.: Designing Connected Products: UX for the Consumer Internet of Things. O'Reilly Media, Inc. (2015)
2. Smit, I.: Designing predictive relations in more-than-human partnerships – Cities of Things. Cities of Things (2021). https://cityofthings.nl/2021/01/05/designing-predictive-relations-in-more-than-human-partnerships/
3. Davis, F.D.: Perceived usefulness, perceived ease of use, and user acceptance of information technology. MIS Q. **13**(3), 319 (1989). https://doi.org/10.2307/249008
4. Wachter, S., Mittelstadt, B., Floridi, L.: Why a right to explanation of automated decision-making does not exist in the general data protection regulation. Int Data Privacy Law **7**(2), 76–99 (2017)
5. Floridi, L., et al.: AI4People—an ethical framework for a good AI society: opportunities, risks, principles, and recommendations. Mind Mach **28**(4), 689–707 (2018)
6. Beer, J.M., Fisk, A.D., Rogers, W.A.: Toward a framework for levels of robot autonomy in human-robot interaction. J. Human-Robot Interaction **3**(2), 74 (2014). https://doi.org/10.5898/jhri.3.2.beer
7. Franklin, S., Graesser, A.: Is it an agent, or just a program? a taxonomy for autonomous agents. In: Proceedings of the Third International Workshop on Agent Theories, Architectures, and Languages, Intelligent Agents, 21–35. Budapest Hungary (1996). https://doi.org/10.1007/BFb0013570
8. Murphy, R.: Introduction to AI Robotics, pp. 1–40. The MIT Press, Cambridge, MA (2000)
9. Thrun, S.: Toward a framework for human-robot interaction. Human-Computer Interaction **19**(1–2), 9–24 (2004)
10. Huang, H.M.: Autonomy levels for unmanned systems (ALFUS) framework volume I: Terminology version 1.1. In: Proceedings of the National Institute of Standards and Technology (NISTSP), Gaithersburg, MD (2004)
11. Sanders, E.B.: Virtuosos of the experience domain. In: Proceedings of the 2001 IDSA Education Conference (2001)
12. Søraa, R.A., Nyvoll, P., Tøndel, G., Fosch-Villaronga, E., Serrano, J.A.: The social dimension of domesticating technology: Interactions between older adults, caregivers, and robots in the home. Technol. Forecast Soc. **167**, 120678 (2021)
13. Berker, T., Hartmann, M., Punie, Y.: Domestication of Media and Technology. McGraw-Hill Education (UK) (2005)
14. Lie, M., Sørensen, K.H. (Eds.): Making Technology Our Own?: Domesticating Technology into Everyday Life. Scandinavian University Press (1996)
15. Forlizzi, J., DiSalvo, C.: Service robots in the domestic environment. In: Proceeding of the 1st ACM SIGCHI/SIGART Conference on Human-Robot Interaction - HRI '06 (2006). https://doi.org/10.1145/1121241.1121286

16. Amershi, S., et al.: Guidelines for human-AI interaction. In: Proceedings of the 2019 CHI Conference on Human Factors in Computing Systems. Published (2019). https://doi.org/10.1145/3290605.3300233
17. Kuijer, L., Giaccardi, E.: Co-performance. In: Proceedings of the 2018 CHI Conference on Human Factors in Computing Systems (2018). https://doi.org/10.1145/3173574.3173699
18. Frey, T.: Google Cloud AI Explanations to increase fairness, responsibility, and trust (2019). https://cloud.google.com/blog/products/ai-machine-learning/google-cloud-ai-explanations-to-increase-fairness-responsibility-and-trust

On Improving the Acceptance of Intelligent Companion Robots Among Chinese Empty-Nesters with the Application of Emotional Design

Kuo-Liang Huang[1](✉), Jinchen Jiang[1], and Yune-Yu Cheng[2]

[1] Department of Industrial Design, Design Academy, Sichuan Fine Arts Institute, Chongqing, China
{shashi,jiangjinchen}@scfai.edu.cn
[2] TAROKO International Co., Ltd., Tainan, Taiwan, China
yuneyu-cheng@taroko-int.com.tw

Abstract. With the number of the elderly population over the age of 65 reaching 190 million (13.5%), China has become the country with the largest number of senior citizens in the world, and its percentage is entering the accelerating period. With the addition of the features of economic society, over half of them are "empty-nesters", so the problem of supporting the elderly at high age has become an important issue that needs to be further solved. However, due to the different national conditions and traditional culture in China, the acceptance of "companion robots for seniors" is significantly lower than that of other countries such as Europe, America and Japan. There are many reasons for this, but the main problem lies in the lack of integration into the user's life, but like a "cold machine" lacking human's emotional temperature. This study aims to use the users' life situation and emotional temperature as the entry point to integrate technology with life, so as to enhance the acceptance of companion robots among Chinese seniors. Based on the concept of User-centered Design (UCD), the author interviewed seniors in the field and interpreted their life patterns, situation skeleton and behavioral patterns with empathy to gain insight into users' emotional needs and expectations. Then, the author designed, defined and conceived 12 different functional programs based on users' needs and expectations. At last, the Kano model was used to confirm the property category and the importance of the value significance of the 12 functional programs to the users.

Keywords: Empty-nesters · Aging · Intelligent companion robots · Demand analysis · Product design

1 Introduction

By 2021, the number of the elderly population over the age of 65 reaches 190 million (13.5%). China has become the country with the largest number of senior citizens in the world, and its percentage is entering the accelerating period. [1], and more than half of

M. Kurosu et al. (Eds.): HCII 2022, LNCS 13519, pp. 257–270, 2022.
https://doi.org/10.1007/978-3-031-17618-0_19

them are empty nesters due to urbanization and economic growth [2]. For the "empty nesters", because their children are mostly working outside the hometown, the function of family supporting is gradually weakening [2, 3], so the issue of "empty nesters" will become a major issue that needs to be further addressed in an aging society. At the same time, a new wave of "artificial intelligence", known as the fourth industrial revolution, is emerging, of which appeals, "artificial intelligence" and "companionship and care", are entering real life from science fiction, providing a solution to the current dilemma of "empty nesters". However, due to the different national conditions and traditional culture in China, the acceptance of "companion robots for the elderly" is significantly lower than that of other countries such as European countries, America and Japan. For Chinese seniors, "robots" are cold devices without emotional temperature. There are many reasons for this, but the main problem is that "cold intelligent products or systems lack human's emotional temperature", and to have personalized emotion, user's life cycle must be properly cross integrated to create more personalized value and increase acceptance [4, 5].

At present when developing and designing cutting-edge products, Technology Driven Innovation (TDI) is usually used, which emphasizes the effectiveness of the product but tends to ignore the real needs of users, thus making it difficult to gain the resonance of users and leading to the failure to increase acceptance [6]. In order to truly realize the "Vision of AI life" and increase people's acceptance of AI, we must start from a "social science" perspective and adopt the concept of User-centred Design (UCD). Only through designs defined by UCD can we truly meet the needs of the elderly, achieve two-way push between the elderly and their children, and tighten the emotional bond between the two generations, thus increasing acceptance and creating value. With the maturity of "intelligent companion robot" technology in recent years, it will gradually shift to "Design Driven" to create innovation value in the future. In order to increase the acceptance of "companion robots for the elderly" among Chinese empty nesters, this paper investigates the following questions: (1) To conduct user research on Chinese empty nesters and identify their Want & Need (W&Ns) based on their life situations; (2) To make functional programs that are urgently needed from and should be provided by the "companion robots for the elderly" effectively meet the needs of the Chinese empty nesters and enhance their acceptance.

The "family" is the most basic structural unit of a society. With the population aging of the society, the problem of empty nesters is expanding. The value of this study is to construct a companion robot program that meets the life and emotional needs of the Chinese people under the context of social development of China in the new era and the life pattern of the Chinese people, which is conducive to Chinese people's satisfaction and acceptance of it, and of which result will help solve the social problems arising from the aging society.

2   Literature Review

2.1   Characteristics of Empty Nesters in China

In terms of the characteristics of empty nesters: (1) in terms of physiology – function degenerating and suffering from chronic diseases; (2) in terms of psychology - prone to psychological disparity and expecting emotional solicitude more than material care; (3) social - mostly living along at home with reduced social life and deepened sense of loneliness [7, 8]. Ian Hosking, an expert in product design for the elderly at the University of Cambridge, argues that the creation of companion robots suitable for the elderly should be guided by the needs of the elderly, rather than the position of the children or the technological orientation to conceive of pseudo-needs that are taken for granted [9].

2.2 User-Centered Design Thinking and Methods

Current design philosophy emphasis on user-centered design (UCD), and through "Design Thinking" advocated by Brown [10], as a way of reasoning/understanding things [11, 12], solving problems [13], and creating meaning and value activities for the design [14]. The products are used by users, so users' needs and expectations shall be understood first through UCD to increase acceptance, UCD consists of four activities: identifying users, analyzing needs, designing, and evaluating and verifying [15, 17], and when a product can truly meet the needs and expectations of users, it can increase "intent to use" and "acceptance" [18]. From the above, it is clear that empty nesters mentally desire emotional care, and human-robot interaction is based on human needs and expectations or human-human-set situations.

2.3 Contextual Inquiry in User Study

UCD emphasizes that design must consider user behavior patterns, needs, attitudes, and possible problems from the user's perspective. According to ISO 9241–11, the definition of "context of use" is shaped by users, products, tasks, and the physical and social environments of use locations. A companion robot must be integrated into the lives of empty nesters, and the design should first understand the entire situation of life and extract users' emotional needs and expectations before proposing a companion robot design that meets those needs. However, traditional user study methods have not been able to clearly and jointly understand the relationship between user "context of use" and "life" and reveal key problems. In practice, when in contextual inquiry, users are already used to behavior pattern, so it is difficult for them to say "why to do" and "how to do" clearly, and the process of obtaining relevant information is laborious.

In view of this, this study utilizes the contextual design technology proposed by Holtzblatt and Beyer [20] to collect and analyze context information. The steps include five stages: (1) field contextual inquiry; (2) interpreting the data; (3) organizing the data; (4) generating ideas; and (5) generating design solutions. In terms of its connotation, in addition to obtaining context of use information, it is emphasized that in the contextual inquiry, the user's context of use is used in a specific task or activity in order to master the behavior pattern and gain insight into the hidden meaning and value behind the user's own needs and behaviors that need to be concerned by the user himself/herself as the core of design [21–23]. In addition, key techniques are proposed for requirement analysis of design teams and design communication of solutions, so that both individuals and design teams can share the thinking process and results, and the time spent is reduced.

2.4 Demand Analysis

In the past, when evaluating product or service functional programs, it was usually assumed that the relationship between the indicator of the performance of products and services and satisfaction was linear [24–26]. However, this is not true for all indicators, as different levels of indicators have different effects on satisfaction [26–29]. In view of this, Kano and Seraku [30] proposed the "Kano model", which borrowed the concept of two-dimensional, with "availability functional programs" as the horizontal axis and "psychological satisfaction" as the vertical axis, to classify user needs, according to the correlation between the performance situations of each psychological satisfaction when functional programs are available and not available, into five categories, that are, attractive, one-dimensional, must-be, indifferent, and reverse, and the presented relationships are shown in Fig. 1.

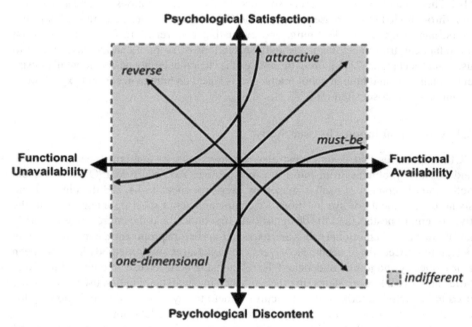

Fig. 1. Coorelation between physical availability and psychological satisfaction of The Kano model

Form *Attractive quality and must-be quality,* by Kano, N., Seraku, N., Takahashi, F., & Tsuji, S., 1984, *The Journal of the Japanese Society for Quality Control,* 14(2), pp39–48.

The horizontal coordinate indicates the degree of availability of a functional program, the more to the right, the higher the degree of availability of the functional program, the more to the left, the lower the degree of availability. The vertical coordinate indicates the degree of customer or user satisfaction, the more upward, the more satisfied, while the more downward, the more dissatisfied. According to the correlation of coordinates, it is divided into five categories.

(1) **Must-be (M)**

It refers to the fact that users consider this product feature as a basic requirement. When the feature is available, users take it for granted; when the feature is not available, user satisfaction declines significantly. Obviously, investing in R&D on such features does not significantly improve user satisfaction, but it is a threshold for building products.

(2) **One-dimensional (O)**

There is a positive linear relationship between this feature and user satisfaction. When the feature is available, the user satisfaction with the product is high; when the feature is not available, the user satisfaction declines. This type of requirement can improve user satisfaction to some extent, and the return-on-investment (ROI) of this aspect is usually approximately linear.

(3) **Indifference (I)**

No matter provided or not, user satisfaction will not change. Because users simply do not care whether the feature is provided or not, and it is something that users are not sensitive to and take no count of. Therefore, such requirements should be ignored in the product design.

(4) **Attractive (A)**

It refers to the element that tends to create a high level of user satisfaction with the feature. When this feature program is available, users are not aware of it; when this element is available, user satisfaction will increase dramatically. This type of requirement should be prioritized in product design by focusing resources on this, which can bring out high satisfaction benefits.

(5) **Reverse (R)**

This function has a negative linear relationship with user satisfaction, that is, this function has negative effect to users that, after providing, user satisfaction will decline; on the contrary, when this function is "insufficient", "user satisfaction" increases by a linear scale. Therefore, to ignore this kind of demand in the product design without providing can achieve a higher satisfaction utility.

Subsequently, the using technology of this concept has been further developed by scholars, for example, when classifying functional programs, the results of Table 1 "Kano model two-way questionnaire" [31] can be defined through a "decision matrix" (see Table 2) to obtain the attribute categories of individual functional programs [25, 32].

Table 1. Kano model two-way questionnaire

Function1: XXX	
Description of the function inclusion	
What do you think if **this feature is provided?**	☐ I like it that way It ☐must be that way ☐ I am neutral☐ I can live with it that way ☐ I dislike it that way
What do you think if **this feature is not provided?**	☐ I like it that way It ☐must be that way ☐ I am neutral☐ I can live with it that way ☐ I dislike it that way

Table 2. Decision Matrix for Functional Attribute Discrimination

Functional from of the question		Dysfunctional from of the question				
		Satisfied	It must be that way	It is indifferent	I can live with it	Dissatisfied
	Satisfied	Q	A	A	A	O
	It must be that way	R	I	I	I	M
	It is indifferent	R	I	I	I	M
	I can live with it	R	I	I	I	M
	Dissatisfied	R	R	R	R	Q

Note. From *How to make product development projects more successful by integrating Kano's model of customer satisfaction into quality function deployment,* by Matzler, K., & Hinterhuber, H. H., 1998, *Technovation, 18*(1), pp. 25–38

Q, questionable quality; A, attractive quality; M, must-be quality; O, one-dimensional quality; R, reverse quality; I, indifferent quality.

3 Method

This study aims to take the user's life situation and emotional temperature as the entry point, integrate technology with life and enhance the acceptance of companion robots by Chinese seniors. Based on the concept of UCD, the author interviewed seniors in the field and interpreted their life patterns, situation skeleton and behavioral patterns with empathy to gain insight into users' emotional needs and expectations. Then, the author designed, defined and conceived users' needs and expectations to generate different functions and values. At last, the Kano model was used to confirm the property category and the importance of the value significance of the functional programs to users. Based on the contextual design approach proposed by Holtzblatt and Beyer [20], this study integrates qualitative and quantitative techniques, and is carried out by three stages (see Fig. 2).

Fig. 2. Research Procedures and Framework

3.1 User Study

In the front-end analysis section, the analysis of related literature is firstly carried out; then, a survey by questionnaire is conducted, of which respondents were divided into two parts: seniors (empty nesters over the age of 65) and family members (whose family has empty nesters over the age of 65). The purpose of the division was to understand the lifestyle, living habits, behavioral characteristics and opinions related to C of senior citizens in China and to obtain a profile of the characteristics of senior citizens in China.

In the Diary Study section, 12 participants were recruited to conduct a 7-day User Study to further understand typical lifestyle, living habits, behavioral characteristics, and patterns of emotional bond with family members. In this study, taking into account the diversity and representativeness of the participants, the Sampling was conducted in the Balance means according to their characteristics based on the analysis of relevant literature and the population profile of the questionnaire in the front-end analysis.

In the Contextual Inquiry section, field investigation was conducted to the same 12 participants in the Diary Study. Through empathy, the following three points were mainly understood: (1) to understand users' lifestyles and values in order to anticipate and design products that meet their expectations of their living situation; (2) to understand users' mental models, contextual situation, operational behaviors and processes in using products, to discover difficulties or obstacles in using them, and to analyze ways to solve these problems and improvement measures; (3) to understand what kind of products users need, what kind of functions they want, how the operational processes of tasks shall be set, and what specific expectations they have about problems. To understand the daily life of the empty nesters, the psychological, physical and social characteristics of the empty nesters, and to obtain the "experience/story/behavior/reason" of the seniors through the three techniques of context immersion, show me and 5 whys.

No	时间	地点	人物	活动状态（娱乐/工作）	健康	情感状态	备注
				居家日志记录表			
1	例4.12/8:30	自家	我/家人/朋友	看电视/做饭/听广播/聊天…	疾病/药品	😄 😊 😐 😕 😣	
2						😄 😊 😐 😕 😣	
3						😄 😊 😐 😕 😣	
4						😄 😊 😐 😕 😣	
5						😄 😊 😐 😕 😣	
6						😄 😊 😐 😕 😣	
7						😄 😊 😐 😕 😣	
8						😄 😊 😐 😕 😣	
9						😄 😊 😐 😕 😣	
10						😄 😊 😐 😕 😣	

Fig. 3. The record table used in the Diary Study

In the Contextual Interview Interpretation section was conducted by the design team in the form of group meetings. First, the design team analyzed the valuable information from the fragmented opinions, situational observations, or direct quotes from users based on the collected data and respectively wrote them on Note Card. The Affinity Diagram method was used to sort out data and generalize the structure. After that, the design team will generalize the structure with Affinity Diagram and respectively interpret needs, intentions, and behaviors to extract the common Contextual Find and obtain the consensus of the team.

3.2 Insight

First, based on the Contextual Interview Interpretation and the consensus gradually formed on each point, the design team presented the "insights" and list the relevant evidence from the user research one by one, and then Identify Design Opportunities after the design team's confirmation. Then, the design team proposes the W&Ns design solutions through Brainstorming in accordance with different design opportunities.

3.3 Want & Need Analysis

In order to clarify the relationship between the availability of individual functional programs and satisfaction, firstly, a set of "relative" question group [31] was used to classify individual W&N functional programs through the Two-Dimensional concept of Kano Model, and participants checked the question cards with their feelings when the function was "available" and "not available" respectively. Then, according to each participant's opinion about a certain function, Table 2 was used to identify each participant's classification of each functional program. Finally, the results of all participants' categorization were accumulated in a frequency-based manner, and the "Mode" was taken as the "W&N functional attribute category" [31].

Therefore, when using the Kano model concept for design evaluation, both the usability of the product and the psychological level of the user can be taken into account, so that the decision for the design can be more detailed. In the Establish importance section, firstly, the degree of "satisfaction" or "dissatisfaction" of the users when the "function is available or not" is calculated, that is, "Satisfaction" (S_i) when the "function is available" and "Dissatisfaction" (D_i) when the "function is not available" [33], the formula mode is calculated by using the frequency of each classification result as the base data. The equation is as follows [31].

$$\text{Extent of satisfaction} : S_i = \frac{A_i + O_i}{A_i + O_i + I_i + M_i} \tag{1}$$

$$\text{Extent of dissatisfaction} : D_i = \frac{M_i + O_i}{A_i + O_i + I_i + M_i(-1)} \tag{2}$$

where the closer to 1 it is, the greater the impact; the closer to 0 it is, the smaller the impact; if it is close to -1, the impact on user dissatisfaction is particularly great when the product features are not met.

Next, in order to make the Kano Model usable to create individual functional program importance rankings, a more thorough understanding of the individual functional programs that affect satisfaction can be further developed in order to facilitate focusing on the demands of higher satisfaction utility when assessing design decision [31]. The evaluation method proposed by Sireli and Kauffmann [24] was used in the study by taking the absolute value of the larger value of Si and Di as the importance score (w_i) and calculating the relative importance score (W_i) using the following equation.

$$\text{Satisfaction contribution weight} : W_i = \text{Max}\left(\frac{S_i}{\sum_{i=1}^{m} S_i}, \frac{D_i}{\sum_{i=1}^{m} D_i} \right) \tag{3}$$

As for the design decision, the quantitative Establish Importance can be obtained as the basis of assessment based on the questionnaire results and calculation equation [24, 29].

4 Results

4.1 User Research Interpreting Basic Ideas and Conclusions

Empty nesters generally have regular lifestyles. As for companion robots, people are in a state of ignorance and resistance to an extent, but most people can accept intelligent companion robots as an emotional hub rather than a replacement for their children's responsibilities. In addition, the elderly clearly feel being "out of time" in their characteristics the physical, psychological, and social levels. They can basically take care of themselves, but they often forget about things, and they usually feel lonely mostly at night, hoping there is someone to talk to. The most exciting things in their lives are communications with family members, such as children's phone calls, video calls or returning home on holidays. However, scrupling to bring trouble to their children's busy life, they do not want to disturb them too much that they are unable to concentrate on their work. The top three things that family members of empty nesters (parents/grandparents) mostly concern about are: (1) health, (2) daily self-care, and (3) mood.

4.2 W&Ns Functional Attribute and Importance Rankings

A total of 22 design opportunities were identified, and the design team proposed the corresponding W&Ns design solutions through Brainstorming, and finally, after feasibility and other assessments, 12 functional programs were selected (Table 3).

Table 3. 12 functional programs and contents.

No.	Function	Content
1	Humanization	Have a name/ have a memory like human/high intelligence/autonomous emotions/ personality
2	User emotional state recognition	Recognize the user's changes in face, voice pitch, manner of speaking, behavior, and movement, and take them as emotional calculation and analysis data
3	Vivid emotional expression	Present different facial expressions, intonation, and gesture according to different emotions
4	Friendly voice interaction	Intuitive voice interaction, can listen/speak various accent through artificial voice recognition and synthesis,
5	Lovely appearance	Rounded profile, simple structure, have self-moving capability
6	Multimedia display	Can display different media, network communication, touch and gesture control for multimodal interaction
7	Accompanying	A new member of the family that will accompany and give support
8	Recreation	Chat, talk back, do gymnastics and sing with seniors, provide fun and ease their loneliness

(continued)

Table 3. (*continued*)

No.	Function	Content
9	Little butler of life	Serve as a family information center, record the senior's daily living behavior for online access by family members, and adapts to give personalized reminders to the senior at appropriate times, scenarios and situations (e.g. taking medication, having meals, handling things, reminding dressing more for cold weather, etc.) according to a self-set and joint-set calendar with families
10	Emotional hub	Proactively build family emotional connections at the right time for both parties to facilitate emotional communication
11	Health data detection and monitoring	Detect and monitor vital signs, and automatically notify family members immediately when reasonable values are exceeded
12	Emergency network alarm	When an emergency situation is judged through posture recognition and vital sign detection monitoring, it will immediately alert the police and emergency contacts through the Internet

In the Kano classification stage for individual functional programs, the results were obtained through calculation and classification after the Kano Model two-way questionnaire being answered by 34 participants of empty nest senior citizens (see Table 4).

From the "Cumulative Count" in Table 4, the results of all participants' checks for each function programs can be seen. The "Kano Category" is the Kano Model classification result of for individual function programs. The values of "Si" and "Di" are the degree of impact on "satisfaction" or "dissatisfaction" of the empty nesters when the function is "available" or "not available" (the closer to 1, the greater the effect); if it is close to -1, the impact on user dissatisfaction is particularly great when the product features are not met. The "Wi (%)" value can be used to know the relative weight percentage of each functional program on the satisfaction of the empty nesters and to establish the importance ranking of individual functional programs.

Table 4. Functional program categories and importance rankings

Function	Accumulated Counts				Kano Category[a]	Importance			
	A	O	M	I		S_i	D_i	w_i	W_i (%)
Humanization	14	8	11	1	A	0.647	−0.559	0.647	9.4
User emotional state recognition	15	9	10	0	A	0.706	−0.559	0.706	10.2
Vivid emotional expression	7	18	9	0	O	0.735	−0.794	0.794	10.7
Friendly voice interaction	4	5	23	2	M	0.265	−0.824	0.824	10.3
Lovely appearance	1	12	3	18	I	0.382	−0.441	0.441	5.5
Multimedia display	6	13	10	5	M	0.559	−0.676	0.676	8.5
Accompanying	10	17	5	2	O	0.794	−0.647	0.794	8.1
Recreation	8	15	11	0	O	0.676	−0.765	0.765	9.8
Little butler of life	18	10	5	1	A	0.824	−0.441	0.824	11.9
Emotional hub	12	12	10	0	A	0.706	−0.647	0.706	10.2
Health data detection and monitoring	4	7	22	1	M	0.324	−0.853	0.853	10.7
Emergency network alarm	6	6	20	2	M	0.353	−0.765	0.765	9.6

5   Conclusions and Suggestions

This paper aims to design a design-driven intelligent senior companion robot. Firstly, through the UCD design concept, the author takes the user's life situation and emotional needs as the entry point, understand the senior's life situation through empathy and extract pain points, needs and expectations, find design opportunities, and then carry out design definition and conception through design thinking to convert to different functional programs. Finally, the Kano Model scale was administered to the empty nesters to differentiate the attribute categories of different functional programs and to calculate different functions, whose contribution degrees to the satisfaction of the "intelligent senior companion robot" are obtained. In this way, we can ensure that the value provided by the "intelligent senior companion robot" is what the Chinese empty nesters need and expect, and it is integrated with their life situations, so that such integration of technology and life can enhance the acceptance of the companion robot by the Chinese seniors.

Taking Chinese empty nester seniors as an object, this paper provides 12 functional programs in the context of the life situation of empty nesters in China and the common needs and expectations of their family members, as well as their Kano attribute categories and importance weighting ratios, which can be used as a reference base for academic research, designers and developers. We believe that "Technology Is Connecting To People", products are for people to use, and the design and development should be based on the concept of UCD thinking. Finally, we believe that individuals and society should not use "intelligent companion robots for the elderly" to avoid responsibilities or necessary care for the elderly, but rather to enhance their self-care ability and help them get out of their inner isolation through technology. Using "intelligent companion robots for the elderly" as an emotional hub, it can act as a booster to build emotional connections between individuals, and between individuals and families in the future intelligent life, being a transmitter of emotional support.

Acknowledgments. Supported by the Science and Technology Research Program of Chongqing Mu-nicipal Education Commission (Grant No. 20YB09) and Major Project of Sichuan Academy of Fine Arts (Grant No. No. 202095).

References

1. Office of the Leading Group of the Seventh National Census of the State Council, Communique of the Seventh National Census (No. 5) - Age Composition of the Population, National Bureau of Statistics, Editor. State Council, Beijing (2021)
2. Chen, W., Duan, Y.: Empty-nester life expectancy of the Chinese Elderly. Population Res. **41**(5–15), (2017)
3. Peng, X., Hu, Z.: Population aging in China from a public policy perspective. Social Sci. China **3**(1), 21 (2011)
4. Yonck, R.: Heart of the Machine: Our Future in a World of Artificial Emotional Intelligence. Skyhorse Publishing (2017)
5. Schuller, B.W.: IEEE transactions on affective computing-challenges and chances. IEEE Trans. Affective Comp. **8**(1), 1–2 (2017)
6. Mao, J., et al.: Demand analysis of an intelligent medication administration system for older adults with chronic diseases based on the Kano model. Int. J. Nurs. Sci. **9**(1), 63–70 (2022)
7. Wang, N., Yuan, Y.: Serving system design of accompany robot for the elderly. Packaging Eng. **38**(18), 72–76 (2017)
8. Zheng, D., Liu, X.: Mental health status of empty nesters and its influencing factors. Chin. J. Gerontol. **37**(20), 5174–5175 (2017)
9. Hsu, Y.-L.: Proposals for the future development of applications of intelligent technology in senior living and care. J. Gerontechnology Service Manage. **6**(3), 307–320 (2018)
10. Brown, T.: Design Thinking: Uma metodologia poderosa para decretar o fim das velhas ideias. Alta Books (2020)
11. Lawson, B.: How designers think: The design process demystified. Routledge (2006)
12. Cross, N.: Design Thinking: Understanding How Designers Think and Work. Bloomsbury Academic (2019)
13. Buchanan, R.: Wicked problems in design thinking. Design Issues **8**(2), 5–21 (1992)
14. Krippendorff, K.: The Semantic Turn: A New Foundation for Design. CRC Press (2005)

15. Han, T.: User research and experience design. In: Zhou, W. (ed): Design Theory and Practice Frontiers Series. Shanghai Jiao Tong University Press, Shanghai (2016)
16. Hu, F., Zhang, X.: Designing for population aging: the emergence and evolution of design concepts involving the elderly since 1945. J. Nanjing Arts Institute (Fine Arts & Design) (6), 33–44 (2017)
17. ISO, Iso 13407: Human-Centred Design Processes for Interactive Systems. International Standards Organization, Geneva (1999)
18. Davis, F.D.: Perceived usefulness, perceived ease of use, and user acceptance of information technology. Mis Quarterly 13(3), 319–340 (1989)
19. Standardization, I.O.F.: ISO 9241–11: Ergonomic Requirements for Office Work with Visual Display Terminals (VDTs): Part 11: Guidance on Usability. International Organization for Standardization (1998)
20. Holtzblatt, K., Beyer, H.: Contextual Design: Design for Life. Elsevier Science & Technology Books (2016)
21. Beyer, H., Holtzblatt, K.: Contextual Design: Defining Customer-Centered Systems. Morgan Kaufmann (1998)
22. Holtzblatt, K., Wendell, J.B., Wood, S.: Rapid Contextual Design: A How-to Guide to Key Techniques for User-Centered Design. Elsevier Science (2005)
23. Sharp, H., Rogers, Y., Preece, J.: Interaction Design: Beyond Human-Computer Interaction. Wiley (2007)
24. Sireli, Y., Kauffmann, P., Ozan, E.: Integration of Kano's model into QFD for multiple product design. IEEE Trans. Eng. Manage. 54(2), 380–390 (2007)
25. Yin, S., et al.: Impact of gamification elements on user satisfaction in health and fitness applications: A comprehensive approach based on the Kano. Comput. Hum. Behav. 128, 107106 (2022)
26. Huang, K.-L., Chen, K.-H., Ho, C.-H.: Promoting in-depth reading experience and acceptance: design and assessment of tablet reading interfaces. Behaviour Information Technol. 33(6), 606–618 (2014)
27. Kincl, T., Štrach, P.: Measuring website quality: asymmetric effect of user satisfaction. Behaviour Information Technol. 31(7), 647–657 (2012)
28. Cheung, C.M.K., Lee, M.K.O.: User satisfaction with an internet-based portal: an asymmetric and nonlinear approach. J. American Society Information Science Technol. 60(1), 111–122 (2009)
29. Shi, Y., Peng, Q.: Enhanced customer requirement classification for product design using big data and improved Kano model. Adv. Eng. Inform. 49, 101340 (2021)
30. Kano, N., et al.: Attractive quality and must-be quality. J. Japanese Society Quality Control 14(2), 39–48 (1984)
31. Matzler, K., Hinterhuber, H.H.: How to make product development projects more successful by integrating Kano's model of customer satisfaction into. Technovation 18(1), 25–38 (1998)
32. Bilgili, B., Erciş, A., Ünal, S.: Kano model application in new product development and customer satisfaction (adaptation of traditional art of tile making to jewelries). Procedia. Soc. Behav. Sci. 24, 829–846 (2011)
33. Berger, C., et al.: Kano's methods for understanding customer-defined quality. Center for Quality Manage. J. 2(4), 3–36 (1993)

Human Interpretation of Inter-robot Communication

Masashi Inoue[✉][iD]

Tohoku Institute of Technology, Yagiyama Kasumicho 35-1,
Taihaku-ku, Sendai, Japan
m.inoue@acm.org
https://www.ice.tohtech.ac.jp/inoue/

Abstract. We investigated how a human observer interprets the motion of a robot while communicating with another robot. We generated a variety of motion patterns for a robot running on wheels and evaluated the ease of human interpretability of these motions. The results showed that although the interpretation results for motoins imitating human head gestures were relatively accurate, motions that imitated hand gestures tended to be interpreted less accurately.

Keywords: Robot-to-robot · Recognition of movement · Robot motion

1 Introduction

Once robots are ubiquitous, people become involved in interaction with unknown robots. In the absence of information about robots, interactions between robots should be conducted in a manner that is understandable to humans. This interpretability is achievable by designing the movements of robots. The motion patterns of mobile robots have been studied in terms of the interpretation of robots with human intentionality [2]. However, knowledge on the interpretation of robot behavior when observing inter-robot communication is limited (Fig. 1). In this study, we created several movements that robots used to communicate with other robots and evaluated whether humans can observe and interpret the movements as they were used.

Various manners of communicating between living and artificial entities, such as robots, exist. Communication between robots can be achieved efficiently using telecommunication technologies [5,15]. However, delivered signals are typically unnoticeable to humans without using particular devices. Robots can also communicate through audio channels. If robots use the same verbal speech sounds as humans, interpretation is easy for humans. When the sounds are implicit and nonverbal, the sounds should be properly designed for interpretability [14]. Other media, such as color and vibration, have been examined [16]. Artificial eyeballs attached to the mobile robot were tested to increase the predictability of robot motion [12]. Motions are used for communication purposes in nature. A

M. Kurosu et al. (Eds.): HCII 2022, LNCS 13519, pp. 271–279, 2022.
https://doi.org/10.1007/978-3-031-17618-0_20

well-known example is that of honey bees dancing [1]. Motion patterns can be applied to robot communication. The perception of robot personality has been studied in chess-playing robot arms based on motion patterns [10]. We focused more on the semantic aspect than on the impression of motion. The intention predictability of robot motion was addressed by Stulp [17], but messages were sent from robot to human rather than robot to robot, which we examined in this research. Although there are related concepts to interpretability such as legibility, explicability, and predictability [3], we are concerned here only with the interpretability that is associated with the recognition of ambiguous motions.

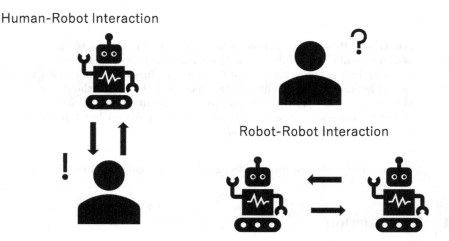

Fig. 1. Interpretation of interactions between robots

2 Method

2.1 Robot

The robot used in this study was iRobot Create2, which is a mobile cleaning robot without a cleaning function for development and educational purposes [11]. The robot runs on wheels. It can be connected to an external PC with a dedicated cable called the Communications Cable for Create2, and controlled via serial communication (Fig. 2). We considered messages that might be practical for communication between robots and their resulting movements.

2.2 Development

This robot is controlled by sending commands through a software interface called Create2 Open Interface. Commands are sent as binary data via serial communication. After establishing serial communication between the robot and PC, a command to start the motion is sent. The interface has two modes: development and control. The user selects the desired mode at the interface.

When using Create2 Open Interface, the amount of moves in each direction can be set in advance to simplify motion design and programming. Variables that have movement speed are defined as parameters. A study on human perception suggests that the speed of gesture motion can alter the interpretation of the gestures [4]. However, to control the experimental condition, we use the fixed speed throughout the development. Motion patterns are defined as the combination of base element motions such as 'move forward' or 'move backward'. When commands are issued to activate a particular movement, the parameter values are called and converted into binary data. Binary data are sent to the robot through the communication cable.

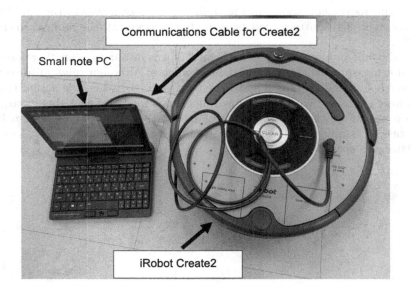

Fig. 2. Experimental results

3 Experiment

3.1 Motion Patterns

We prepared the robot motion patterns for the experiment. Human hand and head movements were used as references to communicate with others. Horizontal human movements were used as the robot's left-right rotation, and vertical human movements were used as the robot's forward-backward movements. For example, in the case of a negative message, the robot rotates 45° to the left and right, as if shaking its head. In general, gestures can be divided into several phases, including preparation, stroke, and retraction [8]. When creating motion patterns, we considered only the stroke, which is the primary phase of the gestures. Head movements play different roles in communication when used repeatedly over a course of time [6]. However, for simplicity, we considered robot motion patterns that represented a single head movement. We created five motion patterns that corresponded to the following messages: 'Follow me,' 'Go right,' 'Go away,' 'No,' and 'Dodge.' Figs. 3 to 7 illustrate the motion patterns. In these figures, the outer circles represent mobile robots when observed from above. The filled circle represents the center of the robot, where the power button is located. A smaller filled circle is placed on the anterior part of the robot, which corresponds to the obstacle sensor. The obstacle sensor was not used in the experiment. Movements are performed from left to right in the figures. For example, in the case of the 'Follow me' movement, shown in Fig. 3, first, the robot moves backward. Subsequently, it moves forward. This pattern repeats; as its final movement, the robot moves in the backward direction. In the case of the 'Turn right' movement, shown in Fig. 4, first, the robot moves to the left. Then, it moves right. This pattern repeats; as its final movement, the robot turns right by 90°.

We did not implement a feedback mechanism in our system; therefore, we could not measure the accuracy of the movements. Although small misdirection and overshoots/undershoots might have been occurred when the actual trajectories were compared with the planned motions, we believe that these marginal gaps do not affect the interpretation of movements. In robot to human handover task, it is reported that the positive impressions given by robots does not correlate with spatial accuracy [9].

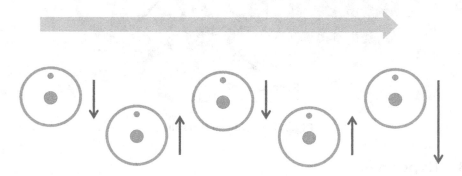

Fig. 3. 'Follow me' movement

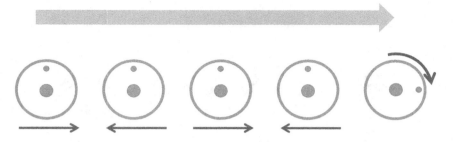

Fig. 4. 'Turn right' movement

3.2   Experiment Procedure

Participants were shown videos of the robots in action and were asked to evaluate them. The robot that sent messages and the robot that received messages faced each other. The videos of the robot sending messages were recorded from a human's eyelevel (Fig. 8). The videos included all movements in their entirety. A small PC was mounted on top of the message-sending robot to control it. Ten male university students participated in the experiment. They watched videos of five movements posted online in a random order. The audio of the videos was removed to avoid the influence of motor sounds on the perception of robot motion [13]. After viewing a video, participants were asked to select what the message-sending robot attempted to convey to the message-receiving robot from options in a questionnaire and to describe the reasons for their selection. Participants were allowed to watch the videos any number of times to confirm their interpretation. The questionnaire included ten options, including five additional messages, and they were presented randomly. The five messages that were not included in the videos but were in questionnaire were 'OK,' 'Hello,' 'Good-bye,' 'See you,' and 'Turn left.' They were meant to have meanings similar to the five movements included in the videos. The degree of agreement between the intention of the motion design and selections made by participants was used to evaluate whether the motion pattern was human-interpretable.

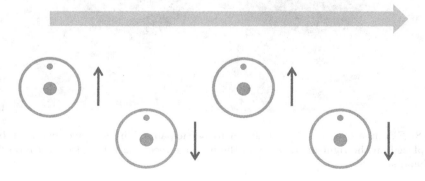

Fig. 5. 'Go away' movement

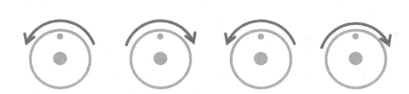

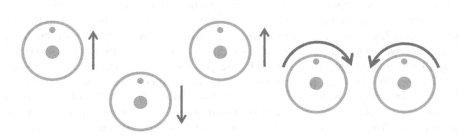

Fig. 6. 'No' movement

Fig. 7. 'Dodge' movement

Fig. 8. Example of video stimuli shown to participants. The message-sending robot was placed on the right-hand side and the message receiving robot stands still on the left-hand side.

4   Results

An analysis of the results showed that the correct response rates were high for 'Turn right' and 'No' (Fig. 9), which were movements created based on the images of movements performed by people using their heads. Many participants responded that they selected these options because they associated them with head movements, indicating that these movements were interpreted as intended by designers. The percentage of correct responses was also high for 'Follow me,' which involved a large motion, and the reasons provided by the correct respondents for their selection were often consistent with the design intention. The unintended option selected by all participants was 'Good-bye,' suggesting that 'Follow me' and 'Good-bye' were conceptually similar in terms of robot movement. The correct response rate was low for 'Go away' and 'Dodge', which were designed to mimic human hand movements.

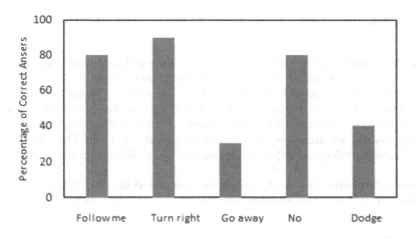

Fig. 9. Equipment used

5   Conclusion

For each message communicated between the robots through their movements, we created motion patterns that could be interpreted by humans. We evaluated the interpretability of the messages. The correct response rate was high for 'Turn right' and 'No,' which were created based on the image of human head movements, and notably, the movements were human-interpretable. 'Go away' and 'Dodge,' which were created based on the image of human hand motions, demonstrated low correct response rates. This may be because human head movements can easily be converted into two-dimensional movements, whereas hand and finger movements are three-dimensional, and ground mobile robots cannot completely reflect this in their movements.

Fig. 10. Message-sending robot from another robot's perspective

In the selection of motion patterns, we considered communicative gestures as references. Investigating non-communicative type gestures [7] would be interesting using this framework. Another point that needs to be addressed is that the motion patterns used were clearly visible to human observers, but not necessarily intelligible for message-receiving robots. Figure 10 illustrates the message-sending robots seen from the message-receiving robots' view. The effectiveness of the motion patterns of other robots should be considered in the future.

Acknowledgments. This work was partially supported by JSPS KAKENHI (grant number 20K11908). The experiment was conducted by Ayato Sampei.

References

1. Barron, A.B., Plath, J.A.: The evolution of honey bee dance communication: a mechanistic perspective. J. Exp. Biol. **220**(23), 4339–4346 (2017)
2. Butler, J.T., Agah, A.: Psychological effects of behavior patterns of a mobile personal robot. Auton. Robot. **10**(2), 185–202 (2001)
3. Chakraborti, T., Kulkarni, A., Sreedharan, S., Smith, D.E., Kambhampati, S.: Explicability? Legibility? Predictability? Transparency? Privacy? Security? The emerging landscape of interpretable agent behavior. In: Proceedings of the International Conference on Automated Planning and Scheduling, vol. 29, pp. 86–96 (2019)
4. Endo, J., Inoue, M.: Speed dependencies of human gesture recognition. In: 2013 International Joint Conference on Awareness Science and Technology & Ubi-Media Computing (iCAST 2013 & UMEDIA 2013), pp. 354–359. IEEE (2013)
5. Gielis, J., Prorok, A.: Improving 802.11p for delivery of safety critical navigation information in robot-to-robot communication networks. IEEE Commun. Mag. **59**(1), 16–21 (2021)

6. Inoue, M., Irino, T., Furuyama, N., Hanada, R.: Observational and accelerometer analysis of head movement patterns in psychotherapeutic dialogue. Sensors **21**(9), 3162 (2021)
7. Inoue, M., Ogihara, M., Hanada, R., Furuyama, N.: Gestural cue analysis in automated semantic miscommunication annotation. Multimed. Tools App. **61**(1), 7–20 (2012)
8. Kita, S., van Gijn, I., van der Hulst, H.: Movement phases in signs and co-speech gestures, and their transcription by human coders. In: Wachsmuth, I., Fröhlich, M. (eds.) GW 1997. LNCS, vol. 1371, pp. 23–35. Springer, Heidelberg (1998). https://doi.org/10.1007/BFb0052986
9. Koene, A., et al.: Relative importance of spatial and temporal precision for user satisfaction in human-robot object handover interactions. In: Third International Symposium on New Frontiers in Human-Robot Interaction (2014)
10. LC, R., et al.: Power chess: robot-to-robot nonverbal emotional expression applied to competitive play. In: 10th International Conference on Digital and Interactive Arts, pp. 1–11 (2021)
11. Mataric, M.J., Koenig, N.P., Feil-Seifer, D.: Materials for enabling hands-on robotics and STEM education. In: AAAI Spring Symposium: Semantic Scientific Knowledge Integration, pp. 99–102 (2007)
12. Matsumaru, T., Iwase, K., Akiyama, K., Kusada, T., Ito, T.: Mobile robot with eyeball expression as the preliminary-announcement and display of the robot's following motion. Auton. Robot. **18**(2), 231–246 (2005)
13. Moore, D., Dahl, T., Varela, P., Ju, W., Næs, T., Berget, I.: Unintended consonances: methods to understand robot motor sound perception. In: Proceedings of the 2019 CHI Conference on Human Factors in Computing Systems, pp. 1–12. Association for Computing Machinery, New York, NY, USA (2019)
14. Robinson, F.A., Bown, O., Velonaki, M.: Implicit communication through distributed sound design: exploring a new modality in human-robot interaction. In: Companion of the 2020 ACM/IEEE International Conference on Human-Robot Interaction, pp. 597–599 (2020)
15. Sanfeliu, A., Hagita, N., Saffiotti, A.: Network robot systems. Robot. Auton. Syst. **56**(10), 793–797 (2008)
16. Song, S., Yamada, S.: Expressing emotions through color, sound, and vibration with an appearance-constrained social robot. In: 2017 12th ACM/IEEE International Conference on Human-Robot Interaction (HRI), pp. 2–11. IEEE (2017)
17. Stulp, F., Grizou, J., Busch, B., Lopes, M.: Facilitating intention prediction for humans by optimizing robot motions. In: 2015 IEEE/RSJ International Conference on Intelligent Robots and Systems (IROS), pp. 1249–1255 (2015)

Conversational Agents and Robot Interaction

Kristiina Jokinen(✉) 🆔

AI Research Center, National Institute of Advanced Industrial Science and Technology (AIST),
Tokyo, Japan
kristiina.jokinen@aist.go.jp

Abstract. The paper concerns conversational interaction for social robots and presents work on combining conversational AI technology and humanoid robot agents. It contributes to designing human-robot interaction with the help of state-of-the-art conversational modelling techniques and discusses issues related to spoken dialogues, social interaction, and context-awareness. The paper explores the use of knowledge graphs in dialogue modelling with the goal of developing interactive robot applications with natural dialogue capabilities. The work thus supports the design of social robot applications where robot agents have capabilities for a more symbiotic relationship with humans.

Keywords: Conversational AI · Robot interaction

1 Introduction

Many different AI agents have appeared providing potentially useful assistance for a variety of everyday tasks. Such agents range from talking heads on phones to situated robots in restaurants and shopping centers, and the agent's role varies from information provider to autonomous robot companion. Conversational AI has produced solutions, culminating in commercial products like IBM Watson, Alexa, Siri, Cortana, and Google Assistant. In fact, Gartner predicts that by 2022, 70% of white-collar workers will interact with conversational AI on a daily basis[1], making the agent's ability to conduct interaction on varied topics, with different users and in different situations, one of the most important aspects of current conversational AI research.

Conversational AI research mostly focuses on text-based interaction powered by big data and deep learning technology. Speech is also included as the conversational agents can be used as apps on a phone or via a speaking head. However, there are no applications that could be used on robots, for instance, there is no obvious way to interact with a humanoid robot using Google Assistant. A notable exception is IBM Watson which was integrated with Softbank's Nao robots to showcase Watson's question answering capability as well as the robot movements.[2] The reason for the apparent vacuum in deploying conversational agent technology in robots may be found in the

---

[1] https://www.gartner.com/smarterwithgartner/chatbots-will-appeal-to-modern-workers/.
[2] https://www.ibm.com/blogs/internet-of-things/doing-the-robot-watson-really-is-all-singing-all-dancing/.

© The Author(s), under exclusive license to Springer Nature Switzerland AG 2022
M. Kurosu et al. (Eds.): HCII 2022, LNCS 13519, pp. 280–292, 2022.
https://doi.org/10.1007/978-3-031-17618-0_21

fact that practically all consumers have mobile phones, whereas having your own social robot at home is still rare and regarded as a curiosity rather than a commodity.

On the other hand, robots and robot interaction have also become hot topics. Robotics has expanded from service automation into areas such as Assistive Robotics and Service Robotics where robots help humans to do daily tasks, or robots and humans try to accomplish tasks together in collaboration. With advances in technology of sensors and motion recognition devices, multimodal dialogues with robot agents have also become feasible: research and development has focused on situated robot agents which can sense their environment, walk and gesture, as well as talk to the user. Moreover, in the vision of Society 5.0[3], AI agents are connected and capable communicating agents, embedded seamlessly into society, and can support AI solutions in service design and decision making by allowing interaction between AI and human users.

As the tasks for robot agents become more complex, the agents' communicative competence must increase, and the area of Social Robotics especially focuses on robot companions that can interact with humans using natural language taking various aspects of social interaction into account. Such social robots aim to offer solutions to societal problems such as lack of human caregivers to help elderly citizens in everyday activities or provide information and assistance in communication between different people and in various situations, especially in dangerous or difficult environments such as disaster areas or hospitals with strict access rules. The global pandemic COVID-19 has also accelerated development for agent interaction.

Dialogue interactions with robot agents are thus likely to become more common and also more complex, since the robots should not only provide useful information but explain their behaviour, instruct human users, and chat about many interesting topics in natural language. The development and design of social robots also face challenges concerning interaction technology and issues of trust, ethics, accessibility, long-term relation, cooperation, etc. In this paper, we will not discuss the ethical challenges but refer to previous work, e.g. 152327, and focus on the main challenge with social robots, namely communication with human users in a natural manner.

In what follows we discuss differences between conversational agent development and social robotics and focus on two aspects: spoken interaction and multimodality. The paper is structured as follows. We first discuss conversational AI and the aspects of communication which are important for human-robot interaction. We then focus on creating situational awareness in dialogue systems and conclude with a short example dialogue related to environmental issues.

2 Conversational Human-Robot Interaction

Conversational interfaces have been much studied (see an overview in 30), and intensive research and development concerns end-to-end dialogue-systems based on big data and deep learning techniques. End-to-end conversational agents are usually directed towards general chatting and conversations, and their use in task-oriented dialogues requires structured knowledge of a particular task to be induced in the learning process.

---

[3] https://www8.cao.go.jp/cstp/english/society5_0/.

Moreover, rich contextual information needs to be included in the dialogue model to address situational interaction management issues such as turn-taking, dialogue history, and creation of mutual knowledge.

Important aspects in current conversational agent development concern integration of spoken language in the chatbot instead of text, as well as the use of ontologies and contextual knowledge. Speech is usually included as a front-end ASR that provides a text transcription as the input for the conversational agent, but such a solution tends to fall short when it comes to natural spoken interaction with disfluencies, false starts, and overlapping speech. Research on end-to-end conversational modelling (283435) uses a similar approach to end-to-end text processing by replacing word2vec 31 with speech2vec 5 embeddings.

Much work is conducted in integrating knowledge graphs into conversational agents. Early works were 39 combining Nao and Pydial 37, and 24 combining knowledge graphs for instruction giving dialogues where Nao robots explain best-practice procedures to novice caregivers in the eldercare domain. The knowledge is structured into a goal-oriented hierarchy modelled in JSON, which shows how the various tasks are interrelated and interdependent. Various dialogue engines exist, with different strengths and weaknesses, see discussion in 32. We chose Rasa open-source conversational AI[4] for dialogue interaction, see discussion in Sect. 4.

2.1 Spoken Communication with Robot Agents

Sophisticated interaction models and robot implementations are critical when developing practical social robot applications. The models are often hand-crafted rule-based scripts for the interaction that focus on providing useful and true information as well as interesting and engaging conversations. Although interaction technology and robotics communities have long worked on spoken conversations and human-robot interaction 213641, integrated approaches to implement spoken conversational dialogues on robot platforms have only recently started to appear. For instance, recent workshops (SLI-VAR[5], ROBOT-DIAL[6]) aim to bring the research communities together, and tutorials 26 and papers 29 have elaborated on the pending issues such as user experience design, adaptivity, robustness, infrastructure, and dynamics.

Active research is going on related to architectures, models, and representations for robots' natural language communication, and pertinent issues concern the embodied nature of robots and interactions that can occur frequently with the same user and are longer than two turns. Friendly-looking humanoid social robots like Nao[7] and Pepper[8] are widely used in research, while android robots 25 with their human-like appearance challenge the limits of natural and comfortable interaction partner. Furhat[9] provides an expressive head and face for various engagement studies.

---

[4] RASA Homepage, https://rasa.com/.

[5] https://www.dagstuhl.de/en/program/calendar/semhp/?semnr=20021.

[6] http://sap.ist.i.kyoto-u.ac.jp/ijcai2020/robotdial/.

[7] https://www.softbankrobotics.com/emea/en/nao.

[8] https://developer.softbankrobotics.com/pepper-qisdk.

[9] https://furhatrobotics.com/.

Considering the need for providing smooth operation and comparison of application among various types, requirements, and domains, much work is related to standards for software interoperability such as OMG[10] and various ISO standards concerning safety management for service robotics[11], personal care robots[12], human-robot collaboration[13], rescue robots[14], ergonomics for human-system interfaces[15], and the campaign for hi-tech standards[16] for new technologies. Standardisation for dialogue interaction has resulted in ISO standard 24617–2[17] for dialogue act annotation 5 and work related to annotation standards for language resources 16 is going on. MPAI (Moving Picture, Audio and Data Coding by Artificial Intelligence) is a community[18] that focuses on standards, interoperability and data sharing for practical interests in human-machine communication, audio, video, etc.

The most important standard for robotics is ROS (Robot Operating System)[19] with a focus on robot vision rather than speech. OpenCV[20] provides standard algorithms for Computer Vision and is used in standard mobile service robots such as Turtlebot for recognizing objects and obstacles, while SLAM 10 (Simultaneous Localisation And Mapping) algorithms are standards for mapping rooms and navigating around.

ROS-based robots do not usually feature spoken interaction due to ROS focusing on vision rather than state-of-the-art speech technology. However, for social robots spoken interaction is necessary, so they use their own platform and OS and resort to proprietary systems such as Nuance in Nao and Pepper, or Google Cloud services for ASR and Amazon Polly for TTS in Furhat. Such open-source speech technologies as Kaldi[21] and ESPNet[22] are good candidates to be part of the ROS-based interactive robots. To this end, a recent integration of open-source technologies is described in 12 who show how ROS, Rasa open-source dialogue framework, and ESPNet speech recognizer can be combined as a platform to support natural interaction with a social robot.

2.2 Multimodal Communication

Besides speech signals, visual signals are effectively used in dialogue management. Communication presupposes awareness of the situation and engagement with the partner, which are signalled by multimodal social signals. Face and body movement, facial

---

[10] Object Management Group https://omg.org.

[11] https://www.iso.org/standard/80886.html.

[12] https://www.iso.org/standard/53820.html.

[13] https://www.iso.org/news/2016/03/Ref2057.html.

[14] https://www.iso.org/news/Ref2169.htm.

[15] https://www.iso.org/standard/80773.html.

[16] https://www.iso.org/sites/hitechstandards/.

[17] https://www.iso.org/standard/76443.html.

[18] https://mpai.community/.

[19] https://www.ros.org/.

[20] https://opencv.org/.

[21] https://kaldi-asr.org/doc/.

[22] https://github.com/espnet/espnet.

expressions, gaze, head and hand gesturing are all important signals in human conversations 11, and crucial in making human-robot interactions more natural 1. The signals manifest the agents' cooperation and indicate their attention to the partner's needs.

According to 19 the main characteristics of social robot interaction are:

- Use of multimodal signals (speech, gaze, gesture, body) to communicate with the human
- Observations of human multimodal behaviour (speech, gaze, gesture, body) to learn human intentions and to react appropriately
- Autonomous decisions about actions
- Independent moving in a 3-dimensional world
- Receiving and sharing information via internet & IoT.

The first two items relate to the robot's communicative capability, the next two items concern its autonomy, and the last one captures the basis for the robot's knowledge.

Detailed analyses of robots' communicative capability are much studied elsewhere, see references above and 4811. This paper ventures into a new area of dialogue modelling, namely studying various environmental sensors and the data they provide for interaction (about temperature, humidity, CO_2 levels, etc.). Advances in sensory device technology have brought new input devices into smart homes, and consequently available for robots to observe their environment and the user 917.

The user can query such information, but the data can also be included in dialogue modelling to produce context-sensitive responses. While the smart home can measure the state of the environment, interactions should be conducted in a particular situation, with a particular partner. Communication with the user needs to be embodied, rather than directed to the walls, remote controllers, or mobile phones. This calls for a social robot powered by conversational AI, which is able to communicate about such information in natural language.

3   Constructing Situational Awareness

3.1 Grounding

In human-robot interaction, the challenges related to situational awareness can be addressed by supplying robots with understanding of the context (context-awareness) and ability to build a shared context with users (grounding). Context-awareness enables the robot agent to behave appropriately in the specific interactive situation and engage with the partner by efficiently using its knowledge to infer the partner's affective state, level of understanding, willingness to continue discussion, etc. Grounding on the other hand is linked to joint meaning creation, i.e., to the agent's ability to understand the meaning of the user's utterance and link the mentioned referents to the current context. In dialogue modelling, predictions of whether the partner refers to the same entity as the agent are important to confirm that the partners are talking about the same thing 7. One of the main means to cooperate in dialogues is to create such shared context in which joint understanding of the goals can be created and the task goals successfully achieved. In robotics, grounding is a related concept but usually associated with the robot's vision studies where symbolic labels are linked to the object in the world 13. A neurocognitive model to integrate the robot's cross-modal sensory and sensorimotor modalities in language grounding is presented in 14.

3.2 Construction of Dialogues

In earlier work, the robot's interaction capability was modelled after the theoretical framework of Constructive Dialogue Model 18, which defines Contact, Perception, Understanding, and Reaction as the basic enablements for cooperative communication. The basic capabilities include the ability to recognize the user's face and gaze (Contact), perceive the user's actions (Perception), provide relevant information (Understanding), and engage with the user (Reaction). In the implemented system, these enablements correspond to different components that perform a particular function, i.e. Contact is implemented via sensors, Perception via various recognizers, Understanding is based on natural language and dialogue components, and Reaction is produced by different generators and output devices.The lower level enablements (Contact, Perception) need to be successful in order for the higher levels to succeed: if there is no contact or perception, there is no point to continue talking. Lower level enablements are thus prerequisites for the higher level enablements. The signals that indicate the partner's contact and perception (awareness and understanding) are stored in the Context Knowledgebase as Boolean values. They are used in the Understanding process of the message. Reaction is produced as the most appropriate action given the current state, and it results in a new dialogue state which represents the knowledge of the system at the time it waits for the user's response.

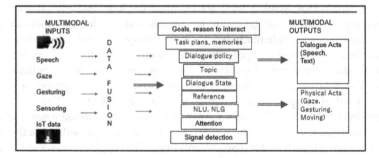

Fig. 1. Subsumption of the enablements of communication in CDM.

The communicative enablements thus form a hierarchy, like the robot's competences in the subsumption architecture for robot control 3. Competences are specifications of desired behaviours for a robot in its environment, and a higher-level competence implies a more specific class of desired behaviours. Enablements in communication are organised analogously as a set of competences which relate to communicative actions rather than physical acts, and control the successful communication. Figure 1 shows a layered set of competences that form the tacit control system for the dialogue model.

3.3 Situational Awareness

As already discussed, communication requires knowledge of what is going on around the agent and is dependent on the level of the agent's autonomous behaviour and the amount of knowledge it has about the world, the situation and the partner. Situational awareness can manifest on many levels, ranging from the dialogue context to the environment in which the communication takes place. For instance, dialogue analysis shows how the interlocutors accurately time their conversational turns and synchronise their behaviour with the partner, as well as giving feedback using social signals such as gaze, gestures, nods, and body movement which indicate the interlocutors' emotion, intent, engagement and attention to the partner's communicative needs.

Considering the enablement of Contact, the participants first need to establish that interaction is possible: that the partners are aware of each other's presence and in the proximity for interaction. Establishing contact also indicates the interlocutors' basic willingness to engage in the conversation, which will then manifest itself in dialogues which are constructed together with the partners as the interaction goes on.

In human-robot interaction, this can be implemented with the help of movement detectors, which can track the user's movements in the rooms and in particular show if the user is in the same room as the robot. They may also be able to tell if the distance to the robot is short enough so that the robot can start talking to the user. Infra-red and touch sensors on the robot itself may help the robot to sense the presence of the users and their distance from the robot. This can be used in dialogue initiation, if the user is close enough to start conversation.

Actual environmental conditions have an impact on the participants' behaviour and indirectly on their interactions with other partners. Weather conditions function not only as a topic for conversation ("It's very hot today") but also affect people's emotional and affective state. Hot weather may not be ideal for long intensive discussions on challenging topics, and it may be useful to communicate to the user about dangerous weather conditions or provide reminders to drink enough to avoid dehydration.

Besides being proactive and providing information about the environmental state, the data from the environmental sensors can be especially used for the initialisation of dialogues. The data from the sensors is collected and a fusion component processes them to the level of categorised information that can be used in the dialogue manager. The system-initiated dialogues form a sensor-based interaction mode where the sensors report the data (e.g. temperature, humidity), possibly combined with proactive recommendations (drink enough water, use dehumidifier). The typical conversational agent dialogues are user-initiated dialogues where the user asks questions, e.g., about the environmental sensors (see the example below in Sect. 4.2).

4 Dialogue Management

4.1 Rasa Dialogue Modelling

This section briefly describes the use of the Rasa conversational AI framework[23] with spoken and multimodal information. Rasa is a popular open-source conversational AI

---

[23] https://rasa.com/.

framework which is scalable and has a modular, extensible architecture, offering the possibility to combine cutting edge natural language processing modules with a transformer-based dialogue manager 38. Rasa supports state-of-the-art natural language understanding, processing user messages in a pipeline of components to interpret user inputs and using rule-based and machine learning-based dialogue policies to determine the system's actions. The pipeline includes the Dual Intent and Entity Transformer (DIET) for entity extraction and intent classification and the Transformer Embedding Dialogues (TED) policy for system responses 2. It also allows the components to be changed from the defaults to a customized configuration.

Dialogue context includes dialogue history, domain information and environmental information obtained via sensors, and is needed for maintaining coherence in long-term interactions. The meaning related to the environmental sensor information is encoded in the appropriate labels and can be stored in Rasa's custom slots which can affect the dialogue. The slot information is mainly used in checking that Contact is still enabled, but it can also play a role in the actual content of the dialogues (e.g. what kind of topics are most likely to be discussed in which room – dialogues in the kitchen are likely to focus on food while those in the living room focus on news, TV programs, and physical activities). As mentioned earlier, the slots are also important in case the user requests room temperature to be changed or if the robot will proactively provide useful recommendations in the current context.

In this work, the contribution to context-aware dialogue modelling is realized by including context knowledge in the form of knowledge graphs in dialogue processing, while grounding is implemented with the help of knowledgebase actions operating on the history of the ongoing dialogue. The model is implemented using Rasa conversational AI, storing recognized entities in the robot's memory and tagging them according to the entity's status in the grounding process. The dialogue model dynamically updates the memory and provides possibilities to study the internal structure of the robot's contextual knowledge and its construction through the interaction. Details can be found in 40. Ongoing work consists of extending the CDM dialogue model with a context model that includes dynamic environmental sensor information and experimenting with the context model to better enable grounding and the shared context construction.

Early dialogue research was task-based in that the system provided information to the user on a particular task domain. Practical conversational chatbot applications are still designed for the task at hand, with the different "intents" and "entities" specific for the application. However, when considering the possibility to apply or reuse chatbots for other domains, the issue of generalisation appears. The problem is similar to the issue in dialogue management research where the domain dependency of dialogue acts is discussed: chatbot development also faces domain dependency in the form of the intents. One approach is to address dialogue intent design as part of the general standardisation and interoperability issues of robots, as discussed in Sect. 2.1. Another approach is to avoid intent classification and instead focus on knowledge-base queries which can find the correct information in the form of entities, predicates, and relations. This recasts the issue as knowledge modelling rather than dialogue management, with the goal of structuring the knowledge for the purpose of providing information. In this paper we aim to structure the domain knowledge in the form of knowledge graphs that model concepts and the relations between them, and thus the goal of the analysis done by the natural language pipeline is not to detect the user's intent and classify it correctly, but rather to extract the entities for the knowledge base search in order to retrieve the content required for a suitable response. Ongoing work is focussed on realising this in appropriate knowledgebase actions.

4.2 Example Dialogue

An extract from a knowledge graph for environmental states including temperature and humidity is shown in Fig. 2. The graph, which was produced using Arrows.app[24], is stored in a Neo4j graph database 33. It shows the connection from an environmental state node to various environmental parameters like humidity and room temperature. These are connected to comfortable and uncomfortable states and also to various recommendations given the sensor measurements at a particular time.

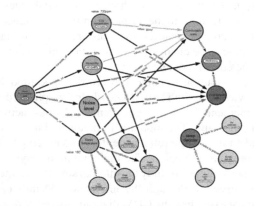

Fig. 2. Example of a knowledge graph for environmental states.

The interaction model is expected to be used with various types of humanoid robots, but we focus on Nao and Furhat robots. In the following example dialogue (Fig. 3), the user asks about recommendations concerning different temperature levels (hot, cold) as well as humidity and noise levels with linguistically varied questions, and finally asks for recommendations for sleep disorder. The bot provides answers based on the knowledge graph. It is interesting to note that the query "what do you recommend for my sleep problem" is answered with the problems that cause sleep disorder rather than recommendations. This is due to the Rasa NLU model picking out "problem" as the object type in the knowledgebase and ignoring the verb "recommend", whereas the similar query "what do you recommend for my sleep disorder" is correctly understood as a question about recommendations with the object type "recommend".

---

[24] Arrows app whiteboard Homepage, https://neo4j.com/labs/arrows/.

```
Bot loaded. Type a message and press enter (use '/stop' to exit):

Your input -> what do you recommend for high temperature
Found the following objects of type 'recommendation':
1: open_window

Your input -> recommend for low temperature
Found the following objects of type 'recommendation':
1: use_heater

Your input -> what is good to do when it's very damp?
Found the following objects of type 'recommendation':
1: use_dehumidifier

Your input -> what's good thing for too cold?
Found the following objects of type 'recommendation':
1: use_heater

Your input -> very cold, what recommend?
Found the following objects of type 'recommendation':
1: use_heater

Your input -> what will help when it's very noisy?
Found the following objects of type 'recommendation':
1: close_window

Your input -> I'm very cold, what will help?
Found the following objects of type 'recommendation':
1: use_heater

Your input -> I have sleep disorder, what will help?
Found the following objects of type 'recommendation':
1: have_regular_lifestyle
2: do_exercises
3: avoid_eating_late

Your input -> what do you recommend for my sleep problem?
Found the following objects of type 'problem':
1: high_noise
2: high_temperature
3: low_temperature
4: sleep_disorder
5: high_humidity

Your input -> what do you recommend for my sleep disorder?
Found the following objects of type 'recommendation':
1: avoid_eating_late
2: have_regular_lifestyle
3: do_exercises

Your input -> thanks
```

Fig. 3. Example dialogue.

5   Conclusions

This paper discusses new opportunities to use AI technology to make human-robot interactions more natural and expressive, thus enabling robots to cross the boundaries from tools to interactive companions 20. The paper argues that human interaction with robots is quite unlike interactions with text-based systems or with other types of mobile devices, and that the conversational agent should take account of the robot's verbal and non-verbal behaviour as well as enable a grounding process in order to create mutual context with the human partner. The context includes the dialogue context as well as the physical environment in which the conversation takes place, and from which information is accessible via environmental sensors. Structured knowledge modelling thus concerns relevant information of the context, of the application domain and the world. Besides the grounding process, another relevant aspect is to exhibit situational awareness which is realised via multimodal processing that indicate context sensitivity with the designated gesturing, pointing and nodding behaviour.

Natural language interaction with humanoid robots can be enabled by conversational AI dialogue modelling. Ongoing work focuses on the Nao humanoid robot and the Rasa conversational AI framework and experiments with conversational dialogues concerning everyday tasks. The contribution of the paper relates to desired functionality by integrating technology from known techniques: the techniques of conversational AI modelling are combined with the robot's capability of sensing the environment and interacting with the user in a multimodal manner. It is expected that this kind of situated agent not only enhances robots' interaction functionality towards natural interaction with humans, but also affects the human view of social robots. More natural conversational interaction between humans and humanoid robots will allow autonomous robots to act as boundary-crossing agents and will thus enable more symbiotic human-robot relations in the future society.

Acknowledgment. I thank all my colleagues and especially Graham Wilcock for fruitful and inspiring conversations. The study is based on results obtained from project JPNP20006 commissioned by the New Energy and Industrial Technology Development Organization (NEDO).

References

1. Baltrusaitis, T., Ahuja, C., Morency, L.-P.: Multimodal machine learning: a survey and taxonomy. IEEE Trans. Pattern Anal. Mach. Intell. (TPAMI) **4**(2) (2019)
2. Bocklisch, T., Faulkner, J., Pawlowski, N., Nichol, A.: Rasa: open source language understanding and dialogue management. arXiv preprint arXiv:1712.05181 (2017)
3. Brooks, R.: A robust layered control system for a mobile robot. IEEE J. Robot. Autom. **2**(1), 14–23 (1986)
4. Broz, F., Lehmann, H., Mutlu, B., Nakano, Y. (eds.): Gaze in Human-Robot Communication. John Benjamins Publishing Company (2015)
5. Bunt, H., et al.: The ISO standard for dialogue act annotation, second edition. In: Proceedings of the 12th Conference on Language Resources and Evaluation (LREC 2020), pp. 549–558. European Language Resources Association (ELRA), licensed under CC-BY-NC 549 (2020)
6. Chung, Y-A., Glass, J.: Speech2vec: a sequence-to-sequence framework for learning word embeddings from speech. In: Proceedisngs of Interspeech, pp. 811–815 (2018)
7. Clark, H., Wilkes-Gibbs, D.: Referring as a collaborative process. Cognition **22**, 1–39 (1986)
8. Csapo, A., et al.: Multimodal conversational interaction with a humanoid robot. In: Proceedings of the 3rd IEEE Conference on Cognitive Infocommunications, Kosice (2012)
9. Dohr, A., Modre-Opsrian, R., Drobics, M., Hayn, D., Schreier, G.D.: The Internet of Things for ambient assisted living. In: The 7th International Conference on Information Technology, pp. 804–809. IEEE (2010)
10. Durrant-Whyte, H., Bailey, T.: Simultaneous localization and mapping: part I. IEEE Robot. Autom. Mag. **13**(2), 99–110 (2006)

11. Feldman, R.S., Rim, B.: Fundamentals of Nonverbal Behavior. Cambridge University Press (1991)
12. Fujii, A., Jokinen, K.: Open source system integration towards natural interaction with robots. In: HRI 2022: ACM/IEEE International Conference on Human-Robot Interaction Late-Breaking Reports (2022)
13. Harnad, S.: The symbol grounding problem. Physica D **42**, 335–346 (1990)
14. Heinrich, S., et al.: Crossmodal language grounding in an embodied neurocognitive model. Front. Neurorobot. **14**, 1662–5218 (2020)
15. Heylen, D., Krenn, B., Payr, S.: Companions, virtual butlers, assistive robots: empirical and theoretical insights for building long-term social relationships. In: Trappl, R. (ed.): Cybernetics and Systems 2010, pp. 539–570. Austrian Society for Cybernetic Studies, Vienna, Austria (2010)
16. Ide, N., Bunt, H.: Anatomy of annotation schemes: mapping to GrAF. In: Proceedings 4th Linguistic Annotation Workshop (LAW IV), Uppsala, pp. 247–255 (2010)
17. Jara, A.J., Zamora, M.A., Skarmeta, A.F.: An internet of things-based personal device for diabetes therapy management in ambient assisted living (AAL). Pers. Ubiquit. Comput. **15**(4), 431–440 (2011)
18. Jokinen, K.: Constructive Dialogue Modelling – Speech Interaction and Rational Agents. John Wiley (2009)
19. Jokinen, K.: Dialogue models for socially intelligent robots. In: Ge, S.S., et al. (eds.) ICSR 2018. LNCS (LNAI), vol. 11357, pp. 127–138. Springer, Cham (2018). https://doi.org/10.1007/978-3-030-05204-1_13
20. Jokinen, K., Watanabe, K.: Boundary Crossing Agents. Societal Impact of Interactions with Socially Capable Agents. ICSR, Springer (2019)
21. Jokinen, K., Wilcock, G.: Next steps for social robots - a robot talking fluently about thousands of topics using English and Japanese Wikipedias. In: The 9th International Conference on Social Robotics (ICSR). sBest Robot Design Award (Software Category), Special Recognition (2017)
22. Jokinen, K., Wilcock, G.: Multimodal open-domain conversations with robotic platforms. In: Alameda-Pineda, X., Ricci, E., Sebe, N. (eds.) Multimodal Behaviour Analysis in the Wild - Advances and Challenges, pp. 9–26. Elsevier/Academic Press (2019)
23. Jokinen, K., Wilcock, G.: Towards long-term relations in social robot interactions. In: HRI (2019)
24. Jokinen, K., Nishimura, S., Watanabe, K., Nishimura, T.: Human-robot dialogues for explaining activities. In: D'Haro, L.F., Banchs, R.E., Li, H. (eds.) The 9th International Workshop on Spoken Spoken Dialogue System Technology. Springer, Singapore https://doi.org/10.1007/978-981-13-9443-0_20
25. Kanda, T., Ishiguro, H.: Human-Robot Interaction in Social Robotics (eBook Published 2017). CRC Press (2013). https://doi.org/10.1201/b13004
26. Kawahara, T., Jokinen, K.: Spoken Dialogue for Social Robots. Tutorial at Interspeech 2020, Shanghai (2020). http://www.interspeech2020.org/index.php?m=content&c=index&a=show&catid=369&id=291
27. Leite, I., Martinho, C., Paiva, A.: Social robots for long-term interaction: a survey. Int. J. Soc. Robot. **5**(2), 291–308 (2013). https://doi.org/10.1007/s12369-013-0178-y
28. Liu, B., Tur, G., Hakkani-Tur, G., Shah, P., Heck, L.: End-to-end optimization of task-oriented dialogue model with deep reinforcement learning. In: NIPS Workshop on Conversational AI (2017)
29. Marge, M., Espy-Wilson, C., Ward, N.: Spoken language interaction with robots: Research issues and recommendations (2020). arXiv: https://arxiv.org/pdf/2011.05533.pdf
30. McTear, M.: Conversational AI: Dialogue Systems, Conversational Agents, and Chatbots. Morgan & Claypool Publishers, Kentfield (2020)

31. Mikolov, T., Chen, K., Corrado, G., Dean J.: Efficient Estimation of Word Representations in Vector Space (2013). arXiv:1301.3781
32. Papangelis, A., Namazifar, M., Khatri, C., Wang, Y-C., Molino, P., Tur, G.: Plato Dialogue System: A Flexible Conversational AI Research Platform (2020)
33. Robinson, I., Webber, J., Eifrem, E.: Graph Databases (2nd edition). O'Reilly Media (2015)
34. Sarikaya, R., et al.: An overview of end-to-end language understanding and dialog management for personal digital assistants. In: Workshop on Spoken Language Technology. IEEE (2016)
35. Serban, I.V., Sordoni, A., Bengio, Y., Courville, A., Pineau, J.: Building end-to-end dialogue systems using generative hierarchical neural network models. In: Proceedings of the Thirtieth AAAI Conference on Artificial Intelligence (AAAI-16) (2016)
36. Sidner, C., Rich, C., Shayganfar, M., Bickmore, T., Ring, L., Zhang, Z.: A robotic companion for social support of isolated older adults. In: Proceedings of the Tenth Annual ACM/IEEE International Conference on Human-Robot Interaction Extended Abstracts (HRI 2015 Extended Abstracts), pp. 289–289. ACM, New York (2015)
37. Ultes, S., et al.: PyDial: a multi-domain statistical dialogue system toolkit. In: Proceedings of ACL 2017, System Demonstrations, pp. 73–78 (2017)
38. Vlasov, V., Mosig, J.M.E., Nichol, A.: Dialogue transformers (2019). ArXiv:1910.00486
39. Wilcock, G.: Using a deep learning dialogue research toolkit in a multilingual multi-domain practical application. In: Proceedings of the Twenty-Seventh International Joint Conference on Artificial Intelligence (IJCAI 2018), Stockholm, Sweden, pp. 5880–5882 (2018)
40. Wilcock, G., Jokinen, K.: Conversational AI and Knowledge Graphs for Social Robot Interaction. In: HRI 2022: ACM/IEEE International Conference on Human-Robot Interaction, Sapporo, Japan (2022)
41. Wrede, B., et al.: Research issues for designing robot companions: BIRON as a case study. In: Proceedings of the IEEE Conference of Mechatronics & Robotics (2004)

Surgical Human-Robot Interaction: A Bibliometric Review

Marian Obuseh$^{(\boxtimes)}$ and Vincent G. Duffy

School of Industrial Engineering, Purdue University, West Lafayette, IN 47906, USA
{mobuseh,duffy}@purdue.edu

Abstract. The purpose of this study was to explore human-robot interaction in surgical contexts using bibliometric analyses. We demonstrate the use of various scientometric tools for a bibliometric review and discuss some trends in robotic surgeries. Metadata was extracted from three databases: Scopus, Web of Science, and Google Scholar through Publish or Perish software. A one-way analysis of variance and Tukey's post hoc test were used to observe any significant differences in database publication yields. Different trend analyses were conducted on metadata with tools including Vicinitas and Google NGram, Co-citation network analyses were also carried out with VOSviewer and CiteSpace. Finally, MAXQDA was used for a content analysis using a subset of 27 articles. The review showed that surgical robotics is a heavily growing field as seen with the uptake of robotic surgeries over other conventional techniques. Findings of current trends in the field are also presented. Finally, we discuss ideas for future work on both technical and non-technical aspects of surgical robotics.

Keywords: Robotic-surgery · Human-robot interaction · Bibliometric analysis · Co-citation analysis

1 Introduction

There has been an uptake of robotic-assisted surgeries (RAS) across many surgical procedures because surgical robotics technology addresses the ergonomic challenges of traditional laparoscopy and open surgeries by improving the surgeon's wrist dexterity, three-dimensional visualization, and magnification (Schiff et al. 2016). However, one of the main issues in ensuring the safe and effective use of the robotic technology in surgeries is the interaction between the user (typically a surgeon) and the robotics system (Abdelaal et al. 2020). The effective design of surgical human-robot interaction (HRI) should address the salient challenges surgeons may face during surgical procedures (Aaltonen et al. 2018). Some of these challenges can affect surgery outcomes, and they include decision-making at each step of the surgery, navigation inside the patient's body, and object recognition (Abdelaal et al. 2020).

Surgical HRI also affects the human aspects of RAS. In RAS, the surgeon sits behind the console in a remote position from the surgical field and mostly gazes at the console visual displays while teleoperating the robot arms (Tiferes et al. 2019; Randell et al.

© The Author(s), under exclusive license to Springer Nature Switzerland AG 2022
M. Kurosu et al. (Eds.): HCII 2022, LNCS 13519, pp. 293–312, 2022.
https://doi.org/10.1007/978-3-031-17618-0_22

2015). Consequently, the spatial separation and lack of physical connection between the surgeon, patient, and team creates challenges for coordination and communication within the surgical team in the operating room (Tiferes et al. 2016). Finally, the robotic system must be designed such that the interaction maintains or enhances the patient's safety. Specifically, surgical robots should be designed with high degrees of compliance between the robotic manipulators to reduce the risk of unintentional excessive force on tissues (Ficuciello et al. 2016).

In the United States, the number of robotic surgeries increased by a factor of 8.4 from 2012 to 2018 (Liu et al. 2021), and the adoption of the da Vinci robot (a commonly used surgical robot) increased by 18% in 2018 when compared to 2017 (Khalafallah et al. 2021). Despite these statistics, a 2013 survey showed that 46% of general surgery residents (most of which were senior residents) believed robot-assisted cases interfered with their participation in the surgical procedures and could impact their overall general surgery training (Farivar et al. 2015). However, the use of the da Vinci robot in general surgery has increased by a factor of 3 since that survey (Intuitive Surgical Inc 2016). Consequently, more studies have investigated HRI within surgical contexts. Hence, the following are the aims of this study:

1. To summarize the efforts made at studying surgical HRI, including trends of such efforts
2. To identify collaborative networks and major scholarly communities, as well as analyze the research status in the field of surgical HRI

2 Methods

2.1 Data Collection

Metadata was extracted from various databases including Scopus, Web of Science (WoS), and Google Scholar (GS) via Harzing's Publish or Perish (PoP) software (Harzing 2006). All searches were done on the 28th of April 2022. Table 1 shows the keywords that were used in the database search, the publication counts per database search, and the timespan per search. The timespan of the search was not set, and this was intentionally done to capture the oldest and newest published articles in the research area. To further elucidate the reader on the keywords used for the search, we define them as follows. HRI is an interdisciplinary field of study concerned with understanding, designing, and evaluating robotic systems for use by or with humans (Goodrich and Schultz 2008). The American College of Surgeons define surgery as a practice of medicine performed to structurally alter the human body by incision or destruction of tissues (American College of Surgeons 2007). Surgery is also the diagnostic or therapeutic treatment of conditions or disease by any instruments causing localized alteration or transportation of live human tissue. Beyond surgery, the role of robots in healthcare has become more diverse in different applications including physical and cognitive rehabilitation therapy (Burgar et al. 2000), drug delivery (Mapara and Patravale 2017), and mental health care (Riek 2016).

Table 1. Keyword search, publication yield, and timespan of search in different databases

Database	Keywords used (without quotes)	Publication counts	Timespan
Scopus	"Surgery" AND "Human-robot interaction"	254	1994–Date
Web of Science	"Surgery" AND "Human-robot interaction"	308	1992–Date
Google Scholar	"Surgery" AND "Human-robot interaction"	980	1989–Date

2.2 Data Analysis

After downloading the metadata from all three databases as either comma separated value or plain text files, they were used for different analyses to address the aims of this study. As part of efforts to address the first aim of this study, we conducted a one-way analysis of variance (ANOVA) and Tukey's post hoc test on publication yields over time from all three databases to determine if there was a significant difference among databases. Table 2 is an emergence indicator summarizing all publication counts over 30 years across the three databases. All statistical analyses were done with Minitab statistical software (Minitab Inc. 2010). Given the high-stakes, time-limited, complicated, and intense nature of surgical operating rooms, research on HRI in surgery is burgeoning. Hence, we conducted a series of analyses with different tools to explore current trends and engagements in the field. Vicinitas is a tool that tracks and analyzes real-time and historical tweets of social media campaigns and brands on Twitter (Vicinitas 2022). As an initial effort to confirm the increasing research trends, we used Vicinitas to measure the engagement level of research on RAS based on Twitter activity within the last 10 days from the search date. We also conducted a trend analysis to study publication trends in the field. The metadata collected from GS via PoP was analyzed to capture the interest of the scientific community pursuing research related to HRI in surgery. GS's metadata was specifically chosen because it had the highest publication count as seen in Table 1. Using Scopus' metadata, we also analyzed publications by location, authors, and author affiliations. Since RAS has been adopted to address some of the challenges associated with both laparoscopic and open surgeries, we conducted a trend analysis with Google Ngram viewer (Google Books 2010) to compare popularity of the three types of surgeries over time. Google Ngram viewer is an online search engine that charts the frequencies of any set of search strings using a yearly count (up to 2019) of n-grams found in a corpus of books for a specified time frame (Michel et al. 2011). A search was done from 1980–2019 using the keywords "robotic surgery", "laparoscopic surgery", and "open surgery".

To address the second aim of this study, we first conducted a co-citation network analyses using two different bibliometric software. Co-citation is the frequency with which two documents are cited together by other documents (Small 1973). If at least one document cites two other documents in common, these two documents are said to be co-cited. The more co-citations two documents receive, the higher their co-citation strength, and the more likely they are semantically related (Small 1973). A co-citation network was first created with VOSviewer, a software tool for constructing and visualizing bibliometric networks (van Eck and Waltman 2019). However, a co-citation network created by VOSviewer does not have its clusters labelled by a unique keyword. We circumvented this limitation by generating a co-citation network with CiteSpace, a computer program for visualizing and analyzing trends and patterns in scientific literature (Chen 2006). From the CiteSpace co-citation network, clusters were then extracted by keywords. To get a broader reach of articles, the keyword used for the search that generated the co-citation analysis metadata was "robotic-assisted surgery". The search was done for 1994–2022 on the WOS Core Collection database, a database that allows researchers to download the metadata of full record and cited reference of each article found from a keyword search. We used the same metadata for the co-citation network generated by both VOSviewer and CiteSpace. In this paper, we used the g-index selection criteria with a scale factor (k) of 1 for the co-citation network with CiteSpace. g-index is an author level metric that represents the largest number such that the top g articles received together at least g^2 citations (Egghe 2006). For example, a g-index of 5 means the top 5 publications of the author have been cited at least 25 times (5^2). k is directly proportional to the size of the network. CiteSpace also supports burst detection on several types of events including the number of citation counts of cited references over time. In bibliometric literature, a burst refers to the frequency surge of an event. Finally, we conducted a content analysis on select articles used in this review using MAXQDA, a software for qualitative and mixed methods data analysis (VERBI Software 2021). From the content analysis, a word cloud depicting the most recurring keywords in the articles was generated.

Table 2. Publication counts over 30 years across the three databases search

Year	Count per database		
	Scopus	Web of science	Google scholar
2022	14	5	40
2021	34	29	134
2020	24	25	131
2019	30	36	93
2018	30	26	99
2017	15	27	74
2016	17	29	53
2015	8	21	60
2014	22	15	45
2013	10	28	37
2012	10	27	30
2011	6	10	22
2010	5	11	22
2009	5	4	20
2008	4	5	17

(*continued*)

Table 2. (*continued*)

Year	Count per database		
	Scopus	Web of science	Google scholar
2007	5	2	11
2006	3	2	16
2005	1	2	10
2004	3	0	9
2003	3	1	2
2002	1	1	5
2001	2	1	4
2000	0	0	4
1998	0	0	1
1997	0	0	1
1995	1	0	1
1994	1	0	0
1993	0	0	1
1992	0	1	3
1989	0	0	1

3 Results

3.1 Statistical Analyses

In this section, we assessed if there were any significant differences between means of publication counts for the keyword search term across Scopus, WoS, and GS. We conducted a one-way analysis of variance (ANOVA) using Minitab. We defined our null and alternative hypothesis (see Eqs. 1 and 2 below) and hypothesized that there is a significant difference in publication counts across the three databases.

$$H_0 : \mu_{scopus} = \mu_{WoS} = \mu_{GS} \text{ (Means of publication counts across all databases are equal)} \tag{1}$$

$$H_1 : at\ least\ one\ \mu\ is\ different\ from\ the\ others \tag{2}$$

Our analysis showed that there was sufficient evidence to reject the null hypothesis ($p < 0.05$) and conclude that at least one database had a different mean of publication count from the other two. To determine which databases' mean publication count was significantly different, we conducted a Tukey's post hoc test for multiple pairwise comparisons. The mean publication count of WoS was greater than that of Scopus (WoS > Scopus). However, the difference was not statistically significant ($p < 0.05$). There was a statistically significant difference between the mean publication count of GS and Scopus (GS > Scopus, $p < 0.05$). Finally, there was also a statistically significant difference between the mean publication count of GS and WoS (GS > WoS, p < 0.05). Since GS > WoS > Scopus, we can conclude that GS had the highest publication count of all databases (p < 0.05).

3.2 Trend Analyses

Using Vicinita's free tool for hashtag/keyword tweets analysis, a search was carried on the keyword "robotic-assisted surgery". Figure 1 shows both engagement and posts timelines for the keyword.

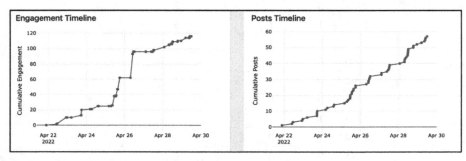

Fig. 1. Results from Vicinitas analysis based on the Twitter feed for the keyword "robotic-assisted surgery"

The trend analysis with GS's metadata to visualize the publication yield over the years are as seen in Fig. 2. Figure 3 also shows the top 10 countries with "surgical human-robot interaction" publications (using data from Scopus). The top 3 countries with the most publications are United States (61), China (48), and the United Kingdom (29). Finally, using the Scopus "analyze search result" tool, Figs. 4 and 5 visualize the top 10 leading authors and affiliations of articles published in the field respectively.

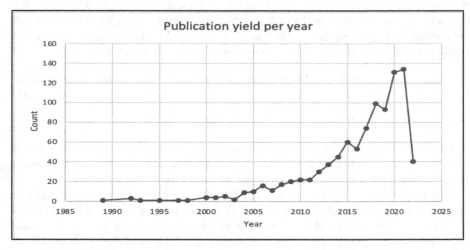

Fig. 2. Publication yield per year based on Google scholar's metadata search

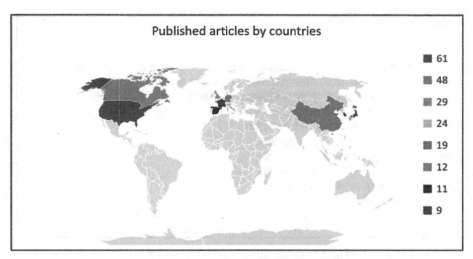

Fig. 3. Top 10 countries with "surgical human-robot interaction" publications on a global map

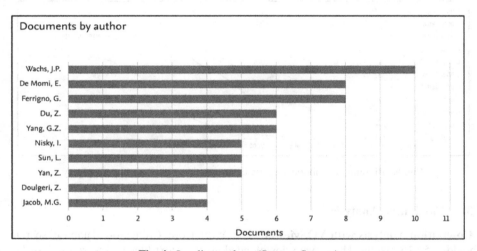

Fig. 4. Leading authors (Source: Scopus)

Figure 6 is the output of the Google Ngram analysis. The output has three bigrams and what the y-axis shows is this: of all the bigrams contained in Google Ngram viewer's sample of books written in English and published in the United States, what percentage of them are "robotic surgery", "laparoscopic surgery", or "open surgery"?

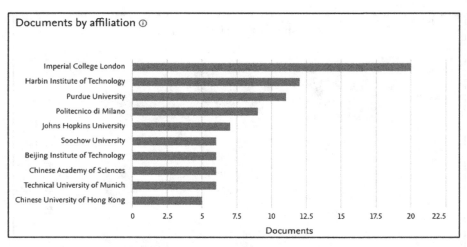

Fig. 5. Leading affiliations (Source: Scopus)

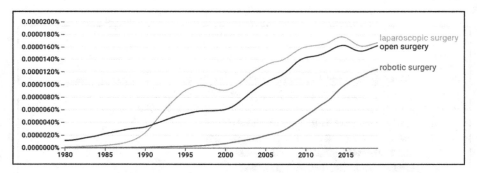

Fig. 6. Bigrams for robotic surgery, laparoscopic surgery, and open surgery

3.3 Co-citation Analysis

Co-citation Analysis with VOSviewer. The WoS Core Collection database search yielded 5,815 results. These were downloaded as plain text files and were used as the input data for the co-citation analysis with VOSviewer. From the 5,815 articles found, there were 74,535 cited references. For the co-citation network, the inclusion criterion was that the article must have been co-cited at least 100 times. Of all the articles found, seven met the criterion. Figure 7 shows the network visualization of the co-citations analysis using the seven articles that met the inclusion criterion.

Each article is represented by a node, and the node size corresponds to the number of times the article was cited in the network (Fig. 7). The network also has three clusters grouped by node colors: cluster 1 (red nodes), cluster 2 (green nodes), and cluster 3 (blue node). Table 3 below shows details of the seven articles used for the co-citation network. For each cited reference in Table 3, VOSviewer also calculates the total strength of its co-citation links with other cited references.

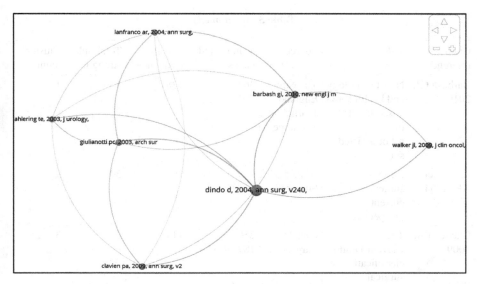

Fig. 7. Co-citation network with VOSviewer (Color figure online)

Table 3. Articles used for VOSviewer co-citation network

Cited reference	Title	Source	Volume and pages	Co-cited frequency	Total link strength	Cluster number
Dindo D, 2004	Classification of surgical complications: a new proposal with evaluation in a cohort of 6336 patients and results of a survey	Annals of Surgery	240, 205–213	347	63	1
Giulianotti PC, 2003	Robotics in general surgery: personal experience in a large community hospital	Archives of Surgery	138, 777–784	121	59	2

(continued)

Table 3. (*continued*)

Cited reference	Title	Source	Volume and pages	Co-cited frequency	Total link strength	Cluster number
Barbash GI, 2010	New technology and health care costs-the case of robot-assisted surgery	The New England Journal of Medicine	363, 701–704	128	34	1
Lanfranco AR, 2004	Robotic surgery: a current perspective	Annals of Surgery	239, 14–21	100	30	2
Clavien PA, 2009	The Clavien-Dindo classification of surgical complications: five-year experience	Annals of Surgery	250, 187–196	114	28	3
Ahlering TE, 2003	Successful transfer of open surgical skills to a laparoscopic environment using a robotic interface: initial experience with laparoscopic radical prostatectomy	The Journal of Urology	170, 1738–1741	101	27	2
Walker JL, 2009	Laparoscopy compared with laparotomy for comprehensive surgical staging of uterine cancer: Gynecologic Oncology Group Study LAP2	Journal of Clinical Oncology	27, 5331–5336	108	11	1

Co-citation Analysis with CiteSpace. The co-citation network created using CiteSpace and clustered by keywords yielded seven clusters (Fig. 8). Each cluster name was auto generated, representing sub-topics within the broader search term used to generate the metadata. CiteSpace generates these keywords (or cluster names) from citing papers by log-likelihood ratios (LLR) and mutual information (MI). Each cluster was identified by a unique identifier (ID) from 0 to 6. Table 4 shows details of each keyword representative of a cluster in the network. The size of the cluster represents the number of publications within each cluster. Our analysis identified 110 citation bursts from 1994 to date. Table 5 shows the top 10 references with the strongest citation bursts.

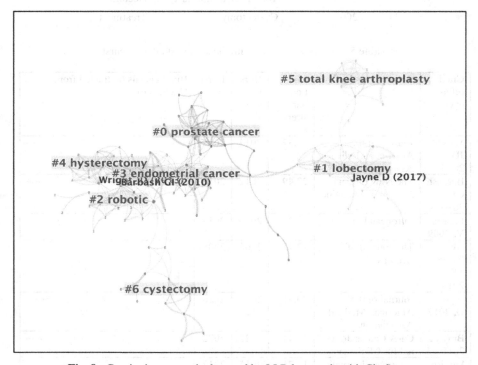

Fig. 8. Co-citation network clustered by LLR keywords with CiteSpace

Table 4. Co-citation network keyword-based cluster information

Cluster ID	Size	Mean (year)	Keyword (LLR)	Keyword (MI)
0	24	2002	Prostate cancer	Robotic technology
1	23	2016	Lobectomy	Artificial intelligence
2	17	2010	Robotic	Hysterectomy
3	17	2007	Endometrial cancer	da Vinci surgery
4	13	2012	Hysterectomy	Utilization of minimally invasive surgery
5	11	2016	Total knee arthroplasty	Accuracy
6	11	2007	Cystectomy	Treatment

Table 5. Top 10 references with the strongest citation burst

Cited reference	Source	Citation burst strength	Burst start	Burst end	Burst visuals (extracted from CiteSpace)
Wright JD, 2013	Journal of the American Medical Association	23.37	2014	2017	
Barbash GI, 2010	The New England Journal of Medicine	22.49	2012	2015	
Ficarra V, 2009	European Urology	22.35	2010	2013	
Ahlering TE, 2013	The Journal of Urology	22.13	2006	2008	
Jayne D, 2017	Journal of the American Medical Association	20.51	2018	2020	
Bray F, 2018	Ca-A Cancer Journal for Clinicians	16.44	2020	2022	
Paraiso MFR, 2013	American Journal of Obstetrics and Gynecology	15.71	2015	2017	
Swanson SJ, 2014	The Journal of Thoracic and Cardiovascular Surgery	15.40	2017	2019	
Hu JC, 2009	Journal of the American Medical Association	14.44	2012	2014	
Menon M, 2007	European Urology	14.43	2008	2010	

3.4   Content Analysis

Twenty-seven articles were downloaded (including the seven that made up the VOSviewer clusters) and used for a content analysis with MAXQDA. From the content analysis, a word cloud showing the most recurring keywords in the articles was generated (Fig. 9). Irrelevant words (prepositions, conjunctions, pronouns, etc.) were removed from the analysis. The most recurring 100 words with a minimum frequency of 3 were used for the word cloud. Table 6 shows the top 10 recurring words (some of which are further reviewed in the discussion section) and their frequencies.

Fig. 9. Word cloud generated from content analysis

Table 6. Top 10 most recurring words and their frequencies from content analysis

	Word	Frequency
1	Surgery	816
2	Robot	796
3	Human	543
4	System	534
5	Control	474
6	Interaction	380
7	Use	338
8	Data	322
9	Research	308
10	Robotics	300

4   Discussion

Robotic-assisted surgery is a form of minimally invasive surgery that is rapidly gar-
nering popularity in different academic and research disciplines including medicine,
engineering, robotics, and design. One of the core concepts of human-centered design
is to actively involve end-users and appropriate stakeholders in the engineering design
process (Margetis et al. 2021). This is especially important in the case of surgical robotics
due to the complex and critical nature of surgeries. As surgical robots evolve from tools
to being a major part of surgical teams, the dynamics of human-human and human-
robot interactions might evolve as necessary to meet the demands of surgical procedures
(Chen and Barnes 2021). Technical and non-technical skills play a key role in seamless
surgical HRI. In this work, we analyze the scientific literature for trends in the field from
a technical and non-technical stance and attempt to summarize such efforts. Similar
bibliometric analyses have also been used to explore scientific trends in other healthcare
contexts (Chen et al. 2018; Liu et al. 2020).

In this study, we found that GS had the highest publication count among all three
databases for the same search keywords "Surgery" AND "Human-robot interaction" (p
< 0.05). One huge limitation of the one-way ANOVA conducted in this study was that its
input data failed the Shapiro-Wilk's normality test (Shapiro and Wilk 1965). However,
research has shown that the one-way ANOVA, in terms of Type 1 error, remains a valid
statistical procedure under slight, moderate, and robust deviations from non-normality
(Blanca et al. 2017). Furthermore, a recent study found that from 2,448,055 citations of
2,299 highly-cited publications in English-language from 252 subject categories published in 2006, GS consistently found the largest percentage of citations across all areas
(93%–96%), ahead of Scopus (35%–77%) and WoS (27%–73%) (Martín-Martín et al.
2018).

The Vicinitas results show timelines depicting an increasing interest in the field of
RAS on Twitter. Research has shown that the most common Twitter analysis consists of
examining trends and peaks in discussion activity about a given topic over time (Kim
et al. 2013). An increasing trend might be due to an increase in tweet volume and/or an
increase in Twitter users for the given timeframe. The goal of our Twitter analysis was to
initially explore trends and confirm that research in the field is rapidly growing. Hence,
we limited the timeframe of the Twitter analysis to 10 days. Consequently, the increased
trend in our results is more likely associated with an increase in tweet volume related to
"robotic-assisted surgery" than an increase in Twitter users the 10 days period.

Publication yield in the surgical HRI was low and plateaued in the 20th century
as seen in the plot of publication yield per year based on Google scholar's metadata
search (see Fig. 3). From the 21st century, we see a steady yield increase from 2010 and
a more drastic increase from 2016. This might suggest that there's been an increased
adoption of RAS, and subsequently, more research is being done on surgical HRI. The
trend analysis with Google Ngram shows that the phrase "robotic surgery" started rising
in the late 20th century while both phrases "laparoscopic surgery" and "open surgery"
have been around before then. The use of robotic systems is still an emerging technology in surgical procedures. This emergence is very likely associated with the lower
popularity of robotic surgery compared with that of laparoscopic and open surgery as
seen from Google Ngram. However, as of 2019, the phrase "laparoscopic surgery" was

more popular than "open surgery". At its most basic level, a robotic-assisted surgery is a robotic-assisted laparoscopic surgery in which surgeon-teleoperated robotic arms perform the laparoscopic surgery. Hence, the exclusion of the phrase "robotic-assisted laparoscopic surgery" might have affected the lower trends of the "robotic surgery" bigram.

The co-citation network with VOSviewer was created with seven articles that met the inclusion criterion of the analysis. Two of these articles were also shown by CiteSpace to have strong citation bursts (Barbash and Glied 2010; Ahlering et al. 2003). Since VOSviewer does not provide additional details on clusters, we attempt to figure out why. The first cluster in the network consists of (Barbash and Glied 2010; Dindo et al. 2004; Walker et al. 2009). These studies looked at the effect of different surgical procedures (hernia repairs, hysterectomies, cholecystectomy, gastric bypass, etc.) and technologies used (robotic, laparoscopic, open or laparotomy) on surgical costs and patient outcomes including but not limited to surgical complications, 6-weeks morbidity and mortality, and hospital length of stay. The second cluster in the network consists of articles that focused on studying surgical robotic systems in different contexts (Ahlering et al. 2003; Giulianotti et al. 2003; Lanfranco et al. 2004). These include: 1) the transfer of open surgery skills to robotic systems, 2) the feasibility of successfully using robotic systems in large community hospitals, and 3) the history, development, and applications of surgical robotic systems. Finally, the third cluster had just one article (Clavien et al. 2009). This study critically evaluated an existing classification of surgical complications (Dindo et al. 2004) from the perspective of its use in the literature. The authors concluded that the classification is valid and applicable worldwide in many fields of surgery and any modification to the classification is unnecessary. Given that this study built off Dindo, Demartines, and Clavien's work in 2004, it makes sense that they are co-cited (although in different clusters: 1 and 3).

In this study, we reported two sets of keywords from the CiteSpace co-citation network of seven clusters (Table 4). The first set of keywords was generated by LLR. Of these, two keywords depict different types of reproductive cancers: prostate (a common cancer that occurs in the prostate, a small walnut-shaped gland in males that produces seminal fluid) and endometrial (a cancer that occurs in the uterus, the hollow, pear-shaped organ where a baby grows in a woman's body). In the United States, the adoption of robotic-assisted radical prostatectomy (a procedure to remove the prostate gland and seminal vesicles after a prostate cancer diagnosis) increased from 0.7% to 42% from 2003 to 2010 (Chang et al. 2015). One study reviewed data of adult patients who underwent hysterectomy (a surgical procedure to remove the uterus) for endometrial cancer in the US between 2008 and 2015 and found that the incidence of robotic-assisted hysterectomy increased from 9.5% to 56.8%. (Casarin et al. 2020). Unsurprisingly, hysterectomy was a cluster keyword generated by both LLR and MI. Another group of LLR keywords are types of surgical procedures: lobectomy, hysterectomy, cystectomy, and total knee arthroplasty (TKA). Lobectomy involves the removal one of the lobes of the lungs, cystectomy is the removal of all or part of the urinary bladder, while a TKA resurfaces a knee damaged by arthritis. From 2011 to 2015, one study found that the number of robotic-assisted lobectomies saw an absolute increase of 10% (Oh et al. 2017) while the use of robotic-assisted radical cystectomy across 279 US hospitals increased from 0.6%

to 12.8% between 2004 and 2010 (Leow et al. 2014). Robotic-assisted TKA has been found to be significantly more accurate for component positioning when compared to other conventional techniques (Deckey et al. 2021) and alluding to this, accuracy was one of the MI cluster keywords. In New York State alone, robotic-assisted TKA increased by 500% from 2009 to 2013 (Naziri et al. 2019). Other keywords (from both LLR and MI) include robotic, robotic technology, artificial intelligence, da Vinci surgery, utilization of minimally invasive surgery, and treatment. These keywords all allude to the growing popularity of the robotic technologies in surgeries.

Of the top 10 articles with the strongest citation bursts, 3 were published in the Journal of the American Medical Association, a medical journal published by the American Medical Association (Wright et al. 2013; Jayne et al. 2017; Hu et al. 2009) while 2 were published in European Urology, a medical journal covering urology (Ficarra et al. 2009; Menon et al. 2007). The top 10 articles with the strongest citation bursts showed strong relationship with some of the CiteSpace cluster keywords. Of these articles, 4 covered robot-assisted prostatectomies (Menon et al. 2007; Ahlering et al. 2003; Ficarra et al. 2009; Hu et al. 2009), 2 of them were on robotic-assisted hysterectomy (Paraiso et al. 2013; Wright et al. 2013), while 1 focused on lobectomy (Swanson et al. 2014). The remaining 3 articles covered robotic-assisted resection for rectal cancer (Jayne et al. 2017), cost of RAS (Barbash and Glied 2010), and statistics of 36 types of cancers in 185 countries (Bray et al. 2018).

Finally, the results of the content analysis carried out in this study further contributes to the literature on the different facets of surgical HRI. Words like "robot", "control", and "robotics" might allude to the technical aspects of RAS while words like "human", "system", and "interaction" might point to the human aspects of RAS. Research has revealed a range of human factors and socio-technical systems issues associated with RAS (Pennathur et al. 2013; Blandford et al. 2014; Catchpole et al. 2019), and some studies have specifically focused on non-technical skills of surgeons in RAS (Manuguerra et al. 2021; Schreyer et al. 2022). To better design seamless and effective surgical HRIs, more collaboration between medical, robotics, and Human Factors research communities would be beneficial. The development of tools and frameworks that enable rapid prototyping and testing of research ideas in surgical robotics would also be helpful. For example, the National Science Foundation recently funded a proposal to develop adaptive control algorithms for teleoperated robotic surgical systems that can respond to, ignore, and/or augment human motor control inputs depending on the output of user-centric models of behavior and task difficulty (National Science Foundation 2020). This work (Boehm et al. 2021; Battaglia et al. 2021), as well as others, could lead to significant improvements in the design of surgical robotic systems while considering the abilities, limitations, and capabilities of surgeons and the environment of use.

5   Conclusion

In this work, we conducted several analyses to study bibliometric trends in the field of surgical HRI. Our findings highlight the growing literature from this interdisciplinary field while emphasizing the importance of both technical and non-technical aspects of surgical robotics.

References

Aaltonen, L.E, Wahlström, M., Ja, J., Wihurin, A., Suomen Akatemia, R.: Envisioning robotic surgery: surgeons' needs and views on interacting with future technologies and interfaces. Int. J. Med. Robot. Comput. Assist. Surg.**14**(6), e1941 (2018) https://doi.org/10.1002/RCS.1941

Abdelaal, A.E., Mathur, P., Salcudean, S.E.: Robotics in vivo: a perspective on human–robot interaction in surgical robotics. **3**(May), 221–242 (2020). https://doi.org/10.1146/ANNUREV-CONTROL-091219-013437

Ahlering, T.E., Skarecky, D., Lee, D., Clayman, R.V.: Successful transfer of open surgical skills to a laparoscopic environment using a robotic interface: initial experience with laparoscopic radical prostatectomy. J. Urology **170**(5), 1738–1741 (2003)https://doi.org/10.1097/01.ju.000 0092881.24608.5e

American College of Surgeons. American College of Surgeons Definition of Surgery Legislative Toolkit (2007). https://www.facs.org/-/media/files/advocacy/state/definition-of-surgery-legisl ative-toolkit.ashx

Barbash, G.I., Glied, S.A.: New technology and health care costs-the case of robot-assisted surgery. N. Engl. J. Med. **363**(8), 701–704 (2010)

Battaglia, E., Boehm, J., Zheng, Y., Jamieson, A.R., Gahan, J., Fey, A.M.: Rethinking autonomous surgery: focusing on enhancement over autonomy. Eur. Urol. Focus **7**(4), 696–705 (2021). https://doi.org/10.1016/J.EUF.2021.06.009

Blanca, M.J., Alarcón, R., Arnau, J., Bono, R., Bendayan, R.: Non-normal data: is ANOVA still a valid option? Psicothema **29**(4), 552–557 (2017). https://redined.educacion.gob.es/xmlui/bit stream/handle/11162/151020/Psicothema%202017%2c%20Vol.%2029%2c%20No.%204% 2c%20552-557.pdf?sequence=1&isAllowed=y

Blandford, A., Furniss, D., Vincent, C.: Patient safety and interactive medical devices: realigning work as imagined and work as done. Clin. Risk **20**(5), 107–110 (2014). https://doi.org/10.1177/ 1356262214556550

Boehm, J.R., Fey, N.P., Fey, A.M.: Online Recognition of Bimanual Coordination Provides Important Context for Movement Data in Bimanual Teleoperated Robots. In: IEEE International Conference on Intelligent Robots and Systems, pp. 6248–55 (2021). https://doi.org/10.1109/ IROS51168.2021.9636272

Bray, F., Ferlay, J., Soerjomataram, I., Siegel, R.L., Torre, L.A., Jemal, A.: Global Cancer Statistics 2018: GLOBOCAN Estimates of Incidence and Mortality Worldwide for 36 Cancers in 185 Countries. Cancer J. Clin. **68**(6): 394–424 (2018). https://doi.org/10.3322/CAAC.21492

Burgar, C.G., Lum, P.S., Shor, P.C., Machiel van der Loos, H.F.: Development of robots for rehabilitation therapy: the Palo Alto VA/Stanford experience. J. Rehabil. Res. Dev. **37**(6), 663–673 (2000)

Casarin, J., et al.: Implementing robotic surgery for uterine cancer in the United States: better outcomes without increased costs. Gynecol. Oncol. **156**(2), 451–458 (2020). https://doi.org/ 10.1016/J.YGYNO.2019.11.016

Catchpole, K., et al.: Human factors in robotic assisted surgery: lessons from studies 'in the Wild.' Appl. Ergon. **78**, 270–276 (2019). https://doi.org/10.1016/J.APERGO.2018.02.011

Chang, S.L., Kibel, A.S., Brooks, J.D., Chung, B.I.: The impact of robotic surgery on the surgical management of prostate cancer in the USA. BJU Int. **115**(6), 929–936 (2015). https://doi.org/ 10.1111/BJU.12850

Chen, C.: CiteSpace II: detecting and visualizing emerging trends and transient patterns in scientific literature. J. Am. Soc. Inform. Sci. Technol. **57**(3), 359–377 (2006). https://doi.org/10.1002/ asi.20317

Chen, J.Y.C., Barnes, M.J.: Human-Robot Interaction. In: Salvendy, G., Karwowski, W. (eds.) Handbook of Human Factors and Ergonomics, pp. 1121–1142. Wiley, New Jersey (2021) https://doi.org/10.1002/9781119636113.CH44

Chen, X., Haoran Xie, F., Wang, L., Liu, Z., Juan, X., Hao, T.: A bibliometric analysis of natural language processing in medical research. BMC Med. Inform. Decis. Mak. **18**(1), 1–14 (2018). https://doi.org/10.1186/S12911-018-0594-X/TABLES/10

Clavien, P.A., et al.: The Clavien-Dindo classification of surgical complications: five-year experience. Ann. Surg. **250**(2), 187–196 (2009). https://doi.org/10.1097/SLA.0b013e3181b13ca2

Deckey, D.G., et al.: Robotic-assisted total knee arthroplasty improves accuracy and precision compared to conventional techniques. Bone Joint J. **103-B**(7), 74–80 (2021). https://doi.org/10.1302/0301-620X.103B6.BJJ-2020-2003.R1/ASSET/IMAGES/LARGE/BJJ-2020-2003.R1-GALLEYFIG1.JPEG

Dindo, D., Demartines, N., Clavien, P.A.: Classification of surgical complications: a new proposal with evaluation in a cohort of 6336 patients and results of a survey. Ann. Surg. **240**(2), 205–213 (2004). https://doi.org/10.1097/01.sla.0000133083.54934.ae

van Eck, N.J., Waltman, L.: VOSviewer: visualizing scientific landscapes. VOSviewer (2019). https://www.vosviewer.com/

Egghe, L.: Theory and practise of the G-Index. Scientometrics **69**(1), 131–152 (2006)

Farivar, B.S., Flannagan, M., Michael Leitman, I.: General surgery residents' perception of robot-assisted procedures during surgical training. J. Surg. Educ. **72**(2), 235–242 (2015). https://doi.org/10.1016/J.JSURG.2014.09.008

Ficarra, V., et al.: Retropubic, laparoscopic, and robot-assisted radical prostatectomy: a systematic review and cumulative analysis of comparative studies. Eur. Urol. **55**(5), 1037–1063 (2009). https://doi.org/10.1016/J.EURURO.2009.01.036

Ficuciello, F., Siciliano, B., Villani, L.: Impedance control of redundant manipulators for safe human-robot collaboration. Acta Polytechnica Hungarica **13**(1), 223–38 (2016). https://doi.org/10.12700/APH.13.1.2016.1.15

KGiulianotti, P.C., et al.: Robotics in General Surgery: per-sonal experience in a large community hospital. Arch. Surg. **138**(7), 777–784 (2003). https://doi.org/10.1007/978-1-4614-8739-5

Goodrich, M.A., Schultz, A.C.: Human-Robot Interaction: A Survey. Now Publishers Inc. (2008)

Google Books. 2010: Google Ngram Viewer (2010). https://books.google.com/ngrams

Harzing, A.: Publish or Perish (2006). http://www.harzing.com/pop/htm

Hu, J.C., et al.: Comparative effectiveness of minimally invasive vs open radical prostatectomy. JAMA **302**(14), 1557–1564 (2009). https://doi.org/10.1001/JAMA.2009.1451

Intuitive Surgical Inc.: Intuitive Surgical, Inc. 2016 Annual Report (2016). http://www.intuitivesurgical.com/

Jayne, D., et al.: Effect of robotic-assisted vs conventional laparoscopic surgery on risk of conversion to open laparotomy among patients undergoing resection for rectal cancer: the ROLARR randomized clinical trial. JAMA **318**(16), 1569–1580 (2017). https://doi.org/10.1001/JAMA.2017.7219

Khalafallah, Y.M., et al.: Residents' views on the impact of robotic surgery on general surgery education. J. Surg. Educ. **78**(3), 1007–1012 (2021). https://doi.org/10.1016/J.JSURG.2020.10.003

Kim, A.E., Hansen, H.M., Murphy, J., Richards, A.K., Duke, J., Allen, J.A.: Methodological considerations in analyzing twitter data. JNCI Monographs **2013**(47), 140–146 (2013). https://doi.org/10.1093/JNCIMONOGRAPHS/LGT026

Lanfranco, A.R., Castellanos, A.E., Desai, J.P., Meyers, W.C.: Robotic surgery: a current perspective. Ann. Surg. **239**(1), 14–21 (2004)

Leow, J.J., et al.: Propensity-matched comparison of morbidity and costs of open and robot-assisted radical cystectomies: a contemporary population-based analysis in the United States. Eur. Urol. **66**(3), 569–576 (2014). https://doi.org/10.1016/J.EURURO.2014.01.029

Liu, C., et al.: A scientometric analysis and visualization of research on Parkinson's disease associated with pesticide exposure. Front. Public Health **8**(April), 91 (2020). https://doi.org/10.3389/FPUBH.2020.00091/BIBTEX

Liu, R., Liu, Q., Wang, Z.: Worldwide diffusion of robotic approach in general surgery. Updat. Surg. **73**(3), 795–797 (2021). https://doi.org/10.1007/s13304-020-00914-3

Manuguerra, A., et al.: Non-technical skills in robotic surgery and impact on near-miss events: a multi-center study. Surg. Endosc. **35**(9), 5062–5071 (2021). https://doi.org/10.1007/S00464-020-07988-5/TABLES/6

Mapara, S.S., Patravale, V.B.: Medical capsule robots: a renaissance for diagnostics, drug delivery and surgical treatment. J. Control. Release **261**(September), 337–351 (2017). https://doi.org/10.1016/J.JCONREL.2017.07.005

Margetis, G., Ntoa, S., Antona, M., Stephanidis, C.: Human-centered design of artificial intelligence. In: Salvendy, G., Karwowski, W. (eds.) Handbook of Human Factors and Ergonomics, pp. 1085–1106. Wiley, New Jersey (2021). https://doi.org/10.1002/9781119636113.CH42

Martín-Martín, A., Orduna-Malea, E., Thelwall, M., López-Cózar, E.D.: Google scholar, web of science, and scopus: a systematic comparison of citations in 252 subject categories. J. Informet. **12**(4), 1160–1177 (2018). https://doi.org/10.1016/J.JOI.2018.09.002

Menon, M., et al.: Vattikuti Institute prostatectomy: contemporary technique and analysis of results. Eur. Urol. **51**(3), 648–658 (2007). https://doi.org/10.1016/J.EURURO.2006.10.055

Michel, J.B., et al.: Quantitative analysis of culture using millions of digitized books. Science **331**(6014), 176–182 (2011). https://doi.org/10.1126/SCIENCE.1199644/SUPPL_FILE/MICHEL.SOM.REVISION.2.SOM_DATA.XLSX

Minitab Inc: Minitab 17 Statistical Software. State College (2010). www.minitab.com

National Science Foundation: CAREER: Human-Centric Control for Teleoperated Surgical Robots (2020). https://nsf.gov/awardsearch/showAward?AWD_ID=2109635&HistoricalAwards=false

Naziri, Q., et al.: The trends in robotic-assisted knee arthroplasty: a statewide database study. J. Orthop. **16**(3), 298–301 (2019).https://doi.org/10.1016/J.JOR.2019.04.020

Oh, D.S., Reddy, R.M., Gorrepati, M.L., Mehendale, S., Reed, M.F.: Robotic-assisted, video-assisted thoracoscopic and open lobectomy: propensity-matched analysis of recent premier data. Ann. Thorac. Surg. **104**(5), 1733–1740 (2017). https://doi.org/10.1016/J.ATHORACSUR.2017.06.020

Paraiso, M.F.R., et al.: A randomized trial comparing conventional and robotically assisted total laparoscopic hysterectomy. Am. J. Obstetrics Gynecol. **208**(5), 368.e1–368.e7 (2013)https://doi.org/10.1016/J.AJOG.2013.02.008

Pennathur, P.R.: Technologies in the Wild (TiW): human factors implications for patient safety in the cardiovascular operating room. **56**(2), 205–219 (2013). https://doi.org/10.1080/00140139.2012.757655

Randell, R., et al.: Impact of robotic surgery on decision making: perspectives of surgical teams. In: AMIA Annual Symposium Proceedings (2015). 1057./pmc/articles/PMC4765621/

Riek, L.D.: "Robotics technology in mental health care. Artif. Intell. Behav. Mental Health Care, 185–203 (2016). https://doi.org/10.1016/B978-0-12-420248-1.00008-8

Schiff, L., Tsafrir, Z., Aoun, J., Taylor, A., Theoharis, E., Eisenstein, D.: Quality of communication in robotic surgery and surgical outcomes. JSLS : Journal of the Society of Laparoendoscopic Surgeons **20**(3) (2016). https://doi.org/10.4293/JSLS.2016.00026

Schreyer, J., et al.: RAS-NOTECHS: validity and reliability of a tool for measuring non-technical skills in robotic-assisted surgery settings. Surg. Endosc. **36**(3), 1916–1926 (2022). https://doi.org/10.1007/S00464-021-08474-2/FIGURES/2

Shapiro, S.S., Wilk, M.B.: An Analysis of variance test for normality (complete samples). Biometrika **52**(3/4), 591 (1965). https://doi.org/10.2307/2333709

Small, H.: Co-citation in the scientific literature: a new measure of the relationship between two documents. J. Am. Soc. Inf. Sci. **24**(4), 265–269 (1973). https://doi.org/10.1002/ASI.463024 0406

Swanson, S.J., et al.: Comparing robot-assisted thoracic surgical lobectomy with conventional video-assisted thoracic surgical lobectomy and wedge resection: results from a multihospital database (premier). J. Thorac. Cardiovasc. Surg. **147**(3), 929–937 (2014). https://doi.org/10.1016/J.JTCVS.2013.09.046

Tiferes, J., et al.: Are gestures worth a thousand words? Verbal and nonverbal communication during robot-assisted surgery. Appl. Ergon. **78**(July), 251–262 (2019). https://doi.org/10.1016/J.APERGO.2018.02.015

Tiferes, J., et al.: The loud surgeon behind the console: understanding team activities during robot-assisted surgery. J. Surg. Educ. **73**(3), 504–512 (2016). https://doi.org/10.1016/J.JSURG.2015.12.009

VERBI Software: MAXQDA 2022. Berlin (2021). https://www.maxqda.com

Vicinitas: Understand How Twitter Users Engage with Your Content (2022). https://www.vicinitas.io/

Walker, J.L., et al.: Laparoscopy compared with laparotomy for comprehensive surgical staging of uterine cancer: gynecologic oncology group study LAP2. J. Clin. Oncol. **27**(32), 5331–5336 (2009)

Wright, J.D., et al.: Robotically assisted vs laparoscopic hysterectomy among women with benign gynecologic disease. JAMA **309**(7), 689–98 (2013). https://doi.org/10.1001/JAMA.2013.186

Human Intention Recognition for Safe Robot Action Planning Using Head Pose

Luka Orsag$^{(\boxtimes)}$ ⓘ, Tomislav Stipancic ⓘ, Leon Koren ⓘ, and Karlo Posavec

Faculty of Mechanical Engineering and Naval Architecture, University of Zagreb,
Zagreb, Croatia
orsagluka@gmail.com

Abstract. An efficient collaborative work between a person and technical system requires a deeper understanding of the human nature including social, cognitive, emotional or any other relationship that the person could have toward the technical system. Such relationships depend also on the case or specific knowledge about the current task they are performing together. Due to safety reasons, increased variability of new products, flexibility, and demands for defect-resistant production, a contemporary production lack such applications where people and robots operate together using social signals or contextual information.

The new paradigms that connect vision of Industry 4.0 with artificial intelligence, robotics, and computer networks are inevitably starting the new era of emerging ubiquitous production cells that will be used in factories of the future.

Authors propose an addition to a safety framework using a worker intention recognition with head pose information. As an indicator of intentions of a person in everyday communication, besides the experiences that represent a priori knowledge, humans are relying on social signals.

Keywords: Human-robot collaboration · Intention recognition · Action recognition · Deep neural networks · LSTM

1 Introduction

Mutual understanding between a man and the system can allow a robust, a self-healing and a self-configurable production, enabling a survival of such productions on the market while making a profit. The problem is focused not only on intention but also on action recognition where the system should recognize the signs that could make the overall interaction more natural and efficient [1].

An efficient collaborative work between a person and a technical system requires a deeper understanding of the human nature including social, cognitive, emotional or any other relationships that the person could have toward the technical system [2]. Such relationships depend also on the case or specific knowledge about the current task they are performing together [3]. Due to safety reasons, increased variability of new products, flexibility, and demands for defect-resistant production, contemporary productions lack such applications where people and robots operate together using social signals or contextual information [4, 5].

M. Kurosu et al. (Eds.): HCII 2022, LNCS 13519, pp. 313–327, 2022.
https://doi.org/10.1007/978-3-031-17618-0_23

Head pose is regularly used in everyday communication on many occasions; for example, to start, control or to stop the social interaction; to focus a person's attention, to express emotions, to confirm or support expressions generated by some other body parts, etc. [6, 7].

Combined with activity recognition [8, 9], an intelligent agent displays active safety features presented as online task switching. Classification of human actions is an ongoing research problem in computer vision [10]. Face alignment is the process of determining the face shape, i.e., the location of characteristic facial features or landmarks (points that delineate eyes, nose, mouth, eyebrows, chin, and face contour) given a face image [1, 11].

Since the motion of a person's head pose and gaze direction are closely related to intention and attention of a person, detection of such information can be utilized to control the robot movements.

Models developed in this work enable an effective classification of intentions that allows the robot to robustly recognize social behaviors of the human co-worker based on a head pose intention recognition [12, 13]. These insights are then used to plan the robot movements during the joint operations within the shared environment [14–16].

2 System Design

The entire system is designed around belief that human action is followed by intention. Authors aim to test the hypothesis that human intention precedes action and can be recognized as a set of subsequent head movements. Visual head pose estimation is already well known in research and practice so it can be used for systems where real-time processing must be taken into consideration, as shown in Fig. 1.

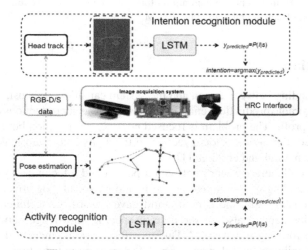

Fig. 1. Intention recognition system proposal

Some authors therefore employ a custom-made method for autonomous detection and adaptation of the light settings, as reported in [17]. For this work LSTM [18] networks are used because of their ability to process and reason spatiotemporal signals such as head pose (represented as Euler angles). Ground truth (GT) is acquired from InHARD dataset which provides motion capture (MOCAP) data stored in BVH files (BioVision Hierarchy), which are a way of storing the skeletal tree-like structures represented as human joints along with their motion data. The Buman-Robot Collaboration (HRC) Interface is implemented and visualized in CoppeliaSim environment.

2.1 Head Pose Estimation

Two methods for head pose data acquisition were investigated: The first one is using the OAK-D platform and the second one is using the visage|SDK face tracking capabilities.

OAK-D is a spatial AI powerhouse, capable of simultaneously running advanced neural networks while providing depth from two stereo cameras and color information from a single 4K camera in the center as presented in Fig. 2.

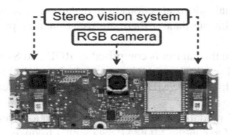

Fig. 2. OAK-D camera

For this approach authors exploit the possibility to use a pre-trained OpenVINO model available online and porting it to the platform. The algorithm is implemented in python programming language using libraries available for OAK-D programming. Proposed model implements a face detector based on SqueezeNet light (half-channels) as a backbone with a single Single Shot Detection (SSD) for indoor/outdoor scenes shot by a front-facing camera.

The second method of head pose data acquisition, as mentioned, is using the visage|SDK's face tracking and analysis features (Fig. 3).

The method is investigated since the SDK provides a convenience of quick and effortless head tracking. Other than being lightweight, fast and accurate another reason for using it in investigation is its proven use in various fields of industry and is more likely to be used for HRC applications in industrial sector where real-time capabilities are of interest and vital importance.

Both methods show head tracking capabilities with world coordinate system translations and Euler angles as output.

Fig. 3. Single shot head pose estimated and visualized using visage|SDK

2.2 InHARD Dataset

The InHARD dataset [19] is a large-scale RGB +Skeleton action recognition dataset named "Industrial Human Action Recognition Dataset". It includes 4804 different action samples spread over 38 videos collected from 14 industrial action classes. In comparison with other existing action recognition datasets, which are comprised of daily activities, Authors of propose actual industrial actions from real use-case scenarios in an industrial environment. Along with the dataset there are usage metrics proposed for algorithm evaluation.

As mentioned above the dataset is comprised of RGB and Skeleton data. The RGB data is recorded from three different angles (top, left side and right side) to capture the complete action and help improve ML algorithm performance in cases where occlusion occurs.

For the "Skeleton" modality a "Combination Perception Neuron 32 Edition v2" motion sensor was used to capture MOCAP data with a frequency of 120 Hz. Skeleton data comprizes the 3D locations (Tx, Ty and Tz) of 17 major body joints along with their rotations (Rx, Ry and Rz). Skeleton data is saved in standard BVH file format (Fig. 4).

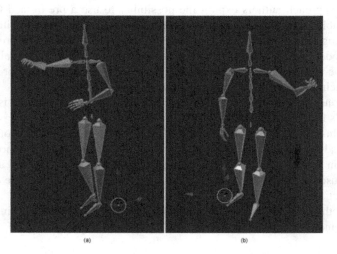

Fig. 4. InHARD dataset examples visualized using Blender: (a) Picking in front (b) Picking left

Authors have identified 14 different low-level classes, as presented in Table 1, and 72 high level classes where actions are a lot more accurate.

Table 1. InHARD dataset low level action classes

ID	Meta action label
0	No action
1	Consult sheets
2	Turn sheets
3	Take screwdriver
4	Put down screwdriver
5	Picking in front
6	Picking left
7	Take measuring rod
8	Put down measuring rod
9	Take component
10	Put down component
11	Assemble system
12	Take subsystem
13	Put down subsystem

Each class mentioned in Table 1 is annotated as a time interval for each sequence of data and represent human activity. The data as such cannot be used for training ML algorithms to recognize intent. However, since the work is based on belief that for each of the actions an intention can be measured, the existing annotations were artificially augmented thus creating a new annotation list as described in Fig. 5.

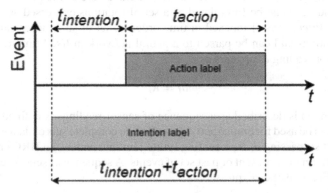

Fig. 5. Dataset augmentation by labels time interval expansion

2.3 Human Intention Recognition

Human Action Recognition (HAR) aims to understand human behaviors which enable the computing systems to proactively assist users based on their requirement [20]. Formally speaking, suppose a user is performing activities belonging to a predefined intention set A. Like HAR we define a set of intentions I in order to formulate the problem of Human Intention recognition (HIR).

$$I = \{i_i\}_{i=1}^{m} \tag{1}$$

where m denotes the number of activity classes. There is a sequence of sensor reading that captures the activity information

$$s = \{d_1, d_2, \cdots, d_t, \cdots, d_n\} \tag{2}$$

where d_t denotes the sensor reading at time t. We need to build a model $\mathcal{F}$ to predict the activity sequence based on sensor reading s

$$\hat{I} = \left\{\hat{i}_j\right\}_{j=1}^{n} = \mathcal{F}(s), \hat{i}_j \in I \tag{3}$$

while the true activity sequence, or the ground truth (GT), is denoted as

$$I^* = \left\{i_j^*\right\}_{j=1}^{n}, i_j^* \in A \tag{4}$$

given that $n \geq m$.

We then chose a positive loss function $\mathcal{L}(\mathcal{F}(s), I^*)$ to minimize the discrepancy between $\hat{I}$ and I^*. In this work a multi-class categorical cross-entropy loss function is used

$$\mathcal{L}\big(\mathcal{F}(s), I^*\big) = - \sum_{c=1}^{n} i_c^* \log\big(P\big(\hat{i}_c\big)\big) \tag{5}$$

The list of output classes is comprised of twelve actions adopted from InHARD dataset forming an output vector I. The actions included are as mentioned in Table 1.

Every head pose can be formulated as a set of rotations expressed as Euler angles $R_k = \{Roll_k, Pitch_k, Yaw_k\}$ indexed in time order. A set of such poses can be used to describe intentions and can be parsed to a neural network in fixed timeframes. In that case one sensor reading d_t appears as

$$d_t = R_t \tag{6}$$

Vector s in (1) is described as a sequence of sensor readings is defined as a sliding window and can be used for human activity analysis in complete sets of data where d_n is in fact a moment surpassing d_t representing future joint movement. In HRC environments sensors can obtain only present or past set of events. A sequence of sensor readings [21], presented in Fig. 6, is then expressed as

$$s = \{d_{t-n}, \cdots, d_{t-2}, d_{t-1}, d_t\} \tag{7}$$

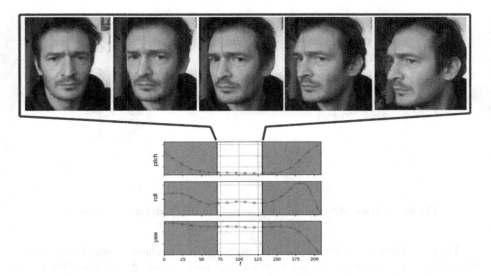

Fig. 6. A set of sensor readings representation for neural network's input layer

The chosen model implements a deep neural network (DNN) with hidden LSTM layers (Fig. 7). We use rectified linear activation function (ReLu) since it overcomes vanishing gradient problems present in RNNs [22] and allows models to learn faster and perform better and the *Softmax* function (Fig. 8) is used as an output layer from the NN since the desired output is a vector of probabilities. The probabilities of each value are proportional to the relative scale of each value in the vector and are interpreted as probabilities of membership of each class.

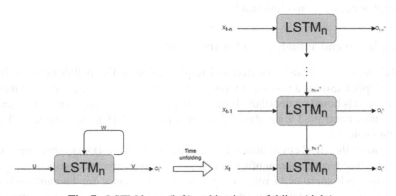

Fig. 7. LSTM layer (left) and its time unfolding (right)

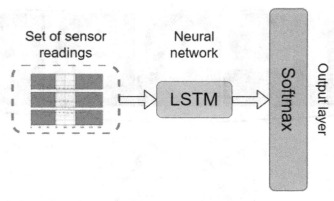

Fig. 8. Overview of the entire LSTM network model for intention recognition

The probabilities of each value are proportional to the relative scale of each value in the vector and are interpreted as probabilities of membership of each class. The $\hat{i}_{class}$ takes the shape of (8).

$$\hat{i}_{class} = P(i|s) \tag{8}$$

The final output is calculated as follows

$$\hat{y} = argmax\left(\hat{I}\right) \tag{9}$$

Metric for model performance evaluation is accuracy but since the problem has a multi-class output it is important to evaluate how well the model differentiates the classes, so the confusion matrix was also calculated, and the training graphs are included as well which display accuracy and loss results.

2.4   Simulation and Visualization Environment

The HRC environment was modeled and implemented in CoppeliaSimEdu software package. CoppeliaSim is a robotic environment simulator, with integrated development environment. It is based on distributed control architecture, meaning that each object can be individually controlled via embedded script, a plugin, ROS node, remote API client or a custom solution.

In this work the HRC environment is modeled as shared workspace between human and robot partner forming a manufacturing team. The workspace consists of two tables representing work surfaces, a robot on a mount and a space for human worker. As presented in Fig. 9. The human worker is represented as a set of joints acquired from InHARD dataset. The topmost joint represents the head, and the red line describes the head pose vector. Green boxes are placed on top of work surfaces to represent the intention activated safety zones.

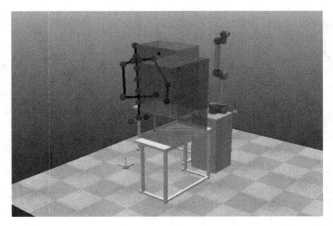

Fig. 9. HRC environment modelled in CoppeliaSim software package (Color figure online)

3   Results

In this section authors present the training and simulation results. After training intention recognition network (and in similar way action recognition), accuracy and confusion matrices were generated. The overall results were also evaluated through visual
inspection in CoppeliaSim environment.

3.1   Intention Recognition

Two networks were trained: (1) a network with three hidden layers, and (2) a network
with 5 hidden layers. The networks were trained in 100 epochs with batch sizes of 32.

Neural network with 5 hidden layers scored 75.344% accuracy on validation data
while the network with 3 layers scored ~ 65% as presented in Figs. 10 and 11. The
confusion matrix was also calculated and is presented in Fig. 12.

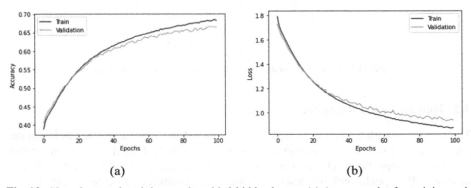

(a)   (b)

Fig. 10. Neural network training results with 3 hidden layers: (a) Accuracy plot for training and
validation, (b) Training and validation loss plot

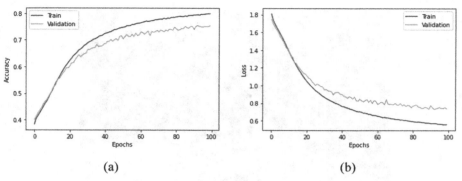

(a)   (b)

Fig. 11. Neural network training results with 5 hidden layers: (a) Accuracy plot for training and validation, (b) Training and validation loss plot

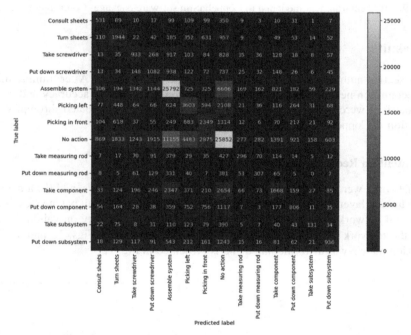

Fig. 12. Confusion matrix for intention recognition network

3.2 Human Action Recognition

The neural network for action recognition was trained in a similar manner as intention recognition but with human worker joint positions and only 4 labels were used for the Proof of Concept (PoC). The network scored ~ 93% accuracy on validation data. It was trained in 500 epochs with batch sizes of 64 and the results are presented in Fig. 13.

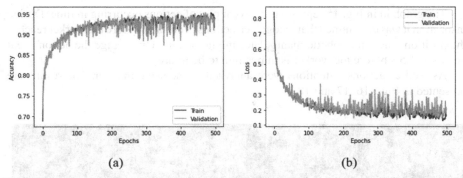

Fig. 13. Neural network for action recognition training results with 5 hidden layers: (a) Accuracy plot for training and validation, (b) Training and validation loss plot

The confusion matrix was also calculated and is presented in Fig. 14.

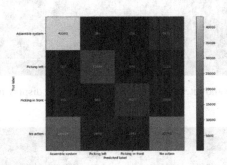

Fig. 14. Confusion matrix for action recognition network

3.3 Overall System Results

Finally, in this section, overall system results are discussed. As mentioned at the beginning of this section the overall results are visually inspected in CoppeliaSim environment. The basis for evaluation was to examine the ability of the system to detect certain intentions before subsequent member actions occur. Inspection was done by examining graphs implemented in environment.

Fig. 15. Action events visualized in CoppeliaSim graph

The graph in in Fig. 15 represents an event plot of actions occurring in time. During inspection it was determined that recognized actions occur well before the worker reaches the position where the robotic manipulator might operate. On average the action event occurs 1–1.5 s before the worker is in position to be injured.

As well as actions, intentions were analyzed in the same manner. The results are presented in Figs. 16, 17 and 18.

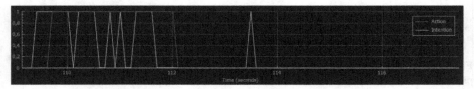

Fig. 16. Action and intention events in CoppeliaSim graph

Fig. 17. Action and intention events where intentions display noisy behavior

Fig. 18. Action and intention events where intentions are detected at the same time as action events

While there are instances where intentions occur at the same time as actions, there are also a lot of events where intentions are detected before actions. On average intention events occur 0.5 s before actions. Using that information as fused, overall safety system response is a lot quicker.

4   Conclusions and Discussion

The main goal of this work is to show how combining predictions from activity recognition and intention algorithms can give good results regarding the overall safety system performance of HRC. This work presents a PoC and a step in a development of a larger system that ensures the safety and efficiency of robotic cells teamed-up with human co-workers.

While investigating the training results and confusion matrices it was concluded that data augmentation in a manner done in this work is not a reliable one. There are a lot of actions that occur subsequently and augmentation in this way undermines the overlapping ones. This results in bad labeling in some cases which could explain poor performance of the intention recognition algorithm.

Online performance displays several issues that result in false positives. One of the issues is that actions are performed in longer time intervals than we allow the system to sample in each time step. That poses a problem since the intentions sampled (5 time steps in this case) appear as one another. To better mitigate this issue, further research on human actions and intentions is required.

Another problem that results display are noisy detections which can bring down the efficiency of the manufacturing cell since the robot has to act on that information. The problem can be solved by increasing the sampling window or by filtering output predictions frequency. Since it is not clear if the noisy data is true positive or false positive a filter that takes intention duration into account should be implemented.

While performance reveals several issues, the results display promise for this method and for future work. Performance of these algorithms can be increased by tunning algorithm hyperparameters or other methods of spatiotemporal information classification can be applied. As opposed to [23] where authors explore safety of a human worker based on detected poses, this system reacts before the pose occurs and becomes hazardous. The HRC context should be better investigated to fully grasp the requirements for collaborative robotic cells and workspaces.

Further work will include new information acquisition and data collection. The requirements for context recognition from visual inputs will be investigated to efficiently explore other modalities and human gestures present during assembly operations in factories of the future. In this way a robust computational mechanism can be designed and implemented.

Acknowledgements. This research is partially supported by Visage Technolgies AB and by the Croa-tian Science Foundation under the project "Affective Multimodal Interaction based on Constructed Robot Cognition—AMICORC (UIP-2020–02-7184)".

References

1. Mollaret, C., Mekonnen, A.A., Ferrané, I., Pinquier, J., Lerasle, F.: Perceiving user's intention-for-interaction: a probabilistic multimodal data fusion scheme. In: 2015 IEEE International Conference on Multimedia and Expo (ICME), pp. 1–6 (2015). https://doi.org/10.1109/ICME. 2015.7177514
2. Conte, D., Furukawa, T.: Autonomous robotic escort incorporating motion prediction and human intention. In: 2021 IEEE International Conference on Robotics and Automation (ICRA), pp. 3480–3486 (2021). https://doi.org/10.1109/ICRA48506.2021.9561469
3. Stipancic, T., Koren, L., Korade, D., Rosenberg, D.: PLEA: a social robot with teaching and interacting capabilities. J. Pacific Rim Psychol. 15. (2021). https://doi.org/10.1177/183449 09211037019

4. Koren, L., Stipancic, T., Ricko, A., Orsag, L.: Person localization model based on a fusion of acoustic and visual inputs. Electronics **11**(3), 440 (2022). https://doi.org/10.3390/electroni cs11030440

5. Stipancic, T., Jerbic, B., Curkovic, P.: A context-aware approach in realization of socially intelligent industrial robots. Robot. Comput. Integrated Manuf. **37**, 79–89 (2016). https://doi. org/10.1016/j.rcim.2015.07.002

6. Matsumoto, Y., Zelinsky, A.: An algorithm for real-time stereo vision implementation of head pose and gaze direction measurement. In: Proceedings Fourth IEEE International Conference on Automatic Face and Gesture Recognition (Cat. No. PR00580), pp. 499–504 (2000). https:// doi.org/10.1109/AFGR.2000.840680

7. Matsumoto, Y., Ogasawara, T., Zelinsky, A.: Behavior recognition based on head pose and gaze direction measurement. In: Proceedings. 2000 IEEE/RSJ International Conference on Intelligent Robots and Systems (IROS 2000) (Cat. No.00CH37113), vol. 3, pp. 2127–2132 (2000). https://doi.org/10.1109/IROS.2000.895285

8. Murad, A., Pyun, J.Y.: Deep recurrent neural networks for human activity recognition. Sensors **17**(11), 2556 (2017). https://doi.org/10.3390/s17112556

9. Banos, O., Galvez, J.M., Damas, M., Pomares, H., Rojas, I.: Window size impact in human activity recognition. Sensors **14**(4), 6474–6499 (2014). https://doi.org/10.3390/s140406474

10. Shaikh, M.B., Chai, D.: RGB-D data-based action recognition: a review. Sensors **21**(12), 4246 (2021). https://doi.org/10.3390/s21124246

11. Liu, X., Liang, W., Wang, Y., Li, S., Pei, M.: 3D head pose estimation with convolutional neural network trained on synthetic images. In: 2016 IEEE International Conference on Image Processing (ICIP), pp. 1289–1293 (2016). https://doi.org/10.1109/ICIP.2016.7532566

12. Huang, Y., Cui, J., Davoine, F., Zhao, H., Zha, H.: Head pose based intention prediction using Discrete Dynamic Bayesian Network. In: 2013 Seventh International Conference on Distributed Smart Cameras (ICDSC), pp. 1–6 (2013). https://doi.org/10.1109/ICDSC.2013. 6778228

13. Hjelmås, E., Low, B.K.: Face detection: a survey. Comput. Vis. Image Underst. **83**(3), 236–274 (2001). https://doi.org/10.1006/cviu.2001.0921

14. Gogić, I., Ahlberg, J., Pandžić, I.S.: Regression-based methods for face alignment: a survey. Signal Process. **178**, 107755 (2021). https://doi.org/10.1016/j.sigpro.2020.107755

15. Jerbic, B., Stipancic, T., Tomasic, T.: Robotic bodily aware interaction within human environments. In: Proceedings of the SAI Intelligent Systems Conference (IntelliSys 2015), London, UK, 10–11 November 2015. https://doi.org/10.1109/IntelliSys.2015.7361160P

16. Wang, J., Chen, Y., Hao, S., Peng, X., Hu, L.: Deep learning for sensor-based activity recognition: a survey. Pattern Recogn. Lett. **119**, 3–11 (2019). https://doi.org/10.1016/j.patrec.2018. 02.010

17. Stipancic, T., Jerbic, B.: Self-adaptive vision system. In: Camarinha-Matos, L.M., Pereira, P., Ribeiro, L. (eds.) DoCEIS 2010. IAICT, vol. 314, pp. 195–202. Springer, Heidelberg (2010). https://doi.org/10.1007/978-3-642-11628-5_21

18. Liu, J., Wang, G., Hu, P., Duan, L.Y., Kot, A.C.: Global context-aware attention LSTM networks for 3D action recognition. In: Proceedings of the IEEE Conference on Computer Vision and Pattern Recognition, pp. 1647–1656 (2017). https://doi.org/10.1109/cvpr.2017.391

19. Dallel, M., Havard, V., Baudry, D., Savatier, X.: InHARD - industrial human action recognition dataset in the context of industrial collaborative robotics, Zenodo, 2020-09-30 2020. https:// doi.org/10.5281/zenodo.4003541

20. Bulling, A., Blanke, U., Schiele, B.: A tutorial on human activity recognition using body-worn inertial sensors. ACM Comput. Surv. **46**(3), 1–33 (2014)

21. Oresti, B.: Window size impact in human activity recognition. G. Juan-Manuel (2014). https://doi.org/10.3390/s140406474
22. Hu, Y., Huber, A., Anumula, J., Liu, S.C.: Overcoming the vanishing gradient problem in plain recurrent networks. arXiv preprint arXiv:1801.06105 (2018)
23. Liu, H., Wang, L.: Collision-free human-robot collaboration based on context awareness. Robot. Comput. Integrated Manuf. **67**, 101997 (2021)

Mobile Manipulator for Hospital Care Using Firebase

José Varela-Aldás[1,2(✉)] ⓘ, Jorge Buele[1,2] ⓘ, Santiago Guerrero-Núñez[1],
and Víctor H. Andaluz[1,3] ⓘ

[1] SISAu Research Group, Facultad de Ingeniería y Tecnologías de la Información y la
Comunicación, Universidad Tecnológica Indoamérica, Ambato 180103, Ecuador
{josevarela,jorgebuele,victorandaluz}@uti.edu.ec
[2] Department of Electronic Engineering and Communications, University of Zaragoza,
44003 Teruel, Spain
[3] Departamento de Eléctrica y Electrónica, Universidad de las Fuerzas Armadas – ESPE,
171103 Sangolquí, Ecuador
vhandaluz1@espe.edu.ec

Abstract. The COVID-19 pandemic has shown that the use of the technology
in medicine is no longer a luxury, but a necessity. The use of the robotics in the
treatment of diseases and physical therapies is limited in Latin America due to
the high acquisition and maintenance costs. This document proposes the design,
development, and evaluation of a robotic system for the guided monitoring of
patients, through remote control using a mobile application. Within the methodology, four phases were proposed: planning, design, development, and evaluation.
The 3D design is done using the Tinkercad software, which facilitates the construction of the pieces using 3D printing technology. The ESP32 board is the main
element that receives the signals from the sensors and controls the actions of the
actuators through the orders received from Firebase. For the development of the
application, App inventor is used, building a friendly and easy-to-use interface. To
validate this proposal, experimental tests were carried out with two patients in a
medical center. In addition, a parameter compliance questionnaire was applied to
the robot, obtaining a score of 92.6%, and the mobile application obtained 72.5%
in the usability test. All this confirms an efficient care proposal, with a reduced
investment.

Keywords: Hospital care · COVID-19 · Mobile manipulator · ESP32 · Firebase

1 Introduction

The rapid progress of technology has allowed robots to perform human-like tasks [1].
This contributes to the development of new alternatives in the treatment and care of
people [2]. The clinical use of robotic systems that interact with patients has increased
during the last decade, despite little research on their efficacy and effectiveness [3].
In developed countries, robots have been placed in emergency rooms, surgery rooms,
special care, and physiotherapy rooms, as specialized care tools in various medical and

M. Kurosu et al. (Eds.): HCII 2022, LNCS 13519, pp. 328–341, 2022.
https://doi.org/10.1007/978-3-031-17618-0_24

clinical procedures [4]. More specifically, the term "Health care robotics" emerged, focusing on patient care in hospitals around the world [5]. Countries like the USA, China, and Japan are those that build the largest number of mobile robots, humanoid robots, and animals. Research has shown that these types of proposals increase patients' enthusiasm, concentration, and attention. Novel social behaviors such as joint attention and other benefits that are still being studied are also being appreciated [6]. In the USA, for example, a robot was implemented that helps with physical and cognitive therapy for people who have had a stroke [7]. These systems can complement the work of medical personnel, reducing the workload, which is beneficial in emergency situations, as can be seen in [8].

The COVID-19 pandemic has posed an unprecedented challenge to the world's health systems. Its rapid progress has highlighted the need to implement new technological tools that reduce the spread of infections [9]. Surface cleaning and personal disinfection have been biosafety measures that have offered good results [10]. In China, robots are used that carry out this work using ultraviolet light, preventing the spread of the virus and protecting health personnel [11]. Something similar has been used in the US, where robotic systems are used to kill viruses and bacteria using UV-C light [12]. Meanwhile, in England, robots are being developed that use vaporized hydrogen peroxide (VHP) for the deep disinfection of trains [13]. The review by Singh et al. [14] shows how the robots, in addition to executing the disinfection activities of the hospitals, can be in charge of the exercise routines of the patients.

As Wang and Wang mention [15], applications with automata could be a good option for the care of patients with COVID-19. In this way, a contact barrier is established between infected patients and their surroundings, which reduces the probability of contagion [16, 17]. In Norway, an assistance robot is presented that is equipped with cameras and can be operated remotely [18]. In India [19] a robot is presented to distribute medicines to infected patients, restricting contact with other humans. In the same country [20] a nursing robot that controls the patient and their medication consumption is described, to provide greater social distancing to health personnel. In Bangladesh, a robotic system that performs cyclic tasks is proposed, which is designed and calibrated for the drug intake of COVID-19 patients [21]. While in Europe it can see a robot for assistance in oncological surgery in the context of this pandemic [22].

In Latin America, the International Network of Informatics Nursing (RIEI in Spanish) has been created, which emphasizes the implementation of projects and programs that relate medicine to technology. Thus, computer systems will reach hospital spaces to achieve a higher level of patient surveillance and may be used to detect different diseases and pathologies. However, the integration of robotics in medical centers is still very limited, due to the high costs, lack of resources, and socio-economic problems in this particular region. The public sector does not have full availability of these devices, which are generally more used in the private and industrial spheres. To this can be added that health professionals do not have adequate training in information technology and training programs are non-existent.

Based on the above, it can be deduced that the knowledge and limited use of robotic systems in patient care is a problem in the region. Some technologies could enhance the benefits that robots already provide, such as the Internet of Things (IoT). In assistance robotics, it allow remote connections from anywhere in the world in real-time [23], which would improve the previously mentioned research. In this context, this work presents the development of a mobile manipulator for hospital care using a real-time database in Firebase. The robot includes a camera to remotely view the patient and proximity, temperature, and humidity sensors to obtain data from the environment. This entire system is managed from a mobile application.

This document is made up of four sections, including the introduction in Sect. 1. The materials and methods used are described in the Sect. 2 and the results and their discussion in Sect. 3. The conclusions and future work are shown in Sect. 4.

2   Methods and Materials

For the development of the system, the XP methodology was selected, its use aims to produce higher quality software. XP is a specific framework for the execution of engineering practices and software development. Figure 1 shows a diagram of the stages that make up this framework.

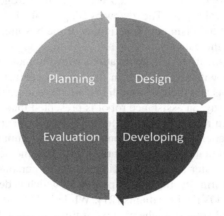

Fig. 1. Development methodology XP.

2.1   Planning

In the planning stage, all the resources and the necessary budget were defined according to the technical feasibility study. After a review of different models, it is analyzed which one has greater mobility, grip, and practicality. For the design of the robot, a mobile manipulator is chosen. It contains a unicycle-like configuration for the mobile part and an anthropomorphic arm for the upper part. Then the sketch of the mobile application is made, considering the form of design and the requirements set out in Table 1.

Table 1. Summary of the requirements considered in the planning.

Robot specific requirements	Application specific requirements
	User validation
Acquire images of the room	View "live" image of the room
Room temperature measurement	View the room temperature in the mobile application
Room humidity measurement	View the amount of humidity in the room in the mobile application
Control the robot movements	Operate the robot manually

2.2 Design

Electronic Design

Figure 2 presents the defined electronic circuit, where the elements are arranged. This stage is the basis for the organization of the design according to the established specifications and the needs of the population. The choice of materials and electronic components is essential for the considerations taken in the mechanical design of the structure. A proximity sensor (HC-SR04) is incorporated for collision avoidance and a temperature and humidity sensor (DHT11) to obtain room conditions. The main element of the system is the ESP32 development board, a low-cost element that has a Bluetooth and WiFi connection. It receives the signals from the sensors, performs the processing, and generates actions in the robot's actuators, based on the established design. The robot actuators are DC motors for locomotion and servo motors for the degrees of freedom of the manipulator. In addition, an ESP32Cam is included for image acquisition through the integrated camera.

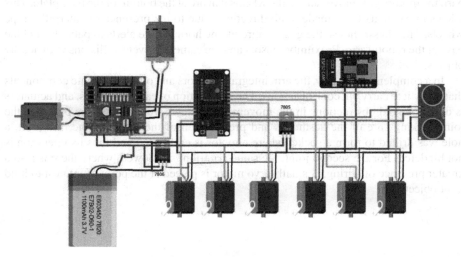

Fig. 2. Electronic circuit diagram.

3D Design

The 3D design of the robot is presented in Fig. 3, made using the Tinkercad software. The metallic, plastic, and prefabricated parts for the robot, are modeled.

- The metal parts include the base of the chassis, star head screws, hex head screws, and the spacer shafts of the bearing wheels.
- The plastic parts include the upper part of the chassis, the robotic arm, and the gripper (point of interest), which is printed in 3D according to the design.
- The prefabricated parts are the roller wheels and the track-type wheels.

Fig. 3. 3D design of the mobile manipulator robot

As previously indicated there are two main parts to this system. As for the moving part, the motors give movement to the wheels that are at the bottom of the base plate. This allows movements to be made in all directions, due to the presence of caterpillar-type wheels. The chassis house the general circuit, the horn to give alerts to patients, and the base of the robotic arm. Proximity sensors and the camera prevent collisions with nearby objects.

In a complementary way, the arm integrates motors and other electronic components that allow it to carry out control actions. The distribution of cables, sensors, and actuators is done to avoid obstructions in the movements. Screws were used in the base and the joints, taking care of the aesthetics and presentation of the robot. In the first joint, a hole was drilled to form a socket where a motor is embedded and thus its operation is not hindered. For the second joint, the same criterion is followed, where there is also a greater presence of wiring. A small servo motor is placed at the point of interest to hold light objects.

Mobile App Design

Figure 4 presents the flowchart of the application to be implemented for the management of the robot. Firebase has been selected, as the Google platform that manages the development of the application connected to a database in real-time. For the presentation to the user, the main screen of the application is designed, with its respective authentication system and hierarchy levels. On the user registration screen, the user can register as an administrator of the mobile application or as a user. After that, it is done at the beginning of the session, where the user can choose the actions to take with the robot. Here the reading of temperature, humidity, and obtaining live images are contemplated, and control buttons are used to move the arm and a joystick is used to control the mobile.

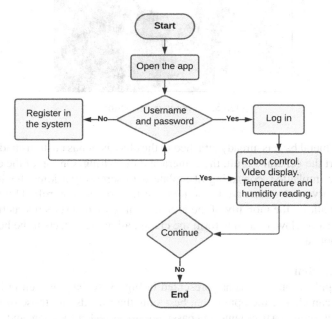

Fig. 4. Mobile App Flowchart.

2.3   Development

Prototype Construction

Using a 3D printer, the construction of the pieces is made with PLA material. It starts at the base until it ends with the claw, which is the point of interest. The body remains fixed and balanced thanks to its differential mechanism. The arm is connected through a metal shaft mounted on the main body of the robot. Figure 5 shows the mobile manipulator robot in the construction process. During the implementation of the mobile part, it is verified that the 10 wheels move inside the plastic tracks that are located on both sides of the robot. On this, there is a metal base that is held to the tracks with screws. The motors located in the lower part of the metal base are inserted inside the main bearing wheel that is located on the track on each side.

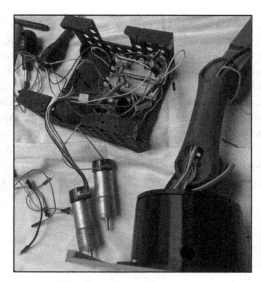

Fig. 5. Robot in construction.

When the metal base is already attached to the chassis, it has custom-made compartments to insert the general circuit, the camera and the wiring. On top of the chassis, the robotic arm is implanted, consisting of a plate with screws that joins the arm and the chassis. The servomotors that are in the joints of the arm are controlled by the general circuit, which allows the mobility of the arm according to the user's instructions. In the point of interest or claw, two ends form the clamp, allowing objects to be held through the mobile application.

Mobile Application

The mobile application screens are presented in Fig. 6. As can be seen in Fig. 6c, the hospital staff can choose the option that best suits their needs and those of the patient. This includes assigning a username and password, locating her location, and designating the robot for service at a specific time. Choosing the "turn on" option (Fig. 6d) shows the motion control options using a joystick as shown in Fig. 6e.

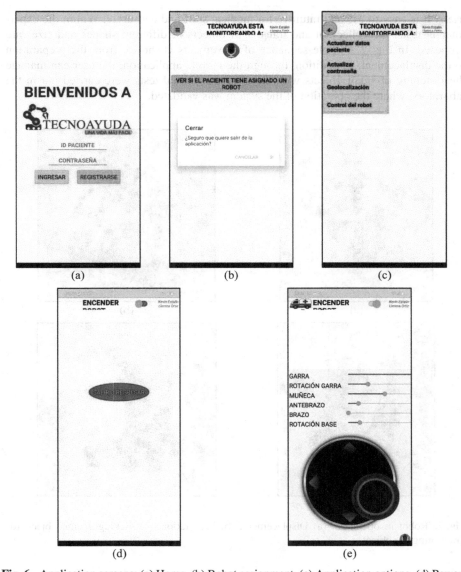

Fig. 6. Application screens: (a) Home. (b) Robot assignment. (c) Application options. (d) Power button. (e) Control options.

3 Results

3.1 Evaluation

The last stage of the methodology is the evaluation, which is carried out with the experimental tests of operation. The built robot shows that its design adapts to the needs of users. It is easy to use and intuitive for medical staff and end-users. Within the experimental tests, the collection and transfer of objects of different shapes and sizes are proposed. In Fig. 7 a whole sequence of movements is shown, from the preparation to the displacement. In addition, through the mobile application, the user can manage the fastening of small objects with the claw. The initial tests were carried out in the laboratory, where the operation of the system was validated.

(a)   (b)

(c)   (d)

Fig. 7. Robot in operation: (a) Displacement. (b) Preparation. (c) Picking up the object. (d) Translating the object.

3.2 Compliance with System Parameters

Figure 8 shows the tests carried out with the mobile manipulator robot in a basic hospital in the city of Ambato in Ecuador. The robot was tested by two patients who agreed voluntarily. Table 2 shows the average score for each test. The rating is made on a range of 1 to 5, where 1 is not at all satisfactory and 5 is totally satisfactory.

 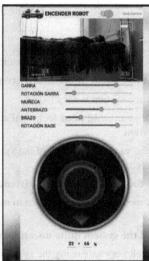

Fig. 8. Tests at the medical center

Table 2. Qualification of system parameters.

Item	Parameter	Qualification
1	Robot structure	5
2	Relevance	4
3	Usefulness	5
4	Benefits	5
5	Ease of use	5
6	Care provided	5
7	Response time	4
8	Mobile app	4
	Mean	4,63

3.3 Usability Test

Based on the literature, the usability of the application that controls this robotic system is evaluated using a questionnaire, as carried out by Danielsson et al. [24]. The questions are based on the SUS test developed by Brooke [25]. The total sum of the results is multiplied by 2.5 obtaining the global value of the SUS. Based on user responses, Table 3 is obtained.

Table 3. Results of SUS.

N°	Question	Score (N = 2)	Operation
1	I think I would like to use this system frequently	4.5	3.5
2	**I find this system unnecessarily complex**	**1.5**	**3.5**
3	I think the system is easy to use	2.5	1.5
4	**I think you would need technical support to make use of the system**	**2**	**3**
5	I find the various functions of the system quite well integrated	4.5	3.5
6	**I have found too much inconsistency in this system**	**1.5**	**3.5**
7	I think most people would learn to make use of the system quickly	3.5	2.5
8	**I found the system quite uncomfortable to use**	**3**	**2**
9	I have felt very safe using the system	4	3
10	**I would need to learn a lot of things before I can manage the system**	**2**	**3**
	Total		29 × 2.5 72.5%

The result of 72.5% in the SUS indicates that the application works correctly and provides a friendly experience to users who had the opportunity to interact with the robot. However, it also shows an opportunity for improvement in some issues related to the ease of operation of the robot.

3.4 Discussion

Robotic systems have demonstrated their importance in the care of human beings. Different investigations have focused on the application of this technology for the cleaning and disinfection of places of mass use [10–14]. This is because the expansion of COVID-19 took place exponentially and the application of biosecurity measures was essential to reduce infections. However, as has been appreciated in the available bibliography, its application goes further. Robotics should currently be seen as a complement to health personnel, which allows the patient to be assisted according to her needs [26].

The use of robots in hospitals makes it possible to take care of people, placing a protective barrier between doctors and nurses. Østvik's proposal [18] presents a fixed robot, which incorporates cameras for remote control, but cannot move like our prototype. Murugan et al. [19] design a robot to help people in hospitals, but it only presents simulation results and there is no evidence of its real application, something contrary to our application. Something similar occurs with the work of Manikandan et al. [20], since there is only a description of the robot's design but its application in a medical center or with a user is not appreciated. Our work is aligned with the research of Oishi et al. [21], although it only proposes a unicycle robot, it demonstrates the use of these systems to mobilize objects that patients require. Although there are studies similar to ours, none of these show a real application of the prototype.

4 Conclusions

The construction of this robot has complied with the feasibility study since the necessary technological resources are found in the local market and are easily accessible. The design is not complex, requires basic elements of 3D printing technology, low-cost electronic materials, and is easy to implement. The development of the mobile application was carried out using a database of a cloud server (Firebase). This shows how industry 4.0 is present in applications of various kinds, and medicine is adapting to new technologies. Computerized design and 3D printing allow ideas to become tangible proposals.

The design of this application is a contribution so that patients who need isolation can be treated remotely. This can even be used for other illnesses or treatments that keep the user in a situation of vulnerability and dependence on a family member or caregiver. Mobile applications are gaining importance, due to their ease and because it has become a daily tool for communication, work, and entertainment. The validation carried out through the different experimental tests within a hospital demonstrates its effectiveness. In addition, a high acceptance was obtained according to the tests carried out, to this is added the comments received that contribute to improving this initial design.

The authors of this study propose future work to improve the design of this prototype with the feedback received from users. It is also proposed to evaluate the robot in other applications in the field of medical care, making adjustments to the original design.

Acknowledgments. Thanks are extended to the Universidad Tecnológica Indoamérica for providing the necessary resources for the development and dissemination of this research.

References

1. Varela-Aldás, J., Buele, J., Jadan-Guerrero, J., Andaluz, V.H.: Teaching STEM competencies through an educational mobile robot. In: Zaphiris, P., Ioannou, A. (eds.) HCII 2020. LNCS, vol. 12206, pp. 560–573. Springer, Cham (2020). https://doi.org/10.1007/978-3-030-50506-6_38
2. Murphy, R.R.: Robots and pandemics in science fiction. Sci. Robot. **5** (2020). https://doi.org/10.1126/SCIROBOTICS.ABB9590
3. Yang, G.Z., et al.: Combating COVID-19-the role of robotics in managing public health and infectious diseases. Sci. Robot. **5**, 5589 (2020). https://doi.org/10.1126/scirobotics.abb5589
4. Varela-Aldás, J., Moreira, A., Criollo, P., Ruales, B.: Body temperature control using a robotic arm. In: Botto Tobar, M., Cruz, H., Díaz Cadena, A. (eds.) CIT 2020. LNEE, vol. 762, pp. 280–293. Springer, Cham (2021). https://doi.org/10.1007/978-3-030-72208-1_21
5. Wazir, H.K., Lourido, C., Chacko, S.M., Kapila, V.: A COVID-19 emergency response for remote control of a dialysis machine with mobile HRI. Front. Robot. AI. **8** (2021). https://doi.org/10.3389/frobt.2021.612855

6. Diehl, J.J., Schmitt, L.M., Villano, M., Crowell, C.R.: The clinical use of robots for individuals with autism spectrum disorders: a critical review. Res. Autism Spectr. Disord. **6**, 249–262 (2012). https://doi.org/10.1016/j.rasd.2011.05.006
7. Lo, A.C., et al.: Robot-assisted therapy for long-term upper-limb impairment after stroke. N. Engl. J. Med. **362**, 1772–1783 (2010). https://doi.org/10.1056/nejmoa0911341
8. Khan, Z.H., Siddique, A., Lee, C.W.: Robotics utilization for healthcare digitization in global COVID-19 management. Int. J. Environ. Res. Public Health. **17**, 3819 (2020). https://doi.org/10.3390/ijerph17113819
9. Talahua, J.S., Buele, J., Calvopiña, P., Varela-Aldas, J.: Facial recognition system for people with and without face mask in times of the covid-19 pandemic. Sustain. **13**, 6900 (2021). https://doi.org/10.3390/su13126900
10. Varela-Aldás, J., Pilla, J., Llugsha, E., Cholota, O.: Application of hand disinfectant gel using a SCARA. In: Rocha, Á., Ferrás, C., López-López, P.C., Guarda, T. (eds.) ICITS 2021. AISC, vol. 1331, pp. 13–23. Springer, Cham (2021). https://doi.org/10.1007/978-3-030-68418-1_2
11. Feng, Q.C., Wang, X.: Design of disinfection robot for livestock breeding. Procedia Comput. Sci. **166**, 310–314 (2020). https://doi.org/10.1016/j.procs.2020.02.093
12. Taylor, W., et al.: DNA damage kills bacterial spores and cells exposed to 222-nanometer UV radiation. Appl. Environ. Microbiol. **86** (2020). https://doi.org/10.1128/AEM.03039-19
13. Bogue, R.: Robots in a contagious world. Ind. Rob. **47**, 673–642 (2020). https://doi.org/10.1108/IR-05-2020-0101
14. Singh, S., Dalla, V.K., Shrivastava, A.: Combating COVID-19: study of robotic solutions for COVID-19. AIP Conf. Proc. **2341**, 020042 (2021). https://doi.org/10.1063/5.0050148
15. Vincent Wang, X., Wang, L.: A literature survey of the robotic technologies during the COVID-19 pandemic. J. Manuf. Syst. **60**, 823–836 (2021). https://doi.org/10.1016/j.jmsy.2021.02.005
16. Sonntag, D.: AI in medicine, Covid-19 and springer nature's open access agreement. KI - Künstliche Intelligenz **34**(2), 123–125 (2020). https://doi.org/10.1007/s13218-020-00661-y
17. Varela-Aldás, J., Pilla, J., Andaluz, V.H., Palacios-Navarro, G.: Commercial entry control using robotic mechanism and mobile application for COVID-19 Pandemic. In: Gervasi, O., et al. (eds.) ICCSA 2021. LNCS, vol. 12957, pp. 3–14. Springer, Cham (2021). https://doi.org/10.1007/978-3-030-87013-3_1
18. Østvik, A., Bø, L.E., Smistad, E.: EchoBot: an open-source robotic ultrasound system. In: Proceedings of the IPCAI 2019 (2019)
19. Murugan, K., Ali Khan, M.A., Kylash, M., Muralidharan, M.: Medicine distribution robot and human less intervention for Covid-19 affected people (AKM Med Assistive Bot). IOP Conf. Ser. Mater. Sci. Eng. **1049**, 012013 (2021). https://doi.org/10.1088/1757-899x/1049/1/012013
20. Manikandan, P., Ramesh, G., Likith, G., Sreekanth, D., Durga Prasad, G.: Smart nursing robot for COVID-19 patients. In: 2021 International Conference on Advance Computing and Innovative Technologies in Engineering, ICACITE 2021, pp. 839–842. Institute of Electrical and Electronics Engineers Inc. (2021). https://doi.org/10.1109/ICACITE51222.2021.9404698
21. Oishi, A.N., Tanjim, M.S.S., Palash, M.M., Barua, S., Sarkar, M.R., Rafi, S.A.: Cyclic task-based affordable robot for medicine-intake purpose of COVID-19 patient. In: 2nd International Conference on Robotics, Electrical and Signal Processing Techniques, pp. 403–407 (2021). https://doi.org/10.1109/ICREST51555.2021.9331070
22. Kimmig, R., Verheijen, R.H.M., Rudnicki, M.: Robot assisted surgery during the COVID-19 pandemic, especially for gynecological cancer: a statement of the society of European Robotic Gynaecological surgery (SERGS). J. Gynecol. Oncol. **31** (2020). https://doi.org/10.3802/jgo.2020.31.e59
23. Mishra, S.S., Rasool, A.: IoT health care monitoring and tracking: a survey. In: Proceedings of the International Conference on Trends in Electronics and Informatics, ICOEI 2019, pp. 1052–1057 (2019). https://doi.org/10.1109/ICOEI.2019.8862763

24. Danielsson, O., Syberfeldt, A., Brewster, R., Wang, L.: Assessing instructions in augmented reality for human-robot collaborative assembly by using demonstrators. Procedia CIRP **63**, 89–94 (2017). https://doi.org/10.1016/j.procir.2017.02.038
25. Brooke, J.: SUS: a retrospective. J. Usability Stud. **8**, 29–40 (2013)
26. Scassellati, B., Vázquez, M.: The potential of socially assistive robots during infectious disease outbreaks. Sci. Robot. **5** (2020). https://doi.org/10.1126/scirobotics.abc9014

Iterative Design Process for HRI: Serving Robot in Restaurant

Yoo Jin Won[✉], Seung Hee Hwang, Serin Ko, and Jungmi Park

Samsung Research, Seoul, Korea
{yoojin.won,seung.hee,serin.ko}@samsung.com

Abstract. We introduces the interactive design process for HRI to derive the robot's key interaction requirement and basic principle. We applied this process in serving robot project in Samsung research and conducted user test on 108 users in the restaurant environment for 4 weeks. We tried to find the awkward moments watching video by week through video ethnography and then updating it in the next week. Through this process, it was possible to discover unexpected awkward moments and continuously upgrade meaningful human-robot-interactions. In conclusion, we found that not-bad interaction is much more important to users than Delightful interaction.

Keywords: HRI design method · HRI testing · Iterative design process · Human-robot interaction

1 Introduction

This research introduces the new HRI design methodology that can provide robust interactions between users and serving robots in restaurants. More specifically, the methodology enables an iterative user testing for serving robots and testing environments similar to the actual restaurants (Fig. 1).

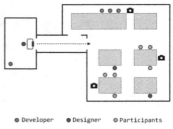

● Developer ● Designer ◎ Participants

Fig. 1. Test environment

For four weeks, 108 users have experienced the serving robots. From the survey, they answered, we had derived key interaction requirements and basic privacy for the robot. To design robot's interaction, it includes setting practical tasks in accordance with given roles and designing detailed interaction algorithm [1]. For example, serving robots need to know which tasks to be done other than food serving, then detailed interactions and process should be established fits for new tasks. In order to know whether the tasks and interactions are actually satisfying the users, it is essential to evaluate through the user test. The robot's user test should consider not only the robot's appearance but also all modalities such as gaze, voice, gesture, and screen along with scenario. This experiment rather relies on the survey or analysis on users' reaction based on each modality than analyses video ethnography that enables figuring awkward moments out of interactions between users and robots. By this method, it was possible to study instant interaction and to concentrate more on users' behavior than on their opinion.

So how will we efficiently) conduct the experiment in order to discover the meaningful insight for the interactions? We conducted a user test with a large number of participants with Samsung Bot Public (Fig. 2), and interaction requirements were derived from the iterative design process for HRI and its process. The gist of iterative design process for HRI is to separate main and sub tasks of robots and to update them continuously. We recruited 108 participants to conduct iterative design process. And finally, we could have derived interaction requirements of serving robots.

Fig. 2. Samsung Bot Public

2 Iterative Design Process for HRI

Through the series of user tests, we identified usability problem and users' satisfaction from quantitative and qualitative data. The design thinking process consists of empathizing, defining, ideating, prototyping [3, 4]. By using the design thinking to test the actual users with the prototype, we could find the solution to improve the product. Double Diamond method consists of four stages that are to discover, to define, to develop, and to deliver. Delivering is the last stage in the Double Diamond method and this stage aims to test and to evaluate concepts in the production and to launch processes [5]. Such traditional design methodology focus on completing whole concept before release the product.

On the contrary, Lean UX is the light and faster version of conducting a collaborative cross-functional way. Even if there is a lack of evidence to support the product right away, the MVP (minimum viable products) is evaluated on the market. As Jeff's lean UX process shows, the most important point is to gradually develop core functions by repeating the steps which is consists of 1)making a hypothesis, 2) designing it, 3) creating an MVP, 4) researching and learning. Based on lean UX, we proposed an iterative design process for HRI to develop core functions for robot interactions.

Based on the iterative design process for HRI (Figs. 3, 4), we organized the main task and the sub tasks of the robot including interactions and conducted 4 different tests which are improved every week. The main task of the serving robot was to deliver food and it was the key function. And the other features such as ordering, promotion games, calling robots for additional order and so on were considered as sub tasks of the robot.

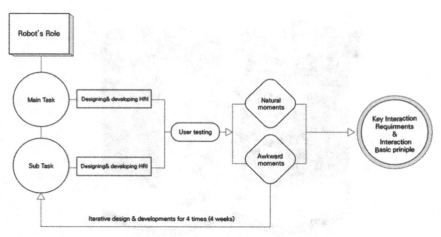

Fig. 3. Iterative design process for HRI

When customer first faces a serving robot in the restaurant, they have no clue about what interaction or functions the robots provide. The robots can also be arranged not only one specific task but also other various tasks at the same time. To observe all the participants' reactions throughout the user testing session, we filmed the test process from

3 different angles. By filming at various angles simultaneously, we wanted to capture awkward moments through video ethnography. After that, designers and developers gathered to find ways to solve these awkward moments (Fig. 5) through discussions and updated them iteratively. In this way, the main tasks could be gradually updated. It was possible to examine whether unexpected issue arises from sub-task or if it meets the user expectations. In addition, in the last week of the test, the robot's appearance and hardware were updated and were re-tested to solve the overall interaction problems found in the first three weeks.

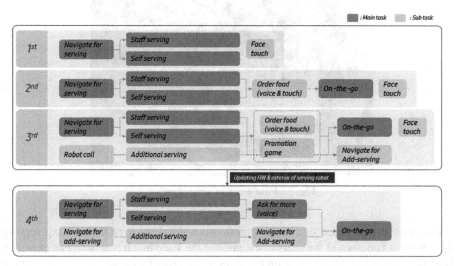

Fig. 4. Serving robot's task by week

3   User Test

3.1   Participants

For this experiment, an in-house survey system was used to recruit executives and employees interested in prior products. External participants were not include due to the security issues. Participants were selected after answering three questions.

Q1. Have you ever experienced a serving robot at a restaurant?

Q2. Do you have a positivity that there will be robots in restaurants in the near future?

Q3. Are you willing to participate in the UT?

Among the 140 survey participants, 108 participants who answered that they were willing to participate in UT were selected. A pilot test conducted with three people a day every week. After that, a group of six people conducted the test twice a day, twice a week, for a total of four weeks.

3.2 Weekly Procedure

First Week User Test
Task: Serving, which is the most important function of serving robots, is divided into two main functions. 1) Staff serving; which is delivering food with the staff, 2) Self-serving; which is delivering food without the staff.

Fig. 5. First week of serving robot

Based on the evidence that users tend to touch the display of the existing serving robots a lot, it is designed for users to experience the Face touch reaction. For example, when the serving robot is touched on the display part, robot's facial expressions change and also it starts to say things like "it's ticklish!".

Result of observation: As a result of observation, participants found that they had questions or felt uncomfortable with the robot's arrival location for Staff serving and Self-serving. In the case of Staff serving, the arrival location was designed so that the staff could naturally take out the food, but from the user's point of view, they were often surprised by the robot which suddenly arrived behind them and made a sound. In the case of Self-serving, there was a notice to the users to take the food out after arriving with the front part of the robot, which the food was invisible. The participants became confused about which and when to take. Finally, in the case of face touch, no one touched the face of the serving robot. For reference, preemptive guidance was provided to participants that they could freely touch, push, or interact with the robot. However, despite such experience guidance, no one touched the robot's face.

Second Week User Test
Task: In the second week, Staff serving and Self-serving, were carried out as before, and after the first week of experiment, the wrong arrival location found as a major problem was improved. Subtitle was also changed, "It's hard to respond now," was changed to "I'll visit you soon" on the display of the robot. In addition, each serving had a special improvement. Staff serving's arrival location became little farther than before, and an

Fig. 6. Second week of serving robot

indicator played "Arrival Soon" in order to prevent users from surprising by the sudden appearance.

In case of self-serving, people could not find food directly in week 1. To improve, we modified the robots' route so that people can see which food is located on the robots.

In week 2, we added new function that users could make an additional order after their first serving had completed. This function has two different interaction; first, additional orders by voice, second, by touching screen. However, the display part did not locate in the center of the table rather one-sided since the robot changed to route in order to show served food. This led to the biased users' experience that people on the other part had more difficulty in additional orders (Fig. 6).

The other test also conducted to analyze the reaction from robots to users on the way to serve dishes. When encountering users, robots were designed to recognize the distance from the users. If the distance is about 80 cm, robots stops immediately, while it is about 1.5 m, robot would bypass them.

Result of observation: In case of additional orders, users showed higher satisfaction with screen touch than voice order, since most restaurant has noisy environment.

The Face touch function was still provided in the second week, participants attempted more interactions such as waving their hands or greeting aloud rather than touching the face of the serving robot.

In addition, the participants did not seem to expect any other functions other than serving, and for this reason, the participants did not continue to interact with the robot after serving.

About the situation that robots and users meeting in hallway, the participant was surprised or wondered why the robot suddenly stopped driving.

Third Week User Test
Task: Three tasks were added as below; additional serving, promotion game, and driving tests. The additional serving is the function which robots ask users about new order or inquiry. In test environment, we set hand sanitizers and wet tissues on serving tray of a robot. Then users were allowed to call the wandering robot any time (Fig. 7).

Fig. 7. Third week of serving robot

About promotion game, we deployed Korean traditional game called 'Cham-Cham-Cham'. The rule is to guess the robot's head direction with user's hand at the same time the robot spin its head. Winning the bet, user got candy.

Next, the driving tests improved robots' reaction ability that they could get out of the stuck situation in narrower distance. Immediate stop distance has shortened for 80 to 50 cm, bypassing distance has shorten 1.5 m to 1.0 m. And when robot encounters the user, TTS utterance "Hold on," "Excuse me," and "Move away" changed to "Go ahead," "I'll wait," and "Pass" to prevent them from feeling negative.

Observing a multi-robot situation, we analyzed users' reaction when robots met in hallway, which actually led rare recognition.

Result of observation: As a result, we found that the users called the robot using both gestures and voices for additional serving. However, gestures took the first place.

In addition, when playing the promotion game, some participants had fun and interacted with robots but the majority of users could not grasp the reason and goal of the game. Users who visited the restaurant actually preferred to focus on eating or talking with the people.

Lastly, Participants were curious about the robots' motions under multi robot situation whether they stopped or passed by each robot. Some participants starred whether robots would bump into each other.

Last Week User Test

Main task: In order to experience interactions that are difficult to experiment in the existing form factor, the interaction of the serving robot was experimented using a skeleton structure with different form factor (Fig. 8).

Existing robots form factor causes users to expect a "high level of intelligence" due to GUI elements, gaze functions, and voice utterance functions that used "moving eye visual motions" from facial display. And it eventually provided a disappointing user experience as it did not reach users mental model, which was highly intelligent robot expectation.

Fig. 8. Last week of serving robot

Therefore, the new form factor was changed so that the display could be used only for employees by touching it from the back. And by removing the display for users, [gazing] was indicated by front LEDs with simple and intuitive reactions while notifying that the user is recognized.

It was intended to change the specific voice speech to a shorter and simpler sentence to provide only essential information and allow users to focus more on the restaurant experience.

Previously, a serving guide was provided through Display, while in Week 4, a serving guide was provided by applying the motion of the tray and the driving of the robot. Each of the three serving methods, which are Staff serving, Self serving, and Additional serving were provided differently. For Staff serving, the tray came out forward. For Self serving the robot just moved 15 cm forward. And for additional serving, the robot moved and the tray came out. The purpose was to minimize the latency that occurs in existing displays and voice-provided serving guides, so that the robot can improve the serving function for users to quickly and intuitively takeout food. In the existing form factor, since it was a fixed tray without a motor and could not be provide any tray motions, a new robot was used for the user test by attaching a motor to the tray.

Driving tests were also conducted with skeleton robots, but the statements that the robot utters when it encounters the user were excluded with the new form factor.

In the fourth week, designers participated in the role of employees and experimented with the cleaning function. The cleaning function was composed by following the patrolling robot together, and when the robot reaches the place to clean, staff touches the "Stop" button on the display. After removing the tableware from the table, the employee touches the "Go" button again to continue patrol to the next place to clean.

Result of observation: As a result of observation, the skeleton type form factor showed high satisfaction as the user could receive food faster.

Especially, the skeleton type makes user to feel more agile and smooth even at the same driving speed, which indicates that the existing form factor can be improved a lot. However, by conducting the experience as a form factor in the development stage, not as a finished product, it was hard for users to accept the experience as a whole serving robot experience in real restaurants.

In addition, by observing employees (designers) who participated in the cleaning function, we found out that the speed and process for cleaning was much easier and faster than before.

4 Results

4.1 Awkward Moments in Video Ethnography

During video ethnography, the most important thing was to discover awkward moments. "Awkward moment" is defined as [the moment when customer engages in stressful situation]. In order to discover the moment, we categorized 4 modalities; movement, touch, speech, and gesture. Under these modalities, we added the list of the moments during whole observation rather preselected the list in advance (Fig. 9). Referring to Fig. 9, the user's awkward moments were observed the most in [Movement]. And the followings were Speech, Touch, and Gesture.

Fig. 9. Awkward moments Frequency total

In Fig. 10, the awkward moments were the most in week 3 even though we deleted the week 3 day 1 data because of technical issue. In the first week, movement's awkward moments (A) were observed in Staff serving and Self/additional serving, and the biggest reason was that Staff serving's POI (Point of Interest) was too close to customers, and no food or tray were seen in Self-serving's POI. In the second week, the POI location was updated to resolve the awkward moment, and the count actually decreased significantly.

However, the largest awkward moment (B) was observed in the on-the-go situation, as the stop distance was too close to the user.

In addition, in the third week, awkward moment was observed, especially in Speech and Gesture (C, D). Overall, after calling the robots and re-ordering food, users' attempts to interact with robots increased.

In the last week, there was an increase in awkward moment (E) in Movement type, where people reached out their hand to the trays before the robots arrived because they could see trays and food better than before.

Type	Category	Awkward moments details	Frequency	Total
Movement	First engagement	Surprised, awkward posture after robot arrival	3	45
	Taking out food from robot tray	Hand reach difficulty	1	
		Wait and take it out	4	
		Don't know what to pull out, hesitating	6	
		Waiting for or commanding the robot to leave	1	
		Take out food and crash hand	1	
	On-the-go (2-4 weeks)	surprised that it almost clash	16	
		keep stopping and hesitating	5	
		Keep testing the Stuck (some users block it)	4	
		Passing or avoiding uncomfortable passages between the robot and the hallway	4	
Touch	-	Find the Cancel button, touch the screen	6	11
		Touch the face at the end	5	
Speech	-	Speaks at a point where it is not recognized (before Mic open, during return)	14	25
		Hesitating or not speaking	2	
		Unrecognizable words, asking questions	6	
		voice volume is too small	3	
Gesture	-	beckon from a distance	2	10
		Beckoning from the back, side of the robot	4	
		Beckoning in an impossible situation (to another table, returning)	4	

Fig. 10. Awkward moments Frequency total

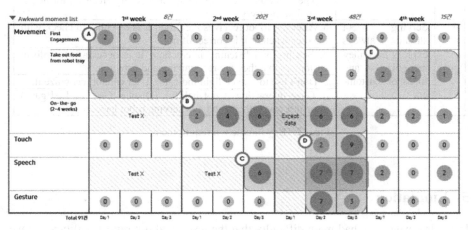

Fig. 11. Awkward moments Frequency per week

4.2 Key Interaction Requirements

In conclusion, the summary of the interaction requirements of the serving robot is as below;

First, it should be physically comfortable.

Second, you should be able to act naturally without any cognitive effort.

Third, you should always express how you recognize and focus on customers.

In conclusion, we found that not-bad interaction is much more important to users than Delightful interaction.

No	Category	Interaction requirements
1	Serving robot should be physically comfortable	a. Serving robot should inform the user before reaching the table
		b. Serving robot should drive in a food-specific driving way. (When robot starts or stops to move, acceleration and deceleration are important.)
		c. When the tray moves in or out, serving robot should inform through sound.
		d. It is recommended to serve heavy or hot food by staff than the serving robot, and light or cold food by robot.
2	Serving robot should provide guides naturally	a. When the robot is delivering information, robot should not use to much modalities at once in order to make the delay less.
		b. Serving Guide interaction: The serving robot should notify in advance.
		c. Motion-based interaction: The robot posture and motion should naturally inform the intention.
		d. Robot should be able to cancel what the robot is doing at any time.
		e. The function of calling robot for ordering creates a lot of expectation for users
3	Serving robot should always express how they recognize and focus on customers	a. After the robot receives the order, it is essential to check with the user whether it is correct of not.
		b. Sensing and listening interaction: It is necessary to inform customers that they are recognizing and listening.
		c. Don't use too much light indicator. User cannot recognize it.
		d. Gaze interaction is not helpful. (Display Gaze or Led gaze) User just watch their food, not serving robot gaze.

Fig. 12. Key interaction requirements

5 Limitation

In the last week, we had main difficulty that the test could not reflect reality since we conducted it with a skeleton form factor while the other three weeks were done with the complete form factor. Considering this difference, we informed the participants to ignore the appearance and in week 4. Even though with this information, it would have been hard to ignore robots' bare appearances in users' perspective. Therefore, we could not do comparative analysis about the users' favorability.

6 Conclusion

Through this four-week iterative process, a total of 91 awkward moments (Fig. 11) were found, and 70 interactions were updated. Three categories and 13 key interaction requirements were listed (Fig. 12). Through this research, we found that our HRI design process can identify users behavior and also give meaningful insights for the robot designers.

Acknowledgment. This work was supported by SAMSUNG Research, Samsung Electronics Co., Ltd.

References

1. Lee, K.W., Kim, H.R., Yoon, W.C., Yoon, Y.S., Kwon, D.S.: Designing a human-robot inter-action framework for home service robot. In: ROMAN 2005. IEEE International Workshop on Robot and Human Interactive Communication, 2005, pp. 286–293. IEEE, August 2005
2. "Usability Testing". usability.gov, last modified 30 September 2020. https://www.usability.gov/how-to-and-tools/methods/usability-testing.html. Accessed 10 Oct 2021
3. Kimbell, L.: Rethinking design thinking: part I. Des. Cult. **3**(3), 285–306 (2011)
4. Plattner, H.: An Introduction to Design Thinking: Process Guide. Institute of Design at Stanford (2010)
5. Cahya, R.A.D., Handayani, A.N., Wibawa, A.P.: Mobile braille touch application for visually impaired people using double diamond approach. In: MATEC Web of Conferences vol. 197, p. 15007. EDP Sciences (2018)
6. Gothelf, J., Seiden, J.: Lean UX: Designing Great Products with Agile Teams. O'Reilly Media, Inc. (2016)
7. Follett, J. (Ed.): Designing for Emerging Technologies: UX for Genomics, Robotics, and the Internet of Things. O'Reilly Media, Inc. (2014)

Brain-Computer Interfaces

Methodology Design of the Correlation Between EEG Signals and Brain Regions Mapping in Panic Attacks

Julia Elizabeth Calderón-Reyes[1], Francisco Javier Álvarez-Rodríguez[1], María Lorena Barba-González[2], and Héctor Cardona-Reyes[2(✉)]

[1] Autonomous University of Aguascalientes, Aguascalientes, Mexico
al178522@edu.uaa.mx
[2] Center for Research in Mathematics, Zacatecas, Mexico
hector.cardona@cimat.mx

Abstract. While EEG signals provide insight into brain activity, computational methods from software engineering and artificial intelligence can contribute to the development of a wide range of solutions. This research explores the difficulty of monitoring brain activity at the time of a panic attack on a common basis, provided the lack of methodologies to identify correlating factors in brain activity before and after a panic attack to reference the event and provide the healthcare specialist with data-driven tools based on the brain activity. The methodology presented is a transversal proposal of Lean UX as a bridge for the health specialist involvement per the designed stages of software solutions based on a case study to monitor brain activity at the time of a panic attack, leading to common ground solutions to identify its triggers. Additionally, control variables were identified to improve the data quality, and a visualization tool was used to display the results and obtain information on the types of users while improving the UX and UI.

Keywords: Methodology design · Lean UX · Panic attacks · BCI

1 Introduction

The software industry has become a framework of development beyond optimization and data sources, thus powering the design of solutions within a wide spectre of applications across each area of knowledge, reason why a holistic approach provided by software methodologies is key to the deployment of human-based technologies that can range from the use of biometrics such as the ones included in mobile devices to authenticate the user and which can be used for security purposes like bank transactions [29], or even applied for medical purposes to select the most fitted individual for a clinical trial based on monitored biomarkers [8], to the design of interfaces that allow the interconnection between the user with a data source given a digital and physical medium as applied on virtual and

M. Kurosu et al. (Eds.): HCII 2022, LNCS 13519, pp. 357–370, 2022.
https://doi.org/10.1007/978-3-031-17618-0_26

augmented reality [24]; furthermore in a changing world methodologies become adaptable according to the needs to cover either for the industry or the user *per se*, hence leaving behind traditional models like the waterfall development model and instead taking the basis of agile methodologies like design thinking to prioritize the user experience without diminishing the quality of the solutions and paving the way to the development of viable products as is appointed by the Lean UX methodology [12].

Although a methodological approach is the basis for any software project, no blueprint is completed without the proper technology, and in the case of human-computer interaction the user experience (UX) and user interface (UI) principles can be meet more specifically via the implementation of brain-computer interfaces (BCI) tackling problems oriented to information technologies, robotics, artificial intelligence, cognitive sciences and even psychology, [18] given the range of modern applications for electroencephalography and the wavelengths provided by the EEG signals with portable devices that are more accessible to both researchers and the general public to acquire and make use of [22]. In the area of psychology, mental health disorders are one of the main concerns about the overall health of individual mood disorders such as anxiety disorders are estimated to be present in 284 million people around the world with a percentage of 4.7 being women [27], additionally during the pandemic due to COVID-19 data has shown an increase in anxiety disorders in children and adolescents [28] highlighting the importance of data-driven tools to provide solutions.

The methodological design in this article encompasses the working principles of the Lean UX methodology as a basis to shape each minimum viable product within its stages into an accessible software that can provide relevant information of the BCI applied to the analysis and treatment of panic attacks, therefore granting a guideline for case studies and prototypes whilst making the monitoring of the panic attacks more feasible in a common basis with an EEG device.

2   Literary Review

Software engineering is an elemental part of computer sciences as it shapes solutions into well-documented instances and schemes that bring up prototypes to a working environment and monitor the interactions of diverse types of users to make a more accurate assessment of the continuous improvements within the development cycle, likewise, the implementation of software methodologies allows to monitor, optimize, and regulate the process taking place which is why regardless of the application area the methodologies are fitted to satisfy the established need and requirements set.

2.1   Lean UX Methodology

Nowadays Lean and agile methodologies take the leading role for the design, development and implementation of software, however, the merge between traditional iterative models and design focus present in the Lean UX methodology offers a reliable medium to obtain quality products in a timely and cost-wise manner [3] by generating minimum viable products as a target per iteration based on an initial proposal that morphs into it enriched by feedback; its applications extend outside the software industry as empirical studies to reference user behavior and experiences [20] covering the pillars of user interface (UI) and user experience (UX) while facilitating the escalation of software with the knowledge harvested for the work team, in addition to research applications to cover costs and time assets along with the growth of the sector and pressing demands [21].

The core of the Lean UX methodology is composed by its stages as a whole that partakes in the collaborative setting for the team members to act upon [10]; the corresponding purpose for each of its stages is: the approach to the problem that establish a common ground for the strategy to follow, the proposed course of action that approach the problem and helps to contextualize the steps to take, the design of minimum viable products with a potential to be escalated, the execution which can be seen as an experimental design, case study or trial according to the iteration taking place and the degree of advance, and the feedback which propels the advances towards the targeted goal while transitioning to another iteration cycle if required.

2.2 Brain Computer Interfaces (BCI)

Since the invention of perforated cards and later on ENIAC as one of the first computers, the humanity has come a long way from desktop computers to mobile devices and quantum technologies further increasing its performance, needless to say, not only the area of computer sciences have benefited from the technological advances as the increase in logical and operational capability propitiated a suitable environment for scientific and technological advances; the brain, for example, has always been an object of study and research to understand the human behavior and related affections, insights obtained from decades of research have also become part of revolutionary applications like brain-computer interfaces (BCI) that allow to read and interpret the intent from an individual by its brain activity. BCI records brain activity with the possibility to use invasive and non-invasive methods whose objective is to provide real-time interaction between the individual and the computational device, thus generating feedback within the reliant system [13] and establishing a clear connection between the software and the hardware elements.

Within the field of software engineering, the branch of human-computer interaction takes the lead in the UX and UI approach of the BCI as a framework for the development of solutions incurring in the use of the technology while prioritizing the experience of the user and the quality of the interactions held although, aside from the user-centered scheme the logical input provided as feed for data analysis involved is of the utmost importance due to the precision required for the BCI to function optimally, deriving in techniques to read, analyze and process brain signals [15]. The learning curve paired with the increasing demand to update models, devices, and practices with a high acceptance rate and a low margin of error makes it necessary to evaluate the current advances and challenges of the BCI to avoid incurring bias and explore the field of solutions and opportunity areas [25]; particularly with technologies available to the public that generate widespread applications as is the case of EEG signals and its classification [14, 23].

2.3   Mood Disorders: Anxiety Cluster

The human brain can sustain affections denominated mental disorders that can be temporary or permanent, and cause a disruption in the state of mind of an individual affecting its behavior and mental capability; they are classified in several clusters and its diagnosis can differ according to the age group that the individual belongs to since some differential diagnosis make a segmentation not only by how many weeks the symptoms have been present but also by age group given the inherent complexity in early stages and the particular characteristics of the disorder, which coupled with the objective to guarantee the veracity of the psychometric evaluations and studies to have a better quality of life [1]. One of the guidelines for the diagnosis of mental disorders with the most reliable is the Diagnostic and Statistical Manual of Mental Disorders, 4th Edition (DSM-IV) [4], where is worth noting the emotional disorders: depression and anxiety; particularly anxiety disorders that can derive in panic attacks, anxiety disorders are mainly classified in five types: generalized anxiety disorder, compulsive obsessive disorder, panic disorder, post-traumatic stress disorder, and social phobia disorder.

A problem that arises at the moment of making a preliminary analysis or differential diagnosis is the initial conception of the constructs of anxiety, stress, and fear, where anxiety can be defined as a disorder (remnant) or a mood (temporary); however, it frequently tends to be associated with stress in the individual generating confusions with the conceptualization itself, so that is connected to fear. Consequently, Table 1 shows a comparison between anxiety and stress, and anxiety and fear [2, 16] to help with the differentiation.

Table 1. Constructs Characterization

Characteristics	Constructs		
	Anxiety	Stress	Fear
Likability	1. Emotional responses		
	2. Insomnia, difficulty to focus, fatigue, tension and irritability		
	3. Accelerated heartbeat rate and breathing on response to the perceived stimuli		
	4. Physical activity, good eating habits and personal care help to manage stress and anxiety		
Differences	1. Triggered by an internal stimuli	1. Triggered by an external stimuli	1. Triggered by danger in the surrounding environment
	2. It an prevail even without stimuli	2. The stimuli can be temporary	2. The fear mobilizes the body responses, while the anxiety suppress them

3   Related Work

Views on anxiety are portrayed in a multidisciplinary context, although the literature is brimming with the psychiatric and psychological context the range of applications differ in the leading speciality of the research; biomarkers are used within the neuroscience field to provide context, evaluate the success rate of treatments and explore mood-related behavior whereas artificial intelligence techniques contribute to the knowledge representation and the software engineering enables the transference of technologies. To elaborate on the related works Table 2 shows the technologies applied to the constructs of anxiety, post-traumatic stress disorder (PTSD) and fear, in conjunction with the cognitive and emotional processes.

Table 2. Panic attacks: related methodologies and applications

Reference	Technology	Construct	Description	Approach
Kerson, C et al. [19]	Biofeedback	Trauma	Somatic biofeedback for trauma and related comorbidities	Neuropsychology applications
Chen, C et al. [7]	EEG signal	Anxiety	Evaluation of neurofeedback for anxiety relief	Neuropsychiatry applications
Wang, Z et al. [31]	fMRI	PTSD	Connectivity of amygdala subregions associated with PTSD	Neuroimaging applications
Balan, O et al. [5]	Machine learning, deep learning	Fear acrophobia	Research of techniques to automatize fear level detection	Artificial intelligence and virtual reality
Valdes-Sosa et al. [30]	EEG, MRI	Cognition	Neuroimages and cognitive dataset	Neuroimaging applications
Beaurenaut, M et al. [6]	STAI questionnaire	Anxiety	Threat of scream paradigm to study physiological and subjective anxiety	Statistic correlation
Petrescu, L et al. [26]	Virtual reality	Anxiety	Biosignals measurement in a virtual environment to detect anxiety	HCI and virtual reality
Francese, R et al. [11]	Virtual reality	Emotions	User centered methodology for an emotion detection system	User experience

Although the literature review analysis is shown above highlight the technological and methodological applications for anxiety and trauma, the fear response along with the cognitive and emotional process were approached to demonstrate the influence of internal and external stimuli while conducting behavior oriented research whereas trauma was introduced due to the association with the development of PTSD. The current methodological proposal prioritizes the lean approach for the development of software products to integrate the user feedback and the algorithm techniques from artificial intelligence whilst providing a guideline for health specialist based on the insights provided by the methods and iterative products.

4   Methodological Proposal

Considering the Lean UX background along with the hybrid approach of BCI and panic attacks contextualization, the development of the methodology was centered towards an iterative process tailored to user segmentation and requirements fulfillment for testing, prior data recollection for the elaboration of a case study and feedback; shown below Fig. 1 introduces the core stages of the methodology in a linear sequence: segmentation, design, treatment, launching, and evolution, with a breakdown based design in which the segmentation and evaluation stages are linked and all the stages are composed by two correlated subsections.

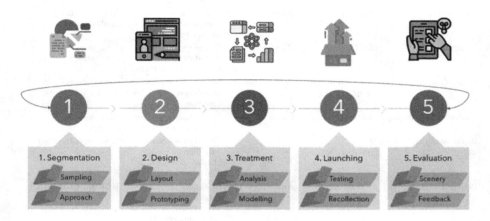

Fig. 1. Methodology design breakdown. Inspired on lean UX [12].

4.1   Segmentation

The segmentation is the opening stage of the methodology and the basis to identify the population, target users, subsequent requirements and needs to be meet within given iterations; to accomplish the projected objectives and allow a margin of time for review and approval of the minimal viable products (MVP) it is divided in sampling and approach:

Sampling. Initial identification of the sample population based on statistical and demographic indicators for further classification. The main objective is to outline a working scheme of the type of users, providing a structure for the assignation of resources and roles to be taken by the multidisciplinary team.

Approach. Type of research and techniques proposed to apply at the target population given the indicators and roles identified in the sampling, with the objective of defining the requirements to cover within each of the following stages and iterations.

4.2   Design

The design stage is the blueprint of the methodology and the MVP's to be delivered at the last stage, it includes the representation of the requirements in layouts and schemes of the main tasks and processes to track down the advances and workflow towards an early deployment of a prototype; it is composed by the layout and prototyping stages:

Layout. Integrates software engineering diagrams and schemes to represent the role of the types of users, the multidisciplinary team and the system/software product as a whole. The objective of the layout is to identify the workflow of the processes, optimize when possible and link the requirements to the processes taking place, hence providing a framework of reference.

Prototyping. Initial development of the software solution to deploy in later stages by taking into account use cases and the progress made towards the requirements, consistently adjusting the working level of the prototype. The objective of prototyping is to shape the MVP advances and obtain further insight from the multidisciplinary team.

4.3   Treatment

The treatment stage involves an exploratory analysis of the data collected from the prototype elaborated in the design stage so that a data model can be obtained and applied for further testing and data recollection prior to launching and while operating. The purpose of the treatment stage lies within the cleaning process in between sub-stages to monitor the margin of error; its sub-stages are analysis and modeling:

Analysis. Processes and techniques oriented towards data that explore a given dataset to identify its structure, composition, and tendencies, its objective is to provide insights into the data obtained from the prototype, monitor the advances, and identify opportunity areas.

Modelling. Transformation of the dataset obtained in the previous stage to match the requirements with the data and insights obtained from the analysis, which objective is to shape the software solution and continuously improve the core model while assigning instances and functions accordingly.

4.4 Launching

The launching stage is the deployment of the software solution that allows to evaluate the hypothesis formulated at the beginning of the process, thus corroborating the objectives of the proposed research space; the software solution must be tested by the users and new data of the interaction is to be collected and stored, its stages are as follows:

Testing. Initial trial of the BCI based software solution to run performance and field tests to monitor both, the human and computational aspects; its objective is to offer a space for observation and analysis to identify adjustment errors that might occur, to suggest changes, optimize areas, or approve the software release.

Recollection. Data gathering with a primary focus on the main user and the connected device that conforms the BCI; objective observation of the behavior to measure the level of interaction with the user, UX, and UI as the pillars of the Lean UX methodology focus.

4.5 Evaluation

The evaluation stage is the culmination of the methodology linear data flow through the five checkpoints, and the beginning of its iterative process as it encompasses the MVP elaborated through each stage and the optimal solution provided as a result of it, hence the sub-stages for the definition of a case study and the incorporation of feedback:

Scenery. Representative data obtained from the testing and recollection processes paired with the statistical and demographic indicator endorsed for the sample population of target users; its objective is to contextualize and create a base for the model of user behavior.

Feedback. Input provided by the users and team members of the disciplinary team regarding the software development, covering an evaluation of the requirements and the suggestions for further iterations; the objective of the feedback is to enable timely changes that can be reflected in the user interaction and assets.

5   MVP Design Guidelines

Introduced by proof of the objectives formulated per stage under the Lean UX premises, an internal iteration was run for the multidisciplinary team members involved in the initial stages of the methodological design: the developer, the health specialist, and the data analyst; MVP were obtained through the process along with corresponding feedback to sustain the knowledge basis of the proposal and the products themselves as a preamble for algorithmic implementation and active case studies of patients with panic attacks. The sub-sections below show the analytical design advances and describe the inquiry for the corresponding stages of the methodology, the MVP target obtained, the accomplishment level, and punctual notes for its improvement and additional filter in between feedback as a whole for further application in psychological interventions at the municipality of Aguascalientes, Mexico on the System for the Integral Development of the Family (Sistema para el Desarrollo Integral de la Familia DIF). It is a governmental entity in Mexico aimed at providing social support to the population in the areas of health, rehabilitation, psychological support and medical care [9,17].

5.1   Segmentation

To validate the sample population and target, the roles from the multidisciplinary team for the software development were defined and assigned accordingly towards the input and output of the data related task to perform, hence after a guided background review on the research topic with a psychologist the sample population was identified and profiled as target user by the developer and data analyst based on the association of the most relevant indicators: age, health condition and associated symptoms; thus the sample population was defined as an age group between 15 to 40 years with anxiety disorder and panic attacks related symptoms, to be approached in a quantitative study process.

5.2   Design

To cover the interactions between the core components involved in the software development a layout of an architectonic classes diagram was elaborated; shown below Fig. 2 represent the interaction between the two main processes of the system in an abstraction level of components with assigned classes to analyze and process the signals respectively, and the user input and output from the health specialist.

The data flow begins in the class of the patient as it integrates the key indicators of age and health condition given the sample population criteria, and the nexus between the processes of the attributed EEG Signals that are to be converted, structured, treated, and subset for the use of the health specialist.

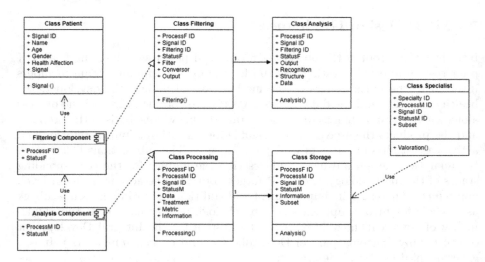

Fig. 2. Classes diagram of the system.

5.3   Treatment

The segmentation of the system functions were outlined in a context diagram shown in Fig. 3 with the main software components to develop and the type of user to exemplify the relationship between each type of user through the components, with the main actor being the patient from whom the EEG Signals come from, and the health specialist as the final user that receives access to the data obtained from the signals once they have been properly processed, filtered and analyzed; therefore offering as result insightful data that can be stored for later access.

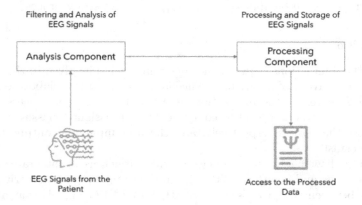

Fig. 3. Context diagram of the system.

5.4   Launching

Complementary to the Context Diagram above in the Fig. 3, the Containers Diagram shown below in the Fig. 4 display the relationship between the software components on a technical level assessing the abstraction in between the data treatment process where data entry from the EEG readings obtained is accessed by the defined classes for the analysis and processing, so that the output generates a dataset accessible for the final user.

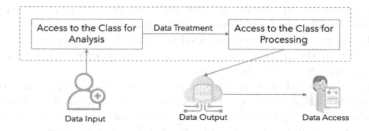

Fig. 4. Containers diagram of the system.

5.5   Evaluation

Based on the user interactions in the system and the abstraction levels identified in the previous sections, the prototype of the system was reviewed, therefore stating the basis of the first exploratory scenery from the methodology; Fig. 5 shows the Python scripts for the analysis and processing components, along with the sampling of the EEG signals dataset under testing and its performance.

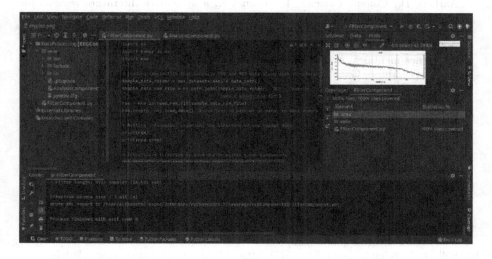

Fig. 5. System evaluation.

6   Conclusions and Future Work

The holistic design and analysis of the proposed methodology and its stages allowed to contrast the formulated hypothesis with the development objectives, the user requirements, and the early MVP designs providing a guideline for upcoming iterations and feedback sessions; subsequently the surrounding processes oriented towards the MVP underlined the importance of their production capacity as well as scalability factoring the exponential growth for the software development scheme while applying the Lean UX approach. Complementary to this the prototyping and feedback sub-stages require a set of standard designs to document the degree of advancement in the case of the prototype, and a metric association for the feedback provided to quantify the user satisfaction and include it within the metrics correspondent to the intervention by the health specialist on anxiety and panic attacks.

To conclude, the data obtained from the designed processes that undergo testing granted the pathway for algorithms applied for data analysis and processing as to obtain further inquires and the level of equipment required to monitor the activity by making it feasible to calibrate an EEG device, process and analyze the signal without significant obstruction by noise; therefore for future works data-based algorithms are to be applied to the key processes incorporating the artificial intelligence as a bridge between the neuroscience application and the guidelines provided by the proposed methodology, enhancing the models within.

References

1. Understanding psychiatric diagnosis in adult mental health. www.bps.org.uk/dcp
2. What's the difference between stress and anxiety? (2019). https://www.apa.org/topics/stress/anxiety-difference
3. Aarlien, D., Colomo-Palacios, R.: Lean UX: a systematic literature review. In: Gervasi, O., et al. (eds.) ICCSA 2020. LNCS, vol. 12254, pp. 500–510. Springer, Cham (2020). https://doi.org/10.1007/978-3-030-58817-5_37
4. Aliño, J.J.L.I., et al.: DSM-IV-TR: Manual diagnóstico y estadístico de los trastornos mentales. American Psychiatric Pub (2008)
5. Bălan, O., Moise, G., Moldoveanu, A., Leordeanu, M., Moldoveanu, F.: An investigation of various machine and deep learning techniques applied in automatic fear level detection and acrophobia virtual therapy. Sensors 20(2), 496 (2020)
6. Beaurenaut, M., Tokarski, E., Dezecache, G., Grèzes, J.: The 'threat of scream' paradigm: a tool for studying sustained physiological and subjective anxiety. Sci. Rep. 10(1), 1–11 (2020)
7. Chen, C., et al.: Efficacy evaluation of neurofeedback-based anxiety relief. Front. Neurosci. 15, 758068 (2021)
8. Cheng, S., Kerr, K.F., Thiessen-Philbrook, H., Coca, S.G., Parikh, C.R.: Biopetsurv: methodology and open source software to evaluate biomarkers for prognostic enrichment of time-to-event clinical trials. PLoS ONE 15(9), e0239486 (2020)
9. DIF: Dif estatal sistema para el desarrollo integral de la familia (2022). https://www.aguascalientes.gob.mx/dif/
10. Follett, J.: What is lean UX? (2017). https://www.oreilly.com/radar/what-is-lean-ux/

11. Francese, R., Risi, M., Tortora, G.: A user-centered approach for detecting emotions with low-cost sensors. Multimed. Tools App. **79**(47), 35885–35907 (2020)
12. Gothelf, J., Seiden, J.: Lean UX. O'Reilly Media, Inc., Sebastopol (2021)
13. Graimann, B., Allison, B.Z., Pfurtscheller, G.: Brain-computer interfaces: revolutionizing human-computer interaction. In: Tan, D., Nijholt, A. (eds) Brain-Computer Interfaces. Human-Computer Interaction Series. Springer, London (2010). https://doi.org/10.1007/978-1-84996-272-8_1
14. Gu, X., et al.: EEG-based brain-computer interfaces (BCIS): a survey of recent studies on signal sensing technologies and computational intelligence approaches and their applications. IEEE/ACM Trans. Comput. Biol. Bioinf. **18**(5), 1645–1666 (2021). https://doi.org/10.1109/TCBB.2021.3052811
15. Hassanien, A.E., Azar, A.: Brain-Computer Interfaces. Springer, Switzerland (2015). https://doi.org/10.1007/978-3-319-10978-7
16. Hendel, H.J.: Anxiety and fear: what's the difference? (2021). https://www.nami.org/Blogs/NAMI-Blog/May-2021/Anxiety-And-Fear-What-s-The-Difference
17. Institutional, E., De Enlace, J.Y.: Sistema nacional para el desarrollo integral de la familia. Titular Del Organismo Dirección General Jurídica y de Enlace Institucional (2006)
18. Kawala-Sterniuk, A., et al.: Summary of over fifty years with brain-computer interfaces-a review. Brain Sci. **11**(1), 43 (2021)
19. Kerson, C.: Biofeedback as a viable somatic modality for trauma and related comorbidities: a new methodology. Int. Body Psychother. J. **18**(2), 196–207 (2019)
20. Kompaniets, V., Lyz, A., Kazanskaya, A.: An empirical study of goal setting in UX/UI-design. In: 2020 IEEE 14th International Conference on Application of Information and Communication Technologies (AICT), pp. 1–5 (2020). https://doi.org/10.1109/AICT50176.2020.9368570
21. Krout, K., Carrascal, J.P., Lowdermilk, T.: Lean UX research at scale: a case study. In: Proceedings of the Conference on Mensch Und Computer, pp. 53–59. MuC 2020, Association for Computing Machinery, New York, NY, USA (2020). https://doi.org/10.1145/3404983.3405587
22. Kübler, A.: The history of BCI: from a vision for the future to real support for personhood in people with locked-in syndrome. Neuroethics **13**(2), 163–180 (2020)
23. Larsen, E.A.: Classification of EEG signals in a brain-computer interface system. Master's thesis, Institutt for datateknikk og informasjonsvitenskap (2011)
24. Lorenz, M., et al.: CAD to VR-a methodology for the automated conversion of kinematic CAD models to virtual reality. Proc. CIRP **41**, 358–363 (2016)
25. Mridha, M., et al.: Brain-computer interface: advancement and challenges. Sensors **21**(17), 5746 (2021)
26. Petrescu, L., et al.: Integrating bio signals measurement in virtual reality environments for anxiety detection. Sensors **20**(24), 7088 (2020)
27. Saloni Dattani, H.R., Roser, M.: Mental health. Our World in Data (2021). https://ourworldindata.org/mental-health
28. Śniadach, J., Szymkowiak, S., Osip, P., Waszkiewicz, N.: Increased depression and anxiety disorders during the COVID-19 pandemic in children and adolescents: a literature review. Life **11**(11), 1188 (2021)
29. Streuter, G.W., Price, W.P.: Methodology for identifying local/mobile client computing devices using a network based database containing records of hashed distinctive hardware, software, and user provided biometric makers for authorization of electronic transactions and right of entry to secure locations, 22 September 2016. US Patent App. 14/693,707

30. Valdes-Sosa, P.A., et al.: The Cuban human brain mapping project, a young and middle age population-based EEG, MRI, and cognition dataset. Sci. Data **8**(1), 1–12 (2021)
31. Wang, Z., et al.: The resting-state functional connectivity of amygdala subregions associated with post-traumatic stress symptom and sleep quality in trauma survivors. Eur. Arch. Psych. Clin. Neurosci. **271**(6), 1053–1064 (2020). https://doi.org/10.1007/s00406-020-01104-3

Establishing Clinical Protocols for BCI-Based Motor Rehabilitation in Individuals Post Stroke - The Impact of Feedback Type and Selected Outcome Measures: A Systematic Review

Elizabeth Clark[1] , Adrienne Czaplewski[1], Khoa Nguyen[1], Patrick Pasciucco[1], Marimar Rios[1], and Milena Korostenskaja[2,3]( )

[1] AdventHealth University, Orlando, FL 32803, USA
[2] AdventHealth, Functional Brain Mapping and BCI Lab, Orlando, FL 32803, USA
Milena.Korostenskaja@gmail.com
[3] The Institute of Neuroapproaches, Winter Springs, FL 32708, USA

Abstract. Stroke is a major cause of disability resulting in multiple system impairments. Limited extended care resulted in prioritizing high level repetitions of task-specific activities to improve function. One such modality is BCI to drive motor rehabilitation. While several systematic reviews and meta-analyses highlight the benefits of utilizing BCIs to enhance motor recovery, it is still unclear how these interventions facilitate rehabilitation of motor function in individuals post-stroke. This systematic review analyzed outcome measures and type of feedback during BCI interventions to inform future protocol development. Included articles were held to rigorous criteria, and potential studies were assessed for methodological quality using the PEDro Scale. Only articles that scored six or greater were included for analysis, and nine randomized controlled trials were included. In brief, the randomized controlled trials demonstrated that BCI enhanced the motor function of the upper extremity as measured by the FMA UE, however no other consistent outcome measures of function or self-efficacy were reported. EEG and ERD of the affected sensorimotor cortices were significantly enhanced in the BCI groups ($p < 0.05$). For those studies that measured retention of function, long-lasting improvements were noted, and BCI coupled to FES elicited significant, clinically relevant motor recovery. Somatosensory/motor and visual feedback were the most common across reviewed studies. While each of the studies had a wide variety of methods, all the evidence suggested that subjects improved. These findings suggest that the most important concept in protocol development may have been the incorporation of principles of motor learning.

Keywords: Brain computer interface (BCI) · Stroke (CVA) · Feedback · Outcome measures

1 Literature Review

1.1 Stroke

Stroke is defined as "a neurological deficit attributed to an acute focal injury of the central nervous system (CNS) by a vascular cause," [1] with the annual incidence in the US of roughly 795,000 individuals [2, 3]. Stroke is a major cause of disability and can result in multiple system impairments, leading to functional deficits in gait and activities of daily living (ADLs). Limited extended care accessibility resulted in a search for therapeutic interventions, prioritizing high level repetitions of task-specific activities to improve function in individuals post-stroke [1–6].

1.2 Brain Computer Interface

One such modality is brain-computer interface (BCI) that utilizes brain signals to drive rehabilitation of motor function [7–13]. The most common type of BCI for motor rehabilitation is based on acquiring the motor imagery-related brain signals and translating them into the device control command. The specific type of brain signal acquired during this process is somatosensory-rhythm (SMR), recorded in the vicinity of the sensorimotor cortex, giving name to its based BCI system (SMR-BCI).

SMR-BCI may facilitate an individual's return to function and improve quality of life [7–13]. The outcomes of the SMR-BCI intervention might be influenced by several internal and external factors, with the closed loop feedback being the major one [7–13]. The integration of specific feedback components has been shown to be an innovative rehabilitation strategy, with potential to reinstitute central motor programs specific to hand function [7–13].

1.3 Feedback Provided During BCI Interventions

The following types of feedback integrated in the SMR-BCIs can be considered: visual, auditory, proprioceptive, haptic, virtual reality, magnetic stimulation, and functional electrical stimulation (FES) [14–23]. Each of these feedback types can influence in different ways the SMR-BCI and affect the outcomes [14–23]. A combination of several feedback modalities can significantly maximize the rehabilitation outcomes [14–23]. Only one systematic review to this day partially considered the effect of feedback on BCI performance, [21] concluding that FES may be a better choice for functional recovery than other kinds of neural feedback [21]. The authors did not aim to specifically answer this question and the information about the use of optimal feedback in the BCI intervention is still missing, thus, impeding the development of the BCI intervention protocols to maximize rehabilitation outcomes.

With the emerging BCI technology, clinicians and scientists can develop protocols based upon theories of experience-dependent neural plasticity principles including specificity of tasks, repetition of functional movements, and incorporation of salient activities [12, 24]. Several systematic reviews and meta-analysis highlight the benefits of utilizing BCIs to enhance motor recovery specifically for upper extremity post-stroke [13–22]. However, it is still unclear how these interventions facilitate the rehabilitation of motor function in individuals post-stroke.

1.4 Measurable Outcomes as a Result of BCI Interventions

In 2017, Monge Pereira et al. analyzed the methodological qualities and impact of SMR-BCI intervention on motor rehabilitation of upper limb function [14]. Their results suggested that BCI interventions may promote motor recovery in individuals post stroke, but randomized controlled trials with well-established criteria for homogeneous subject selection were recommended [14]. Moreover, the use of advanced neurophysiologic assessments, consisting of functional outcome measures aligned with neuroimaging, was recommended to determine how BCI interventions cause change [14].

Functional outcome measures objectively measure how functional tasks are completed. Examples include activities of daily living, mobility related tasks, and may include seeking to understand an individuals' perceived self-efficacy during these functional tasks. To understand the functional outcome measures utilized by researchers, nine systematic reviews and meta-analyses from 2018 to 2022 were critically analyzed [14–22]. All of these reviews sought to understand the impact of BCI interventions on the motor rehabilitation of individuals post stroke.

Across all systematic reviews and meta-analyses, the primary functional outcome measure utilized was the Fugl-Meyer Motor Assessment of the Upper Extremity (FMA-UE) [15, 17–19, 21, 22]. The FMA-UE assesses a wide range of impairments including reflexes, volitional movement (with or without synergy), coordination, sensation, and passive range of movement [25]. While detailed in nature, this examination is exclusive to the objective measurement of impairments, via body structures and function, and does not elaborate on performance of ADLs, mobility, or self-efficacy. Numerous additional functional outcome measures were noted: the manual function test, the Jebsen hand function test, the action research arm test, the box and block test, grip strength, pinch strength, tone via the modified ashworth scale, the wolf motor function test, the motor activity log, and the nine-hole peg test [17, 19, 21, 22]. The emphasis of all of this data collection did not elaborate on functional limitations, community reintegration, or self-efficacy [17, 19, 21, 22].

2 Study Aims

This systematic review (PROSPERO ID: CRD42022298972) had two aims: 1) to understand and categorize recommended outcome measures based on impairment, functional limitations, and self-efficacy for comprehensive assessment of subject outcomes; and 2) to analyze and recommend the type of feedback for BCI intervention that maximizes upper extremity motor rehabilitation in individuals post-stroke.

3 Methods

3.1 Search Strategy

Researchers utilized an extensive electronic search of the literature in both the PubMed and CINAHL databases. Each database was searched using various combinations of a variety of search terms, as viewed in Table 1. MeSH terms were utilized when available to ensure that searches were efficient, comprehensive, and provided researchers with the highest quality of evidence. The last search of the literature was performed on May 20, 2022.

Table 1. Search terms.

brain computer interface (BCI)*, human machine interface, motor imagery based BCI system, human computer interface, sensorimotor rhythm (SMR) BCI
feedback, auditory feedback, visual feedback, sensory feedback, virtual reality feedback, immersive feedback, magnetic stimulation feedback, proprioceptive feedback, haptic feedback
functional electrical stimulation (FES), virtual reality*, motor rehabilitation
stroke*, upper extremity*

* MeSH term

3.2 Selection Criteria

When selecting articles for inclusion, researchers were held to the following criteria: 1) published recently (2010–2022); 2) available in English; 3) randomized controlled trials (RCTs), 4) subjects aged 18 years and older; 5) subjects sustaining their first stroke; 6) primary focus of BCI interventions was on upper extremity motor rehabilitation; 7) research protocols documented feedback provided, and 8) motor rehabilitation was tracked via evidence based outcome measures.

3.3 Methodological Quality Assessment

All potential studies were screened and assessed for methodological quality using the Physiotherapy Evidence Database (PEDro) Scale [26]. This tool has become more prominent within research over the recent years and numerous studies have assessed its credibility and implications with regards to article quality assessment [27–29]. According to Moseley et al., the Cochrane risk of bias and PEDro scales were similar in construct when examining bias of randomized controlled trials [29]. In addition, Cashin et al. suggested that the PEDro score had "fair" to "excellent" inter-rater reliability [27]. The tool consists of 11 criteria, in which criteria 1 is strictly used to assess the external validity and is not taken into consideration when calculating total scoring. The remaining criteria evaluate the internal validity of the article in question, with a maximum score of 10/10. Studies assessed with the PEDro scale result in the following scores: 0–3/10 "poor" quality, 4–5/10 "fair" quality, 6–8/10 "good" quality, and 9–10/10 "excellent" quality. Case reports, case studies, narrative reviews, and expert opinion do not meet PEDro rating criteria and were excluded from this systematic review.

Prior to scoring the included articles, researchers practiced on articles already scored with the PEDro to ensure they could reliably, consistently, and accurately interpret and apply the PEDro scoring criteria. Researchers worked in pairs to analyze articles via the PEDro scale. In the case of any discrepancy, researchers worked to come to a mutually agreeable decision on each PEDro scored item for each article. In some cases, articles had been previously scored and the results were available via PEDro online [26]. Only articles analyzed that scored six or greater were included for further analysis to understand the details surrounding the studies, including: subject demographics, feedback type, outcome measures, and overall researcher recommendations.

4   Results

Based on the search of relevant literature and eligibility of articles established via the PEDro scale, a total of nine randomized controlled trials met the rigorous inclusion criteria and were analyzed. The Preferred Reporting Items for Systematic Review and Meta-Analyses (PRISMA) flow diagram is presented in Fig. 1. The PEDro scale results for included RCTs are displayed in Table 2.

Ultimately, researchers sought to analyze outcome measures utilized to document changes due to the intervention and feedback provided during intervention protocols. Additionally, subject demographics and randomized controlled trial recommendations were summarized.

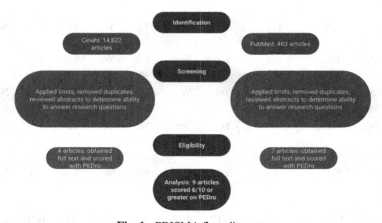

Fig. 1. PRISMA flow diagram.

4.1   Analysis of Outcome Measures Analyzed

When documenting change as the result of an intervention, it is imperative that researchers utilize the evidence to make informed decisions surrounding selection, implementation, and utilization of standardized tests and measures. These outcome measures can provide objective data regarding change via cut-off scores and minimal detectable change (MDC) [38]. While a cut off score may suggest fall risk or functional status change, the MDC is the amount of measurable change necessary to be considered "an actual change" in status or function, that could not be accounted for by chance [38].

Table 2. Assessment of internal validity of RCTs via PEDro scale.

PEDro scale items	Biasiucci [30]	Cantillo Negrete [31]	Chen [32]	Chew [33]	Hu [34]	Kim [12]	Li [35]	Li [36]	Ramos [37]
1 - eligibility criteria (not part of overall score)	Yes	Yes	Yes	Yes	Yes	Yes	Yes	Yes	Yes
2 - random allocation	No	Yes	Yes	Yes	Yes	Yes	Yes	Yes	Yes
3 - allocation was concealed	Yes	Yes	Yes	Yes	Yes	Yes	Yes	No	Yes
4 - baseline comparability	Yes	Yes	Yes	Yes	Yes	Yes	Yes	Yes	Yes
5 - blind subjects	Yes	Yes	Yes	Yes	No	No	No	No	Yes
6 - blind therapists	Yes	Yes	No	No	No	No	No	No	Yes
7 - blind assessors	Yes	Yes	No	Yes	Yes	Yes	Yes	No	No
8 - adequate follow up	Yes	Yes	Yes	Yes	Yes	Yes	Yes	Yes	Yes
9 - intention to treat analysis	Yes	Yes	Yes	Yes	No	No	No	Yes	No
10 - between group comparisons	Yes	Yes	Yes	Yes	Yes	Yes	Yes	Yes	Yes
11 - point estimates and variability	Yes	Yes	Yes	Yes	No	No	Yes	No	Yes
Total score/10	9/10	10/10	8/10	9/10	6/10	6/10	7/10	6/10	8/10

By consistently documenting and observing trends via standardized outcome measures, change as the result of an intervention can be more effectively and objectively tracked over time [39].

The consistent implementation of evidence-based outcome measures in the treatment of adults with neurologic diagnosis is crucial to monitor change, quantify function, enhance communication across an interdisciplinary team, and increase the efficiency of patient care [40]. The International Classification of Functioning, Disability, and Health Model (ICF) classifies outcome measures into categories [41]. These outcome measures can be categorized into categories that assess body function, body structure, and activities/participation [41]. Typically, during a comprehensive assessment in the clinic,

Table 3. Assessment of internal validity of RCTs via PEDro scale.

Outcome measure	ICF category of outcome measured	Biasiucci [30]	Cantillo Negrete [31]	Chen [32]	Chew [33]	Hu [34]	Kim [12]	Li [35]	Li [36]	Ramos [37]
Fugl Meyer (FMA UE) or Modified FMA (cFMA UE)	Body function and structure	Improved at posttest* and follow up*	Improved in both groups*	Improved in both groups*	Improved in both groups*	Improved*	Improved*	Improved*	Improved at 2 wks* (both) and 4 wks* (treatment group)	post2 was improved*
Action Research Arm Test (ARAT)	Activity and participation		Increased in both groups*					Increased*		
Motor Activity Log (MAL)	Activity and participation						Increased*			
Outcome Measure	ICF Category of Outcome Measured	Biasiucci [30]	Cantillo Negrete [31]	Chen [32]	Chew [33]	Hu [34]	Kim [12]	Li [35]	Li [36]	Ramos [37]

(continued)

Table 3. (continued)

Outcome measure	ICF category of outcome measured	Biasiucci [30]	Cantillo Negrete [31]	Chen [32]	Chew [33]	Hu [34]	Kim [12]	Li [35]	Li [36]	Ramos [37]
Wolf Motor Function Test	Activity and participation								Improved at 2 wks* for both groups and 4 wks* for TX group only	
Strength	Body structure	Increased at post1* and follow up* (Medical Research Council Scale)				Increased in both groups* (Motor Status Scale)				
Barthel or Modified Barthel Index	Activity and participation								Improved at 2 wks* for both groups	

* Results were statistically significant and reported as change measured via MDC or $p < 0.05$ in comparison to control group.

clinicians seek to utilize at measures from multiple categories to ensure a thorough assessment of both the impact of pathology on body structure and function, as well as functional status. Therefore, it was our intent during this systematic review to understand statistically significant changes tracked via evidence-based outcome measures. See Table 3 for details.

4.2 Analysis of Feedback Provided

According to the data summarized in Table 4, the most common feedback provided during the BCI interventions was somatosensory/motor. Eight studies out of nine utilized this feedback type [12, 30–33, 35–37]. This finding was expected, as it aligns with the purpose of rehabilitation of motor UE function in patients post-stroke. However, the type of somatosensory/motor feedback varied among the studies. Three studies used FES [12, 30, 35], another three studies used robotic orthosis (all three had different designs) [31, 33, 37], and two studies used exoskeleton as their somatosensory/motor feedback modality [32, 36]. It can be concluded that with rare exceptions, all study protocols agree with using somatosensory/motor feedback as the primary feedback modality for motor UE rehabilitation post-stroke. However, a search for optimal somatosensory/motor feedback devices continues and includes different models and designs of FES devices, exoskeletons, and robotic hand orthoses.

The second most common feedback modality type was visual - more than half of the analyzed studies utilized this as their feedback modality [12, 31, 33, 34, 36]. Visual system plays a crucial role in human sensation and perception. Therefore, the use of visual feedback as a second choice in BCI intervention may stem from the appreciation of the significance of the visual system in humans and the amount of the resources allocated to it in the human brain. It is important to mention that when the movement is being elicited during the somatosensory/motor feedback (e.g., FES, exoskeleton, orthosis), the patients can receive visual feedback by simply looking at their own hands moving. Visual attention requires subjects to keep their attention on their hands during the task execution. For that reason, a different type of visual feedback during BCI-based rehabilitation sessions was provided in three studies, with the goal of engaging the patient in observing the feedback. For example, immersive virtual reality feedback was provided by Hu et al. [34] to avoid external distractors and allow the subjects to concentrate on the visualized hands completely. While in other studies, such as Li et al. [36] and Cantillo Negrete et al. [31], they utilized emotional components in their visual feedback. This was done by providing happy/unhappy faces indicative of the success or failure, respectively, of a patient's intent to perform a movement. When the capacity of the person's ability to process information was exceeded, emotional stimuli were provided as support.

The least common feedback was auditory. Only two of the analyzed studies provided this type of feedback following motor imagery task execution [12, 36]. Similar to visual feedback, the type of auditory feedback was not described in detail by Kim et al. [12] and, therefore, cannot be critically evaluated. The auditory feedback described by Lee et al. [36] was of a verbal nature and included emotionally charged sentences to motivate study participants. For example, when the patient's intent to move was not identified, the "Cheer up! Try again!" was auditorily presented. At the same time the phrase "Congratulations! You got it!" was used when the patient's intent to move was successfully identified.

Here, the auditory feedback serves a purpose of emotional stimuli, performing a similar function as earlier described visual feedback with emotional faces/characters. The reason for underutilizing this feedback type might be easily interfered with by auditory signals present in the environment, including noises, surrounding sounds, voices, commands, and others. Nevertheless, the utility of auditory feedback cannot be underestimated, and we will address this topic in our discussion. In summary, SMR-BCI research for motor rehabilitation post-stroke evaluated in our systematic review study clearly demonstrates that the current use of auditory feedback is limited and mostly reserved for emotionally charged verbal stimuli.

Additionally, multimodal feedback, a combination of two or more types, was used in two studies [12, 36]. However, the type of auditory and visual feedback was not described in detail by Kim et al. [12] and, therefore, cannot be interpreted. This leaves only one study among ten to utilize feedback from three modalities [36]. As described by Li et al. [36], the combination of somatosensory/motor, visual, and auditory components was only provided when the person had a successful intent to perform a movement. When the intent was unsuccessful, the somatosensory/motor feedback component was excluded, and only two feedback modalities were used - visual and auditory. The lack of multimodal feedback can be explained by technically challenging design solutions needed to implement it. In summary, our conducted review demonstrates that despite the evidence of the importance of multimodal feedback, it is very rarely used. Possible hardware and software improvements may shift this situation towards more frequent multimodal feedback implementation.

Finally, more than half of all studies used additional intervention training to the one already provided by BCI [12, 33–36]. In this way, Kim et al. [12] used action observation before the MI-BCI session coupled with FES. In another study, Chew et al. [33] used transcranial direct current stimulation (tDCS) before the MI-BCI intervention coupled with the MIT-Manus robot. Similarly, Hu et al. [34] provided subjects with sensory feedback on the back of both hands prior to attempting the movement prompted by the action of the virtual hand on the screen.

Li et al. [35] used a different approach, where before treatment the subjects in the BCI group were trained to complete MI tasks to effectively perform the MI component of the study; in addition, the authors included five games in the rehabilitation training course - "basic cognition tasks – move eyes, entertainment relaxation – lift a balloon, quick reaction – balance a beam, daily behavior – drink water and compound cognition task – navigate a maze." Whereas Li et al. [36] used video observation for study participants, where they observed the video demonstrating actions of "grabbing the object" or "putting the object down" while imagining performing the action of grabbing the object or putting the object down; importantly, multi-modal feedback, such as visual auditory, and somatosensory, was provided only when the patient's intent to perform movement was successful. Some of the authors refer to these components as feedback, whereas they constitute an additional intervention but not actual feedback. Each of these added interventions can influence the results of the study and have an additive effect on other study components, including feedback. Their contribution to the rehabilitation success still needs to be determined.

Table 4. Feedback provided during BCI interventions.

Feedback provided	Biasiucci [30]	Cantillo Negrete [31]	Chen [32]	Chew [33]	Hu [34]	Kim [12]	Li [35]	Li [36]	Ramos [37]
Visual		Visual feedback from the screen with emotional component: "Patients were shown faces with different degrees of smiling expressions after a defined number of trials had elapsed (a run of the system). This feedback indicated the number of times the system correctly identified MI and activated the robotic hand orthosis."		Visual feedback from the screen: "Indicated the success or failure of MI detection for each MI task."	The movements of virtual hands with VR glasses: "The virtual hand displayed the movements (grasping or extending) according to the MI of the patients."	Yes, but details unknown: "Simultaneously, visual and auditory feedbacks were generated during the process, which allowed patients to adjust their mental state according to the feedback."		Visual feedback from the screen with emotional component: Happy/unhappy face indicated the success or failure, respectively, of the patient's intention to perform a movement (reflected in an ability to generate mu-rhythm)	

(continued)

Table 4. (*continued*)

Feedback provided	Biasiucci [30]	Cantillo Negrete [31]	Chen [32]	Chew [33]	Hu [34]	Kim [12]	Li [35]	Li [36]	Ramos [37]
Auditory						Yes, but details unknown :"Simultaneously, visual and auditory feedback were generated during the process, which allowed patients to adjust their mental state according to the feedback."		Verbal feedback was provided: "Cheer up! Try again!" - when patient's intent to move was not identified; "Congratulations! You got it!" - when the patient's intent to move was identified	

(*continued*)

Table 4. (*continued*)

Feedback provided	Biasiucci [30]	Cantillo Negrete [31]	Chen [32]	Chew [33]	Hu [34]	Kim [12]	Li [35]	Li [36]	Ramos [37]
Somatosensory	FES: "Elicits functional movements; conveys proprioceptive and somatosensory information; massive recruitment of Golgi tendon organs and muscle spindle feedback circuits."	Robotic hand orthosis: "If the processing stage detected MI of the stroke patients' paralyzed hand, a command was sent to a robotic hand orthosis fixed to that hand, which then provided passive flexion and extension of their paralyzed fingers."	Exoskeleton (Omega force feedback device): "When the BCI system correctly recognized the intention of the patients' motor attempt, it would output command and manipulate the Omega force feedback device and drive the patients' affected hands to complete the wrist extension motion."	Robotic hand orthosis (The Inmotion MIT-Manus robot): "Was used to provide unrestricted unilateral passive and active shoulder and elbow movements in the horizontal plane.", "Once motor intention was successfully detected, the robot-assisted motion would be triggered according to the clock exercise therapy of the MIT-Manus robot"		FES: "When patients correctly imagined the movement and their attention level went up the attention threshold, FES was triggered and stimulated wrist extensor muscles of the affected upper extremity."	FES: "Once patients correctly imagined the movement five times in succession, FFS was triggered and stimulated the affected UE's extensor carpus radialis muscles."	Exoskeleton hand: "Would assist the paretic hand in grasping or opening action according to the MI task cued on the video"	Robotic orthosis (two types): "Two movements were practiced, each of them associated with a specific robotic orthosis: (1) open and close the fingers or (2) move the paretic upper limb forward and backward."

4.3 Analysis of Subject Demographics

Often when reviewing published research, clinicians seek to understand if the subject population is truly representative of the general population seen in a clinical environment. At times, due to strict inclusion and exclusion criteria, subject populations are not always representative of the heterogeneity of clients serviced in the clinic.

However, based on the subject recruitment analyzed across all nine studies, the subject demographics seemed to be representative of the population of individuals seen clinically post stroke [12, 30–37]. Each study identified adult subjects with a first-time stroke, inclusive of individuals either post hemorrhagic or ischemic stroke. Additionally, researchers clearly delineated in all studies that treatment and control populations were statistically homogeneous regarding gender and affected hemisphere [12, 30–37].

However, the chronicity of stroke varied widely across the studies, ranging anywhere from subacute (0–6 months) to chronic (>6 months) [12, 30–37]. While this is common clinically to treat clients across a wide range of chronicity, it was difficult to note from these studies which population was optimal for timing of interventions provided. It may be that the chronicity of stroke is not relevant when considering the BCI-based motor rehabilitation, but that cannot be firmly concluded from this analysis.

Additionally, while some studies clearly identified inclusion/exclusion criteria surrounding existing wrist/hand functionality, others did not. It may be of importance to note baseline hand/finger functionality beyond the FMA UE score, to better interpret if changes in the study are due to interventions or may be due to neurologic healing from the stroke itself.

4.4 Analysis of Randomized Controlled Trial Recommendations

In brief, the randomized controlled trials demonstrated that BCI-based motor rehabilitation enhanced the motor function of the upper extremity for stroke patients as measured by the FMA UE due to changes in measured brain function via EEG [12, 30–37]. Additionally, event-related desynchronization (ERD) of the affected sensorimotor cortices (SMCs) were significantly enhanced in the BCI groups ($p < 0.05$) [12, 30–37]. For those studies that measured retention of function at a post-test follow up, BMI-based motor rehabilitation promoted long-lasting improvements in motor function of chronic stroke patients with severe paresis [12, 30–37]. Furthermore, BCI coupled to FES elicited significant, clinically relevant, and lasting motor recovery in chronic stroke survivors more effectively than sham FES, as evidenced by an increase in functional connectivity between motor areas in the affected hemisphere which correlated with functional improvement [12, 30–37]. Finally, FES with VR-based rehabilitation may be more effective than cyclic FES in improving distal upper extremity gross motor performance poststroke [12, 30–37].

5   Discussion

First, it was noted during this systematic review, that while the subject demographics were rather similar and characteristic across all RCTs, and of those post-stroke individuals seen clinically, the wide variability in chronicity of stroke and baseline hand function made it difficult to understand the optimal subject for this intervention.

Second, as a result of systematic review, we noted that researchers utilized a wide variety of outcome measures [12, 30–37]. All studies utilized the Fugl-Meyer Assessment (FMA UE or cFMA UE) as this evidence-based outcome measure tracked active range of motion, passive range of motion, reflexes, and tone over time with each administration of the tool [12, 30–37]. However, while not all outcome measures captured statistically significant change, in total, fifteen different clinically relevant standardized outcome measures were utilized across nine studies [12, 30–37]. Across the nine randomized controlled trials, the outcome measures utilized most consistently measured impairment (body structure or body function), with little emphasis on function (activity and participation) or self-efficacy of subjects.

While the researchers were clear in their presentation of data analysis including use of relevant cut-off scores, MDC, and/or statistical analysis, it is difficult to ascertain from this systematic review, outside of the FMA, which outcome measures and standardized tests should be included in future research for a comprehensive assessment, as many did not show clinically or statistically relevant change, and no other measures were consistent across randomized controlled trials.

Additionally, there was great variability in follow up measurement time points [12, 30–37]. While five studies utilized outcome measures for pre and post testing only, the other four studies included a follow-up time point after the conclusion of the intervention, to further understand retention of changes as a result of intervention [12, 30–37]. However, the final measurement for follow up was anywhere from two weeks post intervention to 12 months post intervention [12, 30–37].

Furthermore, when seeking to understand the outcome measure selection process, most researchers and protocols selected standardized tests and measures which focused on body structure and function, without seeking to understand functional implications and subject self-efficacy. Only four of the nine studies evaluated subject self-efficacy via either the Barthel (statistically significant), modified Barthel, Stroke Impact Scale, and European Stroke Scale, while the rest overlooked this variable [12, 30–37]. Moore et al. [40] suggested a core set of clinical outcome measures that is comprehensive across all ICF domains of body structure, body function, and activities/participation. It would be important for researchers moving forward with BCI protocols to ensure inclusion of clinical outcome measures that seek to understand subject improvement across all domains, as well as at timepoints in the future to assess retention of improvements long-term [40, 41].

In this systematic review, we explored the type of feedback included in BCI-based protocols for UE motor rehabilitation in patients post-stroke. The importance of including feedback in the BCI-based rehabilitation protocols cannot be underestimated. The evidence of improved SMR-BCI performance comes from a number of studies, including those demonstrating changes in the brain network activity, and topology, in response to neurofeedback [42]. A high correlation between event-related coherence and SMR-BCI performance with classical visual feedback, auditory feedback, or functional electrical stimulation feedback has been demonstrated [43]. Moreover, improved SMR-BCI performance associated with provided feedback also resulted in elevated motor cortical excitability and an optimized state of functional brain networks [23].

As a result of our review, we found that current studies are united in their intent to utilize at least one form of feedback. They preferentially use somatosensory/motor feedback in their SMR-BCI-based motor rehabilitation studies. We speculated that the main reason for the unanimous choice of this particular feedback type stemmed from the nature of rehabilitation itself, which attempts to improve motor and sensory function. However, there is evidence from several research studies to support the use of additional feedback. For example, the effect of proprioceptive feedback seems more prominent than visual feedback. For the subjects' attention to stay focused, using their own hands as stimuli may not always be significant enough, as a portion of attention is already allocated for task execution (e.g., imagining closing and opening a hand). Moreover, the external distractors, including patients' surroundings, may also deter their attention from their hands and decrease MI-BCI performance [23]. For example, researchers described how Darvishi et al. [44] examined the effect of proprioceptive feedback by using two mechanical hand orthoses manipulated by the motor imagery task performed by the user [23]. Proprioceptive feedback improved motor imagery-related operant learning, evident in SMR beta-band modulation. Vukelic and Gharabaghi [45] demonstrated similar findings. When proprioceptive feedback was used, an advanced degree of functional coupling of theta and beta-band modulation was demonstrated than with visual feedback.

Whereas the somatosensory/motor feedback type seems to be an obvious choice to include in BCI-based motor rehabilitation protocols, there is still some discrepancy about using other feedback types, such as visual and auditory. The latter, especially, remains underutilized. At the same time, scientific evidence points towards reevaluating the underutilization of auditory feedback for improved SMR-BCI performance. Auditory feedback may improve SMR-BCI performance either combined with visual feedback or independently [23]. For example, when SMR-BCI were presented with initial auditory feedback, their average classification accuracy, and average peak classification accuracy consistently improved [46]. The exact technology of auditory feedback (mono, stereo, or 3-D auditory) does not play a major role [46]. Therefore, an exploration into integrating the auditory feedback into the SMR-based BCI protocols for motor function rehabilitation is warranted. Additionally, the inclusion of emotional feedback in BCI-based rehabilitation protocols can be considered, especially in patients with difficulties processing information and resource allocation. In conclusion, the use of the visual system as a second feedback route for BCI-based motor rehabilitation proves to be legitimate from the cognitive neuroscience perspective. Moreover, the use of immersive visual feedback can be especially recommended.

6   Recommendations

Based upon our analysis, while each of the studies included in this systematic review had a wide variety of methods, with varying intervention modalities, outcome measures, and timepoints for follow up, all the researchers suggested that the subjects improved in their outcomes. These findings, across all methodologies, suggest that the most important concept in protocol development may have been the incorporation of the principles of motor learning [42]. As previously described by Clark et al. in 2019, "Some of the most common principles that appear to have a significant impact on the alteration of neuronal wiring include the following: specificity of the task, repetition of functional movements, and the incorporation of salient activities for each individual" [24]. Similarly, each of the authored articles analyzed in this systematic review incorporated principles of motor learning resulting in improved outcomes in subjects, irrespective of dosage or type of modality. Researchers should consider the principles of motor learning as paramount to their theoretical construct during protocol design and intervention implementation.

Second, while researchers consistently utilized and demonstrated statistically significant change via the FMA UE, this outcome measure only provides part of the picture of rehabilitation in individuals post stroke. Researchers should seek to consistently include measures of function and self-efficacy, at both pre/post timepoints, as well as timepoints into the future, to determine if these changes as a result of the BCI interventions are retained and maintained over time.

The inclusion of somatosensory/motor feedback in the BCI-based protocols for motor rehabilitation seems paramount. There is also a need to consider the inclusion of multimodal feedback, including underutilized auditory feedback. Emotional feedback may be warranted, especially in cognitively compromised patient populations. An immersive environment can be used as a tool to improve SMR-based BCI performance for patients post-stroke. The effect of additional interventions, such as tDCS and others, to accompany BCI-based rehabilitation protocols requires further exploration.

Finally, while a variety of sensory feedback options are implemented in existing protocols, the most consistent type of feedback provided was FES during the BCI intervention. It is not clear from the literature that providing feedback before or after the intervention has immediate or lasting effects on individuals post stroke, but there may be opportunity for multimodal approaches to feedback provided during BCI based motor rehabilitation of individuals post stroke.

References

1. Sacco, R.L., Kasner, S.E., Broderick, J.P., et al.: An Updated definition of stroke for the 21st century. AHA J. **44**(7), 2064–2089 (2013)
2. Go, A.S., Mozaffarian, D., Roger, V.L., et al. Heart disease and stroke statistics—2013 update: a report from the American Heart Association. PMC **127**(1) (2013)
3. Tsao, C.W., Aday, A.W., Almarzooq, Z.I., et al.: Heart disease and stroke statistics - 2022 update: a report from the American Heart Association. Circulation **145**, e153–e639 (2022)
4. Girotra, T., Lekoubou, A., Bishu, K.G., et al.: A contemporary and comprehensive analysis of the costs of stroke in the United States. J. Neurol. Sci. **410**, 116643 (2020)
5. Stroke CDC, https://www.cdc.gov/stroke/facts.htm. Accessed 24 Oct 2018
6. Benjamin, E.J., et al.: Heart disease and stroke statistics—2017 update: a report from the American Heart Association. Circulation **135**(10), e146–e603 (2017)
7. Cervera, M.A., et al.: Brain-computer interfaces for post-stroke motor rehabilitation: a meta-analysis. Ann. Clin. Transl. Neurol. **5**, 651–663 (2018)
8. Zhang, X., et al.: Combining mental training and physical training with goal-oriented protocols in stroke rehabilitation: a feasibility case study. Front. Hum. Neurosci. **12**, 125 (2018)

9. Mrachacz-Kersting, N., Aliakbaryhosseinabadi, S.: Comparison of the efficacy of a real-time and offline associative brain-computer-interface. Front. Neurosci. **12**, 455 (2018)
10. Frolov, A.A., et al.: Post-stroke rehabilitation training with a motor-imagery-based brain-computer interface (BCI)-controlled hand exoskeleton: a randomized controlled multicenter trial. Front. Neurosci. **11** (2017)
11. Irimia, D.C., et al.: Brain-computer interfaces with multi-sensory feedback for stroke rehabilitation: a case study. Artif. Org. **41**, E178–E184 (2017)
12. Kim, T., Kim, S., Lee, B.: Effects of action observational training plus brain-computer interface-based functional electrical stimulation on paretic arm motor recovery in patient with stroke: a randomized controlled trial. Occup. Ther. Int. **23**(1), 39–47 (2016)
13. Pichiorri, F., et al.: Brain–computer interface boosts motor imagery practice during stroke recovery. Ann. Neurol. **77**, 851–865 (2015)
14. Monge-Pereira, E., et al.: Use of electroencephalography brain-computer interface systems as a rehabilitative approach for upper limb function after a stroke: a systematic review. PMR **9**(9), 918–932 (2017)
15. Cervera, M.A., Soekadar, S.R., Ushiba, J., Millán, J.d.R., et al. Brain-computer interfaces for post-stroke motor rehabilitation: a meta-analysis. Ann. Clin. Transl. Neuro. **5**, 651–663 (2018)
16. Carvalho, R., Dias, N., Cerqueira, J.J.: Brain-machine interface of upper limb recovery in stroke patients rehabilitation: a systematic review. Physiother. Res. Int. **24**(2), e1764 (2019)
17. Bai, Z., Fong, K.N.K., Zhang, J.J., Chan, J., Ting, K.H. Immediate and long-term effects of BCI-based rehabilitation of the upper extremity after stroke: a systematic review and meta-analysis. [Meta-Analysis Research Support, Non-U.S. Gov't Systematic Review]. J Neuroeng. Rehabil. **17**(1) (2020)
18. Kruse, A., Suica, Z., Taeymans, J., Schuster-Amft, C.: Effect of brain-computer interface training based on non-invasive electroencephalography using motor imagery on functional recovery after stroke - a systematic review and meta-analysis. BMC Neurol. **20**(1) (2020)
19. Baniqued, P.D.E., et al.: Brain-computer interface robotics for hand rehabilitation after stroke: a systematic review. J. Neuroeng. Rehabil. **18**(1) (2021)
20. Camargo-Vargas, D., Callejas-Cuervo, M., Mazzoleni, S.: Brain-computer interfaces systems for upper and lower limb rehabilitation: a systematic review. Sensors **21**(13), 4312 (2021)
21. Mansour, S., Ang, K.K., Nair, K.P.S., Phua, K.S., Arvaneh, M.: Efficacy of brain-computer interface and the impact of its design characteristics on poststroke upper-limb rehabilitation: a systematic review and meta-analysis of randomized controlled trials. Clin. EEG Neurosci. **53**(1), 79–90 (2022)
22. Yang, W., Zhang, X., Li, Z., Zhang, Q., Xue, C., Huai, Y.: The effect of brain-computer interface training on rehabilitation of upper limb dysfunction after stroke: a meta-analysis of randomized controlled trials. Front. Neurosci. **15**, 766–879 (2022)
23. Horowitz, A.J., Guger, C., Korostenskaja, M. What external variables affect sensorimotor rhythm brain-computer interface (SMR-BCI) performance? HCA Healthc. J. Med. **2**(3) (2021)
24. Clark, E., et al.: Brain-computer interface for motor rehabilitation. In: Stephanidis, C. (ed.) HCII 2019. CCIS, vol. 1032, pp. 243–254. Springer, Cham (2019). https://doi.org/10.1007/978-3-030-23522-2_31
25. Fugl-Meyer, A.R., Jaasko, L., Leyman, I., Olsson, S., Steglind, S.: The post-stroke hemiplegic patient. A method for evaluation of physical performance. Scand. J. Rehabil. Med. **7**, 13–31 (1975)
26. Physiotherapy Evidence Database. https://pedro.org.au/english/summary-of-measurement-properties-of-the-pedro-scale/. Accessed 20 May 2022
27. Cashin, A.G., et al.: Measurement properties of the PEDro scale (2020): clinimetrics: physiotherapy evidence database (PEDro) scale. J. Physiother. **66**(1), 59 (2020)

28. Maher, C.G., et al.: Reliability of the PEDro scale for rating quality of randomized controlled trials. Phys. Ther. **83**(8), 713–721 (2003)
29. Moseley, A.M., et al.: Agreement between the Cochrane risk of bias tool and physiotherapy evidence database (PEDro) scale: a meta-epidemiological study of randomized controlled trials of physical therapy interventions. PLoS ONE **14**(9), e0222770 (2019)
30. Biasiucci, A., Leeb, R., Iturrate, I., et al.: Brain-actuated functional electrical stimulation elicits lasting arm motor recovery after stroke. Nat. Commun. **9**(1) (2018)
31. Cantillo-Negrete, J., et al.: Brain-computer interface coupled to a robotic hand orthosis for stroke patients' neurorehabilitation: a crossover feasibility study. Front. Hum. Neurosci. **15**, 656–975 (2021)
32. Chen, S., et al.: Longitudinal electroencephalography analysis in subacute stroke patients during intervention of brain-computer interface with exoskeleton feedback. Front. Neurosci.**14** (2020)
33. Chew, E., et al.: Using transcranial direct current stimulation to augment the effect of motor imagery-assisted brain-computer interface training in chronic stroke patients-cortical reorganization considerations. Front. Neurol. **11** (2020)
34. Hu, Y.Q., et al.: Motor imagery-based brain-computer interface combined with multimodal feedback to promote upper limb motor function after stroke: a preliminary study. Evid. Based Complement. Alternat. Med. **3** (2021)
35. Li, M., Liu, Y., Wu, Y., Liu, S., Jia, J., Zhang, L.: Neurophysiological substrates of stroke patients with motor imagery based brain-computer interface training. Int. J. Neurosci. **124**, 403–415 (2014)
36. Li, X., et al.: Sensorimotor rhythm-brain computer interface with audio-cue, motor observation and multisensory feedback for upper-limb stroke rehabilitation: a controlled study. Front. Neurosci. **16** (2021)
37. Ramos-Murguialday, A., Broetz, D., Rea, M., et al.: Brain-machine interface in chronic stroke rehabilitation: a controlled study. Ann. Neurol. **74**(1), 100–108 (2013)
38. Furlan, L., Sterr, A.: The applicability of standard error of measurement and minimum detectable change to motor learning research - a behavior study. Front. Hum. Neurosci. **12** (2018)
39. Portney, L.G., Watkins, M.P.: Foundations of Clinical Research: Applications to Practice, 3rd edn. Pearson/Prentice Hall, Upper Saddle River (2009)
40. Moore, J.L., et al.: A core set of outcome measures for adults with neurologic conditions undergoing rehabilitation. A clinical practice guideline. J. Neurol. Phys. Therapy **42**, 74–220 (2018)
41. Salter, K., Jutai, J.W., Teasell, R., Foley, N.C., Bitensky, J., Bayley, J.: Issues for selection of outcome measures in stroke rehabilitation: ICF activity. Disabil. Rehabil. **27**(6), 315–340 (2015)
42. Pichiorri, F., Fallani, F.D.V., Cincotti, F., Babiloni, F., Molinari, M., et al.: Sensorimotor rhythm-based brain–computer interface training: the impact on motor cortical responsiveness. J. Neural. Eng. **8**, 025020 (2011)
43. Angulo-Sherman, I.N., Gutierrez, D.: A link between the increase in electroencephalographic coherence and performance improvement in operating a brain-computer interface. Comput. Intell. Neurosci. **2015**, 824175 (2015)
44. Darvishi, S., Gharabaghi, A., Boulay, C.B., Ridding, M.C., Abbott, D., Baumert, M.: Proprioceptive feedback facilitates motor imagery-related operant learning of sensorimotor beta-band modulation. Front. Neurosci. **11**, 60 (2017)
45. Vukelic, M., Gharabaghi, A.: Oscillatory entrainment of the motor cortical network during motor imagery is modulated by the feedback modality. Neuroimage **111**, 1–11 (2015)

46. McCreadie, K.A., Coyle, D.H., Prasad, G.: Learning to modulate sensorimotor rhythms with stereo auditory feedback for a brain-computer interface. In: Conference Proceedings: Annual International Conference of the IEEE Engineering in Medicine and Biology Society IEEE Engineering in Medicine and Biology Society Annual Conference 2012, pp. 6711–6714 (2012)
47. Kleim, J.A., Jones, T.A.: Principles of experience-dependent neural plasticity: implications for rehabilitation after brain damage. J. Speech Lang. Hear. Res. **51**, S225–S239 (2008)
48. Clark, E, et al.: Computer Interface for Motor Rehabilitation. In: Stephanidis, C. (eds) HCI International 2019 - Posters. HCII 2019. Communications in Computer and Information Science, vol. 1032. Springer, Cham (2019). https://doi.org/10.1007/978-3-030-23522-2_31

Training CNN to Detect Motor Imagery in ECoG Data Recorded During Dreaming

Taisija Demchenko[1]([✉])[ID] and Milena Korostenskaja[1,2][ID]

[1] Vilnus University, Universiteto g. 3, 01513 Vilnius, Lithuania
dtaisija@gmail.com
[2] The Institute of Neuroapproaches, Winter Springs, FL, USA

Abstract. Dreams are often forgotten despite their impact on our emotions and memory. In our pursuit of developing an objective dream-content recording methodology (reaDream), we focused on the motor imagery (MI)-related dream component, which is reported to be present in dreams along with other sensory, perceptual, and cognitive phenomena. It has been shown that brain activation during dreamed actions corresponds to the brain activation for the same actions in a wakeful state. This allows one to decode electrocorticographic (ECoG) brain activity during sleep using a machine learning (ML) model trained on wakeful data. ECoG data is very specific to each individual and not generalized between subjects; deep ML models are prone to overfit on small amounts of data. We propose to generalize ECoG data by combining recordings from several subjects. For that, we developed a Convolutional Neural Network (CNN)-based classifier that discriminates between hand and tongue movements in different subjects. We tested a hypothesis on whether a MI classifier can be trained on motor execution (ME) data. We demonstrate that ME types are easier to distinguish compared to MI. We showed that power features are more informative than temporal features. Finally, we demonstrated how our trained models could be used to predict MI during Rapid Eye Movement (REM) sleep.

Keywords: Dream research · ECoG · Motor imagery · CNN

1 Introduction

People spend about one-third of their lives sleeping, and the absolute majority see dreams, which are often forgotten [21]. Even when remembered, there is a significant probability that the memory of the dream was altered [3], with one of the reasons for that being the active dream forgetting [24]. Currently, dream research resorts to dream reports collected right after awakening. However, the reporting process can have multiple interferences, including poor cognitive performance of the subjects due to sleep inertia [22]. In addition, dream reports can be biased by laboratory setting and socio-cognitive factors [15,44,54]. Our proposed dream recording methodology reaDream [9] would allow recording dreams

© The Author(s), under exclusive license to Springer Nature Switzerland AG 2022
M. Kurosu et al. (Eds.): HCII 2022, LNCS 13519, pp. 391–414, 2022.
https://doi.org/10.1007/978-3-031-17618-0_28

directly from the sleeping brain, thus removing barriers and allowing for more accurate and objective dream reports (brain data-based dream reports). Moreover, dream recording methodologies, such as reaDream [9], have great potential to add to the neuroscience of consciousness, possibly pinpointing the role of dreaming. Accurate brain data-based dream reports can be used more confidently for improving people's mental health by psychotherapists and other mental health professionals [5,6,38] or be a source of leisure and creativity.

During dreaming, brain activation is observed in humans, which overlaps with brain areas responsible for sensory and perceptual phenomena happening in dreams [4,12,46,51]. Still, brain activity patterns are not yet researched enough to be accurately decoded into dream contents, which are shown to be complex and multi-sensory [5,15,32,47]. Moreover, as dream phenomena cannot be observed by people other than the dreamer, besides rare exceptions such as certain disorders [49] and lucid dreaming [12,26], it is difficult to verify whether brain activity patterns during dream experiences are the same as in corresponding wakeful experiences. Nevertheless, brain activation during dreamed movements was shown to correspond to motor imagery (MI) in a wakeful state [12,14,39,48]. Because of that, we focus on the MI-related dream component.

There are plenty of studies on decoding MI, as it is often used in brain-computer interfaces (BCIs) for fully or partially paralyzed patients [35]. Many of them are based on unilateral or bilateral hand movements, while many other types of movement can happen in dreams, such as running and flying. A multi-class model and high-resolution data are needed to classify various movements accurately. Electrocorticography (ECoG) has the potential to record complex brain activity associated with dreams because of its high temporal and spatial resolution [19,23]. Deep machine learning (ML) methods facilitate easier feature extraction and can achieve high accuracy in classifying brain data [31,37,40,45,50], but can overfit when the training data set is too small [41]. This makes using ECoG data in deep ML models difficult, as such data is relatively rare and not generalized between subjects. ECoG recording requires craniotomy for electrodes/grid implantation, which introduces health risks [29]; therefore, ECoG data is recorded only from patients with a certain severity of a condition (e.g., medically intractable epilepsy). In these cases, ECoG electrodes are placed only over the areas of interest, which differs from patient to patient.

To overcome the challenges described above, we propose a method that combines data from several subjects by introducing electrode location information into the data. Moreover, we utilize the main advantage of Convolutional Neural Network (CNN) models, which can detect patterns in data by observing differences between neighboring data values [10,20]. CNN models were already successfully used with brain activity data in studies [7,33].

Dreaming mostly happens in rapid eye movement (REM) sleep [5,32], during which muscle atonia (paralysis) takes place on the level of the brainstem [51,52]. When muscle atonia is disrupted, subjects act out of their dreams, including kicking and punching [1,49]. Because of that, MI during dreaming may be more similar to motor execution (ME) in a wakeful state rather than MI in a wakeful state. [39] in their paper show that applying transcranial direct cortical stimulation (tDCS) over the sensorimotor cortex lowers the amount of dream movement in REM sleep, and [43] in their functional magnetic resonance imaging (fMRI) study show that the sensorimotor cortex was activated during ME but not MI. On the other hand, ME is affected by the weight applied to muscles and other constraints [17,53], which are mostly absent during motionless dreaming. When comparing awake brain activity during MI and ME, the latter was shown to have higher activation levels but, other than that, be quite similar to MI [2,36]. This activation is more clearly detectable in spectral than in temporal space [31]; nevertheless, in the current work, we train classifiers on both feature spaces (spectral and temporal) to confirm these findings. Certain differences remain, e.g., during MI, a motor suppression happens [8,18,42] on the cortical level [11,55], which further differentiates MI during REM sleep and wakefulness. Both MI and ME data were used to train classifiers for REM sleep data to compare their results, as ME data has a higher potential to be accurately differentiated due to its higher activation. Moreover, it is easier to verify that ME data was correctly collected as movements are directly observable, which is not the case with MI.

This work was the first step toward the reaDream project: developing a system for decoding and visualizing human dreams directly from recorded brain cortical activity. The decoding process would be done in real-time, as certain decisions can be made based on predictions, and the brain can be stimulated, for example, to wake the user from a nightmare [9]. For this reason, we also simulated real-time dream decoding by giving the model data fragments cropped using the rolling window method.

2   Materials and Methods

2.1   Motor Data

MI and ME data were obtained from the open library of human electrocorticographic data and analyses [34]. All data samples were taken from the experiment described by [36] and consist of 7 subjects (see Table 1 and Fig. 1), two data files each: one with a recording made during ME tasks, and another - during MI tasks. Data is labeled by cues that were shown to subjects on a monitor as a written word. The movements were either simple and repetitive flexion and extension of all hand fingers or opening a mouth with protrusion and retraction of the tongue. A number of channels per subject is either 48 or 64, with one subject having 46 channels, as two channels were removed due to contamination.

Cues lasted 3 s, with rest intervals (blank screen) in between for 3 or more seconds. Each MI or ME task has 30 repetitions in each recording. Recordings have slightly different lengths (from 376.6 to 390.9 s), the difference coming solely from the varying length of resting intervals.

Data were sampled at 1000 Hz and filtered by a bandpass filter from 0.15 200 Hz but contained powerline noise at 60, 120, 180 Hz. Data were scaled so that 1 amplifier unit equals 0.0298 µV. Epileptiform electrical activity was not

Table 1. Summary of recordings in motor data. For two patients, some electrodes were dropped due to their bad positions on the standardized brain.

Subject	Hemisphere	Channels	Dropped
BP	Left	46	
FP	Left	64	4
HH	Right	48	
JC	Left	48	
JM	Left	64	8
RH	Right	64	
RR	Right	64	

removed from this data, nor were recordings with unsuccessful motor imagery. Electrode coordinates are in Talairach space, and a triangular surface model of the Talairach brain is provided in the library [34].

2.2   REM Sleep Data

REM sleep stage data was obtained from MNI Open iEEG Atlas (described in [13]). As the Atlas contains readings from different types of electrodes, recordings were downloaded only for subjects with subdural grids or strips placed over either frontal or parietal cortices. Finally, 6 subjects were chosen (see Table 2 and Fig. 2). The REM sleep stage was detected by electrooculogram and chin electromyogram or with simultaneous video recording.

Table 2. Summary of selected recordings in REM sleep data.

Subject	Hemisphere	Channels
94	Right	10
99	Right	12
100	Right	17
103	Left	32
106	Right	7
110	Right	10

Data consists of 60 s recordings which were filtered by a bandpass filter from 0.5 80 Hz and downsampled 200 Hz, and a notch filter was applied to remove the powerline noise. No epileptic activity was in the data. Electrodes coordinates were provided in MNI space, so they were transformed to Talairach space using Lancaster transform matrix [28]:

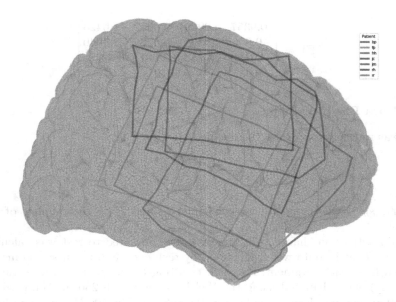

Fig. 1. ECoG grid locations on Talairach brain in motor data. Grids initially placed on the left hemisphere are mirrored on the right hemisphere.

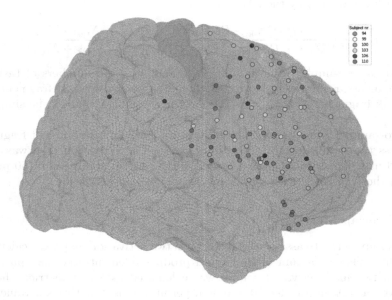

Fig. 2. Electrode locations on Talairach brain in REM sleep data. The precentral gyrus (primary motor cortex) is tinted in orange and green. The orange part is commonly activated during hand movements, and the green part is during tongue movements [16]. (Color figure online)

$$\text{MTT} = \begin{bmatrix} 0.9357 & 0.0029 & -0.0072 & -1.0423 \\ -0.0065 & 0.9395 & -0.0726 & -1.3940 \\ 0.0103 & 0.0752 & 0.8967 & 3.6475 \\ 0 & 0 & 0 & 1 \end{bmatrix} \tag{1}$$

2.3 Data Pre-processing

Data was re-referenced using the mean CAR filter [30]:

$$s'_h = s_h - \frac{1}{H} \sum_{i=1}^{H} s_i \cdot s_h \tag{2}$$

Here, s_h is the signal for each channel h, and H is the number of total channels.

Brain activation change from motor tasks compared to rest was calculated as in [36]. That is, data was fragmented by task cues, and the first 500 ms were removed from each fragment. For each resulting fragment, power spectral density (PSD) was calculated using the Welch method with 250 ms Hann window and 100 ms overlap. From calculated PSD, 8–32 and 76–100 Hz averaged broadbands were calculated, and the signed r-squared cross-correlation was calculated between PSDs of task and rest fragments (with rest fragments happening right after task fragments) by the formula [36]:

$$R = \frac{(PSD_{\text{task}} - PSD_{\text{rest}})^3}{|PSD_{\text{task}} - PSD_{\text{rest}}| \cdot s^2_{PSD_{\text{task}} \cup PSD_{\text{rest}}}} \cdot \frac{N_{\text{task}} \cdot N_{\text{rest}}}{(N_{\text{task}} + N_{\text{rest}})^2} \tag{3}$$

Here, s^2 is sample variance, and N_{task} and N_{rest} are numbers of task and rest fragments, respectively. Note that there was exactly one rest fragment after each task fragment, so $N_{\text{task}} = N_{\text{rest}}$, and the second fraction can be simplified to $\frac{1}{4}$.

Two-sample T-test was calculated between PSDs of task and rest fragments to assess the significance of activation change. The activation map was interpolated using spherical Gaussian kernels with a size of about 5 mm (50 points) only in those channels with significant activation or deactivation.

2.4 Overlap Metric

The overlap metric to assess overlap between two activation maps was calculated as in [36]. That is, a sum of Hadamard product (element-wise multiplication) between two map activation values was calculated as a test metric. The distribution of test metrics for 10^6 random permutations of activation values was generated. P-value was calculated as the probability that a test metric achieved after permutation is larger than without permutation. P-values less than 0.05 were chosen to indicate the significance of the non-permuted test metric. Z-score (from distribution's mean) of the test metric was the overlap strength value.

To assess the overlap between labels predicted by different models, a similar method was used. First, predicted labels from each of the models were collected into a $M \times N$ matrix (M is the number of models and N is the number of samples). The number of samples with the same label predicted by all models was calculated. Then, predicted labels were permuted for each model separately to repeat the agreeing label counting and get the random distribution. Two p-values were calculated from each side of the distribution.

2.5   Pre-training Feature Extraction

Data was first fragmented by task cues, and the first 500 ms were removed from each fragment. Resulting 2500 ms fragments were additionally split into 200 ms fragments with a 100 ms overlap. The REM sleep data was first up-sampled to 1000 Hz to have the same sample rate as the motor data. Because the REM data is unlabeled, it was split into fragments using a 200 ms window with a 100 ms overlap instead; this method was also used to generate an additional data set from motor data.

After that, fragments were either left in temporal space (for time-only models) or transformed into spectral space (for power-only models). 8–80 Hz bands were extracted:

- For time-only data representation, it was filtered using a Butterworth band-pass filter to get 8–80 Hz, then a notch filter to remove the 60 Hz band.
- For power-only data representation, power spectral density was obtained from the data using the Welch method, and only values for 8–59 Hz and 61–80 Hz bands were left.

Additional models using the 8–100 Hz frequency range were trained to assess the importance of 80–100 Hz for better classification of movement types in motor data. Same as for 8–80 Hz data, 60 Hz band was removed. They were not used to make predictions on REM sleep data, as its highest frequency left 80 Hz.

2.6   Spatial Transformation

Several steps were done to add a signal location to the training data:

1. Electrode coordinates (x, y, and z) from all subjects were joined into one group. Electrodes placed on the left hemisphere were mirrored on the right hemisphere.
2. One dimension of coordinates was removed with Principal Component Analysis (PCA), leaving each electrode with two new coordinates, a and b.
3. The resulting coordinates were divided by δ and rounded to whole numbers. The distances between smallest and largest a and b were taken as A and B, respectively. The δ parameter value was chosen by measuring the error

between non-rounded and rounded coordinates to keep the error, A, and B as low as possible, as the resulting spatial dimensions of data samples will be $A \times B$.

4. $A \times B$ matrix was initiated with zeros. Each channel data was placed into a matrix cell by its a and b coordinates while leaving many cells with zeros.
5. Gaussian blur was applied on the resulting matrix along the A and B dimensions. This filled empty cells with values calculated from neighboring cells. The size of the Gaussian kernel was chosen according to the grid size, so its radius would be about 5 mm.

To check whether spatial dimensions provide useful information, for additional training sets, the electrode locations were permuted, resulting in the same data shape while rendering the spatial information meaningless.

The δ parameter was chosen by calculating $A \times B$ grid size and distance error ratios for each δ between 1 and 10, while ensuring that simplified electrode positions do not overlap in the same subject. The biggest possible δ for motor data was 6.21, producing a grid of size 21×18, reducing unique electrode locations by about 46%, and achieving a mean distance error of 39.3% (SD = 14.4%) from the minimum distance between two electrodes in any ECoG grid. A smaller $\delta = 5.12$ was chosen to lower this error to 31% (SD = 12.1%). The resulting grid size was 25×21.

The result of the spatial transformation on motor data electrodes is visualized in Fig. 3.

2.7 CNN Model Architecture

The main model architecture which was used in this work consists of 4 layers: two CNN and two linear layers. In the case of this model, CNN layers extract either temporal or spectral activation patterns regardless of their location and condense the data. In contrast, linear layers pay attention to where patterns were found. All layers were initialized with normal He initialization [20]. For model regularization, Batch Regularization (with learnable parameters) and Dropout (with 30% probability) techniques were used [41]. A simplified scheme of the used model architecture is provided in Fig. 4.

Leaky ReLU is a variation of a ReLU activation function that is popular to use with CNNs [20]:

$$f(x) = \begin{cases} x, & \text{if } x > 0 \\ ax, & \text{if } x \le 0 \end{cases} \tag{4}$$

Here, a is a fixed value which controls the slope of the negative part of the ReLU function. In the case of Leaky ReLU, it is 0.01.

Adam optimizer with default parameters [25] was used with a learning rate $5 \cdot 10^{-4}$ and weight decay $5 \cdot 10^{-6}$. As a loss function, Cross Entropy was used:

$$L_{\text{CE}} = -\sum_{m=1}^{M} w_m y_{o,m} \ln(p_{o,m}) \tag{5}$$

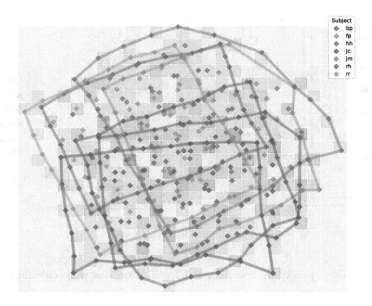

Fig. 3. Motor data electrode locations for each subject after spatial transformation.

Here, M is the number of classes; y and p are the binary indicator and the predicted probability that observation o is of class m, respectively; w_m is the weight for class m. L_{CE} is the loss calculated for one data sample, while the final loss value for all data is the average of all individual loss values.

Models which receive and transform temporal data are called time-only models, and models which work with spectral data are called power-only models.

2.8   Model Evaluation

During the training process, train and test loss values were saved for every 5 epochs. The training speed was calculated as the difference between the first train loss value and the last 5 train loss values, divided by the number of train epochs. The test loss values were used to decide whether the model was overfitting.

After models were trained, class predictions on the test data were obtained, and multi-class confusion matrices were calculated. For each class m, the correct predictions are called True Positives (TP), and incorrect predictions are called False Negatives (FN). Samples of different classes which were predicted as class m are called False Positives (FP). Lastly, all samples which were not of class m and were not predicted as class m are called True Negatives (TN). Baseline metrics were obtained by labeling each sample with the most abundant class (the "rest" class, two times more abundant than "tongue" or "hand" classes).

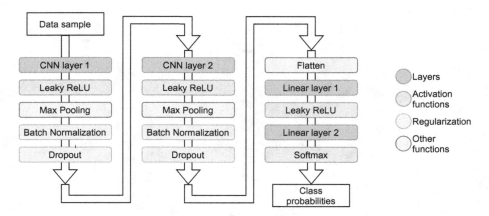

Fig. 4. The model architecture.

The accuracy, precision, recall, and F1 score metrics were calculated as follows:

$$F_{\text{Accuracy}} = \frac{\text{TP} + \text{TN}}{N} \tag{6}$$

$$F_{\text{Precision}} = \frac{\text{TP}}{\text{TP} + \text{FP}} \tag{7}$$

$$F_{\text{Recall}} = \frac{\text{TP}}{\text{TP} + \text{FN}} \tag{8}$$

$$F_{\text{F1}} = 2\frac{F_{\text{Precision}} \cdot F_{\text{Recall}}}{F_{\text{Precision}} + F_{\text{Recall}}} \tag{9}$$

Here, N is the total number of samples.

2.9   Data and Software Availability

Both data sets are openly available:

- Motor data was taken from: https://exhibits.stanford.edu/data/catalog/zk881ps0522,
- REM sleep data was taken from: https://mni-open-ieegatlas.research.mcgill.ca.

All codes were written in Python and are available here: https://github.com/Tallivm/readream-motor.

2.10   Ethics Statement

The ethics statement was included with the motor data: All patients participated in a purely voluntary manner, after providing informed written consent, under experimental protocols approved by the Institutional Review Board of the University of Washington (#12193). Portions of these data originally appeared in the manuscript "Cortical activity during motor execution, motor imagery, and imagery-based online feedback," published in Miller et al. (2010). Portions of these patient data were anonymized according to the IRB protocol, in accordance with HIPAA mandate. It was made available through the library described in "A Library of Human Electrocorticographic Data and Analyses" by Miller (2016), freely available at https://searchworks.stanford.edu/view/zk881ps0522.

3 Results and Discussion

MI Samples are Less Generalized in Temporal Space than ME. MI models overfit after about 20 epochs, and their test losses were higher than test losses of ME models (see Fig. 7). However, train losses steadily decrease, which means that models can find and use differences between train samples. This indicates that the model architecture may be too deep, although it consists of only 4 layers. Previously, 2-layered models were trained to classify the same data, but their learning speed dropped down significantly after about 10 epochs, which was the reason to try deeper models. Stronger regularization techniques and a bigger data set must be used to prevent model overfitting. For each subject, the ME model performed better than MI, with one exception (see Table 3). For the HH subject, the MI model performed better than ME, but the HH model trained on ME data had the worst performance among the ME models. The reason is that the HH model showed the biggest overfit on ME data.

There is No Consensus Between Models on Which Frequencies are More Informative. For 5 out of 7 subjects, low-frequency activation maps significantly overlap between tasks in both MI and ME, so it was expected that these models would concentrate on higher (63–80 Hz) frequencies. To evaluate this, the weights of the first CNN layers were visualized for each model (see Fig. 5). In the case of MI, only 2 models show large weights in high frequencies, while others paid the most attention to 26–34 Hz. On the other hand, in ME models, 5 out of 7 models show large weights in higher frequencies (63–80 Hz), while 2 models remained on low frequencies. Models tend to choose either low or high frequencies, but the reason for this is unclear, as there is no obvious correlation with any other observation.

High-Frequency Patterns are More Informative. BP, HH, JC, and JM subjects show no significant overlap in 76–100 Hz MI, and only they scored the "tongue" class better than the baseline. Additionally, HH, FP, and JM are the only subjects with overlaps in 76–100 Hz ME activity, and they are among the worst ME models if ranked by accuracy. To further investigate the impact of frequencies, it can be noted that ME models for FP and JM subjects were the only ones who had low CNN weights on high frequencies, and they performed

Table 3. Power-only MI and ME model metrics. Spectral data (8–80 Hz) was used for both training (100 epochs) and testing.

Subject	MI			
	Accuracy	F1 for "rest"	F1 for "hand"	F1 for "tongue"
BP	0.49	0.59	0.39	0.44
FP	0.44	0.56	0.34	0.33
HH	0.56	0.69	0.51	0.54
JC	0.49	0.55	0.38	0.53
JM	0.57	0.70	0.45	0.43
RH	0.49	0.60	0.34	0.36
RR	0.47	0.58	0.42	0.31
Mean	0.50	0.61	0.40	0.42
Baseline	0.50	0.67	0.40	0.40
Subject	ME			
	Accuracy	F1 for "rest"	F1 for "hand"	F1 for "tongue"
BP	0.71	0.69	0.69	0.76
FP	0.50	0.62	0.41	0.39
HH	0.45	0.55	0.43	0.34
JC	0.74	0.76	0.70	0.75
JM	0.65	0.76	0.53	0.58
RH	0.55	0.67	0.34	0.50
RR	0.74	0.70	0.69	0.84
Mean	0.62	0.68	0.54	0.59
Baseline	0.50	0.67	0.40	0.40

relatively lower than other ME models. The significant overlap in high-frequency activation maps may be why FP and JM models chose to concentrate on the low frequencies.

Models are Robust in Their Assessment of Frequency Range Importance. Weights of 8–100 Hz models were almost identical to 8–80 Hz models, with 80–100 Hz weights being highly similar to neighboring 72–80 Hz weights. Power-only 8–100 Hz models show slightly better average metrics than 8–80 Hz for ME, which means that 80–100 Hz frequencies are also informative. Still, the increase is only about 2% at most. MI models' performance after adding 80–100 Hz frequencies showed both increase and decrease in different scores, which can be explained by the overall lower performance (higher overfit) of MI models.

ME and MI Data are Substantially Different. On average, the activation overlap was higher between MI and ME than between hand and tongue (see Table 5), and was significant almost for each activation map type. Nevertheless, as it was shown above, MI and ME models were different in both weights and

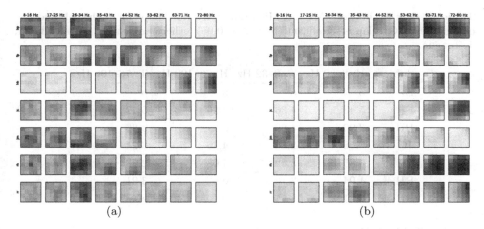

(a)   (b)

Fig. 5. Averaged absolute weights of single-subject power-only models (first CNN layers). Weights are normalized per subject, and the color intensity corresponds to the weight value (white is 0, dark red is the maximum weight). Although models were initiated with the same weights, they differentiated after 100 epochs. (a) models trained on MI, (b) models trained on ME. (Color figure online)

performance. Cross-predictions between MI and ME models were made to ensure that they are not interchangeable. Results are included in Table 6. The average performance in both ME on MI and MI on ME was lower than the baseline. When comparing them, ME models used on MI data show better F1 scores for "rest", while MI models used on ME data show better scores for "hand" and "tongue." This was expected, as the brain activation during ME was found to be stronger than MI, which means MI models are more sensitive to power values than ME models, which over-predicted the "rest" class in MI data.

Tongue Movements are Easier to Identify than Hand Movements. The overlap between brain activation maps from hand and tongue MI and ME tasks was calculated for each subject in motor data (see Table 4). For all subjects

Table 4. Overlap between brain activation map after either hand or tongue movement (MI or ME), in either low or high frequencies. Overlap is significant (p-value < 0.05), otherwise denoted by ø.

Subject	MI, 8–32 Hz	ME, 8–32 Hz	MI, 76–100 Hz	ME, 76–100 Hz
BP	ø	ø	ø	ø
FP	2.59	4.22	2.76	1.74
HH	3.50	4.99	ø	2.05
JC	1.96	2.63	ø	ø
JM	3.72	4.78	ø	3.55
RH	ø	ø	1.60	ø
RR	4.23	2.82	4.23	ø

Table 5. Overlap between MI and ME brain activation maps for each task and frequency range, Overlap is significant (p-value < 0.05), otherwise denoted by ø. H: hand, T: tongue.

Subject	H, 8–32 Hz	T, 8–32 Hz	H, 76–100 Hz	T, 76–100 Hz
BP	ø	ø	ø	ø
FP	5.43	4.36	4.26	5.42
HH	3.90	4.60	ø	3.86
JC	5.50	2.80	4.46	3.24
JM	5.85	3.82	4.08	2.23
RH	1.94	3.15	ø	3.21
RR	3.31	5.71	ø	ø

Table 6. Metrics for each model type averaged between subjects.

	Accuracy	F1 for "rest"	F1 for "hand"	F1 for "tongue"
Power-only MI	0.50	0.61	0.40	0.42
Power-only permuted MI	0.46	0.61	0.30	0.32
Time-only MI	0.41	0.54	0.26	0.29
Power-only ME	**0.62**	**0.68**	**0.54**	**0.59**
Power-only windowed ME	0.59	0.66	0.52	0.50
Power-only MI on ME	0.44	0.55	0.34	0.33
Power-only ME on MI	0.48	0.63	0.28	0.26

except the BP subject, the overlap is significant for at least one task. Although the overlap numbers are consistent with the ones in [36] (as we reproduced the same study results), large overlaps mean that it can be difficult for the model to discriminate between hand and tongue movements.

On average, the "tongue" class received higher F1 scores than the "hand" class in both MI and ME (see Table 3). This can be explained by the fact that each subject's ECoG grid covered the approximate "tongue" activation area. In contrast, only three subjects' (BP, JC, and RH) grids covered the approximate "hand" area. Nevertheless, these models still show higher F1 scores on "tongue" rather than "hand" data. In all cases where the "hand" class received a higher score than "tongue," both scores were close to the baseline, negating this difference's significance.

Hand and Tongue Movements are Less Similar to Each Other than to the "Rest" State. It was initially thought that models would be able to differentiate between any movement and "rest" better than between movement types by simply detecting a decrease in low-frequency power and an increase in high-frequency power. Nevertheless, both MI and ME models had bigger F1

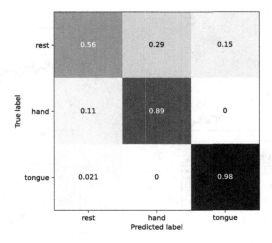

Fig. 6. The confusion matrix for the RR model trained on ME data (numbers are normalized by true labels). There is no mixing between the "hand" and "tongue" class (zeros), and all incorrect predictions for movement samples were labeled as "rest," not another movement type.

scores (compared to the baseline) for "tongue" than for "rest." Confusion matrices were calculated to understand better how models predicted the "rest" class. 5 out of 7 MI models predicted almost the same or bigger ratio of "hand" samples as "rest" compared with the correct class, and 4 out of 7 MI models did the same with "tongue" samples. In comparison, only 2 MI models had similar ratios of "hand" and "tongue" predictions with either "hand" (the BP model) or "tongue" (the FP model) samples. This was opposed to the initial expectation that movements would be more mixed between each other than with the "rest" class. We included a confusion matrix for the best ME model (see Fig. 6). The second and third best ME models (BP and JC) had a similar tendency to mistake the movement with rest rather than another movement type.

Correct Spatial Information Helps Models to Learn (and Overfit). When a model was trained on data with permuted locations, it stopped learning after about 20 epochs. In comparison, a model trained on non-permuted data overfitted after about 20 epochs, and the training loss continued to decrease (see Fig. 7). Although the data were permuted in exactly the same way each epoch, the incorrect spatial location prevented any learning. This suggests that CNN layers find and extract specific patterns that help discriminate between sample types, although these patterns are not common to all data samples.

The "Rest" Class Patterns are Not Affected by the Spatial Permutation. Although the overall performance of models trained on permuted MI data is much worse, the F1 score for the "rest" class was similar to the non-permuted

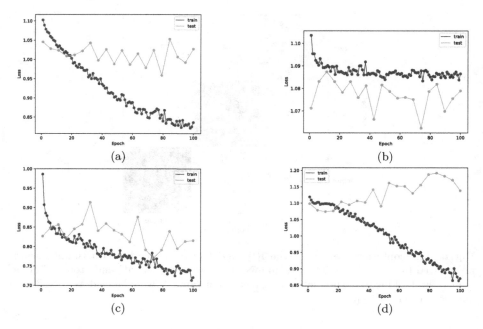

Fig. 7. Comparison of losses between various BP models trained on 8–80 Hz data. For other subjects, the loss curves of respective models are very similar to this example. The scale of y axis is different for each plot. (a) a power-only model trained on MI data. (b) a power-only model trained on permuted MI data. (c) a power-only model trained on ME data. (d) a time-only model trained on MI data.

models. This means that spatial information is not helpful for the "rest" class, while it is important for "tongue" and "hand" classes. This was expected as movement activity is localized in the motor cortex, while the pauses between motor tasks should not induce any localized activity.

Activation Patterns are Easier to Classify in Spectral Space Rather than Temporal. When comparing loss changes for time-only and power-only models, both were able to train and overfit, achieving similar losses after 100 epochs. On the other hand, time-only models showed substantially worse performance in all metrics, scoring much lower than the baseline. This means that the overfit was stronger in time-only models, which was expected, as time-only models had a bigger number of learnable parameters (200 values in a time-only sample compared to 72 values in the power-only sample).

Combining Subjects with Similar Activation Maps Does Not Always Help the Model. To estimate whether combining subjects' data would result in better model scores, for each pair of subjects, electrodes covering the same grid cells were chosen (see Table 7), and activation overlap between them only

Table 7. Number of electrodes covering the same grid cells for both subjects. The diagonal shows the total number of electrodes for individual subjects.

	BP	FP	HH	JC	JM	RH	RR
BP	46	9	5	2	8	15	3
FP	9	60	4	5	19	6	20
HH	5	4	48	7	2	4	10
JC	2	5	7	48	3	13	6
JM	8	19	2	3	56	12	12
RH	15	6	4	13	12	64	6
RR	3	20	10	6	12	6	64

was calculated for each task. The results are shown in Fig. 8. The most significantly overlapping activation maps are for ME in 8–32 Hz, in both hand and tongue tasks. It was expected that models trained on subject pairs with significant overlap would perform better on both subjects compared to single-subject models.

The results were mixed. Some pair models had better results for both subjects; others were significantly worse; in some pairs, one subject received better results while the other was worse. For instance, the JC-RH pair had 13 overlapping electrodes and overlap in MI of hand in low frequencies. The model trained on this pair's MI data performed the worst among all pair models, making no "hand" or "tongue" predictions at all. On the other hand, the FP-RR pair had 20 electrodes in common but no significant overlap in any MI task; nevertheless, both subjects received significantly better predictions from the pair MI model rather than respective single-subject models (the accuracy was 52% and 59% compared to 44% and 47%, respectively). The best MI model for movement classes (HH) boosted "tongue" predictions for 5 out of 6 and "hand" predictions for 3 out of 6 subjects in pairs while lowering the respective scores for itself in almost all cases. As the last example, the BP-JC model got the highest F1 scores for both movements in all MI models when predicting JC: 61% for "hand" and 66% for "tongue." However, BP got somewhat worse predictions from this model than the respective single-subject model. When using pair models, on average, two subjects (FP and RR) got better scores in all classes, two subjects (HH and RH) got worse scores, and the rest got mixed changes.

There was a Significant Overlap Between ME but Not MI Model Predictions on REM Sleep Subjects. Three model types were used to classify REM sleep data samples: MI, ME, and windowed ME. As all models have different parameters and scores, high variability in assigned labels was expected. For each model type, all assigned labels were compared for each REM sleep sample. Not a single sample received "tongue" or "hand" labels from all models, although some samples were predicted as "rest" by all models (133 by MI models, 407 by ME models, and 206 by windowed ME models). The biggest consensus with

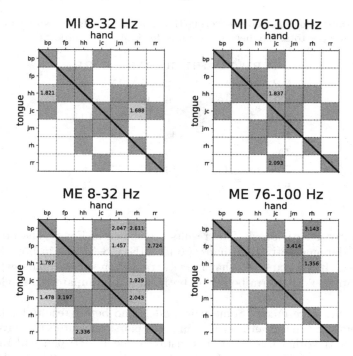

Fig. 8. Overlap metrics for each task and frequency range. Top-right corners of tables are for hand tasks, and the bottom-left corners are for tongue tasks. Only significant (p-value < 0.05) overlap metrics are provided. Irrelevant pairs (less than 5 electrodes in common) are colored in light blue, otherwise white or brown. Brown color intensity corresponds to the overlap metric value. (Color figure online)

movement predictions was in ME models (5 out of 7 models predicted 42 samples as "tongue").

The significance of each consensus was calculated using the permutation method. All ME and some windowed ME models show a significant consensus in predicting the "rest" class, but none of the MI models. For two MI models, p-values show significantly smaller classification label overlap than random. This means that the difference between MI models is too large to combine their predictions in the search for the "most popular" classification labels. On the other hand, ME models show a significant agreement, but only on the "rest" class, while "tongue" and "hand" are rarely predicted. The windowed ME models were similar in predictions to the ME models, although with less consensus. Moreover, ME and windowed ME models predicted about 19% more "tongue" and 48% less "hand" than MI models. In REM sleep data, all subjects had at least one EGoG electrode positioned over or very close to the classical "tongue" area (see Fig. 2), but only one subject had an electrode positioned over the classical "hand" area. This makes any "hand" class predictions in the REM data doubtful. Moreover, as it was mentioned before, the "hand" class is harder to find in the data. This increases the reliability of ME model predictions.

3.1 Limitations

In this work, we proposed a method to introduce spatial information into the EcoG brain activity data. All electrodes in the data were combined with preserving the electrodes' positions on the brain to find the simplified spatial grid. When ECoG grid data taken from different subjects and covering different brain areas are used, the spatial grid increases in size to cover the whole brain area of interest. This means that some grid cells are unfilled for each subject. Currently, they are filled with zeros; however, CNNs cannot determine whether these zeros are unknown values and discriminate them from a zero power. Techniques to impute unknown values must be developed to improve this generalization method.

All subjects, whose motor data was used in this study, had medically refractory epilepsy, which could affect the functional areas of their brain, including motor function. The seizure-related activity was not removed from the motor data set. This increases the chance that a substantial part of the variability between models trained on individual subjects comes from the differences in brain activation for these subjects, which can be bigger in patients than in healthy subjects. From another perspective, fragments with seizures add noise to the data, but seizures happen randomly, while motor activity is present in all respective fragments. Thus, the impact of seizures, if present, can be assumed as minimal.

A problem specific to REM dream decoding is the abundance of saccadic eye movements during REM sleep. Ocular activity may introduce additional noise into the data, especially if electrodes are placed near the eyes, and confuse the models trained on data with less ocular activity [27]. Removing possible ocular activity artifacts is an important step that was out of scope for this work, but should be addressed in future work.

4   Conclusion

We trained CNN models to classify motor imagery or motor execution activity in awake subjects using various ECoG data transformations and applied them to REM sleep data to identify motor imagery-related activity during dreaming. We demonstrated that motor imagery and motor execution-related ECoG activity in awake subjects can be used to identify motor imagery-related ECoG activity during sleep. CNN models trained on motor imagery and motor execution achieved substantially different parameters and scores. Motor execution data had more generalized features allowing CNNs to train better than on motor imagery data. This finding suggests that motor execution-related ECoG activity (rather than motor imagery-related ECoG activity) in awake subjects can be a better source for creating CNN models to classify motor imagery-related ECoG activity during REM sleep. ME models show bigger consensus than MI models with predictions on the REM sleep data. Combining data from several subjects increased the accuracy of several but not all models trained on subject pairs. Four-layered neural networks with two CNN layers easily overfit on motor data; thus, better feature extraction or stronger regularization of models is needed to achieve better results.

Acknowledgements. We want to thank Kai Miller for making the data available to the community and making this work possible. We greatly appreciate the assistance and support provided by Osvaldas Rukšėnas, Audronė Jakaitienė, Robertas Guzulaitis, and Tadas Danielius to the Taisija's Demchenko Master Thesis titled "A neural network to detect motor imagery in ECoG data recorded during dreaming," that became a stepping stone for this original research article.

References

1. Barone, D.A., Henchcliffe, C.: Rapid eye movement sleep behavior disorder and the link to alpha-synucleinopathies. Clin. Neurophys. Off. J. Int. Feder. Clin. Neurophysiol. **129**(8), 1551–1564 (2018). https://doi.org/10.1016/j.clinph.2018.05.003. https://www.ncbi.nlm.nih.gov/pmc/articles/PMC6495539/
2. Batula, A.M., Mark, J.A., Kim, Y.E., Ayaz, H.: Comparison of brain activation during motor imagery and motor movement using fNIRS. Comput. Intell. Neurosci. **2017**, 5491296 (2017). https://doi.org/10.1155/2017/5491296. https://www.ncbi.nlm.nih.gov/pmc/articles/PMC5435907/
3. Beaulieu-Prévost, D., Zadra, A.: When people remember dreams they never experienced: a study of the malleability of dream recall over time. Dreaming **25**(1), 18–31 (2015). https://doi.org/10.1037/a0038788
4. Blake, Y., Terburg, D., Balchin, R., van Honk, J., Solms, M.: The role of the basolateral amygdala in dreaming. Cortex **113**, 169–183 (2019). https://doi.org/10.1016/j.cortex.2018.12.016. https://www.sciencedirect.com/science/article/pii/S0010945218304404
5. Carr, M., Nielsen, T.: Daydreams and nap dreams: content comparisons. Conscious. Cogn. **36**, 196–205 (2015). https://doi.org/10.1016/j.concog.2015.06.012
6. Caviglia, G.: Working on dreams, from neuroscience to psychotherapy. Res. Psychother. Psychopathol. Process Outcome **24**(2), 540 (2021). https://doi.org/10.4081/ripppo.2021.540.   https://www.ncbi.nlm.nih.gov/pmc/articles/PMC8451212/
7. Choi, H., Lee, J., Park, J., Cho, B.H., Lee, K.M., Jang, D.P.: Movement state classification for bimanual BCI from non-human primate's epidural ECoG using three-dimensional convolutional neural network. In: 2018 6th International Conference on Brain-Computer Interface (BCI), pp. 1–3 (2018). https://doi.org/10.1109/IWW-BCI.2018.8311534
8. Dahm, S.F., Rieger, M.: Is there symmetry in motor imagery? Exploring different versions of the mental chronometry paradigm. Atten. Percept. Psychophys. **78**(6), 1794–1805 (2016). https://doi.org/10.3758/s13414-016-1112-9
9. Demchenko, T.: READREAM design idea (2022). https://www.youtube.com/watch?v=FZZuVqiJpzQ

10. Deshpande, A., Estrela, V.V., Patavardhan, P.: The DCT-CNN-ResNet50 architecture to classify brain tumors with super-resolution, convolutional neural network, and the ResNet50. Neurosci. Inform. 1(4), 100013 (2021). https://doi.org/10.1016/j.neuri.2021.100013. https://www.sciencedirect.com/science/article/pii/S2772528621000133

11. Di Rienzo, F., Guillot, A., Daligault, S., Delpuech, C., Rode, G., Collet, C.: Motor inhibition during motor imagery: a MEG study with a quadriplegic patient. Neurocase 20(5), 524–539 (2014). https://doi.org/10.1080/13554794.2013.826685

12. Dresler, M., et al.: Dreamed movement elicits activation in the sensorimotor cortex. Curr. Biol. CB 21(21), 1833–1837 (2011). https://doi.org/10.1016/j.cub.2011.09.029

13. von Ellenrieder, N., et al.: How the human brain sleeps: direct cortical recordings of normal brain activity. Ann. Neurol. 87(2), 289–301 (2020). https://doi.org/10.1002/ana.25651. https://onlinelibrary.wiley.com/doi/abs/10.1002/ana.25651

14. Erlacher, D., Schredl, M.: Do REM (lucid) dreamed and executed actions share the same neural substrate? Int. J. Dream Res., 7–14 (2008). https://doi.org/10.11588/ijodr.2008.1.20. https://journals.ub.uni-heidelberg.de/index.php/IJoDR/article/view/20

15. Fosse, R., Larøi, F.: Quantifying auditory impressions in dreams in order to assess the relevance of dreaming as a model for psychosis. PLOS ONE 15(3), e0230212 (2020). https://doi.org/10.1371/journal.pone.0230212. https://journals.plos.org/plosone/article?id=10.1371/journal.pone.0230212

16. Ghimire, P., et al.: Intraoperative mapping of pre-central motor cortex and subcortex: a proposal for supplemental cortical and novel subcortical maps to Penfield's motor homunculus. Brain Struct. Funct. 226(5), 1601–1611 (2021). https://doi.org/10.1007/s00429-021-02274-z

17. Gravano, S., Zago, M., Lacquaniti, F.: Mental imagery of gravitational motion. Cortex 95, 172–191 (2017). https://doi.org/10.1016/j.cortex.2017.08.005. https://www.sciencedirect.com/science/article/pii/S0010945217302526

18. Guillot, A., Di Rienzo, F., Macintyre, T., Moran, A., Collet, C.: Imagining is not doing but involves specific motor commands: a review of experimental data related to motor inhibition. Front. Hum. Neurosci. 6, 247 (2012). https://doi.org/10.3389/fnhum.2012.00247

19. Haufe, S., et al.: Elucidating relations between fMRI, ECoG, and EEG through a common natural stimulus. NeuroImage 179, 79–91 (2018). https://doi.org/10.1016/j.neuroimage.2018.06.016. https://www.ncbi.nlm.nih.gov/pmc/articles/PMC6063527/

20. He, K., Zhang, X., Ren, S., Sun, J.: Delving deep into rectifiers: surpassing human-level performance on ImageNet classification. arXiv:1502.01852 [cs] (2015). http://arxiv.org/abs/1502.01852

21. Herlin, B., Leu-Semenescu, S., Chaumereuil, C., Arnulf, I.: Evidence that non-dreamers do dream: a REM sleep behaviour disorder model. J. Sleep Res. 24(6), 602–609 (2015). https://doi.org/10.1111/jsr.12323

22. Hilditch, C.J., McHill, A.W.: Sleep inertia: current insights. Nat. Sci. Sleep 11, 155–165 (2019). https://doi.org/10.2147/NSS.S188911. https://www.ncbi.nlm.nih.gov/pmc/articles/PMC6710480/

23. Hill, N.J., et al.: Recording human electrocorticographic (ECoG) signals for neuroscientific research and real-time functional cortical mapping. J. Vis. Exp. JoVE (64), 3993 (2012). https://doi.org/10.3791/3993

24. Izawa, S., et al.: REM sleep-active MCH neurons are involved in forgetting hippocampus-dependent memories. Science **365**(6459), 1308–1313 (2019). https://doi.org/10.1126/science.aax9238. https://www.science.org/doi/10.1126/science.aax9238

25. Kingma, D.P., Ba, J.: Adam: a method for stochastic optimization. arXiv (2017). https://doi.org/10.48550/arXiv.1412.6980. http://arxiv.org/abs/1412.6980

26. Konkoly, K.R., et al.: Real-time dialogue between experimenters and dreamers during REM sleep. Curr. Biol. CB **31**(7) (2021). https://doi.org/10.1016/j.cub.2021.01.026

27. Kovach, C.K., Tsuchiya, N., Kawasaki, H., Oya, H., Howard, M.A., Adolphs, R.: Manifestation of ocular-muscle EMG contamination in human intracranial recordings. NeuroImage **54**(1), 213–233 (2011). https://doi.org/10.1016/j.neuroimage.2010.08.002. https://www.sciencedirect.com/science/article/pii/S1053811910010694

28. Lancaster, J.L., et al.: Bias between MNI and talairach coordinates analyzed using the ICBM-152 brain template. Hum. Brain Mapp. **28**(11), 1194–1205 (2007). https://doi.org/10.1002/hbm.20345

29. Leuthardt, E.C., Moran, D.W., Mullen, T.R.: Defining surgical terminology and risk for brain computer interface technologies. Front. Neurosci. **15**, 599549 (2021). https://doi.org/10.3389/fnins.2021.599549

30. Liu, Y., Coon, W.G., Pesters, A.d., Brunner, P., Schalk, G.: The effects of spatial filtering and artifacts on electrocorticographic signals. J. Neural Eng. **12**(5), 056008 (2015). https://doi.org/10.1088/1741-2560/12/5/056008. https://doi.org/10.1088/1741-2560/12/5/056008

31. Lu, N., Li, T., Ren, X., Miao, H.: A deep learning scheme for motor imagery classification based on restricted Boltzmann machines. IEEE Trans. Neural Syst. Rehabil. Eng. **25**(6), 566–576 (2017). https://doi.org/10.1109/TNSRE.2016.2601240

32. Martin, J.M., et al.: Structural differences between REM and non-REM dream reports assessed by graph analysis. PLOS ONE **15**(7) (2020). https://doi.org/10.1371/journal.pone.0228903. https://journals.plos.org/plosone/article?id=10.1371/journal.pone.0228903

33. Meng, L., Xiang, J.: Brain network analysis and classification based on convolutional neural network. Front. Comput. Neurosci. **12** (2018). https://www.frontiersin.org/article/10.3389/fncom.2018.00095

34. Miller, K.J.: A library of human electrocorticographic data and analyses. Nat. Hum. Behav. **3**(11), 1225–1235 (2019). https://doi.org/10.1038/s41562-019-0678-3. https://www.nature.com/articles/s41562-019-0678-3

35. Miller, K.J., Hermes, D., Staff, N.P.: The current state of electrocorticography-based brain-computer interfaces. Neurosurg. Focus **49**(1), E2 (2020). https://doi.org/10.3171/2020.4.FOCUS20185

36. Miller, K.J., Schalk, G., Fetz, E.E., Nijs, M.d., Ojemann, J.G., Rao, R.P.N.: Cortical activity during motor execution, motor imagery, and imagery-based online feedback. Proc. Natl. Acad. Sci. **107**(9), 4430–4435 (2010). https://doi.org/10.1073/pnas.0913697107. https://www.pnas.org/content/107/9/4430

37. Moon, S.E., Jang, S., Lee, J.S.: Convolutional neural network approach for EEG-based emotion recognition using brain connectivity and its spatial information. In: 2018 IEEE International Conference on Acoustics, Speech and Signal Processing (ICASSP), pp. 2556–2560 (2018). https://doi.org/10.1109/ICASSP.2018.8461315. ISSN 2379-190X

38. Mota, N.B., Furtado, R., Maia, P.P.C., Copelli, M., Ribeiro, S.: Graph analysis of dream reports is especially informative about psychosis. Sci. Rep. **4**(1), 3691 (2014). https://doi.org/10.1038/srep03691. https://www.nature.com/articles/srep03691

39. Noreika, V., et al.: Modulating dream experience: noninvasive brain stimulation over the sensorimotor cortex reduces dream movement. Sci. Rep. **10**(1), 6735 (2020). https://doi.org/10.1038/s41598-020-63479-6. https://www.nature.com/articles/s41598-020-63479-6

40. RaviPrakash, H., et al.: Deep learning provides exceptional accuracy to ECoG-based functional language mapping for epilepsy surgery. Front. Neurosci. **14** (2020). https://doi.org/10.3389/fnins.2020.00409. https://www.frontiersin.org/article/10.3389/fnins.2020.00409

41. Rice, L., Wong, E., Kolter, Z.: Overfitting in adversarially robust deep learning. In: Proceedings of the 37th International Conference on Machine Learning, pp. 8093–8104. PMLR (2020). https://proceedings.mlr.press/v119/rice20a.html

42. Rieger, M., Dahm, S.F., Koch, I.: Inhibition in motor imagery: a novel action mode switching paradigm. Psychon. Bull. Rev. **24**(2), 459–466 (2016). https://doi.org/10.3758/s13423-016-1095-5

43. Sauvage, C., Jissendi, P., Seignan, S., Manto, M., Habas, C.: Brain areas involved in the control of speed during a motor sequence of the foot: real movement versus mental imagery. J. Neuroradiol. J. De Neuroradiologie **40**(4), 267–280 (2013). https://doi.org/10.1016/j.neurad.2012.10.001

44. Schredl, M.: Dream content analysis: basic principles. Int. J. Dream Res. (2010). https://doi.org/10.11588/IJODR.2010.1.474. http://journals.ub.uni-heidelberg.de/index.php/IJoDR/article/view/474

45. Shen, G., Horikawa, T., Majima, K., Kamitani, Y.: Deep image reconstruction from human brain activity. PLOS Comput. Biol. **15**(1) (2019). https://doi.org/10.1371/journal.pcbi.1006633. https://journals.plos.org/ploscompbiol/article?id=10.1371/journal.pcbi.1006633

46. Siclari, F., et al.: The neural correlates of dreaming. Nat. Neurosci. **20**(6), 872–878 (2017). https://doi.org/10.1038/nn.4545. https://www.nature.com/articles/nn.4545

47. Speth, C., Speth, J.: A new measure of hallucinatory states and a discussion of REM sleep dreaming as a virtual laboratory for the rehearsal of embodied cognition. Cogn. Sci. **42**(1), 311–333 (2018). https://doi.org/10.1111/cogs.12491. https://onlinelibrary.wiley.com/doi/abs/10.1111/cogs.12491

48. Speth, J., Speth, C.: Motor imagery in REM sleep is increased by transcranial direct current stimulation of the left motor cortex (c3). Neuropsychologia **86**, 57–65 (2016). https://doi.org/10.1016/j.neuropsychologia.2016.04.010

49. St Louis, E.K., Boeve, B.F.: REM sleep behavior disorder: diagnosis, clinical implications, and future directions. Mayo Clin. Proc. **92**(11), 1723–1736 (2017). https://doi.org/10.1016/j.mayocp.2017.09.007. https://www.ncbi.nlm.nih.gov/pmc/articles/PMC6095693/

50. Sun, P., Anumanchipalli, G.K., Chang, E.F.: Brain2char: a deep architecture for decoding text from brain recordings. J. Neural Eng. (2020). https://doi.org/10.1088/1741-2552/abc742

51. Torontali, Z.A., Fraigne, J.J., Sanghera, P., Horner, R., Peever, J.: The sublaterodorsal tegmental nucleus functions to couple brain state and motor activity during REM sleep and wakefulness. Curr. Biol. CB **29**(22), 3803–3813.e5 (2019). https://doi.org/10.1016/j.cub.2019.09.026

52. Valencia Garcia, S., Luppi, P.H., Fort, P.: A particular medullary-spinal inhibitory pathway is recruited for the expression of muscle atonia during REM sleep. J. Exp. Neurosci. **12**, 1179069518808744 (2018). https://doi.org/10.1177/1179069518808744. https://doi.org/10.1177/1179069518808744
53. White, O., Gaveau, J., Bringoux, L., Crevecoeur, F.: The gravitational imprint on sensorimotor planning and control. J. Neurophysiol. **124**(1), 4–19 (2020). https://doi.org/10.1152/jn.00381.2019. https://journals.physiology.org/doi/10.1152/jn.00381.2019
54. Windt, J.: Reporting dream experience: why (not) to be skeptical about dream reports. Front. Hum. Neurosci. **7** (2013). https://www.frontiersin.org/article/10.3389/fnhum.2013.00708
55. Yoo, P.E., et al.: Distinct neural correlates underlie inhibitory mechanisms of motor inhibition and motor imagery restraint. Front. Behav. Neurosci. **14** (2020). https://www.frontiersin.org/article/10.3389/fnbeh.2020.00077

Time Majority Voting, a PC-Based EEG Classifier for Non-expert Users

Guangyao Dou[1]([✉]) [iD], Zheng Zhou[1] [iD], and Xiaodong Qu[1,2] [iD]

[1] Brandeis University, Waltham, MA 02453, USA
{guangyaodou,zhengzhou}@brandeis.edu
[2] Swarthmore College, Swarthmore, PA 19081, USA
xqu1@swarthmore.edu

Abstract. Using Machine Learning and Deep Learning to predict cognitive tasks from electroencephalography (EEG) signals is a rapidly advancing field in Brain-Computer Interfaces (BCI). In contrast to the fields of computer vision and natural language processing, the data amount of these trials is still rather tiny. Developing a PC-based machine learning technique to increase the participation of non-expert end-users could help solve this data collection issue. We created a novel algorithm for machine learning called Time Majority Voting (TMV). In our experiment, TMV performed better than cutting-edge algorithms. It can operate efficiently on personal computers for classification tasks involving the BCI. These interpretable data also assisted end-users and researchers in comprehending EEG tests better.

Keywords: Brain-machine interface · Machine learning · Ensemble methods · Voting · Time series · Interpretable AI

1 Introduction

Researchers from Computer Science, Neuroscience, and Medical fields have applied EEG-based Brain-Computer Interaction (BCI) techniques in many different ways [2,15,19,22,24,26,34], such as diagnosis of abnormal states, evaluating the effect of the treatments, seizure detection, motor imagery tasks [4–6,17,23,27], and developing BCI-based games [14]. Previous studies have demonstrated the great potential of machine learning, deep learning, and transfer learning algorithms [1,3,7,8,12,16,18,20,21,25,28,29,37–42] in such clinical and non-clinical data analysis.

However, the data size of such experiments is still relatively small compared to the areas of computer vision or natural language processing. Thus, some deep learning or big data approaches still struggling with the limitation of small dataset size. Also, EEG signals have noise issues, partly because of the contact of sensors and skin for several current non-invasive consumer-grade devices. The outlier issue is also a concern for the EEG data because of the difficulties subjects have in concentrating on the experimental tasks during the entire session. Current machine learning and deep learning algorithms are more for clinical experiments and less for the possible experiment for non-expert user to conduct at home.

Our research questions are: Can we develop a PC-based machine learning algorithm for non-expert end-users to do EEG classification at home? Can we achieve reasonably high accuracy while keeping the run time in an acceptable range? Can we make the machine learning classification results explainable to the end-users? To answer these questions, we proposed a new machine learning classification algorithm, Time Majority Voting (TMV). We found TMV outperformed other state-of-the-art classifiers. Also, its run time on a PC is still acceptable compared to the deep learning algorithms. The classification results are adequately interpretable to the end-users.

The paper is organized as follows: section two discusses several most frequently used classification algorithms for BCI research, then present our new algorithm. Section three presents our experiment conducted to test the new algorithm. Section four elaborates our result followed by sedition five, which discusses the limitation and future work. Lastly, section six concludes the study and summarized our answers to the research questions.

2   Algorithms

All of the code was run on a 2018 Macbook Pro with a 2.2 GHz 6-core Intel Core i7 processor and with 16 GB of memory. The Python version is 3.8. The scikit-learn [31] version is 0.24.1. The PyTorch [30] version is 1.10. The code discussed in this paper is available online (https://github.com/GuangyaoDou/Time_Majority_Voting).

2.1   Existing Algorithms

u We reviewed and implemented several machine learning algorithms commonly used in the field [9–11,13]. For examples, Linear Classifiers, Nearest Neighbors, Decision Trees, and Ensemble Methods.

Linear Classifiers: The Shrinkage Linear Discriminant Analysis (Shrinkage LDA) performed adequately on EEG datasets with simple tasks. The Support Vector Machine (SVM), effective in high dimensional spaces, performed reasonably well based on the previous research. These algorithms are simple to implement and are computationally efficient.

Nearest Neighbor: Such a classifier implements the K-Nearest Neighbor (KNN). KNN performs voting to determine an unseen dataset to one of the k nearest neighbors. The KNN performed pretty well compared to most other classifiers on the EEG dataset.

Decision Tree: The Decision Trees classifier is easy to understand, implement, and interpret. The decision tree creates a model that predicts the outcome of a data point based on decision rules. The computational cost is low and can handle both numerical and categorical data. However, it might overfit as trees are too complex.

Ensemble Methods: We used Random Forest and boosting. These are Ensemble Machine Learning algorithms that combine the predictions of several weaker learners and form more robust and more accurate predictions. These have been widely used in EEG-based experiments, and research [24,33,35].

Deep Learning: We implemented CNN with ReLu, and RNN, especially LSTM, mainly using toolsets from the PyTorch platform. [15,34,37]. These DLs performed very well on EEG datasets. However, we excluded these algorithms in this paper due to their high runtime.

2.2   Our New Algorithms

This paper proposed a new voting approach based on the top two individual classifiers. Ensemble methods, especially boosting, bagging, and voting, have demonstrated excellent performance in previous research. [15,24,34,36,37] In EEG-based BCI classification research, the following voting methods have been investigated in several experiments [24,33]: majority voting, weighted voting, and time continuity voting. Here we considered the advantages of both majority voting and time continuity voting and developed our new Time Majority Voting (TMV) algorithm.

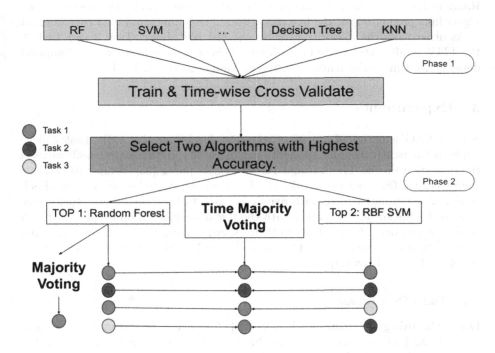

Fig. 1. Our new algorithm: time majority voting

Time Majority Voting (TMV)

Figure 1 demonstrated the concept of the new algorithm. More details are in the Experiment section and the Result section. There are two phases in the new algorithm. First, we investigated the state-of-the-art machine learning algorithms [15,24,34,37] and found the top two performers on average. In our experiments during phase 1, We tested Random Forest (RF), RBF and linear SVM, kNN, Decision Tree, and several boosting algorithms. We found Random Forest performed the best, and RBF SVM performed the second on average. Next, we entered phase two. For each subject, we picked the majority task predicted by the best performing classifier, the Random Forest classifier, for each time interval of each task from each session.

The next step is voting. We used the Random Forest and the RBF SVM to conduct the voting process. The best algorithm is the Random Forest, and the second algorithm is RBF SVM. The voting details are shown in the six examples at the bottom of Fig. 1. If both the Random Forest and the RBF SVM algorithms agree with the results, as shown in the first two rows, the results reflect both algorithms' results. For example, as the second row shows, if both the classifiers predicted the task 2, then the Time Majority Voting will yield task 2 as the result. If the two algorithms do not agree on the prediction results, the results will be labeled as the majority of tasks already determined by the Random Forest classifier, as shown in the last two rows. No matter what the two algorithms predict out of the five tasks, even if they predicted it as two different tasks other than the majority task, as the last row shows, Task 2 and Task 3, the TMV result is still set to be Task one. This concept is based on the temporal dependence time-series features in the previous research [25,36].

3   Experiments

Several EEG experiments focus on the high-level cognitive tasks that college students frequently conduct, as mentioned in Table 1. In this experiment, we used the dataset from the Think-Count-Recall (TCR) paper [33]. Scalp-EEG signals were recorded from seventeen subjects. Each one was tested in six sessions. Each session is five minutes long, with five tasks, each task is one minute. Tasks were selected by the subjects together with the researchers based on frequent tasks in study environments for students in their everyday lives. Each subject completed six sessions over several weeks. The five tasks are Think(T), Count(C), Recall(R), Breathe(B), and Draw(D).

3.1   Data Preprocess

Data Cleaning: As mentioned in [33,35], for each task during each session, the first 30% of the data, which is the first 18 s of each task and during the transition phase, will be removed. Thus, each one-minute task only had 42 s left. This has been proved reasonable during the data cleaning phase. Some electrodes may have temporarily lost contact with the subjects' scalp during

Table 1. Tasks (T) in Experiments (E)

(E) T	1	2	3	4	5
[32]	Math	Close-eye relax	Read	Open-eye relax	None
[36]	Python passive	Math passive	Python active	Math active	None
[35]	Read	Write copy	Write answer	Type copy	Type answer
[33]	Think	Count	Recall	Breathe	Draw

the EEG recording. The result was that multiple sequential spectral snapshots from one or more electrodes had the same value. In this paper, we decide to remove such anomaly when detected for a consecutive 1.4 s. Such a cleaning action caused a different level of loss of the data for each subject.

Subjects: We had a total of seventeen subjects. After the data cleaning actions, subjects who lost more than 65% of the total data will be excluded from the subsequent analysis. In the end, there were twelve subjects left to continue the analysis. Moreover, for the six sessions of each subject, if a session lost more than 65% of the data, then that session will also be excluded for further analysis.

Time-wise Cross-Validation: We adopted time-wise cross-validation. We divided each task into seven subsets, meaning each subset had six seconds, evenly and continuously. Then, we created a total of seven folds. Each fold contained six seconds of data for each task for each session. We checked any folds that lost more than 65% of the original data in each fold and discarded these folds for future analysis. Next, we used one fold for testing and the remaining non-discarded folds for training, and we cross-validated them.

4 Results

4.1 Existing Algorithms

We reported the average accuracy for all subjects and the runtime of each classifier for each subject we trained and tested during phase 1 in Table 2. As we

Table 2. State-of-the-art algorithms with accuracy and run-time

Algorithms	Average accuracy	Average code run-time (s)
Random Forest Phase 1	**0.55**	42.0
RBF SVM	**0.53**	30.5
Nearest Neighbors	0.48	**1.9**
Decision Tree	0.44	0.9
Linear SVM	0.42	23.2
Shrinkage LDA	0.42	0.2
Adaboost Classifier	0.39	47.8
RUSBoost	0.39	28.2
GradientBoost	0.31	24.0

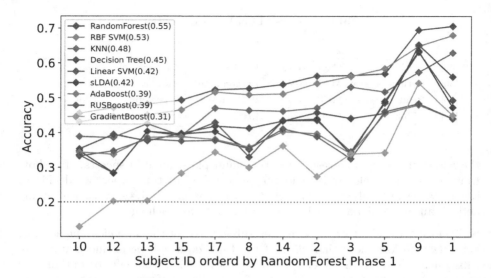

Fig. 2. Accuracy for different algorithms

can see, Random Forest had the highest accuracy of 0.55 in our experiment, and the SVM with RBF kernel performed adequately on the TCR dataset with an average accuracy of 0.53. Though Nearest Neighbors did not perform as well as the Random Forest and the RBF SVM, it was one of the fastest algorithms on personal computers. Other ensemble methods such as Adaboost, RusBoost, and GradientBoosting performed relatively lower than these top three algorithms.

The individual difference may impact the accuracy of each subject. But we can still recognize a general pattern from Fig. 2. We ordered all twelve subjects by prediction accuracy using Random Forest. Most of the algorithms demonstrated consistent patterns for the different algorithms. Random Forest and RBF SVM are above most of the other algorithms. We kept the threshold of maintaining the subject to 35% of the remaining data, as we believed that when a subject has little data left, the high accuracy from that subject contributes little to our research.

4.2 Identify Noisy Sessions

Figure 3 shows what the Random Forest and the RBF SVM in phase 1 predicted during the 42 s of subject 3's task 1 for all six sessions. As we can see, both the Random Forest and the RBF SVM mainly produced results with relatively high accuracy in sessions one, four, and six. On the other hand, session two and three had much noise, and session five predicted task 3 for the majority of the time. To minimize the impact of noisy datasets, we calculated the accuracy compared to the ground truth based on the output of Random Forest for each session for each task in phase 1.

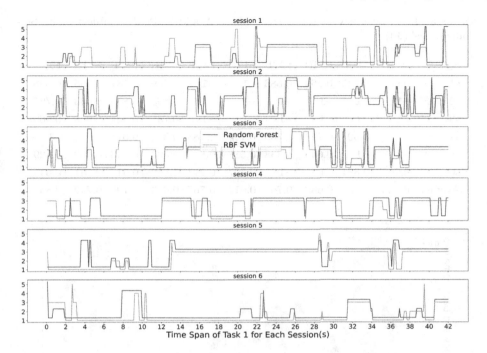

Fig. 3. Subject 3's task 1's RF and SVM in phase 1

We excluded any sessions that yielded an accuracy of less than 50%. In the case of Fig. 3, we excluded sessions two, three, and five for further machine learning analysis. We reported to subject three and started discussing what may have happened in these sessions. With the exclusion of noisy sessions, the new accuracy for the Random Forest in phase 2 is referred to as "Random Forests Phase 2" later in the paper. We also performed Time Majority Voting on this cleaner dataset.

4.3 Time Majority Voting

As shown in Table 3, the Time Majority Voting (TMV) has achieved a higher accuracy for subject three, all the six sessions. A value of -1 means that we excluded that session for that task, as we discussed in the previous section. The Random Forest classifier also reached a higher accuracy after cleaning the noisy sessions. As Fig. 4 and Fig. 5 shows, the pattern is consistent across all the subjects. Figure 5 also shows a clear pattern that not only the Random Forest but also the RBF SVM also increased accuracy in phase 2 across all subjects. Table 4 shows the TMV achieved an 80% average accuracy with an average 74.3 s run time. The runtime consists of 39.1 s of running the Random Forest and 29.5 s of running the RBF SVM. The time for the actual voting is, on average, 5.7 s. The training process is the most time-consuming part of this analysis.

Table 3. TCR, accuracy of top 1 (RF) phase 2, and TMV(T) (subject 3, by Session(S)/Task(T))

S/T	t1 RF	t1 T	t2 RF	t2 T	t3 RF	t3 T	t4 RF	t4 T	t5 RF	t5
s1	0.686	0.745	0.669	0.683	−1	−1	0.569	0.781	0.798	0.898
s2	−1	−1	−1	−1	−1	−1	0.693	0.838	0.633	0.707
s3	−1	−1	−1	−1	−1	−1	0.731	0.824	0.938	0.969
s4	0.543	0.59	0.743	0.869	0.74	0.788	0.521	0.671	−1	−1
s5	−1	−1	0.645	0.738	0.588	0.8	0.593	0.743	0.662	0.829
s6	0.762	0.871	−1	−1	0.507	0.714	0.812	0.917	0.681	0.845
Average	0.663	0.736	0.686	0.763	0.612	0.767	0.653	0.796	0.742	0.85

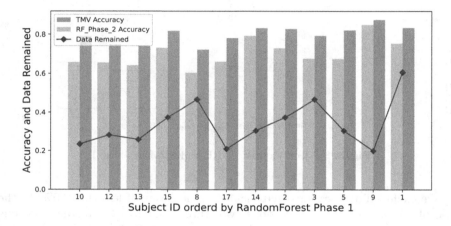

Fig. 4. TMV and RF Phase 2

Table 4. TMV and Random Forest with accuracy and run-time

Algorithms	Average accuracy	Average code run-time (s)
Time Majority Voting	**0.80**	$39.1 + 29.5 + 5.7 = 74.3$
Random Forest Phase 2	0.7	39.1
RBF SVM Phase 2	0.66	29.5
Random Forest Phase 1	0.55	39.1
RBF SVM Phase 1	0.53	29.5

Figure 6 shows what the Time Majority Voting (TMV) predicted during the 42 s of subject 3's task 1 for all six sessions. As you can see, sessions 2, 3, and 5 have values of −1, which means that they have been excluded. Sessions 1, 4, and 6 have less noise than sessions 2, 3, and 6, and the accuracy is relatively high.

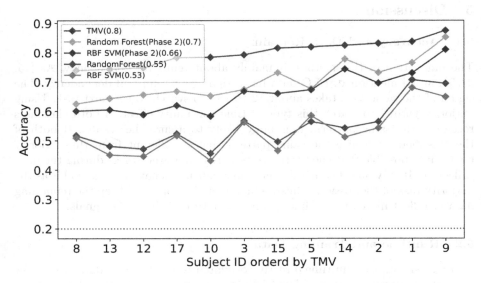

Fig. 5. TMV, RF Phase 2, RBF SVM Phase 2, RF Phase 1, and RBF SVM Phase 1

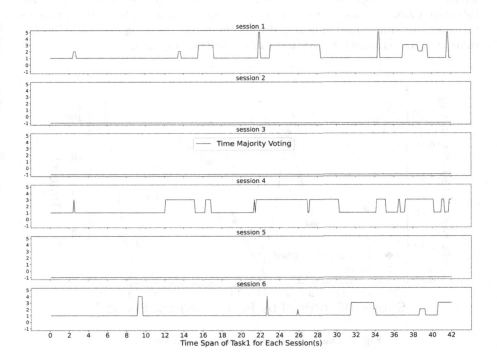

Fig. 6. Subject 3's task 1's TMV

5   Discussion

5.1   Accuracy and Data Remain

The innovation of this method is mainly about temporal dependency. As [15, 24, 34, 36, 37] mentioned, EEG data has a significant temporal dependency. The signal of the same task takes about 12 to 18 s to switch to the next task. Using majority voting can catch this type of time continuity effect. If both classifiers recognize the same pattern, it is more likely to assure the results. If both of the classifiers recognize the same pattern that is different from the majority result, it is possible that the participants were doing other tasks during the data collection. If only one classifier detects some unusual behaviors, we label it as the majority task of the session. Thus we highlight the noise and keep the remaining data to reflect more on the time continuity nature of the EEG signals.

5.2   Runtime and Training Data

As Fig. 7 shows, the run time directly correlated to the training data size. After the data pre-processing, we cleaned up the noise with a plateau longer than a threshold, as mentioned in [24, 32, 34]. We first identified more noisy sessions during the Time Majority Voting process based on the top two classifiers. During this step, more sessions were excluded for further analysis. The training process was the most time-consuming step during the coding running process. Thus the runtime changed together with the size of the training data.

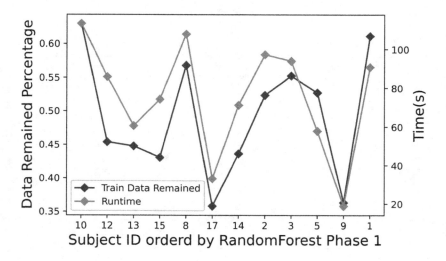

Fig. 7. Data remained for training and run-time

5.3   Interpretability

Figure 3 and 6 shows two examples of the feedback results we present to the end-users. In this Fig. 3, the six sessions of subject three, task one is listed as six horizontal charts. The first chart represents session one. Both the Random Forest and the RBF SVM identified the majority task as task one. And for the results of the different predictions, both of the classifiers agreed at some time spots, but not all of them. Our Time Majority Voting algorithm favorite the majority voting results.

We started with the sessions with good prediction results when demonstrating these figures to each subject. For example, in this Fig. 3, sessions one, four, and six show pretty consistent patterns. The majority of task prediction results were the designed task one. That implies that the subject may spend more time on task one as planned during these sessions. Session two and three had a lot of different prediction results from both classifiers. Thus we suspected some unexpected reason might cause this situation. We referred back to the experiment notes and reached out to subject one. After discussing with the end-user, we figured out that he had many issues with the sensor signals and was adjusting the EEG headset most of the time during the sessions 2 and 3. Thus we had more information to exclude these sessions from further data analysis. Session five is another situation. The data implied that the subject was doing task three, but the experiment notes were missing for that session, and the subject did not remember the details about that session. Thus, we left a question mark for that session, excluded the session for now, and came up with an improvement plan to keep better experiment notes. This type of machine learning result is explainable to the end-user.

Such interpretability could contribute to a better understanding of the results and better design for future experiments.

6   Conclusion

This paper investigated the state-of-the-art machine learning algorithms that can run on mainstream personal computers for EEG-based BCI. We then proposed a new algorithm, Time Majority Voting (TMV). The results demonstrated that TMV outperformed other existing classifiers. The run time for TMV is still within the acceptable range on a PC. The interpretability of TMV can contribute to a better understanding of the machine learning analysis and an improved design for future experiments.

References

1. An, S., Ogras, U.Y.: MARS: mmWave-based assistive rehabilitation system for smart healthcare. ACM Trans. Embed. Comput. Syst. (TECS) **20**(5s), 1–22 (2021)
2. Appriou, A., Cichocki, A., Lotte, F.: Modern machine-learning algorithms: for classifying cognitive and affective states from electroencephalography signals. IEEE Syst. Man Cybern. Mag. **6**(3), 29–38 (2020)

3. Basaklar, T., Tuncel, Y., An, S., Ogras, U.: Wearable devices and low-power design for smart health applications: challenges and opportunities. In: 2021 IEEE/ACM International Symposium on Low Power Electronics and Design (ISLPED), p. 1. IEEE (2021)

4. Bashivan, P., Bidelman, G.M., Yeasin, M.: Spectrotemporal dynamics of the EEG during working memory encoding and maintenance predicts individual behavioral capacity. Eur. J. Neurosci. **40**(12), 3774–3784 (2014)

5. Bashivan, P., Rish, I., Heisig, S.: Mental state recognition via wearable EEG. arXiv preprint arXiv:1602.00985 (2016)

6. Bashivan, P., Rish, I., Yeasin, M., Codella, N.: Learning representations from EEG with deep recurrent-convolutional neural networks. arXiv preprint arXiv:1511.06448 (2015)

7. Bhat, G., Tuncel, Y., An, S., Ogras, U.Y.: Wearable IoT devices for health monitoring. In: TechConnect Briefs 2019, pp. 357–360 (2019)

8. Bird, J.J., Manso, L.J., Ribeiro, E.P., Ekart, A., Faria, D.R.: A study on mental state classification using EEG-based brain-machine interface. In: 2018 International Conference on Intelligent Systems (IS), pp. 795–800. IEEE (2018)

9. Breiman, L.: Bagging predictors. Mach. Learn. **24**(2), 123–140 (1996)

10. Breiman, L.: Random forests. Mach. Learn. **45**(1), 5–32 (2001)

11. Breiman, L.: Classification and Regression Trees. Routledge, London (2017)

12. Chen, L., et al.: Data-driven detection of subtype-specific differentially expressed genes. Sci. Rep. **11**(1), 1–12 (2021)

13. Chevalier, J.A., Gramfort, A., Salmon, J., Thirion, B.: Statistical control for spatio-temporal meg/EEG source imaging with desparsified multi-task lasso. arXiv preprint arXiv:2009.14310 (2020)

14. Coyle, D., Principe, J., Lotte, F., Nijholt, A.: Guest editorial: brain/neuronal-computer game interfaces and interaction. IEEE Trans. Comput. Intell. AI Games **5**(2), 77–81 (2013)

15. Craik, A., He, Y., Contreras-Vidal, J.L.: Deep learning for electroencephalogram (EEG) classification tasks: a review. J. Neural Eng. **16**(3), 031001 (2019)

16. Derby, J.J., et al.: Computational modeling and neutron imaging to understand interface shape and solute segregation during the vertical gradient freeze growth of BaBrCl: EU. J. Cryst. Growth **536**, 125572 (2020)

17. Devlaminck, D., Waegeman, W., Bauwens, B., Wyns, B., Santens, P., Otte, G.: From circular ordinal regression to multilabel classification. In: Proceedings of the 2010 Workshop on Preference Learning (European Conference on Machine Learning, ECML), p. 15 (2010)

18. Gu, J., et al.: Multi-phase cross-modal learning for noninvasive gene mutation prediction in hepatocellular carcinoma. In: 2020 42nd Annual International Conference of the IEEE Engineering in Medicine & Biology Society (EMBC), pp. 5814–5817. IEEE (2020)

19. Kastrati, A., et al.: EEGEyeNet: a simultaneous electroencephalography and eye-tracking dataset and benchmark for eye movement prediction. arXiv preprint arXiv:2111.05100 (2021)

20. Kaya, M., Binli, M.K., Ozbay, E., Yanar, H., Mishchenko, Y.: A large electroencephalographic motor imagery dataset for electroencephalographic brain computer interfaces. Sci. Data **5**(1), 1–16 (2018)

21. Li, S., Zhao, Z., Xu, K., Zeng, Z., Guan, C.: Hierarchical consistency regularized mean teacher for semi-supervised 3d left atrium segmentation. In: 2021 43rd Annual International Conference of the IEEE Engineering in Medicine & Biology Society (EMBC), pp. 3395–3398. IEEE (2021)

22. Lotte, F.: A tutorial on EEG signal-processing techniques for mental-state recognition in brain–computer interfaces. In: Miranda, E.R., Castet, J. (eds.) Guide to Brain-Computer Music Interfacing, pp. 133–161. Springer, London (2014). https://doi.org/10.1007/978-1-4471-6584-2_7

23. Lotte, F.: Signal processing approaches to minimize or suppress calibration time in oscillatory activity-based brain-computer interfaces. Proc. IEEE **103**(6), 871–890 (2015)

24. Lotte, F., et al.: A review of classification algorithms for EEG-based brain-computer interfaces: a 10 year update. J. Neural Eng. **15**(3), 031005 (2018)

25. Lotte, F., Congedo, M., Lécuyer, A., Lamarche, F., Arnaldi, B.: A review of classification algorithms for EEG-based brain-computer interfaces. J. Neural Eng. **4**(2), R1 (2007)

26. Lotte, F., Guan, C.: Regularizing common spatial patterns to improve BCI designs: unified theory and new algorithms. IEEE Trans. Biomed. Eng. **58**(2), 355–362 (2010)

27. Lotte, F., Jeunet, C.: Towards improved BCI based on human learning principles. In: The 3rd International Winter Conference on Brain-Computer Interface, pp. 1–4. IEEE (2015)

28. Lotte, F., Jeunet, C., Mladenović, J., N'Kaoua, B., Pillette, L.: A BCI challenge for the signal processing community: considering the user in the loop (2018)

29. Miller, K.J.: A library of human electrocorticographic data and analyses. Nat. Hum. Behav. **3**(11), 1225–1235 (2019)

30. Paszke, A., et al.: Automatic differentiation in PyTorch. NeurIPS (2017)

31. Pedregosa, F., et al.: Scikit-learn: machine learning in Python. J. Mach. Learn. Res. **12**, 2825–2830 (2011)

32. Qu, X., Hall, M., Sun, Y., Sekuler, R., Hickey, T.J.: A personalized reading coach using wearable EEG sensors-a pilot study of brainwave learning analytics. In: CSEDU (2), pp. 501–507 (2018)

33. Qu, X., Liu, P., Li, Z., Hickey, T.: Multi-class time continuity voting for EEG classification. In: Frasson, C., Bamidis, P., Vlamos, P. (eds.) BFAL 2020. LNCS (LNAI), vol. 12462, pp. 24–33. Springer, Cham (2020). https://doi.org/10.1007/978-3-030-60735-7_3

34. Qu, X., Liukasemsarn, S., Tu, J., Higgins, A., Hickey, T.J., Hall, M.H.: Identifying clinically and functionally distinct groups among healthy controls and first episode psychosis patients by clustering on EEG patterns. Front. Psychiat., 938 (2020)

35. Qu, X., Mei, Q., Liu, P., Hickey, T.: Using EEG to distinguish between writing and typing for the same cognitive task. In: Frasson, C., Bamidis, P., Vlamos, P. (eds.) BFAL 2020. LNCS (LNAI), vol. 12462, pp. 66–74. Springer, Cham (2020). https://doi.org/10.1007/978-3-030-60735-7_7

36. Qu, X., Sun, Y., Sekuler, R., Hickey, T.: EEG markers of stem learning. In: 2018 IEEE Frontiers in Education Conference (FIE), pp. 1–9. IEEE (2018)

37. Roy, Y., Banville, H., Albuquerque, I., Gramfort, A., Falk, T.H., Faubert, J.: Deep learning-based electroencephalography analysis: a systematic review. J. Neural Eng. **16**(5), 051001 (2019)

38. Zeng, Z., et al.: Robust traffic prediction from spatial-temporal data based on conditional distribution learning. IEEE Trans. Cybernet. (2021)

39. Zhang, X., Yao, L., Wang, X., Monaghan, J.J., Mcalpine, D., Zhang, Y.: A survey on deep learning-based non-invasive brain signals: recent advances and new frontiers. J. Neural Eng. **18**, 031002 (2020)

40. Zhao, Z., Chopra, K., Zeng, Z., Li, X.: Sea-net: squeeze-and-excitation attention net for diabetic retinopathy grading. In: 2020 IEEE International Conference on Image Processing (ICIP), pp. 2496–2500. IEEE (2020)

41. Zhao, Z., Qian, P., Hou, Y., Zeng, Z.: Adaptive mean-residue loss for robust facial age estimation. In: 2022 IEEE International Conference on Multimedia and Expo (ICME). IEEE (2022)

42. Zhao, Z., et al.: BiRA-Net: bilinear attention net for diabetic retinopathy grading. In: 2019 IEEE International Conference on Image Processing (ICIP), pp. 1385–1389. IEEE (2019)

It's Easy as ABC Framework for User Feedback

Alexandra Fischmann[✉] and Sydney Levy

Swarthmore College, Swarthmore, PA 19081, USA
{afischm1,slevy1}@swarthmore.edu

Abstract. Improving the interface and training provided to users during data collection could present an important step to solving the reliability issue of Brain-Computer Interfaces (BCIs). We incorporate design principals from human-computer interaction (HCI) and educational research to create an interface for future researchers. Our interface is based on being **A**ttuned to the user (A) by providing **B**iased user feedback (B) and **C**lassification algorithm descriptions (C). This interface can serve as a framework for providing users with feedback according to the experience level and emotional state of the user. Additionally, the interface provides example descriptions of common classification algorithms to better inform users of how their data is being utilized.

Keywords: Human-computer interaction · User feedback design · Brain-computer interfaces · Education

1 Introduction

1.1 Problem Statement

A brain-computer interface (BCI) is a computer system that communicates with a user in an interactive method that translates brain signals into instructions for an application to execute [12]. The common method for receiving these brain signals is the use of electroencephalography (EEG). An online BCI system begins by taking an EEG signal from the user and records the signal being measured [12]. After this, the EEG signals are processed using a variety of filters which extract the important features from the EEG signal [12]. The next step includes classification methods that interpret the EEG features and translate them into the command for the application [12]. Finally, users are informed whether or not the EEG signals were successfully translated into the command for the computer [12]. Machine Learning and Deep Learning algorithms have been implemented in many EEG-based BCI experiments and research [2,6,13,23,27].

Current brain-computer interfaces are not reliable enough to be used consistently outside of laboratory environments [7,14,22,24]. Most BCI research that aims to solve this reliability issue focuses on improving the classification step of

A. Fischmann and S. Levy—Contributed equally to the paper.

© The Author(s), under exclusive license to Springer Nature Switzerland AG 2022
M. Kurosu et al. (Eds.): HCII 2022, LNCS 13519, pp. 429–441, 2022.
https://doi.org/10.1007/978-3-031-17618-0_30

translating the EEG signals effectively into commands for the computer. This has primarily been done through implementing new machine learning techniques.

While this research presents an important step in the right direction for BCI classification algorithms, there has been a lack of research attention devoted to improving the user interface for engaging with BCI systems. Improving the interface and training provided to users could present an important step to solving the reliability issues of BCIs [14].

1.2   Literature Review

The ability to interact with BCIs is not one that comes immediately to the user. The user needs to learn how to operate the BCI while the system simultaneously learns to classify the user's EEG signals [17]. Lotte et al. describe this ability as one that needs to be taught to a user and practiced often [14]. Specifically, the user needs to be able to provide the EEG with consistent and clear brain activity patterns. Without the ability to successfully interpret the user's brain activity, even effective classification algorithms are rendered useless [14]. Current teaching approaches often provide users with uni-modal feedback which fails to adhere to well-known pedagogical design principles [14].

Mladenovic emphasizes the need for a standardization of protocol designs among researchers for how best to train users of BCIs [18]. One attempt to outline effective BCI feedback was created by Kübler et al. [10]. They provide a framework which emphasizes effectiveness, efficiency, and satisfaction [10]. Other frameworks have prioritized motivational factors such as: user's curiosity, relevance to user's values, confidence, and intrinsic and extrinsic rewards [14]. Lotte et al. argue that by focusing on these factors, BCI performance can improve for novice users [14]. Schumacher et al. have explored the potential for providing users of BCIs with explanatory feedback during training [28] and found no deteriorating performance as a result of incorporating multiple forms of feedback. The effective use of feedback has also been studied extensively within educational research. For example, Narciss et al. outline the value of providing learners with details regarding not only the errors they made, but also the flaws in the strategies they used [20].

In addition to these frameworks, Roc et al. provide a review of the feedback, environment, and methods for mental task-based BCI user training [25]. Similarly, Lotte et al. highlight more practical suggestions for the content and type of feedback specific to BCIs [15]. Lotte et al. propose that BCI instructions include both the goals of the training as well as explanations for classifier output [15]. Additionally, Lotte et al. opt for providing the user with detailed information regarding the beneficial or detrimental qualities of their EEG patterns [15].

In terms of the relationship between user characteristics and feedback, a recent study has found that a user's level of tension affects mean BCI performance [21]. Mladenovic et al. found that a user experiencing low initial workload or low anxiety provides the best results when given feedback with a negative bias as opposed to no bias [19]. Research has further suggested providing positive feedback for inexperienced users and more honest feedback for experienced users

[14,15]. This positive feedback can be accomplished through either making the user believe they did better than they actually did, or only providing feedback when the user successfully completed the task [14].

Both interactive visual and tactile forms of user feedback have been explored for BCI training. Lotte et al. advocate for a game-like process for the user to engage with during training and testing for BCIs [15]. Further, researchers have discussed the interplay between EEG-based BCIs and video games [3,9]. Research by Ron-Angevin & AntonioDíaz-Estrella even suggests the use of virtual-reality for increasing user motivation during BCI user training [26]. Additionally, research conducted by Cincotti et al. 2007 explores the potential for vibrotactile user feedback during BCI training [5].

1.3 Purpose of Study

Through our research we hope to bridge the gap between advanced classification methods for BCIs and the feedback that users receive while providing EEG data for these applications. We hope to utilize design principles from human-computer interaction research as well as educational research to improve training protocols for users, increase the effectiveness of communication utilizing BCIs, and improve user motivation during training and testing.

This research has the potential to impact a multitude of user groups who could rely on BCIs [1]. For example, BCIs can serve as a pivotal piece of technology for assessing neurological disorders, providing stroke rehabilitation [16], acting as a communication device for locked-in patients [29], and as a way to detect human drowsiness [8].

1.4 Research Questions

The main research questions that motivate this paper are:

1. What is the most effective interface for providing user training and feedback for BCIs?
2. How can one incorporate pedagogical methods into beneficial feedback for users of BCIs?

2 Experiment

2.1 Experiment Design

Many popular BCI datasets, such as BCI IV Competition 2a dataset, are collected without providing feedback to the users [4]. Although we cannot alter this, we would suggest that to improve EEG data collection, this should have been done. Thus, we will create an interface to provide example feedback for different situations the users might encounter during data collection.

This feedback will be based on the design principles we outline in Table 1. Within our user interface, in order to abide by principle 1, we plan to base feedback on user experience level. For inexperienced users, we will provide feedback

Table 1. Design principles to guide research.

Design principles	Source	Implementation
(1) Positive feedback for inexperienced user and more honest feedback for experienced users	Lotte and Jeunet (2015), Lotte et al. (2013)	Ask the user for their level of experience - provide differing feedback accordingly
(2) Low-anxiety users provide the best result when given feedback with negative bias	Mladenovic et al. (2021)	Ask the users for their anxiety levels and provide biased feedback accordingly
(3) Learners benefit from actively thinking about the strategies they are implementing	Narciss et al. (2004)	Inform users about the classification methods being used for them to better understand the strategies they need to employ during training

with a positive bias whereas feedback for more experienced users will be more honest. To implement design principle 2 from Table 1, we will ask users about their levels of anxiety during training in order to boost confidence for high-anxiety users and provide feedback with a negative bias for low-anxiety users. For design principle 3 from Table 1, we provide classification algorithm descriptions so that users can better understand how their data is being processed and thus come up with improved strategies for providing clear EEG signals. We hope that including these descriptions will make users feel that they are truly a part of the training process and not isolated from the data they provide.

Finally, in order to test the effectiveness of our interface, we had 21 participants answer survey questions as they interacted with our interface and read our classification algorithm descriptions. Users reported their answers via selecting options from a 4-point or 5-point scale via a Google Form.

The questions that made up our survey are:

1. What is your past experience with computer science?
2. What is your past experience with machine learning?
3. What is your past experience with brain-computer interfaces?
4. Are you motivated to learn about machine learning/brain-computer interfaces?
5. Do you get stressed out by computer issues?
6. What is your current understanding of Linear Discriminant Analysis?
7. Here is our description of Linear Discriminant Analysis... After reading this description how would rate your new understanding of Linear Discriminant Analysis?
8. What is your current understanding of Support Vector Machine?

9. Here is our description of Support Vector Machine... After reading this description how would you rate your new understanding of Support Vector Machine?

10. What is your current understanding of Random Forest (classification method)?

11. Here is our description of Random Forest... After reading this description how would you rate your new understanding of Random Forest (classification method)?

12. How would you rate the clarity of our classification algorithm descriptions?

13. If you were providing data for a brain-computer interface, would you find our feedback helpful?

14. How would you rate the ease of use of our interface?

15. How motivated are you to continue learning about brain-computer interfacesmachine learning?

16. Imagine you are providing data for a study involving brain-computer interfaces... After reading the descriptions above and receiving the tailored feedback, would you be more motivated to try your best on the tasks asked of you during the study?

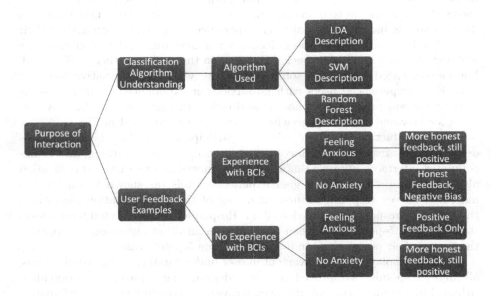

Fig. 1. Interface design flow chart

3   Result

We created an interface that we hope will improve the data that users provide during BCI EEG data collection. Our interface is based on being **A**ttuned to the user (A) by providing **B**iased user feedback (B) and **C**lassification algorithm descriptions (C). Our interface has two main capabilities: (1) Classification Algorithm Descriptions and (2) User Feedback Examples. The code for our interface is publicly available[1].

If a user wants to better understand the classification algorithm that is being used on their data, they can select this option and choose which classification algorithm they are interested in (as shown in Fig. 1). They will then be given a short description of the algorithm they have chosen. To motivate our choice of LDA, SVM, and Random Forest we note that a prominent BCI researcher, Yann LeCun, began his research by focusing on Linear classifiers, K-nearest neighbors and SVMs [11]. Thus, we believe it is important for users of BCIs to begin by understanding the most basic algorithms and can then move onto more advanced and complex algorithms.

The second capability of our interface is to gauge a user's level of anxiety and experience during data collection. In accordance with the design principals noted in Table 1, we provide appropriate feedback tailored to the user. Further, Table 2 shows the feedback we recommend giving to users of brain-computer interfaces during training based on their anxiety, experience level, and the strength of their EEG signal. For experienced users feeling no anxiety during data collection, we will provide more honest feedback depending on the quality of their EEG signal. For inexperienced users with some anxiety, we will provide positive feedback only. For inexperienced users with no anxiety or experienced users with some anxiety, we will provide more honest feedback with slight positive bias. A flow chart for how one might engage with our interface is provided in Fig. 1.

After conducting a survey with 21 participants, we found that respondents with less experience with computer science, machine learning, and brain-computer interfaces improved more in their understanding of the classification algorithms than those with higher experience levels (as shown in Fig. 2). We measured survey respondents understanding of the 3 classification algorithms through their responses to questions 6–11. Respondents first selected their understanding on a 5-point scale, then read our classification algorithm description, then rated their new understanding on the same 5-point scale.

Figure 2 displays the improvement in user understanding on the y-axis. Thus, all survey respondents improved in their understanding of the classification algorithms, but the magnitude of improvement varied according to the participant's experience level with computer science, machine learning, and BCIs. We found that users with less experience had similar improvement levels regardless of classification algorithm type, while users with more experience appeared to have higher increases in understanding for LDA and SVM. Thus, we feel that it is of the utmost importance to provide users who have less experience with ML and

---

[1] https://github.swarthmore.edu/slevy1/ABCUserFramework.

Table 2. Feedback provided to users.

Anxiety level	Experience level	Bias framework	Feedback given
Feeling anxious	Experience with BCIs	Honest feedback, positive bias	**Strong signal**: Your signal looked great. Keep doing what you're doing. **Weak signal**: Your signal wasn't quite right. Good try and keep going
Feeling anxious	No experience with BCIs	Positive feedback only (positive bias)	**Strong signal**: Your signal looked great, fantastic job! Keep doing what you're doing. **Weak signal**: Good try. We think you will improve with practice
No anxiety	Experience with BCIs	Honest feedback, negative bias	**Strong signal**: Good job, your signal is strong but can always be improved. Keep focusing on the task at hand. **Weak signal**: Your signal wasn't clear. Try changing up your strategy
No anxiety	No experience with BCIs	Honest feedback, positive bias	**Strong signal**: Your signal looked great. Keep doing what you're doing. **Weak signal**: Your signal wasn't quite right. Good try and keep going

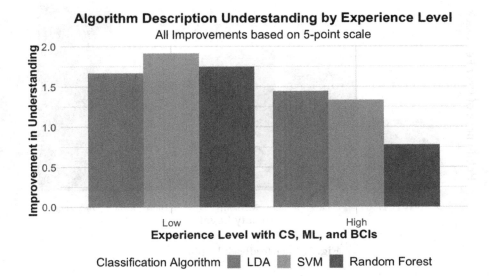

Fig. 2. Improved algorithm understanding

BCIs with classification algorithm descriptions. According to the design principles we outline in Table 1 and our survey results, we believe that an improved classification algorithm understanding could result in increased user motivation during BCI data collection.

We then utilized question 5 as a proxy for a user's anxiety level during BCI data collection. Survey respondents ranked the amount of stress they often feel while using technology on a 5-point scale. We found that respondents with higher anxiety levels found our user feedback more helpful relative to those with lower anxiety surrounding new technology as per Fig. 3. Thus, users with very high anxiety would likely benefit from the more positive feedback we utilize in our interface. Further, these results suggest that users with low or very low anxiety levels would respond well to more negatively biased feedback.

Moreover, users with all levels of experience with computer science, machine learning, and BCIs exhibit a clear increase in motivation after interacting with our interface as per Fig. 4. We measured the survey respondents' motivation to continue learning about machine learning and BCIs as a proxy for their motivation to provide clear EEG signals during BCI training and testing. We based the user's motivation before and after using our interface from questions 4 and 15 in our survey. Thus, users with higher experience levels with CS, ML, and BCIs showed a larger improvement in motivation, on average than respondents with lower experience.

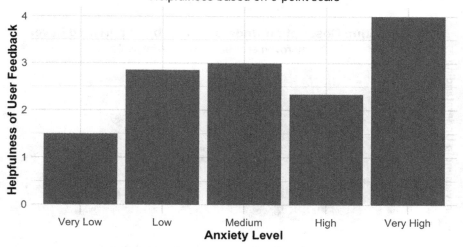

Fig. 3. User feedback helpfulness

Additionally, in question 16, users were asked if they were more motivated to try their best on a BCI data-related task after reading our descriptions. Survey respondents reported an average score of 2.857 (median 3) on a 4 point scale where 1 represented motivation would not change and 4 represented that they were much more motivated. Thus, we believe that users of our interface would have a higher motivation to provide clear EEG signals than users who did not receive biased user feedback and classification algorithm descriptions.

Overall, we did find a statistically significant increase in motivation among all survey respondents after using our interface. When conducting a paired t-test between the motivation of each participant before and after reading our classification algorithm descriptions and using our interface, we found a statistically significant improvement in motivation ($p = 0.008$, $t = 2.65$, $df = 20$).

We recognize that our measure of user motivation before and after using our interface is not a perfect proxy as our survey respondents did not actually use a BCI or provide EEG data. However, we believe our results serve as preliminary evidence of the importance of providing BCI users with feedback based on human-computer interaction as well as educational design principles.

Further, we asked users how easy they found interacting with our interface in question 14. When reporting the ease of use of our interface, the average reported score was 4 (mean 3.905) on a 5 point scale where 1 represented very difficult to use and 5 represented very easy to use. Thus, we believe that the overall framework of our interface can serve as a guide for future researchers.

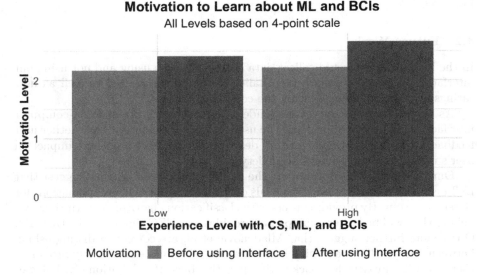

Fig. 4. Motivation before and after utilizing interface

4 Discussion

4.1 Limitations

As our research was conducted during a one-semester undergraduate course, our work was subject to time and complexity limitations. We note that the classification algorithm descriptions provided within our interface give a simplified version of the methods of these algorithms. We implemented the most basic classification algorithms descriptions as a means of demonstrating our interface's algorithm descriptions, but we recognize that future work should implement more advanced classification strategies and more detailed descriptions. Further, we recognize that future researchers may want to further customize these descriptions to their particular work. These descriptions are meant as a sample framework for future research.

Additionally, we provide very brief user feedback that represents the tone and bias that should be implemented for users. We based this biased feedback on the pedagogical and human-computer interaction principles outlined in Table 1. Thus, future researchers should implement more descriptive feedback tailored to their work.

Our research was limited by a lack of time and funding to be able to collect EEG data for a BCI application. Thus, with additional time and resources, we would gather EEG data for users that received feedback based on our interface as compared to no feedback or standardized feedback and measure whether the clarity of the EEG signal or the accuracy of the classification algorithms improved.

4.2 Future Work

In the long term, we would collect data with both users using and not using our interface. We would compare the quality of the data collected as well as user ratings of their experience during the collection process.

As we did not have survey respondents interact with a real brain-computer interface, our survey will primarily be used as a proof of concept for whether user feedback and classification algorithm descriptions can have a positive impact on user's motivation and feelings of anxiety.

Our preliminary results support the findings of Lotte et al. that suggest that BCI instructions include both the goals of the training as well as explanations for classifier output. By providing users with classification algorithm descriptions, we believe they will be better-equipped to provide clear EEG signals to the BCI [15]. Our results further suggest that Mladenovic et al. are correct in distinguishing between users with low and high levels of anxiety, and more specifically providing users with low anxiety feedback with a negative bias [19]. Additionally, Lotte et al. (2015) reviewed a series of studies noting that only providing positive feedback can be beneficial for inexperienced users. By attuning the user's feedback to their level of anxiety and experience, we believe that users will experience higher motivation and enjoyment of the BCI data collection process.

Questions we would like to pose to future researchers include:

1. Does accuracy of classification algorithms improve depending on whether users are provided with biased feedback during data collection?
2. Does accuracy of classification algorithms improve depending on whether users are provided with classification algorithm descriptions before data collection?
3. Does attuning user feedback to the user's emotional state and experience level result in clearer EEG signals and improve user motivation when compared to the same feedback being provided to all users?

5 Conclusion

We created an interface that is **A**ttuned to the user (A) by providing **B**iased user feedback (B) and **C**lassification algorithm descriptions (C). We created an interface where users can better understand classification algorithms that aid in their understanding of how their BCI data will be utilized. Further, this interface provides a framework for how to give biased feedback based on the user's experience and anxiety level. This framework is based on well known pedagogical and human-computer interaction principles that suggest that a user's motivation increases as they better understand the goals of the task at hand. Our interface provides an important step in the direction of improving human computer interaction within the field of machine learning and brain-computer interfaces.

References

1. Allison, B.Z., Wolpaw, E.W., Wolpaw, J.R.: Brain–computer interface systems: progress and prospects. Expert Rev. Med. Dev. **4**(4), 463–474 (2007). https://doi.org/10.1586/17434440.4.4.463. pMID 17605682
2. Bashivan, P., Rish, I., Yeasin, M., Codella, N.: Learning representations from EEG with deep recurrent-convolutional neural networks. arXiv preprint arXiv:1511.06448 (2015)
3. Benaroch, C., et al.: Long-term BCI training of a tetraplegic user: adaptive Riemannian classifiers and user training. Front. Hum. Neurosci. **15** (2021). https://doi.org/10.3389/fnhum.2021.635653. https://www.frontiersin.org/article/10.3389/fnhum.2021.635653
4. Brunner, C., Leeb, R., Müller-Putz, G., Schlögl, A., Pfurtscheller, G.: BCI competition 2008-Graz data set A. Institute for Knowledge Discovery (Laboratory of Brain-Computer Interfaces), Graz University of Technology **16**, 1–6 (2008)
5. Cincotti, F., et al.: Vibrotactile feedback for brain-computer interface operation. Comput. Intell. Neurosci. **2007** (2007)
6. Craik, A., He, Y., Contreras-Vidal, J.L.: Deep learning for electroencephalogram (EEG) classification tasks: a review. J. Neural Eng. **16**(3), 031001 (2019)
7. Ienca, M., Haselager, P., Emanuel, E.J.: Brain leaks and consumer neurotechnology. Nat. Biotechnol. **36**(9), 805–810 (2018)

8. Kastrati, A., et al.: EEGEyeNet: a simultaneous electroencephalography and eye-tracking dataset and benchmark for eye movement prediction. arXiv preprint arXiv:2111.05100 (2021)

9. Kerous, B., Skola, F., Liarokapis, F.: EEG-based BCI and video games: a progress report. Virtual Real. **22**(2), 119–135 (2018)

10. Kübler, A., et al.: The user-centered design as novel perspective for evaluating the usability of BCI-controlled applications. PLoS ONE **9**(12), e112392 (2014)

11. LeCun, Y., Cortes, C., Burges, C.J.: The MNIST database of handwritten digits. http://yann.lecun.com/exdb/mnist/

12. Lotte, F., et al.: A review of classification algorithms for EEG-based brain-computer interfaces: a 10 year update. J. Neural Eng. **15**(3), 031005 (2018)

13. Lotte, F., Congedo, M., Lécuyer, A., Lamarche, F., Arnaldi, B.: A review of classification algorithms for EEG-based brain-computer interfaces. J. Neural Eng. **4**(2), R1 (2007)

14. Lotte, F., Jeunet, C.: Towards improved BCI based on human learning principles. In: The 3rd International Winter Conference on Brain-Computer Interface, pp. 1–4. IEEE (2015)

15. Lotte, F., Larrue, F., Mühl, C.: Flaws in current human training protocols for spontaneous brain-computer interfaces: lessons learned from instructional design. Front. Hum. Neurosci. **7**, 568 (2013)

16. Mane, R., Chouhan, T., Guan, C.: BCI for stroke rehabilitation: motor and beyond. J. Neural Eng. **17**(4), 041001 (2020)

17. McFarland, D.J., Wolpaw, J.R.: Brain-computer interface use is a skill that user and system acquire together. PLOS Biol. **16**(7), 1–4 (2018). https://doi.org/10.1371/journal.pbio.2006719

18. Mladenović, J.: Standardization of protocol design for user training in EEG-based brain-computer interface. J. Neural Eng. **18**(1), 011003 (2021)

19. Mladenovic, J., Frey, J., Pramij, S., Mattout, J., Lotte, F.: Towards identifying optimal biased feedback for various user states and traits in motor imagery BCI. IEEE Trans. Biomed. Eng. **69**, 1101–1110 (2021)

20. Narciss, S., Huth, K.: How to design informative tutoring feedback for multimedia learning. Instruct. Des. Multimedia Learn., 181195 (2004)

21. Pillette, L., Roc, A., N'Kaoua, B., Lotte, F.: Experimenters' influence on mental-imagery based brain-computer interface user training. Int. J. Hum.-Comput. Stud. **149**, 102603 (2021). https://doi.org/10.1016/j.ijhcs.2021.102603. https://www.sciencedirect.com/science/article/pii/S1071581921000215

22. Portillo-Lara, R., Tahirbegi, B., Chapman, C.A., Goding, J.A., Green, R.A.: Mind the gap: state-of-the-art technologies and applications for EEG-based brain-computer interfaces. APL Bioeng. **5**(3), 031507 (2021)

23. Qu, X., Liu, P., Li, Z., Hickey, T.: Multi-class time continuity voting for EEG classification. In: Frasson, C., Bamidis, P., Vlamos, P. (eds.) BFAL 2020. LNCS (LNAI), vol. 12462, pp. 24–33. Springer, Cham (2020). https://doi.org/10.1007/978-3-030-60735-7_3

24. Qu, X., Mei, Q., Liu, P., Hickey, T.: Using EEG to distinguish between writing and typing for the same cognitive task. In: Frasson, C., Bamidis, P., Vlamos, P. (eds.) BFAL 2020. LNCS (LNAI), vol. 12462, pp. 66–74. Springer, Cham (2020). https://doi.org/10.1007/978-3-030-60735-7_7

25. Roc, A., et al.: A review of user training methods in brain computer interfaces based on mental tasks. J. Neural Eng. **18**(1), 011002 (2021)

26. Ron-Angevin, R., Díaz-Estrella, A.: Brain-computer interface: changes in performance using virtual reality techniques. Neurosci. Lett. **449**(2), 123–127 (2009). https://doi.org/10.1016/j.neulet.2008.10.099. https://www.sciencedirect.com/science/article/pii/S0304394008015176
27. Roy, Y., Banville, H., Albuquerque, I., Gramfort, A., Falk, T.H., Faubert, J.: Deep learning-based electroencephalography analysis: a systematic review. J. Neural Eng. **16**(5), 051001 (2019)
28. Schumacher, J., Jeunet, C., Lotte, F.: Towards explanatory feedback for user training in brain-computer interfaces. In: 2015 IEEE International Conference on Systems, Man, and Cybernetics, pp. 3169–3174. IEEE (2015)
29. Vansteensel, M.J., et al.: Fully implanted brain–computer interface in a locked-in patient with ALS. N Engl. J. Med. **375**(21), 2060–2066 (2016). https://doi.org/10.1056/NEJMoa1608085. pMID 27959736

Single-Subject vs. Cross-Subject Motor Imagery Models

Joseph Geraghty$^{(\boxtimes)}$ and George Schoettle

Swarthmore College, Swarthmore, PA 19081, USA
jgeragh1@swarthmore.edu

Abstract. This paper compares the performance of machine learning algorithms trained and tested on single-subject EEG data compared to nine-person cross-subject EEG data from the BCI IV 2a dataset. To compare the performance of single-subject and cross-subject EEG models, we implement eight machine learning algorithms and test them on EEG motor imagery data. Single-subject models had higher average accuracies compared to cross-subject trained models for 7 out of 8 machine learning models.

Keywords: Motor imagery · Single-subject · Cross-subject

1 Introduction

1.1 Problem Statement

A problem in creating accurate EEG motor imagery models is a lack of large datasets [12]. Compared to the computer-vision field, which has many large benchmark datasets like ImageNet [5], the brain-computer interface field does not. Besides a lack of the quantity of EEG data, EEG signals vary significantly from person to person. One study was able to successfully identify individuals based on their EEG signals with 100% accuracy using many machine learning models [11]. Another study used neural networks and EEG signals for system authentication instead of a password, and the researchers achieved 97–98% accuracy [23]. This research proves individual EEG signals are unique, making it challenging to train EEG classification models using EEG data from multiple individuals. These two problems with EEG datasets pose the question should researchers train models on fewer data from just one subject or train models on more data from multiple subjects?

1.2 Research Question

This paper attempts to answer the research question, are single-subject models or nine-person cross-subject models better for classifying motor imagery data from the BCI IV 2a dataset?

© The Author(s), under exclusive license to Springer Nature Switzerland AG 2022
M. Kurosu et al. (Eds.): HCII 2022, LNCS 13519, pp. 442–452, 2022.
https://doi.org/10.1007/978-3-031-17618-0_31

1.3   Literature Review

This paper uses the BCI Competition IV 2a dataset because the dataset is widely used within the brain-computer interface domain [21]. The highest classification accuracy achieved upon the BCI Competition IV 2a dataset is 92.3% using a feature extraction method of LDA-after-PCA with a classification of a voting-based extreme learning machine [6]. Previous research on classification algorithms has shown that there is no single algorithm suitable for all applications and datasets [24]. This research has motivated us to include a variety of classification algorithms in our experiment.

We determined to implement LDA and SVM algorithms because "both LDA and SVM were, and still are, the most popular types of EEG based-BCIs" [16]. Furthermore, SVM often outperformed other algorithms in many studies. We chose to test Random Forest because "shrinkage linear discriminant analysis(LDA with shrinkage) and random forests also appear particularly useful for small training sample settings" [16]. The BCI Competiton IV 2a dataset is relatively small with only nine test subjects, so algorithms that run on small training samples seem beneficial. Furthermore, since the literature recommends LDA generally and with shrinkage for small sample sizes, we implemented three LDA algorithms. We use one LDA algorithm without shrinkage as a baseline and two with different shrinkage methods, Ledoit-Wolf Shrinkage and Oracle Approximating Shrinkage(OAS). Since the random forest is an ensemble learning method and neither LDA nor SVM are, we decided to include an additional ensemble learning algorithm, AdaBoost. AdaBoost has been shown to outperform other classifiers, including SVM, in EEG datasets comprised of driver fatigue data [10]. We included a CNN algorithm because we wanted to include a deep learning algorithm in our experiment. These different algorithms were selected to provide a broad scope to our experiment of subject-specific vs. cross-subject model performance. This will allow further researchers to determine which algorithms may perform well when trained on a subject-specific versus cross-subject basis.The challenge of highly individualized EEG data has been met with research on cross-subject classification architectures. [4] found success with a multi-branch 2d convolutional neural network that achieved a 84.1% accuracy when tested on the eegmmidb dataset (103-subjects). This model was shown to be competitive with three state-of-the-art CNN classifiers: EEGNet, ShallowConvNet, and DeepConvNet. However, the cross-subject model proposed was up to four times more computationally expensive than other state-of-the-art algorithms. A cross-subject workload classifier based on a hierarchical Bayes model was implemented on an 8-subject dataset and was found to have comparable accuracy to benchmark subject-specific classifiers [22]. While our research has yielded many attempts to implement cross-subject architectures, we have not found research that compares a variety of algorithms and compares performance based on cross-subject versus single-subject training.

2   Method

2.1   Data

The BCI IV 2a dataset consists of EEG data collected from 9 subjects [15]. The data consists of cue-based BCI response data, covering four distinct motor imagery tasks. The subjects were asked to imagine the movement of their left hand, right hand, both feet, and tongue. The data was collected for two sessions on differing days for each subject. Each session consisted of 6 runs separated by short breaks, and each run consisted of 48 trials (12 for each specific task). Before each run, researchers recorded subjects for five minutes in order to esti-mate Electrooculography (EOG) influence. EOG signals are electrical signals generated by the eyes. The purpose of estimating EOG signals is to help remove eye movement artifacts from the EEG data. The pre-run five minute record-ing consisted of two minutes with eyes open (looking at a fixation cross on the screen), one minute with eyes closed, and one minute with eye movements (1). The EEG data was collected using twenty-two AG/AgCl Electrodes (2). The EEG signals were sampled 250 Hz and bandpass-filtered between 0.5 Hz and 100 Hz (Figs. 1 and 2).

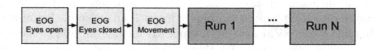

Fig. 1. Per subject timing scheme of each session [15]

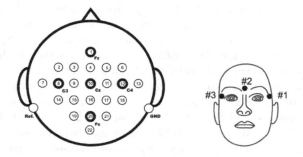

Fig. 2. Left: Electrode montage corresponding to the international 10–20 system. Right: Electrode montage of the three monopolar EOG channels [15].

After data collection, a visual inspection of all data sets was carried out by an EEG expert, and trials containing artifacts were marked accordingly. The BCI IV 2a data set contains GDF files, General Data Format files for biomedical

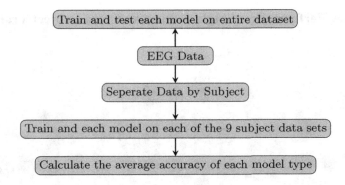

Fig. 3. Experiment flow chart

signals, training and testing file for each of the nine subjects, 18 files total. The files we are using were preprocessed using the open-source BioSig toolbox in MATLAB. Each GDF file was converted to a MAT file, containing binary MATLAB formatted data. The MAT files are then read into our code.

2.2 Experiment

To compare the performance of single-subject and cross-subject EEG models, we implemented eight machine learning algorithms and tested each of them on single-subject subsets of data and all of the cross-subject data (Fig. 3). We defined single-subject models as models trained and tested on data from one subject in the dataset and cross-subject models as trained and tested on data from all nine subjects. The algorithms implemented include LDA without Shrinkage [1], LDA with Ledoit-Wolf Shrinkage [14], LDA with OAS [3], SVM [2], Random Forest with 10 estimators [9], Random Forest with 50 estimators, AdaBoost [7], and CNN [13]. We used the scikit-learn library [20] to implement all of our algorithms except for the CNN. Our CNN model used the Pytorch library [19]. We preprocessed the data using spatial filters [8].

3 Results

Single-subject models achieved higher average accuracies versus cross-subject models for 7 out of 8 machine learning models. The average decrease in accuracy performance amongst the models tested was 11.33% (Table 1, Table 2, Fig. 4). SVM achieved the highest accuracy amongst single-subject models and cross-subject models.

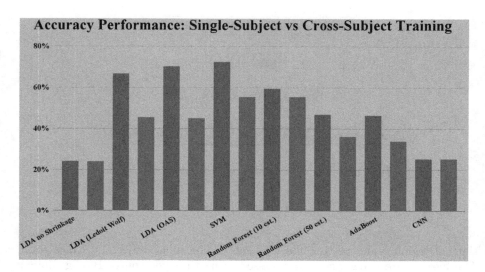

Fig. 4. Comparing single-subject (blue) and cross-subject (red) trained models (Color figure online)

Table 1. Average accuracy single subject models

Algorithm	Accuracy(%)
LDA without shrinkage	24.1
CNN	25.3
AdaBoost	46.4
Random forest 50 estimators	46.9
Random forest 10 estimators	59.5
LDA with ledoit wolf	66.7
LDA with OAS	70.2
SVM	**72.5**

Table 2. Accuracy all subject models

Algorithm	Accuracy(%)
LDA without shrinkage	24.0
CNN	25.3
AdaBoost	33.9
Random forest 50 estimators	36.2
LDA with OAS	45.1
LDA with ledoit wolf	45.5
Random forest 10 estimators	**55.5**
SVM	**55.5**

4   Discussion

4.1   Algorithms

LDA and SVM both employ hyperplanes that separate data points representing different classes. The key distinction between the two algorithms is the means of determining the hyperplane. The LDA models hyperplane is determined by a projection that minimizes the intraclass variance and maximizes the distance between the classes. This method of determining a hyperplane is potentially advantageous for BCI applications as it requires a very low computational requirement [16]. The SVM model's hyperplane is determined by the projection that maximizes the distance from the nearest training points (i.e. margins). In maximizing the margins as opposed to the distance between classes, SVM models tend to be far more generalizable.

Random Forest and AdaBoost are both ensemble learning algorithms that work in slightly different manners. At a high level, Random Forest is implemented by creating many decision trees that take into account features of the data at hand and makes use of a bagging technique. AdaBoost is implemented by creating many decision stumps and making use of boosting techniques. These stumps are decision trees, with only one node and two leaves. Models using these two methods tend to be less prone to overfitting and high variance.

CNN is a deep learning architecture that is modeled after the function of neurons within the human brain. CNN commonly consists of multiple layers including an input, output, multiple convolutional, pooling, fully connected, and normalization layers. CNN is a supervised deep learning algorithm that has been proven to be very successful in several domains including image classification and BCI [16]. We suspect that the relative inaccuracy of the CNN compared to the other algorithms tested is due to the dataset size. Research shows that the accuracy of CNN is positively correlated with the size of the training set [17]. The BCI IV 2a dataset is relatively small and we suspect that the CNN will perform better with the introduction of a larger training set.

One of the main issues within the field of BCI data classification is curse-of-dimensionality. This curse arises in high dimensional data, as the data needed to accurately describe distinct classes grows exponentially. Our SVM model has performed better relative to Adaboost, Random Forest, and the multiple LDA implementations due to the SVM's resilience to the curse-of-dimensionality issue. This resilience allows SVM to achieve greater accuracy with high dimensional feature vectors and a small training set. Moving forward, we plan to implement our algorithms on another dataset to see if our results hold. Furthermore, we plan to test the performance of other algorithms, such as a hybrid SVM-LDA classification algorithm and a kernel-modified SVM on this data set.

4.2   Single Subject versus Cross Subject Models

The substantial accuracy increase from training on a per-subject basis can be attributed to the variability of subjects' EEG data in response to the same stimuli. Signals from the brain are unique in response to the same stimuli, varying from person to person. As a result of this quality of EEG data, the vast majority of EEG classification methods are subject-dependent [18]. The discrepancy of EEG data collected for the same tasks amongst different subjects most likely caused the cross-subject trained models to perform worse. We concluded that single-subject models perform better at classifying motor imagery data from the BCI IV 2a dataset versus nine-person cross-subject models.

4.3 Further Research

We suggest further research comparing single-subject and cross-subject models with larger datasets containing more subjects. Further research could determine how large of a dataset is needed for cross-subject models to outperform single-subject models. We also recommend research into methods to standardize EEG data from different subjects.

5 Conclusion

SVM performed the best for EEG motor imagery classification data out of our subset of selected algorithms. However, almost all cross-subject models exhibited a substantial loss in accuracy relative to the single-subject trained models.

A Appendix

Accuracy for each single-subject model. Bold indicates the highest performing accuracy for a subject. The algorithm order is consistent with previous tables in the paper (Table 3, 4, 5, 6, 7, 8, 9, 10 and 11).

Table 3. Subject 1 model accuracies

Algorithm	Accuracy(%)
LDA without shrinkage	24.9
CNN	25.3
AdaBoost	62.6
Random forest 50 estimators	79.6
Random forest 10 estimators	80.0
LDA with ledoit wolf	83.6
LDA with OAS	83.6
SVM	**85.1**

Table 4. Subject 2 model accuracies

Algorithm	Accuracy(%)
LDA without shrinkage	24.3
CNN	24.4
AdaBoost	44.2
Random forest 50 estimators	10.8
Random forest 10 estimators	5.6
LDA with ledoit wolf	54.8
LDA with OAS	**57.2**
SVM	**57.2**

Table 5. Subject 3 model accuracies

Algorithm	Accuracy(%)
LDA without shrinkage	23.8
CNN	24.9
AdaBoost	53.5
Random forest 50 estimators	73.7
Random forest 10 estimators	76.1
LDA with ledoit wolf	76.2
LDA with OAS	79.9
SVM	**81.0**

Table 6. Subject 4 model accuracies

Algorithm	Accuracy(%)
LDA without shrinkage	20.2
CNN	25.9
AdaBoost	36.7
Random forest 50 estimators	46.3
Random forest 10 estimators	49.5
LDA with ledoit wolf	58.8
LDA with OAS	58.3
SVM	**62.7**

Table 7. Subject 5 model accuracies

Algorithm	Accuracy(%)
LDA without shrinkage	25.4
CNN	23.6
AdaBoost	51.8
Random forest 50 estimators	3.1
Random forest 10 estimators	8.6
LDA with ledoit wolf	43.3
LDA with OAS	60.1
SVM	**64.9**

Table 8. Subject 6 model accuracies

Algorithm	Accuracy(%)
LDA without shrinkage	22.8
CNN	24.7
AdaBoost	28.8
Random forest 50 estimators	27.9
Random forest 10 estimators	30.3
LDA with ledoit wolf	47.4
LDA with OAS	51.1
SVM	**51.2**

Table 9. Subject 7 model accuracies

Algorithm	Accuracy(%)
LDA without shrinkage	26.4
CNN	25.6
AdaBoost	42.2
Random forest 50 estimators	53.6
Random forest 10 estimators	53.3
LDA with ledoit wolf	**92.1**
LDA with OAS	**92.1**
SVM	86.3

Table 10. Subject 8 model accuracies

Algorithm	Accuracy(%)
LDA without shrinkage	21.0
CNN	24.3
AdaBoost	50.1
Random forest 50 estimators	50.5
Random forest 10 estimators	51.4
LDA with ledoit wolf	85.2
LDA with OAS	87.0
SVM	**87.1**

Table 11. Subject 9 model accuracies

Algorithm	Accuracy(%)
LDA without shrinkage	28.0
CNN	24.6
AdaBoost	37.5
Random forest 50 estimators	70.0
Random forest 10 estimators	73.2
LDA with ledoit wolf	68.9
LDA with OAS	0.75
SVM	**85.6**

References

1. Blei, D.M., Ng, A.Y., Jordan, M.I.: Latent Dirichlet allocation. J. Mach. Learn. Res. **3**(Jan), 993–1022 (2003)
2. Boser, B.E., Guyon, I.M., Vapnik, V.N.: A training algorithm for optimal margin classifiers. In: Proceedings of the Fifth Annual Workshop on Computational Learning Theory, pp. 144–152 (1992)
3. Chen, X., Wang, Z.J., McKeown, M.J.: Shrinkage-to-tapering estimation of large covariance matrices. IEEE Trans. Signal Process. **60**(11), 5640–5656 (2012)
4. Cimtay, Y., Ekmekcioglu, E.: Investigating the use of pretrained convolutional neural network on cross-subject and cross-dataset EEG emotion recognition. Sensors **20**(7), 2034 (2020)
5. Deng, J., Dong, W., Socher, R., Li, L.J., Li, K., Fei-Fei, L.: Imagenet: a large-scale hierarchical image database. In: 2009 IEEE Conference on Computer Vision and Pattern Recognition, pp. 248–255. IEEE (2009)
6. Duan, L., Zhong, H., Miao, J., Yang, Z., Ma, W., Zhang, X.: A voting optimized strategy based on elm for improving classification of motor imagery BCI data. Cogn. Comput. **6**(3), 477–483 (2014)
7. Freund, Y., Schapire, R.E.: A decision-theoretic generalization of on-line learning and an application to boosting. J. Comput. Syst. Sci. **55**(1), 119–139 (1997)

8. Hersche, M., Rellstab, T., Schiavone, P., Cavigelli, L., Benini, L., Rahimi, A.: Fast and accurate multiclass inference for mi-bcis using large multiscale temporal and spectral features, pp. 1690–1694 (2018). https://doi.org/10.23919/EUSIPCO.2018.8553378

9. Ho, T.K.: Random decision forests. In: Proceedings of 3rd International Conference on Document Analysis and Recognition, vol. 1, pp. 278–282. IEEE (1995)

10. Hu, J.: Automated detection of driver fatigue based on adaboost classifier with EEG signals. Front. Comput. Neurosci. 11 (2017). https://doi.org/10.3389/fncom.2017.00072,https://www.frontiersin.org/article/10.3389/fncom.2017.00072

11. Jayarathne, I., Cohen, M., Amarakeerthi, S.: Person identification from EEG using various machine learning techniques with inter-hemispheric amplitude ratio. PloS one 15(9), e0238872 (2020)

12. Kastrati, A., et al.: Eegeyenet: a simultaneous electroencephalography and eye-tracking dataset and benchmark for eye movement prediction. arXiv preprint arXiv:2111.05100 (2021)

13. LeCun, Y., Bottou, L., Bengio, Y., Haffner, P.: Gradient-based learning applied to document recognition. Proc. IEEE 86(11), 2278–2324 (1998)

14. Ledoit, O., Wolf, M.: A well-conditioned estimator for large-dimensional covariance matrices. J. Multivariate Anal. 88(2), 365–411 (2004)

15. Leeb, R., Brunner, C., Müller-Putz, G., Schlögl, A., Pfurtscheller, G.: Bci competition 2008-graz data set b. Graz University of Technology, Austria, pp. 1–6 (2008)

16. Lotte, F., et al.: A review of classification algorithms for EEG-based brain-computer interfaces: a 10 year update. J. Neural Eng. 15(3), 031005 (2018)

17. Luo, C., Li, X., Wang, L., He, J., Li, D., Zhou, J.: How does the data set affect CNN-based image classification performance? In: 2018 5th International Conference on Systems and Informatics (ICSAI), pp. 361–366 (2018). https://doi.org/10.1109/ICSAI.2018.8599448

18. Pandey, P., Seeja, K.: Subject independent emotion recognition from EEG using VMD and deep learning. J. King Saud Univ.-Comput. Inf. Sci. (2019)

19. Paszke, A., et al.: Pytorch: an imperative style, high-performance deep learning library. In: Wallach, H., Larochelle, H., Beygelzimer, A., d'Alché-Buc, F., Fox, E., arnett, R. (eds.) Advances in Neural Information Processing Systems, vol. 32, pp. 8024–8035. Curran Associates, Inc. (2019), http://papers.neurips.cc/paper/9015-pytorch-an-imperative-style-high-performance-deep-learning-library.pdf

20. Pedregosa, F., et al.: Scikit-learn: machine learning in python. J. Mach. Learn. Res. 12, 2825–2830 (2011)

21. Roy, Y., Banville, H., Albuquerque, I., Gramfort, A., Falk, T.H., Faubert, J.: Deep learning-based electroencephalography analysis: a systematic review. J. Neural Eng. 16(5), 051001 (2019)

22. Wang, Z., Hope, R.M., Wang, Z., Ji, Q., Gray, W.D.: Cross-subject workload classification with a hierarchical bayes model. NeuroImage 59(1), 64–69 (2012)

23. Zeynali, M., Seyedarabi, H.: Eeg-based single-channel authentication systems with optimum electrode placement for different mental activities. Biomed. J. 42(4), 261–267 (2019)

24. Zhang, C., Liu, C., Zhang, X., Almpanidis, G.: An up-to-date comparison of state-of-the-art classification algorithms. Expert Syst. Appl. 82, 128–150 (2017). https://doi.org/10.1016/j.eswa.2017.04.003,https://www.sciencedirect.com/science/article/pii/S0957417417302397

Hybrid Convolutional, Recurrent and Attention-Based Architectures of Deep Neural Networks for Classification of Human-Computer Interaction by Electroencephalography

Nikita Gordienko$^{(\boxtimes)}$, Oleksandr Rokovyi⬤, Yuri Gordienko⬤, and Sergii Stirenko⬤

National Technical University of Ukraine "Igor Sikorsky Kyiv Polytechnic Institute", Kyiv, Ukraine
nik.gordiienko@gmail.com

Abstract. Nowadays, applications for monitoring physical activity and health are becoming popular, especially for human-computer interaction (HCI) by users with some physical disabilities. Electroencephalography (EEG) data analysis of some HCI-related activities can be useful to support everyday life of such people. Recently several approaches based on artificial intelligence methods, like neural networks (NN), for example, fully connected NN (FCN), convolutional NN (CNN), recurrent NN (RNN), were successfully used for EEG data analysis. Some new attention-based NN (wA) architectures are very promising in various applications. This work is dedicated to the investigation of various hybrid combinations, like FCN-CNN, CNN-RNN, CNN-wA, RNN-wA, CNN-RNN-wA, etc. with regard to EEG data analysis. These hybrid models were trained on the grasp-and-lift (GAL) dataset where users use their arm to manipulate a smartphone.

Keywords: Hybrid deep neural network · Convolutional neural network · Recurrent neural network · Long short-term memory · Grasp-and-lift · Brain-computer interface

1 Introduction

Different approaches of artificial intelligence, for example deep learning (DL) methods based on deep neural networks (DNN), have been used successfully to process different data starting from the very first attempts [9,14–16,24,36] to the recent advances [21,29–31]. Especially, these activities have become very intensive for the processing of data in medical applications, for example, in healthcare and elderly care [6,8]. For example, they have been studied and used for the analysis of temporal sequences such as electroencephalography (EEG) signals obtained from the brain-computer interface (BCI) for various purposes [18,20,28]. This work is devoted to examining EEG data collected by the BCI in order to classify certain bodily actions (here hand movements) using different DNNs.

The structure of this article is as follows: Sect. 2 *Background and Related Work* gives a brief overview of some similar attempts to study the EEG of DNN, Sect. 3 *Methodology* presents the dataset, hand actions with EEG recorded, DNN types and metrics used, the Sect. 4 *Experiment* describes the results on different DNNs, the Sect. 5 *Discussion* contains a summary of all results with the comparative analysis of the applied hybrid DNNs, and the Sect. 6 *Conclusions* gives an overview of the potential directions for further studies.

2   Background and Related Work

The different types of DNNs have been used in EEG-research in medical, educational, operational, and other applications. For example, EEGNet DNN, a compact convolutional neural network (CNN), has been developed for EEG-based BCIs [20]. This EEG-related model uses EEG feature selection concepts by deep and separable convolutions and gives relatively high performance compared to other similar approaches. 3D-CNN has been proposed for the classification of EEG signals by mixture of multidimensional features that improves the accuracy of the classification of tasks activated by the sensorimotor area in the brain [35]. Some combinations of CNNs and recurrent neural networks (RNNs) have been proposed also [23]. Other CNN-linked studies focus on sleep stage classification, stress detection, driver fatigue detection, motor image classification, and emotion detection and classification [13]. Prediction of single-trial EEG hand movement force and velocity from CNN models has also been demonstrated [33].

Recently, some hybridization approaches combining CNNs with various recurrent neural networks (RNNs), including long-term memory (LSTM) blocks, have been proposed for a similar classification problem: identify hand gestures from EEG data using RNN has recently been proposed. Different RNN architectures were compared for performance, where some measures like dropout improved RNN performance [4]. In another work, electrocorticography (EcoG) was used for the detection and prediction of hand movement [34]. The multimodal model with CNN and with short-term memory (LSTM) elements was applied. To estimate hand kinematic parameters from non-invasive EEG time series DL models were used [26]. In particular, several DNNs including components from CNN and LSTM models have been proposed to obtain information about the expected movement of the hand from EEG signals.

In relation to these results, the aim of this work is to analyze the perspectives of combining the components of various NNs, for example, fully connected NN (FCN), CNNs, RNNs, with hidden states (HSs), and with attention (wA) NN architectures that proved to be efficient in various applications.

3   Methodology

In this section some experimental aspects are described, namely: the dataset with recorded brain activities corresponding to 6 basic types of physical action, some types of hybridized FCN, CNN, RNN, HS, and wA models, metrics. They are used to investigate the different types of DNNs applied to time sequences of EEG signals measured with the BCI setup. The main objective was to solve the classification problem: to determine the physical actions (here, the movements of the hand) by analyzing the related brain activity, measured by the corresponding EEG time sequences.

3.1   Dataset

The widely used "grasp-and-lift" (GAL) dataset contains information about brain activity of 12 persons [2,25]: more than 3900 trials (monitored and measured by the sampling rate 500 Hz) in 32 channels of the recorded EEG signals. The persons tried to perform 6 types physical activities, namely: *HandStart* - the person moves a hand to an object (for example, some small size gadget like a smartphone), *FirstDigitTouch* - the person touches the object by a finger (for example, press a button), *BothStartLoadPhase* - the person takes ("grasps") the object by fingers, *LiftOff* - the person raises ("lifts") the object by fingers, *Replace* - the person returns the object by fingers back, *BothReleased* - the person releases fingers. The data pre-processing was used to cut regions of interests (ROIs) that correspond to the actual HCI physical actions of users.The current problem is that some signals overlap and their classification become more complex because they were not presented separately (Fig. 1).

The classes which intersect with other classes were not included in the research. It is another complex task how to correctly classify such overlapping classes. That is why the following 4 classes were selected for the further investigations: *HandStart* (Class 0), *BothStartLoadPhase* (Class 3), *LiftOff* (Class 4), *BothReleased* (Class 5) (Fig. 1).

3.2   Models

Several neural networks (NN) were used as elementary blocks of the proposed hybrid combinations, for example, fully connected NN (FCN), convolutional NN (CNN), recurrent NN (RNN), with hidden states (HSs), and with attention (wA) NN architectures. Various hybrid combinations, like FCN-CNN, CNN-RNN, CNN-wA, RNN-wA, CNN-RNN-wA, etc. were considered:

- the baseline models like: AlexNet, LeNet, VGG16, custom simple CNN, simple RNN (Fig. 2a), GRU, LSTM,
- their convolutional and recurrent (CR-NN) hybrids like: CNN-RNN (Fig. 3a), CNN-GRU, CNN-LSTM, and their more complicated hybrids like: CNN-RNN-CNN (Fig. 3d), CNN-GRU-CNN, CNN-LSTM-CNN,

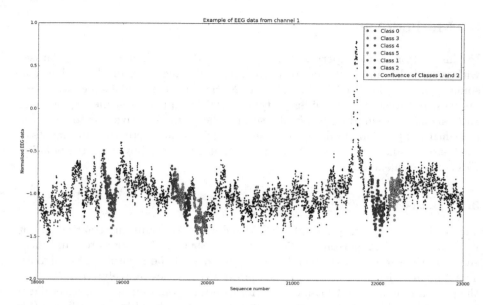

Fig. 1. Example of overlapping EEG data for some hand movement classes (*FirstDigitTouch* and *BothStartLoadPhase*). Class 0 - *HandStart*, Class 1 - *FirstDigitTouch*, Class 2 - *BothStartLoadPhase*, Class 3 - *LiftOff*, Class 4 - *Replace*, Class 5 - *BothReleased*.

– their combinations with attention (wA) and hidden state (HS) hybrids like: RNN-wA (Fig. 2c), GRU-wA, LSTM-HS, RNN-HS (Fig. 2b), GRU-HS, LSTM-HS, and their more complicated hybrids like: CNN-RNN-wA (Fig. 3c), CNN-GRU-wA, CNN-LSTM-wA, CNN-RNN-HS (Fig. 3b), CNN-GRU-HS, CNN-LSTM-HS.

The models with the hidden states (HS) were used where RNN returns the full sequence of hidden states for each input instead of the last state. It gives additional information to the next states. In the next modification additional weights are applied on the hidden states in order to implement the attention mechanism [5]. Recently the dependence between various DNN architectures and their performance in the classification problem for 6 GAL-types of movements was studied for the following types of CNNs described in our previous work [12] for: FCN [27], Lenet-like CNN [22], Alexnet-like CNN [19], VGG-13 CNN [32], "vanilla" DNN [12]. Also some combinations of the following RNNs were researched: "vanilla" LSTM (from Tensorflow-Keras framework [7]) as representation of the classic LSTM architecture [14], and hybrid CNN-LSTM network with 2D convolution operations across all 32 EEG channels for sample of EEG

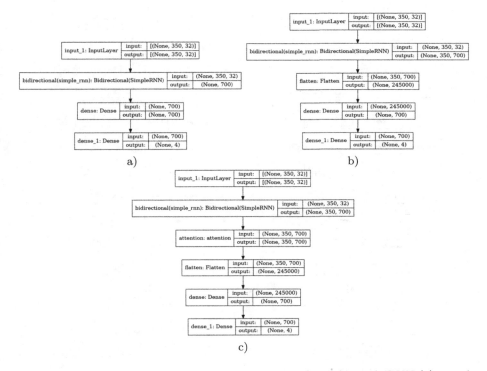

Fig. 2. Some examples of the simple RNN-based models used: simple RNN (a), simple RNN with the hidden states and the flatten layer (b), simple RNN with the hidden states, the attention layer, and the flatten layer (c).

time sequence with LSTM block added [17]. In our previous works, the main idea was to perform convolution operations on an EEG temporal sequence of each EEG channel, assuming that 32 EEG channels are independent. Later, the 32-lead EEG workflows were merged into FCN layers before the classification layer. The other idea was to use 1D convolution operations on the 32 EEG channels for each time step and 2D convolution operations on the 32 EEG channels for an example EEG time sequence in CNN and hybrid CNNs [12,17]. As far as some new attention-based NN (wA) architectures are very promising in various applications, this work is dedicated to the investigation of additional hybrid combinations, like FCN-CNN, CNN-RNN, CNN-wA, RNN-wA, CNN-RNN-wA, etc. with regard to EEG data analysis of 4 classes.

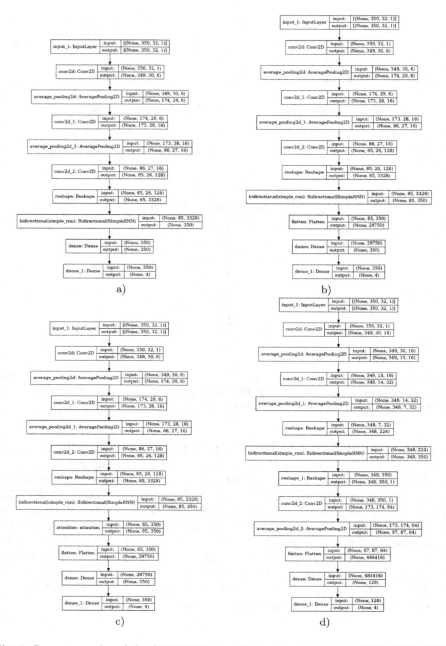

Fig. 3. Some examples of the CNN-RNN-based hybrid models used: CNN-RNN (GRU, LSTM) (a), CNN-RNN hybrid with the hidden states and the flatten layer (b), CNN-RNN hybrid with the hidden states, the attention layer, and the flatten layer (c), CNN-RNN-CNN hybrid with the hidden states, the attention layer, and the flatten layer (d).

3.3 Metrics

Several standard metrics were used like accuracy and loss that were calculated during each run as the minimal value and maximal value of loss and accuracy, respectively. The area under curve (AUC) was measured for receiver operating characteristic (ROC) with their micro and macro versions, and their mean and standard deviation values. In fact, for a given threshold, accuracy measures the percentage of correctly classified objects, regardless of the class they belong to. AUC is threshold-invariant and can measure the quality of the models used here independently of the chosen classification threshold. As far as accuracy depends on the threshold chosen, AUC accounts for all possible thresholds. Because of this, it can sometimes provide a broader view of classifier performance. To determine the basic statistical properties of the metrics obtained (accuracy, loss, AUC) stratified k-fold cross-validation was applied (k = 5) where the folds were created by preserving the percentage of samples for each class.

3.4 Workflow

The before mentioned types of DNNs (Figs. 2 and 3) were used for analysis of time sequences of EEG signals (measured by BCI setup) at training, validation and testing stages. The best trained models were saved after each training iteration as checkpoints for the testing stage. Finally, the models with the maximal validation accuracy were used here for demonstration of the results obtained. The number of signal samples (N) in the input EEG time sequence (TS) was equal to 350 (in contrast to our previous attempts [12,17] where TSs of different sizes in the range from 100 up to 2000 were used). Since the average duration of each stage is 0.3 s, it was decided to use as input data a series of 350 consecutive measurements. 150 measurements before the first label, 150 measurements with labels and 50 measurements after the labeled data. At each epoch, the generators take data from each category from a randomly generated sequence. To diversify the data, it was decided to choose a starting point for the sequence to be used for training, validation and testing in a certain range randomly in the range of 10 measurements. The only present label was set as a ground truth (GT). The training, validation, and testing stages were performed for the GAL-dataset that was divided in proportion of 82.4% (3244 examples)/8.8% (346 examples)/8.8% (346 examples) for training/validation/testing sets, respectively. Finally, it allowed us to obtain trained models, calculate metrics (including AUC, and its micro and macro versions), and plot metrics versus the model types (see below).

4   Experiment

4.1   Exploratory Data Analysis (EDA)

The GAL-dataset [2,25] was used and pre-processed in a standard way (see details in our previous works [12,17]) with taking into account the correspondent time position of physical actions (actually hand movements here) and their duration [3]. In Fig. 1 one example of the time sequences is shown that was obtained after EDA and such pre-processing was performed for all 32 EEG channels. Here the most characteristic parts of EEG signals are shown for the better understanding the details of EEG brain activity. Various combinations of EEG data channels can be used for their processing on the basis of DNNs like simple RNN, GRU, LSTM, and their combinations.

4.2   DNN Training/Validation/Testing Stages

For all settings, the AUC values were measured for each of the hand movements and then their average micro and macro values were also calculated. A macro-average AUC calculates the AUC metric for each class independently and then the average (all classes are treated equally) is computed. A micro-average AUC collects all classes to obtain the average metric. These metrics are very important for multi-class classification problems like here, since the micro-average AUC "takes imbalance into account", i.e. the resulting value is based on the proportion of each class, i.e. the performance of the large class has more influence on the result than the performance of the small class. But the macro-average CSA "does not take into account the imbalance", that is the obtained performance is a simple average across classes, and each class is given equal weight regardless of class proportions.

Baseline Simple RNN, GRU, LSTM. Then 5-fold cross-validation was performed for the simplest ("baseline") RNN, GRU, LSTM (in Tensorflow Keras implementation) models during the single epoch [1]. Then, the mean AUC values were calculated for the different validation subsets and some results for simple RNNs are reported here in Fig. 4.

Table 1. AUC-values, parameters, and training time for the baseline models (RNN, GRU, LSTM) used.

Model	AUC_{macro}	Parameters	Training time, s
SimpleRNN_Dense	0.758	761,604	3,284
GRU_Dense	0.796	1,299,904	1,175
LSTM_Dense	0.793	1,565,904	1,275

CNN-Based hybrids of RNN, GRU, LSTM. The CNN-based hybridization gives the statistically significant impact on increase of the AUC-macro metric Fig. 5.

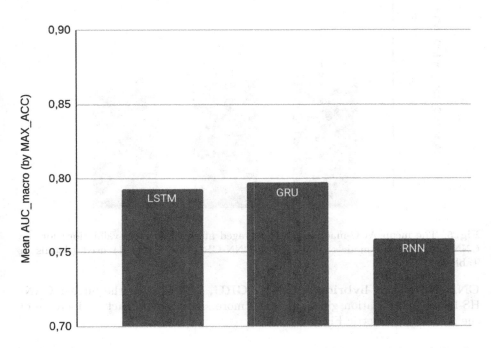

Fig. 4. The mean AUC-macro values (averaged after 5-fold cross-validation) for the baseline models (RNN, GRU, LSTM) used (details in Table 1).

Table 2. AUC-values, parameters, and training time for the CNN-based hybrid models (CNN-RNN, CNN-GRU, CNN-LSTM) used.

Model	AUC_{macro}	Parameters	Training time, s
CNN_SimpleRNN_Dense	0.794	1,359,416	1,666
CNN_GRU_Dense	0.799	3,823,226	899
CNN_LSTM_Dense	0.807	5,038,616	906

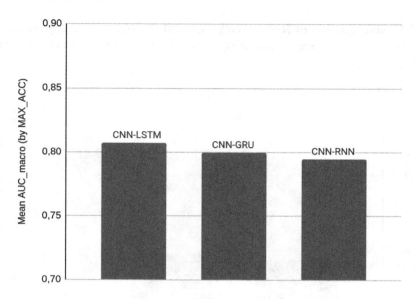

Fig. 5. The mean AUC-macro values (averaged after 5-fold cross-validation) for the CNN-based hybrid models (CNN-RNN, CNN-GRU, CNN-LSTM) used (details in Table 2).

CNN-HS-Based hybrids of RNN, GRU, LSTM. But the further CNN-HS-based hybridization gives the much more significant impact on increase of the AUC-macro metric Fig. 6.

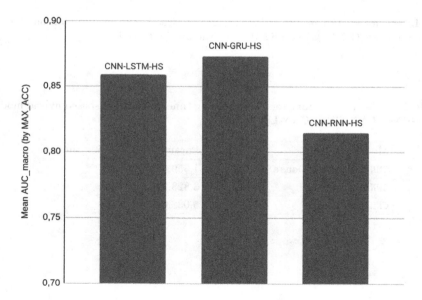

Fig. 6. The mean AUC-macro values (averaged after 5-fold cross-validation) for the CNN-HS-wA-based hybrid models (CNN-RNN-HS, CNN-GRU-HS, CNN-LSTM-HS) used (details in Table 3).

Table 3. AUC-values, parameters, and training time for the CNN-HS-based hybrid models (CNN-RNN-HS, CNN-GRU-HS, CNN-LSTM-HS) used.

Model	AUC_{macro}	Parameters	Training time, s
CNN_SimpleRNN_Hidden_Dense	0.814	11,649,416	1,803
CNN_GRU_Hidden_Dense	0.873	14,103,266	922
CNN_LSTM_Hidden_Dense	0.859	15,328,616	955

The similar tendency was observed for other combinations of CNN, RNN, HS, wA components. The best hybrid models with the highest values of AUCmacro are shown in Fig. 7.

5   Discussion

The results obtained demonstrate the various levels of performance for the different considered DNN architectures, where GRU-wA, CNN-GRU-HS, CNN-GRU-wA, CNN-RNN-wA give the highest AUCs (Fig. 7 and Table 4). The considered attention-based DNNs give the highest AUCs > 0.85, and, actually, they are very close to the values published by others and mentioned above. The higher values of attention-based (wA) models can be explained by the better account of the complex relationships in EEG brain activity which is correlated in time and have causal relationship.

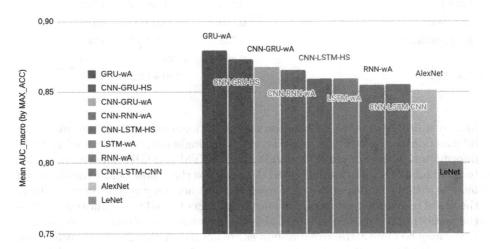

Fig. 7. The hybridized models with the best metrics observed (details in Table 4).

Use of hidden states gives more parameters for analysis and more information about the EEG data than a single output state. Additional attention on the

Table 4. AUC-values (Fig. 6), parameters (Fig. 7), and training time for the models considered (Fig. 2 and 3).

Model	AUC_{macro}	Parameters	Training time, s
CNN_LSTM_CNN_Dense	0.854	62,568,724	1,885
CNN_GRU_CNN_Dense	0.846	62,429,774	1,783
CNN_RNN_CNN_Dense	0.768	62,148,724	4,835
CNN_LSTM_Hidden_Attention_Dense	0.845	15,329,051	946
CNN_GRU_Hidden_Attention_Dense	0.867	15,329,051	985
CNN_SimpleRNN_Hidden_Attention_Dense	0.865	11,649,851	1,766
CNN_LSTM_Hidden_Dense	0.859	15,328,616	955
CNN_GRU_Hidden_Dense	0.873	14,103,266	922
CNN_SimpleRNN_Hidden_Dense	0.814	11,649,416	1,803
CNN_LSTM_Dense	0.807	5,038,616	906
CNN_GRU_Dense	0.799	3,823,226	899
CNN_SimpleRNN_Dense	0.794	1,359,416	1,666
LSTM_Hidden_Attention_Dense	0.859	172,576,954	2,914
GRU_Hidden_Attention_Dense	0.879	172,310,954	4,073
SimpleRNN_Hidden_Attention_Dense	0.854	171,772,654	4,594
LSTM_Hidden_Dense	0.792	172,575,904	3,999
GRU_Hidden_Dense	0.772	172,309,904	3,650
SimpleRNN_Hidden_Dense	0.728	171,772,654	4,907
LSTM_Dense	0.793	1,565,904	1,275
GRU_Dense	0.796	1,299,904	1,175
SimpleRNN_Dense	0.758	761,604	3,284
LeNet	0.800	25,815,476	895
AlexNet	0.851	320,446,212	4,496

hidden states gives more information from additional weights. As a result, more information is given to the dense layers. The single output state may lost the information in the Simple RNN architecture. LSTM and GRU have more ability to accumulate the information in the last state, so they show better results in the models without hidden states. Although the best accuracy was achieved without the use of convolutional layers, convolutional layers helped to significantly reduce the number of parameters (Fig. 8, Table 4). Therefore, models with convolutional layers may be more attractive if resources are limited. Although the convolutional layers helped to significantly reduce the number of parameters in the models, the learning time changed in a similar way, but to a lesser extent. This is because it takes a lot of time to run generators that use a less optimized and slower CPU for this. GPUs are used differently on different models depending on the number of calculations and the ability to use optimized operations. So the GPU is more

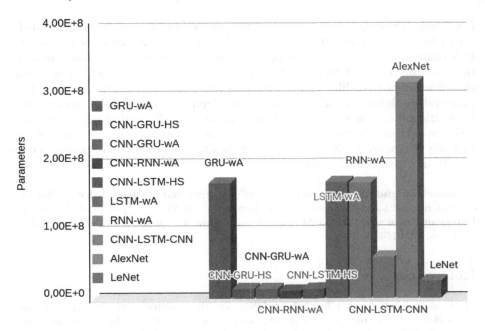

Fig. 8. The number of parameters in the models used (details in Table 4).

efficient on convolutional layers and can take full advantage of the amount of resources on the GPU only when the GPU is loaded more. It is assumed that the lower level of convergence and performance of other DNNs can be interpreted by the worse susceptibility to the distinctive patterns in EEG sequences (that are characteristic for specific physical actions) in comparison to other networks (even after one epoch). This is particularly important considering other work where other combinations of CNN and LSTM blocks were highly effective in detecting and predicting hand movements by analyzing EEG brain activity [26, 34]. Therefore, a more detailed investigation of the specific contributions of FCN, CNN, RNN, HS, wA and other blocks should be investigated.

6   Conclusions

The experimental results suggest that hybrid DNNs based on FCN, CNN, RNN, wA, HS components can be used to classify reliably some hand movements (where AUCs > 0.87 after an epoch) through small and simple combinations of the FCN, CNN, RNN, wA, HS. These results demonstrate the possibility to classify HCI physical actions like GAL hand movements reliably by various combinations of NN components (with AUCs > 0.87 after an epochs). The reliable small-scale models are crucial for porting these hybrid models to Edge Computing devices with low computing resources [10,11]. These results should be verified for larger datasets and with more attention to the contribution of FCN, CNN,

RNN, wA, HS components. Therefore, the next step of this work should be dedicated to the real-time acquisition of the EEG activity measured by the mobile BCI configuration in order to obtain more data and increase the robustness of the measures obtained. In general, such studies can potentially hold promise for classification of GAL-like hand movements and other physical movements. The proposed methods can be used in the development of new EEG devices and applications for various purposes. For example, in health and elderly care apps, assistive devices (like exoskeletons) can provide instant feedback, e.g. supporting that physical actions initiated only by the brain, which cannot be continued due to certain physical disabilities.

Acknowledgements. This work was partially supported by "Knowledge At the Tip of Your fingers: Clinical Knowledge for Humanity" (KATY) project funded from the European Union's Horizon 2020 research and innovation program under grant agreement No. 101017453.

References

1. Cross-validation runs for hybrid DNNs on the preprocessed version of grasp-and-lift EEG detection dataset. https://www.kaggle.com/code/pepsissalom/crossvalidationeegdnncomparison. Accessed on 24 May 2022
2. Grasp-and-lift EEG detection dataset. https://www.kaggle.com/c/grasp-and-lift-eeg-detection/data. Accessed 24 May 2022
3. Preprocessed version of grasp-and-lift EEG detection dataset. https://www.kaggle.com/datasets/pepsissalom/eeg-by-categories. Accessed 24 May 2022
4. An, J., Cho, S.: Hand motion identification of grasp-and-lift task from electroencephalography recordings using recurrent neural networks. In: 2016 International Conference on Big Data and Smart Computing (BigComp), pp. 427–429. IEEE (2016)
5. Bahdanau, D., Cho, K., Bengio, Y.: Neural machine translation by jointly learning to align and translate. arXiv preprint arXiv:1409.0473 (2014)
6. Chen, Y.W., Jain, L.C.: Deep Learning in Healthcare. Springer, Cham (2020). https://doi.org/10.1007/978-3-030-32606-7
7. Chollet, F., et al.: Keras: the Python deep learning library. Astrophysics Source Code Library pp. ascl-1806 (2018)
8. Esteva, A., et al.: A guide to deep learning in healthcare. Nat. Med. **25**(1), 24–29 (2019)
9. Fukushima, K.: Neural network model for a mechanism of pattern recognition unaffected by shift in position-neocognitron. IEICE Tech. Rep. A **62**(10), 658–665 (1979)
10. Gordienko, Y., et al.: Scaling analysis of specialized tensor processing architectures for deep learning models. In: Pedrycz, W., Chen, S.-M. (eds.) Deep Learning: Concepts and Architectures. SCI, vol. 866, pp. 65–99. Springer, Cham (2020). https://doi.org/10.1007/978-3-030-31756-0_3
11. Gordienko, Y., et al.: "Last mile" optimization of edge computing ecosystem with deep learning models and specialized tensor processing architectures. In: Advances in Computers, vol. 122, pp. 303–341. Elsevier (2021). https://doi.org/10.1016/bs.adcom.2020.10.003

12. Gordienko, Y., Kostiukevych, K., Gordienko, N., Rokovyi, O., Alienin, O., Stirenko, S.: Deep learning for grasp-and-lift movement forecasting based on electroencephalography by brain-computer interface. In: Hu, Z., Zhang, Q., Petoukhov, S., He, M. (eds.) ICAILE 2021. LNDECT, vol. 82, pp. 3–12. Springer, Cham (2021). https://doi.org/10.1007/978-3-030-80475-6_1

13. Gu, X., et al.: EEG-based brain-computer interfaces (BCIS): a survey of recent studies on signal sensing technologies and computational intelligence approaches and their applications. IEEE/ACM Trans. Comput. Biol. Bioinf. (2021). https://doi.org/10.1109/TCBB.2021.3052811

14. Hochreiter, S., Schmidhuber, J.: Long short-term memory. Neural Comput. 9(8), 1735–1780 (1997)

15. Ivakhnenko, A.G., Lapa, V.G.: Cybernetic predicting devices. Purdue Univ Lafayette IND School Of Electrical Engineering (1966). https://apps.dtic.mil/sti/citations/AD0654237

16. Kelley, H.J.: Gradient theory of optimal flight paths. ARS J. 30(10), 947–954 (1960)

17. Kostiukevych, K., Stirenko, S., Gordienko, N., Rokovyi, O., Alienin, O., Gordienko, Y.: Convolutional and recurrent neural networks for physical action forecasting by brain-computer interface. In: 2021 11th IEEE International Conference on Intelligent Data Acquisition and Advanced Computing Systems: Technology and Applications (IDAACS), vol. 2, pp. 973–978. IEEE (2021)

18. Kotowski, K., Stapor, K., Ochab, J.: Deep learning methods in electroencephalography. In: Tsihrintzis, G.A., Jain, L.C. (eds.) Machine Learning Paradigms. LAIS, vol. 18, pp. 191–212. Springer, Cham (2020). https://doi.org/10.1007/978-3-030-49724-8_8

19. Krizhevsky, A., Sutskever, I., Hinton, G.E.: Imagenet classification with deep convolutional neural networks. Adv. Neural. Inf. Process. Syst. 25, 1097–1105 (2012)

20. Lawhern, V.J., Solon, A.J., Waytowich, N.R., Gordon, S.M., Hung, C.P., Lance, B.J.: EEGNet: a compact convolutional neural network for EEG-based brain-computer interfaces. J. Neural Eng. 15(5), 056013 (2018)

21. LeCun, Y., Bengio, Y., Hinton, G.: Deep learning. Nature 521(7553), 436–444 (2015)

22. LeCun, Y., et al.: LeNet-5, convolutional neural networks 20(5), 14 (2015). http://yann.lecun.com/exdb/lenet

23. Lin, B., Deng, S., Gao, H., Yin, J.: A multi-scale activity transition network for data translation in EEG signals decoding. IEEE/ACM Trans. Comput. Biol. Bioinf. (2020). https://doi.org/10.1109/TCBB.2020.3024228

24. Linnainmaa, S.: Taylor expansion of the accumulated rounding error. BIT Numer. Math. 16(2), 146–160 (1976)

25. Luciw, M.D., Jarocka, E., Edin, B.B.: Multi-channel EEG recordings during 3,936 grasp and lift trials with varying weight and friction. Sci. Data 1(1), 1–11 (2014)

26. Pancholi, S., Giri, A., Jain, A., Kumar, L., Roy, S.: Source aware deep learning framework for hand kinematic reconstruction using EEG signal. arXiv preprint arXiv:2103.13862 (2021)

27. Rosenblatt, F.: The perceptron: a probabilistic model for information storage and organization in the brain. Psychol. Rev. 65(6), 386 (1958)

28. Roy, Y., Banville, H., Albuquerque, I., Gramfort, A., Falk, T.H., Faubert, J.: Deep learning-based electroencephalography analysis: a systematic review. J. Neural Eng. 16(5), 051001 (2019)

29. Schmidhuber, J.: Deep learning: our miraculous year 1990–1991. arXiv preprint arXiv:2005.05744 (2020)

30. Schmidhuber, J.: Deep learning in neural networks: an overview. Neural Netw. **61**, 85–117 (2015)

31. Schmidhuber, J., Blog, A.: The 2010s: our decade of deep learning/outlook on the 2020s. The recent decade's most important developments and industrial applications based on our AI, with an outlook on the 2020s, also addressing privacy and data markets (2020)

32. Simonyan, K., Zisserman, A.: Very deep convolutional networks for large-scale image recognition. arXiv preprint arXiv:1409.1556 (2014)

33. Vahid, A., Mückschel, M., Stober, S., Stock, A.K., Beste, C.: Applying deep learning to single-trial EEG data provides evidence for complementary theories on action control. Commun. Biol. **3**(1), 1–11 (2020)

34. Wang, N., Farhadi, A., Rao, R., Brunton, B.: AJILE movement prediction: Multimodal deep learning for natural human neural recordings and video. In: Proceedings of the AAAI Conference on Artificial Intelligence, vol. 32 (2018)

35. Wei, M., Lin, F.: A novel multi-dimensional features fusion algorithm for the EEG signal recognition of brain's sensorimotor region activated tasks. Int. J. Intell. Comput. Cybern. **13**(2), 239–260 (2020)

36. Williams, R.: Complexity of exact gradient computation algorithms for recurrent neural networks (technical report nu-ccs-89-27). Northeastern University, College of Computer Science, Boston (1989)

Predicting the Future: A ML MI Replication Study

Marshall McArthur[✉], Xavier Serrano, and Viktoriia Zakharova

Swarthmore College, Swarthmore, PA 19081, USA
{mmcarth1,xserran1,vzakhar1}@swarthmore.edu

Abstract. The study of electroencephalography (EEG) signals is an important stepping stone to providing neuroscience explanations for various phenomena. In this paper we focus on the interpretation of EEG signals in regards to motor imagery. Specifically, we want to analyze the differences between typical machine algorithms and deep learning algorithms in performing EEG interpretations. Additionally, there have been no unique studies comparing the performance of convolutional neural networks and deep belief networks directly when used on motor imagery data. Therefore, attempting to replicate results in deep learning experiments between the two might give insight into why this research inquiry has been left unanswered.

Keywords: Convolutional neural network · Deep belief network · Support vector machine · Linear discriminant analysis · Machine learning · Motor imagery · Electroencephalography (EEG) · EEG signal classification

1 Introduction

1.1 Literature Review

In the context of feature extraction and classification of EEG signals, deep learning has proven to be an effective tool. Convolutional neural networks (CNNs) provide some of the best classification times and accuracy [6]. CNNs theoretically work so well with EEG signals due to the fact that convolution layers are able to extract EEG effective features quickly across multiple scales [14]. The EEG signals in Tang et al. provided a useful real world application, that being a brain-to-wheelchair online BCI system. It was found that the classification success of EEG signals within such BCI systems highly depends on the experimental setup and to where the CNN is getting its data from. Offline systems like the one we propose may fare better than the online systems like Tang et al. because our data is not subject to noise within the experiment and can be preprocessed. The conditional empirical mode decomposition algorithm presented in Tang et al. is not necessary for our study. However, it is mentioned that the effectiveness of intrinsic modal component (IMF) selection for classification is highly dependent on researcher experience with

EEG classification algorithms. Another study, Abbas et al. used Common Spatial Pattern (CSP) and Fast Fourier Transform Energy Maps (FFTEM) for feature computation and selection whereas a Convolutional Neural Network (CNN) is proposed as a classifier with the novel features. The proposed model has yielded mean kappa value of 0.61 and achieved the best-reported results with lower computational complexity when compared with state-of-the-art methods. As a result, choosing an effective algorithm that correctly selects IMFs is imperative to our study's success.

Deep belief networks have gained large popularity in classifying EEG signals due to their training procedure, which yields great success in deep neural network optimization. [10] describes this optimization as a combination of feature extraction and classification into one pipeline, and explains that it is more computationally efficient than other existing classification methods. They note that using frequency domain input for the DBN algorithm improves performance specifically with motor imagery classification, and that their results were in fact statistically significant. Additionally, it is stated that fine tuning the parameters of the DBN structure is imperative for robust results. It is explained that the best way to proceed with tuning is by conducting experiments and proper pretraining techniques prior to the benchmark tasks. The use of DBNs in BCI research is still relatively new, and the application of deep learning in classification with motor imagery EEG data can be a pivotal stepping stone for better BCI developments. Application of DBN in EEG-based BCI is still not common. The main difficulty is the enormously high feature dimensionality spanning EEG channel, frequency, and time. An et al. study used a deep belief network model for two-class motor imagery classification, and DBN was found to be more successful than conventional SVM [4].

1.2   Background

Motor imagery tasks, a subsection of tasks related to brain-computer interfaces, are those in which a subject imagines doing physical movements without actually performing them [6]. These thoughts can then be measured and classified using EEG data, coupled with neural network classification, with the eventual goal of successfully classifying such thoughts in the use of brain-computer interfaces (see Fig. 1). In other words, the eventual goal of such brain-computer interfaces is to provide control over a computer to a person without the requirement of physical movement [11]. This can provide ease and convenience to the user, using all kinds of software, and can be especially beneficial to those for whom physical movement can be a challenge. As an important and emerging field, it is necessary to investigate and compare algorithms that can serve as useful or useless for future research. Many algorithms that focus on EEG classification for motor imagery tasks involve the use of neural networks [6]. The effectiveness of many such algorithms has been compared and studied in literature reviews [6,9]. **Problem Statement:** However, as recently as 2019, no comparisons have been made between DBNs (Deep Belief Networks) and CNNs (Convolutional Neural Networks) in their application to motor imagery tasks [6]. In order to form a

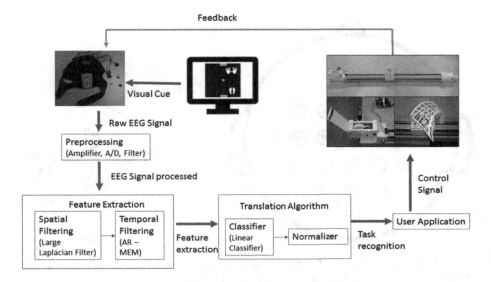

Fig. 1. Process of motor imagery classification [13]

more complete view of the performance of various algorithms in motor imagery classification tasks, in order to provide recommendations for algorithm selection for future work in the field, and in order to offer replication recommendations for newer researchers, further research must be done in order to compare relevant algorithms to one another, which will aid in providing a baseline comparison of the algorithms. **Purpose of Study:** As such, the purpose of this experiment was to focus on the interpretation of EEG signals related to motor imagery. Specifically, we offer a replication of motor imagery studies mentioned in [6,7,9]. We analyze the differences between typical machine algorithms and deep learning algorithms performing EEG interpretations, including the feasibility of doing so given the published studies. Specifically, result replication under the same conditions were attempted in order to form a proper comparison. **Research Question:** Thus, this paper answers the question posed by previous researchers on which type of machine learning algorithm is most feasible for accurate, and/or efficient classification of motor imagery data.

2 Dataset

We have chosen a dataset that was presented in the 2008 article "BCI Competition 2008 - Graz data set A". We specifically chose the dataset based on the credibility of the BCI competition in their respective research practices, and the number of cited references the dataset has had [6,7,9]. This data collection contains EEG data from nine people. The cue-based BCI paradigm included four separate motor imagining tasks: imagination of left hand (class 1), right hand (class 2), both feet (class 3), and tongue movement (class 4). Each subject had

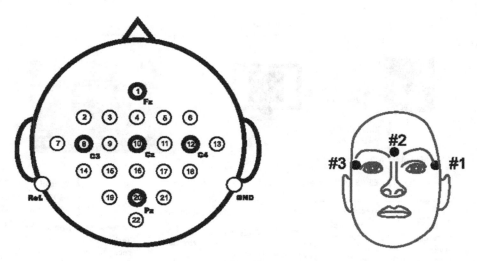

Fig. 2. Left: The worldwide 10–20 system is shown via an electrode montage. Right: The three monopolar EOG channels' electrode montage. [5]

two sessions filmed on different days. Six runs are separated by short rests in each session. A single run has 48 trials (12 for each of the four classes), for a total of 288 trials each session. A recording of around 5 min was made at the start of each session to assess EOG effect. The recording was split into three sections: two minutes with eyes open (looking at a fixation cross on the screen), one minute with eyes closed, and one minute with eye movements. The participants were seated in a plush recliner in front of a computer screen. A fixation cross displayed on the dark screen at the start of each trial (t = 0 s). A brief auditory warning tone was also delivered. A signal in the shape of an arrow pointing left, right, down, or up (corresponding to one of the four classes: left hand, right hand, foot, or tongue) emerged after two seconds (t = 2 s) and lasted on the screen for 1.25 s. The individuals were then encouraged to complete the necessary motor imagery task. There were no responses provided. At t = 6 s, the individuals were instructed to complete the motor imagery task until the fixation cross vanished from the screen. The screen went black for a little moment after that. The EEG was recorded using twenty-two Ag/AgCl electrodes with 3.5 cm inter-electrode intervals (see monatage in Fig. 2). All signals were monopolarly recorded, with the left mastoid acting as the reference and the right mastoid serving as the ground. The data was captured 250 Hz and bandpass filtered between 0.5 100 Hz. The amplifier's sensitivity was set at 100 V. To reduce line noise, an 50 Hz notch filter was activated.

3   Experiment Design

Depending on the outcomes of the algorithm, the machine learning algorithms are classified into various categories i.e. supervised learning, unsupervised learning, semi-supervised learning, and reinforcement learning algorithms. Classification is a supervised learning method, which means both the input and the desired output data are provided. Classification is a process of identifying the particular each instance belongs to a class, which is indicated by the value of a special goal attribute or simply the class attribute. The goal attribute can take on categorical values, each of them corresponding to a class. Each example consists of two parts, namely a set of predictor attribute values and a goal attribute value. The former are used to predict the value of the latter. The predictor attributes should be relevant for predicting the class of an instance. In the classification task the set of examples being mined is divided into two mutually exclusive and exhaustive sets, called the training set and the test set. The classification process is divided into two phases: training, when a classification model is built from the training set, and testing, when the model is evaluated on the test set. In the training phase the algorithm has access to the values of both predictor attributes and the goal attribute for all examples of the training set, and it uses that information to build a classification model. This model represents classification knowledge - essentially, a relationship between predictor attribute values and classes - that allows the prediction of the class of an example given its predictor attribute values. For testing, the test set the class values of the examples is not shown. In the testing phase, only after a prediction is made is the algorithm allowed to see the actual class of the just classified example. One of the major goals of a classification algorithm is to maximize the predictive accuracy obtained by the classification model when classifying examples in the test set unseen during training.

3.1   Algorithm Comparison

Typical Machine Learning Algorithms (LDA, SVM) - Linear Discriminant Analysis is a method used for classification and reducing dimensionality. When presented with different categories of data, LDA maximizes the distance between the categories' data points and minimizes the scatter of the data points withing the category. It then projects the data points onto linear axes (usually two) which presents the category data as nicely separated and easy to differentiate between. LDA can also be used in preprocessing data to reduce the number of features. In BCI, LDA is used to reduce the dimensionality and contrast between the extracted features of cerebral activity. A support vector machine (SVM) is another commonly used machine learning algorithm that aids in classification problems. A support vector machine focuses on linearly separable data. For example, in R2, an SVM would aim to create a line separating two groups of data, with one side of the line corresponding to a certain classification and the other side representing another classification. A good SVM will maximize the distance between points on either side of the linear boundary formed, thus finding the best "middle" separator of the data. More complicated SVMs can also be used on higher dimensional and/or multi-classification problems.

CNNs - Convolutional neural networks are a subcategory of deep learning and neural networks that involve the use of convolutional "layers". The given set of features, often derived from 2D images, is fed through the convolutional neural network. As images, or other data, are fed through the CNN's layers, the important features in determining the class label are weighted more heavily, causing the most attention to be paid to them in future classification. The most unique aspect of CNNs is the "dropout" layers they include, which involve each layer only focusing on a subset of the input features (pixels, etc.). This allows the CNN to accurately label future inputs without overfitting to the training data, allowing it to perform well on unseen data. CNNs also use pooling layers, which group pieces of feature information together to come up with a relationship between them (see Fig. 3). This, like the dropout layer, allows CNNs to come up with meaningful relationships between the input data points (pixels, etc.) without overfitting too much to individual pieces of data. Thus, CNNs are able to focus on the most important parts of the input data and apply that knowledge to future inputs.

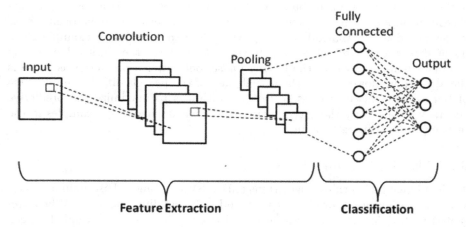

Fig. 3. Depiction of CNN layers [12]

DBNs - Deep belief networks are another subcategory of deep learning and neural networks. DBNs are a generative model which produce the possible outputs for a given feature. DBNs can also be used for both supervised and unsupervised learning. What makes DBNs unique is their method of training, which involves first running through restricted boltzman machine layers (see Fig. 4) and training to find important features for classification, as in typical neural networks, and then using "error back-propagation algorithms to fine-tune the parameters of the DBN" after the training is completed (science direct). This allows the DBN to accurately predict labels (or generate them) for future, unknown, inputs.

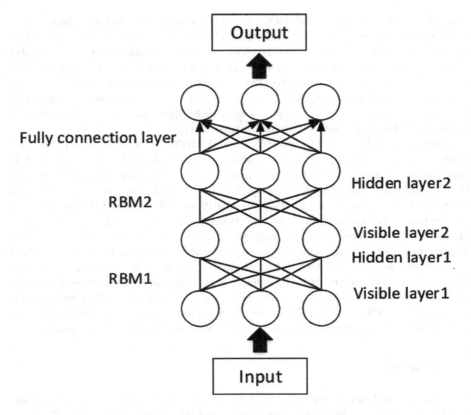

Fig. 4. Depiction of DBN layers [8]

3.2 Experiment Design

Our first experiments will be an attempt at replicating the results found in [7]. This will include using the same code and packages found within the github page associated with Hersche's paper, in order to classify the 2008 BCI competition motor imagery data (as Hersche did). Then, our neural network experiments are designed to replicate the efficiency and effectiveness already proven with CNN and DBN architectures in classification studies, however this time with the EEG results of human motor imagery tasks. In other words, these architectures will form the basis of two algorithms that will be trained and tested on our dataset under a supervised learning approach. Typically, classification algorithms work along the basis of a linear regression algorithm that slowly alters the input parameters of a prediction model (or formula) in order to achieve desirably classified outputs. In terms of our research, classification in this context refers to our models being able to take the results of our chosen motor imagery EEG data and make predictions for future EEG readings (new inputs) based on the sample. As noted in [6], neural networks have gained large popularity in these sorts of classification tasks due to the fact they are also trained in a similar way, with inputs, weights, and desired results. Through our experiments, we want to demonstrate which of the CNN or DBN architectures is more accurate and faster in their predictions. To maintain our experimental validity, both architectures are going to be analyzed prior to their choosing, to make sure that they both can support similar numbers of classification inputs. A direct comparison of this kind can then be very informative as to which algorithm architecture may be more useful for future EEG classification research.

Firstly, we will test different CNNs and DBNs to find architectures that both can handle up to nine input features (the number of samples present in our current dataset). We will do sample runs with smaller input values to ensure the networks are functioning properly. Then, we will begin test trials where we train the two networks on our dataset. Lastly we will measure the accuracy of the networks' predictions, and also the runtime of the predictions of the course of the entire experiment. Measuring the accuracy of the models is the most important aspect of our classification experiment, as it lets us know which model is better at making predictions. The prediction accuracy is the focus for driving new methods of interpreting EEG data, which by specialized person alone is often a slow and meticulous process. This is why the speed of the predictions is important as well, as if the CNN and DBN architectures are accurate but give no relative prediction speed gains, their creation and use is not necessary.

4   Baselines

For testing base level classification examples, we used the support vector machine (SVM), linear discriminant analysis (LDA), and HD models designed by [7]. Both the SVM and LDA models consist of 64 layers. The HD model is a more complex model and involves performing arithmetic on large input hyper vectors. The data is projected to a high dimensional Hamming Space, and the model is trained on this data.

Our CNN model was done in addition to the code by (Hersche 2018). Specifically, we added a program to similarly extract features from the IV-2a data and run a CNN on the data (Fig. 5). Our CNN model aimed to use tensorflow to create a simple CNN using our prior knowledge and implementation tutorials of CNNs for Tensorflow [1]. Ultimately, we were unsuccessful in training and testing CNN on this data. Our problems stemmed from implementing the algorithm, including formatting the data appropriately for inputting into the CNN, along with computational limitations given our personal computers' memory and time restrictions.

```
def run_CNN(self):
    start_train = time.time()
    if self.useCSP:
        w = generate_projection(self.train_data,self.train_label, self.NO_csp,self.filter_bank,self.time_windows)
    else:
        w = generate_eye(self.train_data,self.train_label,self.filter_bank,self.time_windows)

    feature_mat = extract_feature(self.train_data,w,self.filter_bank,self.time_windows)
    eval_feature_mat = extract_feature(self.eval_data,w,self.filter_bank,self.time_windows)

    self.train_label = self.train_label
    self.eval_label = self.eval_label
    y_train = np.empty(219, dtype = float)
    y_test = np.empty(219, dtype = float)
    for i in range(219):
        np.append(y_train[i], self.train_label[i])
        np.append(y_test[i], self.eval_label[i])

    print(y_train.shape, y_test.shape)
    print()
    print(feature_mat.shape, eval_feature_mat.shape)

    cnn = keras.models.Sequential()
    cnn.add(keras.layers.Conv1D(16, 3, activation = 'relu', input_shape = (219, 11352)))
    cnn.add(keras.layers.MaxPooling1D(2))
    cnn.add(keras.layers.Flatten())
    cnn.add(keras.layers.Dense(16, activation='relu'))
    cnn.add(keras.layers.Dense(10))
    cnn.summary()

    cnn.compile(optimizer='adam',
        loss=tf.keras.losses.SparseCategoricalCrossentropy(from_logits=True),
        metrics=['accuracy'])
    history = cnn.fit(feature_mat, y_train, epochs = 2, validation_data = (eval_feature_mat, y_test))
```

Fig. 5. CNN model layers code added to Hersche et al. program.

For the DBN model, two different implementations were attempted [2] and [3]. There were complications with running the code from [2] due to OS errors. The download path, success, and compatibility were all checked on our windows machine, meaning that the code may not be suitable with all environments. The code from [3] also was problematic, as it was built to import image classification files and not EEG signals. Even after alteration to the dataset input information the code could not work. Since this implementation used numerous python files for implementation, it was infeasible for changes to be made at that large a scale while maintaining the implementation's key components. Evidently, no viable results for either of these implementations were producible with the IV-2A motor imagery dataset.

Fig. 6. Average accuracy results for run 1 of (hersche2018) replication of SVM, LDA, HD respectively.

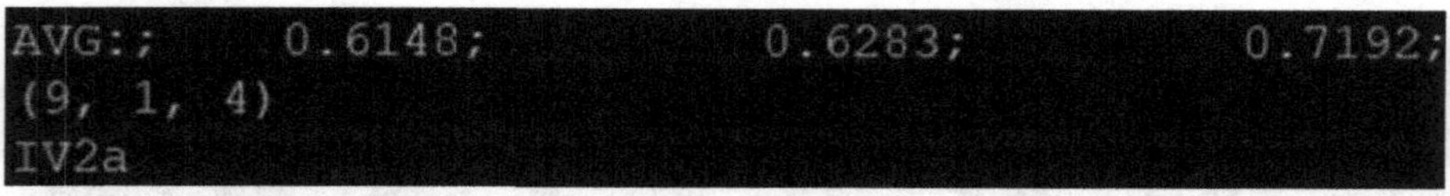

```
AVG:;      0.6148;           0.6283;              0.7192;
(9, 1, 4)
IV2a
```

Fig. 7. Average accuracy results for run 2 of (hersche2018) replication of SVM, LDA, HD respectively.

Table 1. Accuracies of LDA, SVM, and HD model in (hersche2018).

	SVM	LDA	HD
Prediction Accuracy	61.48	62.83	73.5

5 Results

5.1 Typical Algorithm Performance

Figures 6 and 7 represent our reproduction of the results from (Hersche 2018) on two separate runs. Using the authors' provided instructions and code, we recreated the results with the given results. Table 1 provides the results for the same run provided by the original authors themselves. Notably, our results from our replication runs of SVM and LDA classification on the dataset prove to be the exact same (to four decimal places) as the average accuracies reported by the authors for these algorithms. As for the HD model, created by the authors of the Hersche 2018 paper, we achieved similar results to those reported in Table 1. However, there was more variance here than with the previous 2 models. The models differed by approximately 1.6% in terms of accuracy on the shown run, with a variation maximum of 5.55

5.2 CNN/DBN Performance

Our CNN implementation is shown for reference in (Fig. 5). This implementation attempt, along with our attempt to implement a deep belief network, was unsuccessful in producing meaningful results. Implementation, along with memory issues, were problematic for us, which meant that we had no meaningful results for our attempts to run a CNN or DBN (see Fig. 8).

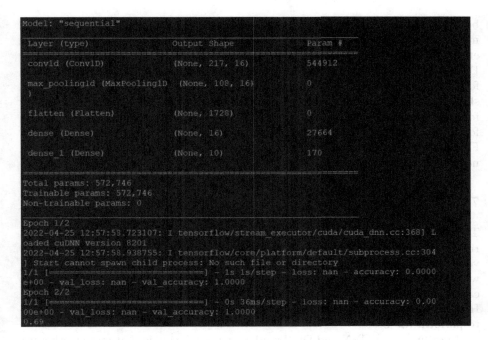

Fig. 8. Erroneous accuracy results for our CNN implementation.

Table 2. Time spent on implementation of algorithms.

	SVM	LDA	HD	CNN	DBN
Time in implementation (hours)	2	2	2	25	25

6   Discussion

Our research is important because it demonstrates the ease of independent researchers in replicating standard machine learning models on motor imagery data, but the expected difficulties encountered in implementing viable neural network implementations. With this in mind, independent researcher such as ourselves can expect to face multiple forms of adversity with replicating the complex neural network applications to motor imagery data, such as machine constraints, research understanding time constraints, and complexities associated with using mixing numerous environment resources into one cohesive implementation. There are multiple tutorials for implementing standard machine learning algorithms on a multitude of different types of datasets and dataset files. These include datasets for motor imagery, emotion recognition, mental workload, seizure detection, sleep stage scoring, and event related potential tasks (Craik et al. 2019). However, with motor imagery specifically there are relatively few research examples for DBNs, alluding that this method of classification might be outdated. The reason being that DBNs are clusters of restricted boltzman machines, which tend to be better optimized for image classification (Larochelle et al. 2012). Nevertheless, it could still be useful, as (An et al. 2014) found their DBN to be more successful than conventional SVM. Meanwhile, CNNs have been found to be useful for motor classification [14], but still also require lots of time, skill, and experience for novel application to motor imagery studies (see Table 2 for time spent on each algorithm) For these reasons, CNNs comparison to DBNs for motor imagery classification is sparse, as identified in (Craik et al. 2019). Future research should take these factors in account when attempting neural network implementations for motor imagery EEG classification.

7   Conclusion

This research project allowed us to replicate and verify the more simple algorithms' (LDA and SVM) performance on motor imagery data. We were able to verify the results provided for these standard machine learning models, along with Hersche et al.'s unique HD model. On this admittedly small dataset, it can be concluded that SVMs perform better than LDAs in terms of accuracy. However a binarized model, like the HD model created by Hersche et al., is able to perform the best.

In terms of our CNN and DBN model, our conclusion is that more work must be done relating to these two algorithms (and perhaps deep learning algorithms in general) when it comes to classifying EEG data. Specifically, future researchers should have experience implementing these algorithms from scratch onto new kinds of data, and be prepared for some of the issues we faced in memory and implementation. Future research into deep learning and EEG data classification should focus on these areas. Providing novel implementations of these commonly used algorithms will provide a starting base for further investigation of the use of deep learning algorithms on EEG classification tasks.

References

1. Abadi, M., et al.: TensorFlow: large-scale machine learning on heterogeneous systems (2015). https://www.tensorflow.org/, software available from tensorflow.org
2. albertbup: a python implementation of deep belief networks built upon NumPy and TensorFlow with scikit-learn compatibility (2017). https://github.com/albertbup/deep-belief-network
3. AmanPriyanshu: deep-belief-networks-in-pytorch (2021). https://github.com/AmanPriyanshu/Deep-Belief-Networks-in-PyTorch
4. An, X., Kuang, D., Guo, X., Zhao, Y., He, L.: A deep learning method for classification of EEG data based on motor imagery. In: Huang, D.-S., Han, K., Gromiha, M. (eds.) ICIC 2014. LNCS, vol. 8590, pp. 203–210. Springer, Cham (2014). https://doi.org/10.1007/978-3-319-09330-7_25
5. Brunner, C., Leeb, R., Muller-Putz, G., Schlogl, A., Competition, B.: Graz Data Set a Institute for Knowledge Discovery, and Institute for HumanComputer Interfaces Graz University of Technology, Austria (2008)

6. Craik, A., He, Y., Contreras-Vidal, J.L.: Deep learning for electroencephalogram (EEG) classification tasks: a review. J. Neural Eng. **16**(3) (2019)
7. Hersche, M., Millán, J.d.R., Benini, L., Rahimi, A.: Exploring embedding methods in binary hyperdimensional computing: a case study for motor-imagery based brain-computer interfaces. arXiv preprint arXiv:1812.05705 (2018)
8. Liu, H., Lang, B.: Machine learning and deep learning methods for intrusion detection systems: a survey. Appl. Sci. **9**, 4396 (2019). https://doi.org/10.3390/app9204396
9. Lotte, F., et al.: A review of classification algorithms for EEG-based brain-computer interfaces: a 10 year update. J. Neural Eng. **15**(3), (2018)
10. Lu, N., Li, T., Ren, X., Miao, H.: A deep learning scheme for motor imagery classification based on restricted Uoltzmann machines. IEEE Trans. Neural Syst. Rehabil. Eng. **25**(6), 566–576 (2016)
11. Park, S., Ha, J., Kim, D.H., Kim, L.: Improving motor imagery-based brain-computer interface performance based on sensory stimulation training: An approach focused on poorly performing users. Front. Neurosci. **15**, 1526 (2021)
12. Phung, V.H., Rhee, E.J., et al.: A high-accuracy model average ensemble of convolutional neural networks for classification of cloud image patches on small datasets. Appl. Sci. **9**(21), 4500 (2019)
13. Quiles, E., Suay, F., Candela, G., Chio, N., Jiménez, M., Álvarez-Kurogi, L.: Low-cost robotic guide based on a motor imagery brain-computer interface for arm assisted rehabilitation. Int. J. Environ. Res. Public Health **17**(3), 699 (2020)
14. Tang, X., Li, W., Li, X., Ma, W., Dang, X.: Motor imagery EEG recognition based on conditional optimization empirical mode decomposition and multi-scale convolutional neural network. Expert Syst. Appl. **149**, 113285 (2020)

High-Powered Ocular Artifact Detection with C-LSTM-E

Ian McDiarmid-Sterling[(✉)] [ID] and Luca Cerbin [ID]

Swarthmore College, Swarthmore, PA 19081, USA
{imcdiar1,lcerbin1}@swarthmore.edu
https://www.swarthmore.edu/computer-science

Abstract. Electroencephalography (EEG) is a technique for examining brain waves through recording devices placed on the scalp. During EEG signal collection, unwanted ocular artifacts (OAs) are frequently introduced and must be removed before the EEG signal can be effectively used. Many deep learning approaches to identifying and correcting OAs attempt to balance prediction accuracy and power consumption, but we introduce a novel high-power ensemble of a Convolutional Neural Network (CNN) and a Long-Short Term Memory network (LSTM), C-LSTM-E. We compare the overall accuracy of C-LSTM-E to previously introduced methods for OA identification and correction, and discover that for certain prevalancies of OAs, C-LSTM-E outperforms previously introduced models. While C-LSTM-E is slightly less accurate than the state-of-the-art OA correction model, it does not require a channel selection algorithm and is robust to changes in OA prevalance. C-LSTM-E is the first CNN and LSTM ensemble method for OA identification.

Keywords: Long Short-Term Memory network · Convolutional Neural Network · Electroencephalography (EEG) · Ocular artifact · High-powered computation · Brain-Computer Interface · Machine learning ensemble · Deep learning

1 Introduction

Electroencephalography recording devices measure electrical impulses between brain cells through a set of electrodes on the scalp. However, because EEG recording devices are sensitive, they also detect electrical impulses generated by muscle movement. These contaminating signals must be identified before the EEG signal can be effectively processed. While many different types of facial muscle movement may contaminate an EEG signal, OAs are frequently the most disruptive signals, caused by high-amplitude patterns (blinks) or low-frequency patterns (eye movement) [1,2]. While statistical and signal analysis methods are effective at OA identification and correction, they are outperformed by deep learning techniques in a variety of situations [3–5]. Specifically, CNNs

---

I. McDiarmid-Sterling and L. Cerbin—Contributed equally to this work.

© The Author(s), under exclusive license to Springer Nature Switzerland AG 2022
M. Kurosu et al. (Eds.): HCII 2022, LNCS 13519, pp. 482–496, 2022.
https://doi.org/10.1007/978-3-031-17618-0_34

and LSTMs are more effective than statistical methods for some types of OA processing [6–11]. Typically these deep learning techniques perform OA correction instead of identification, forcing researchers to use a corrected signal without providing control over how the signal is generated [2, 12–15]. These strategies assume similar incidence and characteristics of OAs across subjects and tasks in a "one size fits all" approach that may be insufficient for any individual research [13]. Additionally, many of these strategies only use a single EEG channel or a subset of EEG channels, further limiting applications for certain kinds of research. Guided by the high accuracy of LSTMs when performing OA identification in low-power contexts [6], we investigated if we could develop a high-power strategy including an LSTM to perform OA identification more accurately than current state-of-the-art techniques.

2 Literature Review

2.1 CNN

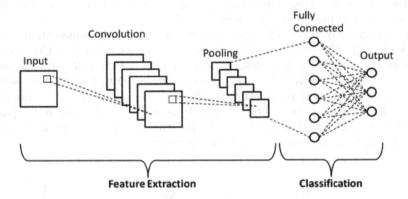

Fig. 1. Typical CNN architecture [16]

Convolutional Neural Networks (CNN) are commonly used to solve classification and regression problems relating to computer vision [11, 17, 18] and brain-computer interfaces [19–21]. Significant work has demonstrated the application of CNN's to a wide array of OA processing problems [6–8]. Typically a CNN consists of several types of layers: convolutional layers, pooling layers, and fully connected layers (Fig. 1). CNN's are trained by optimizing a specified loss function.

The operation of a CNN occurs in several stages. First, a two dimensional convolutional filter takes a raw signal and converts it to a feature map. Next, a pooling layer reduces the data size while preserving the most important features. This allows the CNN to run a single dimensional convolutional filter to further generate features. After this second convolutional filter, a flatten layer modifies the output into a single large vector which is then fed straight into dense layers. The final output from the last dense layer is then compared to the label using mean squared error, categorical cross entropy or annother loss function.

2.2   LSTM

Long Short-Term Memory networks (LSTMs) are proven to work well for a variety of EEG classifications [22,23], and especially for OA detection in low-powered contexts [6]. Since EEG data is a time-series, an LSTMs ability to maintain long-term dependencies across data results in extremely accurate OA identification.

LSTMs are recurrent neural networks (RNNs) designed to handle time-series data. RNNs are neural networks that pass some amount of temporal state through each step of the network [24]. However, classical RNNs suffer from vanishing/exploding gradients. These problems occur when long-term dependency data disappears or explodes as continual iterations throughout the network result in compounding computations on ever growing/shrinking values. LSTMs correct these issues by maintaining long-term dependencies through an additional parameter that is passed through each LSTM layer.

The structure of an LSTM layer is significantly more complex than that of a CNN (Fig. 2). The first sigmoid to x gate (the forget gate) uses the information from the previous cell to determine what parts of the cell state should be forgotten. The results from the second sigmoid are multiplied by the result of the cell state after being passed through the *tanh* function. This operation then updates the cell state for that LSTM layer. Finally, the previous output is passed through a sigmoid function, multiplied by the updated cell state passed through the *tanh* function, and outputted to the next layer.

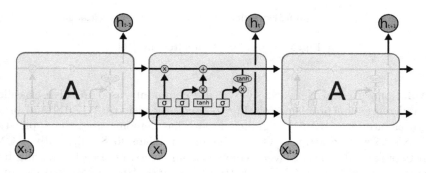

Fig. 2. LSTM cell architecture [25]

2.3 Power Reduction

Previous work has attempted to identify OA's while minimizing power consumption, allowing models to be implemented with field-programmable gate arrays (FPGAs) [8]. While this effectively establishes a strategy for identifying OAs, it requires special hardware and sacrifices overall accuracy for power reduction. As previously published, the electrical energy efficiency of computation almost doubles every year and a half [26]. As a result, the gap between the power consumption of general computation systems like PCs and specialized hardware like FPGA shrinks. As computing power increases, the need for specialized hardware is reduced. As systems become more efficient, industry focus shifts from power reduction to creating more accurate models. The developmental cost of creating models to run on specific hardware outweighs the power savings of these strategies, particularly as mobile computing power increases and the Internet of Things grows.

3 Dataset

We trained our model on a semi-simulated EEG artifact dataset, generating ground truth labels without relying on a labeling expert [27]. The dataset consists of 50 30 s recordings taken from 27 subjects, with 19 electrodes placed on each subject according to the 10–20 international system [28]. Signals were gathered 200 Hz, then band pass filtered at 0.5–40 Hz and notch filtered 50 Hz. The semi-simulated contaminated signal was generated according to:

$$Dirty_{EEG}(i,j) = Pure_{EEG}(i,j) + (a_j)V_{eog} + (b_j)H_{eog}$$

where V_{eog} is the upper minus lower EOG electrode signals, H_{eog} is the left minus right EOG electrode recordings, and a_j, b_j are contamination coefficients as proposed by Klados and Bamidis [27].

By using a semi-simulated dataset we avoided introducing the variance traditionally generated by human data labelers. Since human data labeling is not uniform or objective, training models on human labeled data reduces the generality of the model as it performs similarly to the specific labeler, not the ground-truth.

While the semi-simulated data allows for a more generalizable model, it does not include frequency information about the prevalence of artifacts.

4 Methods

4.1 Rationale

While CNNs have been shown to be effective at identifying OAs, they encode spatial dependence that is not desirable. In the feature extraction stage of a CNN, the CNN kernel sweeps over the input data, encoding information about the order of the channels which is learned by the model. While this is not harmful so long as the order of the channels remains consistent throughout training and testing, it is not relevant information for the OA identification problem. Guided by this, we introduce an LSTM to leverage the temporal dependency of OAs in the EEG signal. By combining a CNN and an LSTM, we capture the temporal forecast of the LSTM and leverage the CNNs ability to create features. Our selection of a nonlinear combination function allows C-LSTM-E to outperform both the LSTM and the CNN individually.

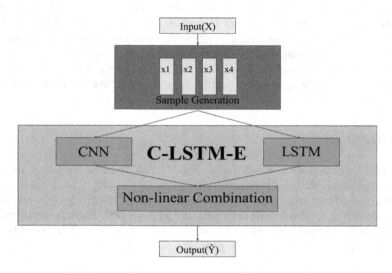

Fig. 3. C-LSTM-E model architecture

4.2   Model Architecture

C-LSTM-E, is an ensemble of a CNN and an LSTM (Fig. 3). Input to C-LSTM-E is a $(20, 19)$ matrix that corresponds to a 20 point window of the larger data sequence, across all 19 channels.

The CNN contains a 2-dimensional convolutional layer of output shape $(18, 17, 20)$, which corresponds to an image height of 18, a width of 17, and 20 channels. This is followed by a max pooling layer that halves the image dimensions to $(9, 8, 20)$. A second 2-dimensional convolutional layer takes the result from the max pooling and outputs a $(7, 6, 38)$ image. This final feature output gets flattened into a vector of size 1596. The model then includes three dense layers: the first with 38 neurons, the second with 16 neurons, and the final layer outputing the regression prediction (Fig. 8).

The LSTM trains on a tensor of shape $(10, 20, 19)$ containing input windows that maintain the temporal flow of the data. The model contains an LSTM layer with 128 units, followed by a 64 neuron dense layer, a 32 neuron dense layer, and a final 19 neuron dense layer for predictions across each channel (Fig. 9).

During training, the CNN and LSTM optimize a prediction threshold to cast their continuous output to binary class labels. This threshold is a function of the percentage of artifacts throughout the dataset and is used as a labeling cutoff.

4.3 Data Processing

To accurately evaluate the performance of C-LSTM-E, we trained the model on 64% of the data, validated on 16% of the data and tested on 20% of the data. We used a standard cross validation structure where 20% of dataset was used for testing and 80% was split into training and validation [29]. The models were trained using the two way mean of residuals calculated by subtracting the clean EEG signal from the dirty EEG signal for each window as labels. We performed min-max normalization across the entire set of windows and normalized all residual means to the unit interval [30].

To generate class labels from the normalized residual means on the unit interval, we set an arbitrary frequency threshold of OAs, n, and marked the top $n\%$ of residuals as artifacts. This allowed us to investigate how C-LSTM-E performed given various contamination percentages.

4.4 Model Training

As demonstrated by other OA identification techniques, we trained C-LSTM-E on all 19 channels of EEG data, broken into windows of 20 data points [6–8]. We trained C-LSTM-E for 30 epochs using the Adam standard optimizer [31].

5 Results

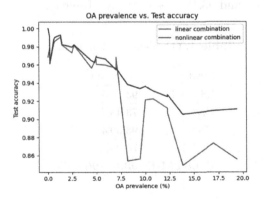

Fig. 4. OA prevalence vs C-LSTM-E accuracy

5.1 Variable Prevalence of OAs

We varied the assumed percentage of artifacts throughout the dataset from 0% (trivial) to 20% to evaluate the performance of C-LSTM-E. While C-LSTM-E performed better when the frequency of OAs was smaller, C-LSTM-E still achieved above 90% accuracy when OAs accounted for 20% of the data (Fig. 4). Therefore C-LSTM-E proved it can classify any EEG recording containing OAs with ≥90% accuracy provided the data remained within our probable upper bound of 20%.

5.2 Fixed Prevalence of OAs

To comparatively assess the performance of C-LSTM-E, we evaluated the performance of the model when artifacts made up 5–10% of the overall dataset, which we believed most accurately simulates many real world experimental conditions. Given these initial conditions, we compared C-LSTM-E to other state-of-the-art models.

We compared C-LSTM-E to OA identification models trained on different datasets because it was the first OA identification model trained using the semi-simulated dataset [32,33]. To benchmark the performance of C-LSTM-E, we compared the final test accuracy when OAs account for 5–10% of the dataset to LSTM-1 [6], CNN-1 [8], CNN-2 [7] and UNET [10] (Table 1).

These models were the state-of-the art OA identification strategies and variations at the time of writing. While we directly compared C-LSTM-E to LSTM-1 and CNN-2, these models explicitly prioritized power efficiency over OA identification accuracy. We also compared the performance of C-LSTM-E to the state-of-the art OA correction strategy, *CNN-3* [11]. C-LSTM-E had an accuracy that ranges from 93.62–96.95% depending on the prevalence of artifacts in the dataset, while the next most accurate models, CNN-2 and LSTM-1, had accuracies of 93.50% and 93.1%, respectively (Table 1).

Table 1. OA identification accuracy

Strategy	Accuracy
LSTM-1	93.10%
CNN-1	73.48%
CNN-2	93.50%
UNET	70.00%
C-LSTM-E	**93.62–96.85%**

5.3   Real-Time Processing

C-LSTM-E required fixed segment size inputs to train both the LSTM and CNN. Real-time predictions should be independent of fixed size segments and C-LSTM-E should be able to process an arbitrarily large artifact size. We removed this dependence on fixed segment size by implementing the following three step procedure.

Given an EEG recording of any length, we generated a window of the fixed segment size starting at every possible point in the recording and then evaluated each window with C-LSTM-E. We flagged each window labeled by C-LSTM-E as an artifact (Figure 5, artifact windows shown as red rectangles). Since many windows containing part of the OA are labeled by C-LSTM-E as artifacts, this generated many overlapping artifact windows.

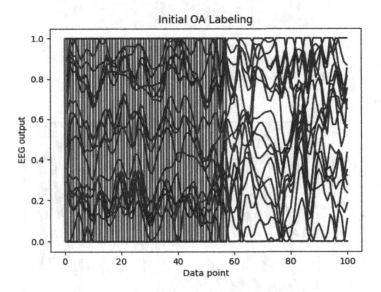

Fig. 5. Initial OA labeled windows (Color figure online)

We then generated a histogram of how many times each point in the EEG recording was included in a window that was labeled as an artifact (Fig. 6). We then found the mean of the OA (Fig. 7, magenta) and used the standard deviation to optimize a bounding box of the OA (Fig. 7, red).

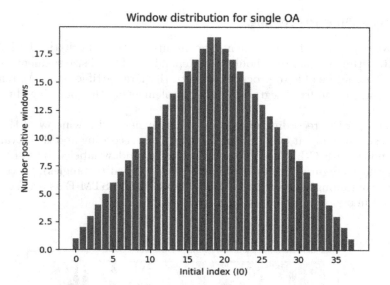

Fig. 6. Histogram of positive OA starting points

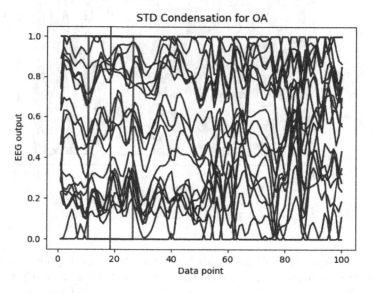

Fig. 7. Mean and confidence interval for OA (Color figure online)

To create an artifact interval we made the assumption each point was independent of one another and then utilized the Central Limit Theorem. Since the points are part of a time-series and therefore dependent, we present this as an approximate artifact interval. We used the properties of the Normal Distribution to approximate 95% of the artifact with an interval equal to $mean \pm 2 * std$. A higher accuracy interval can be used e.g. 99.7%, however, we believed 95% allowed for some inevitable error while still being accurate. We were able to remove the dependence on segment size by reconstructing the total size of the artifact through this artifact interval process.

6 Discussion

6.1 Analysis

It is difficult to directly compare C-LSTM-E to other models because they do not publish what percentage of their dataset consists of OAs. Assuming OAs account for 5–10% of a standard EEG recording, C-LSTM-E is more accurate than LSTM-1, CNN-1, CNN-2, and UNET (Table 1). All of these models use multichannel EEG signals similar to C-LSTM-E but the majority focus on power efficient computations. While this was historically important, with recent advances in processing power and cloud computing, power constraints are now secondary to performance benchmarks, highlighting the importance of high power models [34]. C-LSTM-E demonstrates the significant accuracy improvements of a high-powered model over its low-powered counterparts.

C-LSTM-E is most comparable to LSTM-1 because it utilizes an LSTM to solve a binary-classification problem. While C-LSTM-E is more power intensive, in situations where the inclusion of OAs may result in faulty models, the increase in accuracy provided by C-LSTM-E may be crucial to experimental success.

CNN-1/CNN-2 solve slightly different problems involving more classification classes which makes it difficult to directly compare them to C-LSTM-E. C-LSTM-E outperforms both models but CNN-1 and CNN-2 solve harder classification tasks and so the final accuracies of the models are not directly comparable. In the future, we plan to generalize C-LSTM-E to perform on similar types of classification instead of labeling artifacts in a binary fashion. Unfortunately, the datasets for CNN-1 and CNN-2 are not public to the best of our knowledge, so training C-LSTM-E on these datasets is not possible.

CNN-3 outperforms C-LSTM-E in its binary classification before regression with an accuracy of 99.67%. However, *CNN-3* varies in several ways from C-LSTM-E, which we believe makes C-LSTM-E a more generalizable model. *CNN-3* requires a subset of EEG channels, which must be selected and which greatly simplifies the problem space. By using all available input channels, C-LSTM-E avoids the need for a time intensive and error prone channel selection process [6]. *CNN-3* generates its own synthetic data that is not publicly available so a direct comparison between C-LSTM-E and *CNN-3* is impossible. We believe the semi-simulated dataset used by C-LSTM-E is more similar to real-life EEG data than their synthetic data. The use of a semi-simulated dataset over a simulated one and how C-LSTM-E has proven performance across different OA frequencies makes C-LSTM-E a more generalizable model.

Unlike other models, C-LSTM-E is demonstrated to be effective across a wide range of possible OA frequencies. This means that the effectiveness of the model is not a result of any specific OA distribution, establishing that C-LSTM-E is generalizable to a wide range of research problems where OAs occur with differing frequencies.

6.2   Next Steps

We plan to evaluate C-LSTM-E on a human-labeled dataset to compare the performance to the semi-simulated dataset. This will also provide us with information about possible difficulties generalizing models trained using the semi-simulated dataset to datasets labeled by hand.

To more accurately compare C-LSTM-E to previously published high and low power models we plan to request the source code for a variety of models and train them on the semi-simulated dataset. This will enable a direct comparsion on the same dataset, allowing us to generate more meaningful performance results.

We also plan to evaluate how well C-LSTM-E performs on mobile hardware. By creating a generalized framework to utilize mobile phone computing or cloudlets to perform OA identification on new samples, we plan to offer C-LSTM-E as a portable, highly accurate, solution to the OA identification problem.

7   Conclusion

We present C-LSTM-E, a high-powered ensemble of a CNN and LSTM for OA identification. We then show that our model is more accurate than other state-of-the-art strategies for OA identification using a full set of channels on a semi-simulated dataset. Since using a full set of channels is crucial to applicable models as it avoids the need for lengthy and error-prone pre-processing and channel selection steps, we highlight how C-LSTM-E offers advantages over higher accuracy models that do not use a full set of channels. We also analyze the robustness of C-LSTM-E by varying the OA frequency in the dataset, and show that it performs with $\geq 90\%$ accuracy for all frequencies in the range [0,0.2]. This suggests C-LSTM-E will perform similarly well across different datasets with different frequencies of OAs. We show how C-LSTM-E can be used to estimate total OAs through a reconstructive pipeline. Since C-LSTM-E identifies OAs, it allows for experimental flexibility in their treatment. We also argue the increase in accuracy offered by high-power approaches to OA identification outweigh increased power consumption as mobile systems become increasingly power efficient. We believe high-powered OA identification algorithms are a necessary next step in the future of Brain-Computer Interface research and C-LSTM-E is a powerful addition to the high-powered ecosystem.

A   Appendix

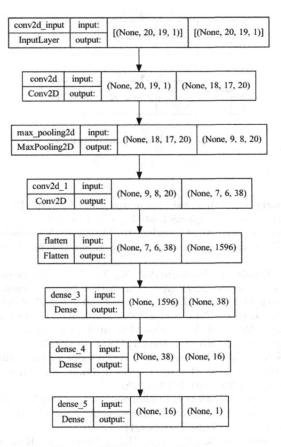

Fig. 8. CNN model architecture

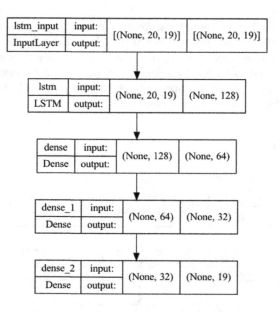

Fig. 9. LSTM model architecture

References

1. Croft, R.J., Barry, R.J.: Removal of ocular artifact from the EEG: a review. Neurophysiol. Clin./Clin. Neurophysiol. **30**(1), 5–19 (2000)
2. Yang, B., Duan, K., Fan, C., Chenxiao, H., Wang, J.: Automatic ocular artifacts removal in EEG using deep learning. Biomed. Signal Process. Control **43**, 148–158 (2018)
3. Qayoom, A., Wahab, A., Kamaruddin, N., Zahid, Z.: Artifacts classification in EEG signals based on temporal average statistics. Jurnal Teknologi **77**(7) (2015)
4. Kotte, S., Kumar Dabbakuti, J.R.K.: Methods for removal of artifacts from EEG signal: a review. J. Phys. Conf. Ser. **1706**, 012093. IOP Publishing (2020)
5. Maddirala, A.K., Veluvolu, K.C.: Eye-blink artifact removal from single channel EEG with k-means and SSA. Sci. Rep. **11**(1), 1–14 (2021)
6. Manjunath, N.K., et al.: A low-power LSTM processor for multi-channel brain EEG artifact detection. In 2020 21st International Symposium on Quality Electronic Design (ISQED), pp. 105–110. IEEE (2020)
7. Khatwani, M., et al.: A flexible multichannel EEG artifact identification processor using depthwise-separable convolutional neural networks. ACM J. Emerg. Technol. Comput. Syst. (JETC) **17**(2), 1–21 (2021)
8. Khatwani, M., Hosseini, M., Paneliya, H., Mohsenin, T., Hairston, W.D., Waytowich, N.: Energy efficient convolutional neural networks for EEG artifact detection. In: 2018 IEEE Biomedical Circuits and Systems Conference (BioCAS), pp. 1–4. IEEE (2018)
9. Garg, P., et al.: Using convolutional neural networks to automatically detect eye-blink artifacts in magnetoencephalography without resorting to electrooculography. In: Descoteaux, M., et al. (eds.) MICCAI 2017. LNCS, vol. 10435, pp. 374–381. Springer, Cham (2017). https://doi.org/10.1007/978-3-319-66179-7_43

10. Komisaruk, O., Nikulchev, E., Malykh, S.: Neural network model for artifacts marking in EEG signals. Cloud Sci. **7** (2020)
11. Jurczak, M., Kołodziej, M., Majkowski, A.: Implementation of a convolutional neural network for eye blink artifacts removal from the electroencephalography signal. Front. Neurosci. **16** (2022)
12. Mashhadi, N., Khuzani, A.Z., Heidari, M., Khaledyan, D.: Deep learning denoising for EOG artifacts removal from EEG signals. In: 2020 IEEE Global Humanitarian Technology Conference (GHTC), pp. 1–6. IEEE (2020)
13. Saba-Sadiya, S., Chantland, E., Alhanai, T., Liu, T., Ghassemi. M.M.: Unsupervised EEG artifact detection and correction. Front. Digit. Health **2**, 57 (2021)
14. Zhang, H., Wei, C., Zhao, M., Liu, Q., Wu, H.: A novel convolutional neural network model to remove muscle artifacts from EEG. In: ICASSP 2021–2021 IEEE International Conference on Acoustics, Speech and Signal Processing (ICASSP), pp. 1265–1269. IEEE (2021)
15. Zhang, H., Zhao, M., Wei, C., Mantini, D., Li, Z., Liu, Q.: Eegdenoisenet: a benchmark dataset for deep learning solutions of EEG denoising. J. Neural Eng. **18**(5) (2021)
16. Van Phung, H., et al.: A high-accuracy model average ensemble of convolutional neural networks for classification of cloud image patches on small datasets. Appl. Sci. **9**(21), 4500 (2019)
17. Qian, P., Zhao, Z., Chen, C., Zeng, Z., Li, X.: Two eyes are better than one: exploiting binocular correlation for diabetic retinopathy severity grading. In: 2021 43rd Annual International Conference of the IEEE Engineering in Medicine & Biology Society (EMBC), pp. 2115–2118. IEEE (2021)
18. Zhao, Z., Chopra, K., Zeng, Z., Li, X.: Sea-Net: squeeze-and-excitation attention net for diabetic retinopathy grading. In: 2020 IEEE International Conference on Image Processing (ICIP), pp. 2496–2500. IEEE (2020)
19. Craik, A., He, Y., Contreras-Vidal, J.L.: Deep learning for electroencephalogram (EEG) classification tasks: a review. J. Neural Eng. **16**(3), 031001 (2019)
20. Roy, Y., Banville, H., Albuquerque, I., Gramfort, A., Falk, T.H., Faubert, J.: Deep learning-based electroencephalography analysis: a systematic review. J. Neural Eng. **16**(5), 051001 (2019)
21. Qu, X., Mei, Q., Liu, P., Hickey, T.: Using EEG to distinguish between writing and typing for the same cognitive task. In: Frasson, C., Bamidis, P., Vlamos, P. (eds.) BFAL 2020. LNCS (LNAI), vol. 12462, pp. 66–74. Springer, Cham (2020). https://doi.org/10.1007/978-3-030-60735-7_7
22. Bashivan, P., Rish, I., Yeasin, M., Codella, N.: Learning representations from EEG with deep recurrent-convolutional neural networks. arXiv preprint arXiv:1511.06448 (2015)
23. Qu, X., Liu, P., Li, Z., Hickey, T.: Multi-class time continuity voting for EEG classification. In: Frasson, C., Bamidis, P., Vlamos, P. (eds.) BFAL 2020. LNCS (LNAI), vol. 12462, pp. 24–33. Springer, Cham (2020). https://doi.org/10.1007/978-3-030-60735-7_3
24. Hochreiter, S., Schmidhuber, J.: Long short-term memory. Neural Comput. **9**(8), 1735–1780 (1997)
25. Olah, C.: Understanding LSTM networks (2015). https://colah.github.io/posts/2015-08-Understanding-LSTMs/. Accessed 5 Oct 2022
26. Koomey, J., Berard, S., Sanchez, M., Wong, H.: Implications of historical trends in the electrical efficiency of computing. IEEE Ann. Hist. Comput. **33**(3), 46–54 (2010)

27. Klados, M.A., Bamidis, P.D.: A semi-simulated EEG/EOG dataset for the comparison of EOG artifact rejection techniques. Data Brief **8**, 1004–1006 (2016)
28. Klem, G.H.: The ten-twenty electrode system of the international federation. The Internanional Federation of Clinical Nenrophysiology. Electroencephalogr. Clin. Neurophysiol. Suppl. **52**, 3–6 (1999)
29. Refaeilzadeh, P., Tang, L., Liu, H.: Cross-validation. Encycl. Database Syst. **5**, 532–538 (2009)
30. Ahsan, Md.M., Mahmud, M.A., Saha, P.K., Gupta, D., Siddique, Z.: Effect of data scaling methods on machine learning algorithms and model performance. Technologies **9**(3), 52 (2021)
31. Kingma, D.P., Ba, J.: Adam: a method for stochastic optimization. arXiv preprint arXiv:1412.6980 (2014)
32. Issa, M.F., Juhasz, Z.: Improved EOG artifact removal using wavelet enhanced independent component analysis. Brain Sci. **9**(12), 355 (2019)
33. Gajbhiye, P., Tripathy, R.K., Pachori, R.B.: Elimination of ocular artifacts from single channel EEG signals using FBSE-EWT based rhythms. IEEE Sensors J. **20**(7), 3687–3696 (2019)
34. Tawalbeh Lo'ai, A., Bakhader, W., Mehmood, R., Song, H.: Cloudlet-based mobile cloud computing for healthcare applications. In: 2016 IEEE Global Communications Conference (GLOBECOM), pp. 1–6. IEEE (2016)

ML vs DL: Accuracy and Testing Runtime Trade-offs in BCI

Anarsaikhan Tuvshinjargal$^{(\boxtimes)}$ ⓘ and Elliot Kim

Swarthmore College, Swarthmore, PA 19081, USA
{atuvshi1,ekim5}@swarthmore.edu

Abstract. Trade-offs between accuracy and runtime are a common phenomenon in the field of computer science, but particularly pose a challenge for online Brain-computer interface (BCI) applications, such as control interfaces for paralysis patients. However, research evaluating the testing runtime of various classifiers is extremely limited. In this study, we assess trade-offs between accuracy and runtime (total and testing) of the classifiers benchmarked in Kastrati et al.'s introduction of EEGEyeNet, as well as sLDA, logistic regression, variants of SVM, and a shallow CNN. For simple BCI tasks requiring binary classification, we find that both simple and ensemble ML algorithms, especially tree-based models, can achieve accuracies comparable to DL networks' while achieving remarkably faster total and testing runtimes. Namely, DecisionTree, RandomForest, and GradientBoost were particularly impressive, and we consider these highly efficient classifiers to be promising machine learning alternatives to slower deep learning classifiers such as CNN in binary motor imagery classification.

Keywords: Machine learning · Deep learning · Runtime · Trade-off

1 Introduction

1.1 Problem Statement

Brain-computer interfaces (BCI) represent an interdisciplinary area of expanding research that relies on neurological, behavioral, and engineering expertise to develop new technologies with an even broader-spanning range of applications [13,20,29,30,32,37], including attention and reaction time evaluation, sleep behavior, neurological disease assessment and diagnosis, communication and motor ability support, advertisement reception in marketing, virtual reality user and video gaming interfaces, and more. Development in this area is rapidly increasing, particularly in enhancing classifier accuracy [19,28,33,36].

Algorithms must not only be accurate, but also efficient with quick runtimes to remain useful for online BCI usages, such as control interfaces for paralysis patients. Trade-offs between accuracy and runtime are a common phenomenon

---

A. Tuvshinjargal and E. Kim—Contributed equally to the paper.

© The Author(s), under exclusive license to Springer Nature Switzerland AG 2022
M. Kurosu et al. (Eds.): HCII 2022, LNCS 13519, pp. 497–511, 2022.
https://doi.org/10.1007/978-3-031-17618-0_35

in the field of computer science, but particularly pose a challenge for online BCI applications, such as control interfaces for paralysis patients. Because of the real-time use cases of online BCI, rapid interpretation of novel user input is critical for BCI devices to seamlessly substitute for normal motor function in impaired users. From machine learning and deep learning perspectives [3,13,31,40], this means that there is a need in the field of BCI to evaluate the testing runtimes of classifiers as well as their accuracies.

1.2   Literature Review

Despite its practical importance, trade-offs between accuracy and testing runtime lacks formal investigation. Trade-offs between accuracy and *training* runtime [24], cost [2], and energy [5,27] are more common.

Eye tracking (ET) is commonly complemented with electroencephalography (EEG) as a non-invasive, flexible, and low-cost method of pairing brain activity with a measurable neurological behavior to develop assessments and technology. The recent assembly of the EEGEyeNet dataset [23] has helped to address the lack of an annotated, synchronized EEG-ET dataset sufficiently large enough for training accurate and generalizable machine learning and, especially, deep learning classifiers. Particularly, they found that their deep learning models performed significantly better than their traditional statistical models, with the average accuracies of their deep learning models ranging from 97.9% to 98.8%, while those of traditional models ranged from 87.7% to 92.0%.

Indeed, one of the main reasons deep learning networks have gained much popularity is their ability to discover intricate patterns and feature representations from given data to achieve high accuracy. This has inspired a growing interest among neuro-engineering researchers to apply deep learning to the development of BCI systems because it largely alleviates the need for manual feature extraction as seen in conventional BCI, which requires domain-specific expertise in the signal [39]. However, deep learning algorithms are highly resource-expensive, taking much more time and computational effort than traditional machine learning algorithms. Additionally, deep learning models require significantly greater numbers of examples in their training datasets, which is especially a challenge in the BCI domain, due to the relatively complex nature of data collection in BCI. The EEGEyeNet dataset goes a significant way to address the latter, but the cost of training deep learning models remains a limitation. Thus, it is valuable to include machine learning models in the assessment of various models' performance on the EEGEyeNet dataset and analyze their performance in comparison to that of deep learning algorithms. This paper particularly focuses on accuracy and runtime (especially testing runtime) as performance metrics in the context of their oft-inverse correlation among many popular algorithms.

The traditional models that Kastrati et al. used included KNN, GaussianNB, LinearSVC, RBF SVM, Linear Regression, Random Forest, AdaBoost, and more [29,34]. However, algorithms such as shrinkage linear discriminant analysis (sLDA) and logistic regression were not mentioned, despite findings indicating that the former is especially useful in the BCI domain [29] and the latter is extremely popular in binary classification tasks.

In addition to the fact that deep learning algorithms make it possible to achieve the already high accuracy of machine learning, it can be noted that people are working on an "inverse problem." Based on fast EEG and MEG (magnetoencephalography) data, one can try to reconstruct the actual activation of neurons in the brain, which is currently shown, for example, by the fMRI method, but with a shallow temporal resolution.

Another problem with BCI based on EEG or MEG is that the activity results in different areas of the brain for the same components differ among users. Researchers have to learn the neural network for each user and task, which complicates the work with the system and makes it more expensive. However, changes are possible here with "learning transfer," when the neural network uses data from different users/in different tasks and is further trained online; as a result, the calibration step can be skipped [41].

1.3 Purpose

In our study, we assess the performances of the sLDA and logistic regression machine learning algorithms. Additionally, in a further step of gradation, we analyze the performance of a shallow convolutional neural network (CNN) classifier, as CNNs have been reported to produce strong accuracy scores while remaining relatively conservative in resource usage, and finally, a CNN classifier with transfer learning [13]. We seek to evaluate the accuracy and runtime performance of Kastrati et al.'s machine learning benchmark models and their expensive deep learning approaches, as well as explore how various machine learning and low-level deep learning algorithms may compare in performance and resource efficiency, with the hopes of highlighting the efficiency of machine learning approaches that produce higher quality outcomes at reduced computational and time cost.

1.4 Research Questions

Two primary questions guide our experiments: 1) How do accuracy-runtime trade-offs compare across machine learning and deep learning models when applied to EEGEyeNet? and 2) What classifiers demonstrate strong performance with minimal accuracy-testing runtime trade-offs when applied to EEGEyeNet?

2 Dataset Description

The EEGEyeNet dataset includes data collected from 356 healthy adults (190 female, 166 male, ages 18–80). They were asked to perform three tasks of increasing difficulty that evaluated for saccades, fixations, and blinks by simultaneously recording EEG and ET data. 47 h of high temporal resolution recordings of such events were captured using a 128-channel EEG Geodesic Hydrocel system and a video-based ET EyeLink 1000 Plus, both with sampling rates 500 Hz. The dataset thus consists of the start and end position of saccades, the average positions of fixations, and the start and end times of each event. Preprocessing was achieved using the openly available toolbox from Pedroni et al. in both minimal and maximal fashion, the former of which includes ocular artifacts and the latter of which isolates specifically neurophysiological information from the data. To date, the EEGEyeNet dataset has the greatest number of hours of any synchronized EEG-ET dataset. For more information, see [23].

We chose to work with the Left-Right task only for our experiment as Kastrati et al. confirmed it to be the easiest task across all three datasets. We also chose to work with minimally preprocessed EEG data as it produces better performance than maximally preprocessed data [23]. The minimally preprocessed LR task dataset size is 62.6 MB.

3   Methods

In this study, we compare the performances of supervised classifiers that are tasked with binary classification in which the models must label each sample "left" or "right."

We use one of the sub-datasets generated for left-right tasks, on the basis of its relatively small size. This allows us to perform several benchmark trials for multiple classifiers in a timely manner, as well as standardize the dataset we are using as a control. The number of trials we run per classifier is five, the performance scores of which are averaged before compared across classifiers. We also measure runtime, which we define as the total training and testing time. We compare the performances of supervised classifiers tasked with binary classification. We analyze both total runtime (training + testing) and testing runtime, emphasizing the latter because online BCI usage lies beyond the training phase. Our hardware and environment specifications are in Table 1.

Table 1. Hardware specifications.

CPU	Intel(R) Core(TM) i5-8600
# of Cores	6
# of Threads	6
RAM	64 GB
GPU	Nvidia GeForce RTX 2080 Ti
OS	Ubuntu 20.04
TF version	TensorFlow 2.6.0

The classifiers include sLDA, logistic regression, and SVM. We select sLDA because it is a simple, fast machine learning classifier. sLDA does have hyperparameters, making it a highly streamlined classifier to use, and it has been used online successfully using standard computers (Lotte 2018). Furthermore, it has been reported to consistently achieve high performance scores for BCI, as well as require much less data [28]. Logistic regression is a classification model that is well-known to perform well in two-class classification tasks, and has been among the best-performing machine learning classifiers previously used in motor imagery tasks [8,21]). SVM-RBF is a classifier that is among the most popular in motor imagery BCI for its better generalization properties as well as its immunity to the curse of dimensionality [1]. A convolutional neural network (CNN) is a powerful deep learning classifier that has been a popular tool in BCI research, thanks to its ability to take advantage of hierarchical patterns in data and its subsequent success in computer vision tasks, including in motor imagery [37]).

4   Results

In Table 2, we provide both the mean accuracies and runtimes of our two machine learning algorithms along with the ones used by Kastrati et al. [23]. We ran each machine learning algorithm five times and recreated the results similar to those in [23].

Table 2. Accuracy and **total runtimes** of various ML models, ensemble methods, and CNN. Accuracies and runtimes were averaged across five trials.

Model	Accuracy	Total runtime (s)
GaussianNB [22]	87.70%	0.1
SVM [11]	89.40%	17.5
KNN [14]	90.73%	1.8
sLDA [26]	91.68%	0.4
Logit regression [12]	91.89%	3.0
LinearSVC	91.99%	7.8
tSVM	93.63%	17.53
bSVM	94.52%	37.26
SVM [11]	94.52%	18.8
CNN [25]	94.57%	161.6
DecisionTree [35]	**96.16%**	**2.4**
AdaBoost	96.27%	54.6
RandomForest [18]	**96.49%**	**8.3**
GradientBoost [15]	97.40%	107.1

Both LDA and Logistic Regression had higher accuracies than GaussianNB, RBF SVC, KNN, scoring 91.7% and 91.9%, respectively. DecisionTree appears to have the smallest accuracy-total runtime trade-off (96.16%, 2.443 s), while sLDA (91.68%, 0.411 s) and GaussianNB (87.70%, 0.055 s) demonstrate exceedingly quick total runtime but sacrifice accuracy. RandomForest (96.49%, 8.256 s) also performs well to achieve the second-highest accuracy, but more than triples DecisionTree's total runtime for its marginal edge in accuracy.

We happened to also include an untuned, RBF SVM. Interestingly, this baseline RBF SVM (henceforth, bSVM) achieved higher accuracies using default hyperparameters than Kastrati et al.'s tuned RBF SVM (simply referred to as SVM). bSVM produced a higher accuracy of 94.5% than SVM's 89.4% in the original study. However, it took over twice as long to run, taking 20.7 s compared to 9.64 s. This shows that differences in runtimes can still be noticeable despite the high performance.

All three models we introduced (sLDA, Logistic Regression, and bSVM) did not get higher scores than tree-based models, which exceeded 96%. LDA performed the LR task the fastest among the three machine learning models we introduced, finishing in 0.477 s.

Table 3. RBF SVM scores and runtimes from hyperparameter tuning. Scores and runtimes were averaged across fifteen trials. Other parameters were set to default values.

Parameters				Performance	
gamma	tol	max_iter	random_state	Score (%)	Runtime (s)
0.01	1e−5	1200	'none'	89.4	29.2
'scale'	1e−3	−1	0	94.5	66.2
'scale'	1e−5	1200	'none'	93.6	30.4
0.01	1e−3	1200	'none'	89.4	19.1
0.01	1e−5	−1	'none'	–	–
0.01	1e−5	1200	0	89.4	19.3
'scale'	1e−5	1200	0	**93.6**	**13.6**

We sought to understand better the performance differences between bSVM and the SVM provided by Kastrati et al. These differences could come down to subset choice and/or the algorithm itself. While bSVM uses default hyperparameter values aside from random_state = 0, Kastrati et al. used gamma = 0.01, tol = 1e−5, max_iter = 1200, and the default random_state = 'none'. We conducted further benchmark tests with varying combinations of hyperparameters and found that gamma was indicative of accuracy: gamma = 0.01 would result in accuracies around 89%, while gamma = 'scale' (default) would yield around 94%. We also found that random_state = 0 coincided with faster runtimes. With these observations, we designed a version of Kastrati et al.'s RBF SVM with gamma = 'scale' instead of 0.01 and random_state = 0 (henceforth, tSVM) that inherited both high accuracy and speed (Table 3). Note that the combination of tol = 1e−5 and max_iter = −1 resulted in extremely long runtimes due to the low tolerance and unlimited iterations, which rules this combination of parameters out of consideration as an efficient classifier.

It became apparent that hyperparameter optimization would be a poor allocation of time. Even if we did find some ideal set of hyperparameters, those values would only apply to the specific dataset and potentially provide little to no generalization value.

While the relatively lengthy total runtime (161.6 s in our study) is one of the greatest downsides of CNN, the testing time is what will be of greatest importance to online BCI usage. We found that CNN's testing time of 0.8807 s, while still in the lower half in testing time performance compared to the other algorithms', was considerably more attractive than its total runtime performance suggested it might be Table 2. However, the classifiers that continued to outperform CNN did so by a great margin - in the case of DecisionTree, its testing time was superior by over thousandfold.

Table 4 demonstrates that testing runtime can widely vary also, but the distribution of classifiers is distinct from that of total runtime. Noteworthy are the performances of ensemble and tree-based machine learning methods, which achieve the highest accuracies and are among the fastest in testing: GradientBoost (97.38%, 0.0073 s) and DecisionTree (96.16%, 0.0021 s) are outstanding, and RandomForest (96.46%, 0.0591 s) also displays high performance (Fig. 1). Algorithms with the best combination of accuracy and testing runtime are in the left upper corner of the graph.

Table 4. Accuracy (%) and **testing runtimes** (s) of various ML models, ensemble methods, and CNN. Accuracies and runtimes were averaged across five trials. The training and testing sets were split at an 85:15 ratio, resulting in a test set of **4820** samples.

Model	Accuracy	Testing runtime (s)
GaussianNB [22]	87.70%	0.0092
SVM [11]	89.40%	2.7444
KNN [14]	90.73%	1.8723
sLDA [26]	91.68%	0.0019
Logit regression [12]	91.89%	0.0014
bSVM	93.63%	1.8809
LinearSVC	91.98%	0.0014
tSVM	93.63%	2.7427
bSVM	94.52%	5.5802
CNN [25]	94.63%	0.8807
DecisionTree [35]	**96.16%**	**0.0021**
AdaBoost	96.27%	0.1549
RandomForest [18]	96.46%	0.0591
GradientBoost [15]	**97.38%**	**0.0073**

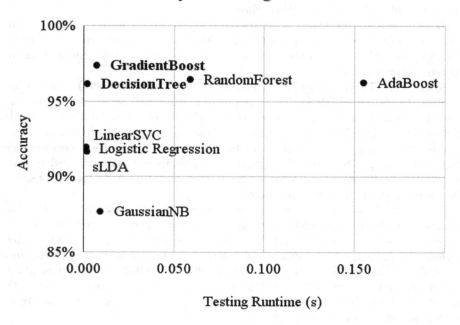

Fig. 1. Accuracy (%) and testing runtimes (s) of various ML models, ensemble methods, and CNN. Accuracies and runtimes were averaged across five trials.

We were further interested if the runtimes would change proportionally to the dataset size in a direct (as opposed to inverse) manner. Thus, we evaluated the total runtimes and testing runtimes using 50% of the original training and testing sets. The results are displayed in Table 5 and Table 6. Note when viewing increases in runtime speed due to reducing the dataset that the converse is true: doubling the size of the dataset leads the classifier's runtime speed to decrease to the observed extent.

As can be observed from Table 5 and Table 6, both the total and testing runtime speeds increased proportionally to the reduction of the dataset's size for most of the algorithms. Notably, while most other classifiers' runtime speeds were about 100% faster, KNN's and bSVM's testing runtime speeds increased dramatically, exhibiting increases of 343% and 341%, respectively.

5   Discussion

5.1   Trade-offs of Baseline ML Algorithms

As can be observed in Table 2, there commonly exists a trade-off between accuracy and total runtime. This is particularly evident across groups of classifiers: simple machine learning models demonstrate the fastest total runtimes at the expense of accuracy, ensemble methods balance both, and DL networks exhibit the highest accuracy at the expense of efficient total runtime. Classifiers that appear to have the best accuracy-total runtime trade-offs on binary classification for the LR task include LDA and DecisionTree.

Table 5. Accuracy and **total runtimes** of various ML models, ensemble methods, and CNN using 50% of the dataset. Accuracies and runtimes were averaged across five trials.

Model	Accuracy	Total runtime (s)	% Increase in speed
GaussianNB [22]	85.85%	0.02	137%
SVM [11]	87.24%	8.5891	104%
KNN [14]	88.45%	0.44	308%
sLDA [26]	88.54%	0.21	92%
LinearSVC	89.26%	3.22	142%
tSVM	91.41%	7.63	130%
bSVM	91.41%	9.14	308%
CNN [25]	91.50%	76.21	112%
DecisionTree [35]	94.94%	1.16	111%
AdaBoost	95.17%	25.99	110%
RandomForest [18]	95.74%	3.88	113%
GradientBoost [15]	96.10%	49.58	116%

5.2   Trade-offs of a Tuned SVM

Tuning the hyperparameters of Kastrati et al.'s RBF SVC allowed us to uncover a set of hyperparameters that achieve both higher accuracy and faster runtimes, the former of which also exceeds those of all other simple machine learning models tested (apart from DecisionTree). However, when comparing Kastrati et al.'s RBF SVC and our improved classifier tSVM, it is unclear how much of this enhanced performance can be attributed to the model's new hyperparameters rather than the smaller size of our dataset. During testing, we also noted a great deal of instability in the runtimes from test session to test session.

5.3   Trade-offs of DL Algorithms

CNN was only able to reach the accuracy of 94.1%, almost similar to the accuracy of bSVM, although it took approximately 50 times more time to train. It could have been that the LR dataset was too small to train the CNN network resulting in underfitting. CNN displayed a classic accuracy-runtime trade-off curve with diminishing returns along the number of epochs: more epochs meant higher

Table 6. Accuracy (%) and **testing runtimes** (s) of various ML models, ensemble methods, and CNN using 50% of the dataset. Accuracies and runtimes were averaged across five trials. The training and testing sets were split at an 85:15 ratio **of 50% of the total dataset**, resulting in a test set of **2410** samples.

Model	Accuracy	Testing runtime (s)	% Increase in speed
GaussianNB [22]	85.85%	0.0037	147%
SVM [11]	87.24%	1.2848	114%
KNN [14]	88.45%	0.4228	343%
sLDA [26]	88.54%	0.0090	−79%
LinearSVC	89.26%	0.0009	64%
CNN [25]	91.26%	0.5099	73%
tSVM	91.41%	1.1300	143%
bSVM	91.41%	1.2639	341%
DecisionTree [35]	94.92%	0.0011	93%
AdaBoost	95.17%	0.0682	127%
RandomForest [18]	95.73%	0.0377	57%
GradientBoost [15]	96.09%	0.0035	108%

accuracy, but also slower total runtime, with smaller increases to accuracy as epochs increase. However, in the context of online BCI usage, a classifier would not be expected to be constantly retraining. Rather, it would be constantly fed novel data to classify (e.g., as a paralysis patient equipped with a BCI device looks left and right), which is more akin to testing. CNN's test-time of 2.6199 s is still unimpressive compared to DecisionTree's 0.0021 s and GradientBoost's 0.0069 s (Table 4). Especially considering the use cases of online BCI to substitute and/or complement neuronal communication for motor function, the classifier used must be exceedingly quick. For example, it takes 0.009 s for a signal to travel from the brain to the hand [1]. Thus, a successful application of BCI to stand in for this rapid process should perform at a similar time scale. Although CNN's high accuracy of 98.75% means CNN may remain in the picture for the time being, DecisionTree and GradientBoost aren't far behind (96.16% and 97.36% respectively) and these results indicate that they may be more useful classifiers than CNN to apply to this problem context.

5.4   Testing Runtime and Tree-Based Models

Testing runtime is important to online BCI usage because after training, the classifier will face novel inputs in regular usage (e.g., in commercial products). Despite their longer total runtimes (evidently due to longer training runtimes), ensembles are more comparable to simple ML models in testing runtime. Our results suggest that tree-based classifiers, ensembles and simple tree methods alike, are highly accurate and quick, and may be a promising area of future research to develop efficient classifiers. Particularly, evaluating whether their level of performance withstands more complex tasks may be interesting.

5.5 Time Complexity of ML Algorithms

A crucial concept that stands at the center of our discussion of total and testing runtimes is the concept of computational complexity, often discussed in terms of Big O. Table 7 shows the various computational complexities of the algorithms used in this paper. Note that Table 7 lacks entries for CNN and sLDA due to the lack of academic documentation online on their computational complexities.

Table 7. Time complexity of ML algorithms in Big O notation. n is the number of examples, k is the number of features, c is the number of classes, d is the tree depth, $m_{support\ vectors}$ is the number of support vectors, and M is the number of iterations or base estimators

Model	Training time complexity	Testing time complexity
GaussianNB [4, 16]	$O(kn)$	$O(cn)$
KNN [14]	$O(1)$	$O(kn)$
Logit Regression [7]	$O(kn)$	$O(k)$
LinearSVC	$O(n)$	?
SVM [10]	$O(kn^2)$ to $O(kn^3)$	$O(km_{support\ vectors})$
DecisionTree [38]	$O(kn \log_2 n)$	$O(\log n)$
	Worst case: $O(dkn)$	Worst case: $O(d)$
AdaBoost [17]	$O(Mdkn \log n)$	$O(Mk)$
RandomForest [6]	$O(Mkn \log n)$	$O(Mk)$
GradientBoost [9]	$O(Mdn \log n)$	$O(Md)$

While our study uses a benchmarking approach to assess the empirical runtimes of the classifiers, a more complete and rigorous evaluation necessitates consideration of the scalability of classifiers' runtime performance. That is, while certain classifiers may outperform others and achieve high accuracy and quick total and/or testing runtimes with a given dataset, their performance may be overtaken by other classifiers when either more complex or more simple data is inputted. In the endeavor to identify classifiers that will perform highly in a given use case, it is important to consider the data that will be supplied.

Here, we can corroborate the results of our empirical total and testing runtime observations. KNN's total runtime and testing runtime is virtually identical (Table 5, Table 6) and this is evidently because training time is constant, meaning that the total runtime is theoretically equal to the testing time. Furthermore, the drastic increase in testing runtime speed compared to other algorithms' can be explained by the fact that KNN's testing time correlates heavily with the number of examples, whereas other algorithms' testing runtimes are associated with other factors such as the number of features of the data or the number of base estimators. GradientBoost's outstanding testing time compared to other boosting methods like AdaBoost may have to do with the fact that Gradient-Boost's testing time complexity correlates with the depth of its trees rather than the number of features.

Referring to the time complexities of classifiers can be a useful method of identifying classifiers that may be promising or less promising for future use cases. For example, AdaBoost's testing time complexity is associated with the number of features of the input data - this could suggest that AdaBoost may be a poorer candidate classifier in the future as input data complexity increases, unless methods of dimensionality reduction are considered as well.

5.6   Limitations and Future Directions

Crucially, this dataset is preprocessed and Hilbert-transformed, which 1) deprives DL methods of information to learn on and results in lower accuracies and 2) means that these runtimes do not represent the entire signal interpretation process in online BCI usage, which begins with raw input data. A more holistic approach we propose for the future might compare preprocessing runtime + ML testing runtime vs. DL testing runtime using raw data. Another aspect to consider for online BCI is that the input data is a stream of examples rather than a dataset, so Big O considerations have to do with the complexity/resolution of the input data (e.g., number of electrodes) rather than the size of datasets. Thus, measuring how test (and preprocessing) runtime scales alongside raw data complexity may be an important consideration for future analyses. Contextualizing testing runtimes in neurophysiology would also better-inform future work on what constitutes "good" runtime.

In the future, GridSearchCV can be used to attempt more complex hyperparameter configurations and uncover the best hyperparameters. A larger dataset can be used to test whether the performance optimizations continue to apply beyond small datasets. Finally, a novel implementation of adaptive transfer learning methods upon CNN represents an opportunity to develop a classifier that is exceedingly accurate, faster, and need not rely on a large, labeled dataset.

6   Conclusion

For simple BCI tasks such as LR, traditional machine learning algorithms can achieve an accuracy as high as DL networks. When it comes to trade-offs, not only can machine learning models produce accuracies as high as simple DL models can, but also they take a significantly shorter time to train. Namely, DecisionTree, RandomForest, and GradientBoost were particularly impressive and we consider these far more efficient than CNN in binary motor imagery classification by virtue of their relatively small accuracy-runtime trade-offs. Hyperparameter tuning for machine learning models can further cut down a considerable amount of runtime as well as significantly improve their performance.

References

1. Aggarwal, S., Chugh, N.: Signal processing techniques for motor imagery brain computer interface: a review. Array **1–2**, 100003 (2019). https://doi.org/10.1016/j.array.2019.100003
2. Ahmad, Z., Shahid Khan, A., Wai Shiang, C., Abdullah, J., Ahmad, F.: Network intrusion detection system: a systematic study of machine learning and deep learning approaches. Trans. Emerg. Telecommun. Technol. **32**(1), e4150 (2021). https://doi.org/10.1002/ett.4150, https://onlinelibrary.wiley.com/doi/abs/10.1002/ett.4150
3. Bashivan, P., Rish, I., Yeasin, M., Codella, N.: Learning representations from EEG with deep recurrent-convolutional neural networks. arXiv preprint arXiv:1511.06448 (2015)
4. Bermejo, P., Gámez, J.A., Puerta, J.M.: Speeding up incremental wrapper feature subset selection with Naive Bayes classifier. Knowl.-Based Syst. **55**, 140–147 (2014)
5. Brownlee, A.E., Adair, J., Haraldsson, S.O., Jabbo, J.: Exploring the accuracy - energy trade-off in machine learning. In: 2021 IEEE/ACM International Workshop on Genetic Improvement (GI), pp. 11–18, May 2021. https://doi.org/10.1109/GI52543.2021.00011
6. Buczak, A.L., Guven, E.: A survey of data mining and machine learning methods for cyber security intrusion detection. IEEE Commun. Surv. Tutorials **18**(2), 1153–1176 (2015)
7. Bulso, N., Marsili, M., Roudi, Y.: On the complexity of logistic regression models. Neural Comput. **31**(8), 1592–1623 (2019)
8. Camacho, J., Manian, V.: Real-time single channel EEG motor imagery based brain computer interface, pp. 1–6 (07 2016). https://doi.org/10.1109/WAC.2016.7582973
9. Chen, T., Guestrin, C.: XGBoost: a scalable tree boosting system. In: Proceedings of the 22nd ACM SIGKDD International Conference on Knowledge Discovery and Data Mining, pp. 785–794 (2016)
10. Claesen, M., De Smet, F., Suykens, J.A., De Moor, B.: Fast prediction with SVM models containing RBF Kernels. arXiv preprint arXiv:1403.0736 (2014)
11. Cortes, C., Vapnik, V.: Support-vector networks. In: Machine Learning, pp. 273–297 (1995)
12. Cox, D.: The regression analysis of binary sequences, vol. Series B, pp. 20, 215–242 (1958)
13. Craik, A., He, Y., Contreras-Vidal, J.L.: Deep learning for electroencephalogram (EEG) classification tasks: a review. J. Neural Eng. **16**(3), 031001 (2019). https://doi.org/10.1088/1741-2552/ab0ab5
14. Fix, E., Hodges, J.L.: Discriminatory analysis. Nonparametric discrimination: consistency properties. Int. Stat. Rev./Revue Internationale de Statistique **57**(3), 238–247 (1989)
15. Friedman, J.: Greedy function approximation: a gradient boosting machine. Ann. Stat. **29**, 1189–1232 (2000). https://doi.org/10.1214/aos/1013203451
16. Hand, D.J., Yu, K.: Idiot's Bayes-not so stupid after all? Int. Stat. Rev. **69**(3), 385–398 (2001)
17. Hastie, T., Rosset, S., Zhu, J., Zou, H.: Multi-class adaboost. Stat. Interface **2**(3), 349–360 (2009)
18. Ho, T.: Random decision forests, vol. 1, pp. 278–282, September 1995. https://doi.org/10.1109/ICDAR.1995.598994

19. Hosseini, M.P., Hosseini, A., Ahi, K.: A review on machine learning for EEG signal processing in bioengineering. IEEE Rev. Biomed. Eng. **14**, 204–218 (2020)
20. Ienca, M., Haselager, P., Emanuel, E.J.: Brain leaks and consumer neurotechnology. Nat. Biotechnol. **36**(9), 805–810 (2018)
21. Isa, N., Amir, A., Ilyas, M., Razalli, M.: Motor imagery classification in brain computer interface (BCI) based on EEG signal by using machine learning technique. Bull. Electr. Eng. Inform. **8**, 269–275 (2019). https://doi.org/10.11591/eei.v8i1.1402
22. John, G.H., Langley, P.: Estimating continuous distributions in Bayesian classifiers. arXiv preprint arXiv:1302.4964 (2013)
23. Kastrati, A., et al.: EEGEyenet: a simultaneous electroencephalography and eye-tracking dataset and benchmark for eye movement prediction. In: Thirty-Fifth Conference on Neural Information Processing Systems Datasets and Benchmarks Track (Round 1) (2021). https://openreview.net/forum?id=Nc2uduhU9qa
24. Kulyukin, V., Mukherjee, S., Amlathe, P.: Toward audio beehive monitoring: deep learning vs. standard machine learning in classifying beehive audio samples. Appl. Sci. **8**(9), 1573 (2018). https://doi.org/10.3390/app8091573, https://www.mdpi.com/2076-3417/8/9/1573
25. LeCun, Y., Bottou, L., Bengio, Y., Haffner, P.: Gradient-based learning applied to document recognition. Proc. IEEE **86**(11), 2278–2324 (1998)
26. Ledoit, O., Wolf, M.: A well-conditioned estimator for large-dimensional covariance matrices. J. Multivar. Anal. **88**(2), 365–411 (2004)
27. León, J., et al.: Deep learning for EEG-based motor imagery classification: accuracy-cost trade-off. PLOS ONE **15**(6), 1–30 (2020). https://doi.org/10.1371/journal.pone.0234178
28. Lotte, F.: Signal processing approaches to minimize or suppress calibration time in oscillatory activity-based brain-computer interfaces. Proc. IEEE **103**(6), 871–890 (2015). https://doi.org/10.1109/JPROC.2015.2404941
29. Lotte, F., et al.: A review of classification algorithms for EEG-based brain-computer interfaces: a 10 year update. J. Neural Eng. **15**(3), 031005 (2018). https://doi.org/10.1088/1741-2552/aab2f2
30. Qu, X., Hall, M., Sun, Y., Sekuler, R., Hickey, T.J.: A personalized reading coach using wearable EEG sensors-a pilot study of brainwave learning analytics. In: CSEDU (2), pp. 501–507 (2018)
31. Qu, X., Liu, P., Li, Z., Hickey, T.: Multi-class time continuity voting for EEG classification. In: Frasson, C., Bamidis, P., Vlamos, P. (eds.) BFAL 2020. LNCS (LNAI), vol. 12462, pp. 24–33. Springer, Cham (2020). https://doi.org/10.1007/978-3-030-60735-7_3
32. Qu, X., Liukasemsarn, S., Tu, J., Higgins, A., Hickey, T.J., Hall, M.H.: Identifying clinically and functionally distinct groups among healthy controls and first episode psychosis patients by clustering on EEG patterns. Front. Psychiatry **11**, 541659 (2020)
33. Qu, X., Mei, Q., Liu, P., Hickey, T.: Using EEG to distinguish between writing and typing for the same cognitive task. In: Frasson, C., Bamidis, P., Vlamos, P. (eds.) BFAL 2020. LNCS (LNAI), vol. 12462, pp. 66–74. Springer, Cham (2020). https://doi.org/10.1007/978-3-030-60735-7_7
34. Qu, X., Sun, Y., Sekuler, R., Hickey, T.: EEG markers of stem learning. In: 2018 IEEE Frontiers in Education Conference (FIE), pp. 1–9. IEEE (2018)
35. Quinlan, J.R.: Induction of decision trees. Mach. Learn. **1**, 81–106 (1986)
36. Roc, A., et al.: A review of user training methods in brain computer interfaces based on mental tasks. J. Neural Eng. **18**, 011002 (2020)

37. Roy, Y., Banville, H., Albuquerque, I., Gramfort, A., Falk, T.H., Faubert, J.: Deep learning-based electroencephalography analysis: a systematic review. J. Neural Eng. **16**(5), 051001 (2019)
38. Sani, H.M., Lei, C., Neagu, D.: Computational complexity analysis of decision tree algorithms. In: Bramer, M., Petridis, M. (eds.) SGAI 2018. LNCS (LNAI), vol. 11311, pp. 191–197. Springer, Cham (2018). https://doi.org/10.1007/978-3-030-04191-5_17
39. Zhang, K., Robinson, N., Lee, S.W., Guan, C.: Adaptive transfer learning for EEG motor imagery classification with deep convolutional neural network. Neural Netw. **136**, 1–10 (2020). https://doi.org/10.1016/j.neunet.2020.12.013
40. Zhang, X., Yao, L., Wang, X., Monaghan, J.J., Mcalpine, D., Zhang, Y.: A survey on deep learning-based non-invasive brain signals: recent advances and new frontiers. J. Neural Eng. **18**, 031002 (2020)
41. Zubarev, I., Zetter, R., Halme, H.L., Parkkonen, L.: Robust and highly adaptable brain-computer interface with convolutional net architecture based on a generative model of neuromagnetic measurements, May 2018

CNN with Self-attention in EEG Classification

Xuduo Wang and Ziji Wang[✉]

Swarthmore College, Swarthmore, PA 19081, USA
{xwang5,zwang6}@swarthmore.edu

Abstract. In this paper, we explored the implementation of transformer-based classifiers in electroencephalogram (EEG) classification tasks. We used a segmented portion of a newly-developed rich EEG dataset, EEGEyeNet, and replicated the benchmark deep learning method results that the dataset developers performed. We then combined the transformer-based self-attention mechanism and Convolutional Neural Network (CNN), and proposed a deep learning model that demonstrates both higher classification performance and greater interpretability of results.

Keywords: Brain-computer interface (BCI) · EEG · Deep learning · CNN · Transformer · Attention mechanism · Multi-head self-attention

1 Introduction

1.1 Problem Statement

The choice of brain-computer interface (BCI) models has long been an extensive topic. The rapid development in the fields of deep learning has produced a wide variety of new tools for researchers to work on [6,20,28,31]. The current state-of-the-art research [7,15,24,26,36,37,40] report high performances in electroencephalography (EEG) classification. However, as a new type of architecture that has proven to be highly effective on a wide range of tasks, including text processing and image classification as the two best representatives, [2,3,8,12,38] transformers-based models have not been fully explored in the field of EEG classification. Compared to traditional deep learning models, transformer-based models have the addition of a multi-head self-attention mechanism to utilize the most relevant information in the input sequence flexibly with parallel computing capacities, which is one of the primary reasons behind its success [4,17,19].

1.2 Purpose of Study

We are particularly interested in how the following two instances from the two fields might work together: CNN with an additional transformers-based self-attention layer, and large EEG datasets such as the EEGEyeNet dataset. We

---

X. Wang and Z. Wang—Contributed equally to this work.

M. Kurosu et al. (Eds.): HCII 2022, LNCS 13519, pp. 512–526, 2022.
https://doi.org/10.1007/978-3-031-17618-0_36

aim to bring these two together in an attempt to study both of them simulta-neously: namely, we would like to know which aspects of them work well with the other field, and which do not. This information will allow us to then aug-ment them to better work with each other, and either produce results that surpass the current state-of-the-art procedures or produce a list of aspects that should be avoided in choosing future datasets and classifiers to work together with. We assessed that the self-attention mechanism (Fig. 1) [41] could prove useful for Electroencephalography (EEG) data, which usually contains multiple cross-spatial relationships within the data entries themselves. Additionally, the absence of transformer-based models in EEG leaves the possibility of improving upon the current state-of-the-art results [6, 20, 31]. In our research, we attempt to combine CNN [1, 16] and self-attention modules [5, 17, 18, 32, 33], experimenting on a rich novel EEG dataset-EEGEyeNet [11].

1.3 Research Questions

We will first start by directly applying the CNN model with a self-attention layer to the EEGEyeNet dataset. Then we will compare the results with the current state-of-the-art models on EEGEyeNet. We aim at discussing several questions targeted at the underlying features, such as: how does the self-attention mecha-nism work in BCI, and how does it improve upon the CNN model? Additionally, how much does self-attention improve the base CNN model, and what specific parts does it improve? What theoretical differences, if any, can be found between self-attention and the CNN model? In particular, we also plan to answer the ques-tion "how can we integrate and tune a self-attention module with a traditional CNN network in EEG classification, so that the model inherits the advantages of both self-attention and CNN?"

2   Dataset

The EEGEyeNet dataset by Kastrati et al. consists of correspondence of high-density EEG data and eye movement data from 356 healthy individuals between the age of 18 and 80 (Fig. 2). The high-density EEG data were recorded at a sam-pling rate 500 Hz, with midline central recording reference, using a 128-channel EEG Geodesic Hydrocel system. The raw data is then preprocessed to reduce environmental factor noise using an open toolbox from Pedroni et al. [23]. Two different standards, minimally and maximally, are used, the difference between which is mainly illustrated by how many artifacts are removed. Annotations in the form of the event start and end time, saccade position, and fixation position are provided for each of the featured paradigms. Three paradigms are present in the dataset, each designed to cover a different range of information: pro and anti-saccade, large grid, and visual paradigm search. The initially proposed bench-mark, utilizing exclusively the minimally preprocessed version of the dataset, is divided into three tasks in increasing order of difficulty: left-right direction of eye movement, angle and amplitude of saccade, and absolute position of gaze.

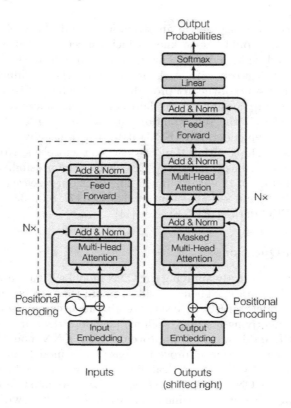

Fig. 1. Attention module in the transformer architecture from [38]

The first task is performed on the saccade paradigm while the latter two are performed on the large grid paradigm.

For our research, we replicated the deep learning benchmark models provided by Kastrati et al. and used the minimally processed left-right classification data. We segmented a random portion of the raw data, amounting to a size of 2000 data entries, to serve as training sets for deep learning models (Fig. 3).

3   Method

3.1   Rationale

CNN is a long-standing neural network algorithm [1,16] that has proven to be a good base for multiple state-of-the-art models in EEG classification research [6,11,11,20,31]. Additionally, CNN has been shown to be compatible with self-attention modules. Li et al. successfully implemented a self-attention-augmented CNN that is capable of processing imagery-related tasks [18]. Another approach that attracted our interests was developed in Cordonnier et al.'s paper [5], which

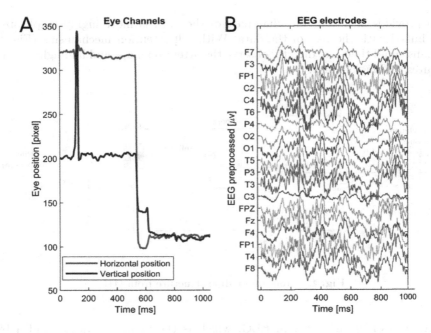

Fig. 2. Gaze data and EEG signal data from [11]

	#Samples			
	Total	Train	Validation	Test
EEGEyeNet Full Dataset	30,842	21,042	4,980	4,820
Segmented Dataset	2,000	1,400	300	300

Fig. 3. Comparison between the segmented data and the original data

replaced the convolutional layer with a multi-head self-attention layer. What Cordonnier et al.'s paper shows us is that the convolution layer of a standard CNN model can be modified and experimented on, while having a safe fallback to the baseline CNN results such that the model will be performing sufficiently well already. However, one drawback of CNN models is the uninterpretability of the feature maps. Humans are unable to directly extract useful information from the feature maps that the CNN models produce. The solution to the uninterpretability problem came out in 2014, when Bahdanau et al. [2] came up with the self-attention mechanism. The self-attention mechanism allows the input data entries to interact with each other and find out who which part of the data they should pay more attention to. The outputs are the aggregates of these matrix interactions and attention scores on an attention map. The residual attention map provides intuitions on what part of the data is most highly emphasized and linked with the rest of the data. With self-attention mechanisms (Fig. 4), humans could therefore directly observe the attention maps and highlight certain features within the data.

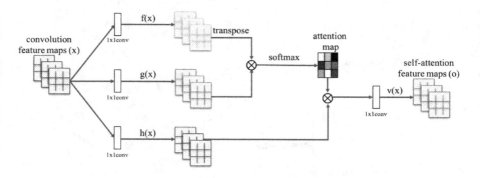

Fig. 4. Attention module structure from [41]

Apart from using CNN in EEG, which is the main innovation and a big collaboration between two novel but under-appreciated fields of study, we also introduce additional innovation here by testing different self-attention modules with or without the convolution layer [4,17,19]. We think that this can tell us what sort of additional information exists in an EEG dataset to be captured beyond the reach of traditional CNN models, and what mechanisms are best suited for capturing them. The interpretability feature is well-captured in the self-attention feature map. This has the potential to not only select the best combination from the models we put to test, but also point out the direction we should optimize the algorithms for EEG in for the greatest improvement in accuracy.

3.2 Implementation

We start with a simple CNN model taken from the original dataset paper [11] and modified it with a series of different layers. The base structure of the model includes two layers of padding, a main pipeline of convolution-batch normalization-pooling, and an activation function layer before pooling takes place. For the attention layer, we choose a gold standard self-attention layer which is also used in the tried-and-successful transformers models [38]. We also attempt to fit several other-purpose attention layers such as ones utilized for image and text classification. For our own baseline that we will use for comparison and further tuning, we simply add the transformer self-attention layer immediately after the convolution layer, as indicated by the orange box in Fig. 3, which is a tried and proven method for integrating the two layers [5]. We then test the results on a segmented dataset of size 2,000 randomly sampled from the full EEGEyeNet dataset, roughly 1/15 of the original size, a choice made due to computation power limitations. The segmented dataset was manually inspected to assure a not overly skewed representation of the original full dataset.

We named our base model CNtention (Fig. 3), a combination of CNN and self-attention. The CNN part of the model used a simple 1-dimensional convolution layer with corresponding 1-dimensional batch normalization and ReLU activation, as well as a MaxPooling layer. Two additional padding modules were also included such that the tensor shapes stay constant when passing through the model. For self-attention, we augmented the model with a 4-head self-attention layer, which was first introduced by Vaswani et al. [38], which was placed directly after the convolution layer due to both input dimension requirements and prior success in [3] using this layout. We also replicated the benchmark deep learning models on the segmented dataset to serve as the control group. For evaluation purposes, we primarily focused on the accuracy of classification as the main performance indicator, but we also included other measures such as precision, recall, and F-score for more in-depth analyses.

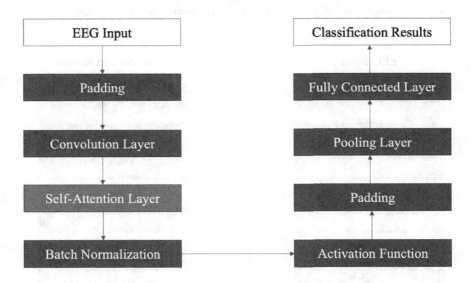

Fig. 5. Proposed CNtention model structure

3.3   Innovation

Apart from using self-attention in EEG, which is the main innovation of our study and a big collaboration between two novel but under-appreciated fields of research, we also tested different variations of the CNtention model on the segmented dataset.

Our primary innovation in varying the base model was testing the impact of the number of self-attention layers on the classification performance. Liu et al. introduced a transformer architecture with two attention layers that aggregate global temporal features with time-series data, extracting high-level temporal features of the EEG signals in the time domain [19]. This brings the possibility that additional self-attention layers in the model, while not able to be clearly defined as in Liu et al.'s paper, could capture additional alternative information to further improve performance. We mimicked their structure and included an extra self-attention layer into CNtention (Fig. 6). We further included a third attention layer into the model and compared the performance of the three variations (Fig. 7).

We venture further from the base CNtention model by varying the layout and individual layers. We tried varying the attention layer performance by changing the number of heads in the attention layer, which is speculated to form a bell curve related to the dataset shape [22, 32]. We also tried a few more conventional methods, namely trying different methods for the pooling and activation function layers, such as switching to average pooling and LP pooling as alternative pooling layers and Sigmoid and SoftMax as alternative activation functions.

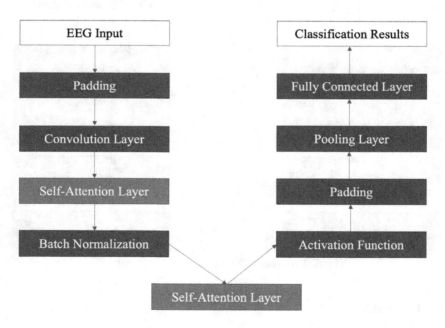

Fig. 6. Proposed 2-layer CNtention model structure

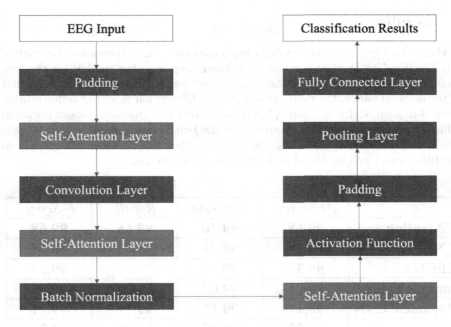

Fig. 7. Proposed 3-layer CNtention model structure

3.4 Connection

We connect our approach to Transformers, a highly rated model collection that excels at NLP and image classification tasks [2,3,8,12,38]. The most notable innovation of Transformers compared to prior methods in the respective fields is the addition of self-attention, which allows for pattern-fitting and filtering across large spatial gaps in the input data. We think that EEG data, which is a type of time-series data [10,21,25], share the same characteristics in terms of patterns with NLP and image classification, and that we could potentially simulate the success of transformers by implementing the same self-attention modules but for EEG baseline models [4,13,17,30,35]. To incorporate the ideals, we use a self-attention layer that is also found in transformers models [38].

We also connect our approach to several successful applications and evaluations of attention layers on EEG data in the BCI domain [8,9,19,32]. Notably none of the approaches make use of a 1-dimensional convolution layer, which we speculate to be due to the dataset they use not performing exceptionally well with it. In our case, the 1-dimensional convolution layer on itself already is gold standard and produces a higher accuracy and f1 score then the better results from among those papers, therefore it is a challenge both in connecting for the first time 1-dimensional convolution and attention, and also in connecting high-performing traditional methods with self-attention.

4   Results

In the control group, we successfully replicated the results shown for the original full EEGEyeNet Dataset for the traditional deep learning models on the segmented dataset. As shown in the table below, our accuracy results mimic that of the original paper. We then ran our default CNtention model (1 self-attention layer, 4-headed, ReLU activated, MaxPooled) on the segmented dataset obtained a higher performance result compared to the benchmark models with a 99.68% prediction accuracy (Fig. 8). The accuracy results for the benchmark models on the full dataset can be found in Table 4 in the original paper.

	Accuracy	*Precision*	*Recall*	*F-Score*
CNtention	**99.68**	**99.70**	**99.66**	**99.68**
CNN	98.74	98.73	98.73	98.73
EEGNet	99.37	99.37	99.37	99.37
InceptionTime	99.05	99.07	99.05	99.05
Pyramidal CNN	99.11	99.13	99.11	99.11
Xception	99.37	99.37	99.37	99.37

Fig. 8. Deep learning models classification performance comparison

Then we ran the CNtention models with different numbers of self-attention layers and observed a slight decrease of classification accuracy as we included more self-attention layers (Fig. 9).

	Baseline CNN	*1 Attention Layer*	*2 Attention Layers*	*3 Attention Layers*
Accuracy	98.74	99.68	99.05	98.44

Fig. 9. Number of self-attention layers vs CNtention performance

We then ran the CNtention models with different numbers of self-attention heads and observed almost no difference in the performance as number of heads vary (Fig. 10).

Results from running the CNtention models with 3 different pooling and 3 different activation layers suggest divergent influence on the classification accuracy. However, with the different pooling layers (Fig. 11) and activation functions (Fig. 12) we used, all of them demonstrated at least as good performances as the plain CNN model.

	2-Head	*4-Head*	*5-Head*	*10-Head*
Accuracy	99.37	99.68	99.68	99.68

Fig. 10. Number of attention heads vs CNtention performance

	Accuracy	*Precision*	*Recall*	*F-Score*
MaxPooling	**99.68**	**99.70**	**99.66**	**99.68**
AvgPooling	99.05	99.10	99.13	99.11
LPPooling	99.26	99.26	99.27	99.26

Fig. 11. Different pooling methods vs CNtention performance

5   Discussion and Future Work

CNN and attention related deep learning approach has demonstrated great potential in computer vision, medical imaging and brain-computer interfaces [6,27,31,42,43].

5.1   Comparison with Benchmarks

In our research, we created a model combining CNN with self-attention mechanism and applied it to EEG classification tasks. We also replicated the benchmark presented by the EEGEyeNet dataset developers on traditional deep learning models, on the segmented minimally processed dataset. We observe in general an extremely high classification accuracy here for all models. We originally speculated this to be a case of overfitting, but after we varied the parameters and tested more models, we come to the conclusion that it is because of the excellent quality of the original dataset rather than a certain flaw: the high base quality of the dataset allows even the simplest models to achieve passable results, and almost any neural network model performs very well without further optimization due to the input being well-formed. However, CNtention still demonstrates extremely strong performances, boasting a full one percent more accuracy compared to the fine-tuned plain CNN model, which translates to roughly 4 more correctly classified examples out of 300 to test, and has additional advantages, namely an increase in the interpretability of the results [9,14,29,39]. For traditional CNN models, humans are unable to extract usable information directly out of the feature maps. With self-attention mechanisms, however, we could therefore observe the attention maps produced and highlight certain features within the data. Researchers in fields other than brain-computer interface, such as pedestrian detection [44], speech enhancement [22], and music theme classification [34], have taken advantage of the interpretability of the attention feature map and improved performance of the traditional CNN model.

	Accuracy	*Precision*	*Recall*	*F-Score*
ReLU	**99.68**	**99.70**	**99.66**	**99.68**
Sigmoid	99.21	99.11	99.15	99.13
SoftMax	98.84	98.88	98.81	98.84

Fig. 12. Different activation methods vs CNtention performance

5.2   Robustness Check

The results from CNtention variants with different numbers of self-attention layers demonstrate the negative relationship between the number of layers and classification accuracy. This might be due to the randomness of our results caused by the lack of 5-fold replication, as well as the lack of fine-tuning for the self-attention layer. But it could also be that we do not have strong support for rationalizing the information gained by those additional layers as relevant, therefore they might act as noise and negatively impact the information extraction. In addition, we found out that the number of heads, the use of different activation functions, and pooling layers have minimum effect on the classification accuracy. We speculate the result to be primarily because of the baseline CNtention model being so powerful that only 1 single example within the test set was misclassified, leaving little wiggle room.

In the current EEG classification research field, transformers-based models are largely absent from the state-of-the-art research, as Craik et al. identified (Fig. 13). Our results have shown the promising future of the combination of transformer-based self-attention layers and other traditional architectures, demonstrated by its ability to raise already high classification accuracies significantly and interpretability of results.

5.3   Future Work

For our future work, we plan to run our default CNtention model and its variants on the entire EEGEyeNet dataset (over 30,000 data entries) and potentially other similar BCI-related datasets for more robust and generalizable results. Future work in this field might also include applying transformer-based multi-headed self-attention modules to other existing traditional deep learning architectures, such as EEGNet-based CNNs, DBNs, and MLPs in order to test the versatility of such self-attention modules.

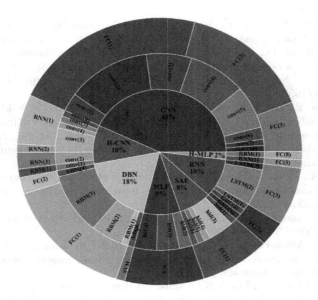

Fig. 13. Deep learning architectures across 90 studies in EEG classification from [6]

6   Conclusion

In our research, we tested a novel architecture called CNtention, a CNN model combined with an additional transformer-based self-attention module on a segmented section of the EEGEyeNet dataset. We achieved high classification results that outperformed the state-of-the-art deep learning models. We reasoned that a CNN model with a self-attention module would work well in EEG classification tasks and has the advantage of capturing additional features in the data. We aim to further validate our conclusions after solving the potential over-optimizing issue and applying our model to other EEG-related datasets.

References

1. Amin, S.U., Alsulaiman, M., Muhammad, G., Mekhtiche, M.A., Hossain, M.S.: Deep learning for EEG motor imagery classification based on multi-layer CNNs feature fusion. Futur. Gener. Comput. Syst. **101**, 542–554 (2019)
2. Bahdanau, D., Cho, K., Bengio, Y.: Neural machine translation by jointly learning to align and translate. arXiv preprint arXiv:1409.0473 (2014)
3. Chung, J., Cho, K., Bengio, Y.: A character-level decoder without explicit segmentation for neural machine translation. arXiv preprint arXiv:1603.06147 (2016)
4. Cisotto, G., Zanga, A., Chlebus, J., Zoppis, I., Manzoni, S., Markowska-Kaczmar, U.: Comparison of attention-based deep learning models for EEG classification. arXiv preprint arXiv:2012.01074 (2020)
5. Cordonnier, J.B., Loukas, A., Jaggi, M.: On the relationship between self-attention and convolutional layers. arXiv preprint arXiv:1911.03584 (2019)

6. Craik, A., He, Y., Contreras-Vidal, J.L.: Deep learning for electroencephalogram (EEG) classification tasks: a review. J. Neural Eng. **16**(3), 031001 (2019)
7. Dai, M., Zheng, D., Na, R., Wang, S., Zhang, S.: EEG classification of motor imagery using a novel deep learning framework. Sensors **19**(3), 551 (2019)
8. Hochreiter, S., Schmidhuber, J.: Long short-term memory. Neural Comput. **9**(8), 1735–1780 (1997)
9. Hu, H., Liu, Y., Yue, K.: Evaluating 3D visual fatigue induced by VR headset using EEG and self-attention CNN. In: 2022 IEEE Conference on Virtual Reality and 3D User Interfaces Abstracts and Workshops (VRW), pp. 784–785. IEEE (2022)
10. Ienca, M., Haselager, P., Emanuel, E.J.: Brain leaks and consumer neurotechnology. Nat. Biotechnol. **36**(9), 805–810 (2018)
11. Kastrati, A., et al.: EEGEyeNet: a simultaneous electroencephalography and eye-tracking dataset and benchmark for eye movement prediction. arXiv preprint arXiv:2111.05100 (2021)
12. Kim, Y., Denton, C., Hoang, L., Rush, A.M.: Structured attention networks. arXiv preprint arXiv:1702.00887 (2017)
13. Kostas, D., Aroca-Ouellette, S., Rudzicz, F.: BENDR: using transformers and a contrastive self-supervised learning task to learn from massive amounts of EEG data. Front. Hum. Neurosci. **15** (2021)
14. Kuo, C.E., Liao, P.Y., Lin, Y.S.: A self-attention-based ensemble convolution neural network approach for sleep stage classification with merged spectrogram. In: 2021 Asia-Pacific Signal and Information Processing Association Annual Summit and Conference (APSIPA ASC), pp. 1262–1268. IEEE (2021)
15. Lawhern, V.J., Solon, A.J., Waytowich, N.R., Gordon, S.M., Hung, C.P., Lance, B.J.: EEGNet: a compact convolutional neural network for EEG-based brain-computer interfaces. J. Neural Eng. **15**(5), 056013 (2018)
16. LeCun, Y., Bengio, Y., et al.: Convolutional networks for images, speech, and time series. Handb. Brain Theory Neural Netw. **3361**(10), 1995 (1995)
17. Lee, Y.E., Lee, S.H.: EEG-transformer: self-attention from transformer architecture for decoding EEG of imagined speech. In: 2022 10th International Winter Conference on Brain-Computer Interface (BCI), pp. 1–4. IEEE (2022)
18. Li, M., Hsu, W., Xie, X., Cong, J., Gao, W.: SACNN: self-attention convolutional neural network for low-dose CT denoising with self-supervised perceptual loss network. IEEE Trans. Med. Imaging **39**(7), 2289–2301 (2020)
19. Liu, X., Shen, Y., Liu, J., Yang, J., Xiong, P., Lin, F.: Parallel spatial-temporal self-attention CNN-based motor imagery classification for BCI. Front. Neurosci. 1157 (2020)
20. Lotte, F., et al.: A review of classification algorithms for EEG-based brain-computer interfaces: a 10 year update. J. Neural Eng. **15**(3), 031005 (2018)
21. Lotte, F., Congedo, M., Lécuyer, A., Lamarche, F., Arnaldi, B.: A review of classification algorithms for EEG-based brain-computer interfaces. J. Neural Eng. **4**(2), R1 (2007)
22. Pandey, A., Wang, D.: Dense CNN with self-attention for time-domain speech enhancement. IEEE/ACM Trans. Audio Speech Lang. Process. **29**, 1270–1279 (2021)
23. Pedroni, A., Bahreini, A., Langer, N.: Automagic: standardized preprocessing of big EEG data. Neuroimage **200**, 460–473 (2019)
24. Phukan, A., Gupta, D.: EEG based emotion classification using Xception architecture. In: Marriwala, N., Tripathi, C.C., Jain, S., Kumar, D. (eds.) Mobile Radio Communications and 5G Networks. LNNS, vol. 339, pp. 95–108. Springer, Singapore (2022). https://doi.org/10.1007/978-981-16-7018-3_7

25. Qu, X., Hall, M., Sun, Y., Sekuler, R., Hickey, T.J.: A personalized reading coach using wearable EEG sensors-a pilot study of brainwave learning analytics. In: CSEDU (2), pp. 501–507 (2018)

26. Qu, X., Liu, P., Li, Z., Hickey, T.: Multi-class time continuity voting for EEG classification. In: Frasson, C., Bamidis, P., Vlamos, P. (eds.) BFAL 2020. LNCS (LNAI), vol. 12462, pp. 24–33. Springer, Cham (2020). https://doi.org/10.1007/978-3-030-60735-7_3

27. Qu, X., Liukasemsarn, S., Tu, J., Higgins, A., Hickey, T.J., Hall, M.H.: Identifying clinically and functionally distinct groups among healthy controls and first episode psychosis patients by clustering on EEG patterns. Front. Psychiatry 938 (2020)

28. Qu, X., Mei, Q., Liu, P., Hickey, T.: Using EEG to distinguish between writing and typing for the same cognitive task. In: Frasson, C., Bamidis, P., Vlamos, P. (eds.) BFAL 2020. LNCS (LNAI), vol. 12462, pp. 66–74. Springer, Cham (2020). https://doi.org/10.1007/978-3-030-60735-7_7

29. Qu, X., Sun, Y., Sekuler, R., Hickey, T.: EEG markers of stem learning. In: 2018 IEEE Frontiers in Education Conference (FIE), pp. 1–9. IEEE (2018)

30. Rajpoot, A.S., Panicker, M.R., et al.: Subject independent emotion recognition using EEG signals employing attention driven neural networks. Biomed. Signal Process. Control **75**, 103547 (2022)

31. Roy, Y., Banville, H., Albuquerque, I., Gramfort, A., Falk, T.H., Faubert, J.: Deep learning-based electroencephalography analysis: a systematic review. J. Neural Eng. **16**(5), 051001 (2019)

32. Siddhad, G., Gupta, A., Dogra, D.P., Roy, P.P.: Efficacy of transformer networks for classification of raw EEG data. arXiv preprint arXiv:2202.05170 (2022)

33. Song, Y., Jia, X., Yang, L., Xie, L.: Transformer-based spatial-temporal feature learning for EEG decoding. arXiv preprint arXiv:2106.11170 (2021)

34. Sukhavasi, M., Adapa, S.: Music theme recognition using CNN and self-attention. arXiv preprint arXiv:1911.07041 (2019)

35. Sun, J., Xie, J., Zhou, H.: EEG classification with transformer-based models. In: 2021 IEEE 3rd Global Conference on Life Sciences and Technologies (LifeTech), pp. 92–93. IEEE (2021)

36. Tang, Z., Li, C., Sun, S.: Single-trial EEG classification of motor imagery using deep convolutional neural networks. Optik **130**, 11–18 (2017)

37. Ullah, I., Hussain, M., Aboalsamh, H., et al.: An automated system for epilepsy detection using EEG brain signals based on deep learning approach. Expert Syst. Appl. **107**, 61–71 (2018)

38. Vaswani, A., et al.: Attention is all you need. Adv. Neural Inf. Process. Syst. **30** (2017)

39. Yuan, Y., et al.: A hybrid self-attention deep learning framework for multivariate sleep stage classification. BMC Bioinform. **20**(16), 1–10 (2019)

40. Zhang, C., Kim, Y.K., Eskandarian, A.: EEG-inception: an accurate and robust end-to-end neural network for EEG-based motor imagery classification. J. Neural Eng. **18**(4), 046014 (2021)

41. Zhang, H., Goodfellow, I., Metaxas, D., Odena, A.: Self-attention generative adversarial networks. In: International Conference on Machine Learning, pp. 7354–7363. PMLR (2019)

42. Zhao, Z., Chopra, K., Zeng, Z., Li, X.: Sea-Net: squeeze-and-excitation attention net for diabetic retinopathy grading. In: 2020 IEEE International Conference on Image Processing (ICIP), pp. 2496–2500. IEEE (2020)

43. Zhao, Z., et al.: BiRA-Net: bilinear attention net for diabetic retinopathy grading. In: 2019 IEEE International Conference on Image Processing (ICIP), pp. 1385–1389. IEEE (2019)
44. Zhou, C., Wu, M., Lam, S.K.: SSA-CNN: semantic self-attention CNN for pedestrian detection. arXiv preprint arXiv:1902.09080 (2019)

Design Thinking the Human-AI Experience of Neurotechnology for Knowledge Workers

Troy R. Weekes$^{(\boxtimes)}$ ⓘ and Thomas. C. Eskridge

L3 Harris Institute for Assured Information, Department of Human-Centered Design,
Florida Institute of Technology, Melbourne, FL 32901, USA
tweekes@fit.edu, teskridge@fit.edu

Abstract. Neurotechnology promises cognitive enhancement as a way
for humanity to extend its information-processing capability without invasive brain surgeries and pharmacological side effects. Notable
advancements in this field have achieved high-bandwidth wireless communication interfaces between human brains and computers. Human-
centered design proposes that human-technology experiences should
focus on human needs. This paper explains how design thinking has been
applied as a methodology to design the user experience of an attention-
based neurotechnology solution that leverages artificial intelligence (AI)
to enhance the flow performance and cognitive well-being of knowledge
workers (KWs). Using the d.school design thinking process, we started
with a mindset that favored empathy, creative confidence, and ambigu-
ity to discover and define the problems confronting KWs. After diverging with deep empathy and converging on user personas and problem
definition, the design thinking process branched into an iterative prototyping cycle that transformed our initial ideas into a human-centered
AI-powered neurotechnology. We utilized the functional prototypes for
testing assumptions and performing a comprehensive design evaluation.
Our final solution incorporated a gamified user interface with visual elements, affordances, and a coherent human-AI experience. Expert software evaluators conducted a series of cognitive walkthroughs and heuristic evaluations by simulating the user personas and performing an end-
to-end user scenario with the prototype. The design thinking process
generated a neurotechnology service with a human-AI experience that
enables KWs to achieve healthy flow performance while enhancing cognitive well-being.

Keywords: Knowledge worker · Neurotechnology · Design thinking

---

Supported by L3 Harris Institute for Assured Information.

M. Kurosu et al. (Eds.): HCII 2022, LNCS 13519, pp. 527–545, 2022.
https://doi.org/10.1007/978-3-031-17618-0_37

1   Introduction

A growing body of literature on neurotechnology recognizes the importance of bio-sensing and biofeedback [17,40,44]. In this paper, the term 'neurotechnology' refers to the methods and instruments that enable a direct connection with the nervous system [34]. Recent studies by computational neuroscientists have shown how neurotechnologies use bio-sensing electrodes to record signals from the brain and transform them into biofeedback displays of useful control commands and stimuli [24,31]. This exploratory research focused on human knowledge workers (KWs) and attention-based neurotechnology-as-a-service shown in Fig. 1.

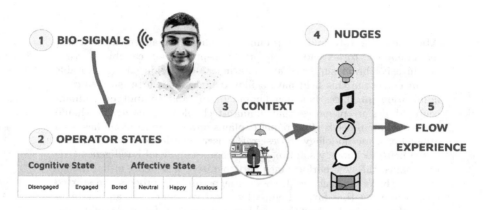

Fig. 1. FCA bio-senses, contextualizes, and nudges KWs into flow

In this work, we design a human-aware and context-aware neurotechnology artificial intelligence (AI) known as the **Flow Choice Architecture (FCA)** that "nudges" [46,51] KWs to increase the healthy time that they spend in the flow state [10,11,13]. Our design thinking story outlines the development of FCA's human-AI experience to strengthen the cognitive abilities of KWs by deepening their levels of cognitive work rather than automating their jobs.

KWs are essential to maintain our standard of living and quality of life. Their well-being is paramount to economic development and human advancement. Since the pandemic caused by the coronavirus disease, KWs have experienced an accelerated shift towards remote working [3] in virtual and hybrid work environments [49] that are augmented by AI [54]. To remain competitive, KWs need to create more value in less time while improving their performance and maintaining their well-being.

In Sect. 2, "Background," we review the literature on cognitive enhancement, neurofeedback, and healthy flow performance. This section analyzes how neurofeedback can be adopted to help KWs effortlessly focus their attention on the task stimulus during knowledge work.

In Sect. 3, "Design Thinking," we describe the phases of the design thinking process used in this paper. We empathize by conducting remote, semi-structured interviews with 12 KWs to generate qualitative results, quotes, and insights about their personal experiences, expectations, and preferences related to knowledge work. We validate the interview results by conducting an online survey with 468 participants. We articulate the results from a need-finding synthesis, which were consistent problem statements evidenced by supporting user personas. These data-driven design assets guided the future steps of the design thinking process. We explore the qualitative dataset to discover commonly used vocabulary and consolidate an intuitive information architecture. We adopt rapid prototyping techniques to build a functional FCA for testing and evaluation.

In Sect. 4, "Evaluation," we conduct cognitive walkthroughs and heuristic evaluations of the prototype with six evaluators who are subject matter experts in knowledge work and software engineering. The evaluation results generated improvements for future development.

In Sect. 5, "Results," we present the findings from the cognitive walkthroughs and heuristic evaluations. The evaluation results highlight how FCA succeeded on the tasks and identify areas for improvement.

In Sect. 6, "Discussion," we explain the implications of the findings and discuss recommendations for improving the learnability and usability of FCA.

In Sect. 7, "Conclusion," we conclude with the research outcomes. We discuss the next steps to advance the FCA neurotechnology prototype to become a beneficial tool for the cognitive enhancement of KWs.

2   Theoretical Background

FCA is a bio-sensing and contextual bio-feedback nudging system that enhances KW flow performance and cognitive well-being. FCA contributes to bridging the gap of growing global demand for more creative and productive human output in knowledge-based industries by helping KWs perform their cognitive work with fewer distractions and attentional load. The references synthesized in this section identify relevant findings from scholarly sources on cognitive enhancement, neurofeedback, and healthy flow performance.

2.1   Cognitive Enhancement

Cognitive enhancement aims to reach one's personal best without necessarily outperforming others [9]. Bostrom and Sandberg [7] define cognitive enhancement as "the amplification or extension of core capacities of the mind through improvement or augmentation of internal or external information processing systems." Contemporary cognitive enhancement methods involve an array of nootropics, brain implants, brain training games, neurofeedback, and transcranial electric stimulation devices for modifying brain function [19,21].

Despite the many positive effects of cognitive enhancement, there are likely negative aspects to be considered. Given that cognitive enhancements are likely to be used for extended periods across the lifespan, the long-term effectiveness and safety are crucial concerns to be determined.

In the knowledge economy, the value of human capital far outweighs more traditional, tangible forms, such as plants and equipment [35]. For this primary reason, we regarded the cognitive performance and well-being of KWs as quintessential elements of organizational success. We value the KW's happiness before, during, and after knowledge work in terms of its immediate and long-term impacts on the KW. By doing so, we designed FCA to guide KWs towards the flow state and enhance cognitive well-being through well-timed nudges and psychological flexibility routines that cultivate mindfulness and commitment.

2.2 Healthy Flow Performance

Csikszentmihalyi [10] defined flow as a state of concentration so focused that it amounts to absolute absorption in an activity. Concentration is a trainable cognitive state that may aid in the activation and maintenance of flow during goal-directed behaviors [48]. We hypothesize that concentration during knowledge work tends to activate flow. To this end, we designed FCA to train KWs to regulate their concentration and benefit from the positive effects experienced during and after flow.

On the contrary, fatigue is the debilitating cognitive state associated with feeling exhausted, sleepy, and tired, which diminishes the ability to function efficiently on a task [18]. Although work may be completed under conditions of high cognitive fatigue, the quality of performance and the quality of work outcomes tend to decrease [29]. Basic research found that an increase in cognitive fatigue correlated with increased reaction times, misses and false alarms, and time-on-task in an attention-dependent task [6]. Matthews and Desmond [32] observed the detrimental impact of cognitive fatigue on performance during highly demanding cognitive tasks. This observation makes the management of task demand an essential aspect for FCA to perform successfully and effectively.

Despite the rich literature on the topic of flow, these studies have been primarily qualitative inductive analyses [47]. Ambiguities exist in its definitions and inconsistencies are evident in how flow is operationalized [1]. In this research, we operationalized flow with the nine components defined by Csikszentmihalyi [10], which include challenge-skill balance, action-awareness merging, clear goals, unambiguous feedback, concentration on the task at hand, sense of control, loss of self-consciousness, time-transformation, and an autotelic experience.

Flow occurs when individuals, acting solo or in teams, operate with optimal concentration, which yields a heightened sense of satisfaction, intrinsic motivation, and peak performance [10,12,37]. In this work, we claim that healthy flow performance is not the excessive attainment of the flow state, which may lead to exhaustion and burnout, but sufficient flow to accomplish one's work while maintaining cognitive and emotional well-being.

2.3 Neurofeedback

Within the neurofeedback domain, training protocols provide audio-visual signals based on site-specific electroencephalography (EEG) frequency bands or combinations thereof [31]. EEG data make up a reliable bio-signal stream that may reify cognitive performance into measurable neural activity. FCA tests this hypothesis with its neurofeedback AI technology for flow augmentation by building upon other neurofeedback interventions grounded in the training of respondent and operant behaviors [17]. The main distinction between FCA and other neurofeedback tools is the use of intuitive and comprehensible nudges that reduce cognitive workload rather than signals that require monitoring and decoding [40].

There are varied results from experiments that correlate EEG to human performance. In a study by Katahira et al. [24], participants performed arithmetic tasks of varying difficulty levels to induce three conditions: flow, boredom, and overload. The researchers analyzed the variance of EEG data between the three conditions. Results from the study demonstrated that theta power in the brain's frontal areas was higher in the flow and overload conditions compared to the boredom condition. According to Katahira et al. [24], high theta power reflects the subjective states of maximum cognitive control and absorption in the task. The flow condition exhibited decreased alpha activity compared to the overload condition, which suggested a relatively low cognitive load on working memory during flow. This study concluded that the flow state was indicated by high frontal theta power and moderate alpha power [24].

Researchers have explored artificial neural networks and deep learning techniques to classify operator states using EEG signals. Wilson et al. [56] performed two-class cognitive workload classification based on artificial neural networks, and achieved 86% classification accuracy. Tripathi et al. [53] used a deep neural network and a convolutional neural network (CNN) to classify valence and arousal measures using EEG signals from the DEAP dataset [27]. Their neural networks provided 58% and 56% classification accuracy for valence and arousal, respectively, and their CNN model provided 67% and 58% for valence and arousal, respectively. Zheng et al. [57] used a deep neural network architecture to process EEG and eye movement features. The fusion of multimodal bio-signals with deep neural networks significantly enhanced the model's performance compared with a single modality, and the best mean accuracy of 85% was achieved for four emotional states [57]. Eskridge and Weekes [20] used the SEED-IV EEG dataset [57] to run dimensionality reduction on the power spectral density features from five EEG frequency bands using linear discriminant analysis followed by an artificial neural network to gain average overall classification accuracy of 99%.

This paper discusses the use of EEG bio-signals in the form of EEG power indices as reliable indicators for effort, concentration, relaxation, absorption, fatigue, arousal, and valence during knowledge work tasks. We computed seven EEG power indices for use in the analysis from evidence-based correlates in the literature of computational neuroscience [2,4–6,8,14–16,22,23,25,26,30,36,41, 43,45,50,52].

3   Design Thinking the Human-AI Experience

In this work, knowledge workers (KWs) are human workers who perform complex deep work [38] that requires considerable amounts of concentration and creativity. We adopted the d.school design thinking process model [42] in Fig. 2 to actively engage the participation of KWs in the design and evaluation of FCA. The Institutional Review Board (IRB) at Florida Tech approved our research with human subjects.

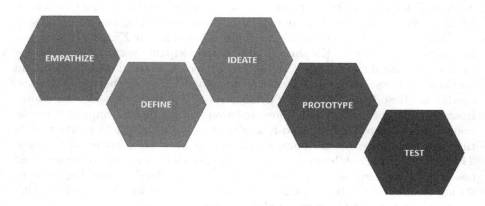

Fig. 2. The five stages of the d.school design thinking process model

3.1   Stage 1 - Empathize

In the "Empathize" stage, we formulated an understanding of potential FCA users, i.e., KWs seeking flow experiences. We conducted remote, semi-structured, one-on-one interviews with KWs and subsequently applied the interview results to develop a cross-sectional survey with KWs to generate quantitative data and validate insights from the interviews.

We conducted the interviews with a sample of 12 KWs (6 females, age M = 29.5 years [SD = 7.91]) who represented KWs from diverse domains in engineering, creative writing, project management, supply chain management, research, and philosophy. The interview study was generative in nature and centered on building a deep empathy with KWs as the starting point for the design thinking method of the innovation process.

The problem under investigation was: how might we describe the flow performance of KWs according to their tasks, workspaces, tools, and heuristics? We hypothesized that KWs explore and exploit their factors of production to maximize performance even though stressors may negatively impact their well-being. To test our claim, we pursued the following research questions. In which domains do KWs work? What types of tasks do KWs perform? Where do KWs perform their work? Which heuristics and tools do KWs use? What is flow at work for

KWs? What is effective work time for KWs? How does KW productivity impact well-being?

The interview questions were derived from the research questions and grouped into the following ten sections: activity tracking, favorite activities, knowledge work, productivity, work tracking scenario, task definition & execution, flow at work, distraction, traction, and changing work states. After the interviews, we applied quantitative content analysis and qualitative thematic analysis to synthesize the results. The process generated a conceptual framework for classifying KWs based on distinct personal traits and work preferences. User personas relevant to productivity multiplier tools help humanize FCA.

The KWs worked in three main work domains, i.e., sciences, business, and arts. The types of knowledge work tasks that the KWs performed included writing, research, coding, design, documentation, reading, finding, visualization, collaboration, and managing subordinates. The types of tasks varied across work domains. The foremost task features that KWs considered included urgency, duration, challenge, importance, sensitivity, and priority.

KWs worked in the office, lab, cubicle, and living room. Participants reported the shift to working from home due to the COVID-19 pandemic. KWs described their efforts to create a distraction-free environment by turning off or stowing phones, wearing headphones, listening to music, and closing or locking doors. They take breaks to relax, relieve stress, refocus, eat, drink, and deflate.

KWs reported that flow was a zone, work mode, or head-space that occurs naturally and is goal-oriented, structure-driven, and distraction-free. The KWs supported the need for clear task goals and complete task absorption to achieve flow. Most of them experience a loss of self-consciousness and a faster passage of time during flow. KWs reported a positive feeling of satisfaction after flow.

KWs identified detrimental impacts of productivity on their well-being, e.g., procrastination, sleep issues, and developing hyper-focus and tunnel vision. Several KWs admitted to missing lunches, not drinking water, ignoring eating, and eating too quickly. Others complained about poor posture, being stationary at the desk, and lack of exercise. On the other hand, KWs identified some positive impacts of productivity on their well-being. KWs reported feeling in a better mood, confident, happy, and more energetic. Some KWs used the positive energy as an opportunity to perform activities outside of work.

A key finding was that KWs considered flow at work in terms of being in a zone and head-space when they are focused on making progress, completing tasks, and achieving results without interruptions and distractions. This finding has significant implications for the design of FCA to increase attention on the task at hand and mitigate external distractions. One of the most important findings to emerge from this study was that KWs balance the positive and negative impacts of productivity with their well-being to seek growth and happiness, which suggests a role for FCA in promoting healthy flow and work-life balance.

We conducted the cross-sectional survey with 468 KWs from MTurk to generate quantitative data, validate earlier insights, and understand what makes flow enjoyable for individual KSs. We used the survey results to identify user preferences and qualify excerpts for the user personas. The survey was randomized and cross-sectional in design to build inclusion across KWs from the three main work domains, i.e., sciences, business, and arts.

The survey yielded significant effects of specific situations on the KW's enjoyment of a task. Success on the initial attempt had an extremely positive effect on the KW's enjoyment of the task. The same positive effect occurred during situations of consistent and unexpected success over time. Contrary to expectations, KWs tended to embrace failure since consistent failure over time also has a significantly positive effect on the KW's enjoyment. The use of incentives for success also had a significantly positive effect on the KW's enjoyment.

In terms of how frequently KWs experienced the state of flow during knowledge work, consistent failure over time had a significantly negative effect on the KW's enjoyment. During flow, KWs felt that failure on the initial attempt had a significantly negative effect on the KW's enjoyment. Similarly, random failure over time had a significantly negative effect on the KW's enjoyment.

3.2   Stage 2 - Define

In the "Define" stage, we synthesized the research from the interviews and survey to discover where KWs were experiencing work-related problems that interfered with their performance and well-being. Our need-finding synthesis generated the user persona in Fig. 3 and a set of user Point-Of-View (POV) problem statements, which guided the remaining stages of the design thinking process.

Fig. 3. The software engineer user persona - kevin small

The following actionable Point-Of-View (POV) statements formulated contextualized problems confronting KWs and identified their needs and insights.

1. Before knowledge work, KWs need a way to prepare for work because they tend to procrastinate and lose focus without precise tasks or goals.
2. During knowledge work, KWs need a way to stay engaged with work because they tend to become distracted and stressed over lost productive time.
3. After knowledge work, KWs need a way to account for and reflect on work accomplishments because there are key work patterns to learn.
4. During boring knowledge work, KWs need a way to stimulate and challenge themselves because they tend to lose motivation and underperform.
5. During overwhelming knowledge work, KWs need a way to relax and calm down because they tend to become anxious and underperform.
6. During enjoyable knowledge work, KWs need encouragement and reinforcement because they tend to perform better and achieve more healthy flow.

3.3 Stage 3 - Ideate

In the "Ideate" stage, we generated creative ideas from the macro-scale to the micro-scale. We used AI to mine the qualitative datasets from the interviews and surveys to discover useful vocabulary, labels, and interactions that were recognizable and appealing to KWs. We abstracted the user scenarios into a generic task list where the interactions and user interface (UI) modeled a "minimalist" version of a task management system. We ideated the FCA through the lens of safe, explainable, and responsible AI.

The design philosophy of FCA's user experience exploited wearable technology that is non-invasive, lightweight, and easy to use. Once we obtained a comfortable hardware setup, the FCA operator needed a simple and effective neurofeedback UI. Our approach to FCA's UI design leveraged research about the operator's biases, behaviors, and preferences. Three **"flow principles"** were incorporated as fundamental tenets of FCA's design philosophy.

1. **Dynamic Flow - In flow, time stands still.** The dynamic visualization of deep flow was represented as minimal motion, whereas shallow flow was moderate motion, and distraction was significant motion.
2. **Cumulative Flow - More flow yields better work.** FCA rewarded the operator with flow points based on the flow state of each epoch. The cumulative visualization of flow applied a heuristic that humans employ, i.e., more is better.
3. **Deep Flow - Never interrupt deep flow.** FCA used a recommender system that delivered nudges based on specific learned criteria or when the system "explored" and tried something novel to learn new knowledge. However, a rule was that FCA would never interrupt "deep flow."

We leveraged the qualitative datasets from the interviews and surveys to construct the information architecture with abstracted keywords, i.e., profile, workspace, device, project, task, and work session, which formed the basis of the functional user requirements for the prototypes.

3.4   Stage 4 - Prototype

In the "Prototype" stage, we incrementally built out FCA by diverging and converging on multiple ideas. We developed four prototypes with different capabilities to answer questions and clarify risky assumptions.

Prototype 1 tested facial expressions as operator state indicators. One of the riskiest components of our research plan was discovering how to classify human bio-signals to provide reliable operator state indicators. This question became a core focus of Prototype 1, which focused on extracting steady streams of facial landmarks and action units to train models that predict the operator's state. Prototype 1 provided insights into which states the predictive model computed from the camera feed overlay of facial landmarks.

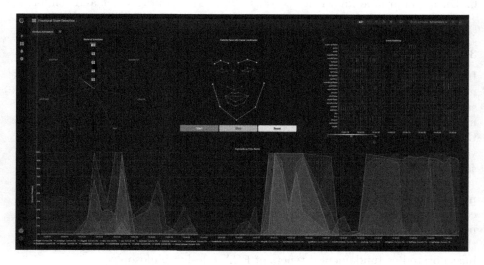

Fig. 4. Prototype 1 classifying facial expression bio-signals

Figure 4 shows the near real-time classification of facial expression bio-signals from an operator performing an experiment watching emotionally-charged videos. This initial prototype demonstrated that it was feasible to classify operator states given the facial expression bio-signal time series vector. After proving that it was possible to classify operator states with a measure of reliability using facial bio-signals, we advanced to the most challenging aspect of our research plan. We needed to discover how to simultaneously classify multiple bio-signals to provide reliable indicators of operator state.

Prototype 2 tested the integration of multimodal bio-signals from wearables devices. We selected two different wearable devices based on their capabilities. Muse headbands are affordable, commercially available off-the-shelf EEG devices developed by InteraXon Inc. Muse headbands aimed to enhance meditation practice by combining instruction and tracking with EEG sensor biofeedback during mindfulness exercises [28]. The Empatica E4 is a wrist-worn photoplethysmography (PPG) bio-sensor device that Empatica Inc developed. The E4 calculated heart rate, inter-beat-interval (IBI), and skin temperature [33].

Prototype 2 demonstrated that it was feasible to classify operator states from multimodal bio-signals. However, Prototype 2 was too slow to reach a consensus due to the various bio-signals with different timescales (Fig. 5).

Fig. 5. Prototype 2 showing an operator performing a mirroring experiment

Prototype 3 in Fig. 6 tested EEG bio-signals as operator state indicators. Prototype 3 proved that it was feasible to compute operator states from EEG bio-signals. This finding supported our decision to focus on neurofeedback.

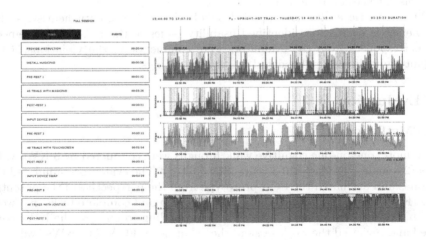

Fig. 6. Prototype 3 showing computed EEG indices & task interval markers

3.5   Stage 5 - Test

In the "Test" stage, we evaluated the effectiveness of the prototypes. We conducted cognitive walkthroughs and heuristic evaluations with KWs to inform the design of the human-AI experience. We developed Prototype 4 in Fig. 7 to evaluate FCA as a gamified neurotechnology in cognitive walkthroughs and heuristic evaluations.

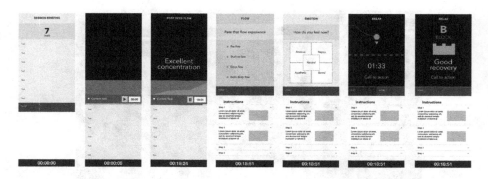

Fig. 7. Prototype 4 showing features of the FCA UI

The cognitive walkthrough was a detailed, step-by-step evaluation of FCA on a set of tasks. The purpose of the walkthrough was to empathize with KWs to uncover design errors in the FCA UI that would interfere with their learning by exploration and cause confusion during interactions. Examples of such errors are poorly worded labels, misguiding layout flows, and inadequate feedback about the consequences of an action.

The heuristic evaluations applied Jakob Nielsen's usability heuristics [39]. The heuristic evaluations identified usability issues in the FCA UI for remediation. Responses from the evaluators were comments on the violations of the usability guidelines supplemented by severity ratings.

4   Evaluation

4.1   Methodology

The remote, one-on-one cognitive walkthroughs were conducted by 3 KW evaluators (2 females, age M = 26.3 years [SD = 4.61]). The evaluators simulated the personas and evaluated the FCA prototype from the perspective of the potential users. KWs started FCA and configured it to plan and complete tasks in a work session. After interpreting FCA's UI and responding to nudges, the KWs completed and reviewed the work session, then shut down FCA. The KWs evaluated FCA by describing how the UI fulfilled each task.

The reseacher administered the cognitive walkthroughs. In the preparatory phase, the evaluator became familiar with the assigned user persona. The user personas from the "Define" phase allowed the evaluators to judge what needs, knowledge, preferences, and limitations the users may have relative to the tasks. During the walkthrough briefing, the researcher discussed the tasks to be analyzed. The evaluator interacted with FCA on the following tasks by describing how the UI performed on each task.

1. Startup FCA
2. Calibrate FCA
3. Plan a new work session
4. Start a work session
5. Complete a task
6. Interpret the signals during a task
7. Respond to the nudges during a task
8. Complete a work session
9. Review a completed work session
10. Shut down FCA

In the analysis phase of the cognitive walkthrough, the evaluators examined each action in the solution path and attempted to tell a credible story that explained why the expected users would choose that action. Credible stories were based on assumptions about the background knowledge of users and the problem-solving process that enables the user to guess the correct action.

If there was a major problem with the UI, the researcher noted the problem and proceeded to the next task as though the correct action had been performed. The state of the UI at the beginning of each action was always assumed to be the correct state and never the state after an incorrect action was performed.

The remote, one-on-one heuristic evaluations were conducted by 3 evaluators (3 males, age M = 39.0 years [SD = 17.32]). The evaluators simulated the Kevin Small persona over ten tasks. The KWs started FCA and configured it to plan and complete a work session. After interpreting FCA's UI and responding to nudges, they completed and reviewed the work session and then shut down FCA. The KWs evaluated FCA by describing how the UI fulfilled each task.

The preparatory phase of the remote heuristic evaluations involved a series of questions about FCA's compliance with Jakob Nielsen's ten usability heuristics. During the evaluation briefing, the researcher discussed the ten tasks above to be analyzed.

During the heuristic evaluations, the evaluators reviewed, interacted with, and evaluated FCA on the given tasks by describing how the UI performed on each task and then performing the correct action sequence to complete each task. In the analysis phase, the evaluators examined each task with each usability heuristic. If there were violations of the design guidelines, the evaluator made a descriptive comment and associated it with the task and the heuristic.

The researcher reviewed the comments with the evaluators where clarity was necessary. If there was a problem with the UI, the researcher noted the problem and proceeded to the next task, as if the correct action had been performed. The UI state at the beginning of each action was always assumed to be the correct state. The evaluators' comments were tabulated and severity ratings were assigned to each comment. In addition to the heuristic, each comment was categorized by the type of design error.

5   Results

The cognitive walkthroughs generated the following key findings and recommendations. We recommended button groups to replace the slider bars in the user profile, which negatively affected the configuration of FCA. We proposed to clarify what the UI does by changing the label "Manage Tasks" to "Plan Worksession." There should be a feedback screen that presents a meaningful summary of the work accomplished in the work session.

Figure 8 shows the tabulated results from the heuristic evaluations. There were 82 design issues covering the ten usability heuristics over the ten tasks. The totals indicated which tasks and heuristics contained a majority of the issues.

					STEPS						
HEURISTICS	1	2	3	4	5	6	7	8	9	10	TOTALS
Visibility of system status	1	3	4	1	3	2	2		4		20
Match between system and the real world	1	2	3		2		1	1	3		13
User control and freedom		3	1	1	1	1	1		1		9
Consistency and standards		1	4	1	1	1			3		11
Error prevention	2	2	1	2			1			1	9
Recognition rather than recall		1							2	1	4
Flexibility and efficiency of use		1				1			1		3
Aesthetic and minimalist design	1										1
Help users recognize, diagnose, and recover from errors	1				1	1					3
Help and documentation	2	1	2	1	1	1	1				9
TOTALS	8	14	15	7	9	6	6	1	14	2	82

Fig. 8. Summary of design issues from the heuristic evaluations

6   Discussion

The relevance of flow among KWs strongly supported our findings. KWs considered flow at work in terms of being in a zone and head-space when they are focused on making progress, completing tasks, and achieving results without interruptions and distractions. The need for flow has significant implications for understanding how to design FCA in a way that increases their focused attention and mitigates distractions.

The cognitive walkthrough rationalized the design problems so that the FCA prototype would promote the discoverability and learnability of its users while providing adequate feedback on their tasks early in the implementation. Overall the cognitive walkthroughs demonstrated that FCA fits the KW's mental model. The concepts of user accounts, profiles, workspaces, devices, and tasks were all very familiar to the evaluators. The streamlined user flows to complete the UI interaction tasks guided the KWs from initial use onward.

The top-3 tasks that contained the majority of the design issues were tasks 3, 2, and 9, i.e., "Plan a new work session," "configure FCA," and "Review a completed work session." The top-3 heuristics that exhibited the highest frequencies were "Visibility of system status," "Match between system and the real world," and "Consistency and standards." The severity of the design issues factored into the prioritization of the fixes.

In addition to uncovering design issues that degrade the learnability and usability of FCA, this design thinking process reinforced the need for FCA to help KWs balance positive and negative impacts of productivity with their well-being. This finding underpins the primary goal of FCA to promote healthy flow performance and work-life balance.

7   Conclusion

This paper discussed the design thinking of a human-centered AI system that seeks to enhance the flow performance and well-being of individual KWs. We effectively applied the d.school design thinking process model to iteratively integrate lessons learned across the entire AI design and development life cycle.

The design thinking process reinforced that system design should start with the correct user to find the right problem. The application of design thinking to the human-AI experience of FCA involved a high level of sensemaking to decide which questions about the KW required clarity [55]. We leveraged samples of KWs and Amazon MTurk's pool of KWs to generate sufficient qualitative and quantitative data to ensure that FCA was developed to fit their needs.

Each prototyping cycle solved specific problems. Prototype 1 visualized outputs from the predictive model as time series and heatmaps. Prototype 2 tested the feasibility of classifying multimodal bio-signals and confirmed the decision to pursue a neurofeedback-based solution. Prototype 3 extended the neurofeedback approach and determined the efficacy of the computed EEG indices. Prototype 4 evaluated FCA in cognitive walkthroughs and heuristic evaluations.

In the context of FCA, an organization may mandate that individual KWs use FCA. The organization may wish to fire specific KWs if they do not achieve a high flow state for more than five hours a day. FCA proposes to protect against this type of misuse and abuse by treating bio-signal data as personal health information, defined as protected information under the Health Insurance Portability and Accountability Act (HIPAA). FCA digitalizes and scales the role of a personal workplace coach who helps KWs work healthier, happier, and more productively of their own volition.

The most challenging aspect of this research plan was developing a multi-modal Prototype 2. This prototype required the simultaneous classification of multiple bio-signals to provide reliable indicators of the KW state. The prototype was too slow to reach a consensus due to various bio-signals with different timescales and inexplicable classifications. Another significant challenge was the downtime to train, test, and tune the AI models that punctuated the rapid exploratory iterations of the prototypes.

Future research includes experiments to streamline protocols, collect self-reports, and compute EEG indices. Other UI-focused advancements will center on a wider variety of flow-inducing conditions. We will continue to collect data from KWs performing measurable knowledge work tasks in randomized controlled trials and longitudinal playtests. These data will help to improve the human-AI experience of FCA for the benefit of KWs.

References

1. Abuhamdeh, S.: Investigating the "flow" experience: key conceptual and operational issues. Front. Psychol. **11**, 158 (2020)
2. Alves, N.T., Fukusima, S.S., Aznar-Casanova, J.A.: Models of brain asymmetry in emotional processing. Psychol. Neurosci. **1**, 63–66 (2008)
3. Amankwah-Amoah, J., Khan, Z., Wood, G., Knight, G.: COVID-19 and digitalization: the great acceleration. J. Bus. Res. **136**, 602–611 (2021)
4. Barwick, F., Arnett, P., Slobounov, S.: EEG correlates of fatigue during administration of a neuropsychological test battery. Clin. Neurophysiol. **123**(2), 278–284 (2012)
5. Berka, C., et al.: EEG correlates of task engagement and mental workload in vigilance, learning, and memory tasks. Aviat. Space Environ. Med. **78**(5), B231–B244 (2007)
6. Boksem, M.A., Meijman, T.F., Lorist, M.M.: Effects of mental fatigue on attention: an ERP study. Cogn. Brain Res. **25**(1), 107–116 (2005)
7. Bostrom, N., Sandberg, A.: Cognitive enhancement: methods, ethics, regulatory challenges. Sci. Eng. Ethics **15**(3), 311–341 (2009)
8. Cheng, S.Y., Hsu, H.T.: Mental fatigue measurement using EEG. IntechOpen (2011)
9. Colzato, L.S., Hommel, B., Beste, C.: The downsides of cognitive enhancement. Neuroscientist **27**(4), 322–330 (2021)
10. Csikszentmihalyi, M.: Flow: the psychology of optimal performance (1990)
11. Csikszentmihalyi, M.: Happiness and creativity. Futurist **31**(5), S8 (1997)

12. Csikszentmihalyi, M.: Play and intrinsic rewards. In: Csikszentmihalyi, M. (ed.) Flow and the Foundations of Positive Psychology, pp. 135–153. Springer, Dordrecht (2014). https://doi.org/10.1007/978-94-017-9088-8_10

13. Csikszentmihalyi, M.: Toward a psychology of optimal experience. In: Csikszentmihalyi, M. (ed.) Flow and the Foundations of Positive Psychology, pp. 209–226. Springer, Dordrecht (2014). https://doi.org/10.1007/978-94-017-9088-8_14

14. Dasari, D., Shou, G., Ding, L.: ICA-derived EEG correlates to mental fatigue, effort, and workload in a realistically simulated air traffic control task. Front. Neurosci. **11**, 297 (2017)

15. De Gennaro, L., et al.: Neurophysiological correlates of sleepiness: a combined TMS and EEG study. Neuroimage **36**(4), 1277–1287 (2007)

16. DeLosAngeles, D., et al.: Electroencephalographic correlates of states of concentrative meditation. Int. J. Psychophysiol. **110**, 27–39 (2016)

17. Demos, J.N.: Getting Started with EEG Neurofeedback. Norton & Company (2019)

18. Dittner, A.J., Wessely, S.C., Brown, R.G.: The assessment of fatigue: a practical guide for clinicians and researchers. J. Psychosom. Res. **56**(2), 157–170 (2004)

19. Dubljević, V., Saigle, V., Racine, E.: The rising tide of tDCS in the media and academic literature. Neuron **82**(4), 731–736 (2014)

20. Eskridge, T.C., Weekes, T.R.: Opportunities for case-based reasoning in personal flow and productivity management. In: Watson, I., Weber, R. (eds.) ICCBR 2020. LNCS (LNAI), vol. 12311, pp. 349–354. Springer, Cham (2020). https://doi.org/10.1007/978-3-030-58342-2_23

21. Farah, M.J.: The unknowns of cognitive enhancement. Science **350**(6259), 379–380 (2015)

22. Freeman, F.G., Mikulka, P.J., Prinzel, L.J., Scerbo, M.W.: Evaluation of an adaptive automation system using three EEG indices with a visual tracking task. Biol. Psychol. **50**(1), 61–76 (1999)

23. Grammer, J.K., Xu, K., Lenartowicz, A.: Effects of context on the neural correlates of attention in a college classroom. npj Sci. Learn. **6**(1), 1–4 (2021)

24. Katahira, K., Yamazaki, Y., Yamaoka, C., Ozaki, H., Nakagawa, S., Nagata, N.: EEG correlates of the flow state: a combination of increased frontal theta and moderate frontocentral alpha rhythm in the mental arithmetic task. Front. Psychol. **9**, 300 (2018)

25. Keller, B.M.: Cognitive avionics toolset for operator state classification based on physiological signals. In: 2007 IEEE/AIAA 26th Digital Avionics Systems Conference, p. 6-A. IEEE (2007)

26. Kim, M.K., Kim, M., Oh, E., Kim, S.P.: A review on the computational methods for emotional state estimation from the human EEG. Comput. Math. Methods Med. **2013** (2013)

27. Koelstra, S., et al.: DEAP: a database for emotion analysis. Using physiological signals. IEEE Trans. Affect. Comput. **3**, 18–31 (2012)

28. Krigolson, O.E., Williams, C.C., Norton, A., Hassall, C.D., Colino, F.L.: Choosing MUSE: validation of a low-cost, portable EEG system for ERP research. Front. Neurosci. **11**, 109 (2017)

29. Langner, R., Steinborn, M.B., Chatterjee, A., Sturm, W., Willmes, K.: Mental fatigue and temporal preparation in simple reaction-time performance. Acta Physiol. (Oxf). **133**(1), 64–72 (2010)

30. Lim, S., Yeo, M., Yoon, G.: Comparison between concentration and immersion based on EEG analysis. Sensors **19**(7), 1669 (2019)

31. Marzbani, H., Marateb, H.R., Mansourian, M.: Neurofeedback: a comprehensive review on system design, methodology and clinical applications. Basic Clin. Neurosci. **7**(2), 143 (2016)
32. Matthews, G., Desmond, P.A.: Task-induced fatigue states and simulated driving performance. Q. J. Exp. Psychol. Sect. A **55**(2), 659–686 (2002)
33. Milstein, N., Gordon, I.: Validating measures of electrodermal activity and heart rate variability derived from the empatica E4 utilized in research settings that involve interactive dyadic states. Front. Behav. Neurosci. **14**, 148 (2020)
34. Müller, O., Rotter, S.: Neurotechnology: current developments and ethical issues. Front. Syst. Neurosci. **11**, 93 (2017)
35. Murray, A.J., Greenes, K.A.: From the knowledge worker to the knowledge economy: six billion minds co-creating the future. Vine (2007)
36. Nacke, L.: Affective ludology: scientific measurement of user experience in interactive entertainment. Ph.D. thesis, Blekinge Institute of Technology (2009)
37. Nakamura, J., Csikszentmihalyi, M.: The concept of flow. In: Csikszentmihalyi, M. (ed.) Flow and the Foundations of Positive Psychology, pp. 239–263. Springer, Dordrecht (2014). https://doi.org/10.1007/978-94-017-9088-8_16
38. Newport, C.: Deep Work: Rules for Focused Success in a Distracted World. Hachette, UK (2016)
39. Nielsen, J.: Enhancing the explanatory power of usability heuristics. In: Proceedings of the SIGCHI Conference on Human Factors in Computing Systems, pp. 152–158 (1994)
40. Norman, D.: The Design of Everyday Things: Revised and Expanded Edition. Basic Books (2013)
41. Ota, T., Toyoshima, R., Yamauchi, T.: Measurements by biphasic changes of the alpha band amplitude as indicators of arousal level. Int. J. Psychophysiol. **24**(1–2), 25–37 (1996)
42. Plattner, H., Meinel, C., Leifer, L.: Design Thinking Research. Springer, Heidelberg (2012). https://doi.org/10.1007/978-3-642-21643-5
43. Prinzel, L.J., Freeman, F.G., Scerbo, M.W., Mikulka, P.J., Pope, A.T.: A closed-loop system for examining psychophysiological measures for adaptive task allocation. Int. J. Aviat. Psychol. **10**(4), 393–410 (2000)
44. Putze, F., Jarvis, J.P., Schultz, T.: Multimodal recognition of cognitive workload for multitasking in the car. In: 2010 20th International Conference on Pattern Recognition, pp. 3748–3751. IEEE (2010)
45. Reuderink, B., Mühl, C., Poel, M.: Valence, arousal and dominance in the EEG during game play. Int. J. Auton Adapt. Commun. Syst. **6**(1), 45–62 (2013)
46. Sunstein, C.R.: Nudging: a very short guide. In: The Handbook of Privacy Studies, pp. 173–180. Amsterdam University Press (2018)
47. Swann, C., Piggott, D., Schweickle, M., Vella, S.A.: A review of scientific progress in flow in sport and exercise: normal science, crisis, and a progressive shift. J. Appl. Sport Psychol. **30**(3), 249–271 (2018)
48. Tang, Y.Y., Posner, M.I.: Attention training and attention state training. Trends Cogn. Sci. **13**(5), 222–227 (2009)
49. Human Resources Research Team: Redesigning work for the hybrid world, April 2021. https://www.gartner.com/en/documents/4001104/redesigning-work-for-the-hybrid-world. Accessed 03 Nov 2020
50. Teplan, M., Krakovská, A., Špajdel, M.: Spectral EEG features of a short psychophysiological relaxation. Measur. Sci. Rev. **14**(4), 237–242 (2014)
51. Thaler, R.H., Sunstein, C.R.: Nudge: Improving Decisions About Health, Wealth, and Happiness. Penguin (2009)

52. Tomarken, A.J., Davidson, R.J., Henriques, J.B.: Resting frontal brain asymmetry predicts affective responses to films. J. Pers. Soc. Psychol. **59**(4), 791 (1990)
53. Tripathi, S., Acharya, S., Sharma, R.D., Mittal, S., Bhattacharya, S.: Using deep and convolutional neural networks for accurate emotion classification on DEAP dataset. In: Twenty-Ninth IAAI Conference (2017)
54. Vaishya, R., Javaid, M., Khan, I.H., Haleem, A.: Artificial intelligence (AI) applications for COVID-19 pandemic. Diabetes Metab. Syndr. Clin. Res. Rev. **14**(4), 337–339 (2020)
55. Verganti, R., Vendraminelli, L., Iansiti, M.: Innovation and design in the age of artificial intelligence. J. Prod. Innov. Manag. **37**(3), 212–227 (2020)
56. Wilson, G.F., Russell, C.A.: Real-time assessment of mental workload using psychophysiological measures and artificial neural networks. Hum. Factors **45**(4), 635–644 (2003)
57. Zheng, W.L., Liu, W., Lu, Y., Lu, B.L., Cichocki, A.: EmotionMeter: a multimodal framework for recognizing human emotions. IEEE Trans. Cybern. **49**(3), 1110–1122 (2018)

Optimizing ML Algorithms Under CSP and Riemannian Covariance in MI-BCIs

Yang Windhorse⬤ and Nader Almadbooh$^{(\boxtimes)}$⬤

Swarthmore College, Swarthmore, PA 19081, USA
{ylhamo1,nalmadb1}@swarthmore.edu

Abstract. Motor imagery brain-computer interface (MI-BCI) systems face a multitude of challenges, one of which is optimizing multiclass classification of electroencephalography (EEG) signals. Hersche et al. (2018) extracted features from the 4-class BCI competition IV-2a data using Common Spatial Patterns (CSP) and Riemannian Covariance methods which resulted in improved performance speed and accuracy when fed to Support Vector Machines (SVM). We propose testing a variety of classifiers for both feature extraction methods to see their relative performance compared to SVM and to observe the impact of the two different feature extraction methods aforementioned on the different classifiers. SVM performed best, and ensemble algorithms had poor performance- especially AdaBoost. CSP feature extraction resulted in improved accuracy for most algorithms, but consumed more time, whereas the Riemannian feature extraction was twice-faster runtime for all algorithms, as expected. These results provide better understanding of feature extraction using CSP or Riemannian Covariance for MI-BCI data.

Keywords: Evaluation methods and techniques · CSP · Riemannian · SVM · LDA · Random Forest · AdaBoost · GaussianNB · KNN · Bagging

1 Introduction

1.1 Literature Review

A brain-computer interface (BCI) is a system where the human brain and some external device, like a computer, communicate and try to control things. The system tries to recognize and act on human intentions from neural activity that's often recorded through noninvasive electroencephalogram (EEG) electrodes [6–9, 13, 14, 18, 20, 21, 25–27, 30]. Motor-Imagery (MI) is an application of BCI systems where humans think of a motion without actually performing it. By looking into different brain signals and matching EEG signal patterns to motions, MI-BCI systems improve and researchers get closer to improving communication capabilities of people with severe motor disabilities [28].

Y. Windhorse and N. Almadbooh—Contributed equally to the paper.

© The Author(s), under exclusive license to Springer Nature Switzerland AG 2022
M. Kurosu et al. (Eds.): HCII 2022, LNCS 13519, pp. 546–556, 2022.
https://doi.org/10.1007/978-3-031-17618-0_38

MI-BCIs face a multitude of challenges. Among these challenges are the low signal-to-noise ratio in the recorded EEG signals, the limited amount of data available for training, the nonstationarity of EEG sensors between multiple people or the different trial sessions of the same person, and the relatively low accuracy of most BCIs. To mitigate these issues, researchers tried to improve the features extracted from the data like Hersche et al., and others capitalized on the use of adaptive classifiers and ensemble classification algorithms. The former tends to adapt better to the randomness of the data and reflects more accuracy in the model as the weighting of features in the algorithms is more dynamic especially in online operation. The latter also yields good accuracy especially when the training data is limited.

Feature extraction is the process of identifying the most discriminating characteristics in signals. Training machine learning (ML) directly on raw signals/data typically produces poor results due to information redundancy [2,15,17], so feature extraction is pretty much a prerequisite on training any data. There are many feature extraction algorithms, some of which include CSP and Riemannian Covariance methods. CSP is widely used, especially in BCI competitions, due to its efficiency in BCI design [16].

Hersche et al. (2018) state that large amounts of labeled EEG signal data is lacking but needed due to high variance in EEG signal. There is no error-proof way to recognize patterns. Hersche et al. (2018) overcome the difficult obstacle of training complex classifiers with large amounts of parameters by designing feature extractors that can be combined with simpler classifiers. They use common spatial patterns (CSP) algorithm and Riemannian Covariance methods to extract the most discriminative features on the BCI competition IV-2a data [4].

The CSP method was first introduced by Koles [11] to extract abnormal components from EEG, and have since been improved upon to create features for classification of EEG [23] and be more robust against artifacts [12]. CSP learns spatial filters that maximize discriminability of two classes [16]. In other words, CSP finds "spatial filters that maximize the ratio of average variances between two different classes" [29]. We see an example of CSP successfully discriminating neuromodulatory changes in Fig. 4 [29].

Drawbacks of CSP include sensitivity to noise and overfitting with small training sets [24]. As CSP is "highly dependent on the considered operational frequency bands", raw data is first split into frequency bands and then spatially filtered [7]. Spatial filters are used to extract sources, which Riemannian Covariance approaches can improve. In a nutshell, Riemannian geometry is similar to Euclidean geometry, but the former is more suited for Symmetric Positive Definite (SPD) matrices which model Covariance matrices [33].

Since source extraction requires estimation and manipulation of Covariance matrices [33], Hersche and et al. (2018) focus on an additional feature extractor on top of CSP: Riemannian Covariance method. Riemannian Covariance can improve CSP or remove the need for it, reduce calibration time, and optimize distance based EEG classification [33]. Hersche and et al. (2018) enhance CSP and Riemannian Covariance methods to multiscale spectral and temporal features.

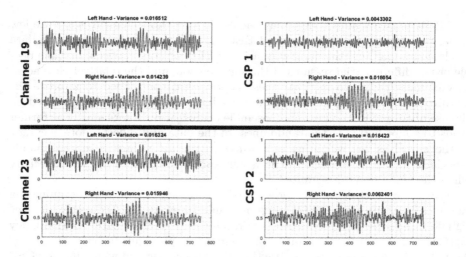

Fig. 1. Effect of CSP filter on patterns. On the left are Channel 19 and 23: two EEG channels referring to the mental tasks of imagining movement of left hand and right hand. There's seemingly little difference between the signals, until CSP filtering is applied (CSP 1 and 2 on the right side). Figure and caption sourced from [29].

Their main goal was to improve the performance of MI-BCIs while maintaining relatively good accuracy. This was accomplished by feeding the extracted features into an SVM classifier.

Although CSP and Riemannian methods are used heavily in classification of imagined movement [5, 24], they have not been robustly compared against many ML algorithms, which is our research focus.

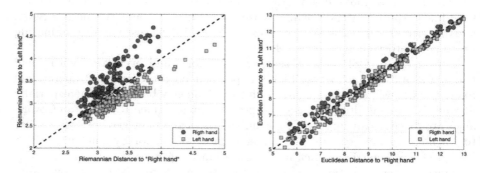

Fig. 2. Riemannian and Euclidean distance to their respective mean for two class-related mean covariance matrices- case of right hand versus left hand. Euclidean distance and it's mean does not tell us information about class membership unlike Riemannian distance and it's mean. Figure and caption sourced from [3].

1.2   Problem Statement

Hersche and et al. (2018) devised improved methods to better extract features from BCI data using CSP and Riemannian Covariance. The major goal was to increase performance of MI-BCI while maintaining relatively good accuracy. They used the support of SVM in order to test the speed and accuracy of their aforementioned work and found that their Riemannian method was superior in both. However, while their work does optimize MI-BCIs, it would be interesting to know which classifiers work best with their extracted features, and whether models other than SVM, especially ensemble algorithms (Random Forest, AdaBoost, Bagging), can provide better accuracy within the same range of speed when analyzing their motor-imagery EEG signals. Our interest in ensemble methods stem from the methods' goal of combining predictions from multiple models to ideally create a single superior model. It would also be of value to see which feature extraction method, CSP or Riemannian Covariance, improve the accuracy of what machine learning models and if ensemble classifiers can outperform other classifiers given the the improvement in feature extraction, and despite the limited number of subjects and trials but with.

1.3   Research Questions

Which classifiers work better for the analysis of MI-BCIs? Which classifiers' performance is improved by the proposed CSP and Riemannian feature extraction methods? Can ensemble classifiers give results that are comparable to LDA and SVM which are still the most heavily used for MI-BCIs, especially with aforementioned feature extraction adjustments?

2   Methods

2.1   Dataset Source

Dataset 2a, titled "Four class motor imagery (001-2014)," from BCI Competition IV was collected by researchers in Institute for Knowledge Discovery and Institute for Human-Computer Interfaces in Graz University of Technology [4]. This dataset is open access and available online.

Hersche and et al. (2018) build off this dataset by running CSP and Riemannian covariance methods. The researchers come from ETH Zurich, University of Bologna, and University of California Berkeley. Their paper, published in the 26th European Signal Processing Conference, links their GitHub code, https://github.com/MultiScale-BCI/IV-2a, which we utilize.

2.2   Dataset Description

The overarching goal of BCI Competition IV was to "validate signal processing and classification methods for BCIs," and datasets in the second class address "classification of EEG signals affected by eye movement artifacts" [1]. Dataset

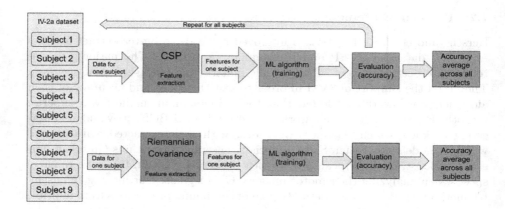

Fig. 3. The different stages of processing the data.

2a consists of EEG data from nine participants who carried out four different motor-imagery tasks like imagining moving their left hand, right hand, and feet and tongue [4]. In one session, each participant had 72 trials per class, totaling 288 trials. There were two sessions in total: one for training and the other for testing. Signals were recorded using 22 EEG electrodes/channels. There were also three Electrooculography (EOG) channels that gave information about the eye movement, from which an expert determined if a trial had artifacts, leading to 9.41% of the trials being removed [7].

Hersche and et al. (2018) calculate the average covariance matrix of the EEG signals, and find a spatial filter that maximizes the Rayleigh quotient by solving the generalized eigenvalue decomposition (GEVD) problem. A set of spatial filters is built, and feature fl is set as the logarithm of the spatial filtered and normalized variances. EEG signals are divided into multiscale temporal and spectral components before CSP is applied. The robustness of this feature extraction is increased through the temporal windows and the spectral bands inducing redundant information [7]. For the Riemannian covariance method, the geometric mean is used to find a point that minimizes the sum of all squared Riemannian distances [7]. The covariance matrix is vectorized for SVM, and a matrix kernel where the Riemannian distance is factored is built [7].

2.3   Experiment Design

This paper compares the performance of seven different classifiers on the BCI Competition IV 2a dataset: LDA, SVM, KNN, AdaBoost, BaggingClassifier, GaussianNB and RandomForest [4]. Thus, the algorithms span multiple types of classifiers: ensemble, naive-bayes, discriminant analysis, and nearest neighbors [13, 15, 19, 22, 34]. The dataset and feature extraction methods were not altered nor was the format of the data. Apart from linear SVM, all other algorithms were added to the original code provided for the paper [7].

Figure 1 shows that each algorithm was run twice, once with the features extracted using CSP, and the other with the features extracted from the Riemannian Covariance method. The scoring and comparison of each algorithm depended on 3 parameters: the success rate (accuracy), training time, and evaluation time (scoring). All of these parameters were provided as averages across the 9 subjects of the trial. The calibration of each algorithm is the default provided by the sklearn library.

3   Results

As shown in Fig. 3, SVM and LDA are still relatively superior to other algorithms achieving a success rate of 75% and 60% respectively with the Riemannian extracted features, and 74% and 69% respectively with the CSP extracted features. The ensemble algorithms had a poorer performance, especially AdaBoost, which is the least accurate and the slowest of all seven for both CSP and Riemannian methods. However, RandomForest and GaussianNB were very similar in performance to LDA for both methods. RandomForest, GaussianNB, KNN, LDA, and Bagging all achieved better performance with CSP compared to Riemannian covariance. RandomForest's performance, particularly, was boosted with CSP, reaching a success rate of 70%, which is close to SVM's success rate of 74%. Figure 3 is ordered in increasing differences of success rate between CSP and Riemannian Covariance with RandomForest experiencing the greatest difference. Finally, as seen in Fig. 2, Riemannian results were, as expected, about two times faster than CSP for all algorithms. CSP feature extraction generally provided more accurate results for all models except SVM, but consumed more time.

4   Conclusion

CSP and Riemannian Covariance methods were reported to improve feature extraction for MI-BCI data. Upon applying a battery of ML classifiers to the extracted features for training and testing, multiple patterns were noticed. CSP extracted features generally resulted in better performance for all algorithms except SVM and AdaBoost, which performed almost the same regardless. SVM and LDA performed best, with ensemble models, except AdaBooster, accomplishing results that are similar to LDA. All algorithms applied with CSP took approximately twice the time compared to when they were applied with Riemannian Covariance. These findings can provide a guide for MI-BCI researchers who plan to use CSP and the Riemannian Covariance with ML (Fig. 4).

Algorithm	Average success rate (%)		Difference (%)	Training average time (s)		Evaluation average time (s)	
	Riemannian	CSP	CSP - Riemmanian	Riemannian	CSP	Riemannian	CSP
AdaBoost	42	40	-2	32	61	6	30
SVM (linear kernel)	75	74	-1	23	60	6	29
GaussianNB	59	62	3	25	50	7	31
Bagging	54	62	8	26	53	6	30
KNN	58	66	8	23	49	7	30
LDA	60	69	9	24	52	7	31
RandomForest	57	**70**	**13**	26	52	7	33

Fig. 4. Summary of results: Average success rate, difference, training and evaluation time for Riemannian and CSP features tested with different classifiers. The greatest difference is highlighted.

5   Discussion

Hersche et al. (2018) used novel feature extraction methods to revolutionize the performance of machine learning algorithms by improving their inputs. Our work is an extension of their efforts attempting to create a guide as to how different ML algorithms are affected by the improved feature extraction methods, and which of those algorithms respond to them with more accuracy and speed (Fig. 5).

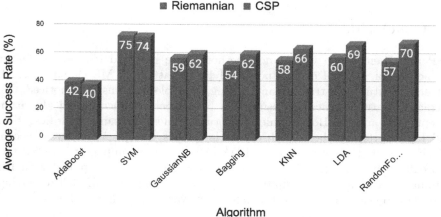

Fig. 5. Average success rate (%) ordered in increasing difference of CSP and Riemannian Covariance.

Previous work in the field indicated that KNN and ensemble methods had promising performances that could compete with LDA and SVM [10]. We expand these results by implementing a variety of algorithms. We conclude that Hersche et al.'s (2018) improved CSP algorithm boosted the accuracy of most of our algorithms, especially RandomForest, LDA, and KNN.

References	Feature Extractor	Classifier	Mean Accuracy
H. Yang et al. [31]	CSP	CNN	69%
A. Barachant et al. [3]	Riemannian Covariance	LDA	70%
M. Hersche et al. [7]	CSP	SVM	73.70%
	Riemannian Covariance	SVM	74.77%
P. Yang et al. [32]	CSP	MLP	68%
	Riemannian Covariance	MLP	76%
Our proposal	CSP	LDA	69%
	CSP	RandomForest	70%

Fig. 6. Mean accuracy comparisons to other published results. All studies used BCI competition IV dataset. This figure is adjusted from [32] to include our best results.

Figure 6 shows that our best results are with the CSP feature extractor, and meet eye-to-eye with other results. For instance, our LDA and RandomForest performs about the same as CNN with CSP, MLP with CSP, and LDA with Riemannian Covariance. We didn't get to run CNN due to our limited timeframe, so it's helpful to see studies that ran CNN on the same dataset. Our LDA with Riemannian Covariance performed more poorly than Barachant et al. (2011)- we got an average success rate of 60% compared to Barachant et al.'s (2011) 70%, which is achieved through Tangent Space Linear Discriminant Analysis (TSLDA). Barachant et al. (2011) writes that "the improvements brought upon by TSLDA are mainly due to a better handling of critical cases, resulting in a 7% improvement classification for both left hand and foot classes."

P. Yang et al.'s (2020) result had the greatest mean accuracy with Riemannian Covariance. From our study, we thought that CSP, compared to Riemannian Covariance, generally had a tradeoff of longer execution time for greater accuracy. However, we do not see shorter execution time, or computation power, with P. Yang et al.'s (2020) model. They state that their model required more time, up to three times as SVM, and memory than SVM [32]. In this sense, SVM is most well-rounded in terms of execution time and mean accuracy, but MLP with Riemannian Covariance has the greatest accuracy in classifying MI-BCI EEG signals.

Our work provides value in a multitude of ways. First, it allows researchers who are familiar with the common ML models to use Hersche et al.'s (2018) work more robustly in order to delve into MI-BCI research and development without the need for a rigid background in data science and signal processing. It provides them with a concrete direction as to what algorithms have better chances of success when employing CSP or the Riemannian Covariance and allows them to go beyond the use of SVM. Second, if the purpose of CSP and the Riemannian Covariance is to increase the efficiency of MI-BCIs such that they can reach a level of speed and accuracy to work both online and offline, then understanding which types of machine learning algorithms works faster and performs better with them can indeed serve said purpose. Our work provides a glimpse into what algorithms are promising to work with, develop further, or calibrate better to improve MI-BCI learning using the aforementioned latest methods of feature extraction in the field. Third, CSP and the Riemannian Covariance are concepts adapted by Hersche et al. (2018) for MI-BCI feature extraction, but these concepts can be generalized for other types of data.

Thus, our work's usefulness can be extendable to signal processing ventures of the same nature as EEG signals that may attempt to use CSP and the Riemannian Covariance on Machine Learning data. Our future work will focus on implementing deep learning models in addition to already-implemented ML models. Increasing the total number of tested algorithms will allow us to observe more patterns and relationships between their performances.

References

1. https://www.bbci.de/competition/iv/
2. Feature extraction. https://www.mathworks.com/discovery/feature-extraction. html
3. Barachant, A., Bonnet, S., Congedo, M., Jutten, C.: Multiclass brain-computer interface classification by Riemannian geometry. IEEE Trans. Biomed. Eng. **59**(4), 920–928 (2011)
4. Brunner, C., Leeb, R., Müller-Putz, G., Schlögl, A., Pfurtscheller, G.: BCI competition 2008-Graz data set a. Institute for Knowledge Discovery (Laboratory of Brain-Computer Interfaces), vol. 16, pp. 1–6. Graz University of Technology (2008)
5. Congedo, M., Barachant, A., Bhatia, R.: Riemannian geometry for EEG-based brain-computer interfaces; a primer and a review. Brain Comput. Interfaces **4**(3), 155–174 (2017)
6. Craik, A., He, Y., Contreras-Vidal, J.L.: Deep learning for electroencephalogram (EEG) classification tasks: a review. J. Neural Eng. **16**(3), 031001 (2019)
7. Hersche, M., Rellstab, T., Schiavone, P.D., Cavigelli, L., Benini, L., Rahimi, A.: Fast and accurate multiclass inference for MI-BCIs using large multiscale temporal and spectral features, pp. 1690–1694 (2018). https://doi.org/10.23919/EUSIPCO. 2018.8553378
8. Hosseini, M.P., Hosseini, A., Ahi, K.: A review on machine learning for EEG signal processing in bioengineering. IEEE Rev. Biomed. Eng. **14**, 204–218 (2020)
9. Ienca, M., Haselager, P., Emanuel, E.J.: Brain leaks and consumer neurotechnology. Nat. Biotechnol. **36**(9), 805–810 (2018)

10. Khan, G., Hashmi, M., Awais, M., Khan, N., Basir, R.: High performance multi-class motor imagery EEG classification. In: Proceedings of the 13th International Joint Conference on Biomedical Engineering Systems and Technologies, vol. 4: BIOSIGNALS, pp. 149–155. INSTICC, SciTePress (2020). https://doi.org/10.5220/0008864501490155

11. Koles, Z.J.: The quantitative extraction and topographic mapping of the abnormal components in the clinical EEG. Electroencephalogr. Clin. Neurophysiol. **79**(6), 440–447 (1991)

12. Lemm, S., Blankertz, B., Curio, G., Muller, K.R.: Spatio-spectral filters for improving the classification of single trial EEG. IEEE Trans. Biomed. Eng. **52**(9), 1541–1548 (2005)

13. Lotte, F.: Signal processing approaches to minimize or suppress calibration time in oscillatory activity-based brain-computer interfaces. Proc. IEEE **103**(6), 871–890 (2015)

14. Lotte, F., et al.: A review of classification algorithms for EEG-based brain-computer interfaces: a 10 year update. J. Neural Eng. **15**(3), 031005 (2018)

15. Lotte, F., Congedo, M., Lécuyer, A., Lamarche, F., Arnaldi, B.: A review of classification algorithms for EEG-based brain-computer interfaces. J. Neural Eng. **4**(2), R1 (2007)

16. Lotte, F., Guan, C.: Regularizing common spatial patterns to improve BCI designs: unified theory and new algorithms. IEEE Trans. Biomed. Eng. **58**, 355–362 (2011). https://doi.org/10.1109/TBME.2010.2082539

17. Lotte, F., Jeunet, C., Mladenović, J., N'Kaoua, B., Pillette, L.: A BCI challenge for the signal processing community: considering the user in the loop (2018)

18. Qu, X., Hall, M., Sun, Y., Sekuler, R., Hickey, T.J.: A personalized reading coach using wearable EEG sensors-a pilot study of brainwave learning analytics. In: CSEDU (2), pp. 501–507 (2018)

19. Qu, X., Liu, P., Li, Z., Hickey, T.: Multi-class time continuity voting for EEG classification. In: Frasson, C., Bamidis, P., Vlamos, P. (eds.) BFAL 2020. LNCS (LNAI), vol. 12462, pp. 24–33. Springer, Cham (2020). https://doi.org/10.1007/978-3-030-60735-7_3

20. Qu, X., Liukasemsarn, S., Tu, J., Higgins, A., Hickey, T.J., Hall, M.H.: Identifying clinically and functionally distinct groups among healthy controls and first episode psychosis patients by clustering on EEG patterns. Front. Psychiatry 938 (2020)

21. Qu, X., Mei, Q., Liu, P., Hickey, T.: Using EEG to distinguish between writing and typing for the same cognitive task. In: Frasson, C., Bamidis, P., Vlamos, P. (eds.) BFAL 2020. LNCS (LNAI), vol. 12462, pp. 66–74. Springer, Cham (2020). https://doi.org/10.1007/978-3-030-60735-7_7

22. Qu, X., Sun, Y., Sekuler, R., Hickey, T.: EEG markers of stem learning. In: 2018 IEEE Frontiers in Education Conference (FIE), pp. 1–9. IEEE (2018)

23. Ramoser, H., Muller-Gerking, J., Pfurtscheller, G.: Optimal spatial filtering of single trial EEG during imagined hand movement. IEEE Trans. Rehabil. Eng. **8**(4), 441–446 (2000)

24. Reuderink, B., Poel, M.: Robustness of the common spatial patterns algorithm in the BCI-pipeline. No. DTR08-9/TR-CTIT-08-52 in CTIT Technical report Series, Centre for Telematics and Information Technology (CTIT), Netherlands, July 2008

25. Robinson, N., Vinod, A.P., Ang, K.K., Tee, K.P., Guan, C.T.: EEG-based classification of fast and slow hand movements using wavelet-CSP algorithm. IEEE Trans. Biomed. Eng. **60**(8), 2123–2132 (2013)

26. Roc, A., et al.: A review of user training methods in brain computer interfaces based on mental tasks. J. Neural Eng. (2020)

27. Roy, Y., Banville, H., Albuquerque, I., Gramfort, A., Falk, T.H., Faubert, J.: Deep learning-based electroencephalography analysis: a systematic review. J. Neural Eng. **16**(5), 051001 (2019)

28. Schalk, G., McFarland, D., Hinterberger, T., Birbaumer, N., Wolpaw, J.: BCI 2000: a general-purpose brain-computer interface (BCI) system. IEEE Trans. Biomed. Eng. **51**(6), 1034–1043 (2004). https://doi.org/10.1109/TBME.2004.827072

29. Virgilio Gonzalez, C.D., Sossa Azuela, J.H., Rubio Espino, E., Ponce Ponce, V.H.: Classification of motor imagery EEG signals with CSP filtering through neural networks models. In: Batyrshin, I., Martínez-Villaseñor, M.L., Ponce Espinosa, H.E. (eds.) MICAI 2018. LNCS (LNAI), vol. 11288, pp. 123–135. Springer, Cham (2018). https://doi.org/10.1007/978-3-030-04491-6_10

30. Wu, W., Chen, Z., Gao, X., Li, Y., Brown, E.N., Gao, S.: Probabilistic common spatial patterns for multichannel EEG analysis. IEEE Trans. Pattern Anal. Mach. Intell. **37**(3), 639–653 (2014)

31. Yang, H., Sakhavi, S., Ang, K.K., Guan, C.: On the use of convolutional neural networks and augmented CSP features for multi-class motor imagery of EEG signals classification. In: 2015 37th Annual International Conference of the IEEE Engineering in Medicine and Biology Society (EMBC), pp. 2620–2623. IEEE (2015)

32. Yang, P., Wang, J., Zhao, H., Li, R.: MLP with Riemannian covariance for motor imagery based EEG analysis. IEEE Access **8**, 139974–139982 (2020)

33. Yger, F., Berar, M., Lotte, F.: Riemannian approaches in brain-computer interfaces: a review. IEEE Trans. Neural Syst. Rehabil. Eng. **25**(10), 1753–1762 (2017). https://doi.org/10.1109/TNSRE.2016.2627016

34. Zhang, X., Yao, L., Wang, X., Monaghan, J.J., Mcalpine, D., Zhang, Y.: A survey on deep learning-based non-invasive brain signals: recent advances and new frontiers. J. Neural Eng. (2020)

Author Index

Printed in the United States
by Baker & Taylor Publisher Services